CISCO SYSTEMS

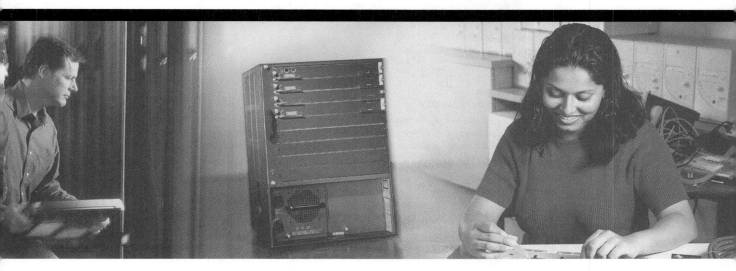

Cisco Networking Academy Program

CCNP 3: Multilayer Switching
Companion Guide

Second Edition

Wayne Lewis, Ph.D.

Cisco Networking Academy Program

Cisco Press

800 East 96th Street

Indianapolis, Indiana 46240 USA

www.ciscopress.com

Cisco Networking Academy Program

CCNP 3: Multilayer Switching Companion Guide

Second Edition

Cisco Systems, Inc.

Cisco Networking Academy Program

Copyright © 2005 Cisco Systems, Inc.

Published by:
Cisco Press
800 East 96th Street
Indianapolis, Indiana 46240 USA

Printed in the United States of America 1 2 3 4 5 6 7 8 9 0

Library of Congress Cataloging-in-Publication Number: 2003114385

ISBN: 1-58713-143-9

Trademark Acknowledgments

All terms mentioned in this book that are known to be trademarks or service marks have been appropriately capitalized. Cisco Press or Cisco Systems, Inc. cannot attest to the accuracy of this information. Use of a term in this book should not be regarded as affecting the validity of any trademark or service mark.

Warning and Disclaimer

This book is designed to provide information about the Cisco Networking Academy Program CCNP 3: Multilayer Switching course. Every effort has been made to make this book as complete and accurate as possible, but no warranty or fitness is implied.

The information is provided on an "as is" basis. The author, Cisco Press, and Cisco Systems, Inc. shall have neither liability nor responsibility to any person or entity with respect to any loss or damages arising from the information contained in this book or from the use of the disks or programs that might accompany it.

The opinions expressed in this book belong to the author and are not necessarily those of Cisco Systems, Inc.

This book is part of the Cisco Networking Academy® Program series from Cisco Press. The products in this series support and complement the Cisco Networking Academy Program curriculum. If you are using this book outside the Networking Academy program, then you are not preparing with a Cisco trained and authorized Networking Academy provider.

For information on the Cisco Networking Academy Program or to locate a Networking Academy, please visit www.cisco.com/edu.

CISCO SYSTEMS

Corporate and Government Sales

Cisco Press offers excellent discounts on this book when ordered in quantity for bulk purchases or special sales.

For more information please contact:
U.S. Corporate and Government Sales   1-800-382-3419 corpsales@pearsontechgroup.com

For sales outside the United States please contact:
International Sales international@pearsoned.com

Feedback Information

At Cisco Press, our goal is to create in-depth technical books of the highest quality and value. Each book is crafted with care and precision, undergoing rigorous development that involves the unique expertise of members of the professional technical community.

Reader feedback is a natural continuation of this process. If you have any comments on how we could improve the quality of this book, or otherwise alter it to better suit your needs, you can contact us through e-mail at feedback@ciscopress.com. Please be sure to include the book title and ISBN in your message.

We greatly appreciate your assistance.

Publisher	John Wait
Editor-in-Chief	John Kane
Executive Editor	Mary Beth Ray
Cisco Representative	Anthony Wolfenden
Cisco Press Program Manager	Nannette M. Noble
Production Manager	Patrick Kanouse
Senior Development Editor	Christopher Cleveland
Project Editor	Marc Fowler
Copy Editor	Gayle Johnson
Technical Editors	Mark Gallo, Stanford M. Wong, Jim Yoshida
Book/Cover Designer	Louisa Adair
Compositor	Octal Publishing, Inc.
Indexer	Larry Sweazy

CISCO SYSTEMS

leaddquarters
s, Inc.
sman Drive
, 95134-1706

om
6-4000
3-NETS (6387)
6-4100

European Headquarters
Cisco Systems International BV
Haarlerbergpark
Haarlerbergweg 13-19
1101 CH Amsterdam
The Netherlands
www-europe.cisco.com
Tel: 31 0 20 357 1000
Fax: 31 0 20 357 1100

Americas Headquarters
Cisco Systems, Inc.
170 West Tasman Drive
San Jose, CA 95134-1706
USA
www.cisco.com
Tel: 408 526-7660
Fax: 408 527-0883

Asia Pacific Headquarters
Cisco Systems, Inc.
Capital Tower
168 Robinson Road
#22-01 to #29-01
Singapore 068912
www.cisco.com
Tel: +65 6317 7777
Fax: +65 6317 7799

Systems has more than 200 offices in the following countries and regions. Addresses, phone numbers, and fax numbers are listed on the
Cisco.com Web site at www.cisco.com/go/offices.

Australia • Austria • Belgium • Brazil • Bulgaria • Canada • Chile • China PRC • Colombia • Costa Rica • Croatia • Czech Republic
Dubai, UAE • Finland • France • Germany • Greece • Hong Kong SAR • Hungary • India • Indonesia • Ireland • Israel • Italy
rea • Luxembourg • Malaysia • Mexico • The Netherlands • New Zealand • Norway • Peru • Philippines • Poland • Portugal
, • Romania • Russia • Saudi Arabia • Scotland • Singapore • Slovakia • Slovenia • South Africa • Spain • Sweden
• Taiwan • Thailand • Turkey • Ukraine • United Kingdom • United States • Venezuela • Vietnam • Zimbabwe

About the Author

Wayne Lewis is the Cisco Academy manager for the Pacific Center for Advanced Technology Training, based at Honolulu Community College. Since 1998, he has taught routing and switching, remote access, troubleshooting, network security, and wireless networking to instructors from universities, colleges, and high schools in Australia, Canada, Central America, China, Hong Kong, Indonesia, Japan, Mexico, Singapore, South America, Taiwan, and the United States, both onsite and at Honolulu Community College. Before teaching computer networking, Wayne began teaching math at age 20 at Wichita State University, followed by the University of Hawaii and Honolulu Community College. He received a Ph.D. in math from the University of Hawaii in 1992. He works as a contractor for Cisco Systems, developing curriculum for the Cisco Networking Academy Program. He enjoys surfing the North Shore of Oahu when he's not distracted by work.

About the Technical Reviewers

Mark Gallo is a technical manager with America Online, where he leads a group of engineers responsible for the design and deployment of the domestic corporate intranet. His network certifications include Cisco CCNP and Cisco CCDP. He has led several engineering groups responsible for designing and implementing enterprise LANs and international IP networks. He has a bachelor of science in electrical engineering from the University of Pittsburgh. He resides in northern Virginia with his wife, Betsy, and son, Paul.

Stanford M. Wong, CCIE No. 8038, CCAI, MCSE, received his bachelor of science electrical engineering from the University of Hawaii and his master of business administration from the University of Phoenix. He is the owner and founder of Complete Network Solutions Corporation (CNSC). He is responsible for providing global enterprise networking solutions to the U.S. Government and commercial customers. He has 20 years in the networking industry; recently his work has focused on MPLS, VPN, and VoIP technologies. In addition, he instructs CCNP Cisco Networking Academy courses at Honolulu Community College.

Jim Yoshida, CCDA, CCNP, is the Cisco Networking Academy Program main contact and a CCNA and CCNP instructor at Hawaii Community College. He has more than 20 years of teaching experience and has been involved with the Cisco Networking Academy Program since 1998. In addition to being responsible for overseeing the Cisco Networking Academy Program and conducting classes, he has worked closely with members of the Cisco World Wide Education team on CCNP curriculum development.

Overview

Table of Contents

Cisco Systems Networking Icon Legend

Cisco Systems, Inc. uses a standardized set of icons to represent devices in network topology illustrations. The following icon legend shows the most commonly used icons you will encounter throughout this book.

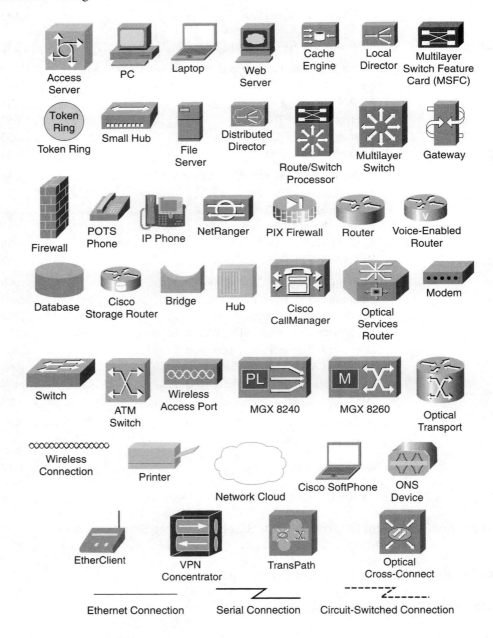

Command Syntax Conventions

The conventions used to present command syntax in this book are the same conventions used in the Cisco IOS software Command Reference. The Command Reference describes these conventions as follows:

- **Bold** indicates commands and keywords that are entered exactly as shown.

- *Italic* indicates arguments for which you supply values.

- Vertical bars (|) separate alternative, mutually exclusive elements.

- Square brackets ([ ]) indicate an optional element.

- Braces ({ }) indicate a required choice.

- Braces within brackets ([{ }]) indicate a required choice within an optional element.

Foreword

Throughout the world, the Internet has offered tremendous new opportunities for individuals and their employers. Companies and other organizations are seeing dramatic increases in productivity by investing in robust networking capabilities. Some studies have shown measurable productivity improvements in entire economies. The promise of enhanced efficiency, profitability, and standard of living is real and growing.

Such productivity gains aren't achieved by simply purchasing networking equipment. Skilled professionals are needed to plan, design, install, deploy, configure, operate, maintain, and troubleshoot today's networks. Network managers must ensure that they have planned for network security and continued operation. They need to design for the required performance level in their organization. They must implement new capabilities as the demands of their organization, and its reliance on the network, expand.

To meet the many educational needs of the internetworking community, Cisco Systems established the Cisco Networking Academy Program. The Networking Academy is a comprehensive learning program that provides students with the Internet technology skills that are essential in a global economy. The Networking Academy integrates face-to-face teaching, web-based content, online assessment, student performance tracking, hands-on labs, instructor training and support, and preparation for industry-standard certifications.

The Networking Academy continually raises the bar on blended learning and educational processes. The Internet-based assessment and instructor support systems are some of the most extensive and validated systems ever developed, including a 24/7 customer service system for Networking Academy instructors. Through community feedback and electronic assessment, the Networking Academy adapts the curriculum to improve outcomes and student achievement. The Cisco Global Learning Network infrastructure designed for the Networking Academy delivers a rich, interactive, personalized curriculum to students worldwide. The Internet has the power to change how people work, live, play, and learn, and the Cisco Networking Academy Program is at the forefront of this transformation.

This Cisco Press book is one in a series of best-selling companion titles for the Cisco Networking Academy Program. Designed by Cisco Worldwide Education and Cisco Press, these books provide integrated support for the online learning content that is made available to Academies all over the world. These Cisco Press books are the only books authorized for the Networking Academy by Cisco Systems. They provide print and CD-ROM materials that ensure the greatest possible learning experience for Networking Academy students.

I hope you are successful as you embark on your learning path with Cisco Systems and the Internet. I also hope that you will choose to continue your learning after you complete the Networking Academy curriculum. In addition to its Cisco Networking Academy Program titles, Cisco Press publishes an extensive list of networking technology and certification publications that provide a wide range of resources. Cisco Systems has also established a network of professional training companies—the Cisco Learning Partners—that provide a full range of Cisco training courses. They offer training in many formats, including e-learning, self-paced, and instructor-led classes. Their instructors are Cisco-certified, and Cisco creates their materials. When you are ready, please visit the Learning & Events area at Cisco.com to learn about all the educational support that Cisco and its partners have to offer.

Thank you for choosing this book and the Cisco Networking Academy Program.

The Cisco Networking Academy Team
Cisco Systems, Inc.

Introduction

This companion guide is designed as a desk reference to supplement your classroom and laboratory experience with version 3 of the CCNP 3 course in the Cisco Networking Academy Program.

CCNP 3: Multilayer Switching is the third of four courses leading to the Cisco Certified Network Professional certification. CCNP 3 teaches you how to design, configure, maintain, and scale multilayer switched networks. You will learn to use VLANs, STP, VTP, inter-VLAN routing, redundancy, QoS, and security on Catalyst switches. While taking the course, use this companion guide to help you prepare for the Building Cisco Multilayer Switched Networks (BCMSN) 642-811 BCMSN exam, which is one of the four required exams to obtain the CCNP certification.

This Book's Goal

The goal of this book is to build on the switching concepts you learned while studying for the CCNA exam and to teach you the foundations of advanced switching concepts. The topics are designed to prepare you to pass the Building Cisco Multilayer Switched Networks (BCMSN) exam (642-811 BCMSN).

The Building Cisco Multilayer Switched Networks exam is a qualifying exam for the CCNP, CCDP, and CCIP certifications. The 642-811 BCMSN exam tests materials covered under the new Building Cisco Multilayer Switched Networks course and exam objectives. The exam certifies that the successful candidate has the knowledge and skills necessary to use multilayer switching to implement campus networks with Catalyst switches. The exam covers campus network design, STP, VTP, inter-VLAN routing, redundancy techniques, basic Cisco IP BCMSN Telephony, QoS, and security.

The key methodologies used in this book are to help you discover the exam topics you need to review in more depth, to help you fully understand and remember those details, and to help you prove to yourself that you have retained your knowledge of those topics. This book does not try to help you pass by memorization; it helps you truly learn and understand the topics. This book focuses on introducing techniques and technology for enabling WAN solutions. To fully benefit from this book, you should be familiar with general networking terms and concepts and should have basic knowledge of the following:

- Basic Cisco router and Catalyst switch operation and configuration
- TCP/IP operation and configuration
- VLANs, STP, VTP, and inter-VLAN routing

This Book's Audience

This book has a few different audiences. First, it is intended for students who are interested in multilayer switching technologies. In particular, it is targeted toward students in the Cisco Networking Academy Program CCNP 3: Multilayer Switching course. In the classroom, this book serves as a supplement to the online curriculum. This book is also appropriate for corporate training faculty and staff members, as well as general users.

This book is also useful for network administrators who are responsible for implementing and troubleshooting enterprise Cisco routers and router configuration. Furthermore, it is valuable for anyone who is interested in learning advanced switching concepts and passing the Building Cisco Multilayer Switched Networks (BCMSN) exam (642-811 BCMSN).

This Book's Features

Many of this book's features help facilitate a full understanding of the topics covered in this book:

- **Objectives**—Each chapter starts with a list of objectives that you should have mastered by the end of the chapter. The objectives reference the key concepts covered in the chapter.

- **Figures, examples, tables, and scenarios**—This book contains figures, examples, and tables that help explain theories, concepts, commands, and setup sequences that reinforce concepts and help you visualize the content covered in the chapter. In addition, the specific scenarios provide real-life situations that detail the problem and its solution.

- **Chapter summaries**—At the end of each chapter is a summary of the concepts covered in the chapter. It provides a synopsis of the chapter and serves as a study aid.

- **Key terms**—Each chapter includes a list of defined key terms that are covered in the chapter. The key terms appear in color throughout the chapter where they are used in context. The definitions of these terms serve as a study aid. In addition, the key terms reinforce the concepts introduced in the chapter and help you understand the chapter material before you move on to new concepts.

- **Check Your Understanding questions and answers**—Review questions, presented at the end of each chapter, serve as a self-assessment tool. They reinforce the concepts introduced in the chapter and help test your understanding before you move on to a new chapter. An answer key to all the questions is provided in Appendix A, "Check Your Understanding Answer Key."

- **Certification exam practice questions**—To further assess your understanding, you will find on the companion CD-ROM a test bank of questions exclusive to Cisco Press that covers the full range of exam topics published by Cisco Systems for the CCNP BCMSN # 642-811 exam. The robust test engine is powered by Boson Software, Inc.

- **Skill-building activities**—Throughout the book are references to additional skill-building activities to connect theory with practice. You can easily spot these activities by the following icons:

Interactive Media Activities

Interactive Media Activities included on the companion CD are hands-on drag-and-drop, fill-in-the-blank, and matching exercises that help you master basic networking concepts.

Lab Activity

The collection of lab activities developed for the course can be found in the *Cisco Networking Academy Program CCNP 3: Multilayer Switching Lab Companion Guide,* Second Edition.

How This Book Is Organized

Although you could read this book cover to cover, it is designed to be flexible and to allow you to easily move between chapters and sections of chapters to cover just the material you need to work with more. If you do intend to read all the chapters, the order in which they are presented is the ideal sequence. This book also contains three appendixes. The following list summarizes the topics of this book's elements:

- **Chapter 1, "Campus Networks and Design Models"**—Good design is the key to the operation and maintenance of a multilayer switched network. Campus networks can be described in terms of component building blocks. Campus network design includes correct placement of Layer 2, Layer 3, and multilayer devices in a campus network. Basic network management command-line operations with Catalyst switches are introduced.

- **Chapter 2, "VLANs and VTP"**— This chapter explores the role of VLANs and VLAN protocols in modern campus networks. You learn how to configure VLANs on Catalyst switches. Trunk encapsulation types are discussed as well as trunk negotiation with DTP. You learn how to understand and use VLAN management tools, such as VLAN Trunking Protocol (VTP).

- **Chapter 3, "Spanning Tree Protocol (STP)"**—IEEE 802.1D specifies Spanning Tree Protocol. STP uses a number of variables to calculate the shortest-path tree for a Layer 2 switched network. You learn what these variables are and how STP is affected by them. Cisco enhanced the 802.1D standard with the PortFast, UplinkFast, and BackboneFast extensions. A brief history of STP leading to the present is given. Vendor-neutral RSTP and MST are introduced. Load sharing with EtherChannel is also described.

- **Chapter 4, "Inter-VLAN Routing"**—Inter-VLAN routing can be configured with various physical and logical topologies. A router with several physical LAN interfaces can route between distinct connected VLANs. A router connected to a switch via an ISL or IEEE 802.1Q trunk can route between VLANs. A multilayer switch can route between VLANs without the intervention of a router. Finally, Catalyst multilayer switch ports can be configured as Layer 3 ports (router interfaces), in which case they do not participate in any VLANs. On chassis-based Catalyst switches, inter-VLAN routing is performed by a number of different line cards and daughter cards, depending on the platform.

- **Chapter 5, "Multilayer Switching"**—Two methods of multilayer switching, also known as wire-speed routing, have been employed by Catalyst switches in the past. Cisco's MLS was used for several years before CEF was invented. MLS operation and configuration are discussed in this chapter. CEF is now a standard feature on Catalyst switches and Cisco routers. It provides a method for wire-speed routing by using dedicated ASICs and two data structures (adjacency table and FIB).

- **Chapter 6, "Redundancy"**—Redundancy in network design is critical to organizations being able to maintain services to customers and internal users. Redundancy, resiliency, and availability are all terms used to describe a network's ability to deliver services even when devices or interfaces fail. The goal is to reach the "five nines" of redundancy—maintaining uptime of 99.999%, during which the network is continuously operating. Redundancy is explored in the following cases:

  — Router redundancy with IRDP, HSRP, VRRP, and GLBP

  — Redundant uplinks in Catalyst switches

  — Power module redundancy in chassis-based Catalyst switches

  — Supervisor engine redundancy in Catalyst 6500 switches with SRM

  — Server redundancy via SLB

- **Chapter 7, "Cisco AVVID"**—Architecture for Voice, Video, and Integrated Data (AVVID) is Cisco's hardware and software solution for the integration of voice, video, and data. AVVID has largely been driven by IP telephony and the push to be an industry leader in the migration to an IP-based world of communication. This chapter touches on the various aspects of AVVID in general and IP telephony in particular. Whenever

IP telephony is discussed, QoS is brought into the conversation, because QoS smoothes the integration of voice, video, and data; without QoS, IP telephony on an Internet scale would never be realized. QoS and its role in AVVID is introduced.

Multicasting allows for sending data from one source to many receivers without burdening hosts or network devices that do not need to receive the traffic. Multicast traffic optimizes bandwidth utilization by using only the links necessary to get the traffic from the source to the destination. This chapter explains multicasting from scratch and builds to discussing the three major function areas for multicast protocols: between hosts and routers, between routers and switches, and between routers.

- **Chapter 8, "Quality of Service"**—QoS lets network engineers prescriptively optimize traffic utilization on network links. The primary force behind the growing dependence on QoS is the integration of voice, video, and data on IP networks. Service providers also use QoS to provide various classes of service to their customers. Cisco divides QoS subject matter into the following six areas:

  — Classification
  — Congestion management
  — Congestion avoidance
  — Policing and shaping
  — Signaling
  — Link efficiency mechanisms

QoS models fall under either the IntServ model or the DiffServ model. This chapter deals almost entirely with the DiffServ model, which is by far the most common model used in real-world QoS implementations.

- **Chapter 9, "Monitoring and Security"**—Monitoring refers to any software or hardware technology that lets the network engineer monitor network traffic. SPAN, VSPAN, and RSPAN are software technologies used on Catalyst switches for traffic monitoring. The network analysis module for the Catalyst 6500 is a dedicated link card used as a LAN monitoring tool.

Security is just as important in a switched network as it is in any other part of an enterprise or campus network. Cisco has a growing list of technologies available on Catalyst switches to ensure the integrity and confidentiality of data traversing the switched network. This chapter explores the most common network security options deployed in switched networks.

The content in this chapter roughly falls under the categories of SPAN technologies, basic Catalyst switch security options, securing remote management of Catalyst switches, and securing user access via ACLs, AAA, and 802.1X authentication.

- **Chapter 10, "Transparent LAN Services"** — Transparent LAN services are employed in metropolitan-area networks to provide geographically remote Ethernet service, VLAN sanctity over MANs, and integration with various high-speed Layer 1 and Layer 2 fiber-optic transports. Cisco's ONS product line, along with the Catalyst 3550 and Catalyst 6500 switches and the Cisco 7600 routers, comprise a collection of network devices that can deliver state-of-the-art TLS.

- **Appendix A, "Check Your Understanding Answer Key"** — This appendix lists the solutions to the Check Your Understanding Questions in each chapter.

- **Appendix B, "Gigabit Ethernet and 10 Gigabit Ethernet Standards and Operation"** — This appendix introduces the Gigabit and 10 Gigabit Ethernet standards.

- **Appendix C, "Using the Catalyst Operating System"** — This appendix introduces the Catalyst operating system. Companies over the years have deployed Catalyst switches, such as the 4000, 5000, and 6000 family switches, using the CatOS. Many of these companies opt not to migrate to the IOS-based alternatives to the CatOS, so Cisco continues to support CatOS options for these switches. This appendix describes how to configure common LAN switching features using the Catalyst OS.

- **Glossary** — The glossary lists all the key terms that appear throughout the book.

About the CD-ROM

The CD-ROM included with this book contains eighteen Interactive Media Activities from Cisco Systems, Inc. The Interactive Media Activities are hands-on drag-and-drop, fill-in-the-blank, and matching exercises that help you master basic networking concepts. The CD-ROM also contains a test engine by Boson Software, Inc. with a total of 200 multiple choice, drag and drop, and fill in the blank practice exam questions that are exclusive to Cisco Press. The questions cover the full range of exam topics published by Cisco Systems for the CCNP BCMSN # 642-811 exam. Boson Software, Inc. is a software and training company specializing in test preparation and hands-on skills acquisition product development. Boson was among the first software vendors to support Cisco certifications, and is now an authorized Cisco Learning Partner as well as Premier Reseller. Additional Boson practice tests, simulation products, and other study aids are available at www.boson.com.

Objectives

After completing this chapter, you will be able to perform tasks related to the following:

- Understand the multilayer switching approach to campus networking.
- Explain the correct placement of Layer 2, Layer 3, and multilayer devices on a campus network.
- Develop a logical design for the network irrespective of any product that might be implemented to guarantee continued scalability.
- Perform basic command-line interface (CLI) operations on Cisco Catalyst switches, such as command-line recall, command editing, and uploading and downloading code images and configuration files.

Chapter 1

Campus Networks and Design Models

As corporate intranets continue to evolve, network managers and architects are faced with a multitude of options in building and modifying their networks. Starting from a premise that the existing environment already has a combination of switches and routers within the network, this chapter shows you how to scale the campus intranet to meet the ever-increasing demands of the business. In this chapter, you learn about the approach to campus networking called *multilayer switching*. This chapter discusses the correct placement of Layer 2, Layer 3, and multilayer devices on a campus network.

This chapter also describes a set of building blocks, which presents a logical design for the network irrespective of any product that might be implemented. The success of any campus intranet is based on the placement of network services that, when applied correctly, guarantee continued scalability.

Finally, this chapter describes the command-line interface (CLI) on Cisco switches, including aspects such as command-line recall, command editing, uploading and downloading code images, and configuration files.

Overview of a Campus Network

Here, traditional campus networks and their traffic patterns are described, followed by a discussion of the evolving traffic patterns in modern campus networks and their requirements.

Traditional Campus Networks

In the early days of networking, primarily research universities and the military experimented with computer networks. The term *campus network* derives from networks built on university campuses. Today, the term is used more broadly to include networks that span corporate "campuses," consisting of buildings, portions of a building, or a collection of colocated buildings. Campus size is an important factor in network design. A large campus has several or many colocated buildings, a medium campus has one or several colocated buildings, and a small campus resides within a single building.

Historically, campus networks consisted of a single LAN to which new users were added simply by connecting anywhere on the LAN. Because of the distance limitations of the networking media, campus networks usually were confined to a building or several buildings in close proximity, as shown in Figure 1-1.

Figure 1-1 Traditional Campus Networks Connected Small Groups of Users to Share Local Resources

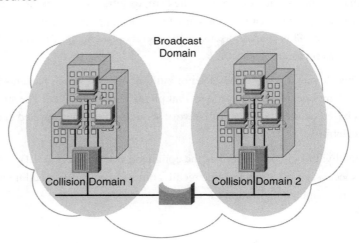

The LAN was a physical network that connected the devices. In the case of Ethernet, all the devices shared the available half-duplex 10-Mbps network. Because of the carrier sense multiple access collision detect (CSMA/CD) access method used by Ethernet, the whole LAN was a single *collision domain* (such as Collision Domain 1 in Figure 1-1).

Few design considerations were needed to provide user access to the network backbone. Because of Ethernet's inherent limitations, physically adjacent users were sometimes connected to a single access device to minimize the number of taps into the backbone. Although hubs (see Figure 1-2) met this requirement and became standard devices for multiple network access, increased user demand quickly slowed network performance.

Figure 1-2 Traditional Campus Networks Typically Used Hubs to Connect Users

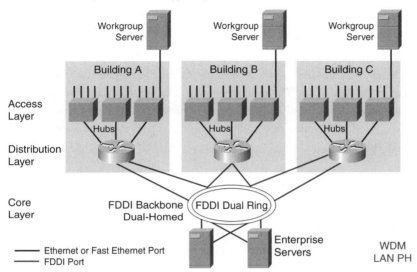

Issues with Traditional Campus Network Designs

The two major problems with traditional networks have always been availability and performance. These two problems are both affected by the amount of bandwidth available. In a single collision domain, frames are visible to all devices on the LAN and are free to collide.

Multiport Layer 2 devices, such as bridges and switches, are used to segment the LAN into discrete collision domains and forward Layer 2 data frames to only the segment of the network that contains the destination address. For example, a 48-port switch has 48 collision domains. Because the Layer 2 ports separate the LAN into distinct physical segments, they also help resolve issues related to Ethernet's distance limitations.

However, frames containing the broadcast Media Access Control (MAC) address are still flooded throughout the entire *broadcast domain*. A single network device could malfunction and flood the network with "noise," and this could bring down the network. This is where routers come in. Because routers operate at Layer 3 of the Open System Interconnection (OSI) model, they can make intelligent decisions about the flow of data to and from a network segment. Routers do not forward broadcasts, so if noise from excessive broadcasts cripples one logical segment, the router does not forward those broadcasts to other logical segments.

Traffic that polls the network about component status or availability and that advertises network component status or availability can affect network performance. Two common types of broadcasts that poll the network are IP Address Resolution Protocol (ARP) requests and

NetBIOS name requests. These broadcasts are normally propagated across an entire subnet and expect the target device to respond directly to the broadcast.

In addition to broadcasts, multicast traffic can also consume a large amount of bandwidth. Multicast traffic is propagated to a specific group of users, so if deployed correctly, it actually conserves bandwidth relative to broadcast traffic. Depending on the number of users in a multicast group or the type of application data contained in the multicast packet, multicast traffic can consume most, if not all, of the network resources. An example of a multicast implementation is the Cisco IP/TV solution, which uses multicast packets to transport multimedia such as audio and video.

As networks grow, so does the amount of broadcast traffic on the network. Excessive broadcasts reduce the bandwidth available to the end users and force end-user nodes to waste CPU cycles on unnecessary processes. In a worst-case scenario, broadcast storms can effectively shut down the network by monopolizing the available bandwidth.

Two methods can address the broadcast issue for large switched LAN sites:

- Using routers to create many subnets and logically segment the traffic
- Implementing virtual LANs (VLANs) within the switched network

With the option to use routers (see Figure 1-3), broadcasts do not pass through routers. Although this approach contains broadcast traffic, the CPU of a traditional router has to process each packet. This scenario can create a bottleneck in the network. If a router has an interface on a subnet in which a broadcast storm is occurring, the router CPU might be interrupted to the extent that the router is unable to process packets destined for other networks in a timely fashion.

Figure 1-3 Routers Segment Traffic into Independent Broadcast Domains

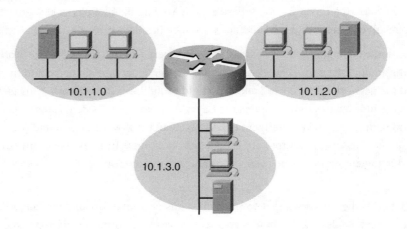

10.1.1.0

10.1.2.0

10.1.3.0

Figure 1-4 depicts the option to implement VLANs within the switched network. For the purpose of this curriculum, VLANs are basically defined as broadcast domains. A VLAN includes a group of end devices that populate multiple physical LAN segments and switch ports. They communicate as if they were on a single LAN segment. One of the primary benefits of LAN switches with VLANs is that they can be used to effectively contain broadcast traffic and manage traffic flows. A router is required for traffic to traverse between VLANs. Although routers are almost always part of a network where VLANs exist, a switch also prevents broadcast traffic from one VLAN from affecting another VLAN.

Figure 1-4 VLANs Allow for More Flexible Arrangements of Broadcast Domains

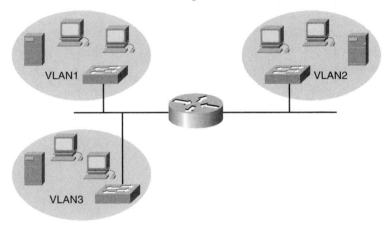

Traditional 80/20 Rule of Network Traffic

Ideally, end users with common interests or work patterns are placed in the same logical network as the servers they access most. Most of the traffic within these logical networks is contained on the local LAN segment. This simple task effectively minimizes the load on the network backbone.

As shown in Figure 1-5, the 80/20 rule (pertinent through much of the 1990s) states that in a properly designed network, 80 percent of the traffic on a given network segment is local. No more than 20 percent of the network traffic should move across the network's backbone. Backbone congestion indicates that traffic patterns are not meeting the 80/20 rule. In this case, rather than adding switches or replacing hubs with switches, network administrators can improve network performance by doing one of the following:

- Moving resources such as applications, software programs, and files from one server to another to contain traffic locally within a workgroup
- Moving users logically, if not physically, so that the workgroups more closely reflect the actual traffic patterns
- Adding servers so that users can access them locally without having to cross the backbone

Figure 1-5 The 80/20 Rule of Network Traffic

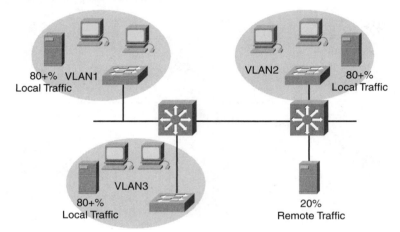

The New 20/80 Rule of Network Traffic

In today's networks, traffic patterns are moving toward what is called the 20/80 model (see Figure 1-6). In the 20/80 model, only 20 percent of traffic remains local to the workgroup LAN, and 80 percent of the traffic leaves the local network.

Two factors have contributed to these changing traffic patterns:

- **The Internet**—With web-based computing and Internet applications, a PC can be a tool for both publishing and accessing information. So information can now come from anywhere in the network, potentially creating massive amounts of traffic crossing subnet boundaries. Users hop transparently between servers across the enterprise by using hyperlinks, without having to worry about where the data is located.
- **Server farms**—The second factor leading to the decline of local-centric networks is the move toward server consolidation. Enterprises are deploying centralized server farms for security purposes, ease of management, and reduced cost of ownership. All traffic from the client subnets to these servers must travel across the campus backbone.

Figure 1-6 The 20/80 Rule of Network Traffic

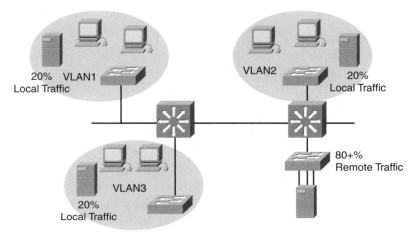

However, this change in traffic patterns requires the Layer 3 performance to approximate the Layer 2 performance. Because routing is a CPU-intensive process, this Layer 3 processing can create network bottlenecks. This increased reliance on Layer 3 processing is an important factor driving the continued increase in requirements on campus networks.

Key Requirements of the Evolving Campus Structure

The key requirements placing pressure on the emerging campus designs are as follows:

- **Fast convergence**—This requirement stipulates that the network must be able to adapt very quickly to changes in the network topology, such as failed links and insertion of new devices on the network. Fast convergence becomes even more critical as the campus network grows in geographic scope.

- **Deterministic paths**—This requirement allows a device or administrator to make a decision based on the desirability of a given path to a destination for certain applications or user groups.

- **Redundancy**—This requirement specifies that a mechanism, such as redundant links, devices, or modules, is in place to ensure that the network is operational at all times.

- **Scalable**—This requirement states that as the network grows and new applications are added, the infrastructure must be able to handle the increased traffic demands.

- **Centralized applications**—This requirement dictates that centralized applications must be available to support most or all users on the network. The server farm is in a centralized location using the same hop count for each area of the network.

- **The new 20/80 rule**—This requirement focuses on the shift in traditional traffic patterns.

- **Multiprotocol support**—This requirement specifies that campus networks must be able to support multiprotocol environments, such as mixed Internet Protocol (IP) and Internetwork Packet Exchange (IPX) environments.

- **Multicasting**—This requirement demands that campus networks be able to support IP multicast traffic in addition to IP unicast traffic.

Evolving Campus Structure

Increased user demands and complex applications have forced network designers to focus on the network's actual traffic patterns. Networks can no longer be divided into subnetworks based only on the number of users. The emergence of enterprise servers that run applications serving all users also has a direct effect on the load across the network. A higher traffic load across the entire network results in the need for more efficient routing and switching techniques. In the new campus model, traffic patterns dictate the placement of the services required by the end user. To service the local traffic, Layer 2 switches have moved to the edge of the network and into the wiring closets. These switches connect end-user devices and servers into a common workgroup. Services can be separated into three categories:

- Local services
- Remote services
- Enterprise services

A local service is one in which the entities that provide the service reside on the same subnet and, therefore, the same virtual network as the user. Local services remain in specific areas of the network. Traffic to and from local services is confined to links between the server, the switches, and the end users. Local traffic does not enter the network backbone or pass through a router.

A remote service is an entity that might be geographically close to the end user but that is not on the same subnet or VLAN as the user. Traffic to and from remote services might or might not cross the backbone. Requests for the remote services have to cross broadcast domain boundaries because these services are remote to the requesting end user. Therefore, switches must connect to Layer 3 devices to allow for access to remote services.

Enterprise services are services common to all users. Examples of enterprise services are e-mail, Internet access, and videoconferencing. Because all users need to access enterprise services, these servers and services exist within a separate subnet placed close to the backbone. Because enterprise services exist outside the end user's broadcast domain, Layer 3 devices are required to access these services. The enterprise services might or might not be grouped by Layer 2 switches.

Assuming a hierarchical design, placing the enterprise servers close to the backbone ensures the same distance from each user. It also means that all traffic going to an enterprise server indeed crosses the network backbone.

 Interactive Media Activity   Drag and Drop: Evolving Campus Structure

This activity helps you understand local, remote, and enterprise services.

Key Characteristics of Various Switching Technologies

Two primary factors govern a switched network's success:

- Availability
- Performance

Other factors include

- Reliability
- Scalability
- Cost

The range and variety of services now available on modern switches are extensive, can be overwhelming, and will continue to evolve over time because these services are driven by customer needs. Focus on the core concepts of these technologies instead of expecting to master each one. Many of these technologies will be replaced by completely independent solutions in the coming years.

Overview

Modern networks should support data, voice, and video. This means the network devices must support *quality of service (QoS)* and multicast technologies. QoS is needed to provide acceptable levels of service to the end user. During periods of congestion, a QoS policy ensures that certain types of traffic, defined by the network engineer, receive preferential treatment over other types of traffic. In addition, QoS is not effective when chronic congestion exists. QoS is better suited to handle occasional periods of congestion.

The network should also have a high-speed, reliable backbone. This means that one or more switches need to support large capacities on the switch backplane and offer significant Gigabit Ethernet port densities.

The network should be scalable. This means having devices that can be upgraded without needing to replace them with completely new equipment. Each switch purchased for the backbone must have a chassis containing sufficient slots to reasonably support module upgrades over time that are appropriate for the network. Backbone switches should have *nonblocking* back-planes. A switch that supports high-speed switching at Layer 3 to Layer 7 is needed. This means that the switches should support technologies such as Cisco Express Forwarding (CEF).

Finally, the network should have redundancy. This means that the switches need to support such features as *Hot Standby Router Protocol (HSRP)*, Internet Control Message Protocol (ICMP) Router Discovery Protocol (IRDP), *VLAN Trunking Protocol (VTP)*, trunking, chan-neling, *Internet Group Management Protocol (IGMP)*, *Cisco Group Management Protocol (CGMP)*, and *Spanning Tree Protocol (STP)*.

These features are just some of the considerations you need to keep in mind when purchasing a switch. Modern switches support a variety of other features.

The OSI model provides a convenient way to describe processes that take place in a network-ing environment. Each layer in the OSI model relates to a set of specific functions. This book focuses on Layers 2, 3, and 4 of the OSI model.

Protocols normally can be categorized into one or more of the OSI layers. Each protocol exchanges information called protocol data units (PDUs) between peer layers of network devices. Table 1-1 shows the specific name for each PDU at each layer and the device type that traditionally processes the PDU.

Table 1-1 Generic Names for PDUs at Each OSI Layer

Layer	PDU Type	Device Type
Data link (Layer 2)	Frames	Layer 2 switch or bridge
Network (Layer 3)	Packets	Router, Layer 3 switch
Transport (Layer 4)	Segments	Router or server (TCP or UDP port), Layer 4 switch

The underlying layer services each protocol peer layer. For example, TCP segments are encapsulated in Layer 3 packets, which are encapsulated in Layer 2 frames. A layer-specific device processes only those PDUs for which it is responsible by inspecting the PDU header. Each device treats the higher-level information as payload. For example, a switch processes Layer 2 information and considers the Layer 3 information payload and merely forwards it without processing it.

Switches are available that can make decisions based on PDU header information at Layers 2, 3, and 4. Content service switches, such as the Cisco CSS 11800, make switching decisions based on Layer 2 to Layer 7 header information.

Layer 2 Switching

Bridges and switches analyze incoming frames, make forwarding decisions based on information contained in the frames, and forward the frames toward the destination. Upper-layer protocol transparency is a primary advantage of both bridging and switching. Because both bridges and switches operate at the data link layer, they are not required to examine upper-layer information. Bridges also can filter frames based on any Layer 2 fields.

Although bridges and switches share most relevant attributes, several distinctions differentiate these technologies. Switches are significantly faster because they switch in hardware. Switches also can support higher port densities than bridges. Some switches support cut-through switching, which reduces latency and delays in the network by processing only the MAC address portion of the frame. Bridges support only store-and-forward traffic switching (where the entire frame is processed before forwarding). The main differences are that bridges perform switching through software, as opposed to hardware, and switches have a higher port density.

Layer 2 switching is basically hardware-based bridging, as shown in Figure 1-7. In a switch, frame forwarding is handled by specialized hardware called *Application-Specific Integrated Circuits (ASICs)*. The ASIC technology engineered for switches allows for scalability up to gigabit speeds, with low latency at costs significantly lower than Ethernet bridges.

Figure 1-7 Layer 2 Switching Is Hardware-Based Bridging

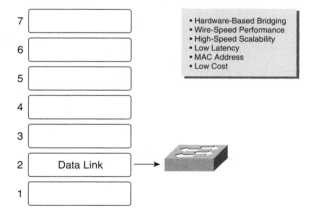

Layer 2 switches let network managers increase bandwidth without adding complexity to the network. Layer 2 data frames consist of both control information, such as MAC addresses, and end-user content. At Layer 2, no modification of the frame control information is required when moving between similar Layer 1 interfaces, such as Ethernet and Fast

Ethernet. However, changes to control information might occur when bridging between unlike media types, such as Fiber Distributed Data Interface (FDDI), Asynchronous Transfer Mode (ATM), and Ethernet.

Workgroup connectivity and network segmentation are the two primary uses for Layer 2 switches. The high performance of a Layer 2 switch allows for network designs that significantly decrease the number of hosts per physical segment, creating a flatter design with more segments in the campus network.

Despite the advantages of Layer 2 switching, it still has all the same characteristics and limitations of legacy bridging. Broadcast domains are unaffected by the incorporation of Layer 2 switches. The same scaling and performance issues exist as in the large bridged networks of the past. The broadcast and multicast radius increases with the number of hosts, and broadcasts are still propagated across the network. Also, STP issues are proportional to the size of the Layer 2-only network.

It is evident that Layer 3 functionality is still needed within the network. The next section introduces Layer 3 switching.

Layer 3 Switching

Layer 3 switching is hardware-based routing, as illustrated in Figure 1-8.

Figure 1-8 Layer 3 Switching Is Hardware-Based Routing

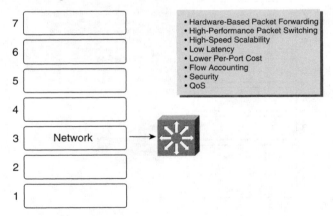

The packet forwarding is handled by specialized hardware ASICs. The goal is to capture the speed of switching and the scalability of routing. A Layer 3 switch acts on a packet in the same way a traditional router does:

- Determines the forwarding path based on Layer 3 information

- Validates the integrity of the Layer 3 header via checksum
- Verifies packet expiration and updates accordingly
- Processes and responds to any option information
- Updates forwarding statistics in the Management Information Base (MIB)
- Applies security controls if required
- Implements QoS

The primary difference between the packet-switching operation of a router and a Layer 3 switch lies in the physical implementation. In general-purpose routers, microprocessor-based engines typically perform software-based packet switching. A Layer 3 switch performs packet switching with hardware. Because it is designed to handle high-performance LAN traffic, a Layer 3 switch can be placed anywhere within the network, offering a cost-effective alternative to the traditional router.

Layer 4 Switching

Layer 4 switching refers to Layer 3 hardware-based routing that accounts for Layer 4 control information, as shown in Figure 1-9. Information in packet headers typically includes Layer 3 addressing, the Layer 3 protocol type, and more fields relevant to Layer 3 devices, such as Time-To-Live (TTL) and checksum. The packet also contains information relevant to the higher layers within the communicating hosts, such as the protocol type and port number.

Figure 1-9 Layer 4 Switching Is Hardware-Based, or Wire-Speed Routing That Accounts for Layer 4 Control Information

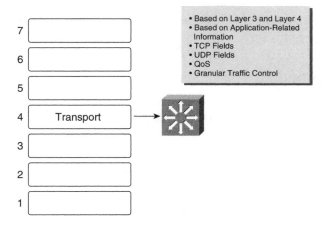

The term *Layer 4 switching* is sometimes used to describe switching frames based on flows characterized by a combination of source/destination MAC addresses, IP addresses, and port

numbers. One advantage of Layer 4 switching is that it allows QoS to be applied to traffic. QoS is typically applied to classes of traffic defined by port numbers, so it can be said to provide application-based prioritization.

Routers can control traffic based on Layer 4 information. One method of controlling Layer 4 traffic is by using extended access lists. Another method of providing Layer 4 accounting of flows, NetFlow switching, is used on the Cisco 7200 and 7500 router platforms and the Catalyst 5000 and 6000 family switches.

Finally, when performing Layer 4 functions, a switch reads the TCP and UDP fields in the headers to determine what type of information the packet is carrying. The network manager can program the switch to prioritize traffic by application. This function allows network managers to define a QoS for end users. When used for QoS purposes, Layer 4 switching might mean that a videoconferencing application is granted more bandwidth than an e-mail message or FTP packet.

Layer 4 switching is necessary if the organization's policy dictates granular control of traffic by application or if the organization requires accounting of traffic itemized in terms of applications. However, it should be noted that switches performing Layer 4 switching need the capability to identify and store large numbers of forwarding-table entries, especially if the switch is within the core of an enterprise network. Many Layer 2 and Layer 3 switches have forwarding tables that are sized in proportion to the number of network devices.

With Layer 4 switches, the number of network devices must be multiplied by the number of different application protocols and conversations in use in the network. Thus, the size of the forwarding table can grow quickly as the numbers of end devices and types of applications increase. This large table capacity is essential to creating a high-performance switch that supports wire-speed Layer 4 forwarding of traffic.

Multilayer Switching

The term *multilayer switching* is used for two distinct things. On one hand, multilayer switching is a general network design term used to refer to hardware-based PDU header rewrite of PDUs based on information specific to one or more OSI layers. On the other hand, *multilayer switching* when referenced by the acronym MLS refers to a specific technology employed by various Cisco devices to perform wire-speed PDU header rewrites.

Multilayer switching combines Layer 2 switching, routing, and caching of Layer 4 port information, as shown in Figure 1-10. Multilayer switching provides wire-speed (hardware-based) switching enabled by ASICs within a switch, which share the duties normally assumed by the CPU.

Figure 1-10 Multilayer Switching

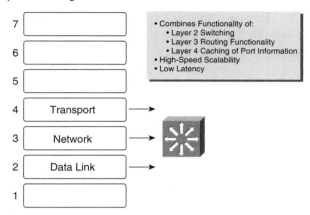

With MLS, the switch caches information about a given flow of data through the switch, inspecting the PDU header information of the first frame in the flow and switching the remaining data at wire speed based on the information from the first frame (see Figure 1-11). This explains the phrase used with MLS—"route once, switch many." The figure shows the pertinent Layer 2 and Layer 3 information used as the frame moves from Host A to Host B. MLS stores this information to circumvent the router for subsequent frames in the same flow.

NOTE

The term *flow* loosely describes a stream of data between two end-points across a network. The flow can be based on Layer 2 and 3 information or a combination of Layer 2, 3, and 4 information.

Figure 1-11 "Route Once, Switch Many" Switching Mechanism Provided by MLS

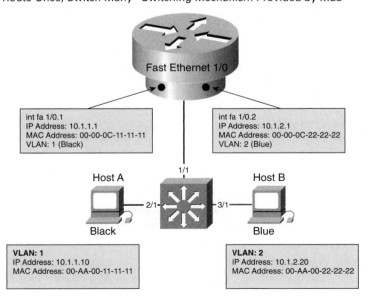

Quality of Service (QoS)

Quality of service (QoS) refers to a network's capability to provide better service to selected network traffic. QoS maps well to the multilayer campus design. Packet classification is a multilayer service that is applied at the wiring closet switch, the ingress point to the network. Table 1-2 outlines the QoS options available with Cisco IOS software.

Table 1-2 QoS Options Available with Cisco IOS Software

Protocol Group	Protocol
QoS Classification and Marking	Distributed Committed Access Rate (DCAR)
	Multiprotocol Label Switching (MPLS) EXP bit
QoS Configuration and Monitoring	Network-Based Application Recognition (nBAR)
QoS Congestion Avoidance	Random Early Detection (RED)
	Weighted RED (WRED)
	Distributed WRED (D-WRED)
	Flow-based WRED
QoS Congestion Avoidance	Low-Latency Queuing (LLQ)
	Distributed Low Latency Queuing
	Weighted Fair Queuing (WFQ)
	Class-Based Weighted Fair Queuing (CBWFQ)
	First-in, first-out (FIFO) queuing
	IP RTP priority
	Priority Queuing (PQ)
QoS Link Efficiency Mechanisms	Multilink Point-to-Point Protocol (MLPPP)
QoS Policing and Shaping	Committed Access Rate (CAR)
	CAR rate limiting
QoS Signaling	Resource Reservation Protocol (RSVP)

QoS for voice or video over IP consists of providing minimal packet loss and minimal delay so that voice/video quality is unaffected by conditions in the network. A brute-force solution is to simply provide sufficient bandwidth at all points in the network to minimize packet loss and queuing delay. A better alternative is to apply congestion management and congestion avoidance at oversubscribed points in the network. Most modern Layer 3 and above switches support configuration options for congestion management and congestion avoidance.

A reasonable design goal for end-to-end network delay for voice over IP (VoIP) is 150 milliseconds. Providing a separate outbound queue for real-time traffic is sufficient to guarantee low delay for voice at campus speeds. Bursty traffic, such as file transfers, is placed in a different queue from real-time traffic. Low-latency queuing (LLQ) is the preferred method for queuing in this context, giving priority to voice traffic while data traffic is typically governed by weighted fair queuing. Auxiliary VLANs also provide an effective means for optimizing voice traffic in a campus LAN. Another option for achieving low packet loss and high throughput in any queue that experiences bursty data traffic flow is Weighted Random Early Detection (WRED). Note that WRED affects only TCP traffic, so it has no effect on voice traffic, which is UDP-based.

QoS plays a significant role in designing a modern switched network. With VoIP and streaming video now commonplace and videoconferencing on the rise, it is important to understand the particular demands of these types of traffic on the network and how to design the switched network to optimally support it.

Multicast

Multicast is becoming an integral part of network design, although it poses one of the greatest challenges to network engineers. Multicast is configured so that one-to-many and many-to-many communication with voice and video take place. Applications such as Cisco IP/TV depend on multicast functionality in the campus network.

A good multicast network design is fundamentally important for any enterprise that wants to enjoy the many benefits of multicast technology. If the devices in the network are not specifically configured for multicast, this precludes the possibility of end users receiving multicast streams from multicast servers. In addition, the network might be subject to indiscriminate flooding of multicast traffic in portions of the network, which might result in loss of services.

Multicast control is extremely important because of the large amount of traffic involved when several high-bandwidth multicast streams are provided, as illustrated in Figure 1-12. The multilayer campus design is ideal for the control and distribution of IP multicast traffic. Layer 3 multicast control is provided primarily by the Protocol-Independent Multicast (PIM) protocol. Multicast control at the wiring closet is provided by Internet Group Management Protocol (IGMP) and IGMP Snooping or Cisco Group Multicast Protocol (CGMP).

At the wiring closet, IGMP Snooping and CGMP (detailed in Chapter 7, "Cisco AVVID") are multilayer services that prune multicast traffic between switch ports and directly connected routers. Without IGMP Snooping or CGMP, multicast traffic would flood all switch ports. IGMP itself prunes unnecessary multicast traffic on router interfaces connected to client workstations.

Figure 1-12 Multicasting Optimizes Bandwidth Utilization

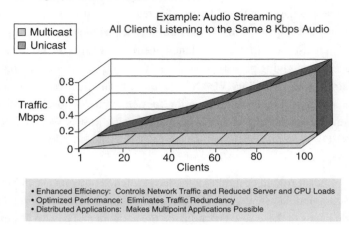

In PIM sparse mode (also discussed in Chapter 7), a rendezvous point is used as a broker or proxy for multicast traffic. A design goal of multicast networks is to place the rendezvous point and backup rendezvous point(s) to affect the shortest path. If this is accomplished, there is no potential for suboptimal routing of multicast traffic. Ideally, the rendezvous point and optional backups should be placed on the Layer 3 distribution switch in the server farm close to the multicast sources. If redundant rendezvous points are configured on routers instead of switches, recovery in the case of one rendezvous point going down is more CPU-intensive.

In any case, it is critical that network design take into account multicast functionality. The switches should support IGMP Snooping or CGMP, as well as the various PIM modes and Multicast Source Discovery Protocol (MSDP), a relatively new protocol that can, among other things, enhance dynamic rendezvous point selection.

Hierarchical Design Model for Campus Networks

A hierarchical network design includes the following three layers, each of which provides different functionality:

- The core layer, which provides optimal connectivity between distribution blocks
- The distribution layer, which provides policy-based connectivity
- The access layer, which provides access layer aggregation and Layer 3 and Layer 4 services

Figure 1-13 shows a high-level view of the various aspects of a hierarchical network design.

Figure 1-13 Hierarchical Design Model: The Core, Distribution, and Access Layers Comprise the Campus Network

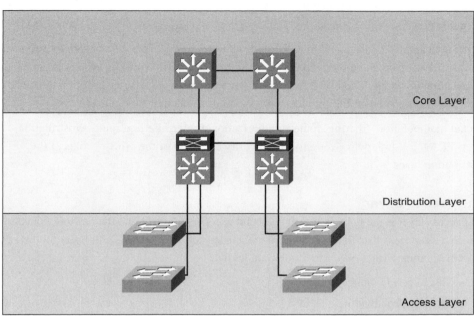

The Core Layer

The core layer is a high-speed switching backbone and should be designed to switch packets as fast as possible between all distribution layer devices in the campus network. The core layer should not perform any packet manipulation (such as filtering with access lists) that would slow down the switching of packets. It is now common for the core layer to be a pure Layer 3 switched environment, which means that VLANs and VLAN trunks (discussed in Chapter 2, "VLANs and VTP") are not present in the core. It also means that spanning tree loops (discussed in Chapter 3, "Spanning Tree Protocol (STP)") are avoided in the core.

The Distribution Layer

The network's distribution layer divides the access and core layers and helps define and differentiate the core. This layer provides a boundary definition and is where packet manipulation takes place. In the campus environment, the distribution layer can serve several functions:

- Address or area aggregation
- Departmental or workgroup access connectivity to the backbone
- Broadcast/multicast domain definition

- Inter-VLAN routing
- Any media transitions that need to occur
- Security

In the noncampus environment, the distribution layer can be a redistribution point between routing domains or the demarcation between static and dynamic routing protocols. It can also be the point at which remote sites access the corporate network. The distribution layer can be summarized as the layer that provides policy-based connectivity.

Packet manipulation, filtering, route summarization, router filtering, route redistribution, inter-VLAN routing, policy routing, and security are some of the primary roles of the distribution layer.

The Access Layer

The access layer is the point at which local end users are allowed into the network. This layer can also use access lists to further optimize the needs of a particular set of users. In the campus environment, access layer functions can include

- Shared bandwidth
- Switched bandwidth
- MAC layer filtering
- Microsegmentation

In the noncampus environment, the access layer can give remote sites access to the corporate network via wide-area technologies, such as Public Switched Telephone Network (PSTN), Frame Relay, Integrated Services Digital Network (ISDN), digital subscriber line (xDSL), and leased lines.

It is often mistakenly thought that the three layers (core, distribution, and access) must exist as clear and distinct physical entities, but this does not have to be the case. The layers are defined to aid successful network design and to represent functionality that must exist in a network. How the layers are implemented depends on the needs of the network being designed. It is important to remember that for a network to function optimally and maintain scalability as growth occurs, hierarchy must be maintained.

 Interactive Media Activity   Drag and Drop: Hierarchical Design Model for Campus Networks

This activity helps you understand the core, distribution, and access layers.

Building-Block Approach

Network building blocks, as shown in Figure 1-14, can be any one of the following fundamental campus elements or contributing variables:

- Campus elements:
  - Switch block
  - Core block
- Contributing variables:
  - Server block
  - WAN block
  - Mainframe block
  - Internet connectivity

Figure 1-14 Network Building Blocks Enable a Hierarchical Multilayer Campus Network Design

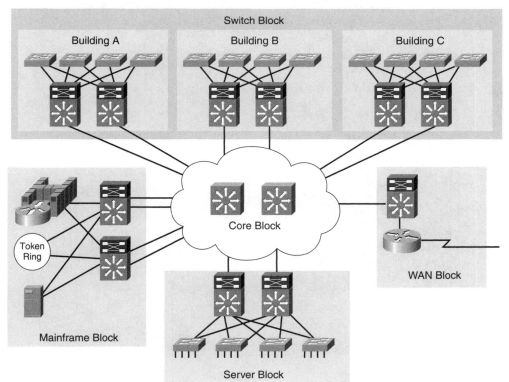

The Switch Block

The switch block contains a set of logically grouped switches and associated network devices. This set provides a balance of Layer 2 and Layer 3 services. Although the current generation of LAN switches has replaced bridges and shared-media hubs, LAN switches are not replacements for Layer 3 devices. Therefore, the switch block consists of both switch and router functionality.

Layer 2 switches in the wiring closets connect users to the network at the access layer and provide dedicated bandwidth to each port. The access layer devices merge into one or more distribution layer devices. The distribution device provides Layer 2 connectivity between access switches and acts as a central connection point for all the switches in the wiring closets. The distribution layer also provides Layer 3 functionality, which supports routing and networking services. The distribution layer shields the switch block against failures in other parts of the network, as shown in Figure 1-15.

Figure 1-15 The Distribution Layer Switches Prevent Propagation of Network Problems, Such as Broadcast Storms, to Other Switch Blocks

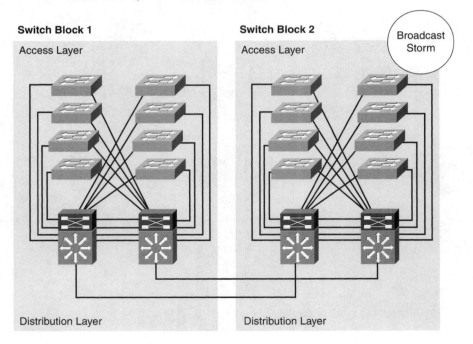

The distribution device can be one of the following:

- A switch and external router combination
- A multilayer switch

If the switch block experiences a broadcast storm, the router prevents the storm from propagating into the core and across the rest of the network. Of course, this assumes that the Cisco-recommended design using local VLANs is in effect. Each block is protected from the other blocks when failures occur. However, the switch block, in which the broadcast storm occurs, still experiences network problems until the device generating the broadcasts is found and removed from the network.

A switch might support one or more subnets. Remember that a subnet must reside within one broadcast domain. This means that all stations residing in or ports configured on the same VLAN are assigned network addresses within the same subnet.

The broadcast-isolation feature of VLANs is the characteristic that allows VLANs to be identified with subnets. For example, the IP ARP propagates only within the VLAN of the originating request. All subnets terminate on Layer 3 devices, such as a router or route processor. To connect to devices in other VLANs, the frame must traverse a Layer 3 device. Using this model, VLANs should not extend beyond the distribution switch.

Access devices have redundant connections, or uplinks, to the distribution switch to maintain resiliency. STP allows these redundant links to exist while preventing undesirable loops in the switch block. STP terminates at the boundary of the switch block.

Scaling the Switch Block

Although the size of a switch block is flexible, certain factors limit its size. How many switches collapse into the distribution layer depends on several factors:

- Different types and patterns of traffic
- Amount of Layer 3 switching capacity at the distribution layer
- Number of users per access layer switch
- Extent to which subnets need to traverse geographic locations within the network
- Size to which the spanning-tree domains should be allowed to grow

Sizing the switch block involves two main factors:

- Traffic types and behavior
- Size and number of workgroups

A switch block is too large if

- A traffic bottleneck occurs in the routers at the distribution layer because of intensive CPU processing resulting from policy-based filters
- Broadcast or multicast traffic slows down the switches and routers

Building the Core Block

A core is required when two or more switch blocks exist. The core block is responsible for transferring cross-campus traffic without any processor-intensive operations. All the traffic going to and from the switch blocks, server blocks, the Internet, and the WAN must pass through the core. Traffic going from one switch block to another also must travel through the core. It follows that the core handles much more traffic than any other block. Therefore, the core must be able to pass the traffic to and from the blocks as quickly as possible.

Different technologies such as frame, packet, or cell-based technologies can be used in the core, depending on the organization's specific needs. The examples shown here use an Ethernet core. Because the distribution switch provides Layer 3 functionality, individual subnets connect all distribution and core devices, as shown in Figure 1-16.

Figure 1-16 The Core Layer Switches Prevent Propagation of Network Problems, Such as Broadcast Storms, to Other Switch Blocks

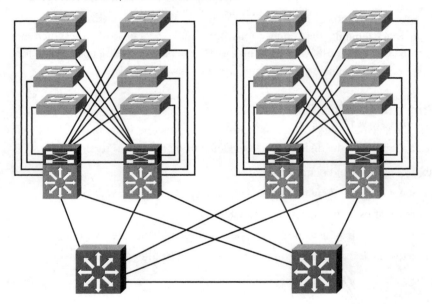

The core can consist of one subnet. However, for resiliency and load balancing, at least two subnets are configured. Because VLANs terminate at the distribution device, core links are not trunk links, and traffic is routed across the core. Therefore, core links do not carry multiple VLANs per link. One or more switches make up a core subnet. It is strongly recommended that a minimum of two devices be present in the core to provide redundancy. The core block can consist of high-speed Layer 2 devices or Layer 3 devices.

At a minimum, the media between the distribution switches and the core layer switches should be capable of supporting the amount of load handled by the distribution switch. Also, at a minimum, the links between core switches in the same core subnet should be sufficient to switch the aggregate amount of traffic with respect to the input aggregation switch traffic. The design of the core should consider average link utilization while allowing for future traffic growth.

There are two basic core designs:

- Collapsed core
- Dual core

Collapsed-Core Design

The collapsed core, shown in Figure 1-17, is characterized by a consolidation of the distribution and core-layer functions into one device. A collapsed-core design is prevalent in small campus networks. Although the functions of each layer are contained in the same device, the functionality remains distinct. In a collapsed-core design, each access layer switch has a redundant link to the distribution layer switch. Each access layer switch might support more than one subnet. However, all subnets terminate at Layer 3 ports on the distribution switch.

Figure 1-17 The Collapsed Core Is Common in Small and Medium Campus Networks

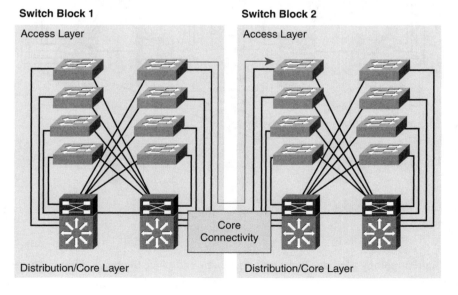

Redundant uplinks provide Layer 2 resiliency between the access and distribution switches. Spanning Tree Protocol blocks the redundant links to prevent loops. Redundancy is provided at Layer 3 by the dual distribution switches with HSRP, providing transparent default gateway operations for IP. If the primary routing process fails, connectivity to the core is maintained.

Dual-Core Design

A dual-core configuration is necessary when two or more switch blocks exist and redundant connections are required. Figure 1-18 shows a dual-core configuration in which the core contains only Layer 2 switches in the backbone.

Figure 1-18 The Dual Core Is Common When the Campus Network Contains Several Switch Blocks

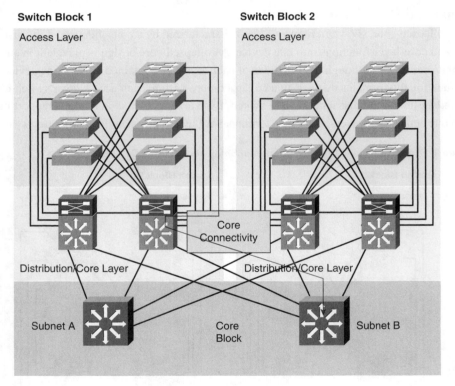

A dual-core topology provides two equal-cost paths and twice the bandwidth. Each core switch carries a symmetrical number of subnets to the Layer 3 function of the distribution device. Each switch block is redundantly linked to both core switches, allowing for two distinct, equal path links. If one core device fails, convergence is not an issue, because the routing tables in the distribution devices already have an established route to the remaining core device. The Layer 3 routing protocol provides the link determination across the core, and HSRP provides quick failover determination. Spanning Tree Protocol is not needed in the core because there are no redundant Layer 2 links between the core switches.

Layer 2 and Layer 3 Backbone Scaling

Switched Layer 2 Ethernet cores are very cost-effective, and they provide high-performance connectivity between switch blocks. The classic design model has several switch blocks, each supporting Layer 2 devices in a wiring closet that terminate into a Layer 3 device. A core composed of Layer 2 devices connects the Layer 3 distribution devices.

Spanning Tree Protocol represents a practical limit to the scale of a Layer 2 switched backbone. As the number of core devices increases, there is a corresponding increase in the number of links from the distribution switches to maintain redundancy. Because routing protocols dictate the number of equal-cost paths, the number of independent core switches is limited. Interconnecting the core switches creates bridging loops. Introducing Spanning Tree Protocol into the core compromises the high-performance connectivity between switch blocks. Ideally, Layer 2 switched backbones consist of two switches with no spanning-tree loops in the topology.

The Layer 2 switched backbone provides redundancy without any spanning-tree loops. Because the two core switches are not linked in Figure 1-19, loops do not occur. Each distribution switch in every switch block has a separate path to each core switch. The dual connection between the core and distribution device provides each Layer 3 device with two equal-cost paths to every other router in the campus.

Figure 1-19 Physical Loops Are Avoided in a Layer 2 Core if the Backbone Switches Are Not Physically Connected

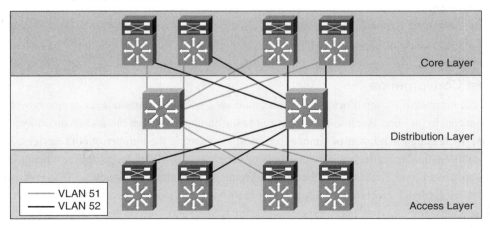

Note that a Layer 2 switched backbone does not preclude connecting the core switches, as long as Spanning Tree Protocol is carefully configured to logically prevent any loops. The advantage of having the core switches physically connected in a Layer 2 backbone is that failover maintains connectivity between switch blocks when uplinks from distribution switches in independent switch blocks fail. The trade-off is increased complexity in Layer 2 configuration and probably is not worth the trouble.

Most of the designs successfully follow the Layer 2/Layer 3/Layer 2 model. However, there are designs where the Layer 2/Layer 3/Layer 3 model is advantageous.

Figure 1-20 shows a Layer 3 core.

Figure 1-20 A Layer 3 Core Is Standard in Modern Campus Networks

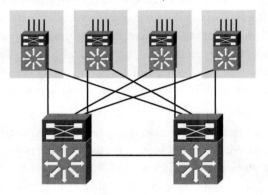

Implement a Layer 3 core for the following reasons:

- Fast convergence
- Automatic load balancing
- Elimination of peering problems

Fast Convergence

As the number of switch blocks and servers increases, each distribution layer device must be connected to the core. Because there is a limit to the number of switch blocks in a dual Layer 2 core, increasing the number of connections means increasing the number of core devices. To maintain redundancy, the core devices must be connected. Bridging loops appear when you interconnect Layer 2 devices. To eliminate bridging loops in the core, Spanning Tree Protocol must be enabled. Unfortunately, Spanning Tree Protocol has a convergence time of more than 50 seconds. If the network core experiences a fault, Spanning Tree Protocol convergence can disable the core for more than 1 minute.

If Layer 3 devices are implemented in the core, Spanning Tree Protocol is unnecessary. In this design, routing protocols are used to maintain the network topology. Convergence for link-state routing protocols takes from 5 to 10 seconds, depending on the routing protocol.

Automatic Load Balancing

Load balancing allows for a traffic-distribution pattern that best uses the multiple links that provide redundancy. With multiple, interconnected Layer 2 devices in the core, the route for using more than one path must be individually selected. The links must then be manually configured to support specific VLAN traffic. With Layer 3 devices in the core, routing protocols can be used to load-balance over multiple equal-cost paths.

Elimination of Peering Problems

Another issue with the Layer 2 core in a very large network is that of router peering. Router peering mandates that the routing protocol running in a router maintain state and reachability information for neighboring routers. In this scenario, each distribution device becomes a peer with every other distribution device in the network. Scalability becomes an issue in the configuration because each distribution device has to maintain state for all other distribution devices.

By implementing Layer 3 devices in the core, a hierarchy is created, and the distribution device is not considered a peer with all other distribution devices. This type of core might appear in very large campus networks where the network supports more than 100 switch blocks.

Performance and Cost Issues

Implementing Layer 3 devices in the core can be expensive, although relatively much less so than in the past. As stated earlier, the main purpose of the core is to move packets as quickly and efficiently as possible. Although Layer 3 devices support switching of routed protocols, both performance and equipment costs weigh in heavily as design considerations.

Advantages of the Building-Block Approach

As shown so far, the implementation of a building-block approach and hierarchical model has many advantages, including redundancy, scalability, loop-free topologies, fast convergence, and load balancing. The examples in Figures 1-21, 1-22, and 1-23 illustrate these advantages.

Figure 1-21 A Campus Network Operating Normally

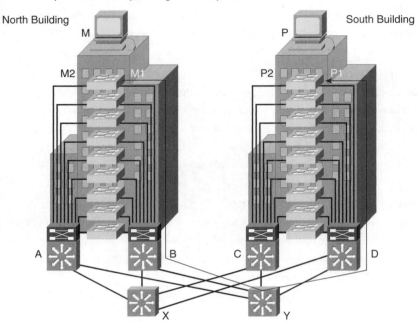

Figure 1-22 Spanning Tree Protocol Provides Redundancy: If One Access Uplink Fails, a Second Uplink Immediately Takes Over

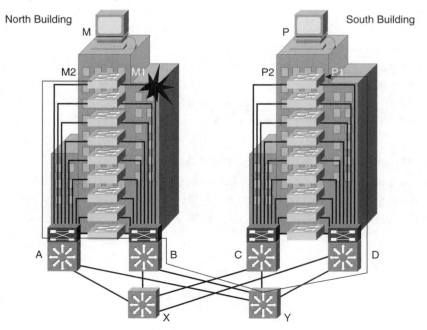

Figure 1-23 Failover Takes Place Via Spanning Tree Protocol or Dynamic Routing if an Uplink
Between a Distribution Switch and Core Switch Fails, Depending on Whether VLAN
Trunks or Routed Links Connect the Distribution and Core Layers

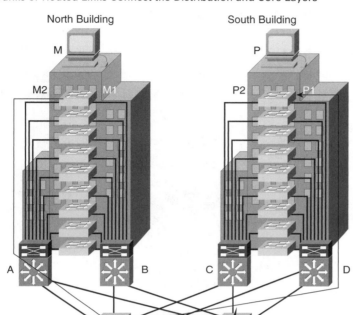

In the sample network, two buildings have an access switch on each floor and redundant connections to a distribution layer switch. Each distribution layer switch has redundant connections into the network core.

In Figure 1-21, notice the flow of traffic from host M to host P. Suppose there is a port failure in the access switch. Notice in Figure 1-22 how the switch immediately chooses an alternative path. Assume in Figure 1-23 that the link between the distribution switch and the core switch fails. As shown, the switches choose an alternative path through the core. The following chapters explain how to configure these behaviors on the switch.

Interactive Media Activity   Drag and Drop: Advantages of the Building-Block Approach

This activity helps you understand the advantages of the building-block approach.

Small Campus Networks

Small campus networks, as shown in Figure 1-24, are the most common and are typically contained within one building. In this design, it is not unusual to have a single multilayer switch servicing the entire network. In most cases, cost effectiveness is the top priority, not network redundancy. Requirements for this design typically include the following:

- High performance for applications such as voice, video, and IP multicast
- Support for applications based on Novell IPX, DECnet, AppleTalk, and Systems Network Architecture (SNA)

Figure 1-24 Small Campus Networks Are the Most Prevalent Type of Network

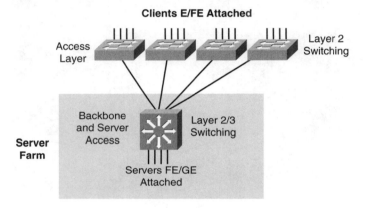

A design solution that meets these requirements provides a high-performance, switched infrastructure for a building-sized intranet with hundreds of networked devices. The network backbone consists of a multilayer switch. The access layer switches provide connectivity to clients and servers.

Medium Campus Networks

Medium campus networks, as shown in Figure 1-25, are characterized by a collapsed backbone, where the distribution layer and core layer merge. Medium campus networks are typically contained within one large building or several buildings. In this design, high availability, performance, and manageability are important. Additional requirements for this design typically include the following:

- High performance and availability for applications such as voice, video, and IP multicast
- Support for applications based on Novell IPX, DECnet, AppleTalk, and SNA

Figure 1-25 Medium Campus Networks Employ a Collapsed Backbone

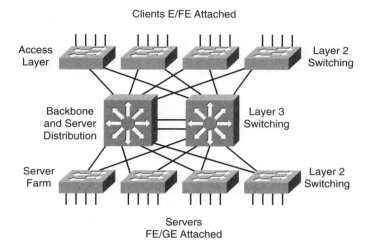

The requirements for medium campus networks parallel those of small campus networks. The major differences are the number of users and the importance of building redundancy into medium campus networks.

A design solution that meets these requirements provides a high-performance, manageable switched infrastructure for a campus intranet with more than 1000 networked devices. The collapsed backbone uses Layer 3 switching, and network redundancy is provided for clients and servers.

Large Campus Networks

Large campus networks have redundancy, high bandwidth, and well-defined core, distribution, and access layers. As Figure 1-26 illustrates, with typical designs, the buildings or different parts of the campus are connected across a high-performance switched backbone. Network redundancy and high availability are provided at each layer, and a high-capacity centralized server farm provides resources to the campus.

Businesses operating large campus networks are increasingly looking for infrastructure upgrades to offer

- Support for high-bandwidth applications such as voice, video, and IP multicast
- Support for applications based on Novell IPX, DECnet, AppleTalk, and SNA
- High availability, performance, and manageability for the company's intranet

Large campus networks use Layer 2, Layer 3, or ATM backbone solutions to expand the network.

Figure 1-26 Large Campus Networks Can Have Layer 2, Layer 3, or ATM Backbones

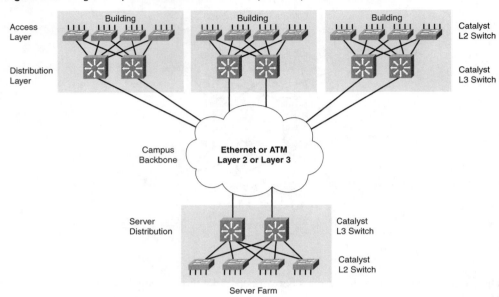

Layer 2 Backbone Designs

Layer 2 backbone designs are commonly used when cost-effectiveness and high availability are high priorities. Businesses operating large campus networks are also increasingly looking for infrastructure upgrades to

- Support high-bandwidth applications based on IP
- Provide high performance and fast recovery from failures
- Support applications based on Novell IPX, DECnet, AppleTalk, and SNA

Campus building blocks and server farms connect to the backbone with redundant Gigabit Ethernet, Gigabit EtherChannel, 10 Gigabit Ethernet, or 10 Gigabit EtherChannel trunks.

In this design, Catalyst 3550, 4500, and 6500 switches are typically used at the distribution layer and Catalyst 6500 switches at the core layer.

Layer 3 Backbone Designs

Layer 3 backbone designs are commonly used when very high performance is desired for supporting multimedia applications based on IP unicast and multicast. Additional requirements of these designs typically include the following:

- Nonblocking campus backbone that scales to many Gigabits per second of throughput
- Broadcast containment

- Very fast deterministic failure recovery campus-wide
- Support for applications based on Novell IPX, DECnet, AppleTalk, and SNA

This design solution provides a manageable switched infrastructure that scales to a huge campus with many buildings and tens of thousands of networked devices.

Buildings connect to a very high-performance, nonblocking Layer 3 switched backbone. Fast failure recovery is achieved campus-wide using a Layer 3 routing protocol such as Enhanced Interior Gateway Routing Protocol (EIGRP), Open Shortest Path First (OSPF), or Intermediate System-to-Intermediate System (IS-IS). One or several high-capacity server farms provide application resources to the campus.

The Layer 3 backbone is ideal for multicast traffic because Protocol-Independent Multicast (PIM) runs on the Layer 3 switches in the backbone. PIM routes multicasts efficiently to their destinations along a shortest-path tree, as opposed to the multicast flooding inherent in a Layer 2 switched backbone design.

In this design, Catalyst 3550, 4500, and 6500 switches are typically used at the distribution layer; Catalyst 6500 switches are often used at the core layer. Although Catalyst 8500 Campus Switch Routers were often used in the core in the past, they have largely been replaced by Catalyst 6500 switches. All these switches can intelligently distribute a load via routing protocols.

ATM Backbone Designs

ATM backbone designs are typically used for a very large switched campus intranet that demands high performance and availability. Requirements of these designs typically include the following:

- High performance and very high availability for IP applications
- Trunking for native real-time voice and video applications
- Fast deterministic failure recovery for high application availability
- Support for applications based on Novell IPX, DECnet, AppleTalk, and SNA

The ATM backbone design solution provides a manageable switched infrastructure for a large campus with thousands of networked devices.

Buildings are connected across a high-performance ATM switched backbone. IP routing protocols as well as ATM routing with Private Network-to-Network Interface (PNNI) provide network redundancy and high availability. One or more high-capacity server farms provide resources to the campus.

In this design, Catalyst 6500 switches and Catalyst 8500 Switch Routers are typically used at the distribution layer; Catalyst 8540 Multiservice Switch Routers are used at the core layer.

Although ATM is still popular in the world of telecommunications, its use as a campus backbone solution is on the decline.

Basic Configuration of the Switch

This section introduces the basic procedures network engineers go through in administering a switched network. These procedures include establishing passwords, password recovery, remote access, and speed and duplex settings.

Cabling the Switch Block

Before switch configuration is begun, physical connectivity between the switch and a workstation must be established. Two types of cable connections are used to manage the switch:

- **Through the console port**—The console port is used to initially configure the switch. The port itself normally does not require configuration.
- **Through the Ethernet port**—To access the switch via the Ethernet port, the switch must be assigned an IP address.

As Table 1-3 documents, when connecting the switch's Ethernet ports to Ethernet-compatible servers, routers, or workstations, use a straight-through unshielded twisted-pair (UTP) cable. When connecting the switch to another switch, you must use a crossover cable.

Table 1-3 Straight-Through and Crossover UTP Connections Used Between Networking Devices, Particularly at the Access Layer

	Host	Switch	Router
Host	Crossover	Straight-through	Crossover
Switch	Straight-through	Crossover	Straight-through
Router	Crossover	Straight-through	Crossover

Fiber-optic cable could also be used for these combinations of devices, provided that the devices support fiber-optic connections.

Connecting to the Console Port

Before starting to configure a switch "out of the box," you need to access the operating system using a console connection from a management terminal. The management terminal is usually a workstation with a terminal emulation program such as HyperTerminal. An RJ-45-to-RJ-45 rollover cable is used to connect the workstation from its serial port to the console port of the Cisco switch, as shown in Figure 1-27.

Figure 1-27 Console, or Rollover, Cables Are Used to Configure Catalyst Switches

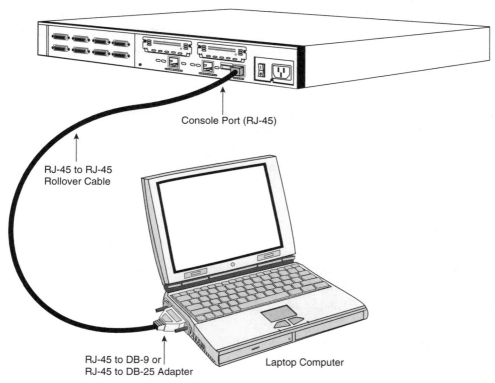

Console Port (RJ-45)

RJ-45 to RJ-45
Rollover Cable

RJ-45 to DB-9 or
RJ-45 to DB-25 Adapter   Laptop Computer

The steps to establish a console connection from a workstation to a switch are as follows:

Step 1   Connect one end of the supplied rollover cable to the console port.

Step 2   Attach one of the following supplied adapters to a management station or modem:

- RJ-45-to-DB-9 female data terminal equipment (DTE) adapter (labeled Terminal) to connect a PC

- RJ-45-to-DB-25 female DTE adapter (labeled Terminal) to connect a UNIX workstation

- RJ-45-to-DB-25 male data communications equipment (DCE) adapter (labeled Modem) to connect a modem

Step 3   Connect the other end of the supplied rollover cable to the adapter.

Step 4   From the management station, start the terminal emulation program.

Connecting to an Ethernet Port

The Catalyst 2900XL, 2950, 3500XL, 3550, 4000, 4500, 5000, 5500, 6000, and 6500 series switches have ports that can be configured for either 10BASE-T, 100BASE-T, or 1000BASE-T connections. Catalyst 6500 series switches also have module options supporting 10 Gigabit Ethernet.

When connecting the switch to servers, workstations, and routers, you must use a straight-through cable. When connecting to other switches or repeaters, you must use a crossover cable. The port status light emitting diode (LED) illuminates when both the switch and the connected device are powered up. If the LED is not illuminated, it is possible that one of the devices might not be turned on, there might be a problem with the adapter on the attached device or with the cable, or the wrong type of cable might be in use.

After setting up the basic IP configuration, you can access the switch through Telnet unless security policy precludes Telnet access.

Many applications, such as Tera Term, QVT Term, HyperTerminal, PUTTY (Pretty Useful TTY), SecureCRT, and Secure Shell, include terminal emulation programs that can be used for console access to a Cisco switch. These applications also provide other access options such as Telnet (TCP port 23) and Secure Shell (TCP port 22).

Clearing a Configuration

Cisco routers run Cisco IOS software. The CLI embedded in Cisco IOS software should be familiar to you by now. Some Cisco Catalyst switches such as the 2950 and 3550 series use an IOS-like operating system that is a hybrid OS that evolved from Cisco's acquisition of Kalpana in 1994. This Catalyst switch OS normally is referred to as command-based or IOS-based. The term *command-based* comes from the fact that hundreds of commands in various modes are used to configure a variety of technologies.

On Cisco Catalyst IOS-based switches, the CLI supports two basic modes of operation that are password-protected and similar to the Cisco routers:

- User EXEC mode
- Privileged EXEC mode

No configuration changes are permitted in user EXEC mode. Changes can be entered only in privileged EXEC mode. Privileged EXEC mode functionally equates to router privileged EXEC mode. In privileged mode, configuration files can be viewed, as with a router. Configuration changes can also be made. Also similar to a router, you enter switch privileged mode using the **enable** command. Table 1-4 describes the main command modes, how to access each one, the prompt for that mode, and how to exit the mode.

Table 1-4 Catalyst IOS Main Command Modes

Command Mode	Access Method	Prompt	Exit or Access Next Mode
User EXEC	This is the first level of access. (For the switch) Change terminal settings, perform basic tasks, and list system information.	Switch>	Enter the **logout** command. To enter privileged EXEC mode, enter the **enable** command.
Privileged EXEC	From user EXEC mode, enter the **enable** command.	Switch#	To exit to user EXEC mode, enter the **disable** command. To enter global configuration mode, enter the **configure** command.
Global configuration	From privileged EXEC mode, enter the **configure** command.	Switch(config)#	To exit to privileged EXEC mode, enter the **exit** or **end** command, or press **Ctrl-Z**. To enter interface configuration mode, enter the **interface** configuration command.
Interface configuration	From global configuration mode, specify an interface by entering the **interface** command.	Switch(config-if)#	To exit to privileged EXEC mode, enter the **end** command, or press **Ctrl-Z**. To exit to global configuration mode, enter the **exit** command.

continues

Table 1-4 Catalyst IOS Main Command Modes (Continued)

Command Mode	Access Method	Prompt	Exit or Access Next Mode
Config-vlan	In global configuration mode, enter the **vlan** *vlan-id* command.	Switch(config-vlan)#	To exit to global configuration mode, enter the **exit** command. To return to privileged EXEC mode, enter the **end** command, or press **Ctrl-Z**.
VLAN configuration	From privileged EXEC mode, enter the **vlan** *database* command.	Switch(vlan)#	To exit to privileged EXEC mode, enter the **exit** command.
Line configuration	From global configuration mode, specify a line by entering the **line** command.	Switch(config-line)#	To exit to global configuration mode, enter the **exit** command. To return to privileged EXEC mode, enter the **end** command, or press **Ctrl-Z**.

Just as with Cisco routers, IOS-based Catalyst switches have a basic and extended configuration dialog that can be used for initial switch setup. A prompt to enter the System Configuration Dialog automatically appears at power-up when no configuration exists in the switch's nonvolatile RAM (NVRAM). To exit and enter the CLI operating mode, respond "No" to the prompt when you're asked if you want to continue with the configuration dialog.

The switch CLI can be accessed through the console interface or through a Telnet session after an IP address has been assigned. Similar to a router, commands in a switch are additive. This means that adding configuration statements to an existing file doesn't completely overwrite the existing operating or running configuration. The only way to replace the running configuration with a configuration from NVRAM is to reboot the switch.

To clear both the running configuration and startup configuration, enter the **erase startup-config** command, and then reboot the switch with the **reload** command or power-cycle the switch. The configuration can be erased with any of the access methods. If the switch is rebooted during a Telnet session, the connection can be lost because the switch interface is shut down.

On the 2950 and 3550 switches, the **erase startup-config** command erases the configuration that is stored in NVRAM, but this does not erase the VLAN information. To erase the VLAN information, use the **delete flash:vlan.dat** command. To ensure absolutely no residual configurations, it is a good idea to erase the startup configuration, VLAN database, and then reboot the switch. See Example 1-1.

Example 1-1 *Delete the startup-config File and the vlan.dat File and Reboot to Ensure That There Are No Residual Configurations on a 2950 or 3550 Switch*

```
3550#erase start
3550#erase startup-config
Erasing the nvram filesystem will remove all files! Continue? [confirm]
[OK]
Erase of nvram: complete
3550#dir
Directory of flash:/
   2  -rwx        270   Mar  16  1993  05:58:00  system_env_vars
   3  drwx         64   Mar  01  1993  00:00:48  crashinfo
  13  -rwx        856   Mar  01  1993  00:01:14  vlan.dat
   5  -rwx          0   Mar  16  1993  05:58:00  env_vars
   6  drwx        192   Mar  16  1993  05:55:44  c3550-i5k212q3-mz.121-12c.EA1a
  11  -rwx        264   Mar  16  1993  05:55:44  info
  12  -rwx        264   Mar  16  1993  05:55:44  info.ver
16128000 bytes total  (9961984 bytes free)
3550#delete flash:vlan.dat
Delete filename [vlan.dat]?
Delete flash:vlan.dat? [confirm]
3550#dir
Directory of flash:/
   2  -rwx        270   Mar  16  1993  05:58:00  system_env_vars
   3  drwx         64   Mar  01  1993  00:00:48  crashinfo
   5  -rwx          0   Mar  16  1993  05:58:00  env_vars
   6  drwx        192   Mar  16  1993  05:55:44  c3550-i5k212q3-mz.121-12c.EA1a
  11  -rwx        264   Mar  16  1993  05:55:44  info
  12  -rwx        264   Mar  16  1993  05:55:44  info.ver
```

continues

Example 1-1 *Delete the startup-config File and the vlan.dat File and Reboot to Ensure That There Are No Residual Configurations on a 2950 or 3550 Switch (Continued)*

```
16128000 bytes total  (9963520 bytes free)
3550#reload


System configuration has been modified. Save? [yes/no]: no
Proceed with reload? [confirm]
```

As addressed previously, Cisco IOS-based switches use the **enable** command to access privileged mode, where extensive configuration parameters can be viewed. However, the switch still cannot be configured in this mode. To configure the switch, enter global configuration mode by using the **configure** command. The **configure** command puts the switch in global configuration mode, where switch configuration is possible.

Configuring the switch through the console port and through Telnet lets you enter commands in real time, but only one at a time. The Cisco IOS-based switch does not immediately store commands in NVRAM. The command **copy running-configuration startup-configuration**, similar to the Cisco IOS router command, must be used. As with a router, a series of commands can be reversed with a **reload** command, provided that the running configuration was not saved to NVRAM. Note that VLAN changes made in VLAN database mode (see Chapter 2) cannot be reversed in this way.

Setting a Password

One of the first tasks to perform when configuring a device is to secure it against unauthorized access. The simplest form of security is to limit access to the switches with passwords. Passwords restrict the level of access or completely exclude a user from logging on to a switch.

Two types of passwords can be applied to switches:

- The login password requires authorization before you access any line, including the console.
- The enable password requires authentication before you set or change switch parameters.

Cisco also provides levels of authority. A privilege level of 1 gives the user normal EXEC-mode user privileges. A privilege level of 15 is the level of access permitted by the enable password.

To set passwords on a Cisco IOS-based switch, enter either one or both of the following commands in global configuration mode:

```
Switch(config)#enable password password
Switch(config)#enable secret password
```

The password should at the very least consist of four alphanumeric characters. The difference between the two commands is that the **enable secret** command encrypts the password, whereas the **enable password** command displays the password in clear text, as shown in Example 1-2. The **service password-encryption** global configuration command prevents all configured passwords from being viewed as plain text in the **show running-config** output.

Example 1-2 *The Enable Password and the Enable Secret Password Are Options for Securing Access to Privileged EXEC Mode*

```
3550#show running-config
Building configuration...

Current configuration : 1518 bytes

!
version 12.1
no service pad
service timestamps debut uptime
service timestamps log uptime
no service password-encryption
!
hostname 3550
!
enable secret 5 $1$Eqe9$ThVz.PdVU538SWkvWPVNLO
enable password cisco
!
ip subnet-zero
!
!
spanning-tree extend system-id
!
!
!
interface FastEthernet0/1
 no ip adress
 --More--
```

Naming the Switch

Every switch arrives from the factory with the same default prompt: Switch>. In a large campus network, it is crucial to establish a coherent naming structure for the switches. This is especially true because most network administrators use Telnet to connect to many switches across the campus.

To set the host or system name on a Cisco IOS-based switch, enter the following command in global configuration mode:

```
Switch(config)#hostname name
```

The *name* parameter can have from 1 to 255 alphanumeric characters.

As soon as the **hostname** command is entered, the system prompt assumes the host name. To remove the system name (to bring it back to the default configuration), enter the **no hostname** command in global configuration mode.

Configuring the Switch for Remote Access

For you to perform Layer 3 operations such as Telnet, ping, or remote switch management, the switch must have a valid IP address associated with the management VLAN. Although LAN switches are essentially Layer 2 devices, these switches do maintain an IP stack for administrative purposes. Assigning an IP address to the switch associates that switch with the management VLAN, provided that the subnet portion of the switch IP address matches the subnet number of the management VLAN.

To assign an IP address to VLAN 1 on a Cisco IOS-based switch, follow these steps:

Step 1 Enter global configuration mode on the switch.

Step 2 Go to interface VLAN 1 by issuing the following command:

```
Switch(config)#interface vlan 1
```

Step 3 Enter the switch IP address and activate the interface with the following commands:

```
Switch(config-if)#ip address address mask
Switch(config-if)#no shutdown
```

Step 4 If you're accessing the switch across a router, you must configure a default gateway on the switch. You can do this in global configuration mode with the following command:

```
Switch(config)#ip default-gateway address
```

Layer 3 switches, such as the Catalyst 3550, let you configure IP addresses on any VLAN interface, also known as a switch virtual interface (SVI). So the "management VLAN" on such a device is whichever one the network engineer decides to separate out for that purpose.

Before Cisco IOS Release 12.1, Catalyst 2950 switches had a **management** command in interface VLAN mode that was used to change the management VLAN to a VLAN other than VLAN 1. VLAN 1 is the default management VLAN. Beginning with Cisco IOS Release 12.1, the management VLAN on a Catalyst 2950 switch is simply determined by configuring an IP address on an alternative VLAN interface, administratively shutting down the VLAN 1 interface, and entering **no shutdown** on the alternative VLAN interface. A 2950 switch can have only one IP address. Without inter-VLAN routing provided by a router or Layer 3 switch, the IP address of the 2950 switch can be accessed only by nodes connected to ports that belong to the management VLAN.

With Step 1 to Step 4 just outlined, a network engineer can Telnet to the switch. Using the additional procedure outlined in the article "Secure Shell Version 1 Support," at http://www.cisco.com/univercd/cc/td/doc/product/software/ios121/121newft/121t/121t1/sshv1.htm#1019743, the switch can be configured for Secure Shell (SSH). On the 2950, this requires the strong cryptographic software image (Cisco IOS Release 12.1(12)c or later). On the 3550, the strong cryptographic software image (Cisco IOS Release 12.1(11)EA1 or later) is required.

The **show interface** command displays the device's IP address and subnet mask. In Example 1-3, the management interface resides in VLAN 1, which is the default management VLAN, and it has a subnet mask of 255.255.255.0.

Example 1-3 *Hosts on VLAN 1 Can Telnet to the Switch*

```
2950#configure terminal
Enter configuration commands, one per line.  End with CNTL/Z.
2950(config)#interface vlan 1
2950(config-if)#ip address 10.1.1.1 255.255.255.0
2950(config-if)#no shutdown
2950(config-if)#
*Apr  8 17:31:19: %LINK-3-UPDOWN: Interface VLAN1, changed state to up
*Apr  8 17:31:20: %LINEPROTO-5-UPDOWN: Line protocol on Interface Vlan1,
  changed state to up
2950(config-if)#exit
2950(config)#ip default-gateway 10.1.1.254
2950(config)#show interface fa0/1
Vlan1 is up, line protocol is up
  Hardware is CPU Interface, address is 0009.430f.a400 (bia 009.430f.a400)
  Internet address is 10.1.1.1/24
  MTU 1500 bytes, BW 1000000 Kbit, DLY 10 usec,
```

continues

Example 1-3 *Hosts on VLAN 1 Can Telnet to the Switch (Continued)*

```
     reliability 255/255, txload 1/255, rxload 1/255
   Encapsulation ARPA, loopback not set
   ARP type: ARPA, ARP Timeout 04:00:00
   Last input 5w3d, output never, output hang never
   Last clearing of "show interface" counters never
   Input queue: 0/75/0/0 (size/max/drops/flushes); Total output drops: 0
   Queueing strategy: fifo
   Output queue :0/40 (size/max)
   5 minute input rate 0 bits/sec, 0 packets/sec
   5 minute output rate 5000 bits/sec, 5 packets/sec
      2258699 packets input, 203684534 bytes, 0 no buffer
      Received 62611 broadcasts, 0 runts, 0 giants, 0 throttles
      0 input errors, 0 CRC, 0 frame, 0 overrun, 16 ignored
      11465385 packets output, 2790388760 bytes, 0 underruns
      0 output errors, 6 interface requests
      0 output buffer failures, 0 output buffers swapped out
--More--
```

To remove the IP address and subnet mask, enter the **no ip address** command on the VLAN interface. You would do this, for example, if you were changing the management VLAN.

Lab 1.6.1   Catalyst 2950T and 3550 Series Basic Setup

In this lab exercise, you configure a Cisco Catalyst 2950T or 3550 series Ethernet switch for the first time using CLI mode. You complete basic first-time tasks such as configuring a switch name and passwords and assigning an IP address to the Management VLAN for remote management purposes.

Identifying Individual Ports

A description added to an interface or port helps identify specific information about that interface. For example, information could include what access or distribution layer device the interface services. The **description** command is very useful in an environment where a switch has numerous connections and the administrator needs to check a link to a specific location. This description is meant solely as a comment to help identify how the interface is being used or where it is connected. It could include the floor number or the office number or name. This description appears in the configuration information output.

To add a unique comment to an interface on a Cisco IOS-based switch, enter the following command in interface configuration mode:

```
Switch(config-if)#description description string
```

The string might be up to 80 characters, as shown in Example 1-4.

Example 1-4 *Standard Operating Procedure Is to Include Descriptions on Switch Ports*

```
3550(config)#interface fa0/1
3550(config-if)#description  :Connection to 3rd Floor"
3550(config-if)#end
3550#
02:07:26: %SYS-5-CONFIG_I: Configured from console by console
3550#show running-config
Building configuration...

Current configuration : 1584 bytes
!
version 12.1
no service pad
service timestamps debug uptime
service timestamps log uptime
no service password-encryption
!
hostname 3550
!
enable secret 5 $1$Eqe9$ThVz.PdVU538SWkvWPVLNLO
enable password cisco
!
ip subnet-zero
!
!
spanning-tree extend system-id
!
!
!
interface FastEthernet0/1
 description :Connection to 3rd Floor"
 --More--
```

To clear a description, enter the **no description** command on the interface in interface configuration mode.

Defining Port Speed and Line Mode on a Switch

Setting the port speed and line mode (duplex) are among the most common configuration requirements for a network engineer. It can be frustrating to see messages constantly appear on the console screen, complaining about speed or duplex mismatches. Although autonegotiation is generally supposed to take care of speed configuration, frequently the setting must be hard-coded. You can avoid much frustration by proactively configuring port speed rather than depending on autonegotiation. If the port speed and duplex are hard-coded, connected devices should be configured with the same parameters.

The order of configuration for speed and duplex is important:

1. Configure the speed for a port.

2. Follow with the duplex configuration.

Full duplex is the simultaneous action of transmitting and receiving data by two devices. This operation can be achieved only if the devices on each end support full duplex.

Full-duplex links not only double potential throughput, but also eliminate collisions and the need for each station to wait until the other station finishes transmitting. If reads and writes on a full-duplex link are symmetric, data throughput theoretically can be doubled. However, in reality, bandwidth improvements are more modest.

Full-duplex links are particularly useful for server-to-server, server-to-switch, and switch-to-switch connections.

The following guidelines can serve as a reference when you configure speed and duplex settings on IOS-based switches:

- Gigabit Ethernet ports should always be set to 1000 Mbps, but they can negotiate full duplex with the attached device. To connect to a remote Gigabit Ethernet device that does not autonegotiate, disable autonegotiation on the local device, and set the duplex parameters to be compatible with the other device. Gigabit Ethernet ports that do not match the settings of an attached device lose connectivity and do not generate statistics.

- To connect to a remote 100BASE-T device that does not autonegotiate, set the duplex setting to full duplex or half duplex, and set the speed setting to autonegotiation. Autonegotiation for the speed setting selects the correct speed even if the attached device does not autonegotiate, but the duplex setting must be explicitly set.

NOTE

Because the behavior of switch ports on Catalyst switches with respect to speed, duplex, default settings, and autonegotiation is specific to the platform and Cisco IOS release, it is not worth memorizing all the rules governing the behavior. Instead, it is recommended that you consult Cisco.com. For example, see http://www.cisco.com/univercd/cc/td/doc/product/lan/cat2950/12114ea1/2950cr/cli2.htm#1027083 for information on the **speed** command on 2950 switches running Cisco IOS Release 12.1(14)EA1.

- 10/100/1000 ports can operate at 10 or 100 Mbps when they are set to half duplex or full duplex, but they operate in full-duplex mode only when set to 1000 Mbps.
- Gigabit Interface Converter (GBIC) module ports operate at only 1000 Mbps.
- 100BASE-FX ports operate at only 100 Mbps in full duplex.

On a Cisco IOS-based switch, you set the port speed using the **speed {10 | 100 | 1000 | auto}** command in interface configuration mode.

To set an interface's duplex mode on a Cisco IOS-based switch, enter the **duplex {auto | full | half}** command in interface configuration mode, as shown in Example 1-5.

Example 1-5 *Configure the Speed Setting First, Followed by the Duplex Setting*

```
2950(config)#interface fa0/1
2950(config-if)#speed 100
2950(config-if)#
*Apr  8 18:40:08: %LINEPROTO-5-UPDOWN: Line protocol on Interface FastEthernet0/1,
  changed state to down
2950(config-if)#
*Apr  8 18:40:09: %LINK-3-UPDOWN: Interface FastEthernet0/1, changed state to up
2950(config-if)#
*Apr  8 18:40:013: %LINEPROTO-5-UPDOWN: Line protocol on Interface
  FastEthernet0/1, changed state to up
2950(config-if)#duplex full
2950(config-if)#
*Apr  8 18:40:29: %LINEPROTO-5-UPDOWN: Line protocol on Interface FastEthernet0/1,
  changed state to down
2950(config-if)#
*Apr  8 18:40:30: %LINK-3-UPDOWN: Interface FastEthernet0/1, changed state to up
2950(config-if)#
*Apr  8 18:40:34: %LINEPROTO-5-UPDOWN: Line protocol on Interface FastEthernet0/1,
  changed state to up
2950(config-if)#end
```

To view the configuration changes, use the **show interface** *interface-id* and **show running-configuration** commands, shown in Examples 1-6 and 1-7.

Example 1-6 *The* **show interface** *Command Displays the Duplex and Speed Settings*

```
2950(config)#show interface fa0/1
FastEthernet0/1 is up, line protocol is up
  Hardware is Fast Ethernet, address is 0009.430f.a401 (bia 009.430f.a401)
  Description: Link to ISP
  MTU 1500 bytes, BW 100000 Kbit, DLY 1000 usec,
    reliability 255/255, txload 1/255, rxload 1/255
  Encapsulation ARPA, loopback not set
  Keepalive set (10 sec)
  Full-duplex, 100Mb/s
  input flow-congrol is off, output flow-control is off
  ARP type: ARPA, ARP Timeout 04:00:00
  Last input 00:00:19, output 00:00:00, output hang never
  Last clearing of "show interface" counters never
  Input queue: 0/75/0/0 (size/max/drops/flushes); Total output drops: 0
  Queueing strategy: fifo
  Output queue :0/40 (size/max)
  5 minute input rate 0 bits/sec, 0 packets/sec
  5 minute output rate 0 bits/sec, 0 packets/sec
     644584 packets input, 68487493 bytes, 0 no buffer
     Received 132743 broadcasts, 0 runts, 0 giants, 0 throttles
     0 input errors, 0 CRC, 0 frame, 0 overrun, 0 ignored
     0 watchdog, 122832 multicast, 0 pause input
     0 input packets with dribble condition detected
     3234255 packets output, 563630304 bytes, 0 underruns
--More--
```

Example 1-7 *The* **show running-config** *Command with the* **interface** *Keyword Provides a Convenient Way to Verify Speed and Duplex Settings*

```
2950#show running-config interface fa0/1
Building configuration...

Current configuration : 124 bytes
!
```

Example 1-7 *The* **show running-config** *Command with the* **interface** *Keyword Provides a Convenient Way to Verify Speed and Duplex Settings (Continued)*

```
interface FastEthernet0/1
 description Link to ISP
 switchport access vlan 10
 no ip address
 duplex full
 speed 100
end
```

Important IOS Features

This section describes further system administration techniques, including command history, password recovery, idle timeouts, verifying connectivity, TFTP transfers, and HTTP access.

Command-Line Recall

When you enter a command on the switch, the command is held in a buffer called the history buffer. On a Cisco IOS-based switch, the history buffer holds the last ten commands by default, like a router does. To access these commands, use the up and down arrows on the keyboard.

Use the **show history** command to see the contents of the history buffer, as shown in Example 1-8.

Example 1-8 *The* **show history** *Command Displays Previously Entered Commands*

```
Switch#show history
enable
show running-configuration
show interface fastethernet 0/2
show vtp status
!!
show history
Switch#
```

To change the size of the history buffer, use the **terminal history size** *size* command, as shown in Example 1-9.

Example 1-9 *The* **terminal history size** *Command Conveniently Sets the Number of Commands Stored in the History Buffer*

```
Switch#terminal history size 100
Switch#

Switch#show history
enable
show running-configuration
show interface fastethernet 0/2
show vtp status
show history
terminal history size 100
show history
Switch#
```

Using the Help Feature

The **help** command on a Cisco IOS-based switch works the same as that on a router. On a switch, you can access help by entering a question mark (**?**) on the command line. The switch then prompts you with all the possible choices for the next parameter. If you enter the next parameter followed by **?**, the switch displays the next set of command-line choices. In fact, the switch displays help on a parameter-by-parameter basis. Additionally, when the switch displays help options, it ends by displaying the portion of the command entered so far. This lets you append commands to the line without needing to reenter the previous portion of the command. See Example 1-10.

Example 1-10 **?** *Is Used to View All Subcommands of a Given Command*

```
Switch#?
Exec commands:
access-enable     Create a temporary Access-List entry
access-template   Create a temporary Access-List entry
archive           manage archive files
cd                Change current directory
clear             Reset functions
clock             Manage the system clock
cns               CNS subsystem
configure         Enter configuration mode
connect           Open a terminal connection
copy              Copy from one file to another
```

Example 1-10 *? Is Used to View All Subcommands of a Given Command (Continued)*

```
debug              Debugging functions (see also 'undebug')
delete             Delete a file
dir                List files on a filesystem
disable            Turn off privileged commands
disconnect         Disconnect an existing network connection
dot1x              IEEE 8021.X commands
enable             Turn on privileged commands
erase              Erase a filesystem
exit               Exit from the EXEC
format             Format a filesystem
fsck               Fsck a filesystem
help               Description of the interactive help system
lock               Lock the terminal
login              Log in as a particular user
logout             Exit from the EXEC
mkdir              Create a new directory
more               Display the contents of a file
mrinfo         Request neighbor and version information from a multicast router
mrm                IP Multicast Routing Monitor Test
mstat              Show statistics after multiple multicast traceroutes
mtrace             Trace reverse multicast path from destination to source
name-connection    Name an existing network connection
no                 Disable debugging functions
ping               Send echo messages
pwd                Display current working directory
rcommand           Run command on remote switch
reload             Halt and perform a cold restart
rename             Rename a file
resume             Resume and active network connection
rmdir              Remove existing directory
rsh                Execute a remote command
send               Send a message to other tty lines
setup              Run the SETUP command facility
--More--
```

Password Recovery

Each networking device has its own procedure for recovering passwords. For Cisco devices, the procedures are conveniently organized by platform in the document "Password Recovery Procedures" (Document ID: 6130) at http://www.cisco.com/warp/public/474/.

As with many security situations, it is extremely important to consider physical security of the equipment. As demonstrated in the password recovery process, an attacker simply needs to be able to reboot the Catalyst switch and access the console to enter privileged mode. When in privileged mode, the attacker can make any changes he or she desires. Keep the wiring closets secured, and minimize access to console ports.

The following steps for recovering passwords apply to Catalyst 2950 and 3550 switches. They assume that a console connection is used:

Step 1 Unplug the power cable.

Step 2 Hold down the MODE button located on the left side of the front panel while reconnecting the power cord to the switch. Release the mode button a second or two after the LED above port 1x is no longer lit. The following instructions appear:

The system has been interrupted prior to initializing the Flash file system. The following commands will initiate the Flash file system, and finish loading the operating system software:

```
flash_init
load_helper
boot
```

Step 3 Enter **flash_init**. This initializes the Flash file system.

Step 4 Enter **load_helper**. This loads and initializes the helper image, which is a minimal IOS image stored in ROM that is typical for disaster recovery.

Step 5 Enter **dir flash:** (do not forget the colon). This displays a list of files and directories in the Flash file system.

Step 6 Enter **rename flash:config.text flash:config.old** to rename the configuration file. This is the file that contains the password definition.

Step 7 Enter **boot** to reboot the system.

Step 8 Enter **n** (for "no") at the prompt to bypass the System Configuration dialog.

Step 9 At the normal switch prompt, enter **enable** to enter privileged mode.

Step 10 Enter **rename flash:config.old flash:config.text** to rename the configuration file to its original name.

Step 11 Copy the configuration file, *config.text,* into the running configuration:

```
Switch#copy startup-config running-config
Destination filename [running-config]? <press ENTER>
1613 bytes copied in 1.316 secs (1613 bytes/sec)
Switch#
```

The configuration is now reloaded.

Step 12 Change the password or passwords:

```
Switch#configure terminal
Switch(config)#no enable password
Switch(config)#enable secret cisco
Switch(config)#^Z
```

Step 13 Save the running configuration to the configuration file:

```
Switch#copy running-configuration startup-configuration
```

This procedure is more complicated than Cisco router password recovery.

 Lab 1.6.3   Catalyst 2950T and 3550 Series Password Recovery

In this lab exercise, you recover passwords while retaining configurations for the Catalyst 2950T and 3550 series Ethernet switches.

Setting an Idle Timeout

If a user is logged into a switch and performs no keystrokes or remains idle for 10 minutes, the switch automatically logs the user out. This feature is called *idle timeout.* If the user doesn't log out and the terminal is left unattended, this feature prevents someone from gaining unauthorized access to the switch by using the terminal. Although the default setting of this feature is 10 minutes, it can be altered with the **exec-timeout** line console command:

```
Switch(config-line)#exec-timeout number of minutes number of seconds
```

This command works just like the router command. Example 1-11 shows the commands to set the timeout on the console port of a Cisco IOS-based switch to 20 minutes.

Example 1-11 *The* **exec-timeout** *Command Logs a User Out After the Specified Idle Timeout*

```
Switch(config)#line console 0
Switch(config-line)#exec-timeout 20
```

Verifying Connectivity

After you assign the switch an IP address and connect at least one switch port to the network and properly configure it, the switch can communicate with other nodes on the network. This communication goes beyond simply switching traffic.

To test connectivity to remote hosts, enter the following command in privileged mode:

`Switch#`**`ping`** `destination ip address`

The **ping** command usually returns one of the following responses:

- **Success rate is 100 percent**—This response occurs in 1 to 10 seconds, depending on network traffic and the number of *Internet Control Message Protocol (ICMP)* packets sent.

- **Destination does not respond**—No answer message is returned if the host does not respond.

- **Unknown host**—This response occurs if the targeted host does not exist.

- **Destination unreachable**—This response occurs if the default gateway cannot reach the specified network.

- **Network or host unreachable**—This response occurs if there is no entry in the route table for the host or network.

Example 1-12 shows that the destination IP address 172.16.1.1 can be reached by the device generating the ping.

Example 1-12 *The* **ping** *Command Verifies Layer 3 Connectivity*

```
Switch#ping 172.16.1.1


Type escape sequence to abort.
Sending 5, 100-byte ICMP Echos to 172.16.1.1, timeout is 2 seconds:
!!!!!
Success rate is 100 percent (5/5), round-trip min/avg/max = 1/2/4 ms
Switch#
```

Backup and Restoration of a Configuration Using a TFTP Server

Most switches have a Trivial File Transfer Protocol (TFTP) client, allowing configuration files to be sent to and retrieved from a TFTP server.

For the switch to obtain the new configuration over the network, after the configuration is cleared, you must configure a valid IP address and default gateway setting.

For complete system recovery, make sure that a copy of the configuration file of each switch has been stored somewhere other than on the switch itself. It is a big mistake to have to rebuild the entire configuration file from scratch during a system outage, especially when a backup copy could have easily been created as a backup on a network-accessible machine.

Through TFTP, a configuration file can be stored on a TFTP server and recovered later when needed.

Transferring Cisco IOS-based switch configuration files via TFTP to another device works the same as with a router. The command **copy startup-config tftp** copies the configuration file to a TFTP server at the location specified by the IP address.

The recovery process works in reverse. To recover a configuration file from a TFTP server, issue the command **copy tftp running-config**. This loads the specified configuration file into the switch's active memory. When the configuration file is retrieved, it can be written to Macromedia Flash, to the startup configuration (NVRAM), or to the running configuration.

 Lab 1.6.2   Catalyst 2950T and 3550 Configuration and IOS Files

In this lab exercise, you upload and download configuration files and IOS system image files.

HTTP Access to the Switch

The Catalyst Web Interface (CWI), shown in Figure 1-28, is a browser-based tool that can be used to configure Catalyst 4000 family switches running CatOS. Note that each Catalyst platform has its own particular flavor of HTTP access. Communication between the client and server usually occurs on a TCP/IP connection. The TCP/IP port number for HTTP is 80. In this client/server mode, the client (browser) opens a connection to the server (switch) and sends a request. The server receives the request, sends a response to the client, and closes the connection.

CAUTION

TFTP servers are inherently weak in security. TFTP uses UDP port 69. It is highly recommended that you not keep your configuration files in a TFTP directory space until you need them. Anyone who compromises the TFTP server can modify the configuration files without approval. A prudent network administrator maintains configuration files in a secure directory space and copies them back to the TFTP directory space only when he or she is ready to use them. Although this adds another step to the recovery process, the security benefits definitely outweigh the procedural disadvantages.

Figure 1-28 The Catalyst Web Interface Includes the CiscoView GUI, Which Permits HTTP Configuration of Catalyst 4000 Family Switches Running CatOS

When you log into the switch via HTTP, a dialog box appears and prompts you for the device's username and password (the default authentication requires a password only). After you provide the correct username and password, the system authenticates the login with the HTTP user authentication method. The system denies access unless the username and password are valid. In the default configuration, verification is enabled for all users of the CWI. The system validates the login password against the enable password.

Note that the enable password is sent over the network in clear text. Therefore, the CWI is not a tool that should be used in a nonsecure environment.

To access the switch using HTTP, enter the switch IP address in the browser's Location field (Netscape) or Address field (Microsoft Internet Explorer), and then enter the switch password when prompted.

An opening screen with various options appears. Click the Web Console option to enter the mode that lets switch configurations be made.

Similar to CWI for 4000 family switches running CatOS, the Cisco Cluster Management Suite (CMS) software is web-based network management software embedded in Cisco Catalyst 2900XL, 2950, 3500XL, and 3550 switches. Also note that many Cisco vulnerabilities have been identified with the HTTP server functionality on Catalyst switches.

Lab 1.6.4   Introduction to Fluke Network Inspector

In this lab exercise, you learn how to use the Network Inspector (NI) from Fluke Networks to discover and analyze network devices in a broadcast domain.

Lab 1.6.5   Introduction to Fluke Protocol Expert

In this lab exercise, you learn how to use the Fluke Networks Optiview Protocol Expert (PE) to analyze network traffic and troubleshoot switched networks.

Summary

After completing this chapter, you should understand the following:

- Broadcasts are useful and necessary traffic. However, too much broadcast traffic can cause network performance problems. Managing broadcast traffic is a critical aspect of campus LAN design.
- The location of common workgroups and servers can have a significant impact on traffic patterns.

- Adding bandwidth is not necessarily the long-term solution to meeting the needs of high-priority traffic.

- Multilayer switching combines Layer 2 switching and Layer 3 routing functionality and caching of Layer 4 port information.

- The multilayer design model is inherently scalable. Layer 3 switching performance scales because it is distributed. Backbone performance scales as you add more links or switches.

- A switch block is the unit that contains distributed network services and network intelligence. A switch block consists of Layer 2 switches, Layer 3 switches, and sometimes distributed servers.

- A core block is the unit that transfers cross-campus traffic. It can consist of Layer 2 or Layer 3 devices.

- The purpose of network link redundancy is to provide alternative physical pathways through the network in case one pathway fails.

- How to make initial connections to the switch, connecting to the console port and an Ethernet port.

- Basic configuration of the switch includes
  - Clearing a configuration
  - Setting a password
  - Naming the switch
  - Configuring the switch for remote access
  - Identifying individual ports
  - Defining link speed and line mode on a switch

- Important IOS features include
  - Command-line recall
  - Using the help feature
  - Password recovery
  - Verifying connectivity
  - Saving the configuration
  - Backup and restoration of a configuration using a TFTP server

Key Terms

Application-Specific Integrated Circuit (ASIC) A chip designed for a particular application (as opposed to the integrated circuits that control functions such as RAM).

broadcast domain The set of all devices that receive broadcast frames originating from any device in the set. Broadcast domains are typically bounded by routers because routers do not forward broadcast frames.

Cisco Group Management Protocol (CGMP) A Cisco-developed protocol that runs between Cisco routers and Catalyst switches to leverage IGMP information on Cisco routers to make Layer 2 forwarding decisions on Catalyst switch ports that are attached to interested receivers.

collision domain In Ethernet, the network area within which frames that have collided are propagated. Repeaters and hubs propagate collisions; LAN switches, bridges, and routers do not.

flow A unidirectional sequence of packets between a particular source and destination that share the same Layer 3 and Layer 4 information.

Hot Standby Router Protocol (HSRP) Provides high network availability and transparent network topology changes. HSRP creates a hot standby router group with a lead router that services all packets sent to the hot standby address. The lead router is monitored by other routers in the group, and if it fails, one of these standby routers inherits the lead position and the hot standby group address.

Internet Control Message Protocol (ICMP) A network layer Internet protocol that reports errors and provides other information relevant to IP packet processing. Documented in RFC 792.

Internet Group Management Protocol (IGMP) Used by IP hosts to report their multicast group memberships to an adjacent multicast router.

nonblocking The ability to switch a packet immediately without encountering a busy condition.

Spanning Tree Protocol (STP) A bridge protocol that uses the spanning-tree algorithm, allowing a learning bridge to dynamically work around loops in a network topology by creating a spanning tree. Bridges exchange Bridge Protocol Data Unit (BPDU) messages with other bridges to detect loops and then remove the loops by shutting down selected bridge interfaces. STP refers to both the IEEE 802.1 Spanning Tree Protocol standard and the earlier Digital Equipment Corporation Spanning Tree Protocol on which it is based. The IEEE version supports bridge domains and allows the bridge to construct a loop-free topology across an extended LAN. The IEEE version is generally preferred over the Digital version.

VLAN Trunking Protocol (VTP)   A Cisco-proprietary protocol that uses Layer 2 trunk frames to communicate VLAN information among a group of switches and to manage the addition, deletion, and renaming of VLANs across the network from a central point of control.

Check Your Understanding

Use the following review questions to test your understanding of the concepts covered in this chapter. Answers are listed in Appendix A, "Check Your Understanding Answer Key."

1. Which of the following are key requirements in a modern campus network?

   A. Redundancy

   B. Scalability

   C. 80/20 rule

   D. Multicasting

2. Which of the following is not a category of service in a campus network?

   A. Local

   B. Geographic

   C. Remote

   D. Enterprise

3. Which of the following layers typically involve Layer 3 switching?

   A. Access

   B. Distribution

   C. Session

   D. Core

4. What layer is the point at which end users are allowed into the network?

   A. Access

   B. Distribution

   C. Session

   D. Core

5. Which of the following are backbone campus network solutions?

  A. Layer 2 switching

  B. Layer 3 switching

  C. Layer 4 switching

  D. ATM

6. What type of cable is used to configure Catalyst 2950 switches through a console connection?

  A. Coaxial

  B. Straight-through

  C. Crossover

  D. Rollover

7. What type of UTP cable can be used to connect FastEthernet ports on two Catalyst 3550 switches?

  A. Coaxial

  B. Straight-through

  C. Crossover

  D. Rollover

8. What two commands are used to restore a Catalyst 3550 switch to a default configuration?

  A. delete startup-config

  B. erase startup-config

  C. delete vlan.dat

  D. erase vlan.dat

9. Which of the following commands are used with password recovery on a Catalyst 2950 switch?

  A. flash_init

  B. load_helper

  C. rename

  D. boot

10. What command is used to set the port speed to 100 on a Catalyst 3550 10/100 interface?

   A. set speed

   B. speed

   C. bandwidth

   D. set bandwidth

Objectives

After completing this chapter, you will be able to perform tasks related to the following:

- Understand and explain the role of virtual LANs (VLANs) and VLAN protocols in modern campus networks.
- Know the definitions and understand the various ways in which VLANs are categorized.
- Configure VLANs.
- Describe situations in which VLANs are appropriate.
- Explain reasons not to use VLANs.
- Understand VLAN Membership Policy Server (VMPS).
- Understand and configure Dynamic Trunking Protocol (DTP).
- Understand and configure VLAN Trunking Protocol (VTP).

Chapter 2

VLANs and VTP

Promotion of *virtual LANs* (VLANs) in the 1990s by the trade journals and the workforce created confusion. Authors used different and inconsistent interpretations of the new network terminology. Vendors also took varied approaches to creating VLANs, which led to further confusion.

VLAN designs have changed over the last decade as a result of advances in technology. In the mid-1990s, deployment of campus-wide VLANs was acknowledged as the best design methodology. Local or geographic VLANs are now considered the better design methodology, because VLANs are separated by geographic location and not by function.

The speed of Layer 2 switching influenced campus-wide VLAN design. Multilayer switches can perform Layer 3 switching at rates approximating that of Layer 2 switching. Hardware-based Layer 3 switching provided speeds of hundreds of millions of packets per second (pps). Although campus-wide VLANs play a role in special circumstances, designing a stable, scalable campus network has become more important.

The CPU-intensive Spanning Tree Protocol (STP) essential to campus-wide VLANs causes convergence and redundancy problems in some large networks, making them susceptible to network instabilities. With the widespread adoption of high-performance Layer 3 switches, the campus-wide model has become obsolete and is no longer recommended in most network designs.

With a local VLAN model, Layer 3 switching allows the users' traffic to be carried based on the network layer address, such as the IP address. VLANs then become a simple mechanism of segmenting an IP subnet at Layer 2. For example, the 172.16.10.0/24 subnet is mapped to VLAN 10, the 172.16.20.0/24 subnet is mapped to VLAN 20, and so forth. A critical tenet of campus design declares that user VLANs terminate at a Layer 3 switch, which is typically located in a data center or basement of a building.

In this chapter, you learn how to do the following:

- Clarify the role of VLANs and VLAN protocols in modern campus networks.
- Present definitions and categorizations for VLANs.
- Explain how to configure VLANs.
- Describe situations in which VLANs are appropriate.
- Clarify misinformation about VLANs.
- Introduce VLAN management tools such as VLAN Trunking Protocol (VTP).

VLAN Basics

VLANs are pervasive in multilayer switched networks. This section introduces VLANs, the motivation for their use, and how they relate to security, broadcast domains, bandwidth utilization, and router latency.

Describe a VLAN

A VLAN is a logical construct that includes a group of hosts with a common set of requirements that communicate as if they were attached to the same wire, regardless of their physical location. A VLAN has the same attributes as a physical LAN, but it allows end stations to be grouped even if they are not located on the same physical LAN segment.

Networks that use the campus-wide or end-to-end VLANs logically segment a switched network based on an organization's functions, project teams, or applications, as shown in Figure 2-1, rather than on a physical or geographic basis. For example, all workstations and servers used by a particular workgroup can be connected to the same VLAN, regardless of their physical network connections or interaction with other workgroups. Network reconfiguration can be done through software instead of physically relocating devices.

Cisco recommends the use of local or geographic VLANs that segment the network based on Internet Protocol (IP) subnets. In Figure 2-2, each wiring closet switch is on its own VLAN or subnet, and traffic between each switch is routed by the router (except for the users in VLAN 10 on distinct access layer switches). The examples shown in Figures 2-1 and 2-2 do not show the entire network model. The reasons for the Layer 3 switch and examples of a larger network using both the campus-wide and local VLAN models are discussed in the later section "VLAN Types." VLAN member hosts are often dedicated to an access layer switch or a cluster of access layer switches.

Figure 2-1 Campus-Wide or End-to-End VLANs Can Span the Entire Campus Network and Are Not Limited by Geography

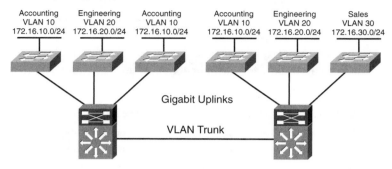

Figure 2-2 Local VLANs Based on Physical Location, in One-to-One Correspondence with IP Subnets, Are Now the Norm

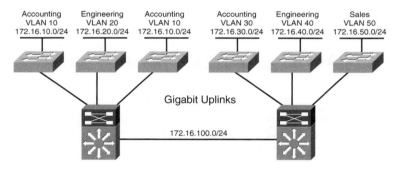

A VLAN can be thought of as a broadcast domain that exists within a defined set of switches. Ports on a switch can be grouped into VLANs to limit unicast, multicast, and broadcast traffic flooding. Flooded traffic originating from a particular VLAN is flooded only out ports belonging to that VLAN, including trunk ports (assuming that the trunk ports are configured to carry that VLAN traffic).

Any switch port can belong to a VLAN. Unicast, broadcast, and multicast packets are forwarded and flooded only to stations in the same VLAN. Each VLAN is a logical network, and packets destined for stations that do not belong to the same VLAN must be forwarded through a router or routing device. Each VLAN can also run a separate instance of STP. The technology that allows Cisco switches to support an independent implementation of STP for each VLAN is called Per-VLAN Spanning Tree (PVST).

VLANs are created to provide flexibility and the segmentation services traditionally provided by routers in LAN configurations. VLANs address scalability, security, and network management issues. Routers in VLAN topologies provide broadcast filtering, security, address summarization, and traffic flow management. By definition, switches cannot bridge IP traffic between VLANs because doing so would violate the integrity of the VLAN broadcast domain (although you can force the issue using Integrated Routing and Bridging). Normally, IP traffic is routed between VLANs.

VLANs are essentially Layer 2 constructs, and IP subnets are Layer 3 constructs. In a campus LAN employing VLANs, a one-to-one relationship often exists between VLANs and IP subnets. It is possible to have multiple subnets on one VLAN, and in some cases one subnet might be spread across multiple VLANs. Such cases are the exception, however, not the rule. VLANs and IP subnets provide an example of independent Layer 2 and Layer 3 constructs that normally map to one another. This correspondence is useful during the network design process. Network designers must consider several key issues when designing and building scalable multilayer switched internetworks. These issues are examined in the section "VLAN Types."

Motivation for VLANs

In a legacy network, administrators assign users to networks based on geography. The administrator attaches the user's workstation to the nearest network cable. If the user belongs to the engineering department and sits next to someone from the accounting department, they both belong to the same network because they attach to the same segment. Topologies such as this create interesting network issues and highlight some of the reasons for using VLANs. For example, the engineering group might require access to simulation and modeling programs that consume a lot of bandwidth, preventing the accountants from accessing relatively small spreadsheet documents. VLANs help resolve many of the problems associated with legacy network designs.

With VLANs, network managers can logically group networks that span all major topologies. This includes high-speed technologies such as

- ATM
- Fast Ethernet
- Gigabit Ethernet
- 10 Gigabit Ethernet

By creating VLANs, system and network administrators can control traffic patterns, react quickly to relocations, and keep up with constant changes in the network caused by moving requirements and node relocation. VLANs provide the flexibility to carry out these actions. The network administrator simply changes the VLAN member list in the switch configuration.

The administrator can add, remove, or move devices or make other changes to the network configuration using software. In addition to simplified administration, VLANs are also implemented for their increased security and their capability to contain broadcasts.

VLANs and Network Security

Almost everything in networking has a connection to security. With VLAN technology, security is essentially a side effect. With the exception of the *private VLANs* that are available on Catalyst 4000 and 6000 family switches, security was not originally a motivating factor for the creation of VLANs.

The shared-media nature of legacy networks is a security issue. Whenever a station transmits in a shared network, such as a legacy half-duplex 10BASE-T system, all stations attached to the segment receive a copy of the frame, even if they are not the intended recipients. This does not prevent the network from functioning, but readily available software packages that monitor network traffic make it possible for anyone to capture passwords, sensitive e-mail, and any other unencrypted traffic on the network.

If the users on the network belong to the same department, this might not be disastrous, but when users from mixed departments share a segment, sensitive information can be compromised. For example, if someone from human resources or accounting sends sensitive data such as salaries, stock options, or health records on the shared network, anyone with a network-monitoring tool on that LAN can intercept the information.

In fact, these problems are not constrained to a single LAN segment. They can occur in multisegment environments interconnected with routers. If the accounting department resides on two isolated segments, packets from one segment must cross the engineering network to reach the other accounting segment, as shown in Figure 2-3. When they cross the engineering segment, it is possible for that information to be intercepted and misused if someone has physical access to the switch on the engineering segment.

Figure 2-3 Traffic Can Be Intercepted When Hosts Reside on Intermediary Segments

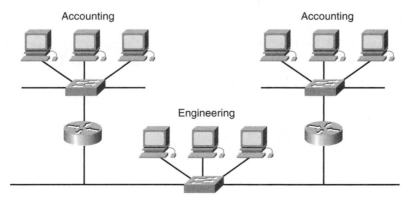

One way to eliminate the problem is to move all accounting users onto the same segment, but that might not be possible. Space limitations might prevent all accountants from sharing a common part of the building. Another reason might be the company's geographic makeup. Users on one segment might be a considerable distance from users on the other segment.

In most cases, assuming physical security of a switch and password-protected remote access, the issue of intercepting data because of shared-media technology should not be a problem. Virtually all hosts in modern networks reside on switched ports, so unicast data normally is not visible to any hosts except the sender and receiver. However, some applications can redirect data in a switched network to a single host. Without physical access to the switches, it should not be possible to intercept data in a switched environment, but a comprehensive security policy should take this possibility into account, especially if the LAN carries sensitive data.

Another approach to securing intersubnet traffic (as shown in Figure 2-3) is through the use of VLANs. VLANs add an additional layer of isolation between hosts and, therefore, make it much more difficult for data to be intercepted. All process-related users can be contained in the same broadcast domain and isolated from users in other broadcast domains. All the accounting users can be assigned to the same VLAN, regardless of their physical location in the facility. In fact, all the users can be assigned to VLANs based on their job function. For example, all the accounting users could go on one VLAN, the marketing users on another VLAN, and engineering on a third.

When VLANs are implemented with switched network devices, another level of protection is added to the network. Switches bridge traffic within a VLAN. When a station transmits, the frame goes to the intended destination. As long as it is a known unicast frame, the switch does not distribute the frame to all users in the VLAN.

Station A transmits a frame to Station B, attached to another switch, as shown in Figure 2-4. Although the frame crosses through a switch, only the destination receives a copy of the frame. The switch does not send the frame to the other stations, whether they belong to a different VLAN or the same VLAN. Assuming that physical access to the switches is not possible, this switch feature limits the opportunity for packets to be captured with a network analyzer.

Hosts on different VLANs cannot communicate with each other unless the network is explicitly configured to allow it. If the network has a one-to-one mapping between IP subnets and VLANs, hosts on different VLANs must communicate through IP routing. In this case, access control lists (ACLs) can filter traffic between VLANs. It is possible to configure VLANs without inter-VLAN routing among user VLANs, but this is rarely done.

Figure 2-4 Normally, Unicast Traffic Cannot Be Intercepted by a Host Connected to the Same
Switch as Unicast Traffic Traversing the Same Switch

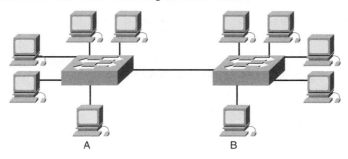

A   B

Another case where VLANs play a definitive role in network security is the capability to configure ACLs on switches. This is discussed in the section "Understanding Switch ACLs" and in Chapter 9, "Monitoring and Security."

Although these security methods might seem excessive, in the corporate network they are crucial. Consider the data transferred within a company's accounting department. This department has salary information, stock option information, personal information, and other sensitive and personal material. It is very important to protect the users' privacy and the data's integrity. VLANs greatly assist in this endeavor.

VLANs and Broadcast Distribution

Practically every network protocol creates broadcast traffic. AppleTalk hosts, Microsoft hosts, and Novell servers create broadcasts to announce or request services. Furthermore, multimedia applications create broadcast and multicast frames that are distributed across the broadcast domain.

Broadcasts are necessary to support protocol operations and, therefore, are acceptable overhead in the network. So why do network administrators dislike broadcast traffic? Broadcasts go to all devices in the broadcast domain and must be processed by the receiving devices. With the exception of multimedia-based traffic, broadcast frames rarely transport user data. Because switches flood broadcasts, they consume bandwidth in the LAN, resulting in a reduction of the bandwidth for productive traffic.

Broadcasts also have a profound effect on the performance of workstations. Any broadcast received by a workstation interrupts the CPU and prevents it from working on user applications. As the number of broadcasts per second increases at the interface, effective CPU utilization diminishes. The actual level of degradation depends on the applications running in the workstation, the type of network interface card and drivers, the operating system, and the workstation platform.

VLANs form broadcast domains. Broadcasts and multicasts are not propagated between VLANs unless the intermediary network devices are specifically configured to do so (see Figure 2-5). If broadcasts and multicasts are creating problems in the network, creating smaller broadcast domains can mitigate the negative effects. This means creating additional VLANs and attaching fewer devices to each one. The effectiveness of this action depends on the source of the broadcast. If a local server is sending broadcast traffic, that server should be isolated in another broadcast domain. If the broadcasts and multicasts come from end stations, creating additional VLANs helps reduce the number of broadcasts in each domain.

Figure 2-5 Broadcasts Originating in a VLAN Do Not Propagate Beyond That VLAN's Boundary

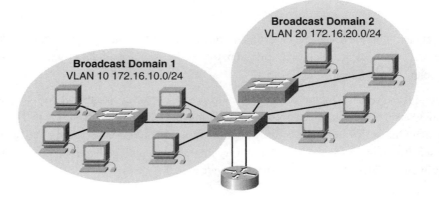

VLANs and Bandwidth Utilization

When users attach to the same shared segment, they all share the segment's bandwidth. With every additional user on the shared medium, less bandwidth is available for each user. User network and application performance begin to diminish if the bandwidth sharing becomes too great. The network administrator needs to take action because the users will be less productive. VLANs can offer more bandwidth to users than is inherent in a shared network; VLANs do this by limiting the size of each broadcast domain.

Remember that each interface on a switch behaves like a port on a legacy bridge. Bridges filter traffic for the source segment. If a frame needs to cross the bridge, the bridge forwards the frame to the correct interface. If the bridge or switch does not know the destination port, it floods the frame to all ports in the broadcast domain (VLAN) except the source port. By assigning ports on a switch to different VLANs, you can limit the number of switch ports to which data traffic is flooded.

In a switched environment, a station usually sees only traffic destined specifically for it. The switch filters most of the other background traffic in the network, which allows the workstation to have full, dedicated bandwidth for sending or receiving traffic. Unlike a shared-hub system, in which only one station can transmit at a time, a switched network allows many concurrent transmissions within a broadcast domain without directly affecting other stations inside or outside the broadcast domain. In Figure 2-6, station pairs A/B, C/D, and E/F can all communicate without affecting the other station pairs.

Figure 2-6 Internal Switched Virtual Circuits Permit Simultaneous Transmissions Between Pairs of Hosts

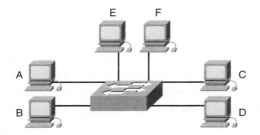

VLANs Versus Router Latency

In a traditional routed network, packets going between networks have to be routed by a router. Every router that handles the data increases the end-to-end latency. Latency constitutes the amount of time necessary to transport a frame from the source port to the destination port. The latency could be reduced by replacing the routers with Layer 2 switches, but the network would then become a single broadcast domain and lose other advantages of Layer 3 segmentation such as security management and traffic filtering. VLANs have the advantages of the decreased latency of Layer 2 switching and the segmentation of Layer 3 routing.

Campus-wide VLANs were once the answer to Layer 3 latency, but they introduced their own complexities into the network. Campus-wide VLANs are still appropriate in some circumstances; however, Cisco recommends designing networks using the local VLAN model. The local VLAN model has VLANs dedicated to each access layer switch cluster, with Layer 3 switching between wiring closets performed at the distribution layer or Main Distribution Facility (MDF). As illustrated in Figure 2-7, inter-VLAN routing is provided by Layer 3 switches, which are connected by IP subnets instead of the traditional VLAN trunks. With both the local VLAN and campus-wide VLAN model, VLANs have many advantages over traditional switched networks, including segmentation of broadcast domains.

Figure 2-7 VLANs in Modern Campus Networks Are Local to Access Layer Switches

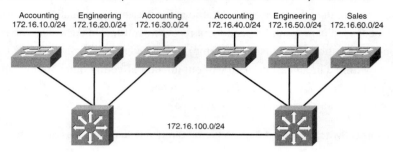

In modern campus operations, Layer 3 latency issues become rare as a result of multilayer switching (MLS). MLS enables hardware-based routing. In Cisco switches that support MLS, the router routes the first packet in software, and the switch handles subsequent packets in hardware. Newer Cisco switches, such as the Catalyst 3550 and 6500, use Cisco Express Forwarding (CEF). CEF uses a method of communicating information between the routing table and CEF tables that allows packets to be forwarded by the switches without routing table lookups. Chapter 5, "Multilayer Switching," discusses MLS and CEF in more detail.

Wrong Motives for Implementing VLANs

The advent of VLANs led many to believe that a network administrator's life would be simplified, which was to be a welcome relief. Many network administrators believed that VLANs would eliminate, to some extent, the need for routers. They also believed that because campus-wide VLANs place all users in one large flat network, many long hours of network administration would be eliminated. This turned out to be far from the truth and, unfortunately, enthusiasm quickly met reality. VLANs do not eliminate Layer 3 issues. They might ease some Layer 3 tasks, such as enabling the use of simpler access lists, but routing is still a necessity. Last, contrary to expectations, network monitoring is more challenging with a VLAN-based network than with a traditional routed network, because VLANs permit much more complex logical designs.

VLAN Security

Network security is becoming more pervasive in network design. VLAN implementation must be factored into the network security policy. This section explores the relationship between VLANs and network security.

Overview

Routers allow administrators to introduce policies that control the flow of traffic in the network. ACLs control traffic flow and provide varied degrees of policy granularity. ACLs can prevent a specific user from communicating with another user or network, or they can prevent an entire network from accessing a user or network. ACLs are sometimes implemented for security reasons, and they are also used to prevent traffic from flowing through a segment to protect local bandwidth.

In any case, the management of ACLs can be quite cumbersome. ACLs in a production network should be based on the organization's business and security needs.

To safeguard the accounting department's data, filters in the routers attached to the engineering segment can include ACLs, allowing the accounting traffic to pass through the engineering segment, but never talk to any engineering devices (see Figure 2-8). That does not prevent engineers from monitoring the traffic (using Catalyst Switched Port Analyzer [SPAN] technology, for example), but it does prevent explicit communication between the engineering and accounting devices. Accounting does not see the engineering traffic, but engineering can see all the accounting transit traffic using Catalyst SPAN technology, introduced in Chapter 9.

Figure 2-8 ACLs Can Prevent Accounting Data from Being Transferred to the Engineering
Department

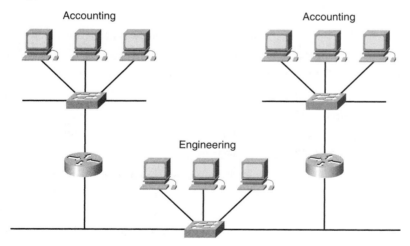

Switches traditionally operate at Layer 2 only, switching traffic within a VLAN, whereas routers route traffic between VLANs. The Catalyst 3550 switch with the Enhanced Multilayer Image (EMI) installed and the Catalyst 6500 switches with the Supervisor Engine 720 can accelerate packet routing between VLANs by using Layer 3 switching. The process of routing traffic between VLANs is as follows:

1. The switch bridges the packet.

2. The packet is routed internally without going to an external router.

3. The packet is bridged again to send it to its destination.

During this process, the switch can enforce ACLs on all packets it switches, including packets bridged within a VLAN.

Layer 3 switching uses the traditional combination of external router and Layer 2 switch, also known as "router-on-a-stick," into a single device. ACLs can be configured on a Layer 3 switch to provide basic security and traffic management for the network.

Understanding Switch ACLs

Packet filtering can help limit network traffic and restrict network use by certain users or devices. ACLs can filter traffic as it passes through a router and permit or deny packets from crossing specified interfaces. An ACL contains an ordered list of access control entries (ACEs), also called access control entities. Each ACE specifies **permit** or **deny** and a set of conditions the packet must satisfy to match the ACE. The meaning of **permit** or **deny** depends on the context in which the ACL is used.

ACLs on switches function very much like those on a router. When a frame is received on an interface, the switch compares the fields in the frame against any applied ACLs to verify that it should be forwarded, based on the criteria specified in the ACLs. It tests frames against the conditions in an ACL one by one.

The first match determines whether the switch accepts or rejects the packets. Because the switch stops testing conditions after the first match, the order of conditions in the list is critical. If no conditions match, the switch rejects the packets.

If a switch is not configured with ACLs, all packets passing it are allowed onto all parts of the network. ACLs can be used to control which hosts can access different parts of a network or to decide which types of traffic are forwarded or blocked at router interfaces. For example, a Layer 3 switch can be configured to allow e-mail traffic to be forwarded but not Telnet traffic. ACLs can be configured to block inbound traffic, outbound traffic, or both.

The Catalyst 3550 and 6500 switches support two types of ACLs:

- IP ACLs filter IP traffic, including Transmission Control Protocol (TCP), User Datagram Protocol (UDP), Internet Group Management Protocol (IGMP), and Internet Control Message Protocol (ICMP).
- Ethernet ACLs filter non-IP traffic.

Catalyst 6500 switches also support Internetwork Packet Exchange (IPX) ACLs. The 2950 switch with the enhanced image supports only IP ACLs.

Catalyst 3550 and 6500 switches support two applications of ACLs to filter traffic:

- Router ACLs
- VLAN ACLs

Catalyst 3550 and 6500 switches also support quality of service (QoS) ACLs, which are used to implement QoS features.

Router ACLs filter routed traffic between VLANs. For a Catalyst 3550 to filter packets routed between VLANs, it must be running EMI.

VLAN ACLs, also called *VLAN maps*, filter both bridged and routed packets. VLAN maps can be used to filter packets exchanged between devices in the same VLAN. Unlike router ACLs, a switch does not need to run EMI software to use VLAN maps. VLAN maps are configured to provide access control based on Layer 3 IP addresses. Frames for non-IP protocols can be filtered based on their Media Access Control (MAC) addresses, using Ethernet ACEs. An ACE is a single line in an ACL.

When a VLAN map is applied to a VLAN, all packets (routed or bridged) entering the VLAN are checked against the VLAN map. Packets can enter the VLAN either through a switch port or through a routed port.

Router ACLs and VLAN Maps

Router ACLs are applied to switch virtual interfaces (SVIs), which are Layer 3 VLAN interfaces. Router ACLs are also applied to physical Layer 3 interfaces and to Layer 3 EtherChannel interfaces. Router ACLs are applied on interfaces as either inbound or outbound.

One ACL can be used with multiple features for a given interface, and one feature can use multiple ACLs. When a single router ACL is used by multiple features, such as for QoS and security, it is examined multiple times.

Standard IP access lists use source addresses for matching operations. Extended IP access lists use source and destination addresses and optional protocol type information for matching operations.

The switch examines ACLs associated with features configured on a given interface with a specific direction. As packets enter the switch on an interface, ACLs associated with all inbound features configured on that interface are examined. After packets are routed and before they are forwarded out to the next hop, all ACLs associated with outbound features configured on the egress interface are examined.

ACLs permit or deny packet forwarding based on how the packet matches the entries in the ACL. For example, ACLs can be used to allow one host to access part of a network but prevent another host from accessing the same part. In Figure 2-9, ACLs applied at the router input allow Host A to access the Human Resources network but prevent Host B from accessing the same network.

Figure 2-9 Router ACLs Are Applied to Switch Virtual Interfaces and Routed Ports

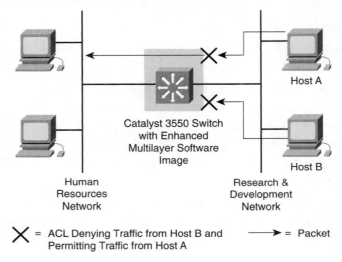

ACLs permit or deny packet forwarding based on how the packet matches the entries in

VLAN maps can filter all traffic received by the switch. VLAN maps are applied to all packets that are routed into or out of a VLAN or are bridged within a VLAN. VLAN maps are used strictly for security packet filtering. Unlike router ACLs, VLAN maps are not defined by direction (inbound or outbound).

VLAN maps can be configured to match Layer 3 addresses for IP traffic. All non-IP protocols are filtered through MAC addresses and Ethertype using MAC VLAN maps. IP traffic is not access-controlled by MAC VLAN maps. VLAN maps can be enforced only on packets going through the switch. They cannot be enforced on traffic between hosts on a hub or on another switch connected to the switch on which the VLAN map is applied.

With VLAN maps, packets are forwarded or dropped based on the action specified in the map. In Figure 2-10, a VLAN map is applied to deny a specific type of traffic from Host A in VLAN 10 from being forwarded.

Figure 2-10 VLAN Maps or VLAN ACLs (VACLs) Can Perform Intra-VLAN Filtering

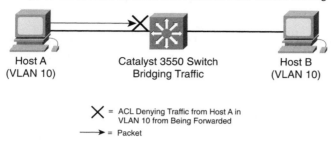

Host A
(VLAN 10)

Catalyst 3550 Switch
Bridging Traffic

Host B
(VLAN 10)

✗ = ACL Denying Traffic from Host A in
    VLAN 10 from Being Forwarded
⟶ = Packet

Configuring Router ACLs

Router ACLs are configured on Layer 3 SVIs with the same commands used to configure ACLs on Cisco routers. The process is briefly described here.

Catalyst 3550 switches do not support all IOS router ACL-related features. They do not support the following:

- Non-IP protocol ACLs
- Bridge-group ACLs
- IP accounting
- Rate limiting (except with QoS ACLs)
- IP packets with a header length of less than 5
- Reflexive ACLs
- Dynamic ACLs (except for certain specialized dynamic ACLs used by the *clustering* feature on the switch)

Standard and extended IP router ACLs are created on the switch just as they are on a router.

In addition to numbered standard and extended ACLs, standard and extended named and time-range ACLs are available.

Here are the basic two steps involved in using ACLs:

Step 1   Create an ACL by specifying an access list number or name and access conditions.

Step 2   Apply the ACL to an interface, terminal line, or VLAN map.

Existing ACLs can be displayed by using **show** commands.

The **show access-lists** command displays information about all IP and MAC ACLs or about a specific ACL.

NOTE

For more detailed information on configuring router ACLs, refer to the Cisco IOS Security Configuration Guide, Release 12.3 at http//www.cisco.com. For detailed information about the commands, refer to the Cisco IOS Security Command Reference, 12.3.

The **show ip access-lists** command displays information about all IP ACLs or about a specific IP ACL.

The **show ip interface** command can be used to view the input and output access groups on the interface, as well as other interface characteristics. If IP is not enabled on the interface, the access groups are not shown.

A Catalyst 3550 switch has a routed port, interface GigabitEthernet 0/2, connected to Server A, as shown in Figure 2-11. Server A has benefits information and other documentation on it that all employees can access. The switch also has routed port 0/3 connected to Server B, which contains confidential payroll data. All users can access Server A, but Server B has restricted access.

Figure 2-11 ACLs on Switches Can Restrict Access Between Subnets Just as They Would on a Router

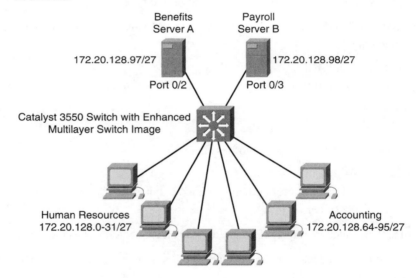

Use router ACLs to do this in one of two ways:

- Create a standard ACL and filter traffic coming to the server from port 0/3.
- Create an extended ACL and filter traffic coming from the server into port 0/3.

Example 2-1 uses a standard ACL to filter traffic coming into Server B from port 0/3, permitting traffic only from hosts in the Accounting department, which have source addresses 172.20.128.64 to 172.20.128.95.

Example 2-1 *A Standard ACL Filters Traffic to Server B*

```
Switch(config)#access-list 6 permit 172.20.128.64 0.0.0.31
Switch(config)#end
Switch#show access-list
Standard IP access list 6 permit 172.20.128.64, wildcard bits 0.0.0.31
Switch#configure terminal
Switch(config)#interface gigabitethernet0/3
Switch(config-if)#ip access-group 6 out
```

The ACL is applied to traffic coming out of routed port 0/3. Only traffic from the specified source address is permitted.

Example 2-2 uses an extended ACL to filter traffic coming from Server B into port 0/3, permitting traffic from any source address (in this case, Server B) to only the Accounting destination addresses 172.20.128.64 to 172.20.128.95.

Example 2-2 *An Extended ACL Filters Traffic to Server B*

```
Switch(config)#access-list 106 permit ip any 172.20.128.64 0.0.0.31
Switch(config)#end
Switch#show access-list
Extended IP access list 106 permit ip any 172.20.128.64 0.0.0.31
Switch#configure terminal
Switch(config)#interface gigabitethernet0/3
Switch(config-if)#ip access-group 106 in
```

NOTE

Refer to the Catalyst 2950 Desktop Switch Software Configuration Guide, Catalyst 3550 Multilayer Switch Software Configuration Guide, and Catalyst 6500 Series Software Configuration Guide for additional information about configuring ACLs and examples.

The ACL is then applied to traffic going into routed port 0/3, permitting it to go only to the specified destination addresses. Remember that with extended ACLs, a protocol must be entered before the source and destination information.

Configuring VLAN Maps

This section briefly describes how to configure VLAN maps, which is the only way to control filtering within a VLAN. VLAN maps have no direction. To filter traffic in a specific direction using a VLAN map, you must configure an ACL with a specific source or destination address. Unlike router ACLs, the default action for VLAN maps is to forward. This action is taken if the packet does not match any of the entries within the map.

Each VLAN map consists of an ordered series of entries. A packet that comes into the switch is tested against the first entry in the VLAN map. If the packet matches the first VLAN map entry, the action specified for that part of the VLAN map is taken. If no action is specified, the default action is to forward. If no match occurs, the packet is tested against the next entry in the map. If no entries match, the implicit forward default applies. Beginning in privileged EXEC mode, follow the steps listed in Table 2-1 to create, add to, or delete a VLAN map entry.

To create a VLAN map and apply it to one or more VLANs, follow these steps:

Step 1 Create the standard or extended IP ACLs or named MAC extended ACLs that will be applied to the VLAN.

Step 2 Enter the **vlan access-map** global configuration command to create a VLAN ACL map entry.

Step 3 In access map configuration mode, optionally enter an action, either drop or forward, and enter the **match** command to match the packet against one or more access lists.

Step 4 Use the **vlan filter** global configuration command to apply a VLAN map to one or more VLANs.

Remember that VLAN maps have an implicit forward feature at the end of the list; a packet is forwarded if it does not match any ACL within the VLAN map.

Follow these guidelines when configuring VLAN maps:

- If no router ACL is configured to deny traffic on a routed VLAN interface, and no VLAN map is configured, all traffic is permitted.
- As with ACLs, the order of entries in a VLAN map is important.
- The system might take longer to boot if a large number of ACLs have been configured.

Use the **no vlan access-map** *name* command to delete a map.

Use the **no vlan access-map** *name number* command to delete a single sequence entry from within the map.

Use the **no action** command to enforce the default action, which is to forward.

VLAN maps do not use the specific **permit** or **deny** keywords. To deny a packet by using VLAN maps, create an ACL that would match the packet, and set the **action** to **drop**. A **permit** in the ACL counts as a match. A **deny** in the ACL means no match.

Example 2-3 shows how to create an ACL and a VLAN map to deny a packet. In this example, any packets that match the ip1 ACL (TCP packets) are dropped. First, create the IP ACL to permit any TCP packet and no other packets; then set the action for packets that match the permit list to be dropped.

Table 2-1 The VLAN Map Syntax Involves Configuring a List of Action and Match Entries for Data

Step	Command	Description
1	**configure terminal**	Enters global configuration mode.
2	**vlan access-map** *name* [*number*]	Changes to access map configuration mode. It creates a VLAN map and gives it a name and (optionally) a number. The number is the sequence number of the entry within the map. When creating VLAN maps with the same name, numbers are created sequentially in increments of 10. When modifying or deleting maps, enter the number of the map entry to be modified or deleted.
3	**action** [**drop** ǀ **forward**]	(Optional) Sets the action for the map entry. The default is to forward.
4	**match** {**ip address** ǀ **mac address**} {*name* ǀ *number*} [*name* ǀ *number*]	Matches the packet (using either the IP or MAC address) against one or more standard or extended ACLs. Note that packets are matched only against ACLs of the correct protocol type. IP packets are matched against standard or extended IP ACLs. Non-IP packets are matched only against named MAC extended ACLs.
5	**end**	Returns to global configuration mode.
6	**show running-config**	Displays the ACL configuration.
7	**copy running-config startup-config**	(Optional) Saves the configuration file.

Example 2-3 *Named ACLs Are Convenient for Use in VLAN Maps to Specify Traffic to Drop or Forward. In This Case, All TCP Traffic Is Dropped.*

```
Switch(config)#ip access-list extended ip1
Switch(config-ext-nacl)#permit tcp any any
Switch(config-ext-nacl)#exit
Switch(config)#vlan access-map map_1 10
Switch(config-access-map)#match ip address ip1
Switch(config-access-map)#action drop
```

Example 2-4 shows how to create a VLAN map to permit a packet. In this example, ip2 permits UDP packets, and any packets that match the ip2 ACL are forwarded.

Example 2-4 *Traffic That Does Not Match an Entry in a VLAN Map Is Forwarded. Continuing from Example 2-3, the Following Results in All Non-TCP Traffic Being Forwarded.*

```
Switch(config)#ip access-list extended ip2
Switch(config-ext-nacl)#permit udp any any
Switch(config-ext-nacl)#exit
Switch(config)#vlan access-map map_1 20
Switch(config-access-map)#match ip address ip2
Switch(config-access-map)#action forward
```

In Example 2-5, any packets that do not match any of the previous ACLs (that is, packets that are not TCP packets or UDP packets) are dropped.

Example 2-5 *Continuing from Examples 2-3 and 2-4, the Following Results in All Traffic Being Dropped Except UDP Traffic*

```
Switch(config)#vlan access-map map_1 30
Switch(config-access-map)#action drop
```

Beginning in privileged EXEC mode, follow the steps listed in Table 2-2 to apply a VLAN map to one or more VLANs.

Table 2-2 VLAN Maps Are Applied to VLANs in Global Configuration Mode

Step	Command	Description
1	**configure terminal**	Enters global configuration mode.
2	**vlan filter** *mapname* **vlan-list** *list*	Applies the VLAN map to one or more VLAN IDs. The list can be a single VLAN ID (**22**), a consecutive list (**10-22**), or a string of VLAN IDs (**12, 22, 30**). Spaces around the comma and hyphen are optional.
3	**show running-config**	Displays the ACL configuration.
4	**copy running-config startup-config**	(Optional) Saves the configuration file.

Example 2-6 shows how to apply VLAN map 1 to VLANs 20 to 22.

Example 2-6 *Applying a VLAN Map Requires Only One Command*

```
Switch(config)#vlan filter map 1 vlan-list 20-22
```

To display information about VLAN access maps or VLAN filters, use the appropriate **show** command from privileged EXEC mode.

The **show vlan access-map** [*mapname*] command displays information about all VLAN access maps or a specified access map.

The **show vlan filter** [**access-map** *name* | **vlan** *vlan-id*] command displays information about all VLAN filters or about a specified VLAN access map or VLAN.

Example 2-7 illustrates some **show** commands for ACLs and VLAN maps.

Example 2-7 *Several* **show** *Commands Are Available for Verifying ACLs and VLAN Maps*

```
Switch#show access-list
Extended MAC access list mac1
deny any any decnet-iv
permit any any
Switch#show vlan access-map
Vlan access-map "map_1" 10
Match clauses:
ip address: ip1
Action:
drop
Vlan access-map "map_1" 20
Match clauses:
mac address: mac1
Action:
forward
Vlan access-map "map_1" 30
Match clauses:
Action:
drop
Switch#show vlan filter
VLAN Map map_1 is filtering VLANs:
20-22
```

Lab 2.9.4   Catalyst 2950 and 3550 Series Intra-VLAN Security

In this lab exercise, you configure intra-VLAN security with ACLs using command-line interface (CLI) mode.

Using VLAN Maps with Router ACLs

To filter both bridged and routed traffic, VLAN maps can be used by themselves or in conjunction with router ACLs. Router ACLs can be applied on both input and output routed VLAN interfaces, and a VLAN map can be used to filter the bridged traffic.

If a packet flow matches a VLAN map deny clause in the ACL, regardless of the router ACL configuration, the packet is dropped.

When using router ACLs with VLAN maps, packets that require logging on the router ACLs are not logged if they are denied by a VLAN map.

Remember, VLAN maps have a default action of forward, so a packet is forwarded if it does not match any VLAN map entry.

These guidelines are for configurations where a router ACL and a VLAN map need to be applied on the same VLAN. These guidelines do not apply to configurations where router ACLs and VLAN maps are used on different VLANs.

The switch hardware provides one lookup for security ACLs for each direction, input and output. As a result, a router ACL and a VLAN map must be merged when they are configured on the same VLAN.

Merging the router ACL with the VLAN map might significantly increase the number of ACEs.

If a router ACL and a VLAN map must be configured on the same VLAN, use the following guidelines for both router ACL and VLAN map configuration:

- Whenever possible, try to write the ACL with all entries having a single action except for the final default action of the other type. That is, write the ACL using one of these two forms:

```
permit...
permit...
permit...
deny ip any any
```

or

```
deny...
deny...
deny...
permit ip any any
```

- To define multiple permit and deny actions in an ACL, group each action type to reduce the number of entries.
- Avoid including Layer 4 information in an ACL.
- Use wildcard masks in the IP address whenever possible.

The best merge results are obtained if the ACLs are filtered based on source or destination IP addresses and not on the full flow (source IP address, destination IP address, protocol, and protocol ports). If the full flow must be specified, and the ACL contains both IP ACEs and TCP/UDP/ICMP ACEs with Layer 4 information, put the Layer 4 ACEs at the end of the list. This gives priority to the filtering of traffic based on IP addresses.

ACL processing in the 3550 switch is done mostly in hardware, but if the hardware exceeds its capacity to store ACL configurations, the switch software attempts to fit a simpler configuration into hardware. This simpler configuration does not do all the filtering that has been configured, but instead sends some or all packets to the CPU to be filtered by software. All configured filtering is accomplished, but performance is greatly decreased when the filtering is done in software.

Any problem in fitting the configuration into hardware is logged, but it is possible that not everyone who configures the switch can see the log messages as they occur. The **show fm** command displays feature manager information for the interface or the VLAN. The **show fm vlan** *vlan-id* and **show fm interface** *interface-id* commands can be executed from privileged mode to determine if any interface or VLAN configuration did not fit into hardware. Example 2-8 shows some sample output.

Example 2-8 *An ACL Configuration Conflict Exists*

```
Switch#show fm vlan 1
Conflicts exist with layer 2 access groups.
Input VLAN Label:1
Output VLAN Label:0 (default)
Priority:normal
```

The **show fm** command is also used to determine what label is used in the hardware for the interface or VLAN configuration. VLAN labels are used for features configured on VLANs, such as router ACLs and VLAN maps. The VLAN label ID range is from 0 to 255. The **show fm vlan-label** *label-id* command displays what features associated with that label cannot fit in the hardware or if configuration conflicts have occurred, as shown in Example 2-9.

Example 2-9 *A Merge Failure on an Input Access Group*

```
Switch#show fm vlan-label 1
Unloaded due to merge failure or lack of space:
  InputAccessGroup
  Merge Fail:input
Input Features:
  Interfaces or VLANs: Vl1
  Priority:normal
  Vlan Map:(none)
  Access Group:131, 6788 VMRs
  Multicast Boundary:(none), 0 VMRs
Output Features:
  Interfaces or VLANs:
  Priority:low
  Bridge Group Member:no
  Vlan Map:(none)
  Access Group:(none), 0 VMRs
```

Applying Router ACLs and VLAN Maps on VLANs

This section contains examples of applying router ACLs and VLAN maps to a VLAN for switched, bridged, routed, and multicast packets. Although the following figures show packets being forwarded to their destination, each time the packet's path crosses a line indicating a VLAN map or an ACL, it is also possible that the packet might be dropped rather than forwarded.

Packets switched within the VLAN without being routed are subject only to the VLAN map of the input VLAN, as shown in Figure 2-12.

For routed packets, the ACLs are applied in the following order, as shown in Figure 2-13:

1. VLAN map for input VLAN

2. Input router ACL

3. Output router ACL

4. VLAN map for output VLAN

Figure 2-12 Switched Packets Are Affected Only by VLAN Maps

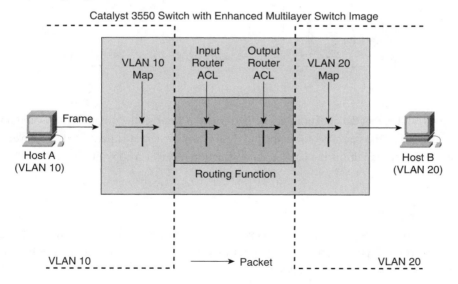

Figure 2-13 Routed Packets Can Be Filtered by Multiple VLAN Maps and Incoming and Outgoing ACLs

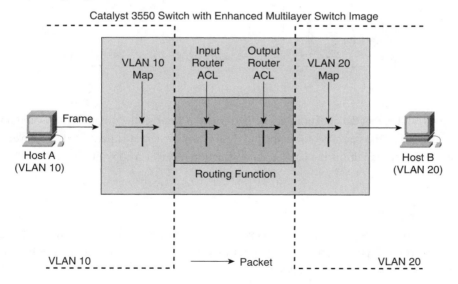

A multicast packet that is being routed has two different types of filters applied:

- One for destinations that are other ports in the input VLAN
- Another for each of the destinations that are in other VLANs to which the packet has been routed

The packet might be routed to more than one output VLAN, in which case a different router output ACL and VLAN map would apply for each destination VLAN, as shown in Figure 2-14.

Figure 2-14 Multicast Packets Are Subject to VLAN Maps and Might Also Be Subject to ACLs, Depending on Their Destination

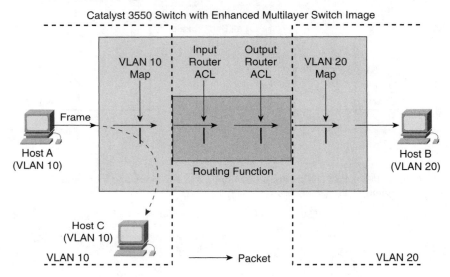

The final result is that the packet might be permitted in some of the output VLANs and not in others. A copy of the packet is forwarded to destinations where it is permitted. However, if the input VLAN map drops the packet, no destination receives a copy of the packet.

VLAN Types

VLANs can be implemented in various ways. This section describes different types of VLAN implementations. First, campus-wide VLANs versus local VLANs are explored, followed by static VLANs versus dynamic VLANs.

VLAN Boundaries

Just as routing protocols are classified in various ways, so are VLANs. VLANs are classified as local (geographic) or end-to-end (campus-wide). Alternatively, VLANs are classified as either port-based (static) or dynamic.

The number of VLANs in the switch block might vary greatly, depending on several factors:

- Traffic patterns
- Types of applications
- Network management needs
- Group commonality

In addition, an important consideration in defining the size of the switch block and the number of VLANs is the IP addressing scheme.

For example, suppose a network uses a 24-bit mask to define a subnet. Given this criterion, a total of 254 host addresses are allowed in one subnet. Because a one-to-one correspondence between VLANs and IP subnets is strongly recommended, there can be no more than 254 devices in any one VLAN. It is further recommended that VLANs should not extend outside the Layer 2 domain of the distribution switch. With many users spread across three departments in one building, four VLANs would be required under the recommended constraints, as shown in Figure 2-15.

Figure 2-15 Modern Campus Networks Employ a One-to-One Correspondence Between IP Subnets and VLANs

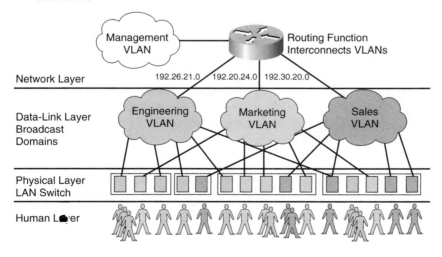

When scaling VLANs in the switch block, there are two basic methods of defining the VLAN boundaries:

- End-to-end VLANs
- Local VLANs

End-to-End VLANs

VLANs can exist either as end-to-end networks (campus-wide) or inside limited geographic (local) boundaries. An *end-to-end VLAN* network has the following characteristics:

- Users are grouped into VLANs independent of physical location and dependent on group or job function.
- All users in a VLAN should have the same 80/20 traffic flow patterns.
- As a user moves around the campus, VLAN membership for that user should not change.
- Each VLAN has a common set of security requirements for all members.

Backbone links in a switched LAN should be faster than access level links, as shown in Figure 2-16. Starting in the wiring closet, 100-Mbps dedicated Ethernet ports are provisioned for each user. Each VLAN corresponds to a subnet and, because people have moved around over time, each switch eventually becomes a member of all VLANs. Fast Ethernet *Inter-Switch Link (ISL)* or IEEE 802.1Q is used to carry multiple VLAN information between the wiring closets and the distribution layer switches.

Figure 2-16 Uplinks Should Provide Greater Bandwidth Than Access Links

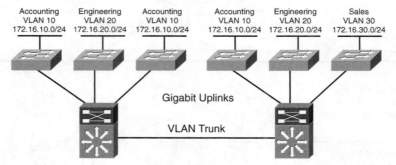

ISL is a Cisco-proprietary protocol that maintains VLAN information as traffic flows between switches and routers. *IEEE 802.1Q* is an open-standard VLAN tagging mechanism that predominates in modern switching installations. VLAN tagging mechanisms are explored later in this chapter in the section "VLAN Identification."

Workgroup servers operate in a client/server model, and attempts have been made to keep users in the same VLAN as their server to maximize the performance of Layer 2 switching, and keep traffic localized.

In the core, a router allows intersubnet communication. The network is engineered in the campus-wide VLAN model, based on traffic flow patterns, to have 80 percent of the traffic within a VLAN and 20 percent crossing the router to the enterprise servers and to the Internet and WAN. End-to-end VLANs allow devices to be grouped based on resource usage. This includes such parameters as server usage, project teams, and departments. The goal of end-to-end VLANs is to maintain 80 percent of the traffic on the local VLAN.

As corporate networks move to centralize their resources, end-to-end VLANs have become more difficult to maintain. Users are required to use many different resources, many of which are no longer in their VLAN. Because of this shift in placement and usage of resources, VLANs now are frequently created around geographic (local) boundaries rather than commonality boundaries.

Local VLANs

The *local VLAN* model has VLANs dedicated to each access layer switch cluster, with Layer 3 switching between wiring closets performed at the distribution layer or Main Distribution Facility (MDF), as shown in Figure 2-17. With the campus-wide VLAN model, users who are in the same department would be in the same VLAN regardless of the location of the VLAN in the network. In the local VLAN model, users in the same department are in the same VLAN only if their access layer switches are connected to the same distribution layer switch (see Figure 2-17). If the access layer switch is connected to a different distribution layer switch, the users are assigned a different VLAN ID and subnet address, regardless of the users' department.

NOTE

If an access layer switch has only users who belong to a single VLAN, it is not necessary to configure those interfaces for the specific VLAN. However, some network administrators assign these interfaces to their proper VLAN in case the switch has other VLANs configured on it in the future (see Figure 2-18).

Figure 2-17 Local VLANs Are Based on Physical Location and Are Dedicated to an Access Layer Switch Cluster. Accounting Users on Different Layer 3 Switches Can Be on Different VLANs.

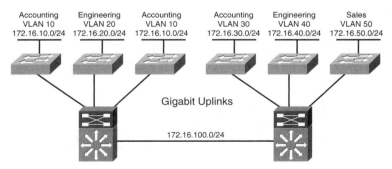

Figure 2-18 Access Uplinks Do Not Carry VLAN Tags, So Access Ports Can Be Left with Their Default VLAN Configuration

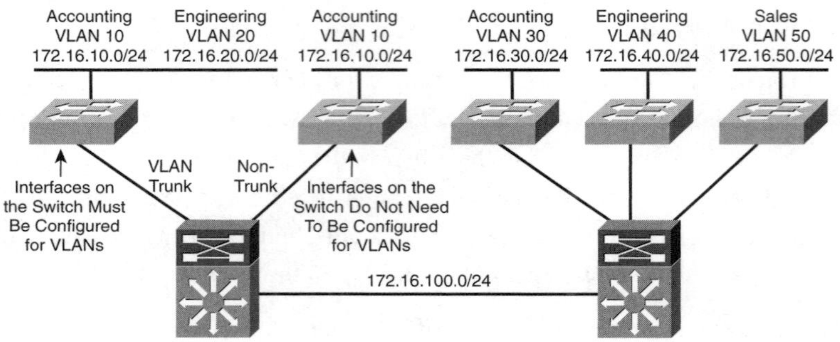

Geographic VLANs are also considerably easier to manage and conceptualize than VLANs that span different geographic areas.

Establishing VLAN Memberships

The two common approaches to assigning VLAN membership are as follows:

- Static VLANs
- Dynamic VLANs

Static VLANs are also called *port-based VLANs*. Static VLAN assignments are created by manually assigning ports to a VLAN. As a device enters the network, the device automatically assumes the port's VLAN. If the user changes ports and needs access to the same VLAN, the network administrator must manually make a port-to-VLAN assignment for the new connection.

Dynamic VLANs are created through the use of software packages such as CiscoWorks 2000. With a *VLAN Management Policy Server (VMPS)*, an administrator can assign switch ports to VLANs dynamically based on information such as the source MAC address of the device connected to the port or the username used to log on to that device. As a device enters the network, the device queries a database for VLAN membership. Figure 2-19 illustrates a VMPS setup.

Port-Based VLAN Membership

With port-based VLAN membership, the port is assigned to a specific VLAN independent of the user or system attached to the port. This means that all users attached to the port should be members of the same VLAN, as shown in Figure 2-20. The network administrator typically performs the VLAN assignment. The port configuration is static and cannot be automatically changed to another VLAN without manual reconfiguration.

Figure 2-19 VMPS Lets Ports Be Automatically Assigned VLAN Membership

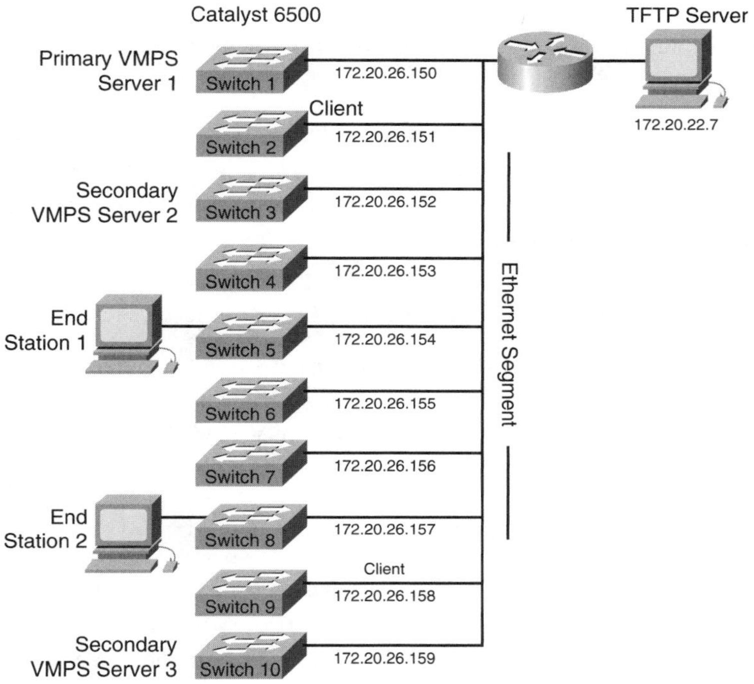

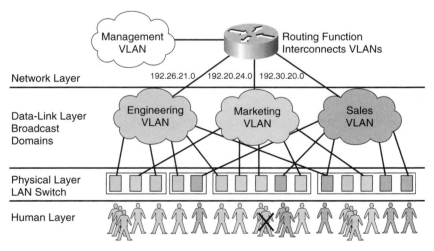

Catalyst 6500

TFTP Server

Primary VMPS
Server 1 — Switch 1 — 172.20.26.150

Client
Switch 2 — 172.20.26.151

Secondary
VMPS Server 2 — Switch 3 — 172.20.26.152

Switch 4 — 172.20.26.153

End
Station 1 — Switch 5 — 172.20.26.154

Switch 6 — 172.20.26.155

Switch 7 — 172.20.26.156

End
Station 2 — Switch 8 — 172.20.26.157

Client
Switch 9 — 172.20.26.158

Secondary
VMPS Server 3 — Switch 10 — 172.20.26.159

172.20.22.7

Ethernet Segment

Figure 2-20 All Users Attached to the Same Switch Port Must Be in the Same VLAN

Management
VLAN

Routing Function
Interconnects VLANs

Network Layer   192.26.21.0   192.20.24.0   192.30.20.0

Data-Link Layer
Broadcast
Domains

Engineering
VLAN

Marketing
VLAN

Sales
VLAN

Physical Layer
LAN Switch

Human Layer

As with other VLAN approaches, the packets forwarded using this method do not leak into other VLAN domains on the network. After a port has been assigned to a VLAN, the port cannot send to or receive from devices in another VLAN without the intervention of a Layer 3 device.

The device that is attached to the port likely doesn't understand that a VLAN exists. The device simply knows that it is a member of a subnet and that the device should be able to talk to all other members of the subnet by simply sending information to the cable segment. The switch is responsible for identifying that the information came from a specific VLAN and for ensuring that the information gets to all other members of the VLAN. The switch is further responsible for ensuring that ports in a different VLAN do not receive the information.

This approach is quite simple, fast, and easy to manage because no complex lookup tables are required for VLAN segmentation. If port-to-VLAN association is done with an application-specific integrated circuit (ASIC), the performance is very good. An ASIC allows the port-to-VLAN mapping to be done at the hardware level.

Dynamic VLANs

With a VMPS, ports can be assigned to VLANs dynamically, based on information entered in the VMPS database. When a host moves from a port on one switch in the network to a port on another switch in the network, the switch assigns the new port to the proper VLAN for that host dynamically.

When VMPS is enabled, a MAC address-to-VLAN mapping database downloads from a TFTP server, and VMPS begins to accept client requests. If the switch is power-cycled or reset, the VMPS database downloads from the TFTP server automatically, and VMPS is reenabled.

VMPS opens a UDP socket to communicate and listen to client requests. When the VMPS server receives a valid request from a client, it searches its database for a MAC address-to-VLAN mapping. Figure 2-21 illustrates primary and secondary VMPS servers.

If the assigned VLAN is restricted to a group of ports, VMPS verifies the requesting port against this group. If the VLAN is allowed on the port, the VLAN name is returned to the client. If the VLAN is not allowed on the port and VMPS is not in secure mode, the host receives an access-denied response. If VMPS is in secure mode, the port is shut down.

If a VLAN in the database does not match the current VLAN on the port and active hosts are on the port, VMPS sends an access-denied or port-shutdown response based on the secure mode of the VMPS.

Figure 2-21 VMPS Servers Process Client Requests for MAC-to-VLAN Maps

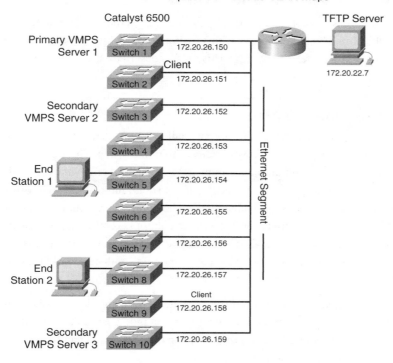

Multiple hosts can be active on a dynamic port if they are all in the same VLAN. If the link goes down on a dynamic port, the port returns to an isolated state. Any hosts that come online through the port are checked again with VMPS before the port is assigned to a VLAN.

The following guidelines and restrictions apply to dynamic port VLAN membership:

- VMPS must be configured before the ports can be configured as dynamic.
- When a port is configured as dynamic, Spanning Tree PortFast is enabled automatically for that port.
- If a port is converted from static to dynamic on the same VLAN, the port connects immediately to that VLAN, but VMPS eventually checks the host's legality on the port.
- Static secure ports cannot become dynamic ports unless security is disabled before the port is made dynamic.
- Static ports that are trunking cannot become dynamic ports unless trunking is disabled on the port before it is changed from static to dynamic.

It is also important to note that the *VLAN Trunking Protocol (VTP)* management domain and the management VLAN of VMPS clients and the VMPS server must be the same.

Configuring VLANs and VMPS

A static VLAN is easy to configure and is by far the most common method of configuring VLAN membership. Dynamic VLANs with VMPS is another option, but Cisco is no longer recommending it as a preferred solution. This section describes static and dynamic VLAN configurations.

Configuring Static VLANs

Static VLANs are ports on a switch that are manually assigned to a VLAN by using a VLAN management application or by working directly within the switch. These ports maintain their assigned VLAN configuration until an administrator changes them. Although static VLANs require manual entry changes, they are secure, easy to configure, and straightforward to monitor. This type of VLAN works well in networks where moves are controlled and managed. Static VLANs are also appropriate for networks that employ robust VLAN management software to configure the ports. Static VLANs are also a consideration if it is undesirable to assume the additional overhead required when maintaining end-station MAC addresses and custom filtering tables.

The creation of a VLAN on a switch is a very straightforward and simple task. If you're using a Cisco IOS-based switch, from interface configuration mode, issue the **switchport** command. The **switchport mode [access | dynamic | trunk]** command can be used to set the interface to access, dynamic, or trunk.

To statically assign an interface to a VLAN, use the **switchport mode access** command followed by the **switchport access vlan** *number* command.

To set interface FastEthernet 0/3 on a Catalyst switch to access mode, use the **switchport mode** IOS command. The port is then assigned to VLAN 2 with the **switchport access vlan** command, as verified in Example 2-10 using the **show running-config** command. The **switchport mode access** command is the default mode for switch interfaces. The mode is not shown in the running configuration.

Example 2-10   *The **switchport access vlan** Command Is Used to Statically Configure a Port for a Particular VLAN*

```
Switch#show running-config
hostname switch
!
ip subnet-zero
!
```

Example 2-10 *The* **switchport access vlan** *Command Is Used to Statically Configure a Port for a Particular VLAN (Continued)*

```
!
!
interface FastEthernet0/1
!
interface FastEthernet0/2
!
interface FastEthernet0/3
    switchport access vlan 2
```

Unlike the earlier 2900XL and 3500XL switches, the 2950 switches with Cisco IOS Release 12.1(6)EA2 or later and the 3550 switches with Cisco IOS Release 12.1(4)EA1 or later have an **interface range** command that lets multiple interfaces be identified for a subsequent operation. For example, several ports can be assigned to a VLAN with one **switchport** command, as shown in Example 2-11.

Example 2-11 *The* **interface range** *Command Is Definitely a Time-Saver!*

```
Switch(config)#interface range fa0/1 - 6
Switch(config-if-range)#switchport access vlan 10
```

These commands assign ports 1 to 6 to VLAN 10 in one command sequence.

Ports on Cisco switches usually default to the *Dynamic Trunking Protocol (DTP)* mode of **dynamic desirable**. This means that another switch connected to this port can cause trunking to occur on this interface. It is recommended that all nontrunking switch ports be configured as *access ports* with the command **switchport mode access**. This helps prevent certain man-in-the-middle attacks from occurring within the network. There are also other reasons why it is important not to have rogue switches attaching to the network in regard to STP. Chapter 3, "Spanning Tree Protocol (STP)," discusses these issues in greater detail.

Lab 2.9.1   Catalyst 2950T and 3550 Series Static VLANS

In this lab exercise, you create and maintain VLANs on a Cisco Catalyst 2950T or 3550 series Ethernet switch using CLI mode.

Verifying VLAN Configuration

As soon as a switch has been configured for VLANs, you should verify the configuration with the **show vlan** or **show vlan brief** command. The output in Example 2-12 shows that VLAN 2 is configured on interface FastEthernet 0/3.

Example 2-12 *The* **show vlan brief** *Command Provides a Quick List of VLANs and Associated Ports*

```
Switch#show vlan brief
VLAN  Name                Status  Ports
----  ----------------    ------  ------------------------_
1     default             active  Fa0/1, Fa0/2, Fa0/4, Fa0/5
                                  Fa0/6, Fa0/7, Fa0/8, Fa0/9
                                  Fa0/10, Fa0/11, Fa0/12, Fa0/13
                                  Fa0/14, Fa0/15, Fa0/16, Fa0/17
                                  Fa0/18, Fa0/19, Fa0/20, Fa0/21
                                  Fa0/22, Fa0/23, Fa0/24,


2     VLAN0002            active  Fa0/3
1002  fddi-default        active
1003  token-ring-default  active
1004  fddinet-default     active
1005  trnet-default       active
```

When configuring VLANs, keep the following in mind:

- A created VLAN remains unused until it is mapped to switch ports.
- The default configuration has all the switch ports on VLAN 1.

Deleting VLANs

When a VLAN is deleted from a switch that is in VTP server mode, the VLAN is removed from all switches in the *VTP domain*. When a VLAN is deleted from a switch that is in VTP transparent mode, the VLAN is deleted only on that specific switch. A VLAN cannot be deleted from a switch that is in VTP client mode. The later section "VLAN Trunking Protocol (VTP)" covers the different VTP modes in greater detail.

The default VLANs for the different media types cannot be deleted. Ethernet VLAN 1, Fiber Distributed Data Interface (FDDI), and Token Ring VLANs 1002 to 1005 cannot be removed from the switch.

Beginning in privileged EXEC mode, follow the steps listed in Table 2-3 to delete a VLAN on the switch.

Table 2-3 VLANs Can Be Removed in VLAN Database Configuration Mode

Step	Command	Description
1	**vlan database**	Enters VLAN configuration mode.
2	**no vlan** *vlan-id*	Removes the VLAN by entering the VLAN ID.
3	**exit**	Updates the VLAN database, propagates it throughout the administrative domain, and returns to privileged EXEC mode.
4	**show vlan brief**	Verifies the VLAN removal.
5	**copy running-config startup-config**	(Optional) Saves the configuration file.

> **CAUTION**
>
> When a VLAN is deleted, any ports assigned to that VLAN become inactive. They remain associated with the deleted VLAN until they are assigned to a new VLAN. Use caution when deleting VLANs. It is possible to cause a major loss of connectivity by accidentally eliminating a VLAN that still has active users on it.

It is important to note that the **no vlan** command must be issued on a switch in VTP server or VTP transparent mode. VLANs cannot be deleted from a VTP client switch. If the switch is configured in transparent mode, you can delete the VLAN. VLANs deleted from a switch in VTP transparent mode are removed from that one switch only and not throughout the VTP domain. VTP domains are covered in the later section "VLAN Trunking Protocol (VTP)."

VMPS Operation

With VLAN Membership Policy Server (VMPS), switch ports can be assigned to VLANs dynamically, based on the source MAC address or user ID of the device connected to the port. When a host or user moves from a port on one switch in the network to a port on another switch in the network, the switch dynamically assigns the new port to the proper VLAN for that host.

When VMPS is enabled, a MAC address-to-VLAN mapping database downloads from a TFTP server to the VMPS server (a Catalyst switch). The VMPS server then begins accepting client requests.

The VMPS client communicates with a VMPS server through the VLAN Query Protocol (VQP). When the VMPS receives a VQP request from a client switch, it searches its database for a MAC-address-to-VLAN mapping.

The server response is based on this mapping and whether the server is in secure mode. Secure mode determines whether the server shuts down the port when a VLAN is not allowed on it or just denies the port access to the VLAN.

In response to a request, the VMPS takes one of these actions:

- If the assigned VLAN is restricted to a group of ports, the VMPS verifies the requesting port against this group and responds as follows:
  - If the VLAN is allowed on the port, the VMPS sends the VLAN name to the client in response.
  - If the VLAN is not allowed on the port and the VMPS is not in secure mode, the VMPS sends an access-denied response.
  - If the VLAN is not allowed on the port and the VMPS is in secure mode, the VMPS sends a port-shutdown response.
- If the VLAN in the database does not match the current VLAN on the port and active hosts exist on the port, the VMPS sends an access-denied or port-shutdown response, depending on the secure mode of the VMPS.

If the switch receives an access-denied response from the VMPS, it continues to block traffic from the MAC address to or from the port. The switch continues to monitor the packets directed to the port and sends a query to the VMPS when it identifies a new address. If the switch receives a port-shutdown response from the VMPS, it disables the port. The port must then be enabled manually.

It is also possible to configure a fallback VLAN name. If a device is plugged into the network and its MAC address is not in the database, VMPS sends the fallback VLAN name to the client. If no fallback VLAN is configured and the MAC address does not exist in the database, VMPS sends an access-denied response. If VMPS is in secure mode, it sends a port-shutdown response.

An administrator can also make an explicit entry in the configuration table to deny access to specific MAC addresses for security reasons by specifying a **--NONE--** keyword for the VLAN name. In this case, VMPS sends an access-denied or port-shutdown response.

Dynamic Port VLAN Membership

A dynamic port on the switch can belong to only one VLAN. When the link comes up, the switch does not forward traffic to or from this port until the VMPS server provides the VLAN assignment. The VMPS client receives the source MAC address from the first packet of a new host connected to the dynamic port and attempts to match the MAC address to a VLAN in the VMPS database via a VQP request to the VMPS server.

If there is a match, the VMPS server sends the VLAN number for that port. If the client switch was not previously configured, it uses the domain name from the first VTP packet it receives on its trunk port from the VMPS. If the client switch was previously configured, it includes its domain name in the query packet to the VMPS to obtain its VLAN number. The VMPS verifies that the domain name in the packet matches its own domain name before accepting the request and responds to the client with the assigned VLAN number for the client. If there is no match, the VMPS either denies the request or shuts down the port, depending on the VMPS secure mode setting.

Multiple hosts can be active on a dynamic port if they are all in the same VLAN, but the VMPS shuts down a dynamic port if more than 20 hosts are active on the port for a Catalyst 2950 or 3550 switch. The total number of allowable hosts varies by platform.

If the link goes down on a dynamic port, the port returns to an isolated state and does not belong to a VLAN. Any hosts that come online through the port are checked again through VQP request with the VMPS before the port is assigned to a VLAN.

VMPS Configuration Guidelines

There are several restrictions for configuring VMPS client switch ports as dynamic. The following requirements apply to dynamic port VLAN membership:

- VMPS must be configured before ports can be set as dynamic.
- The VTP management domain of the VMPS clients and the VMPS server must be the same.
- The management VLAN of VMPS clients and the VMPS server must be the same.
- When a port is configured as dynamic, the Spanning Tree Port Fast feature is automatically enabled for that port.
- After a static port is converted to dynamic on the same VLAN, the port connects immediately to that VLAN until VMPS checks its database for the legality of the specific host on the dynamic port.
- Static ports cannot become dynamic ports.
- Static ports that are trunking cannot become dynamic ports.
- Physical ports in an EtherChannel cannot be configured as dynamic ports.
- VMPS shuts down a dynamic port when too many active hosts connect to a port.

To use VMPS, a VMPS database must be created and stored on a TFTP server.

A VMPS database configuration file is an ASCII text file that is stored on a TFTP server accessible to the switch configured as the VMPS server, as shown in Example 2-13.

Example 2-13 *A TFTP Server Stores the ASCII VMPS Database File. The VMPS Server Pulls the VLAN-to-MAC Address Mappings from the TFTP Server.*

```
!VMPS FILE FORMAT, version 1.1
!Always begin the configuration file with the word "VMPS"
!
!vmps domain <domain-name>
!The VMPS domain must be defined.
!vmps mode {open | secure}
!The default mode is open.
!vmps fallback <vlan-name>
!vmps no domain-req {allow | deny}
!
!The default value is allow. Deny means requests from
!clients with no domain name are rejected.
vmps domain wBU
vmps mode open
vmps fallbackback default
vmps no-domain-req deny
!
!
!MAC Addresses
!
vmps-mac-addrs
!
!address <addr> vlan-name <vlan_name>
!
address 0012.2233.4455 vlan-name hardware
address 0000.6509.a080 vlan-name hardware
address aabb.ccdd.eeff vlan-name Green
address 1223.5678.9abc vlan-name ExecStaff
address fedc.ba98.7654 vlan-name -NONE-
address fedc.ba23.1245 vlan-name Purple
!
!Port Groups
!
```

The VMPS parser is line-based. Each entry in the text file starts on a new line.

Ranges are not allowed for the switch port numbers. It is probably easiest to take a sample VMPS database file and edit it to meet the network's needs.

Although it is rarely done, a VMPS database file can be created from scratch using these rules:

- Begin the configuration file with the word "VMPS" to prevent other types of configuration files from being read incorrectly by the VMPS server.
- Define the VMPS domain.
- Define the security mode as either open (the default) or secure mode.
- Define a fallback VLAN (optional).
- Define the MAC address-to-VLAN name mappings.
- Define port groups to which VMPS will be applied, using groups, individual ports, or the **all-ports** keyword.
- Define VLAN groups to which VLAN port policies will be applied.
- Define VLAN port policies to associate ports with a restricted VLAN.

To review the general mechanism by which VMPS makes policy decisions affecting switch ports and VLAN assignments, review the earlier section "VMPS Operation." Here's a summary of the sample VMPS configuration file:

- The security mode is open.
- The default is used for the fallback VLAN.
- MAC address-to-VLAN name mappings provide the MAC address of each host, and the VLAN to which each host belongs is defined.
- Port groups are defined.
- VLAN groups are defined.
- VLAN port policies are defined for the ports associated with restricted VLANs.

To create a VMPS database, do the following:

Step 1   Determine the MAC addresses of the hosts that will be assigned to VLANs dynamically, and determine the VMPS mode.

Step 2   Map out the port groups, VLAN groups, port policies, and fallback VLAN.

Step 3   Create an ASCII text file that contains the MAC address-to-VLAN mappings and policies.

Step 4   Move the ASCII text file to a TFTP server so that it can be downloaded to the switch that will act as the VMPS server.

As soon as the VMPS database is in place on the TFTP server, the VMPS server and clients can be configured. If a network interface card (NIC) in a PC changes, the VMPS database needs to be updated.

Recall that when VMPS is enabled, the switch downloads the VMPS database from the TFTP server and begins accepting VMPS requests from VMPS clients.

Configure VMPS clients with the commands shown in Example 2-14, starting in global configuration mode.

Example 2-14 *The* **switchport access vlan dynamic** *Command Enables Dynamic VLAN Assignment to a Port*

```
Switch#configure terminal
Switch(config)#vmps server ipaddress primary
Switch(config)#vmps server ipaddress for up to 3 secondary VMPS servers (optional)
Switch(config)#interface interface-id
Switch(config-if)#switchport mode access
Switch(config-if)#switchport access vlan dynamic
```

Repeat the last three commands for each dynamic switch port. To reenable a shut-down dynamic port, enter the interface configuration command **no shutdown**.

Now that all the VMPS components are configured and in place, verify that everything is working correctly.

Use the **show vmps** command to verify the VMPS server entry. This command did not become available on some IOS-based switch platforms until Cisco IOS Release 12.1(6). The **show vmps** command displays the VQP version and the VMPS server IP addresses, including which server is the primary. Use the **statistics** keyword to display client-side statistics.

Use the command **show interface** *interface-id* **switchport** to verify dynamic assignment of VLAN membership to a given port.

After the database has loaded, a VMPS server switch answers queries from VMPS client switches with dynamic ports. The following assumptions apply to the scenario pictured in Figure 2-22:

- The VMPS server and the VMPS client are separate switches.
- Switch 1 is the primary VMPS server.
- Switch 3 and Switch 10 are secondary VMPS servers.
- End stations are connected to these clients:
    - Switch 5
    - Switch 8
- The database configuration file is called Bldg-G.db and is stored on a TFTP server with IP address 172.20.22.7.

Figure 2-22 The TFTP Server, the VMPS Server(s), the VMPS Clients, and the VQP Work in Concert to Provide Dynamic VLAN Assignment to Ports

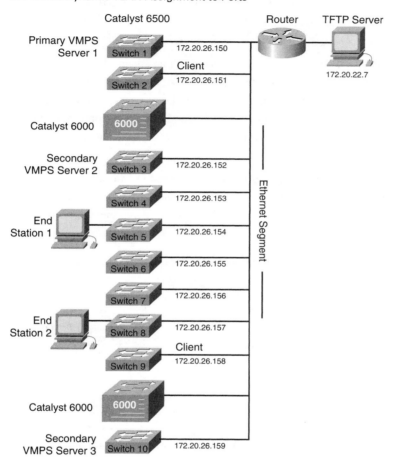

Access Links and Trunk Links

Static switch ports run in either access or trunk mode. Accordingly, the links connected to these switch ports are called *access links* or *trunk links*. In access mode, the port belongs to one and only one VLAN. An access port is a switch port that connects to an end-user device or a server; the frames transmitted on an access link look like any other Ethernet frames.

A *trunk* link differs from an access link in that it can support multiple VLANs. The VLANs are multiplexed over the link with a trunking protocol. The trunk link also does not belong to a specific VLAN. Trunk links are typically used to connect switches to other switches, routers, or a server that uses an IEEE 802.1Q-enabled network card to participate in multiple VLANs.

Trunks can extend VLANs across an entire network. A trunk link can be configured to transport all VLANs or a restricted set of VLANs. Trunk links are typically configured on ports that support the greatest bandwidth for a given switch. Catalyst switches support trunk links on Fast Ethernet, Gigabit Ethernet, and 10 Gigabit Ethernet ports.

To multiplex VLAN traffic, special protocols exist that encapsulate or tag the frames so that the receiving device can determine the frame's VLAN membership. The Cisco-proprietary ISL protocol lets Cisco devices multiplex VLANs between Cisco devices. In multivendor environments, switches must use IEEE 802.1Q, an industry-standard protocol that permits multiplexing of VLANs over trunk links. The Catalyst 3550 switches support both ISL and 802.1Q, and the Catalyst 2950 switch supports only 802.1Q.

Without trunk links, multiple access links would have to be installed to support multiple VLANs between switches (one link per VLAN). This is clearly neither a cost-effective nor scalable solution. Trunking is absolutely essential for interconnecting switches in a campus network. Figure 2-23 illustrates access and trunk links.

Figure 2-23 Access and Trunk Links Link All the Devices in a Campus Network

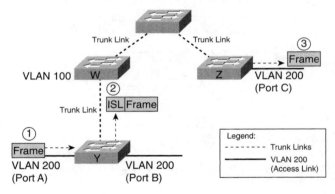

Port A and Port B on Switch Y have been defined as access links on the same VLAN. By definition, they can belong to only VLAN 200 and cannot receive frames with a VLAN identifier. As Switch Y receives traffic from Port A destined for Port B, Switch Y does not add an ISL header to the frame.

Port C is also an access link that has been defined as a member of VLAN 200. If Port A sends a frame destined for Port C, the switch does the following:

  1. Switch Y receives the frame and identifies it as traffic destined for VLAN 200 by the VLAN and port number association.

2. Switch Y encapsulates the frame with an ISL header identifying VLAN 200 and sends the frame through the intermediate switch on a trunk link.

This process is repeated for every switch that the frame must transit as it moves to its final destination of Port C.

3. Switch Z receives the frame, removes the ISL header, and forwards the frame to Port C.

VLAN Trunking and Dynamic Trunking Protocol

Layer 2 switching relies on trunk links between switches. Trunk ports can be configured to autonegotiate trunk links via DTP, or trunk links can be hard-coded. This section explores Ethernet trunks and DTP.

Trunking Overview

When a port is in trunk mode, the trunk link can be configured to transport all VLANs or a restricted set of VLANs across an entire network. Trunk links are typically used to connect switches to other switches, routers, or VLAN-enabled servers.

In basic terminology, a trunk is a point-to-point link that supports several VLANs. The purpose of a trunk is to save ports when creating a link between two devices implementing VLANs, as shown in Figure 2-24.

Figure 2-24 Trunk Links Carry Data Traffic for Multiple VLANs

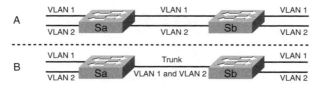

In Portion A of Figure 2-24, two VLANs need to be available on two switches, Sa and Sb. The first easy method of implementation is to create two physical links between the devices, each one carrying the traffic for a separate VLAN.

Of course, this first solution does not scale very well. If the network has a third VLAN, you would need to sacrifice two additional ports. This design is also inefficient in terms of load sharing; the traffic on some VLANs might not justify a dedicated link. A trunk bundles virtual links over one physical link.

In Portion B of Figure 2-24, one physical link between the two switches can carry traffic for any VLAN. To achieve this, each frame sent on the link is tagged by Sa so that Sb knows which VLAN it belongs to. Different tagging schemes exist. The most common protocols for Ethernet segments to follow are the IEEE 802.1Q standard and the Cisco-proprietary ISL protocol.

Configuring a VLAN Trunk

To create or configure a VLAN trunk on a Cisco IOS-based switch, you must configure the port as a trunk and specify the trunk encapsulation. To do this, issue the **switchport mode trunk** and **switchport trunk encapsulation [dot1q | isl]** commands, as shown in Example 2-15.

Example 2-15 *Two Commands Generally Suffice to Configure an Interface for Trunking*

```
Switch(config-if)#switchport mode trunk
Switch(config-if)#switchport trunk?
allowed        Set allowed VLAN characteristics when
               interface is in trunking mode
encapsulation  Set trunking encapsulation when interface
               is in trunking mode
native         Set trunking native characteristics when
               interface is in trunking mode
pruning        Set pruning VLAN characteristics when
               interface is in trunking mode

Switch(config-if)#switchport trunk encap ?
dot1q   Interface uses only 801.1q trunking encapsulation
        when trunking
isl     Interface uses only ISL trunking encapsulation
        when trunking

Switch(config-if)#switchport trunk encapsulation isl
Switch(config-if)#
```

dot1q trunk interfaces use only 802.1q trunking encapsulation when trunking. **isl** trunk interfaces use only ISL trunking encapsulation when trunking.

When configuring switches that allow multiple trunking encapsulations, dot1q or isl, the **switchport trunk encapsulation** command must be used before the **switchport mode trunk** command. By default, the **switchport mode trunk** command trunks all VLANs.

In 802.1Q trunking, all VLAN packets are tagged on the trunk link to indicate the VLAN to which they belong. Frames belonging to the *native VLAN* are sent untagged on the trunk link. The native VLAN contains ports not assigned to other VLANs that by default belong to VLAN 1. VLAN 1 is the native VLAN by default, but VLANs other than VLAN 1 can be designated as the native VLAN. However, the native VLAN must be the same on trunked switches in 802.1Q trunking. If a VLAN other than VLAN 1 is to be the native VLAN, it needs to be identified on the trunk ports. In the interface configuration mode of the trunk port(s), the IOS-based command to designate the native VLAN is **switchport trunk native vlan** *vlan-id*.

The **switchport trunk native vlan** command is necessary only when changing the native VLAN from something other than VLAN 1 or when changing it back to VLAN 1.

Remember that the Catalyst 3550 switch supports both 802.1Q and ISL, whereas the Catalyst 2950 supports only 802.1Q.

Removing VLANs from a Trunk

By default, all VLANs are transported across a trunk link when you issue the **trunk** command. However, in some instances the trunk link should not carry all VLANs. One instance is broadcast suppression. All broadcasts are sent to every port in a VLAN. A trunk link acts as a member port of the VLAN and, therefore, must pass all the broadcasts. Bandwidth and processing time are wasted if no port at the other end of the trunk link is a member of that VLAN. Also, VLANs might also be removed from a trunk as a result of a topology change. Changes that occur in the topology must also be propagated across the trunk link. If the VLAN is not used on the other end of the trunk link, there is no need for the overhead of a topology change.

By default, a Cisco IOS-based switch trunk port sends traffic to and receives traffic from all VLANs in the VLAN database. All VLANs, 1 to 1005, are allowed on each trunk, but some of those VLANs can be removed from the list of allowed VLANs, preventing traffic from those VLANs from passing over the trunk. To restrict the traffic a trunk carries, use the **remove** *vlan-list* parameter with the **switchport trunk allowed vlan** command.

In Example 2-16, the **switchport trunk allowed** command is used to remove VLAN 3 and then remove VLANs 6 to 10 from the trunk. This is verified by using the **show running-config** command.

Example 2-16 *Specifying the VLANs Allowed Over the Trunk Link*

```
Switch(config-if)#switchport trunk allowed vlan remove 3
Switch(config-if)#switchport trunk allowed vlan remove 6-10
Switch#show running-config
<output omitted>
hostname Switch
!
ip subnet-zero
!
!
!
interface FastEthernet0/1
!
interface FastEthernet0/2
!
interface FastEthernet0/3
 switchport trunk allowed vlan 1,2,4,5,11-1005
 switchport mode trunk
```

To remove a large number of VLANs from a trunk link, it is often faster to clear all VLANs from the trunk link before specifying the VLANs that are supposed to be on the link. The command syntax is **switchport trunk allowed vlan** {**add** *vlan-list* | **all** | **except** *vlan-list* | **remove** *vlan-list*}.

Basics of Dynamic Trunking Protocol

Ethernet trunk interfaces support several different trunking modes:

- Access
- Dynamic desirable (the default mode on Catalyst 2950 and 3550)
- Dynamic auto
- Trunk
- Nonnegotiate
- Dot1q-tunnel (not an option on the Catalyst 2950)

Using these different trunking modes, an interface can be set to trunking or nontrunking or can be set to negotiate trunking with the neighboring interface. To automatically negotiate trunking, the interfaces must be in the same VTP domain. Trunk negotiation is managed by DTP, which is a Cisco-proprietary point-to-point protocol.

These various modes are configured using the **switchport mode** interface command, as shown in Example 2-17. Table 2-4 shows the various DTP modes.

Example 2-17 *Configuring Trunking Modes*

```
3550-Switch(config-if)#switchport mode ?
access        Set trunking mode to ACCESS unconditionally
dot1q-tunnel  Set trunking mode to DOT1Q TUNNEL unconditionally
dynamic       Set trunking mode to dynamically negotiate access or trunk mode
trunk         Set trunking mode to TRUNK unconditionally


2950-Switch(config-if)#switchport mode ?
access        Set trunking mode to ACCESS unconditionally
dynamic       Set trunking mode to dynamically negotiate access or trunk mode
trunk         Set trunking mode to TRUNK unconditionally
```

Table 2-4 DTP Modes

Command	Description
switchport mode access	Puts the interface (access port) into permanent nontrunking mode. The interface generates DTP frames, negotiating with the neighboring interface to convert the link into a nontrunk link. The interface becomes a nontrunk interface even if the neighboring interface does not agree to the change.
switchport mode dynamic desirable	Makes the interface actively attempt to convert the link into a trunk link. The interface becomes a trunk interface if the neighboring interface is set to **trunk**, **desirable**, or **auto** mode. This is the default mode for all Ethernet interfaces. If the neighboring interface is set to **access** or **non-negotiate** mode, the link becomes nontrunking.
switchport mode dynamic auto	Makes the interface willing to convert the link to a trunk link if the neighboring interface is set to **trunk** or **desirable** mode. Otherwise, the link becomes nontrunking.

continues

Table 2-4 DTP Modes (Continued)

Command	Description
switchport mode trunk	Puts the interface into permanent trunking mode and negotiates to convert the link into a trunk link. The interface becomes a trunk interface even if the neighboring interface does not agree to the change.
switchport nonegotiate	Prevents the interface from generating DTP frames. You can use this command only when the interface switchport mode is **access** or **trunk**. You must manually configure the neighboring interface as a trunk interface to establish a **trunk** link; otherwise, the link is nontrunking.

DTP Trunk and Access Modes

Using the **switchport mode** interface command, two of the DTP modes set trunking to off or on, as demonstrated in Example 2-18.

Example 2-18 *Trunking Is Turned Off or On Based on the Switchport Mode*

```
Switch(config-if)#switchport mode access
! Sets trunking OFF
Switch(config-if)#switchport mode trunk
! Sets trunking ON
```

Access Mode

In Example 2-19, Switch A and Switch B are connected on their FastEthernet 0/1 interfaces. If both switches are set to access mode, the link is a nontrunking link. Both interfaces must be on the same VLAN, and only that single VLAN is transmitted across the link.

Example 2-19 *The* **switchport mode access** *Command Is Used for Access Links*

```
SwitchA(config)#inter fa 0/1
SwitchA(config-if)#switchport mode access
SwitchB(config)#inter fa 0/1
SwitchB(config-if)#switchport mode access
```

Trunk Mode

If both switches are set to trunk mode, as shown in Example 2-20, the link is a trunking link. By default, all VLANs are transmitted across this trunk.

Example 2-20 *The* **switchport mode trunk** *Command Is Used for Trunk Links*

```
SwitchA(config)#inter fa 0/1
SwitchA(config-if)#switchport mode trunk
SwitchB(config)#inter fa 0/1
SwitchB(config-if)#switchport mode trunk
```

NOTE

For switches such as the Catalyst 3550 that are capable of either 802.1Q or ISL trunking encapsulation, the **switchport trunk encapsulation [dot1q | isl | negotiate]** interface command must be used before the **switchport mode trunk** command.

DTP Combinations

All the DTP modes and their various combinations can be somewhat confusing. Looking at some of the basic combinations can help clarify this.

The Default: Desirable Mode

By default, Ethernet interfaces on most Cisco switches are set to desirable mode. This is true for both the Catalyst 2950 and 3550 switches. Desirable mode creates a trunk link if the neighboring interface is set to desirable, trunk, or auto mode. Because both interfaces by default are in desirable mode, this means a link between two Cisco switches automatically becomes a trunk link unless configured otherwise.

Combinations

Table 2-5 shows the various DTP trunking modes and the results of the different combinations.

One combination that could result in traffic being blocked from transmitting the link is if one interface is in access mode and the neighboring interface is in trunk mode. In this case, the access mode interface only wants to do nontrunking, whereas the trunk mode interface only wants to do trunking. This is not a recommended combination and might create unexpected results. Traffic might or might not be able to transit the link depending on several factors, such as the spanning-tree root bridge location. In some situations, the link works as a non-trunking link even though one interface is in access mode and the other is in trunk mode. In other situations, spanning tree puts the access mode port into blocking mode and traffic does not transit the link to the neighboring trunk mode interface. To get consistent results, regardless of the topology, it is recommended that you never have a combination of access mode and trunk mode on the interfaces of two neighboring switches.

Table 2-5 The DTP Trunking Modes Configured on Either End of a Link Determine the Link's Operational Mode

Administrative Mode	Auto	Desirable	Trunk (On)	Access (Off)	Nonnegotiate (Access)	Nonnegotiate (Trunk)
Auto	Static access (NT)	Trunk	Trunk	Static access	Static access	Unexpected results
Desirable	Trunk	Trunk	Trunk	Static access	Static access	Unexpected results
Trunk (On)	Trunk	Trunk	Trunk	Unexpected results	Unexpected results	Trunk
Access (Off)	Static access	Static access	Unexpected results	Static access	Static access	Unexpected results
Nonnegotiate (Access)	Static access	Static access	Unexpected results	Static access	Static access	Unexpected results
Nonnegotiate (Trunk)	Unexpected results	Unexpected results	Trunk	Unexpected results	Unexpected results	Trunk

The only modes that actually negotiate trunking between adjacent switches are trunk, dynamic desirable, and dynamic auto. Even though the **switchport mode trunk** command does not modify its own interface to be anything other than trunking, it sends out DTP frames to attempt to negotiate the other end of the link to be a trunking interface.

In Example 2-21, the **show interface switchport** command shows the negotiation of trunking set to on. The interface always attempts to negotiate trunking on the link unless the **switchport nonegotiate** command is configured on the interface.

Example 2-21 *Without the* **switchport nonegotiate** *Command, Trunking Negotiation Is Turned On*

```
2950-1(config-if)#switchport mode dynamic auto
2950-1(config-if)#end
2950-1#show interface switchport
Name: Fa0/1
Switchport: Enabled
Administrative Mode: dynamic auto
Operational Mode: static access
Administrative Trunking Encapsulation: dot1q
Operational Trunking Encapsulation: native
Negotiation of Trunking: on
Access mode VLAN: 1 (default)
Trunking Native Mode VLAN: 1 (default)
Administrative private-vlan host-assocation: none
Administrative private-vlan mapping: none
Operational private-vlan: none
Trunking VLANs Enabled: ALL
Pruning VLANs Enabled: 2-1001
```

Nonegotiate

The **switchport nonegotiate** command prevents the interface from generating DTP frames, turning off the negotiation of trunking. This can be viewed with the **show interface switchport** command. Example 2-22 shows the **switchport nonegotiate** interface command, which can be used only on an interface that is in access or trunk mode, previously configured with either the **switchport mode access** command or the **switchport mode trunk** command.

Example 2-22 *The* **switchport nonegotiate** *Command Prevents the Interface from Generating DTP Frames*

```
2950-1(config-if)#switchport mode access
2950-1(config-if)#switchport mode nonegotiate
2950-1(config-if)#end

2950-1#show interface switchport
Name: Fa0/1
Switchport: Enabled
Administrative Mode: static access
Operational Mode: static access
Administrative Trunking Encapsulation: dot1q
Operational Trunking Encapsulation: native
Negotiation of Trunking: Off
Access mode VLAN: 1 (default)
Trunking Native Mode VLAN: 1 (default)
Administrative private-vlan host-assocation: none
Administrative private-vlan mapping: none
Operational private-vlan: none
Trunking VLANs Enabled: ALL
Pruning VLANs Enabled: 2-1001
```

If an interface is configured with both the **switchport mode trunk** command and the **switchport nonegotiate** command, the interface on the neighboring switch must be configured as with the **switchport mode trunk** command to establish a trunk link. Otherwise, the link is a nontrunking link.

To enable trunking to a device that does not support DTP, the **switchport mode trunk** and **switchport nonegotiate** interface configuration commands should be used to cause the interface to become a trunk but not to generate DTP frames. The **switchport mode access** and **switchport nonegotiate** interface configuration commands should be used when configuring a nontrunking interface to another switch that does not support DTP.

Verifying DTP

The **show interface switchport** command, shown in Example 2-23, can be used to verify the following DTP information and status:

- Administrative mode
- Operational mode
- Administrative trunking encapsulation
- Negotiation of trunking

Example 2-23 *The* **show interface switchport** *Command Is Extremely Useful for Verifying LAN Configuration*

```
2950-1(config-if)#switchport mode dynamic auto
2950-1(config-if)#end
2950-1#show interface switchport
Name: Fa0/1
Switchport: Enabled
Administrative Mode: dynamic auto
Operational Mode: static access
Administrative Trunking Encapsulation: dot1q
Operational Trunking Encapsulation: native
Negotiation of Trunking: on
Access mode VLAN: 1 (default)
Trunking Native Mode VLAN: 1 (default)
Administrative private-vlan host-assocation: none
Administrative private-vlan mapping: none
Operational private-vlan: none
Trunking VLANs Enabled: ALL
Pruning VLANs Enabled: 2-1001
```

The Administrative Mode displays the interface's DTP state. The default on most Cisco switches is **dynamic desirable**. The DTP mode can be set using the **switchport mode** interface command.

The Operational Mode shows whether the interface is in a trunking or nontrunking state. If the Operational Mode is **static access**, this interface considers the link nontrunking. If the operational mode is **trunk,** as shown in the output of the **show interface switchport** command in Example 2-24, this interface is considered a trunking link. The **show interface trunk** command can be used to display all the interfaces on the switch that have the Operational Mode set to **trunk**, as shown in Example 2-24.

The Administrative Trunking Encapsulation displays the trunking protocol, 802.1Q or ISL, that is used on this interface if the operational mode is **trunk**. If the switch's Operational Mode is **static access**, nontrunking, the trunking protocol that Administrative Trunking Encapsulation displays is not currently being used on the link.

The Negotiation of Trunking shows whether the interface is willing to negotiate trunking by sending DTP frames. By default, the interface negotiates trunking and the Negotiation of Trunking shows as on. Use the **switchport nonegotiate** interface command to turn off this negotiation.

Example 2-24 *The* **show interface trunk** *Command Displays Useful Details About a Trunking Interface*

```
2950-1#show interface switchport
Name: Fa0/1
Switchport: Enabled
Administrative Mode: dynamic desirable
Operational Mode: trunk
Administrative Trunking Encapsulation: dot1q
Operational Trunking Encapsulation: dot1q
Negotiation of Trunking: on
Access mode VLAN: 1 (default)
Trunking Native Mode VLAN: 1 (default)
Administrative private-vlan host-assocation: none
Administrative private-vlan mapping: none
Operational private-vlan: none
Trunking VLANs Enabled: ALL
Pruning VLANs Enabled: 2-1001


2950-1#show interface trunk


Port      Mode         Encapsulation   Status       Native vlan
Fa0/1     desirable    802.1q          trunking     1


Port      Vlans allowed on trunk
Fa0/1     1-4094


Port      Vlans allowed and active in management domain
Fa0/1     1


Port      Vlans in spanning tree forwarding
          state and not pruned
Fa0/1     1
```

VLAN Identification

Although Ethernet VLAN frames are by far the most common type of tagged Layer 2 LAN traffic, FDDI and Asynchronous Transfer Mode (ATM) also have their own tagging mechanism for transporting traffic for multiple subnets over a single link. This section describes the various tagging mechanisms used in LAN networks.

VLAN Frame Identification

VLAN identification logically identifies which packets belong to which VLAN group. Multiple trunking methods exist (as shown in Table 2-6):

- ISL
- IEEE 802.1Q
- IEEE 802.10
- ATM LAN Emulation (LANE)

Table 2-6 Different LAN Media Use Different VLAN Encapsulation Methods

Identification Method	Encapsulation	Tagging (Insertion into Frame)	Media
802.1Q	No	Yes	Ethernet
ISL	Yes	No	Ethernet
802.10	No	No	FDDI
LANE	No	No	ATM

ISL is a Cisco-proprietary encapsulation protocol for trunking between switches. ISL prepends a 26-byte header and appends a 4-byte cyclic redundancy check (CRC) to each frame. ISL is supported in Cisco switches and routers.

The IEEE 802.1Q protocol is an IEEE standard method for identifying VLANs by inserting a VLAN identifier into the frame header. This process is called frame tagging or internal tagging.

The *IEEE 802.10* standard is a method of transporting VLAN information inside the standard 802.10 frame (FDDI). The VLAN information is written to the Security Association Identifier (SAID) portion of the 802.10 frame. This method is typically used to transport VLANs across FDDI backbones.

LAN Emulation (LANE) is an ATM Forum standard that can be used to transport VLANs over ATM networks, in which case they are called *Emulated LANs (ELANs)*.

Inter-Switch Link (ISL)

ISL is a Cisco-proprietary protocol used to interconnect multiple switches and maintain VLAN information as traffic travels between switches on trunk links. This technology provides one method for multiplexing bridge groups (VLANs) over a high-speed backbone. It is defined for Fast Ethernet and Gigabit Ethernet, as is IEEE 802.1Q. ISL has been available on Cisco routers since Cisco IOS Release 11.1.

With ISL, an Ethernet frame is encapsulated with a header that transports VLAN IDs between switches and routers, as shown in Figure 2-25.

Figure 2-25 The Cisco-Proprietary ISL Frame Format Has a 26-Byte Header

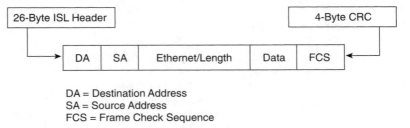

DA = Destination Address
SA = Source Address
FCS = Frame Check Sequence

ISL does add overhead to the packet as a 26-byte header containing a 10-bit VLAN ID. In addition, a 4-byte CRC is appended to the end of each frame, as shown in Figure 2-26. This CRC is in addition to any frame checking that the Ethernet frame requires.

Figure 2-26 The ISL Frame Format Includes a Field for the VLAN ID

40 Bits	4 Bits	4 Bits	48 Bits	16 Bits	24 Bits	24 Bits	15 Bits	1 Bit	16 Bits	16 Bits	Variable Length	32 Bits
DA	TYPE	USER	SA	LEN	SNAP/ LLC	HSA	VLAN ID	BPDU/ CDP	INDX	Reserved	Encapsulated Frame	FCS (CRC)

The fields in an ISL header identify the frame as belonging to a particular VLAN:

- **DA**—A 40-bit multicast address with a value of 0x01-00-0C-00-00 that indicates to the receiving Catalyst switch that the frame is an ISL encapsulated frame.
- **Type**—A 4-bit value indicating the source frame type. Values include 0 0 0 0 (Ethernet), 0 0 0 1 (Token Ring), 0 0 1 0 (FDDI), and 0 0 1 1 (ATM).
- **User**—A 4-bit value usually set to 0. It can be used for special situations when transporting Token Ring.
- **SA**—The 802.3 MAC address of the transmitting Catalyst switch. This is a 48-bit value.
- **Length**—The LEN field is a 16-bit value indicating the length of the user data and ISL header, excluding the DA, Type, User, SA, Length, and ISL CRC bytes.
- **SNAP**—A 3-byte field with a fixed value of 0xAA-AA-03.
- **HSA**—This 3-byte value duplicates the high-order bytes of the ISL SA field.

- **VLAN**—A 15-bit value to reflect the numerical value of the source VLAN that the user frame belongs to. Note that only 10 bits are used.

- **BPDU**—A single-bit value that, when set to 1, indicates that the receiving Catalyst switch should immediately examine the frame at an end station because the data contains either a spanning tree, ISL, VTP, or CDP message.

- **Index**—Indicates what port the frame exited from the source Catalyst switch.

- **Reserved**—Token Ring and FDDI frames have special values that need to be transported over the ISL link. These values, such as AC and FC, are carried in this field. The value of this field is 0 for Ethernet frames.

- **User Frame**—The original user data frame is inserted here, including the frame's frame check sequence (FCS).

- **CRC**—ISL calculates a 32-bit CRC for the header and user frame. This double-checks the message's integrity as it crosses an ISL trunk. It does not replace the User Frame CRC.

A VLAN ID is added only if the frame is forwarded out a port configured as a trunk link. If the frame is to be forwarded out a port configured as an access link, the ISL encapsulation is removed.

The IEEE 802.1Q Protocol

The official name of the IEEE 802.1Q protocol is the Standard for Virtual Bridged Local-Area Networks. It relates to the capability to carry the traffic of more than one subnet down a single cable. The IEEE 802.1Q committee defined this method of multiplexing VLANs in an effort to provide multivendor VLAN support.

Both ISL and IEEE 802.1Q tagging perform explicit tagging, meaning that the frame is tagged with VLAN information explicitly. However, whereas ISL uses an external tagging process that does not modify the existing Ethernet frame, IEEE 802.1Q uses an internal tagging process that does modify the Ethernet frame. This internal tagging process is what allows IEEE 802.1Q tagging to work on both access and trunk links, because the frame appears to be a standard Ethernet frame.

The IEEE 802.1Q frame-tagging scheme also has significantly less overhead than the ISL tagging method. As opposed to the 30 bytes added by ISL, 802.1Q inserts only an additional 4 bytes into the Ethernet frame, as shown in Figure 2-27.

Figure 2-27 IEEE 802.1Q VLAN Encapsulation Is the Most Common Format Currently Used

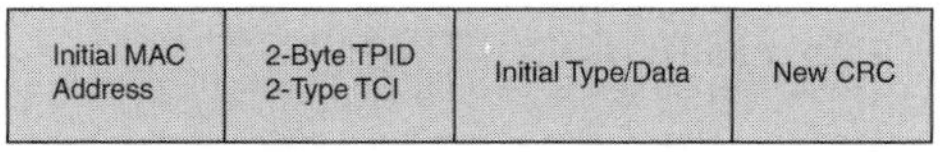

Initial MAC Address	2-Byte TPID 2-Type TCI	Initial Type/Data	New CRC

The IEEE 802.1Q header contains a 4-byte tag header that contains the following:

- A 2-byte tag protocol identifier (TPID) with a fixed value of 0x8100 that indicates that the frame carries the 802.1Q/802.1p tag information.
- A 2-byte tag control information (TCI) that contains the following:
  — 3-bit user priority
  — 1-bit canonical format indicator (CFI)
  — 12-bit VLAN identifier (VID) that uniquely identifies the VLAN to which the frame belongs

The 802.1Q standard can create an interesting scenario on the network. Recalling that the maximum size for an Ethernet frame as specified by IEEE 802.3 is 1518 bytes, this means that if a maximum-sized Ethernet frame gets tagged, the frame size is 1522 bytes, a number that violates the IEEE 802.3 standard. To resolve this issue, the 802.3 committee created a subgroup called 802.3ac to extend the maximum Ethernet size to 1522 bytes. Network devices that do not support a larger frame size process the frame successfully but might report these anomalies as a "baby giant."

The IEEE 802.10 Protocol

VLANs can be multiplexed across an FDDI backbone supporting the IEEE 802.10 protocol. Catalyst 5000 and 6000 family switches support 802.10 trunking.

FDDI interfaces that support 802.10 make selective forwarding decisions within a network domain based on a VLAN identifier. This VLAN identifier is the user-configurable 4-byte IEEE 802.10 SAID. The SAID identifies traffic as belonging to a particular VLAN.

On a Catalyst 5000 or 6000, if an FDDI module receives a packet containing a VLAN SAID that maps to a locally supported Ethernet VLAN on the switch, the FDDI module translates the packet into Ethernet format and forwards it across the switch backplane to the Ethernet module. FDDI modules filter the packets they receive from reaching the backplane if the VLAN SAIDs in the packets do not map to a locally supported VLAN.

A SAID is applied when a frame from an Ethernet VLAN needs to cross an FDDI backbone, as shown in Figure 2-28. Switch 1 must forward a packet from the Ethernet Module, Port 1, Slot 2, to the FDDI Module, Port 1, Slot 5. In this example, the translation of Ethernet VLAN 2 to FDDI VLAN 22 must be specified. The VLAN SAID must be identical on both FDDI modules. Because 802.10 FDDI interface links can also operate as ISL trunks, multiple VLAN translations can take place over a single link.

Figure 2-28 IEEE 802.10 Is the VLAN Encapsulation Method Used with FDDI

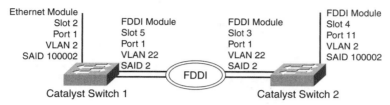

FDDI modules also support one native (nontrunk) VLAN, which handles all non-802.10 encapsulated FDDI traffic.

LAN Emulation (LANE)

ATM LANE is a standard defined by the ATM Forum that gives two stations attached via ATM the same capabilities they normally would have with legacy LANs, such as Ethernet and Token Ring. As the name suggests, the function of the LANE protocol is to emulate a LAN on top of an ATM network. Specifically, the LANE protocol defines mechanisms for emulating either an IEEE 802.3 Ethernet or 802.5 Token Ring LAN.

The LANE protocol defines a service interface for network layer protocols that is identical to that of existing LANs. Data sent across the ATM network is encapsulated in the appropriate LAN MAC format. In other words, the LANE protocols make an ATM network look and behave like an Ethernet or Token Ring LAN, albeit one operating much faster than standard Ethernet or Token Ring LAN networks (see Figure 2-29).

An emulated LAN (ELAN) provides Layer 2 communication between all users on an ELAN. One or more ELANs can run on the same ATM network. However, each ELAN is independent of the others, and users on separate ELANs cannot communicate directly. As with a VLAN, communication between ELANs is possible only through routers or bridges.

Because an ELAN provides Layer 2 communication, it can be equated to a broadcast domain. VLANs can also be thought of as broadcast domains. This makes it possible to map an ELAN to a VLAN on Layer 2 switches with different VLAN multiplexing technologies such as ISL or 802.10. In addition, IP subnets and Internetwork Packet Exchange (IPX) networks that are defined on Layer 3-capable devices such as routers frequently map into broadcast domains. This makes it possible to assign an IP subnetwork or IP network to an ELAN.

Figure 2-29 *LANE Is the Mechanism Used by ATM for VLAN Encapsulation*

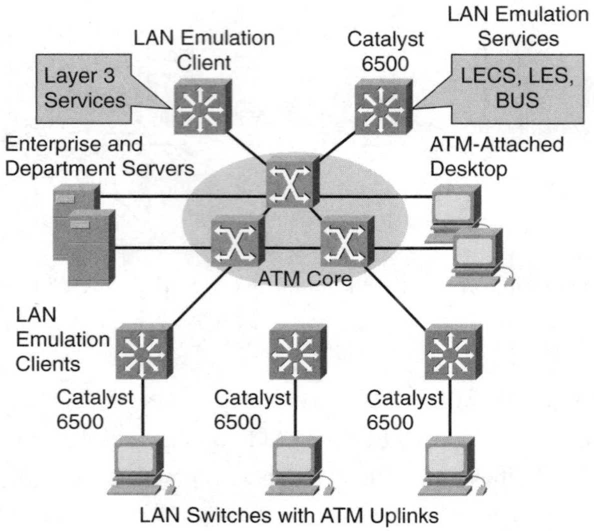

It is important to note that LANE does not attempt to emulate the access method of the specific LAN concerned (that is, carrier sense multiple access collision detect [CSMA/CD] for Ethernet or token passing for IEEE 802.5). LANE requires no modifications to higher-layer protocols to enable their operation over an ATM network. Because the LANE service presents the same service interface of existing MAC protocols to network layer drivers, such as a network driver interface specification (NDIS) or Open Data-Link Interface (ODI) driver interface, no changes are required for these drivers.

VLAN Trunking Protocol (VTP)

The role of VTP is to maintain VLAN configuration consistency across the entire network. VTP is a messaging protocol that uses Layer 2 trunk frames to manage the addition, deletion, and renaming of VLANs on a network-wide basis from a centralized switch that is in VTP server mode. VTP is responsible for synchronizing VLAN information within a VTP domain. This reduces the need to configure the same VLAN information on each switch.

VTP Benefits

VTP minimizes the possible configuration inconsistencies that arise when changes are made. These inconsistencies can result in security violations, because VLANs can crossconnect when duplicate names are used. VLANs also could become internally disconnected when they are mapped from one LAN type to another, such as Ethernet to *ATM LANE* ELANs or FDDI 802.10 VLANs. VTP provides a mapping scheme that enables seamless trunking within a network employing mixed-media technologies.

VTP provides the following benefits:

- VLAN configuration consistency across the network
- Mapping scheme that allows a VLAN to be trunked over mixed media
- Accurate tracking and monitoring of VLANs
- Dynamic reporting of added VLANs across the network
- Plug-and-play configuration when adding new VLANs

As beneficial as VTP can be, it does have disadvantages that are normally related to STP. The greatest risk is a bridging loop propagating throughout the entire campus network. Because Cisco switches run an instance of STP for each VLAN, and because VTP propagates VLANs across the campus LAN, VTP effectively creates more opportunities for a bridging loop to occur. Network designers and administrators must balance the ease of administration made possible by VTP with the risk of a large, potentially unstable STP domain.

Before you create VLANs on the switch that will be propagated via VTP, you must set up a VTP domain. A VTP domain for a network is a set of all contiguously trunked switches with the same VTP domain name. All switches in the same management domain share their VLAN information with each other, and a switch can participate in only one VTP management domain. Switches in different domains do not share VTP information.

Using VTP, each Catalyst family switch advertises the following on its trunk ports:

- Management domain
- Configuration revision number
- Known VLANs and their specific parameters

VTP Operation

A VTP domain is made up of one or more interconnected devices that share the same VTP domain name. A switch can be configured to be in one VTP domain only. Global VLAN information is propagated across the network by way of connected switch trunk ports.

When VTP messages are transmitted to other switches in the network, the VTP message is encapsulated in a trunking protocol frame such as ISL or IEEE 802.1Q, as shown in Figure 2-30.

Figure 2-30 VTP Messages Are Encapsulated in ISL or IEEE 802.1Q Frames

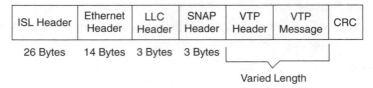

The VTP header varies, depending on the type of VTP message, but generally, four items are found in all VTP messages:

- **VTP protocol version**—Either version 1 or 2.
- **VTP message type**—Indicates one of four types (summary advertisement, subset advertisement, advertisement request, and/or join message).
- **Management domain name length**—Indicates the size of the name that follows.
- **Management domain name**—The name configured for the management domain.

It is important to note that switches can be configured not to accept VTP information. These switches forward VTP information on trunk ports to ensure that other switches receive the update, but the switches do not modify their database, nor do they send an update indicating a change in VLAN status. This is called transparent mode.

By default, management domains are set to a nonsecure mode, meaning that the switches interact without using a password. Adding a password automatically sets the management domain to secure mode. A password must be configured on every switch in the management domain to use secure mode.

Detecting the addition of VLANs within the advertisements notifies the switches that they should be prepared to receive traffic on their trunk ports with the newly defined VLAN IDs, emulated LAN names, or 802.10 SAIDs.

For example, in Figure 2-31, C6500-3 transmits a VTP database entry with additions or deletions to C6500-1 and C6500-2. The configuration database has a revision number that is notification +1. A higher configuration revision number indicates that the VLAN information that is being sent is more current than the stored copy. Any time a switch receives an update that has a higher configuration revision number, the switch overwrites the stored information with the new information being sent in the VTP update.

Figure 2-31 The VTP Configuration Revision Number Iterates When VLAN Information Is Changed on a VTP Server

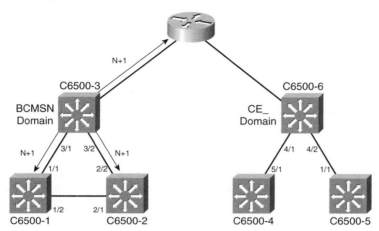

To use VTP, a VTP domain name must be assigned to each switch. VTP domain names are case-sensitive. VTP information remains in the VLAN management domain. The following are conditions for a VTP domain:

- Each Catalyst switch in a domain must have the same VTP domain name, whether learned or configured.
- The Catalyst switches must be adjacent, meaning that all switches in the VTP domain form a contiguous tree in which every switch is connected to every other switch in the domain via the tree.
- Trunking must be enabled between all Catalyst switches.

If any one of these conditions is not met, the VTP domain becomes disconnected, and information does not travel between the separate parts of the network.

VTP Modes

Switches can operate in any one of the following three VTP modes, as described in Table 2-7 and the following sections:

- Server
- Client
- Transparent

Table 2-7 VTP Mode Characteristics

Feature	Server	Client	Transparent
Source VTP messages	Yes	Yes	No
Listen to VTP messages	Yes	Yes	No
Create VLANs	Yes	No	Yes[*]
Remember VLANs	Yes	No	Yes[*]

[*] Locally significant only

VTP Server Mode

By default, a Catalyst switch is in VTP server mode and in the "no management domain" state until the switch receives an advertisement for a domain over a trunk link or a VLAN management domain is configured. A switch that has been put in VTP server mode and that has a domain name specified can create, modify, and delete VLANs. VTP servers can also specify other configuration parameters, such as VTP version and *VTP pruning* for the entire VTP domain. VTP information is stored in nonvolatile RAM (NVRAM).

VTP servers advertise their VLAN configuration to other switches in the same VTP domain and synchronize the VLAN configuration with other switches based on advertisements received over trunk links. When a change is made to the VLAN configuration on a VTP server, it is propagated to all switches in the VTP domain. VTP advertisements are transmitted out all trunk connections, including ISL, IEEE 802.1Q, IEEE 802.10, and ATM LANE trunks.

A critical parameter governing VTP function is the VTP configuration revision number. This 32-bit number indicates the particular revision of a VTP configuration. A configuration revision number starts at 0 and increments by 1 with each modification until it reaches 4294927295, at which point it cycles back to 0 and starts incrementing again. Each VTP device tracks its own VTP configuration revision number; VTP packets contain the sender's VTP configuration number. This information determines whether the received information is more recent than the current version. To reset a configuration revision number to 0, simply disable trunking, change the VTP domain name, change it back to the original name, and reenable trunking.

If the switch receives a VTP advertisement over a trunk link, it inherits the VTP domain name and configuration revision number. The switch ignores advertisements that have a different VTP domain name or an earlier configuration revision number.

VTP Client Mode

The VTP client maintains a full list of all VLANs within the VTP domain, but it does not store the information in NVRAM. VTP clients behave the same way as VTP servers, but it is not possible to create, change, or delete VLANs on a VTP client. Any changes made must be received from a VTP server advertisement.

VTP Transparent Mode

VTP transparent switches do not participate in VTP. A VTP transparent switch does not advertise its VLAN configuration and does not synchronize its VLAN configuration based on received advertisements. However, in VTP version 2, transparent switches do forward VTP advertisements that the switches receive out their trunk ports. VLANs can be configured on a switch in VTP transparent mode, but the information is local to the switch (VLAN information is not propagated to other switches) and is stored in NVRAM.

There is also an "off" VTP mode in which switches behave the same as in VTP transparent mode, except that VTP advertisements are not forwarded.

Adding a Switch to a VTP Domain

Use caution when inserting a new switch into an existing domain. To prepare a switch to enter an existing VTP domain, follow these steps:

Step 1   Delete the VLAN database, erase the startup configuration, and power-cycle the switch. This avoids potential problems resulting from residual VLAN configurations or from adding a switch with a higher VTP configuration revision number that could result in the propagation of incorrect VLAN information. From privileged mode, issue the **delete vlan.dat** and **erase startup-config** commands, and then power-cycle the switch.

Step 2   Determine the switch's VTP mode of operation and include it when setting the VTP domain name information on the switch. If you leave the switch in server mode, be sure to verify that the configuration revision number is set to 0 before adding the switch to the VTP domain. It is generally recommended that you have several servers in the domain, with all other switches set to client mode for the purposes of controlling VTP information.

Step 3   It is also highly recommended that you use secure mode in your VTP domain. Assigning a password to the domain accomplishes this. It prevents unauthorized switches from participating in the VTP domain. From privileged mode or VLAN configuration mode, use the **vtp password** *password* command.

VTP Advertisements

Periodic VTP advertisements are sent out each trunk port with the multicast destination MAC address 01-00-0C-CC-CC-CC. VTP advertisements contain the following configuration information:

- VLAN IDs (ISL and 802.1Q)
- Emulated LAN names (ATM LANE)
- 802.10 SAID values (FDDI)
- VTP domain name
- VTP configuration revision number
- VLAN configuration, including the maximum transmission unit (MTU) size for each VLAN
- Frame format

VTP messages are encapsulated in either ISL frames or IEEE 802.1Q frames.

VTP messages are sent with the following Ethernet frame field values:

- Multicast destination MAC address 01-00-0C-CC-CC-CC
- Destination Service Access Point (DSAP) 0xAA in the Logical Link Control (LLC) header
- Source Service Access Point (SSAP) 0xAA in the LLC header
- Organizational Unique Identifier (OUI) of 00-00-0C (for Cisco) in the Subnetwork Access Protocol (SNAP) header
- Ethertype of 2003 in the SNAP header

VTP packets can be encapsulated into an ISL frame. The VTP header's format varies, depending on the type of VTP message. However, all packets contain the following fields in the header:

- VTP protocol version—1 or 2
- VTP message type
- Management domain length
- Management domain name

VTP uses the following message types:

- Summary advertisements
- Subset advertisements
- Advertisement requests
- VTP join messages

VTP join messages, which rely on the VTP pruning protocol, are examined in the "VTP Configuration and VTP Pruning" section.

Advertisements on factory-default VLANs are based on media types. User ports should not be configured as VTP trunks.

There are two types of advertisements:

- Requests from clients that want information at bootup
- Response from servers

Figure 2-32 illustrates advertisement requests, summary advertisements, and subset advertisements.

Figure 2-32 Advertisement Requests, Summary Advertisements, and Subset Advertisements Are Used with VTP Operation

Advertisement Request			
1	2	3	4
Version	Code	Rsvd	MgmtD Len
Management Domain Name (Zero-Padded to 32 Bytes)			
Start Value			

Summary Advertisement			
1	2	3	4
Version	Code	Followers	MgmtD Len
Management Domain Name (Zero-Padded to 32 Bytes)			
Configuration Revision Number			
Updater Identity			
Update Timestamp (12 Bytes)			
MD5 Digest (16 Bytes)			

Subset Advertisement			
1	2	3	4
Version	Code	Seq-Num	MgmtD Len
Management Domain Name (Zero-Padded to 32 Bytes)			
Configuration Revision Number			
VLAN-Info Field 1			
Updater Identity			
Update Timestamp (12 Bytes)			
VLAN-Info Field N			

Advertisement Requests

A switch issues a VTP advertisement request in the following situations:

- The switch has been reset.
- The VTP domain name has been changed.
- The switch has received a VTP summary advertisement with a higher configuration revision number than its own.

The server responds with summary and subset advertisements (refer to Figure 2-32):

- Code is 0x03 for advertisement request (type 3).
- Rsvd is reserved and always set to 0.
- Start-Value is used in cases in which there are several subset advertisements. If subset advertisements *n* is the first advertisement that has not been received in a sequence of advertisements, an advertisement request is sent for advertisements starting with *n*. If the start value is 0, all subset advertisements are sent for the particular management domain.

Summary Advertisements

By default, Catalyst switches issue summary advertisements every 5 minutes. They inform neighbor switches of the current domain name and the configuration revision number.

When the switch receives a summary advertisement packet, as shown in Figure 2-33, it compares the VTP domain name. If the name is different, the switch simply ignores the packet. If the name is the same, the switch then compares the configuration revision. If its own configuration revision is higher or equal, the packet is ignored. If it is lower, an advertisement request is sent.

Figure 2-33 Summary Advertisements Include the VTP Domain Name and the Configuration Revision Number

Version	Code	Number of Subset Advertisement Messages	Domain Name Length
Management Domain Name (Zero-Padded to 32 Bytes)			
Configuration Revision Number			
Updater Identity			
Update Timestamp (12 Bytes)			
MD5 Digest (16 Bytes)			

The fields illustrated in Figure 2-33 are defined as follows:

- Version indicates the VTP version, which is either 1 or 2.
- Code indicates which of the four VTP message types is included. Here, 0x01 or type 1 indicates summary advertisements.
- Number of Subset Advertisement Messages (type 2) follows the Code field. The value can range from 0 to 255; 0 indicates that no subset advertisements follow. A Catalyst transmits the subset advertisement only if there is a change in the system or as a response to an advertisement request.

- Domain Name Length specifies the length of the VTP domain name.

- Management Domain Name specifies the VTP domain name.

- The Configuration Revision Number field is 32 bytes.

- The Updater Identity is the IP address of the last switch that incremented the configuration revision.

- Update Timestamp is the date and time of the last increment of the configuration revision.

- MD5 Digest consists of a message-digest hash—a function of the VTP password and the VTP header contents (excluding the MD5 Digest field). If the receiving Catalyst hash computation does not match, the packet is discarded.

Subset Advertisements

When a VLAN is added, changed, or deleted on a VTP server, the configuration revision number is incremented, and a summary advertisement is issued, followed by one or several subset advertisements. Subset advertisements are also triggered by suspending or activating a VLAN, changing its name, or changing the MTU. A subset advertisement contains a list of VLANs and corresponding VLAN information. If there are several VLANs, as shown in Figure 2-34, more than one subset advertisement might be required to advertise all the information.

Figure 2-34 Multiple VLANs Might Require Several VTP Subset Advertisements

Version	Code	Seq-Number	Domain Name Length
Management Domain Name (Zero-Padded to 32 Bytes)			
Configuration Revision Number			
VLAN-info Field 1			
:			
VLAN-info Field N			

The VLAN-info Field Contains Information for Each VLAN and Is Formatted as Follows:

Info Length	Status	VLAN-Type	VLAN-Name Len
ISL VLAN-ID		MTU Size	
802.10 Index			
VLAN-Name (Padded with Zeros to Multiple of 4 Bytes)			

The fields in a VTP subset advertisement are as follows:

- Code is 0x02 for subset advertisement (type 2).

- Seq-Number represents the packet's sequence number in the stream of subset advertisements following a summary advertisement. The sequence starts with 1. The receiving Catalyst uses this value to ensure that it receives all subset advertisements. If it does not receive all the subsets, it requests a resend, starting with a specific subset advertisement.

VLAN-info fields each contain the following information:

- The VLAN's status (active or suspended)
- VLAN-Type (Ethernet, Token Ring, FDDI, or otherwise)
- VLAN-Name Len—Length of the VLAN name
- ISL VLAN-ID—VLAN number of this named VLAN
- MTU size—Maximum frame size supported for this VLAN
- 802.10 Index—SAID value used if the frame passed over an FDDI trunk
- VLAN-name

The VTP subset advertisement lists this information for each individual VLAN, including default VLANs.

VTP Configuration and VTP Pruning

Basic Configuration Steps

The following basic tasks should be carried out before implementing VTP on a network:

Step 1   Determine the version number of VTP that will be running.

Step 2   Decide if this switch is to be a member of an existing management domain or if a new domain should be created. If a management domain does exist, determine the domain's name and password.

Step 3   Choose a VTP mode for the switch.

Remember too that for VTP to function, ports designated as trunk links also need to be configured.

VTP Configuration Options

VTP can be configured using the following configuration modes:

- Global configuration mode.
- VLAN configuration mode. VLAN configuration mode is accessed by entering the **vlan database** privileged EXEC command.

Example 2-25 demonstrates VTP configuration in global configuration mode.

Example 2-25 *VTP Configuration in Global Configuration Mode*

```
Switch#config terminal
Switch(config)#vtp version 2
Switch(config)#vtp mode server
Switch(config)#vtp domain cisco
Switch(config)#vtp password mypassword
Switch(config)#end
```

NOTE

The **exit** or **end** command can be used to leave VLAN global configuration mode. The **exit** command must be used to leave VLAN database configuration mode.

Example 2-26 illustrates VTP configuration in VLAN database configuration mode.

Example 2-26 *VTP Configuration in VLAN Database Configuration Mode*

```
Switch#vlan database
Switch(vlan)#vtp v2-mode
Switch(vlan)#vtp server
Switch(vlan)#vtp domain cisco
Switch(vlan)#vtp password mypassword
Switch(vlan)#exit
```

 Lab 2.9.2   Catalyst 2950T and 3550 Series VTP Domain and VLAN Trunking

In this lab exercise, you configure a VLAN trunk between two Cisco Catalyst WS-C2950T-24-EI switches and a Cisco Catalyst WS-C3550-24-EMI switch in CLI mode.

Configuring the VTP Version

Two different versions of VTP can run in the management domain: VTP version 1 and VTP version 2. The two versions are not interoperable in the same VTP domain. The major difference between the two versions is that version 2 introduces support for Token Ring VLANs.

If all switches in a VTP domain can run VTP version 2, version 2 needs to be enabled on only one VTP server switch. The version number is propagated to the other VTP version 2-capable switches in the VTP domain. Version 2 should not be enabled unless every switch in the VTP domain supports version 2.

The VTP version can be configured from global configuration mode or VLAN database mode on a Cisco IOS-based switch. From there, the VTP version can be changed with the **vtp** command.

Example 2-27 specifies the VTP version in global configuration mode.

Example 2-27 *Specifying the VTP Version in Global Configuration Mode*

```
Switch#config terminal
Switch(config)#vtp version 2
```

Example 2-28 specifies the VTP version in VLAN database configuration mode.

Example 2-28 *Specifying the VTP Version in VLAN Database Configuration Mode*

```
Switch#vlan database
Switch(vlan)#vtp v2-mode
```

Configuring the VTP Domain

If the switch being installed is the first switch in the network, the management domain needs to be created. However, if the network has other switches running VTP, the new switch joins an existing management domain. Verify the name of the management domain. If the management domain has been secured, verify and configure its password.

To create a management domain or to add a switch to a management domain, use the **vtp domain** command in global configuration mode or VLAN configuration mode.

If a VTP password is in use, it needs to be configured on all switches in the domain. The VTP password is translated using an algorithm resulting in a 16-byte MD5 value carried in all summary advertisements. From privileged mode or VLAN configuration mode, use the **vtp password** command. To remove the password, use the **no vtp password** command.

The domain name can be up to 32 characters, and the password must be between 8 and 64 characters.

Example 2-29 configures the VTP domain and password in global configuration mode.

Example 2-29 *Specifying the VTP Domain and Password in Global Configuration Mode*

```
Switch#config terminal
Switch(config)#vtp domain cisco
Switch(config)#vtp password mypassword
```

Example 2-30 demonstrates that the VTP domain and password can also be configured in VLAN database configuration mode.

Example 2-30 *Specifying the VTP Domain and Password in VLAN Database Configuration Mode*

```
Switch#vlan database
Switch(vlan)#vtp domain cisco
Switch(vlan)#vtp password mypassword
```

Configuring the VTP Mode

Here are some general guidelines for choosing a switch's VTP mode:

- If this is the first switch in the management domain and additional switches will be added, set the mode to server.
- If there are any other switches in the management domain, set the switch mode to client to prevent the new switch from accidentally propagating the incorrect information to your existing network.
- If a new switch needs to be set up as a VTP server, change the switch's mode to server after it has learned the correct VLAN information from the network while in client mode.
- If the switch won't share VLAN information with any other switch on the network, set it to transparent mode.

To set the correct mode of a Cisco IOS-based switch in global configuration mode, use the **vtp mode** command, as demonstrated in Example 2-31.

Example 2-31 *Specifying the VTP Mode in Global Configuration Mode*

```
Switch#config terminal
Switch(config)#vtp mode [client | server | transparent]
```

To set the correct mode of a Cisco IOS-based switch in VLAN database configuration mode, use the **vtp** command, as demonstrated in Example 2-32.

Example 2-32 *Specifying the VTP Mode in VLAN Database Configuration Mode*

```
Switch#vlan database
Switch(vlan)#vtp [client | server | transparent]
```

Verifying VTP Configuration

The **show vtp status** command, shown in Example 2-33, is used to verify VTP configuration settings on a Cisco IOS-based switch.

Example 2-33 *The* **show vtp status** *Command Displays Important VTP Information*

```
Elmhurst#show vtp status
VTP Version                     : 2
Configuration Revision          : 0
Maximum VLANs supported locally : 250
Number of existing VLANs        : 9
VTP Operating Mode              : Transparent
VTP Domain Name                 : CIT
VTP Pruning Mode                : Enabled
VTP V2 Mode                     : Disabled
VTP Traps Generation            : Disabled
MD5 digest                      : 0x61 0xEB 0x7B 0x1E 0xX4 0x2D 0x24 0x58
Configuration last modified by 0.0.0.0 at 3-1-93 00:02:53
```

The **show vtp counters** command, shown in Example 2-34, can also be used to verify VTP advertisement messages sent and received, as well as configuration errors detected. This command is useful when troubleshooting VTP.

Example 2-34 *The* **show vtp counters** *Command Displays the Number of VTP Advertisement Requests, Summary Advertisements, Subset Advertisements, and Join Messages Sent and Received*

```
Elmhurst#show vtp counters
VTP statistics:
Summary advertisements received    : 0
Subset advertisements received     : 0
Request advertiements received     : 0
Summary advertisements transmitted : 0
Subset advertisements transmitted  : 0
Request advertisements transmitted : 0
Number of config revision errors   : 0
Number of config digest errors     : 0
Number of V1 summary errors        : 0
```

Example 2-34 *The* **show vtp counters** *Command Displays the Number of VTP Advertisement Requests, Summary Advertisements, Subset Advertisements, and Join Messages Sent and Received (Continued)*

```
VTP pruning statisitcs:


Trunk            Join Transmitted Join Received   Summary advts received from
                                                  non-pruning-capable device

---------------- ---------------- ---------------   -------------------------
Fa0/2                   0                0                   0
Po6                     0                0                   0
```

Default Behavior of a Switch

A switch's default behavior is to propagate broadcast and unknown packets across the network. This behavior results in a large amount of unnecessary traffic crossing the network.

VTP pruning increases bandwidth efficiency by reducing unnecessary flooding of traffic, such as broadcast, multicast, unknown, and flooded unicast packets. VTP pruning increases available bandwidth by restricting flooded traffic to those trunk links that the traffic must use to access the appropriate network devices. By default, VTP pruning is disabled.

In a switched network that does not have VTP pruning enabled, broadcasts are sent to switches that do not need to receive them. In Figure 2-35, Port 1 on Switch 1 and Port 2 on Switch 4 are assigned to VLAN 10. A broadcast is sent from the host connected to Switch 1.

Figure 2-35 Ethernet Frames Are Propagated According to How VTP Pruning Is Configured

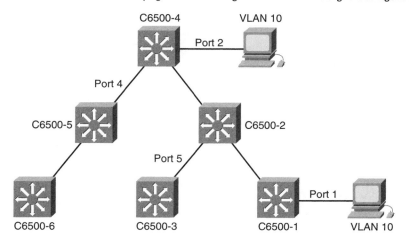

Switch C6500-1 floods the broadcast. Every switch in the network receives this broadcast, even though Switches C6500-3, C6500-5, and C6500-6 have no ports in VLAN 10.

With VTP pruning enabled, the broadcast traffic from Switch C6500-1 is not forwarded to Switches C6500-3, C6500-5, and C6500-6 because traffic for VLAN 10 has been pruned on Port 5 on Switch C6500-2 and Port 4 on Switch C6500-4.

Configuring VTP Pruning

Enabling VTP pruning on a VTP server enables pruning for the entire management domain. VTP pruning takes effect several seconds after it is enabled. By default, VLANs 2 to 1000 or 2 to 1001 are pruning-eligible, depending on the platform. VTP pruning does not prune traffic from VLANs that are pruning-ineligible. VLAN 1 is always pruning-ineligible, and it cannot be removed from a trunk. However, the "VLAN 1 disable on trunk" feature available on Catalyst 4000, 5000, and 6000 family switches enables the pruning of user traffic, but not protocol traffic, such as CDP and VTP, for VLAN 1 from a trunk. Use the **vtp pruning** VLAN database configuration command to make VLANs pruning-eligible on a Cisco IOS-based switch.

As soon as pruning is enabled, use the **switchport trunk pruning** interface configuration command to make a specific VLAN pruning-ineligible. Example 2-35 shows how to enable pruning for all VLANs except VLANs 5 to 10 (VLANs 5 to 10 are pruning-ineligible).

Example 2-35 *VTP Pruning Is Enabled on a VTP Server. The Specific VLANs That Are Pruned Can Be Configured on an Interface*

```
Switch(vlan)#vtp pruning
Pruning switched ON
Switch#configure terminal
Enter configuration commands, one per line. End with CNTL/Z
Switch(config)#interface fastethernet 0/3
Switch(config-if)#switchport trunk pruning vlan remove 5-10
Switch(config-if)#
```

Lab 2.9.3   Catalyst 2950T and 3550 Series VTP Pruning

In this lab exercise, you configure VTP pruning between two Cisco Catalyst WS-C2950T-24-EI switches and a Cisco Catalyst WS-C3550-24-EMI switch using CLI mode.

Verifying VTP Pruning

To verify the VLANs that are either pruned or not pruned on a Cisco IOS-based switch, use either the **show running-config** or **show interface** *interface-id* **switchport** command, as shown in Example 2-36.

Example 2-36 *Verifying VTP Pruning*

```
Switch#show running-config

<output omitted>

hostname Switch
!
ip subnet-zero
!
!
!
interface FastEthernet0/1
!
interface FastEthernet0/2
!
interface FastEthernet0/3
 switchport trunk allowed vlan 1,2,4,5,11-1005
 switchport trunk pruning vlan 2-4, 11-1001
 switchport mode trunk
!
interface FastEthernet0/4
Switch#show interface fastethernet 0/3 switchport
Name: Fa0/2
Switchport: Enabled
Administrative mode: trunk
Operational Mode: trunk
Administrative Trunking Encapsulation: isl
Operational Trunking Encapsulation: isl
Negotiation of Trunking: Disabled
```

continues

Example 2-36 *Verifying VTP Pruning (Continued)*

```
Access Mode VLAN: 0 ((Inactive))
Trunking Native Mode VLAN: 1 (default)
Trunking VLANs Enabled: 1,2,4,5,11-1005
Trunking VLANs Active: 1,2
Pruning VLANs Enabled: 2-4,11-1001

Priority for untagged frames: 0
Override vlan tag priority: FALSE
Voice VLAN: none
Appliance trust: none
Switch#
```

The **show vtp counters** and **debug sw-vlan vtp pruning** commands can also be useful for verifying VTP pruning.

Summary

The following concepts were covered in this chapter:

- VLANs solve many of the issues found in Layer 2 environments, including broadcast control, isolation of problem components in the network, security, and load balancing through the use of a Layer 3 protocol between VLANs.

- VLAN identification allows different VLANs to be carried on the same physical link, called a trunk link. Four major trunking technologies exist: ISL, IEEE 802.1Q, IEEE 802.10, and ATM LANE. ISL encapsulates Ethernet frames, and IEEE 802.1Q embeds a tag in the Ethernet header.

- The VLAN Trunking Protocol (VTP) provides support for dynamic reporting of the addition, deletion, and renaming of VLANs across the switch fabric.

- VTP pruning permits the dynamic pruning of unnecessary VLAN traffic within the management domain.

Key Terms

access port   A switch port that connects to an end-user device or a server.

ATM LAN Emulation (ATM LANE)   A standard defined by the ATM Forum that gives two stations attached via ATM the same capabilities they normally have with Ethernet and Token Ring.

clustering   A method of managing a group of switches without having to assign an IP address to every switch.

Dynamic Trunking Protocol (DTP)   A Cisco-proprietary protocol that autonegotiates trunk formation for either ISL or 802.1Q trunks.

Dynamic VLAN   A VLAN in which end stations are automatically assigned to the appropriate VLAN based on their MAC address. This is made possible via a MAC address-to-VLAN mapping table contained in a VLAN Management Policy Server (VMPS) database.

Emulated LAN (ELAN)   A logical construct, implemented with switches, that provides Layer 2 communication between a set of hosts in a LANE network. See *ATM LAN Emulation (ATM LANE)*.

end-to-end VLAN   Also known as a campus-wide VLAN. An end-to-end VLAN spans a campus network. It is characterized by the mapping to a group of users carrying out a similar job function (independent of physical location).

IEEE 802.10   The IEEE standard that provides a method for transporting VLAN information inside the IEEE 802.10 frame (FDDI). The VLAN information is written to the security association identifier (SAID) portion of the 802.10 frame. This allows for transporting VLANs across FDDI backbones.

IEEE 802.1Q   The IEEE standard for identifying VLANs associated with Ethernet frames. IEEE 802.1Q trunking works by inserting a VLAN identifier into the Ethernet frame header.

Inter-Switch Link (ISL)   A Cisco-proprietary encapsulation protocol for creating trunks. ISL prepends a 26-byte header and appends a 4-byte CRC to each data frame.

LAN Emulation (LANE)   An ATM Forum standard used to transport VLANs over ATM networks.

local VLAN   Also known as a geographic VLAN. A local VLAN is defined by a restricted geographic location, such as a wiring closet.

native VLAN   The VLAN that a trunk port reverts to if trunking is disabled on the port.

port-based VLAN   Also known as a static VLAN. A port-based VLAN is configured manually on a switch, where ports are mapped, one by one, to the configured VLAN. This hard-codes the mapping between ports and VLANs directly on each switch.

private VLAN   A VLAN you configure to have some Layer 2 isolation from other ports within the same private VLAN. Ports belonging to a private VLAN are associated with a common set of supporting VLANs that create the private VLAN structure.

trunk   A point-to-point link connecting a switch to another switch, router, or server. A trunk carries traffic for multiple VLANs over the same link. The VLANs are multiplexed over the link with a trunking protocol.

virtual LAN (VLAN)   A group of end stations with a common set of requirements, independent of their physical location, that communicate as if they were attached to the same wire. A VLAN has the same attributes as a physical LAN but allows you to group end stations even if they are not located physically on the same LAN segment.

VLAN Management Policy Server (VMPS)   A Cisco-proprietary solution for enabling dynamic VLAN assignments to switch ports within a VTP domain.

VLAN map   Referred to as a VLAN access control list (VACL) in the context of Catalyst 6500 switches. A generalized access control list applied on a Catalyst switch that permits filtering of both intra-VLAN and inter-VLAN packets.

VLAN Trunking Protocol (VTP)   A Cisco-proprietary protocol used to communicate information about VLANs between Catalyst switches.

VTP domain   Also called a VLAN management domain. A network's VTP domain is the set of all contiguously trunked switches with the same VTP domain name.

VTP pruning   A switch feature used to dynamically eliminate, or prune, unnecessary VLAN traffic.

Check Your Understanding

Use the following review questions to test your understanding of the concepts covered in this chapter. Answers are listed in Appendix A, "Check Your Understanding Answer Key."

1. For which of the following VTP modes does a Catalyst switch listen to VTP advertisements?

    A. Client

    B. Server

    C. Transparent

    D. Peer

2. Which of the following are Cisco-proprietary protocols?

  A. CDP

  B. VQP

  C. VTP

  D. ISL

3. Which of the following are VLAN trunking methods?

  A. ATM LANE

  B. IEEE 802.10

  C. IEEE 802.1Q

  D. ISL

4. Two devices in the same VLAN require a Layer 3 switch to communicate. What campus design model is used?

  A. Remote VLANs

  B. Campus VLANs

  C. Local VLANs

  D. End-to-end VLANs

5. Which of the following are required for dynamic VLAN assignment to ports with VMPS?

  A. VQP

  B. VMPS server

  C. VMPS client

  D. TFTP server

6. Which VLAN database configuration mode command is used to remove VLAN 20?

  A. **erase vlan 20**

  B. **clear vlan 20**

  C. **delete vlan 20**

  D. **no vlan 20**

7. What is the operational mode of a link when both ends are configured as dynamic desirable?

   A. Trunk

   B. Static access

8. What three commands are used to restore a Catalyst 3550 switch to a default configuration?

   A. copy running-config startup-config

   B. erase startup-config

   C. delete vlan.dat

   D. reload

9. Which construct can be used to filter both intra-VLAN and inter-VLAN traffic?

   A. Router ACL

   B. VLAN map

   C. IOS ACL

   D. Port ACL

10. Which of the following messages are used with VTP?

    A. Join messages

    B. Advertisement requests

    C. Subset advertisements

    D. Summary advertisements

Objectives

After completing this chapter, you will be able to perform tasks related to the following:

- Explain the evolution of Spanning Tree Protocol (STP).
- Understand and have the knowledge and skills to configure basic STP operations, processes, and enhancements.
- Have a basic understanding of Rapid Spanning Tree Protocol (RSTP).
- Configure basic STP functions, operations, and tuning.
- Verify and troubleshoot STP configuration.
- Differentiate between Mono Spanning Tree and Multiple Spanning Tree, both of which are abbreviated MST.
- Configure EtherChannel.

Chapter 3

Spanning Tree Protocol (STP)

Of all the protocols that network engineers spend time learning about and planning for, the one that is probably overlooked the most is *Spanning Tree Protocol (STP)*. As routers became popular in the early 1990s, STP faded into the background as a "less-important protocol that just worked." However, with switching technology now in the forefront, STP has once again earned its place as an important consideration in network design.

A poorly planned initial implementation of STP can mean that an inordinate proportion of the configuration, troubleshooting, and maintenance effort on a campus network becomes devoted to STP. This chapter explains the mechanics of STP, detailing its loop-prevention function in switched networks. Understanding these mechanics enables a proactive rather than reactive approach to configuring STP on the target switched network.

STP is one of the most technical subjects in LAN switching. The challenge of understanding STP is similar to that of understanding the underlying operation of Open Shortest Path First (OSPF) or Enhanced Interior Gateway Routing Protocol (EIGRP) in a campus network (timers, packet types, algorithms, and so on). It is essential to gain this understanding. STP serves as a fundamental logical building block in every campus network, and it plays a key role in network design and implementation.

This chapter discusses Layer 2 techniques and technologies designed to optimize network reliability, resiliency, and redundancy within a campus network. In particular, this chapter explores scaling issues with STP as they pertain to virtual LANs (VLANs).

STP Operation

Broadcast storms and bridge table corruption are primary motivators for the use of STP in a switched network. STP parameters such as Bridge Priority, Path Cost, and Port ID govern STP's behavior. This section discusses the motivators for STP and the parameters affecting its behavior.

STP Concepts

STP is a Layer 2 protocol that uses a special-purpose algorithm to discover physical loops in a network and effect a logical loop-free topology. STP creates a loop-free tree structure consisting of leaves and branches that span the entire Layer 2 network. The actual mechanics of how bridges communicate and how the STP algorithm works are discussed at length in this chapter. Note that the terms *bridge* and *switch* are used interchangeably when discussing STP, because with respect to the IEEE 802.1D STP specifications, there is no distinction between bridges and switches. In addition, unless otherwise indicated, connections between switches are assumed to be trunks.

The greater discussion of STP concerns its behavior on trunk connections, which form the spanning tree. Loops can occur in a network for a variety of reasons. Usually, loops in a network are the result of a deliberate attempt to provide redundancy. However, loops can also result from configuration errors. Figure 3-1 shows a typical switched network and how physical loops can be intentionally used to provide redundancy. Without STP, looping network traffic would degrade performance to the extent that the network would be effectively unusable.

Physical loops without proper STP design can be disastrous. Two problems that can result are broadcast storms and bridge table corruption. These phenomena are discussed in the next two sections.

Broadcast Loops

Broadcasts and physical loops are a dangerous combination. Figure 3-2 shows how broadcast loops are generated. Two switches, Cat-1 and Cat-2, have STP disabled. Host A and Host B are connected to Cat-1 and Cat-2 by hubs.

Figure 3-1 Physical Loops Provide Redundancy in Switched Networks

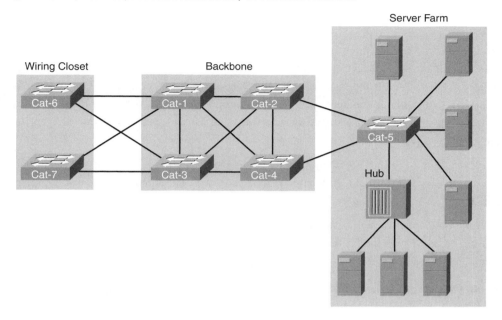

Figure 3-2 Broadcast Loops Would Occur in This Scenario Because STP Is Disabled

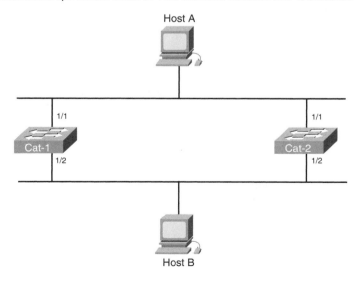

Host A sends a frame to the broadcast Media Access Control (MAC) address FF-FF-FF-FF-FF-FF, which travels to both Cat-1 and Cat-2. When the frame arrives at Port 1/1 on Cat-1, Cat-1 follows the standard transparent bridging algorithm and floods the frame out all the other ports, including Port 1/2. The frame exiting Port 1/2 travels to all nodes on the lower Ethernet segment, including Port 1/2 on Cat-2. Cat-2 floods the broadcast frame out all the other ports, including Port 1/1, and, once again, the frame shows up at Port 1/1 on Cat-1. Oblivious to the loop, Cat-1 sends the frame out Port 1/2 for the second time, and a broadcast loop is now in effect. Recall that a switch does not forward a frame out the same port through which it entered the switch.

The discussion so far has not mentioned that not only would Cat-1 have received the initial broadcast from Host A, but Cat-2 would receive it as well. The same problem would propagate in the reverse direction as a result. The "feedback" loop would occur in both directions.

An important conclusion to be drawn is that bridging loops are much more dangerous than routing loops. Why is this? Suppose the initial broadcast frame were an Ethernet version II frame, as shown in Figure 3-3.

Figure 3-3 The Format for the Ethernet Version II Frame Was Developed by Digital, Intel, and Xerox

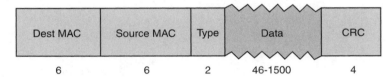

The Ethernet version II frame contains only two MAC addresses, a Type field, the network-layer packet as data, and a cyclic redundancy check (CRC). In contrast, an IP header contains a Time-To-Live (TTL) field that is set by the source and is decremented at each router. By discarding packets that reach TTL = 0, routers prevent "runaway" datagrams. Unlike IP, Ethernet does not have a TTL field. Therefore, after a frame starts to loop in the network, as just described, it continues until a switch is turned off or a link is broken. The network shown in Figure 3-2 is extremely simple. Feedback loops of this type grow exponentially as additional switches and links are incorporated into the network. A single broadcast can render a network unusable, all because STP is disabled or configured incorrectly.

Bridge Table Corruption

A less-understood problem than broadcast storms is unicast frames causing network bottlenecks. Figure 3-4 illustrates how a unicast packet can cause such a problem.

Figure 3-4 The MAC Address-to-Port Associations for Host A Flip-Flop on Cat-1 and Cat-2

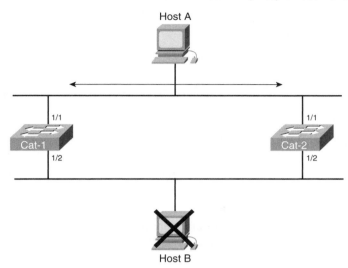

Host A possesses a prior Address Resolution Protocol (ARP) entry for Host B and wants to ping Host B. However, Host B has been temporarily removed from the network, and the corresponding bridge-table entries in the switches have been flushed for Host B. Assume that neither switch is running STP. As with the previous example, the frame travels to Port 1/1 on both switches. Consider the scenario relative to Cat-1 alone. Cat-1 does not have an entry for the MAC address of Host B, BB-BB-BB-BB-BB-BB, in its bridging table; as a result, it floods the frame to all other ports. Cat-2 then receives the frame on Port 1/2.

Two things happen at this point:

1. Cat-2 floods the frame because MAC address BB-BB-BB-BB-BB-BB is not in its bridging table.

2. Cat-2 notices that it received a frame on Port 1/2 with a source MAC address of AA-AA-AA-AA-AA-AA (from Host A).

As a result, Cat-2 changes its bridging table entry for the MAC address of Host A to the wrong port.

As frames loop in the reverse direction (the feedback loop goes both ways), the MAC address of Host A flip-flops between Port 1/1 and Port 1/2 on the switches. In short, not only does this permanently saturate the network with the unicast ping packet, but it also corrupts the bridging tables and drives the switch CPU utilization to 100 percent (which prevents the switch from forwarding traffic). This example demonstrates that broadcasts are not the only types of frames that can bring down a network.

Bridge Priority

An algorithm is a formula or set of steps for solving a particular problem. Algorithms rely on a set of rules. They have a clear beginning and end. The Spanning Tree Algorithm is no exception.

The IEEE 802.1D standard defines the Spanning Tree Algorithm that characterizes STP. This algorithm relies on the BID, Path Cost, and Port ID parameters to make decisions (the following sections cover Path Cost and Port ID in greater detail).

The *Bridge ID (BID)* is the first parameter used by the Spanning Tree Algorithm. STP uses the BID to determine the center of the bridged network, known as the *Root Bridge* or *Root Switch*. The BID parameter is an 8-byte field consisting of an ordered pair of numbers, as shown in Figure 3-5. The first is a 2-byte decimal number called the *Bridge Priority*, and the second is a 6-byte (hexadecimal) MAC address. The Bridge Priority is a decimal number used to measure the preference of a bridge in the Spanning Tree Algorithm. The possible values range between 0 and 65,535. The default setting is 32,768.

Figure 3-5 The BID Consists of an Ordered Pair of Numbers, the Bridge Priority, and the MAC Address

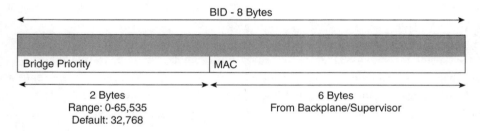

The MAC address in the BID is one of the switch's MAC addresses. Each switch has a pool of MAC addresses, one for each instance of STP, used as BIDs for the VLAN spanning-tree instances (one per VLAN). For example, Catalyst 6000 switches each have a pool of 1024 MAC addresses assigned to the Supervisor module or backplane for this purpose.

The way to compare BIDs is as follows:

Let (s,t) and (u,v) represent two BIDs, where the first coordinate is the Bridge Priority and the second coordinate is the MAC address (Priority, MAC address). Then (s,t) < (u,v) if and only if

- $s < u$

or

- $s = u$ and $t < v$

Two BIDs cannot be equal, because Catalyst switches are assigned unique MAC addresses. In terms of the Spanning Tree Algorithm, when a comparison is made between two values of a given STP parameter, the lower value is always preferred.

Path Cost

The Path Cost is the second parameter used by the Spanning Tree Algorithm to determine the path to the Root Switch.

Path Cost is a measure of how close bridges are to each other. Path Cost is the sum of the costs of the links in a path between two bridges. It is not a measure of hop count. The hop count for Path A might be greater than the hop count for Path B, while the cost of Path A is less than the cost of Path B. Closeness is not necessarily reflected by hop count.

Switches use the Path Cost to determine the best path to the Root Switch. The lowest combination of links has the lowest cumulative Path Cost and is the best path to the Root Switch.

The IEEE 802.1D standard originally defined the cost of a link as 1000 Mbps divided by the link's bandwidth in Mbps. For example, a 10BASE-T link has a cost of 100 (1000/10), and Fast Ethernet and Fiber Distributed Data Interface (FDDI) each have a cost of 10 (1000/100). With the advent of Gigabit Ethernet and other high-speed technologies, a problem with this definition evolved.

The cost is stored as an integer value, not as a floating-point value. For example, 10 Gbps results in 1000 Mbps/10000 Mbps = .1, an invalid cost value. To solve this problem, the IEEE changed the "inverse proportion" definition. Table 3-1 shows the definition of the STP cost for a link exceeding 1 Gbps on a CatOS switch (short mode). Table 3-2 shows the definition of the STP cost for a link of 10 Gbps or higher on a CatOS switch (long mode). The default cost mode for a CatOS switch can be manually configured; all switches in a network must use the same default. On newer IOS-based switches such as the Catalyst 2950 and Catalyst 3550, the valid range from which the STP cost can be assigned is 1 to 200,000,000.

Table 3-1 The CatOS STP Cost Definition Was Updated to Account for Links with Speeds Up to 10 Gbps (Short Mode)

Bandwidth	STP Cost
4 Mbps	250
10 Mbps	100
16 Mbps	62
45 Mbps	39

continues

Table 3-1 The CatOS STP Cost Definition Was Updated to Account for Links with Speeds Up to 10 Gbps (Short Mode) (Continued)

Bandwidth	STP Cost
100 Mbps	19
155 Mbps	14
622 Mbps	6
1 Gbps	4
10 Gbps	2

Table 3-2 The CatOS STP Cost Definition Was Again Updated to Account for Links with Speeds Up to 10 Tbps (Long Mode)

Bandwidth	STP Cost
4 kbps	200,000,000
1 Mbps	20,000,000
10 Mbps	2,000,000
100 Mbps	200,000
1 Gbps	20,000
10 Gbps	2000
100 Gbps	200
1 Tbps (terabits per second)	20
10 Tbps	2

Port ID

The *Port ID* is the third parameter used by the Spanning Tree Algorithm to determine the path to the Root Switch. Figure 3-6 illustrates the Port ID, which is a 2-byte STP parameter consisting of an ordered pair of numbers, the Port Priority and the Port Number.

Figure 3-6 The Port ID

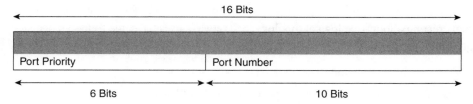

On a CatOS switch, the Port Priority is 6 bits and the Port Number is 10 bits. On an IOS-based switch, both numbers are 8 bits.

Port ID should not be confused with the Port Number. The Port Number is just part of the Port ID. Lower Port IDs are preferred over higher Port IDs in the STP decision process. The order relation for Port IDs is explained in the following example.

If (s,t) and (u,v) represent two Port IDs (the first coordinate being the Port Priority and the second coordinate being the Port Number), (s,t) < (u,v) if and only if

- $s < u$
- $s = u$ and $t < v$

Two Port IDs cannot be equal, because Port Numbers uniquely identify the switch ports on a Catalyst switch.

The *Port Priority* is a configurable STP parameter (unlike the Port Number), with values ranging from 0 to 255 on an IOS-based switch (the default value is 128).

Port Numbers are numerical identifiers used by Catalyst switches to enumerate the ports. The Port Number leaves room for 2^8 (256) ports on an IOS-based switch (Cisco routers also use the 8-bit/8-bit Port ID definition).

STP Processes

This section provides details of exactly how IEEE 802.1D STP works by describing the three steps of STP convergence, as well as the election of the Root Switch, Root Port, and Designated Port. Furthermore, this section explores STP timers and the process of topology change.

STP Decisions and BPDU Exchanges

The Spanning Tree Algorithm operates as a function of the BID, Path Cost, and Port ID. When creating a loop-free logical topology, STP always uses the same four-step decision sequence:

Step 1   Determine the Root Switch.

Step 2   Calculate the lowest Path Cost to the Root Switch.

Step 3   Determine the lowest sender BID.

Step 4   Determine the lowest Port ID.

Figure 3-7 illustrates this sequence.

Figure 3-7 The Four-Step Decision Process of STP

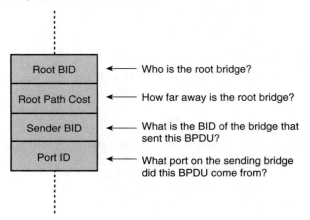

As a clarification, Step 1 is essentially the election of the switch that has the lowest BID when compared with other switches in the topology. This is fully discussed in the following sections.

To make good decisions, STP needs to ensure that the participating bridges have the correct information. The bridges need to communicate the STP information between them. Bridges pass spanning-tree information between them using Layer 2 frames called *bridge protocol data units (BPDUs)*. A bridge uses the four-step decision sequence to determine the "best" BPDU seen on each port. The bridge determines the best BPDU based on the four-step STP process. The bridge stores the best BPDU it receives for each port. When making this evaluation, it considers all the BPDUs received on the port, as well as the BPDU it would send on that same port.

As each BPDU arrives at the switch port, it is checked against this four-step sequence to see if it is more attractive than the existing BPDU saved for that port. If the new BPDU (or the locally generated BPDU) is more attractive, the old value is replaced.

Additionally, this "saving-the-best-BPDU" process also controls the sending of BPDUs. When a bridge first becomes active, all its ports send BPDUs every 2 seconds (the default *Hello Time*). However, if a port hears about a BPDU from another bridge that is more attractive than the BPDU it has been sending, the local port eventually stops sending BPDUs. If the more-attractive BPDU stops arriving from a neighbor for 20 seconds (the default Max Age), the local port resumes sending BPDUs. Max Age is the time it takes for the best BPDU to time out.

Three Steps of STP Convergence

The Spanning Tree Algorithm is somewhat complex, but the initial process used to converge on a loop-free topology consists of three election steps:

Step 1   Elect a Root Switch.

Step 2   Elect Root Ports.

Step 3   Elect Designated Ports.

Figure 3-8 illustrates Root Port election.

NOTE

The default configuration for Catalyst switches is to run one instance of the Spanning Tree Algorithm per VLAN.

Figure 3-8 Root Port Election is the Second Step

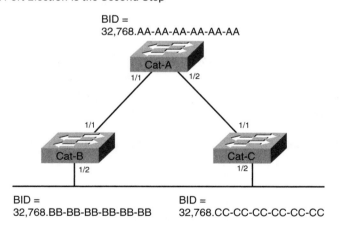

When the network first "starts," all the bridges flood it with a mixture of BPDU information. The bridges begin applying the STP four-step decision sequence discussed in the preceding section. This allows the bridges to hone in on a set of BPDUs that enable the formation of a single spanning tree for the entire network or VLAN.

A single Root Switch is elected to act as the central point of this network (Step 1). All the remaining bridges calculate a set of Root Ports (Step 2) and Designated Ports (Step 3) to build a loop-free topology. The resulting topology is a tree, with the Root Switch as the trunk and loop-free active paths radiating outward as tree branches. In a steady-state network, BPDUs flow from the Root Switch outward along these loop-free branches to every segment in the network. After the network has converged on a loop-free active topology using this three-step process, changes are handled using the spanning-tree topology change process. The following sections consider the three steps of STP convergence in detail.

Electing the Root Switch

As a first step in the STP process, the switches need to elect a single Root Switch by looking for the bridge with the lowest BID. This process of selecting the bridge with the lowest BID is sometimes called the "root war."

As discussed in the earlier "Bridge Priority" section, a BID is an 8-byte identifier that is composed of two subfields, the Bridge Priority and a MAC address. As Figure 3-8 illustrates, Cat-A has a default BID of 32,768.AA-AA-AA-AA-AA-AA, Cat-B assumes a default BID of 32,768.BB-BB-BB-BB-BB-BB, and Cat-C uses 32,768.CC-CC-CC-CC-CC-CC. Because all three bridges use the default Bridge Priority of 32,768, the lowest MAC address, AA-AA-AA-AA-AA-AA, serves as the tiebreaker, and Cat-A becomes the Root Switch. The process of how to configure a switch to become the Root Switch is examined in the following sections. Normally, the default settings should not be allowed to determine the location of the Root Switch. How did the bridges learn that Cat-A has the lowest BID? This is accomplished through the exchange of BPDUs. As discussed earlier, BPDUs are special frames that bridges use to exchange spanning-tree information with each other. By default, BPDUs are sent every 2 seconds. BPDUs propagate between bridges, which includes switches and all routers configured for bridging. BPDUs do not carry end-user traffic. Figure 3-9 illustrates the layout of a BPDU.

Figure 3-9 A BPDU Includes Root BID, Root Path Cost, Sender BID, and Port ID Information

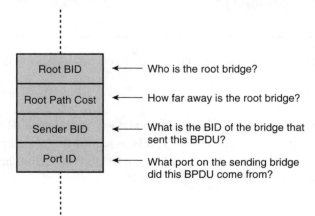

For the purposes of the root war, this discussion involves only the Root BID and Sender BID fields. When a bridge generates a BPDU every 2 seconds, the bridge places what it thinks is the Root Switch at that instant in the Root BID field. The bridge always places its own BID in the Sender BID field. Initially, before the switch knows any better, it populates the Root BID field with its own BID. Suppose that Cat-B boots first and starts sending out BPDUs announcing itself as the Root Switch every 2 seconds. A few minutes later, Cat-C boots and announces itself as the Root Switch. When the Cat-C BPDU arrives at Cat-B, Cat-B discards the BPDU because it has a lower BID saved on its ports (its own BID). As soon as Cat-B transmits a BPDU, Cat-C learns that it is not as important as it initially thought. At this point, Cat-C starts sending BPDUs that list Cat-B as the Root BID and Cat-C as the sender BID. The network now agrees that Cat-B is the Root Switch. Five minutes later, Cat-A boots. Cat-A initially thinks it is the Root Switch and starts advertising this fact via BPDUs. As soon as these BPDUs arrive at Cat-B and Cat-C, the switches hand over the Root Switch position to Cat-A. All three switches now send BPDUs that announce Cat-A as the Root Switch and themselves as the sender BID.

Electing Root Ports

At the conclusion of the root war, the switches move on to selecting Root Ports. A bridge's **Root Port** is the port that is closest to the Root Switch in terms of Path Cost. Every non-Root Switch must select one Root Port. Again, bridges use the concept of cost to measure closeness. As with some routing metrics, the measure of closeness using STP is not necessarily reflected by hop count. Specifically, bridges track the **Root Path Cost**, the cumulative cost of all links to the Root Switch. Figure 3-10 illustrates how this value is calculated across multiple bridges and the resulting Root Port election process.

Figure 3-10 Root Ports Are Elected After the Root Switch Is Elected

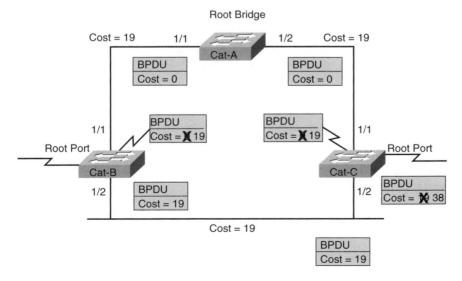

When Cat-A (the Root Switch) sends out BPDUs, they contain a Root Path Cost of 0. When Cat-B receives these BPDUs, it adds the Path Cost of Port 1/1 to the Root Path Cost contained in the received BPDU. Assume that the network is running Fast Ethernet:

1. Cat-B receives a Root Path Cost of 0 and adds in the Port 1/1 cost of 19.

2. Cat-B uses the value of 19 internally and sends BPDUs with a Root Path Cost of 19 out Port 1/2.

3. When Cat-C receives these BPDUs from Cat-B, it increases the Root Path Cost to 38 (19 + 19).

4. However, Cat-C is also receiving BPDUs from the Root Switch on Port 1/1.

5. These BPDUs enter Port 1/1 on Cat-C with a cost of 0, and Cat-C increases the cost to 19 internally. Cat-C has a decision to make.

6. Cat-C must select a single Root Port—the port that is closest to the Root Switch.

7. Cat-C sees a Root Path Cost of 19 on Port 1/1 and 38 on Port 1/2. Port 1/1 on Cat-C becomes the Root Port.

8. Cat-C begins advertising this Root Path Cost of 19 to downstream switches.

Cat-B goes through a similar set of calculations. Port 1/1 on Cat-B can reach the Root Switch at a cost of 19, whereas Port 1/2 on Cat-B calculates a cost of 38. Port 1/1 becomes the Root Port for Cat-B. The costs increment as BPDUs are received on a port, not as they are sent out the port. For example, BPDUs arrive on Port 1/1 on Cat-B with a cost of 0 and get increased to 19 "inside" Cat-B.

Electing Designated Ports

At this point, the Spanning Tree Algorithm still has not eliminated any loops. This is taken care of after the *Designated Ports* and non-Designated Ports are determined. Each segment in a bridged network has one Designated Port. A Designated Port for a segment is the bridge port connected to that segment that both sends traffic toward the Root Switch and receives traffic from the Root Switch over that segment. The idea behind this is that if only one port handles traffic for each link, all the loops have been broken. The *Designated Bridge* for a segment is the bridge containing the Designated Port for that segment.

With the Root Port selection, the Designated Ports are chosen based on the Root Path Cost to the Root Switch, as shown in Figure 3-11.

Figure 3-11 Designated Ports Are Elected After the Root Switch and Root Ports Are Elected

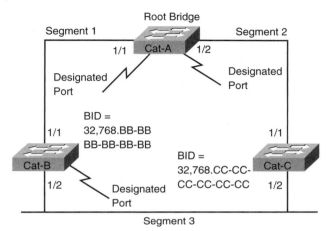

The Root Path Cost is the cumulative cost of all links leading to the Root Switch. Segment 1 forms a link between Cat-A and Cat-B. This segment has two bridge ports, Port 1/1 on Cat-A and Port 1/1 on Cat-B. Port 1/1 on Cat-A has a Root Path Cost of 0 because Cat-A is the Root Switch. Port 1/2 on Cat-A has a Root Path Cost of 0 because Cat-A is the Root Switch. Port 1/1 on Cat-B has a Root Path Cost of 19—the value 0 received in BPDUs from Cat-A plus the Path Cost of 19 assigned to Port 1/1 on Cat-B. Because Port 1/1 Cat-A has the lower Root Path Cost, it becomes the Designated Port for this link. For Segment 2, the Cat-A-to-Cat-C link, a similar election takes place. Port 1/2 on Cat-A has a Root Path Cost of 0, whereas Port 1/1 on Cat-C has a Root Path Cost of 19. Port 1/2 on Cat-A has the lower cost and becomes the Designated Port. Notice that every active port on the Root Switch becomes a Designated Port.

Examining Segment 3, the link from Cat-B to Cat-C, both Port 1/2 on Cat-B and Port 1/2 on Cat-C have a Root Path Cost of 19, resulting in a tie. When faced with a tie, STP always uses the STP four-step decision sequence discussed earlier. Recall that the four steps are as follows:

Step 1   Determine the Root Switch.

Step 2   Calculate the lowest Root Path Cost.

Step 3   Determine the lowest sender BID.

Step 4   Determine the lowest Port ID.

All three bridges shown in Figure 3-11 agree that Cat-A is the Root Switch, so the algorithm checks Root Path Cost next. However, both Cat-B and Cat-C have a cost of 19, so the algorithm resorts to the lowest sender BID. Because the Cat-B BID (32,768.BB-BB-BB-BB-BB-BB) is lower than the Cat-C BID (32,768.CC-CC-CC-CC-CC-CC), Cat-B:Port 1/2 becomes the Designated Port for Segment 3. Cat-C:Port 1/2 becomes a non-Designated Port. Note that access ports do not play a role in the election of Designated Ports. Trunk ports are used to connect to other switches. Access ports are used to connect to hosts or routers. The process described here involves communication of STP parameters over trunk links.

STP States

After the bridges have determined which ports are Root Ports, Designated Ports, and non-Designated Ports, STP is ready to create a loop-free topology. To do this, STP configures Root Ports and Designated Ports to forward traffic. STP sets non-Designated Ports to block traffic. Although Forwarding and Blocking are the only two states commonly seen in a stable network, there are actually five STP states, as described in Table 3-3.

Table 3-3 STP States

State	Description
Forwarding	Sends and receives user data
Learning	Builds the bridging table
Listening	Builds the "active" topology
Blocking	Receives BPDUs only
Disabled	Administratively down

The STP states can be viewed hierarchically in that bridge ports start at the Blocking state and work their way up to the Forwarding state. The *Disabled state* is the administratively shut down STP state. It is not part of the normal STP port processing. After the switch is initialized, ports start in the Blocking state. The Blocking state is the STP state in which a bridge listens for BPDUs.

Blocking State

A port in the *Blocking state* has the following characteristics and functions:

- It discards frames received from the attached segment or internally forwarded through switching.

- It receives BPDUs and directs them to the system module.
- It has no address database.
- It does not transmit BPDUs received from the system module.
- It receives and responds to network management messages but does not transmit them.

Listening State

If a bridge thinks it is the Root Switch immediately after booting or in the absence of BPDUs for a certain period of time, the port transitions into the *Listening state*. The Listening state is the STP state in which no user data is being passed, but the port is sending and receiving BPDUs in an effort to determine the active topology.

A port in the Listening state has the following characteristics and functions:

- It discards frames received from the attached segment or frames switched from another port.
- It has no address database.
- It receives BPDUs and directs them to the system module.
- It processes BPDUs received from the system module. (Processing BPDUs is a separate action from receiving or transmitting BPDUs.)
- It receives and responds to network management messages.

The three initial convergence steps—electing a Root Switch, Root Ports, and Designated Ports—take place during the Listening state. Ports that lose the Designated Port election become non-Designated Ports and drop back to the Blocking state. Ports that remain Designated Ports or Root Ports after 15 seconds—the default Forward Delay STP timer value—progress into the Learning state.

Learning State

The *Learning state* is the STP state in which the bridge is doesn't pass user data frames but builds the bridging table and gathers information, such as the source VLANs of data frames. As the bridge receives a frame, it places the source MAC address and port into the bridging table. The Learning state reduces the amount of flooding required when data forwarding begins. The lifetime of the Learning state is also governed by the Forward Delay timer of 15 seconds, the default setting.

A port in the Learning state has the following characteristics and functions:

- It discards frames received from the attached segment.
- It discards frames switched from another port for forwarding.
- It incorporates station location into its address database.

- It receives BPDUs and directs them to the system module.
- It receives, processes, and transmits BPDUs received from the system module.
- It receives and responds to network management messages.

Forwarding State

If a port is still a Designated Port or Root Port after the Forward Delay timer expires for the Learning state, the port transitions into the Forwarding state. The *Forwarding state* is the STP state in which data traffic is both sent and received on a port. It is the "last" STP state. At this stage, it finally starts forwarding user data frames.

A port in the Forwarding state has the following characteristics and functions:

- It forwards frames received from the attached segment.
- It forwards frames switched from another port for forwarding.
- It incorporates station location information into its address database.
- It receives BPDUs and directs them to the system module.
- It processes BPDUs received from the system module.
- It receives and responds to network management messages.

Transitions Between STP States

Figure 3-12 illustrates the transitions between STP states. The scenario in Figure 3-13 shows Root Ports, Designated Ports, and non-Designated Ports and the associated STP states.

Figure 3-12 Various Events Trigger Transitions Between STP States

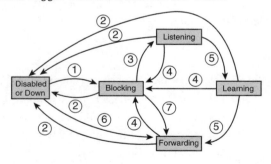

Legend of Events:
1. Port Enabled or Initialized
2. Port Disabled or Fails
3. Port Selected as Root or Designated Port
4. Port Ceases to be a Root or Designated Port
5. Forwarding Timer Expires
6. PortFast
7. UplinkFast

Figure 3-13 Root Ports, Designated Ports, and Non-Designated Ports and the Associated STP
States in a Stable STP Topology

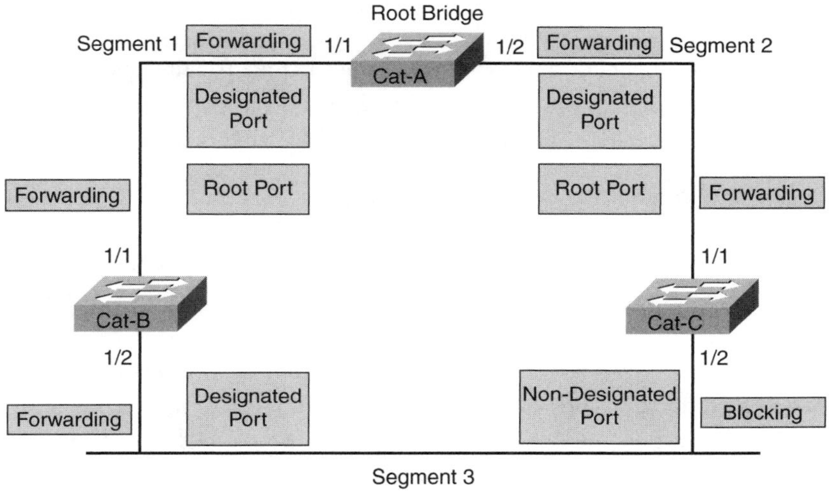

STP Timers

STP operation is controlled by three timers, as described in Table 3-4.

Table 3-4 Three Timers Used with STP

Timer	Primary Purpose	Default
Hello Time	The amount of time between the sending of Configuration BPDUs by the Root Switch	2 seconds
Forward Delay	The duration of the Listening and Learning states	15 seconds
Max Age	How long a BPDU is stored	20 seconds

The Hello Time is the amount of time between the sending of Configuration BPDUs. The
802.1D standard specifies a default value of 2 seconds. This value controls Configuration
BPDUs as the Root Switch generates them. Other bridges propagate BPDUs from the Root
Switch as they are received.

If BPDUs stop arriving for the time interval ranging from 2 to 20 seconds because of a network disturbance, or if the Root Switches stop sending periodic BPDUs during this time,
the timer expires. The range between the expected receipt of a BPDU and the expiration of

the Max Age time is 2 to 20 seconds. If the outage lasts for more than 20 seconds (the default Max Age time), the bridge invalidates the saved BPDUs and begins looking for a new Root Port.

Forward Delay is the amount of time the bridge spends in the Listening and Learning states. This is a single value that controls both states. The default value of 15 seconds was originally derived assuming a maximum network size of seven bridge hops, a maximum of three lost BPDUs, and a Hello Time of 2 seconds. The Forward Delay timer also controls the bridge table age-out period after a change in the active topology.

Max Age is the STP timer that controls how long a bridge stores a BPDU before discarding it. Max Age is an issue only when the link failure is not on a directly connected link. When a failure occurs on a directly connected link, the switch knows that no BPDUs will be coming in on that link, so Max Age is not considered in transitioning the port to Forwarding state. Recall that each port saves a copy of the best BPDU it has seen. As long as the bridge receives a continuous stream of BPDUs every 2 seconds, Max Age does not come into play. However, if the device sending this best BPDU fails, a mechanism must exist to allow other bridges to take over.

For example, assume that the Segment 3 link shown in Figure 3-14 uses a hub and that Port 1/2 on the Cat-B transceiver fails. Cat-C receives no immediate notification of the failure, because it still has an active Ethernet link to the hub. The only thing Cat-C knows is that BPDUs stop arriving. Twenty seconds (Max Age) after the failure, Port 1/2 on Cat-C ages out the BPDU information that lists Cat-B as having the best Designated Port for Segment 3. This forces Port 1/2 on Cat-C to transition to the Listening state in an effort to become the Designated Port. Because Port 1/2 on Cat-C now offers the most attractive access from the Root Switch to this link, it eventually transitions all the way into Forwarding state. In this example, with a hub between Cat-B and Cat-C, it takes approximately 50 seconds (20 Max Age + 15 Listening + 15 Learning) for Cat-C to take over after the failure of Port 1/2 on Cat-B. In some situations, switches can detect topology changes on directly connected links and immediately transition into the Listening state without waiting Max Age seconds.

For example, in Figure 3-15, Port 1/1 on Cat-C fails. Because the failure results in a loss of link on the Root Port, there is no need to wait 20 seconds for the old information to age out. Note the difference between this scenario and the one in Figure 3-14, where link integrity was maintained because of the presence of a hub. When Port 1/1 on Cat-C fails, Port 1/2 on Cat-C immediately goes into Listening state in an attempt to become the new Root Port. The STP convergence time decreases from 50 seconds to 30 seconds (15 Listening + 15 Learning). So the port moves into Forwarding state within 30 seconds.

Figure 3-14 A Hub Connects Cat-B and Cat-C in a Converged STP Topology

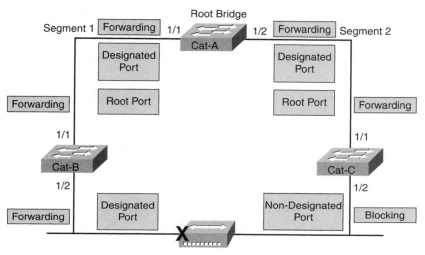

Figure 3-15 Port 1/1 on Cat-C Fails

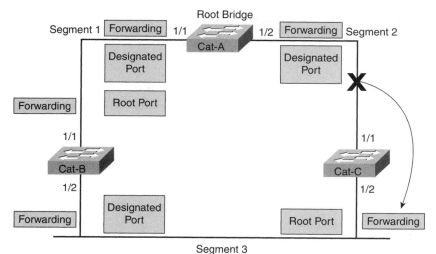

There are two key points to remember about using the STP timers:

- Default timer values should not be changed without careful consideration.
- If timer tuning is attempted, modify the STP timers only from the Root Switch, because the BPDUs contain three fields with timer values that can be passed from the Root Switch to all other bridges in the network. If every bridge were locally configured, some bridges could work their way up to the Forwarding state before other bridges ever left the Listening state. This chaotic approach could quickly lead to an unstable network. By providing timer fields in the BPDUs, the single bridge acting as the Root Switch can dictate the timing parameters for the entire bridged network.

BPDU Format

The format of a STP BPDU frame varies depending on the type of protocol used. Figure 3-16 shows the format of an IEEE 802.1D Spanning Tree Protocol BPDU frame. Figure 3-17 shows the format of a Cisco STP BPDU frame.

Figure 3-16 IEEE 802.1D Is the Original Specification for STP

Frame Control (1 Byte)	Destination Address (6 Bytes)	Source Address (6 Bytes)	Logical Link Control (3 Bytes)	IEEE BPDU

Figure 3-17 Cisco Catalyst Switches Use a Proprietary BPDU Frame Format

Frame Control (1 Byte)	Destination Address (6 Bytes)	Source Address (6 Bytes)	Routing Information Field (Variable)	Logical Link Control (3 Bytes)	IEEE BPDU

The fields shown in both Figures 3-16 and 3-17 are as follows:

- The Frame Control field is always 01.
- The Destination Address field indicates the destination address as specified in the Bridge Group Address table. For IEEE STP BPDU frames, the address is 0x800143000000.
- The Source Address field indicates the base MAC address used by the switch. For Cisco STP BPDU frames, the multicast bit is set to indicate the presence of a Routing Information Field (RIF) in the header.

- The Routing Information field is applicable only to Cisco STP BPDU frames. The RIF must be set to 0x0200.
- The Logical Link Control field controls all types of STP BPDU frames. This field is set to 0x424203.

Figure 3-18 shows the format of the fields inside a BPDU. All fields in the BPDU are common to all STPs except for the Port ID field. For IEEE and Cisco STP BPDU frames, the Port ID field specifies the transmitting Port Number of the originating bridge.

Figure 3-18 Fields in the BPDU

Protocol Identifier (2 Bytes)	Version (1 Byte)	Message Type (1 Byte)	Flags (1 Byte)	Root ID (8 Bytes)	Root Path Cost (4 Bytes)	Bridge ID (8 Bytes)	Port ID (2 Bytes)	Message Age (2 Bytes)	Maximum Age (2 Bytes)	Hello Time (2 Bytes)	Forward Delay (2 Bytes)

The Protocol Identifier, Version, and Message Type fields are all set to 0.

The Flags field includes one of the following:

- A Topology Change (TC) bit, which signals a topology change and designates this BPDU as a Topology Change Notification (TCN) BPDU. Without this bit set, the BPDUs are Configuration BPDUs.
- A Topology Change Acknowledgment (TCA) bit, which is set to acknowledge receipt of a configuration message with the TC bit set.

The remaining fields contained in a BPDU frame are as follows:

- The Root ID field indicates the Root Switch by listing its 2-byte priority followed by its 6-byte ID.
- The Root Path Cost field indicates the path's cost from the bridge sending the configuration message to the Root Bridge.
- The BID field indicates the priority and ID of the bridge sending the message.
- The Port ID field indicates the Port Number (IEEE or Cisco STP BPDU) from which the configuration message was sent. This field allows loops created by multiple attached bridges to be detected and corrected.
- The Message Age field indicates how much time has elapsed since the root sent the configuration message on which the current configuration message is based.
- The Maximum Age field indicates when the current configuration message should be deleted.
- The Hello Time field indicates the time between Root Bridge configuration messages.

■ The Forward Delay field indicates how long bridges should wait before transitioning to a new state after a topology change. If a bridge transitions too soon, it is possible that not all network links will be ready to change their state, and loops can result.

Topology Changes and STP

STP implements a series of timers to prevent bridging loops from occurring within the network. It can take from 30 to 50 seconds for a network to converge to a new topology when a change occurs in an otherwise stable STP process.

While the network is converging, physical addresses that can no longer be reached are still listed in the switch table. Because these addresses are in the table, the switch attempts to forward frames to devices it cannot reach. Fortunately, the STP change process requires the switch to clear the table faster to get rid of unreachable physical addresses.

Figure 3-19 illustrates a link failure between Switch D and Switch E, which in turn triggers a topology change condition. This topology change condition triggers a Topology Change Notification BPDU to be generated and sent toward the Root Switch. For this BPDU to reach the Root Switch, each switch forwards the update out the Root Port (RP in the figure) and toward the Designated Port (DP in the figure) of each Designated Bridge along the path to the Root Switch.

Figure 3-19 A Link Failure Triggers a Topology Change, Which STP Handles Via Built-in Mechanisms

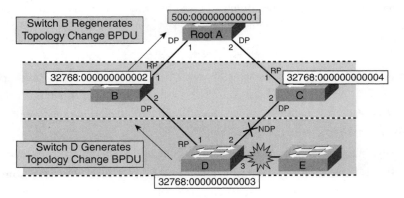

The topology change in this spanning-tree network triggers the following steps:

Step 1   Switch D notices that a change to a link has occurred.

Step 2   Switch D sends a Topology Change Notification (TCN) BPDU out the Root
Port destined ultimately for the Root Switch. The TCN BPDU is indicated by
the value 0x80 in the BPDU's 1-byte Type field. The bridge sends out the TCN
BPDU until the Designated Bridge for that segment responds with a TCA Configuration BPDU, indicated by the high-order bit in the 1-byte Flag field.

Step 3   The Designated Bridge (Switch B) for that segment sends out a TCA Configuration BPDU to the originating bridge (Switch D). Switch B also sends a TCN
BPDU out the Root Port destined for the Root Switch.

Step 4   When the Root Switch receives the (upstream) TCN BPDU, it sends Configuration BPDUs to indicate that a topology change is occurring (using the low-
order bit in the Flag field). The Root Switch sets the topology change in the
configuration for a period of time equal to the sum of the Forward Delay and
Max Age parameters.

Step 5   A bridge receiving a (downstream) topology change configuration message
from the Root Switch uses the Forward Delay timer (15 seconds) to age out
entries in the address table. This allows the device to age out entries faster than
the normal 5-minute default so that stations that are no longer available are
aged out faster. The bridge continues this process until it no longer receives
topology change configuration messages from the Root Switch.

STP Enhancements

Cisco implemented several proprietary improvements to IEEE 802.1D STP to speed convergence in certain situations. PortFast allows immediate conversion to the Forwarding state on
ports connected to workstations, servers, or routers (access ports). UplinkFast speeds up STP
convergence on uplink trunk ports when redundant uplinks are available and one of them
fails. BackboneFast speeds up STP convergence when an indirect trunk link goes down.

Delay in STP Updates

The current IEEE 802.1D STP standard was designed at a time when recovering connectivity
after an outage within a minute or so was considered adequate performance. With the advent
of Layer 3 switching in LAN environments, Layer 2 switching (as illustrated in Figure 3-20)
competes with routed solutions where protocols, such as OSPF and EIGRP, can provide an
alternate path in less time.

Figure 3-20 A Traditional Switched Campus Network Was Layer 2 Switched Throughout

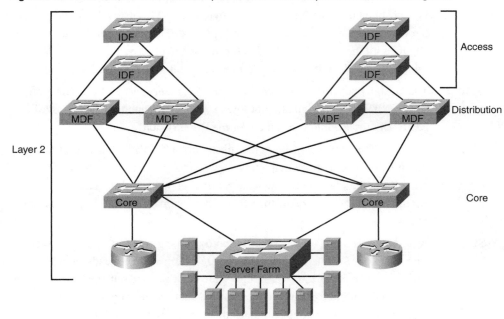

Enhancements to the IEEE 802.1D specification have been developed in an attempt to speed up STP alternate path selection. These areas are discussed in the following sections.

PortFast

STP *PortFast* is a Catalyst feature that causes a switch or trunk port to enter the STP Forwarding state immediately, bypassing the Listening and Learning states. IOS-based switches use PortFast only on access ports connected to end stations, as shown in Figure 3-21.

When a device is connected to a port, the port normally enters the Listening state. When the Forward Delay timer expires, the port enters the Learning state. When the Forward Delay timer expires a second time, the port is transitioned to the Forwarding or Blocking state. When PortFast is enabled on a switch or trunk port, the port is immediately transitioned to the Forwarding state. As soon as the switch detects the link, the port is transitioned to the Forwarding state (less than 2 seconds after the cable is plugged in).

Figure 3-21 PortFast Is an Extremely Useful Option for Access Switch Ports Connected to Hosts

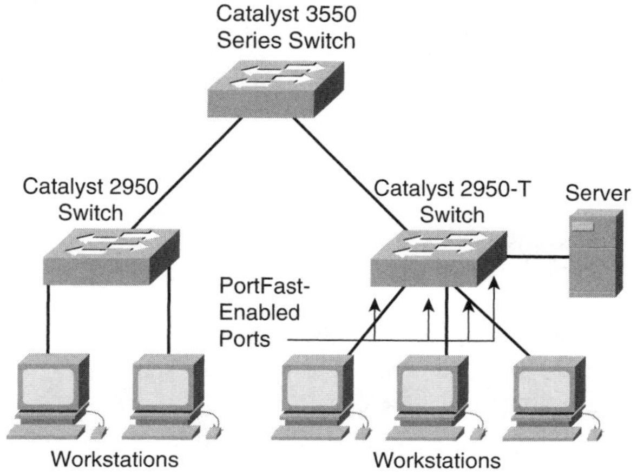

If a loop is detected and PortFast is enabled, the port is transitioned to the Blocking state. It is important to note that PortFast begins only when the port first initializes. If the port is forced into the Blocking state for some reason and later needs to return to the Forwarding state, the usual Listening and Learning processes are performed. (Note the difference here from the usual PortFast operation when a link first initializes.)

A primary reason for enabling PortFast is in cases where a PC boots in a period less than the 30 seconds it takes for a switch to put a port into Forwarding state from Disconnected state. Some network interface card (NICs) do not enable a link until the MAC layer software driver is actually loaded. Most operating systems try to use the network almost immediately after the driver is loaded, as in the case of Dynamic Host Configuration Protocol (DHCP). This can create a problem, because the 30 seconds of STP delay from listening to Forwarding states begins right when the IOS begins trying to access the network. In the case of DHCP, the PC does not obtain a valid IP address from the DHCP server. This problem is common with PC Card (PCMCIA) NICs used in laptop computers. Additionally, there is a race between operating systems and CPU manufacturers. CPU manufacturers keep making the chips faster while operating systems keep slowing down, but the chips are speeding up at a greater rate than the operating systems are slowing down. As a result, PCs are booting faster than ever. In fact, modern machines are often finished booting and need to use the network before the STP 30-second delay is over.

This problem motivates some network administrators to disable STP altogether. This certainly fixes any STP booting problems, but it can easily create other problems. If this strategy is employed, all physical loops must be eliminated, meaning no redundancy. STP cannot be disabled for a single port, so the PortFast feature should be considered. The PortFast feature gives the best of both worlds—immediate end-station access and the safety net of STP. The later section "Configuring PortFast" details the procedures for configuring this feature on a Catalyst switch.

UplinkFast

During the time it takes for STP to converge, some end stations might become inaccessible, depending on the STP state of the switch port to which the station is attached. This disrupts network connectivity, so it would be advantageous to decrease STP convergence time and reduce the length of the disruption. *UplinkFast* was developed to facilitate fast STP convergence. UplinkFast is a Catalyst feature that accelerates the choice of a new Root Port when a link or switch fails.

Switches in hierarchical networks can be grouped into core layer switches, distribution layer switches, and access layer switches. Figure 3-22 shows a portion of a campus network in which distribution switches and access switches each have at least one redundant link that STP blocks to prevent loops. If a switch loses connectivity on a link, it begins using the alternative paths as soon as STP selects a new Root Port. When STP reconfigures the new Root Port, other interfaces flood the network with multicast packets, at least one for each address that was learned on the interface.

Figure 3-22 Redundancy Is Critical for a Robust Network Design

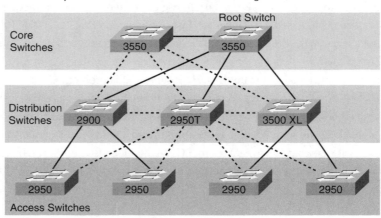

UplinkFast accelerates the choice of a new Root Port when a link or switch fails or when STP reconfigures itself. The Root Port transitions to the Forwarding state immediately without going through the Listening and Learning states, as it would with the usual STP process. UplinkFast also limits the burst of multicast traffic by reducing the max-update-rate, which specifies the maximum rate (in packets per second) at which update packets are sent. For IOS the default for this parameter is 150 packets per second.

UplinkFast is most useful in wiring closet switches at the edge of the network. It is inappropriate for backbone (core) devices. UplinkFast provides fast convergence after a direct link failure and achieves load sharing between redundant links using uplink groups. An uplink group is a set of interfaces (per VLAN), only one of which is forwarding at any given time. Specifically, an uplink group consists of the Root Port (which is forwarding) and a set of Blocked Ports.

The uplink group provides an alternative path in case the currently forwarding link fails. Figure 3-23 shows a sample topology with no link failures and a Blocked Port on Switch C.

Figure 3-23 A Blocked Port Is in Effect When Physical Loops Are Present in a Network Running STP

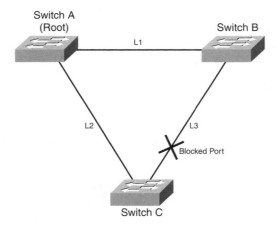

Switch A, the Root Switch, is connected directly to Switch B over link L1 and to Switch C over link L2. The interface on Switch C that is connected directly to Switch B is in a Blocking state. Switch C is configured with UplinkFast.

If Switch C detects a link failure on the currently active link L2 on the Root Port (a direct link failure), UplinkFast unblocks the Blocked Port on Switch C and transitions it to the Forwarding state without going through the Listening and Learning states, as illustrated in Figure 3-24.

Figure 3-24 *UplinkFast Enables a Quick Transition to Forwarding State for an Alternate Uplink Upon Primary Link Failure*

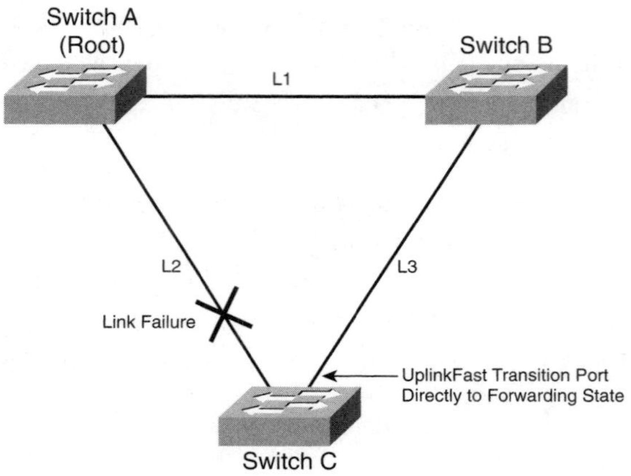

The change affected by UplinkFast takes approximately 1 to 5 seconds. As soon as a switch transitions an alternative port to the Forwarding state, the switch begins transmitting dummy multicast frames on that port, one for each entry in the local bridge table (except entries that are associated with the failed Root Port). By default, approximately 15 dummy multicast frames are transmitted per 100 milliseconds.

Each dummy multicast frame uses the station address in the bridge table entry as its source MAC address and a dummy multicast address (01-00-0C-CD-CD-CD) as the destination MAC address. Switches receiving these dummy multicast frames immediately update their bridge table entries for each source MAC address to use the new port, allowing the switches to begin using the new path almost immediately.

In the event that connectivity on the original Root Port is restored, the switch waits for a period equal to twice the Forward Delay time plus 5 seconds before transitioning the port to the Forwarding state to give the neighbor port time to transition through the Listening and Learning states to the Forwarding state. Configuring UplinkFast on Catalyst switches is straightforward, as you will see in the section "Configuring UplinkFast."

BackboneFast

BackboneFast is a Catalyst feature that is initiated when a Root Port or Blocked Port on a switch receives inferior BPDUs from its Designated Bridge. An inferior BPDU identifies one switch as both the Root Switch and the Designated Bridge. When a switch receives an inferior BPDU, it means that a link to which the switch is not directly connected (an indirect link) has failed. That is, the Designated Bridge has lost its connection to the Root Switch. Under STP rules, the switch ignores inferior BPDUs for the configured Max Age (the default is 20 seconds).

The role of BackboneFast is essentially to cheat this 20-second delay. When the switch receives the inferior BPDU, the switch tries to determine if it has an alternative path to the Root Switch.

There are two cases to consider:

- If the inferior BPDU arrives on a Blocked Port, the Root Port and other Blocked Ports on the switch become alternative paths to the Root Switch.
- If the inferior BPDU arrives on the Root Port, all Blocked Ports become potential alternative paths to the Root Switch.

If the inferior BPDU arrives on the Root Port and there are no Blocked Ports, the switch assumes that it has lost connectivity to the Root Switch, causing the Max Age on the root to expire, and it becomes the Root Switch according to normal STP rules. If the switch has alternative paths to the Root Switch, it uses these alternative paths to transmit a new kind of protocol data unit (PDU) called the Root Link Query PDU. The switch sends the Root Link Query PDU on all potential alternative paths to the Root Switch.

If the switch determines that it still has an alternative path to the root, it causes the Max Age on the ports on which it received the inferior BPDU to expire. The switch then makes all ports on which it received an inferior BPDU its Designated Ports and moves them out of the Blocking state (if they were in the Blocking state), through the Listening and Learning states, and into the Forwarding state. On the other hand, if the switch learns via the Root Link Query process that all the alternative paths to the Root Switch have lost connectivity to the root, the switch causes the Max Age on the ports on which it received inferior BPDUs to expire, and a new STP topology is calculated. To illustrate this process, Figure 3-25 shows a sample topology with no link failures. Switch A, the Root Switch, connects directly to Switch B over link L1 and to Switch C over link L2. The interface on Switch C that connects directly to Switch B is in the Blocking state.

Figure 3-25 A Converged Spanning-Tree Topology Is in Place

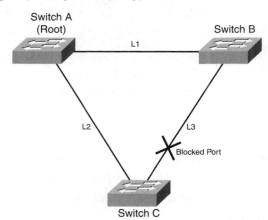

If link L1 fails, Switch C cannot directly detect this failure, because it is not directly connected to link L1. Switch B is directly connected to the Root Switch over L1, detects the failure, elects itself as the root, and begins sending BPDUs to Switch C. When Switch C receives the inferior BPDUs from Switch B, Switch C assumes that an indirect failure has occurred. At that point, BackboneFast allows the Blocked Port on Switch C to move immediately to the Listening state without waiting for Max Age on the port to expire. BackboneFast then transitions the interface on Switch C to the Forwarding state, providing a path from Switch B to Switch A. This switchover takes approximately 30 seconds, twice the Forward Delay time if the default Forward Delay time of 15 seconds is set. This saves up to 20 seconds. Figure 3-26 shows how BackboneFast reconfigures the topology to account for the failure of link L1.

Figure 3-26 BackboneFast Permits Rapid STP Reconvergence When a Remote Link Fails

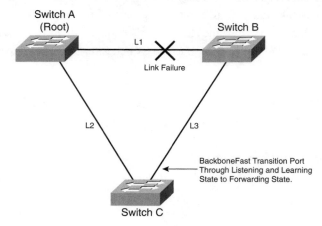

The later section "Configuring BackboneFast" details the procedures for configuring this feature on a Catalyst switch.

802.1w Rapid STP

Rapid Spanning Tree Protocol (RSTP) IEEE 802.1w can be seen as more of an evolution of the 802.1D standard than a revolution (see Figure 3-27). The 802.1D terminology remains primarily the same, and most parameters have been left unchanged so that users familiar with 802.1D can rapidly configure the new protocol comfortably. In most cases, RSTP performs better than Cisco's proprietary extensions without any additional configuration. 802.1w also can revert to 802.1D to interoperate with legacy bridges (thus, dropping the benefits it introduces) on a per-port basis. This section briefly explains the enhancements RSTP adds to the previous 802.1D standard.

Figure 3-27 Trying to Keep All the STPs and Their Features in Perspective Is Challenging

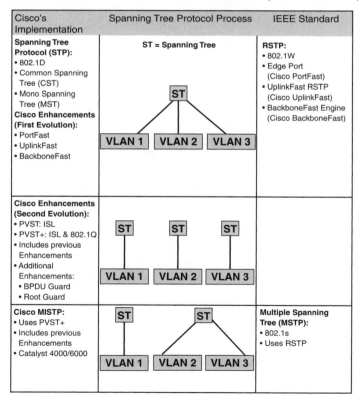

RSTP States

802.1D defined five different port states:

- Disabled
- Listening
- Learning
- Blocking
- Forwarding

Table 3-5 compares the 802.1D STP states with the 802.12 RSTP states.

Table 3-5 IEEE 802.1w Has Three Port States Versus the Five Port States Used in IEEE 802.1D

STP (802.1D) Port State	RSTP (802.1w) Port State	Is the Port Included in the Active Topology?	Is the Port Learning MAC Addresses?
Disabled	Discarding	No	No
Blocking	Discarding	No	No
Listening	Discarding	No	No
Learning	Learning	No	Yes
Forwarding	Forwarding	Yes	Yes

IEEE 802.1D STP was a bit confusing in that it mixed a port's state (whether it blocks or forwards traffic) and the role it plays in the active topology (Root Port, Designated Port, and so on). For example, from an operational point of view, there is no difference between a port in Blocking state and a port in Listening state. They both discard frames and do not learn MAC addresses. The real difference lies in the role the spanning tree assigns to the port. It can be safely assumed that a port in Listening state is either Designated or Root and is on its way to the Forwarding state. Unfortunately, once in Forwarding state, there is no way to infer from the port state whether the port is Root or Designated, which demonstrates the weakness of this state-based terminology. RSTP addresses this by decoupling a port's role and state.

Only three port states in RSTP correspond to the three possible operational states. The 802.1D states Disabled, Blocking, and Listening have been merged into a unique 802.1w Discarding state, as shown in Table 3-5.

Rapid transition to Forwarding state is the most important feature introduced by 802.1w. The legacy Spanning Tree Algorithm passively waited for the network to converge before turning a port into the Forwarding state. Achieving faster convergence was a matter of tuning the conservative default parameters (Forward Delay and Max Age timers), often putting the network's stability at stake. RSTP can actively confirm that a port can safely transition to the Forwarding state without relying on any timer configuration. RSTP provides a real feedback mechanism that takes place between RSTP-compliant bridges. To achieve fast convergence on a port, the protocol relies on two new variables—edge ports and link type.

The *edge port* concept is already well known to the Cisco implementation of STP, because it basically corresponds to the PortFast feature. All ports directly connected to end stations cannot create bridging loops in the network and, thus, can directly transition to the Forwarding state, skipping the Listening and Learning states. Neither edge ports nor PortFast-enabled ports generate topology changes when the link toggles. Unlike PortFast, an edge port that receives a BPDU immediately loses its edge port status and becomes a normal spanning-tree port. At this point, the edge port state has a user-configured value and an operational value. Cisco implementation maintains the **portfast** keyword to be used for edge port configuration, thus making the transition to RSTP simpler.

RSTP link type, point-to-point or shared, can achieve rapid transition to the Forwarding state only on edge ports and on point-to-point links. The link type is automatically derived from a port's duplex mode. A port operating in full duplex is assumed to be point-to-point, whereas a half-duplex port is considered a shared port by default. This automatic link type setting can be overridden by explicit configuration. In today's switched networks, most links operate in full-duplex mode and, therefore, are treated as point-to-point links by RSTP. This makes them candidates for rapid transition to the Forwarding state.

RSTP Port Roles

The RSTP role is now a variable assigned to a given port. The Root Port and Designated Port roles remain, but the Blocking Port role is now split into backup and Alternate Port roles. The Spanning Tree Algorithm determines a port's role based on BPDUs. To keep things simple, the thing to remember about a BPDU is that there is always a way to compare any two of them and to decide whether one is more useful than the other. This is based on the values stored in the BPDU and occasionally on the port on which they are received. This considered, the following paragraphs explain practical approaches to port roles.

As in standard STP, the port receiving the best BPDU on a bridge is the Root Port. This is the port that is the closest to the Root Bridge in terms of Path Cost, as shown in Figure 3-28.

Figure 3-28 RSTP Also Uses Root Ports

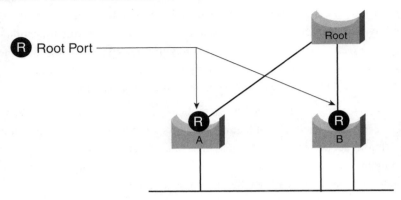

If a port can send the best BPDU on the segment to which it is connected, the port is considered a Designated Port (see Figure 3-29). As with 802.1D, bridges create a bridged domain by linking different segments. A given segment can have only one path to the Root Switch. Multiple paths would create a bridging loop in the network.

Figure 3-29 RSTP Uses Designated Ports as Well

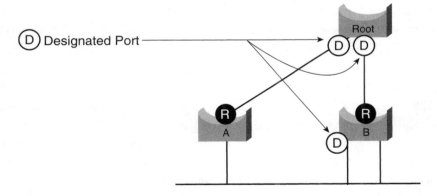

Alternate Port and Backup Port roles correspond to the Blocking state of 802.1D. A Blocked Port is defined as not being the Designated or Root Port. A Blocked Port receives a more useful BPDU than the one it would send out on its segment. Remember that a port absolutely needs to receive BPDUs to stay blocked. RSTP introduces these two roles for this purpose. An Alternate Port is a port blocked by receiving more useful BPDUs from another bridge, as shown in Figure 3-30.

Figure 3-30 An Alternate Port Is a Port Blocked by Receiving More Useful BPDUs from
Another Bridge

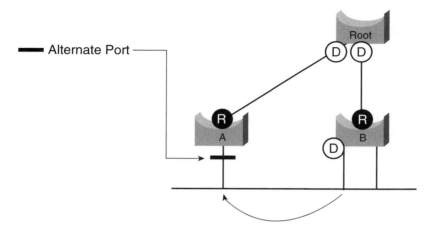

A Backup Port is a port blocked by receiving more useful BPDUs from the same bridge it is
on, as shown in Figure 3-31.

Figure 3-31 A Backup Port Is a Port Blocked by Receiving More Useful BPDUs from the
Same Bridge

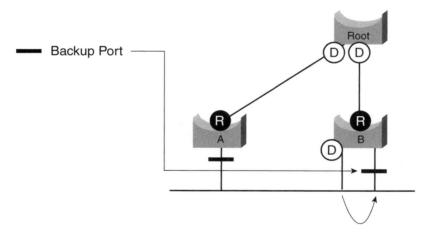

This Backup Port distinction was already made internally within 802.1D and is essentially
how Cisco UplinkFast functions. The rationale behind 802.1w is that an Alternate Port provides an alternate path to the Root Bridge and, therefore, could replace the Root Port should it
fail. A Backup Port provides redundant connectivity to the same segment and cannot guarantee
alternate connectivity to the Root Switch. Therefore it was excluded from the uplink group.

RSTP calculates the final topology for the spanning tree using exactly the same criteria as 802.1D. There is absolutely no change in how the different bridge and port priorities are used. The term Blocking is used for the Discarding state in Cisco implementation. With RSTP, there is a difference between the role the protocol has determined for a port and its current state. For example, with RSTP it is perfectly valid for a port to be both a Designated Port and a Blocking Port at the same time. Although this typically happens for very short periods of time, it simply means that this port is in a transitory state toward designated forwarding.

RSTP Timers

When the Spanning Tree Algorithm selects a port to become a Designated Port, 802.1D still waits twice the Forward Delay number of seconds (2 * 15 seconds by default) before transitioning it to the Forwarding state. In RSTP, this condition corresponds to a port with a designated role but a Blocking state. Figures 3-32 to 3-36 illustrate how fast transition is achieved step by step. If a new link is created between the root and Switch A, both ports on the link are put in a Discarding state until they receive a BPDU from their counterpart.

When a Designated Port is in Discarding or Learning state, and only in this case, it sets the proposal bit on the BPDUs it sends out. This is what happens for port p0 of the Root Switch, as shown in Step 1 of Figure 3-32. Because Switch A receives superior information, it immediately knows that p1 will be its new Root Port. Switch A then starts a sync to ensure that all its ports are in sync with this new information.

Figure 3-32 RSTP Uses a Sync Mechanism That Does Not Depend on Timers

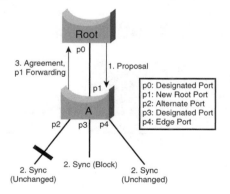

A port is in sync if it meets either of the following criteria:

- It is in a Blocking state (which means Discarding in a stable topology)
- It is an edge port

To illustrate the effect of the sync mechanism on different kinds of ports, suppose there exists an Alternate Port p2, a designated forwarding port p3, and an edge port p4 on Switch A, as illustrated in Figure 3-32. Notice that p2 and p4 already meet one of the criteria just listed. To be in sync, Switch A needs to block port p3, assigning it the Discarding state. Now that all of its ports are in sync, Switch A can unblock its newly selected Root Port p1, and reply to the root by sending an agreement message. This message is a copy of the proposal BPDU, with the agreement bit set instead of the proposal bit. This ensures that port p0 knows exactly to which proposal the agreement it receives corresponds.

After p0 receives that agreement, it can immediately transition to the Forwarding state, as shown in Figure 3-33. Notice that port p3 was left in a designated Discarding state after the sync. In Step 4, that port is in the same situation as was port p0 during Step 1 (in Figure 3-32). It then starts proposing to its neighbor, attempting to quickly transition to forwarding.

Figure 3-33 p0 Immediately Transitions to Forwarding

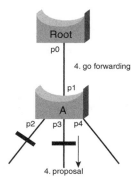

The proposal agreement mechanism is very fast, because it does not rely on any timers. This wave of handshakes propagates quickly toward the edge of the network and quickly restores connectivity after a change in the topology.

If a designated discarding port does not receive an agreement after having sent a proposal, it falls back to the traditional 802.1D Listening-Learning sequence. This could happen if the remote bridge does not understand RSTP BPDUs or if the remote bridge port is blocking, as with Switch C in Figure 3-34.

UplinkFast RSTP incorporates an automatically enabled feature similar to the Cisco UplinkFast proprietary STP extension. The 802.1w topology change mechanism clears the appropriate entries in the Content Addressable Memory (CAM) tables of the upstream bridges, removing the need for UplinkFast's dummy multicast generation process.

Figure 3-34 If a Remote Bridge Does Not Support RSTP, the Sync Mechanism Will Not Work, and the Switches Resort to Traditional 802.1D STP

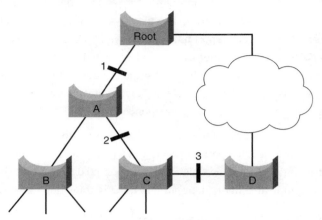

When an 802.1D bridge detects a topology change, it first notifies the Root Bridge using a reliable mechanism, as shown in Figure 3-35. As soon as the Root Bridge is aware of a change in the network topology, it sets the TC flag on the BPDUs it sends out, which are then relayed to all the bridges in the network. When a bridge receives a BPDU with the TC flag bit set, it reduces its bridging table aging time to forward delay seconds, ensuring a relatively quick flushing of stale information.

Figure 3-35 An 802.1D Bridge Reacts to a Topology Change by Notifying the Root Switch with a Reliable Mechanism

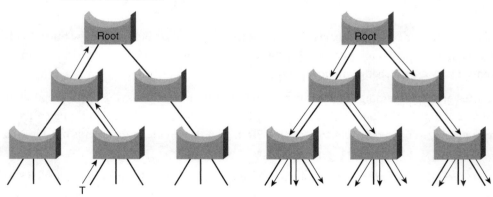

This topology change mechanism has been deeply remodeled in RSTP. Both the detection of a topology change and propagation through the network have evolved.

In RSTP, only non-edge ports moving to the Forwarding state cause a topology change. This means that a loss of connectivity is not considered a topology change, contrary to 802.1D (that is, a port moving to blocking no longer generates a TC).

When a RSTP bridge detects a topology change, the following happens:

- The RSTP bridge starts the TC While timer with a value equal to twice the Hello Time for all its non-edge Designated Ports and its Root Port if necessary.
- The RSTP bridge flushes the MAC addresses associated with all of these ports.
- As long as the TC While timer is running on a port, the BPDUs sent out that port have the TC bit set. BPDUs are also sent on the Root Port while the timer is active.

Topology change propagation with RSTP is handled differently with RSTP. When a bridge receives a BPDU from a neighbor with the TC bit set, the following happens:

- The bridge clears the MAC addresses learned on all of its ports except the one that received the topology change.
- The bridge starts the TC While timer and sends BPDUs with the TC set on all of its Designated Ports and Root Port. (RSTP no longer uses the specific TCN BPDU unless a legacy bridge needs to be notified.)

This way, the TCN is flooded very quickly across the whole network, as shown in Figure 3-36.

Figure 3-36 The Initiator of the Topology Change Floods the Information Throughout the Network

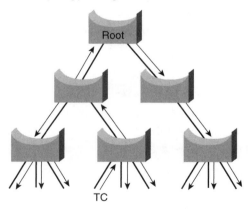

With RSTP, the TC propagation is a one-step process. In fact, the initiator of the topology change floods this information throughout the network (as opposed to 802.1D, where only the root could do so). This mechanism is much faster than the 802.1D equivalent. There is no need to wait for the Root Bridge to be notified and then maintain the topology change state for the whole network for Max Age plus Forward Delay seconds. In just a few seconds (a small multiple of Hello Time), most of the entries in the CAM tables of the entire network (VLAN) are flushed. This approach results in potentially more temporary flooding, but on the other hand, it clears potential stale information that prevents rapid connectivity restitution.

RSTP is fully compatible with and capable of interoperating with legacy (802.1D) STP protocols. However, it is important to note that 802.1w inherent fast convergence benefits are lost when interacting with legacy bridges.

RSTP BPDU Format

RSTP has introduced a few changes to the BPDU format. Only two flags, Topology Change (TC) and TC Acknowledgment (TCA), were defined in 802.1D. As shown in Figure 3-37, RSTP uses all 6 remaining bits of the flag byte to do the following:

- Encode the role and state of the port originating the BPDU
- Handle the proposal/agreement mechanism

Figure 3-37 The RSTP BPDU Uses All the Bits in the Flag Byte

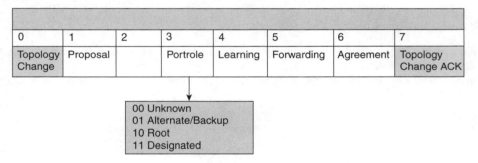

Another important change is that the RSTP BPDU is of type 2, version 2. The implication is that legacy bridges must drop this new BPDU. This property makes it easy for an 802.1w bridge to detect legacy bridges connected to it.

BPDUs are sent every Hello Time (not simply relayed, as with 802.1D). With 802.1D, a non-Root Switch generated BPDUs only when it received one on its Root Port. In fact, with 802.1D, a bridge relays BPDUs more than actually generating them. This is not the case with 802.1w, where a bridge sends a BPDU with its current information every Hello Time seconds (2 by default), even if it does not receive any BPDUs from the Root Bridge.

On a given port, if hellos are not received for three consecutive times (or if Max Age expires), protocol information can be immediately aged out. Because of the previously mentioned protocol modification, BPDUs are now used as a keepalive mechanism between bridges. A bridge decides it has lost connectivity to its direct neighboring root or designated bridge if it misses three BPDUs in a row. This fast aging of the information allows quick failure detection. If a bridge fails to receive BPDUs from a neighbor, it is certain that the connection to that neighbor has been lost, as opposed to 802.1D, where the problem could be anywhere on the path to the root. Note that with RSTP, failures are detected much faster in case of physical link failures than with 802.1D.

The concept of accepting inferior BPDUs is what makes up the core of the BackboneFast engine. The IEEE 802.1w committee decided to incorporate a similar mechanism into RSTP. When a bridge receives inferior information from its Designated or Root Switch, it immediately accepts it and replaces the one previously stored.

In Figure 3-38, Bridge C still knows the root is alive and well and immediately sends a BPDU to Bridge B containing information about the Root Switch. As a result, Bridge B stops sending its own BPDUs and accepts the port leading to Bridge C as its new Root Port.

Figure 3-38 Bridge B Stops Sending Its Own BPDUs and Accepts the Port Leading to Bridge C as Its New Root Port

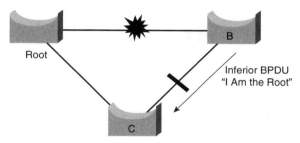

Evolution of Spanning Tree

Several options are now available with STP on Catalyst switches, as described in this section. PVST+ is still the default setting on Catalyst switches, but RSTP and MST are now viable alternatives. The legacy 802.1D implementations of spanning tree are also described here.

PVST (Per-VLAN Spanning Tree), PVST+, and Mono Spanning Tree Modes

Common Spanning Tree (CST) is specified in the IEEE 802.1Q standard. CST defines a single instance of spanning tree for all VLANs. BPDUs are transmitted over VLAN 1. *Per-VLAN Spanning Tree (PVST)* is a Cisco-proprietary implementation requiring Interlink

Switch (ISL) trunk encapsulation. PVST runs a separate instance of STP for each VLAN. Among other things, this lets you configure distinct Root Switches for each VLAN and configure Layer 2 load sharing, as shown in Figure 3-39.

Figure 3-39 PVST Enables Layer 2 Load Sharing by Running a Separate Instance of Spanning Tree for Each VLAN

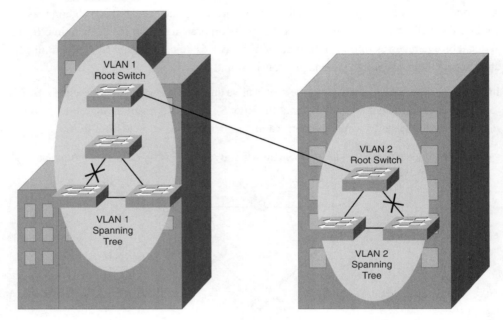

Having a separate spanning tree instance for each VLAN reduces the recovery time for STP recalculation and, hence, increases network reliability in the following ways:

- It reduces the overall size of the spanning-tree topology.
- It improves scalability and decreases convergence time.
- It provides faster recovery and better reliability.

Disadvantages of a spanning tree for each VLAN include the following:

- Use of switches (such as CPU load) to support spanning tree maintenance for multiple VLANs
- Use of bandwidth on trunk links to support BPDUs for each VLAN

PVST+ is a Cisco-proprietary STP mode that allows CST and PVST to exist on the same network.

PVST+ supports 802.1Q trunks and the mapping of multiple spanning trees to the single spanning tree of non-Cisco 802.1Q switches. PVST+ is automatically enabled on Catalyst 802.1Q trunks. It runs one instance of STP per VLAN when Catalyst switches are connected by 802.1Q trunks. PVST+ is the default STP used on all Ethernet, Fast Ethernet, and Gigabit Ethernet port-based VLANs on the Catalyst 4000 and 6000 family of switches. PVST+ runs on each VLAN on the switch, ensuring that each has a loop-free path through the network.

PVST+ provides Layer 2 load sharing for the VLAN on which it runs. Different logical topologies can be created using the VLANs on a network to ensure that all links are used, but no single link is oversubscribed.

Each instance of spanning tree has a single Root Switch. This Root Switch propagates the spanning tree information associated with that VLAN to all other switches in the network. Because each switch has the same knowledge about the network, this process ensures that the network topology is maintained.

The PVST+ architecture distinguishes three types of zones or regions:

- A PVST zone or region
- A PVST+ zone or region
- A mono spanning tree zone or region

Mono Spanning Tree (MST) is the spanning tree implementation used by non-Cisco 802.1Q switches. One instance of STP is responsible for all VLAN traffic. Each zone or region consists of a homogenous type of switch. Connecting two ISL ports can connect a PVST region to a PVST+ region. Similarly, connecting two 802.1Q ports can connect a PVST+ region to an MST region. Note that an MST and PVST region cannot be connected via a trunk link. Although it is possible to provide a nontrunk connection between the two regions by using an access link, this is of limited use in real-world networks. Figure 3-40 illustrates the three types of STP regions and how they are linked.

At the boundary between a PVST region and a PVST+ region, the mapping of spanning trees is one-to-one. At the boundary between an MST region and a PVST+ region, the spanning tree in the MST region maps to one PVST in the PVST+ region. The one it maps to is the CST. The default CST is VLAN 1.

All PVSTs, except the CST, are tunneled through the MST region. Tunneling means that BPDUs are flooded through the MST region along the single spanning tree that is present in the MST region. Do not confuse this use of the term tunnel with the point-to-point tunnels configured on Cisco routers and PIX firewalls. In general, a tunnel refers to a mechanism that enables the propagation of packets or frames through a series of devices in such a way that the contents of the packets or frames are not changed in transit.

Figure 3-40 PVST+ Allows for Interoperation Between PVST Switches and Non-Cisco 802.1Q Mono Spanning Tree Switches

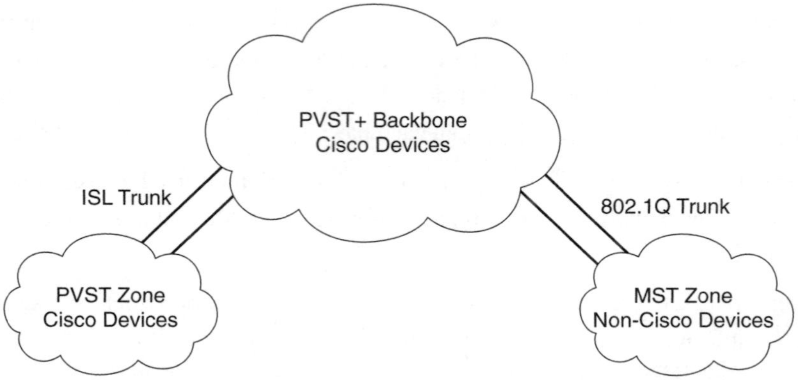

Enhanced PVST+

Enhanced PVST+ permits interoperability between PVST+ and MST. MISTP mode is a Cisco-proprietary implementation of MST on some Catalyst switches. MISTP-PVST+ allows the use of MISTP functionality of the Catalyst 4000 and 6000 series switches while continuing to communicate with the older Catalyst switches in the network that use PVST+. The MISTP options are implemented under Catalyst OS (CatOS).

MISTP Mode

After the development of PVST+, someone got the idea that it would be useful to have an STP mode that allows for a compromise between PVST+ and MST. *Multiple Instances of Spanning Tree Protocol (MISTP)* lets you group multiple VLANs under a single instance of spanning tree. MISTP combines the Layer 2 load-balancing benefits of PVST+ with the lower CPU load of IEEE 802.1Q.

MISTP is an optional STP mode that runs on the Catalyst 4000 and 6000 switch families. A MISTP instance is a virtual logical topology defined by a set of bridge and port parameters. An MISTP instance becomes a real topology when VLANs are mapped to it. Each MISTP instance has its own Root Switch and a different set of forwarding links (that is, different bridge and port parameters). This Root Switch propagates the information associated with that instance of MISTP to all other switches in the network. This process ensures that the network topology is maintained, because each switch has the same knowledge about the network.

MISTP builds MISTP instances by exchanging MISTP BPDUs with peer entities in the network. There is only one BPDU for each MISTP instance, rather than for each VLAN as in PVST+. There are fewer BPDUs in a MISTP network, so there is less overhead in the network. MISTP discards any PVST+ BPDUs it sees.

A MISTP instance can have any number of VLANs mapped to it, but a VLAN can be mapped to only a single MISTP instance. VLANs can be easily moved in a MISTP topology to another MISTP instance if they have converged. However, if ports are added at the same time the VLAN is moved, additional convergence time is required.

MISTP-PVST+ Mode

MISTP-PVST+ is a transition STP mode that allows the use of MISTP functionality of the Catalyst 4000 and 6000 series switches while continuing to communicate with the older Catalyst switches in the network that use PVST+. A switch using PVST+ mode and a switch using MISTP mode that are connected cannot see the BPDUs of the other switch, a condition that can cause loops in the network. MISTP-PVST+ allows interoperability between PVST+ and MISTP, because it detects the BPDUs of both modes. To convert a network to MISTP, MISTP-PVST+ can be used to transition the network from PVST+ to MISTP to avoid problems. MISTP-PVST+ conforms to the limits of PVST+.

MST (802.1s)

The acronym MST stands for two things:

- Mono Spanning Tree
- Multiple Spanning Tree

Be careful to differentiate between the two in context. The *Multiple Spanning Tree* feature was originally released for Catalyst 4000 and 6000 series switches. MST is specified in IEEE 802.1s, an amendment to IEEE 802.1Q. MST extends the IEEE 802.1w Rapid Spanning Tree (RST) Algorithm to multiple spanning trees, as opposed to the single CST of the original IEEE 802.1Q specification.

This extension provides for both rapid convergence and load sharing in a VLAN environment. Cisco implementation of MST is backward-compatible with 802.1D STP, the 802.1w RSTP, and the Cisco PVST+ architecture. MST can be thought of as a standards-based MISTP. The IEEE 802.1w specification, RSTP, provides for subsecond reconvergence of STP after failure of one of the uplinks in a bridged environment. 802.1w provides the structure on which the 802.1s feature operates.

Table 3-6 describes support for MST on Cisco switches.

Table 3-6 MST Is Supported on All New Catalyst Switches

Catalyst Platform	MST with RSTP Support
Catalyst 2900 XL and 3500 XL	Unavailable
Catalyst 2950 and Catalyst 3550	Cisco IOS Release 12.1(9)EA1
Catalyst 2955	All Cisco IOS software releases
Catalyst 2948G-L3 and Catalyst 4908G-L3	Unavailable
Catalyst 4000, Catalyst 2948G, and Catalyst 2980G (Catalyst OS)	Catalyst OS version 7.1
Catalyst 4000 and Catalyst 4500 (Cisco IOS)	Cisco IOS Release 12.1(12c)EW
Catalyst 5000 and Catalyst 5500	Unavailable
Catalyst 6000 and Catalyst 6500 (Catalyst OS)	Catalyst OS version 7.1
Catalyst 6000 and Catalyst 6500 (Cisco IOS)	Cisco IOS Releases 12.1(11b)EX, 12.1(13)E, and 12.2(14)SX
Catalyst 8500	Unavailable

The IEEE 802.1s Multiple Spanning Tree specification allows a user to build multiple spanning trees over VLAN trunks. Fast convergence of the MST topology is achieved using a modified version of the RSTP protocol. VLANs can be grouped and associated to spanning-tree instances. Each instance can have a topology independent of other spanning-tree instances. This new architecture provides multiple forwarding paths for data traffic and enables load sharing. Network fault tolerance is improved, because a failure in one instance does not affect other instances.

In large networks, having different VLAN spanning-tree instance assignments located in different parts of the network makes it easier to administer and use redundant paths. However, a spanning-tree instance can exist only on bridges that have compatible VLAN instance assignments. Therefore, MST requires the configuration of a set of bridges with the same MST configuration information, allowing them to participate in a given set of spanning-tree instances. Interconnected bridges that have the same MST configuration are called MST regions. MST, like MISTP (see Figure 3-41), provides interoperability with PVST+ regions.

Figure 3-41 MISTP Is a Cisco-Proprietary Implementation of MST

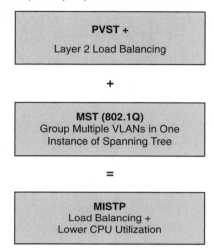

Load Sharing

Load sharing can be accomplished using a couple of different methods. The most common method of load sharing is through Root Bridge placement on a per-VLAN basis. This distributes traffic for separate VLANs across separate paths to different Root Switches. A separate method divides the bandwidth supplied by parallel trunks connecting switches. To avoid loops, STP normally blocks all but one parallel link between switches.

Using load sharing, traffic can be divided between the links according to which VLAN the traffic belongs to.

Load sharing can be configured on trunk ports using one of the following methods:

- **STP port priorities**—Both load-sharing links must be connected to the same switch.
- **STP path costs**—Each load-sharing link can be connected to the same switch or to two different switches.

The following sections examine each of these methods in greater detail. For detailed configuration information, consult the "Configuring Load Sharing" section later in this chapter.

Load Sharing Using STP Port Priorities

When two ports on the same switch form a loop, the STP Port Priority setting determines which port is enabled and which port is in a blocking state. The priorities on a parallel trunk port can be set so that the port carries all the traffic for a given VLAN. The trunk port with the higher priority (lower values) for a VLAN forwards traffic for that VLAN. The trunk port with the lower priority (higher values) for the same VLAN remains in a Blocking state for that VLAN. One trunk port sends or receives all traffic for the VLAN.

Figure 3-42 shows two trunks connecting supported switches configured as follows:

- VLANs 8 to 10 are assigned a Port Priority of 10 on Trunk 1.
- VLANs 3 to 6 retain the default Port Priority of 128 on Trunk 1.
- VLANs 3 to 6 are assigned a Port Priority of 10 on Trunk 2.
- VLANs 8 to 10 retain the default Port Priority of 128 on Trunk 2.

Figure 3-42 Port Priorities Can Be Used to Affect STP Load Sharing

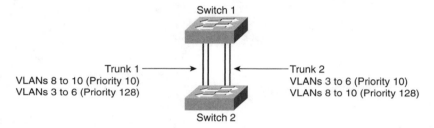

In the configuration shown in Figure 3-42, Trunk 1 carries traffic for VLANs 8 to 10, and Trunk 2 carries traffic for VLANs 3 to 6. If the active trunk fails, the trunk with the lower priority takes over and carries the traffic for all the VLANs. No duplication of traffic occurs over any trunk port.

Load Sharing Using STP Path Cost

Parallel trunks can be configured to share VLAN traffic by setting different Path Costs on a trunk and associating them with different sets of VLANs. The VLANs keep the traffic separate. Because no loops exist, STP does not disable the ports, and redundancy is maintained in the event of a lost link.

Figure 3-43 shows that trunk ports 1 and 2 are 100BASE-T ports. The Path Costs for the VLANs are assigned as follows:

- VLANs 2 to 4 are assigned a Path Cost of 30 on Trunk Port 1.
- VLANs 8 to 10 retain the default 100BASE-T Path Cost of 19 on Trunk Port 1.
- VLANs 8 to 10 are assigned a Path Cost of 30 on Trunk Port 2.
- VLANs 2 to 4 retain the default 100BASE-T Path Cost of 19 on Trunk Port 2.

Figure 3-43 Path Costs Can Be Used to Affect STP Load Sharing

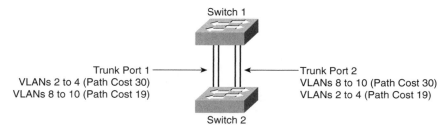

In the configuration shown in Figure 3-43, Trunk 1 carries traffic for VLANs 8 to 10, and Trunk 2 carries traffic for VLANs 2 to 4. If the active trunk fails, the trunk with the higher Path Cost takes over and carries the traffic for all the VLANs. No duplication of traffic occurs over any trunk port.

Switchport Tuning Using BPDU Guard

STP configures a meshed topology into a loop-free, tree-like topology. When the link on a bridge port goes up, STP calculation is done on that port. The result of the calculation is the transition of the port into the Forwarding or Blocking state, depending on the port's position in the network and the STP parameters. This calculation and transition period usually takes about 30 to 50 seconds. At this time, no user data passes via the port. Some user applications might time out during this period.

To allow immediate transition of the port into the Forwarding state, the STP PortFast feature is enabled. PortFast transitions the port into the STP Forwarding state immediately upon linkup. The port still participates in STP in the event that the port is to be a part of a loop; if so, the port eventually transitions into STP blocking mode.

As long as the port is participating in STP, there is a possibility that some device attached to that port and also running STP with a lower Bridge Priority than that of the current Root Switch will assume the Root Bridge function and affect active STP topology, thus rendering the network suboptimal. Permanent STP recalculation caused by the temporary introduction and subsequent removal of STP devices with low (0) Bridge Priority represents a simple form of Denial of Service (DoS) attack on the network.

The STP PortFast BPDU guard enhancement is designed to allow network designers to enforce the STP domain borders and keep the active topology predictable. The devices behind the ports with STP PortFast enabled are not allowed to influence the STP topology. This is achieved by disabling the port with PortFast configured upon receipt of BPDU. The port is transitioned into Errdisable state, and a message appears on the console. The following is an example of the message that appears as a result of BPDU guard operation:

```
2000 May 12 15:13:32 %SPANTREE-2-RX_PORTFAST:Received BPDU on PortFast enable
   port. Disabling 2/1
2000 May 12 15:13:32 %PAGP-5-PORTFROMSTP:Port 2/1 left bridge port 2/1
```

On the left side of Figure 3-44, Bridge A has priority 8192 and is the root for the VLAN. Bridge B has priority 16384 and is the backup Root Switch for the same VLAN. Bridges A and B, connected by a Gigabit Ethernet link, make up the network core. Bridge C is an access switch and has PortFast configured on the port connected to Device D. Given that the other STP parameters are the default, the Bridge C port that connects to Bridge B is in STP Blocking state. Device D (a PC) is not participating in STP. The red arrows indicate the flow of STP BPDUs.

Figure 3-44 BPDU Guard Prevents Rogue Devices from Affecting the STP Topology

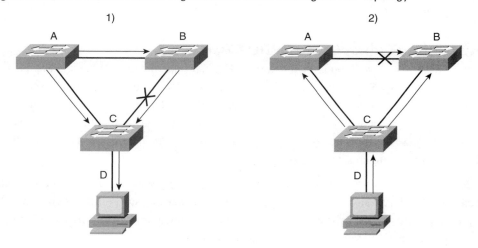

Now, suppose that Device D starts participating in STP (for example, if a Linux-based bridge application were launched on a PC), as shown on the right side of Figure 3-44. If the software bridge's priority is 0 or any value below that of the Root Switch, the software bridge takes over the Root Bridge function (as the bridge with the lowest priority). The Gigabit link connecting the two core switches transitions into blocking mode, causing all the data in that particular VLAN to flow via the 100-Mbps link. If more data is flowing via the core in the VLAN than the link can accommodate, dropping of frames occurs, leading to a connectivity outage. The STP PortFast BPDU guard feature would prevent such a situation by disabling the port as soon as an STP BPDU is received from Device D.

Switchport Tuning Using Root Guard

Traditional 802.1D STP does not provide any means for the network administrator to securely enforce the switched Layer 2 network topology. This might become especially important in networks with shared administrative control (for example, one switched network controlled by different administrative entities or companies).

The switched network's forwarding topology is calculated based on, among other parameters, the Root Switch position. Although any switch can be the Root Switch in the network, it is better to place the Root Bridge manually (somewhere in the core layer) so that the forwarding topology is optimal. The standard 802.1D STP does not allow the administrator to enforce the Root Switch's position. If a bridge is introduced into the network with a lower Bridge Priority, it takes the role of the Root Bridge.

The root guard ensures that the port on which root guard is enabled is the Designated Port. (Normally, Root Bridge ports are all designated unless two or more ports of the Root Bridge are connected.) If the bridge receives superior STP BPDUs on a root guard-enabled port, this port is moved to a root-inconsistent STP state (effectively equal to the Listening state), and no traffic is forwarded across this port. The position of the Root Switch is enforced, as shown in Figure 3-45.

NOTE

Even if the administrator sets the Root Bridge Priority to 0 in an effort to secure the Root Bridge position, there is still no guarantee, because there might be a bridge with priority 0 and a lower BID. The Root Guard feature is designed to provide a way to enforce the Root Switch placement in the network.

Figure 3-45 The Root Guard Feature Enforces the Placement of the Root Switch in a Network

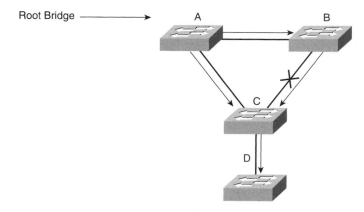

Consider an example of why a rogue Root Bridge can cause problems on the network and how root guard can help:

- Switches A and B comprise the core of the network, and Switch A is the Root Switch for a VLAN.
- Switch C is an access layer switch.
- The link between Switches B and C is blocking on the C side. The flow of STP BPDUs is shown with arrows.

In Figure 3-46, Device D begins to participate in STP. If the priority of Bridge D is 0 or any value lower than that of the Root Switch, the software bridge is elected as a Root Switch for this VLAN. In turn, the Gigabit link connecting the two core switches blocks, causing all the data in that particular VLAN to flow via a 100-Mbps link across the access layer. If more data is flowing via the core in that VLAN than this link can accommodate, some frames are dropped, causing performance loss or a connectivity outage.

Figure 3-46 Root Guard Prevents Device D from Becoming the Root Switch

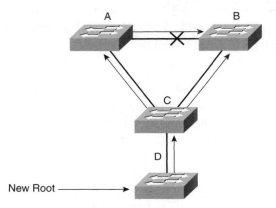

The root guard feature is designed to protect the network from such issues. Root guard is configured on a per-port basis and does not allow the port to become an STP Root Port. This means that the port is always STP-designated. If a better BPDU is received on this port, BPDU guard disables the port rather than taking the BPDU into account and electing a new STP root.

Root guard needs to be enabled on all ports where the Root Switch should not appear. In Figure 3-46, root guard should be enabled as follows:

- Switch A: the port connecting to Switch C
- Switch B: the port connecting to Switch C
- Switch C: the port connecting to Switch D

In this configuration, Switch C blocks the port connecting to Switch D as soon as it receives a better (superior) BPDU. The port is put in a special STP state (root-inconsistent) that is effectively the same as the Listening state. No traffic passes through the port in this state. As soon as Device D stops sending superior BPDUs, the port is unblocked again and goes, via STP, into the Listening and Learning states, and eventually transitions to the Forwarding state. Recovery is automatic—no human intervention is required.

The following message appears when root guard blocks a port:

```
%SPANTREE-2-ROOTGUARDBLOCK: Port 1/1 tried to become non-designated in VLAN 77.
  Moved to root-inconsistent state
```

STP Configuration

Configuring PVST+ on Catalyst switches involves configuring the Root Switches for each VLAN and optionally configuring load sharing via Port Cost and Port Priority. The default STP timers can be tuned in specialized situations.

Default STP Configuration

Table 3-7 shows the default STP (PVST/PVST+) configuration settings.

Table 3-7 The Default PVST+ Settings Include the Bridge Priority, Port Priority, and Port Cost

Feature	Default Setting
enable state	Enabled on VLAN 1. Up to 64 spanning-tree instances can be enabled.
switch priority	32768
spanning-tree port priority (Can be configured on a per-interface basis and used on interfaces configured as Layer 2 access ports)	128
spanning-tree port cost (Can be configured on a per-interface basis and used on interfaces configured as Layer 2 access ports)	1000 Mbps: 4 100 Mbps: 19 10 Mbps: 100
spanning-tree vlan port priority (Can be configured on a per-VLAN basis and used on interfaces configured as Layer 2 trunk ports)	128
spanning-tree vlan port cost (Can be configured on a per-VLAN basis and used on interfaces configured as Layer 2 trunk ports)	1000 Mbps: 4 100 Mbps: 19 10 Mbps: 100

continues

Table 3-7 The Default PVST+ Settings Include the Bridge Priority, Port Priority, and
Port Cost (Continued)

Feature	Default Setting
Hello Time	2 seconds
Forward Delay Time	15 seconds
Max Age Time	20 seconds

Lab 3.10.1   STP Default Behavior

In this lab exercise, you observe STP's default behavior.

Lab 3.10.2   Use Network Inspector to Observe STP Behavior

In this lab exercise, you observe STP behavior with the Network Inspector switch
trace feature.

NOTE

In Cisco IOS Release
12.1(9)EA1 and later,
Catalyst 2950 switches
support the IEEE 802.1t
STP extensions. Some
of the bits previously
used for the switch pri-
ority are now used as
the VLAN identifier.
The result is that fewer
MAC addresses are
reserved for the switch,
and a larger range of
VLAN IDs can be sup-
ported, all while main-
taining the uniqueness
of the BID. The 2 bytes
previously used for
the switch priority are
reallocated into a
4-bit priority value and
a 12-bit extended sys-
tem ID value equal to
the VLAN ID.

Enabling and Disabling STP

STP is enabled by default on VLAN 1 and on all newly created VLANs up to the spanning-
tree limit as specified. Disable STP only if the network topology has no loops. When STP is
disabled and loops are present in the topology, excessive traffic and indefinite packet duplication can drastically reduce network performance.

To re-enable STP, use the **spanning-tree vlan** *vlan-id* global configuration command.

Modifying the Root Switch

By default, switches with Cisco PVST and PVST+ maintain a separate spanning-tree
instance for each active VLAN configured on them. A BID consisting of the switch priority
and the switch MAC address is associated with each instance. For each VLAN, the switch
with the lowest BID becomes the Root Bridge for that VLAN.

To configure a switch to become the root for the specified VLAN, use the **spanning-tree vlan**
vlan-id **root primary** global configuration command to change the switch priority from the
default value (32768) to a significantly lower value. When this command is entered, the switch
checks the switch priority of the Root Switches for each VLAN. Because of the extended system ID support, the switch sets its own priority for the specified VLAN to 24576 if this value
will cause this switch to become the root for the specified VLAN.

If any Root Bridge for the specified VLAN has a switch priority lower than 24576, the switch sets its own priority for the specified VLAN to 4096 less than the lowest switch priority. 4096 is the value of the least-significant bit of a 4-bit switch priority value.

Beginning in privileged EXEC mode, follow the steps listed in Table 3-8 to configure a switch to become the root for the specified VLAN.

NOTE

The **spanning-tree vlan** *vlan-id* **root primary** global configuration command fails if the value necessary to be the Root Switch is less than 1.

Table 3-8 A Single Command Is Used to Configure a Switch to Be the Root of the Spanning Tree for a Particular VLAN

Step	Command	Description
1	**configure terminal**	Enters global configuration mode.
2	**spanning-tree vlan** *vlan-id* **root primary** [**diameter** *net-diameter* [**hello-time** *seconds*]]	Configures a switch to become the root of the specified VLAN. For *vlan-id,* the range is 1 to 4094 when the Enhanced Image is installed and 1 to 1005 when the Standard Image is installed. Do not enter leading 0s. (Optional) For **diameter** *net-diameter,* specify the maximum number of switches between any two end stations. The range is 2 to 7. (Optional) For **hello-time** *seconds,* specify the interval in seconds between the generation of configuration messages by the Root Bridge. The range is 1 to 10 seconds; the default is 2 seconds.
3	**end**	Returns to privileged EXEC mode.
4	**show spanning-tree detail**	Verifies the entries.

Before Cisco IOS Release 12.1(9)EA1, entering the **spanning-tree vlan** *vlan-id* **root primary** global configuration command on a Catalyst 2950 switch (no extended system ID) caused it to set its own switch priority for the specified VLAN to 8192 if this value caused this switch to become the root for the specified VLAN.

If any Root Switch for the specified VLAN has a switch priority lower than 8192, the switch sets its own priority for the specified VLAN to 1 less than the lowest switch priority.

The following examples show the effect of the **spanning-tree vlan** *vlan-id* **root primary** command with and without the extended system ID support:

- For Catalyst 2950 switches with the extended system ID (Release 12.1(9)EA1 and later), if all network devices in VLAN 20 have the default priority of 32768, entering the **spanning-tree vlan 20 root primary** command on the switch sets the switch priority to 24576, which causes this switch to become the Root Switch for VLAN 20.

- For Catalyst 2950 switches without the extended system ID (software earlier than Release 12.1(9)EA1), if all network devices in VLAN 100 have the default priority of 32768, entering the **spanning-tree vlan 100 root primary** command on the switch sets the switch priority for VLAN 100 to 8192, which causes this switch to become the Root Switch for VLAN 100.

If the network consists of switches that both do and do not support the extended system ID, it is unlikely that the switch with the extended system ID support will become the Root Switch. The extended system ID increases the switch priority value every time the VLAN number is greater than the priority of the connected switches running older software.

The Root Switch for each spanning-tree instance should be a backbone or distribution switch. Do not configure an access switch as the spanning-tree primary root.

Use the **diameter** keyword to specify the Layer 2 network diameter (that is, the maximum number of switch hops between any two end stations in the Layer 2 network). When the network diameter is specified, the switch automatically sets an optimal hello time, forward-delay time, and maximum-age time for a network of that diameter, which can significantly reduce the convergence time. The **hello-time** keyword can be used to override the automatically calculated hello time.

After configuring the switch as the Root Switch, the recommended practice is to avoid manual configuration of the hello time, forward-delay time, and maximum-age time using the **spanning-tree vlan** *vlan-id* **hello-time**, **spanning-tree vlan** *vlan-id* **forward-time**, and **spanning-tree vlan** *vlan-id* **max-age** global configuration commands.

To return the switch to its default setting, use the **no spanning-tree vlan** *vlan-id* **root** global configuration command.

Setting the Priority for Ports and VLANs

If a loop occurs, STP uses the Port Priority when selecting an interface to put into the Forwarding state. Assign higher-priority values (lower numerical values) to interfaces that the network administrator prefers to have selected first and lower-priority values (higher numerical values) to interfaces that the network administrator wants selected last. If all interfaces have the same priority value, STP puts the interface with the lowest interface number in the Forwarding state and blocks the other interfaces.

Cisco IOS uses the Port Priority value when the interface is configured as an access port and uses VLAN Port Priority values when the interface is configured as a trunk port.

Beginning in privileged EXEC mode, follow the steps listed in Table 3-9 to configure an interface's Port Priority.

Table 3-9 Port Priority Can Be Configured on Interfaces to Influence the Spanning-Tree Topology

Step	Command	Description
1	**configure terminal**	Enters global configuration mode.
2	**interface** *interface-id*	Enters interface configuration mode and specifies an interface to configure.
		Valid interfaces include physical interfaces and port-channel logical interfaces (**port-channel** *port-channel-number*).
3	**spanning-tree vlan port-priority** *priority*	Configures the Port Priority for an interface that is an access port.
		For *priority,* the range is 0 to 255; the default is 128. The lower the number, the higher the priority.
4	**spanning-tree vlan** *vlan-id* **port-priority** *priority*	Configures the VLAN Port Priority for an interface that is a trunk port.
		For *vlan-id,* the range is 1 to 4094 when the Enhanced Image is installed and 1 to 1005 when the Standard Image is installed. Do not enter leading 0s.
		For *priority,* the range is 0 to 255; the default is 128. The lower the number, the higher the priority.
5	**end**	Returns to privileged EXEC mode.
6	**show spanning-tree interface** *interface-id* or **show spanning-tree vlan** *vlan-id*	Verifies the entries.

The **show spanning-tree interface** *interface-id* privileged EXEC command displays information only if the port is in a link-up operative state. Otherwise, use the **show running-config interface** privileged EXEC command to confirm the configuration.

To return the interface to its default setting, use the **no spanning-tree** [**vlan** *vlan-id*] **port-priority** interface configuration command.

 Lab 3.10.3   Advanced PVST+ Configuration

In this lab exercise, you modify the default PVST+ configuration to control the spanning-tree behavior.

Setting the Port Cost

The spanning-tree Path Cost default value is derived from an interface's media speed. If a loop occurs, STP uses cost when selecting an interface to put in the Forwarding state. Assign lower-cost values to interfaces that the network administrator prefers to have selected first and higher-cost values to interfaces that the network administrator wants selected last. If all interfaces have the same cost value, STP puts the interface with the lowest interface number in the Forwarding state and blocks the other interfaces.

STP uses the cost value when the interface is configured as an access port and uses VLAN port cost values when the interface is configured as a trunk port.

Beginning in privileged EXEC mode, follow the steps listed in Table 3-10 to configure an interface's cost.

Table 3-10 Port Cost Can Be Configured on Interfaces to Influence the Spanning-Tree Topology

Step	Command	Description
1	**configure terminal**	Enters global configuration mode.
2	**interface** *interface-id*	Enters interface configuration mode and specifies an interface to configure. Valid interfaces include physical interfaces and port-channel logical interfaces (**port-channel** *port-channel-number*).
3	**spanning-tree cost** *cost*	Configures the cost of an interface that is an access port. If a loop occurs, STP uses the Path Cost when selecting an interface to place in the Forwarding state. A lower Path Cost represents higher-speed transmission. For cost, the range is 1 to 200000000; the default value is derived from the interface's media speed.

Table 3-10 Port Cost Can Be Configured on Interfaces to Influence the Spanning-Tree
           Topology (Continued)

Step	Command	Description
4	**spanning-tree vlan** *vlan-id* **cost** *cost*	Configures the VLAN cost for an interface that is a trunk port.
		If a loop occurs, STP uses the Path Cost when selecting an interface to place in the Forwarding state. A lower Path Cost represents higher-speed transmission.
		For *vlan-id,* the range is 1 to 4094 when the Enhanced Image is installed and 1 to 1005 when the Standard Image is installed. Do not enter leading 0s.
		For *cost,* the range is 1 to 200000000; the default value is derived from the interface's media speed.
5	**end**	Returns to privileged EXEC mode.
6	**show spanning-tree interface** *interface-id* or **show spanning-tree vlan** *vlan-id*	Verifies the entries.

The **show spanning-tree interface** *interface-id* privileged EXEC command displays information only for ports that are in a link-up operative state. Otherwise, use the **show running-config** privileged EXEC command to confirm the configuration.

To return the interface to its default setting, use the **no spanning-tree** [**vlan** *vlan-id*] **cost** interface configuration command.

Configuring Switch Priority of a VLAN

You can configure the switch priority to make it more likely that the switch will be chosen as the Root Switch. For most situations, the recommended practice is to use the **spanning-tree vlan** *vlan-id* **root primary** and **spanning-tree vlan** *vlan-id* **root secondary** global configuration commands to modify the switch priority.

However, beginning in privileged EXEC mode, you can follow the steps outlined in Table 3-11 to configure a VLAN's switch priority.

Table 3-11 Bridge Priority Can Be Configured to Influence the Spanning-Tree Topology

Step	Command	Description
1	**configure terminal**	Enters global configuration mode.
2	**spanning-tree vlan** *vlan-id* **port-priority** *priority*	Configures a VLAN's switch priority. For *vlan-id*, the range is 1 to 4094 when the Enhanced Image is installed and 1 to 1005 when the Standard Image is installed. Do not enter leading 0s. For *priority*, the range is 0 to 61440 in increments of 4096; the default is 32768. The lower the number, the more likely the switch will be chosen as the Root Switch. Valid priority values are 4096, 8192, 12288, 16384, 20480, 24576, 28672, 32768, 36864, 40960, 45056, 49152, 53248, 57344, and 61440. All other values are rejected.
3	**end**	Returns to privileged EXEC mode.
4	**show spanning-tree vlan** *vlan-id*	Verifies the entries.

To return the switch to its default setting, use the **no spanning-tree vlan** *vlan-id* **priority** global configuration command.

Modifying Default Timers

IEEE 802.1D STP parameters can be individually configured in specialized situations. These parameters include hello time, forward delay, and VLAN maximum aging time.

Hello Time

Changing the hello time configures the interval period of configuration messages generated by the Root Switch. For most situations, it is recommended that you use the **spanning-tree vlan** *vlan-id* **root primary** and **spanning-tree vlan** *vlan-id* **root secondary** global configuration commands to modify the hello time.

However, beginning in privileged EXEC mode, you can follow the steps outlined in Table 3-12 to configure the hello time for a VLAN.

Table 3-12 The Default STP Hello Time Is 2 Seconds

Step	Command	Description
1	**configure terminal**	Enters global configuration mode.
2	**spanning-tree vlan** *vlan-id* **hello-time** *seconds*	Configures a VLAN's hello time. The hello time is the interval between the generation of configuration messages by the Root Switch. These messages mean that the switch is alive. For *vlan-id,* the range is 1 to 4094 when the Enhanced Image is installed and 1 to 1005 when the Standard Image is installed. Do not enter leading 0s. For *seconds,* the range is 1 to 10; the default is 2.
3	**end**	Returns to privileged EXEC mode.
4	**show spanning-tree vlan** *vlan-id*	Verifies the entries.

To return the switch to its default setting, use the **no spanning-tree vlan** *vlan-id* **hello-time** global configuration command.

Forward Delay

Use the global configuration command **spanning-tree vlan** *vlan-id* **forward-time** *seconds* command to configure the Forward Delay for a VLAN.

The forwarding time determines how long each of the Listening and Learning states last before the interface begins forwarding. The range is 4 to 30 seconds.

To return the switch to its default setting, use the **no spanning-tree vlan** *vlan-id* **forward-time** global configuration command.

VLAN Maximum Aging Time

Use the global configuration command **spanning-tree vlan** *vlan-id* **max-age** *seconds* command to configure the Max Age for a VLAN.

This command sets the interval between messages the spanning tree receives from the Root Switch. If a switch does not receive a BPDU message from the Root Switch within this interval, it recomputes the spanning-tree topology. The range is 6 to 40 seconds.

To return the switch to its default setting, use the **no spanning-tree vlan** *vlan-id* **max-age** global configuration command.

Tuning, Verifying, and Troubleshooting STP

Cisco added several features to its PVST+ STP implementation. Configuring these options can significantly enhance convergence time in switched networks. PortFast speeds up the amount of time it takes an access port to transition to Forwarding state when a workstation or router is attached. UplinkFast and BackboneFast speed up STP convergence when an uplink trunk link or indirect trunk link fails, respectively. BPDU guard and root guard prevent rogue devices or unintended devices from influencing spanning-tree behavior. This section also explores spanning-tree load sharing.

Configuring PortFast

A port with the PortFast feature enabled is moved directly to the STP Forwarding state without waiting for the standard forward-time delay.

Use PortFast only when connecting a single end station to an access or trunk port. Enabling this feature on a port connected to a switch or hub could prevent STP from detecting and disabling loops in the network, which could cause broadcast storms and address-learning problems.

When the voice VLAN feature is enabled, the PortFast feature is automatically enabled. When voice VLAN is disabled, the PortFast feature is not automatically disabled.

Enable PortFast if the switch is running PVST or Multiple Spanning Tree Protocol (MSTP). Note that MSTP is available only if the EI is installed on the switch.

Beginning in privileged EXEC mode, follow the steps outlined in Table 3-13 to enable PortFast.

Use the **spanning-tree portfast** global configuration command to globally enable the Port-Fast feature on all nontrunking ports.

To disable the PortFast feature, use the **no spanning-tree portfast** interface configuration command.

Table 3-13 PortFast Is Disabled by Default and Can Be Configured Per Interface

Step	Command	Description
1	**configure terminal**	Enters global configuration mode.
2	**spanning-tree portfast [trunk]**	Enables PortFast on an access port connected to a single workstation or server. By specifying the **trunk** keyword, you can enable PortFast on a trunk port.
3	**end**	Returns to privileged EXEC mode.
4	**show spanning-tree interface** *interface-id* **portfast**	Verifies the entries.

Configuring UplinkFast

UplinkFast RSTP incorporates an automatically enabled feature similar to the Cisco UplinkFast proprietary STP extension. The 802.1w topology change mechanism clears the appropriate entries in the CAM tables of the upstream bridges, removing the need for UplinkFast's dummy multicast generation process.

UplinkFast cannot be enabled on VLANs that have been configured for switch priority. To enable UplinkFast on a VLAN with switch priority configured, first restore the switch priority on the VLAN to the default value by using the **no spanning-tree vlan** *vlan-id* **priority** global configuration command.

When UplinkFast is enabled, it affects all VLANs on the switch. UplinkFast cannot be configured on an individual VLAN.

The UplinkFast feature is supported only when the switch is running PVST. Beginning in privileged EXEC mode, follow the steps outlined in Table 3-14 to enable UplinkFast.

Table 3-14 UplinkFast Can Be Configured Only for All VLANs on a Switch; It Cannot Be Configured on a Per-VLAN Basis

Step	Command	Description
1	**configure terminal**	Enters global configuration mode.
2	**spanning-tree uplinkfast** [**max-update-rate** *pkts-per-second*]	Enables UplinkFast. (Optional) For *pkts-per-second,* the range is 0 to 65535 packets per second; the default is 150. If you set the rate to 0, station-learning frames are not generated, and the spanning-tree topology converges more slowly after a loss of connectivity.
3	**end**	Returns to privileged EXEC mode.
4	**show spanning-tree summ**ary	Verifies the entries.

When UplinkFast is enabled, the switch priority of all VLANs is set to 49152. If the Path Cost is changed to a value less than 3000 and then UplinkFast is enabled, or if UplinkFast is already enabled, the Path Cost of all interfaces and VLAN trunks is increased by 3000. (If the Path Cost is changed to 3000 or greater, the Path Cost is not altered.) The changes to the switch priority and the Path Cost reduce the chance that the switch will become the Root Switch.

When UplinkFast is disabled, the switch priorities of all VLANs and Path Costs of all interfaces are set to default values unless the defaults have been modified.

To return the update packet rate to the default setting, use the **no spanning-tree uplinkfast max-update-rate** global configuration command. To disable UplinkFast, use the **no spanning-tree uplinkfast** command.

Configuring BackboneFast

Accepting inferior BPDUs is what makes up the core of the BackboneFast engine. The IEEE 802.1w committee decided to incorporate a similar mechanism into RSTP. When a bridge receives an inferior BPDU from its Designated or Root Switch, the bridge immediately accepts this BPDU and replaces the one previously stored.

BackboneFast can be enabled to detect indirect link failures and to start the spanning-tree reconfiguration sooner. You must enable BackboneFast on all switches in the network for it to work properly. BackboneFast is not supported on Token Ring VLANs; however, Backbone-Fast is supported for use with third-party switches.

The BackboneFast feature is supported only when the switch is running PVST. Beginning in privileged EXEC mode, follow the steps outlined in Table 3-15 to enable BackboneFast.

Table 3-15 BackboneFast Must Be Configured on All Switches in the Network

Step	Command	Description
1	**configure terminal**	Enters global configuration mode.
2	**spanning-tree backbonefast**	Enables BackboneFast.
3	**end**	Returns to privileged EXEC mode.
4	**show spanning-tree summary**	Verifies the entries.

To disable the BackboneFast feature, use the **no spanning-tree backbonefast** global configuration command.

Configuring BPDU Guard

When BPDU guard is enabled globally on ports that are PortFast-enabled (the ports are in a PortFast-operational state), STP shuts down PortFast-enabled ports that receive BPDUs.

In a valid configuration, PortFast-enabled ports do not receive BPDUs. Receiving a BPDU on a PortFast-enabled port signals an invalid configuration, such as the connection of an unauthorized device, and the BPDU guard feature puts the port in the error-disabled state. The BPDU guard feature provides a secure response to invalid configurations because the port must be manually put back into service. Use the BPDU guard feature in a service provider network to prevent an access port from participating in the spanning tree.

Configure PortFast only on ports that connect to end stations; otherwise, an accidental topology loop could cause a data packet loop and disrupt switch and network operation.

Use the **spanning-tree bpduguard enable** interface configuration command to enable BPDU guard on any port without also enabling the PortFast feature. When the port receives a BPDU, it is put in the error-disabled state.

The BPDU guard feature can be enabled if the switch is running PVST or MSTP. MSTP is available only if the Enhanced Image is installed on the switch.

Beginning in privileged EXEC mode, follow the steps outlined in Table 3-16 to globally enable the BPDU guard feature on all access ports and to enable PortFast on all access ports.

Table 3-16 BPDU Guard Can Be Globally Configured, But PortFast Must Also Be Configured on the Interfaces Connected to End Stations

Step	Command	Description
1	**configure terminal**	Enters global configuration mode.
2	**spanning-tree portfast bpduguard default**	Globally enables BPDU guard. By default, BPDU guard is disabled.
3	**interface** *interface-id*	Enters interface configuration mode and specifies the interface connected to an end station.
4	**spanning-tree portfast**	Enables the PortFast feature.
5	**end**	Returns to privileged EXEC mode.
6	**show running-config**	Verifies the entries.

To disable BPDU guard on all access ports, use the **no spanning-tree portfast bpduguard default** global configuration command. You can override this command on a particular interface by using the **spanning-tree bpduguard enable** interface configuration command.

Lab 3.10.7   Port-Level Tuning to Control STP Behavior

In this lab exercise, you use PortFast, UplinkFast, BPDU guard, root guard, and UDLD to control STP behavior on a port.

Configuring Root Guard

Root guard enabled on an interface applies to all the VLANs to which the interface belongs.

Do not enable the root guard on interfaces to be used by the UplinkFast feature. With Uplink-Fast, the backup interfaces (in the blocked state) replace the Root Port in case of a failure. However, if root guard is also enabled, all the backup interfaces used by the UplinkFast feature are placed in the root-inconsistent state (blocked) and are prevented from reaching the Forwarding state. Root guard and loop guard cannot both be enabled at the same time.

Loop guard can be used to prevent alternate or Root Ports from becoming Designated Ports because of a failure that leads to a unidirectional link. This feature is most effective when it is configured on the entire switched network. Loop guard operates only on ports that the spanning tree considers point-to-point.

Root guard can be enabled if the switch is running PVST or MSTP. Recall that the MSTP feature is available only if the Enhanced Image is installed on the switch.

Beginning in privileged EXEC mode, follow the steps listed in Table 3-17 to enable root guard on an interface.

Table 3-17 Root Guard Is Configured on Interfaces to Prevent Inadvertent Root Switch Election

Step	Command	Description
1	**configure terminal**	Enters global configuration mode.
2	**interface** *interface-id*	Enters interface configuration mode and specifies the interface to configure.
3	**spanning-tree guard root**	Enables root guard on the interface. By default, root guard is disabled on all interfaces.
4	**end**	Returns to privileged EXEC mode.
5	**show running-config**	Verifies the entries.

To disable root guard, use the **no spanning-tree guard** interface configuration command.

Configuring Load Sharing

Load sharing divides the bandwidth supplied by parallel trunks connecting switches. To avoid loops, STP normally blocks all but one parallel link between switches. Using load sharing, divide the traffic between the links according to which VLAN the traffic belongs to.

Configure load sharing on trunk ports by using STP port priorities or STP Path Costs. For load sharing using STP port priorities, both load-sharing links must be connected to the same switch. For load sharing using STP Path Costs, each load-sharing link can be connected to the same switch or to two different switches.

Load Sharing Using STP Port Priorities

When two ports on the same switch form a loop, the STP Port Priority setting determines which port is enabled and which port is in a Blocking state. The priorities on a parallel trunk port can be set so that the port carries all the traffic for a given VLAN. The trunk port with the higher priority (lower Port Priority values) for a VLAN forwards traffic for that VLAN.

The trunk port with the lower priority (higher Port Priority values) for the same VLAN remains in a Blocking state for that VLAN. One trunk port sends or receives all traffic for the VLAN.

Figure 3-47 shows two Gigabit Ethernet trunks connecting supported switches. In this example, the switches are configured as follows:

- VLANs 8 to 10 are assigned a Port Priority of 10 on Trunk 1.
- VLANs 3 to 6 retain the default Port Priority of 128 on Trunk 1.
- VLANs 3 to 6 are assigned a Port Priority of 10 on Trunk 2.
- VLANs 8 to 10 retain the default Port Priority of 128 on Trunk 2.

Figure 3-47 Port Priority Can Be Configured to Enable STP Load Sharing

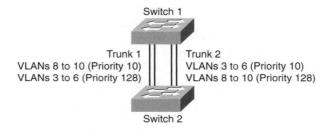

In this way, Trunk 1 carries traffic for VLANs 8 to 10, and Trunk 2 carries traffic for VLANs 3 to 6. If the active trunk fails, the trunk with the lower priority takes over and carries the traffic for all the VLANs. No duplication of traffic occurs over any trunk port.

Beginning in privileged EXEC mode, follow the steps shown in Table 3-18 to configure the network shown in Figure 3-47.

Table 3-18 Port Priority Can Be Configured on Interfaces to Affect STP Load Sharing

Step	Command	Description
1	**interface gigabitethernet0/1**	Enters interface configuration mode and defines the interface to set the STP Port Priority.
2	**spanning-tree vlan 8 port-priority 10**	Assigns a Port Priority of 10 for VLAN 8.
3	**spanning-tree vlan 9 port-priority 10**	Assigns a Port Priority of 10 for VLAN 9.

Table 3-18 Port Priority Can Be Configured on Interfaces to Affect STP Load Sharing (Continued)

Step	Command	Description
4	**spanning-tree vlan 10 port-priority 10**	Assigns a Port Priority of 10 for VLAN 10.
5	**exit**	Returns to global configuration mode.
6	**interface gigabitethernet0/2**	Enters interface configuration mode and defines the interface to set the STP Port Priority.
7	**spanning-tree vlan 3 port-priority 10**	Assigns a Port Priority of 10 for VLAN 3.
8	**spanning-tree vlan 4 port-priority 10**	Assigns a Port Priority of 10 for VLAN 4.
9	**spanning-tree vlan 5 port-priority 10**	Assigns a Port Priority of 10 for VLAN 5.
10	**spanning-tree vlan 6 port-priority 10**	Assigns a Port Priority of 10 for VLAN 6.
11	**end**	Returns to privileged EXEC mode.

Load Sharing Using STP Path Cost

Parallel trunks can be configured to share VLAN traffic by setting different Path Costs on a trunk and associating the Path Costs with different sets of VLANs. The VLANs keep the traffic separate. Because no loops exist, STP does not disable the ports, and redundancy is maintained in the event of a lost link.

In Figure 3-48, trunk ports 1 and 2 are 100BASE-T ports. The Path Costs for the VLANs are assigned as follows:

- VLANs 2 to 4 are assigned a Path Cost of 30 on Trunk Port 1.
- VLANs 8 to 10 retain the default 100BASE-T Path Cost of 19 on Trunk Port 1.
- VLANs 8 to 10 are assigned a Path Cost of 30 on Trunk Port 2.
- VLANs 2 to 4 retain the default 100BASE-T Path Cost of 19 on Trunk Port 2.

Figure 3-48 Port Cost Can Be Configured to Enable STP Load Sharing

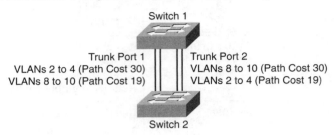

Beginning in privileged EXEC mode, follow the steps outlined in Table 3-19 to configure the network shown in Figure 3-48.

Table 3-19 Port Cost Can Be Configured on Interfaces to Affect STP Load Sharing

Step	Command	Description
1	**configure terminal**	Enters global configuration mode on Switch 1.
2	**interface fastethernet 0/1**	Enters interface configuration mode and defines Fast Ethernet port 0/1 as the interface to be configured as a trunk.
3	**switchport trunk encapsulation dot1q**	Configures the trunk encapsulation.
4	**switchport mode trunk**	Configures the port as a trunk port.
5	**exit**	Returns to global configuration mode.
6		Repeat Steps 2 to 4 on Switch 1 interface Fast Ethernet 0/2.
7	**end**	Returns to privileged EXEC mode.
8	**show running-config**	Verifies your entries. In the display, make sure that interfaces Fast Ethernet 0/1 and Fast Ethernet 0/2 are configured as trunk ports.
9	**show vlan**	When the trunk links come up, Switch 1 receives the VLAN Trunking Protocol (VTP) information from the other switches. Verify that Switch 1 has learned the VLAN configuration.

Table 3-19 Port Cost Can Be Configured on Interfaces to Affect STP Load Sharing (Continued)

Step	Command	Description
10	**configure terminal**	Enters global configuration mode.
11	**interface fastethernet 0/1**	Enters interface configuration mode and defines Fast Ethernet port 0/1 as the interface to set the STP cost.
12	**spanning-tree vlan 2 cost 30**	Sets the spanning-tree Path Cost to 30 for VLAN 2.
13	**spanning-tree vlan 3 cost 30**	Sets the spanning-tree Path Cost to 30 for VLAN 3.
14	**spanning-tree vlan 4 cost 30**	Sets the spanning-tree Path Cost to 30 for VLAN 4.
15	**end**	Returns to global configuration mode.
16		Repeat Steps 9 to 11 on the Switch 1 interface Fast Ethernet 0/2 and set the spanning-tree Path Cost to 30 for VLANs 8, 9, and 10.

Lab 3.10.6   Per-VLAN Spanning-Tree Load Sharing

In this lab exercise, you modify spanning tree's default behavior for VLAN load sharing using Cisco IOS commands.

Verifying STP, RSTP, and MSTP Configuration

Table 3-20 lists and describes the privileged EXEC commands for displaying spanning-tree status.

Table 3-20 show Commands for Verifying Spanning-Tree Configuration

Command	Description
show spanning-tree active	Displays spanning-tree information on active interfaces only.
show spanning-tree detail	Displays a detailed summary of interface information.

continues

Table 3-20 **show** Commands for Verifying Spanning-Tree Configuration (Continued)

Command	Description
show spanning-tree interface *interface-id*	Displays spanning-tree information for the specified interface.
show spanning-tree mst interface *interface-id*	Displays MST information for the specified interface.
show spanning-tree summary [**totals**]	Displays a summary of port states or displays the total lines of the STP state section.

NOTE

Within each MST region, the MSTP maintains multiple spanning-tree instances. Instance 0 is a special instance for a region, known as the internal spanning tree (IST). All other MST instances are numbered from 1 to 15. The IST is the only spanning-tree instance that sends and receives BPDUs.

A common and internal spanning tree (CIST) is a collection of the internal spanning trees in each MST region and the common spanning tree (CST) that interconnects the MST regions and single spanning trees.

The spanning tree computed in a region appears as a subtree in the CST that encompasses the entire switched domain. The CIST is formed as a result of the Spanning Tree Algorithm running between switches that support the 802.1w, 802.1s, and 802.1D protocols. The CIST inside an MST region is the same as the CST outside a region.

For information about other keywords for the **show spanning-tree** privileged EXEC command, refer to the command reference for the particular Cisco IOS release.

RSTP and MSTP Configuration

RSTP and MSTP can be used in place of the default PVST+ to improve Layer 2 convergence in the network and to improve Catalyst switch CPU and memory utilization. Configuring MST involves defining instances and assigning Layer 2 properties to each instance. Here you learn how to enable RSTP, how to enable MST, and how to configure the MST Root Switch, MST Bridge Priority, MST Path Cost, MST Port Priority, MSTP timers, and maximum hop count.

Default RSTP and MSTP Configuration

The switch uses the default settings of PVST/PVST+, as shown in Table 3-21. By default, RSTP/MST are not enabled.

Table 3-21 The Default Settings for RSTP/MST Are Exactly the Same as Those for PVST+ Because RSTP/MST Is Disabled by Default

Feature	Default Setting
Spanning-tree mode	PVST (MSTP and RSTP are disabled)
switch priority (Can be configured on a per-CIST interface basis)	32768
spanning-tree port priority (Can be configured on a per-CIST interface basis)	128

Table 3-21 The Default Settings for RSTP/MST Are Exactly the Same as Those for PVST+ Because RSTP/MST Is Disabled by Default (Continued)

Feature	Default Setting
spanning-tree port cost (Can be configured on a per-CIST interface basis)	1000 Mbps: 4 100 Mbps: 19 10 Mbps: 100
Hello Time	2 seconds
Forward Delay Time	15 seconds
Max Age Time	20 seconds
Maximum hop count	20 hops

RSTP and MSTP Configuration Guidelines

The configuration guidelines for RSTP and MSTP are as follows:

- Per-VLAN RSTP (PVRST) is not supported. When MST is enabled using the **spanning-tree mode mst** global configuration command, RSTP is enabled.

- PVST, PVST+, and MSTP are supported, but only one version can be active at any time: all VLANs run PVST, or all VLANs run MSTP.

- VTP propagation of the MST configuration is not supported. Manually configure the MST configuration (region name, revision number, and VLAN-to-instance mapping) on each switch within the MST region by using the command-line interface (CLI) or through the SNMP support.

- For load sharing across redundant paths in the network to work, all VLAN-to-instance mapping assignments must match. Otherwise, all traffic flows on a single link.

- All MST boundary ports must be forwarding for load sharing between a PVST+ and an MST cloud. For this to happen, the IST master of the MST cloud should also be the root of the CST. If the MST cloud consists of multiple MST regions, one of the MST regions must contain the CST root, and all the other MST regions must have a better path to the root contained with the MST cloud than a path through the PVST+ cloud. It might be necessary to manually configure the switches in the clouds.

- Partitioning the network into a large number of regions is not recommended. However, if this situation is unavoidable, it is recommended that the switched LAN be partitioned into smaller LANs interconnected by routers or non-Layer 2 devices.

TIP

Cisco.com includes an extensive set of technical information describing RSTP and MSTP operation and configuration, which you can find at http://www.cisco.com/univercd/cc/td/doc/product/lan/c3550/12120ea2/3550scg/swmstp.htm.

Enabling RSTP and MSTP

For two or more switches to be in the same MST region, they must have the same VLAN-to-instance mapping, the same configuration revision number, and the same name.

A region can have one member or multiple members with the same MST configuration. Each member must be capable of processing RSTP BPDUs. There is no limit to the number of MST regions in a network, and each region can support up to 16 spanning-tree instances. A VLAN can be assigned to only one spanning-tree instance at a time.

Beginning in privileged EXEC mode, follow the steps outlined in Table 3-22 to specify the MST region configuration and enable MSTP.

Table 3-22 Up to 16 Spanning-Tree Instances Can Be Configured with MST

Step	Command	Description
1	**configure terminal**	Enters global configuration mode.
2	**spanning-tree mst configuration**	Enters MST configuration mode.
3	**instance** *instance-id* **vlan** *vlan-range*	Maps VLANs to an MST instance. For *instance-id*, the range is 1 to 15. For **vlan** *vlan-range*, the range is 1 to 4094. When you map VLANs to an MST instance, the mapping is incremental, and the range of VLANs specified is added to or removed from the existing ones. To specify a range, use a hyphen. For example, **instance 1 vlan 1-63** maps VLANs 1 through 63 to MST instance 1. To specify a series, use a comma. For example, **instance 1 vlan 10, 20, 30** maps VLANs 10, 20, and 30 to MST instance 1.
4	**name** *name*	Specifies the configuration name. The *name* string has a maximum length of 32 characters and is case-sensitive.
5	**revision** *version*	Specifies the configuration revision number. The range is 0 to 65535.
6	**show pending**	Verifies your configuration by displaying the pending configuration.

Table 3-22 Up to 16 Spanning-Tree Instances Can Be Configured with MST (Continued)

Step	Command	Description
7	**exit**	Applies all changes and returns to global configuration mode.
8	**spanning-tree mode mst**	Enables MSTP. RSTP is also enabled. Caution: Changing spanning-tree modes can disrupt traffic because all spanning-tree instances are stopped for the previous mode and restarted in the new mode.
9	**end**	Returns to privileged EXEC mode.
10	**show running-config**	Verifies your entries.

To return to the default MST region configuration, use the **no spanning-tree mst configuration** global configuration command. To return to the default VLAN-to-instance map, use the **no instance** *instance-id* [**vlan** *vlan-range*] MST configuration command. To return to the default name, use the **no name** MST configuration command. To return to the default revision number, use the **no revision** MST configuration command.

To re-enable PVST, use the **no spanning-tree mode** or the **spanning-tree mode pvst** global configuration command.

Example 3-1 demonstrates how to enter MST configuration mode, map VLANs 10 to 20 to MST instance 1, name the region region1, set the configuration revision to 1, display the pending configuration, apply the changes, and return to global configuration mode. MST information is not propagated in VTP updates, so this configuration must be done on all the appropriate switches.

Example 3-1 *Mapping VLANs 10 to 20 to MST Instance 1*

```
Switch(config)#spanning-tree mst configuration
Switch(config-mst)#instance 1 vlan 10-20
Switch(config-mst)#name region1
Switch(config-mst)#revision 1
Switch(config-mst)#show pending
Pending MST configuration
Name [region1]
Revision 1
```

continues

Example 3-1 *Mapping VLANs 10 to 20 to MST Instance 1 (Continued)*

```
Instance Vlans Mapped
-------- -----------------------
0   1-9, 21-4094
1   10-20
--------------------------------
Switch(config-mst)#exit
Switch(config)#
```

Configuring the MST Root Switch

The switch maintains a spanning-tree instance for the group of VLANs mapped to it. A BID, consisting of the switch priority and the switch MAC address, is associated with each instance. The switch with the lowest BID becomes the Root Switch for the group of VLANs.

To configure a switch to become the root, use the **spanning-tree mst** *instance-id* **root** global configuration command to modify the switch priority from the default value (32768) to a significantly lower value so that the switch becomes the Root Switch for the specified spanning-tree instance. When this command is issued, the switch checks the switch priorities of the Root Switches. Because of the extended system ID support, the switch sets its own priority for the specified instance to 24576 if this value will cause this switch to become the root for the specified spanning-tree instance.

If any Root Switch for the specified instance has a switch priority lower than 24576, the switch sets its own priority to 4096 less than the lowest switch priority. 4096 is the value of the least-significant bit of a 4-bit switch priority value.

Catalyst 2950 switches running Cisco IOS software earlier than Release 12.1(9)EA1 do not support the extended system ID. Catalyst 2950 switches running Cisco IOS software earlier than Release 12.1(9)EA1 do not support the MSTP.

If the network consists of switches that both do and do not support the extended system ID, it is unlikely that the switch with the extended system ID support will become the Root Switch. The extended system ID increases the switch priority value every time the VLAN number is greater than the priority of the connected switches running older software.

The Root Switch for each spanning-tree instance should be a backbone or distribution switch. Do not configure an access switch as the spanning-tree primary root.

Use the **diameter** keyword, which is available only for MST instance 0, to specify the Layer 2 network diameter (that is, the maximum number of switch hops between any two end stations in the Layer 2 network). When specifying the network diameter, the switch automatically sets an optimal hello time, forward-delay time, and maximum-age time for a network of that diameter, which can significantly reduce the convergence time. Use the **hello** keyword to override the automatically calculated hello time.

The recommended practice is that you avoid manually configuring the hello time, forward-delay time, and maximum-age time. In other words, the recommended practice is to avoid using the **spanning-tree mst hello-time**, **spanning-tree mst forward-time**, and **spanning-tree mst max-age** global configuration commands after configuring the switch as the Root Switch.

Beginning in privileged EXEC mode, follow the steps outlined in Table 3-23 to configure a switch as the Root Switch.

Table 3-23 Configuring the Root Switch with MST Is Done Per Instance Instead of Per VLAN

Step	Command	Description
1	**configure terminal**	Enters global configuration mode.
2	**spanning-tree mst** *instance-id* **root primary** [**diameter** *net-diameter* [**hello-time** *seconds*]]	Configures a switch as the Root Switch. For *instance-id*, the range is 0 to 15. (Optional) For **diameter** *net-diameter*, specify the maximum number of switches between any two end stations. The range is 2 to 7. This keyword is available only for MST instance 0. (Optional) For **hello-time** *seconds*, specify the interval in seconds between the generation of configuration messages by the Root Switch. The range is 1 to 10 seconds; the default is 2 seconds.
3	**end**	Returns to privileged EXEC mode.
4	**show spanning-tree mst** *instance-id*	Verifies your entries.

To return the switch to its default setting, use the **no spanning-tree mst** *instance-id* **root** global configuration command.

Lab 3.10.4 Implementing MST

In this lab exercise, you implement MST in a switched network.

Configuring MST Switch Priority

The switch priority can be configured to make it more likely that the switch will be chosen as the Root Switch. Exercise care when using the **spanning-tree mst** *instance-id* **priority** global configuration command. For most situations, it is recommended that you use the **spanning-tree mst** *instance-id* **root primary** and **spanning-tree mst** *instance-id* **root secondary** global configuration commands to modify the switch priority.

Beginning in privileged EXEC mode, follow the steps outlined in Table 3-24 to configure the switch priority.

Table 3-24 MST Bridge Priority Can Also Be Used to Influence Root Bridge Election

Step	Command	Description
1	**configure terminal**	Enters global configuration mode.
2	**spanning-tree mst** *instance-id* **priority** *priority*	Configures the switch priority for an MST instance.
		For *instance-id,* the range is 0 to 15.
		For *priority,* the range is 0 to 61440 in increments of 4096; the default is 32768. The lower the number, the more likely the switch will be chosen as the Root Switch.
		Valid priority values are 0, 4096, 8192, 12288, 16384, 20480, 24576, 28672, 32768, 36864, 40960, 45056, 49152, 53248, 57344, and 61440. All other values are rejected.
3	**end**	Returns to privileged EXEC mode.
4	**show spanning-tree mst** *instance-id*	Verifies your entries.

To return the switch to its default setting, use the **no spanning-tree mst** *instance-id* **priority** global configuration command.

Configuring MST Path Cost

The MST Path Cost default value is derived from an interface's media speed. If a loop occurs, the MSTP uses cost when selecting an interface to put in the Forwarding state. Assign lower-cost values to interfaces that the network administrator wants selected first and higher-cost values to interfaces that the administrator wants selected last. If all interfaces have the same cost value, the MSTP puts the interface with the lowest interface number in the Forwarding state and blocks the other interfaces.

Beginning in privileged EXEC mode, follow the steps outlined in Table 3-25 to configure an interface's MSTP cost.

Table 3-25 MST Port Cost Can Be Configured to Alter the Default MST Topology

Step	Command	Description
1	**configure terminal**	Enters global configuration mode.
2	**interface** *interface-id*	Enters interface configuration mode and specifies an interface to configure. Valid interfaces include physical ports and port channels. Valid port-channel numbers are 1 to 6.
3	**spanning-tree mst** *instance-id* **cost** *cost*	Configures the cost of an MST instance. If a loop occurs, MSTP uses the Path Cost when selecting an interface to place in the Forwarding state. A lower Path Cost represents higher-speed transmission. For *instance-id,* the range is 0 to 15. For *cost,* the range is 1 to 200000000; the default is derived from the interface's media speed.
4	**end**	Returns to privileged EXEC mode.
5	**show spanning-tree mst interface** *instance-id* or **show spanning-tree mst** *instance-id*	Verifies your entries.

The **show spanning-tree mst interface** *interface-id* privileged EXEC command displays information only for ports that are in a link-up operative state. Otherwise, use the **show running-config** privileged EXEC command to confirm the configuration.

To return the interface to its default setting, use the **no spanning-tree mst** *instance-id* **cost** interface configuration command.

Configuring MST Port Priority

If a loop occurs, MSTP uses the Port Priority when selecting an interface to put in the Forwarding state. Assign higher-priority values (lower numerical values) to interfaces that the network administrator wants selected first and lower-priority values (higher numerical values) to interfaces that the administrator wants selected last. If all interfaces have the same priority value, the MSTP puts the interface with the lowest interface number in the Forwarding state and blocks the other interfaces.

Beginning in privileged EXEC mode, follow the steps outlined in Table 3-26 to configure an interface's MSTP Port Priority.

Table 3-26 MST Port Priority Can Be Configured to Alter the Default MST Topology

Step	Command	Description
1	**configure terminal**	Enters global configuration mode.
2	**interface** *interface-id*	Enters interface configuration mode and specifies an interface to configure. Valid interfaces include physical ports and port channels. Valid port-channel numbers are 1 to 6.
3	**spanning-tree mst** *instance-id* **port-priority** *priority*	Configures the Port Priority for an MST instance. For *instance-id,* the range is 0 to 15. For *priority,* the range is 0 to 255; the default is 128. The lower the number, the higher the priority.
4	**end**	Returns to privileged EXEC mode.
5	**show spanning-tree mst interface** *instance-id* or **show spanning-tree mst** *instance-id*	Verifies your entries.

The **show spanning-tree mst interface** *interface-id* privileged EXEC command displays information only if the port is in a link-up operative state. Use the **show running-config interface** privileged EXEC command to confirm the configuration.

To return the interface to its default setting, use the **no spanning-tree mst** *instance-id* **port-priority** interface configuration command.

Configuring MSTP Timers

The MSTP Hello time, MSTP Forward Delay time, and MSTP Maximum Aging time can be configured. This section explores the steps to configuring these timers.

MSTP Hello Time

You can change how often the Root Switch generates configuration messages by adjusting the hello time. Exercise care when using this command. For most situations, the recommended practice is to use the **spanning-tree mst** *instance-id* **root primary** and **spanning-tree mst** *instance-id* **root secondary** global configuration commands to modify the hello time.

Beginning in privileged EXEC mode, follow the steps outlined in Table 3-27 to configure the hello time for all MST instances.

Table 3-27 The MST Hello Time Can Be Configured to Alter the Default Value of 2 Seconds

Step	Command	Description
1	**configure terminal**	Enters global configuration mode.
2	**spanning-tree mst hello-time** *seconds*	Configures the hello time for all MST instances. The hello time is the interval between the generation of configuration messages by the Root Switch. These messages mean that the switch is alive. For *seconds,* the range is 1 to 10; the default is 2.
3	**end**	Returns to privileged EXEC mode.
4	**show spanning-tree mst**	Verifies your entries.

To return the switch to its default setting, use the **no spanning-tree mst hello-time** global configuration command.

MSTP Forward Delay Time

Beginning in privileged EXEC mode, follow the steps shown in Table 3-28 to configure the forward delay time for all MST instances.

Table 3-28 The MST Forward Delay Can Be Configured to Alter the Default Value of 15 Seconds

Step	Command	Description
1	**configure terminal**	Enters global configuration mode.
2	**spanning-tree mst forward-time** *seconds*	Configures the forward time for all MST instances. The forward time is the number of seconds a port waits before changing from its STP Learning and Listening states to the Forwarding state. For *seconds,* the range is 4 to 30; the default is 15.
3	**end**	Returns to privileged EXEC mode.
4	**show spanning-tree mst**	Verifies your entries.

To return the switch to its default setting, use the **no spanning-tree mst forward-time** global configuration command.

MSTP Maximum Aging Time

Beginning in privileged EXEC mode, follow the steps outlined in Table 3-29 to configure the maximum aging time for all MST instances.

Table 3-29 The MST Max Age Can Be Configured to Alter the Default Value of 20 Seconds

Step	Command	Description
1	**configure terminal**	Enters global configuration mode.
2	**spanning-tree mst max-age** *seconds*	Configures the maximum aging time for all MST instances. The maximum aging time is the number of seconds a switch waits without receiving spanning-tree configuration messages before attempting a reconfiguration. For *seconds,* the range is 6 to 40; the default is 20.
3	**end**	Returns to privileged EXEC mode.
4	**show spanning-tree mst**	Verifies your entries.

To return the switch to its default setting, use the **no spanning-tree mst max-age** global configuration command.

Configuring Maximum Hop Count

Beginning in privileged EXEC mode, follow the steps outlined in Table 3-30 to configure the maximum hop count for all MST instances.

Table 3-30 The MST Maximum Hop Count Can Be Configured to Alter the Default Value of 20 Hops

Step	Command	Description
1	**configure terminal**	Enters global configuration mode.
2	**spanning-tree mst max-hops** *hop-count*	Specifies the number of hops in a region before the BPDU is discarded and the information held for port is aged. For *hop-count,* the range is 1 to 40; the default is 20.
3	**end**	Returns to privileged EXEC mode.
4	**show spanning-tree mst**	Verifies your entries.

To return the switch to its default setting, use the **no spanning-tree mst max-hops** global configuration command.

EtherChannel

EtherChannel is a Cisco-proprietary technology that, by aggregating links into a single logical link, provides incremental trunk speeds ranging from 10 Mbps to 160 Gbps (full duplex). EtherChannel comes in four flavors:

- Standard EtherChannel
- Fast EtherChannel (FEC)
- Gigabit EtherChannel (GEC)
- 10-Gigabit EtherChannel

The term EtherChannel encompasses all these technologies. EtherChannel combines up to eight standard Ethernet links (160 Mbps on a Catalyst 3000), up to eight Fast Ethernet links (1.6 Gbps), up to eight Gigabit Ethernet links (16 Gbps), and up to eight 10 Gigabit Ethernet links (160 Gbps).

EtherChannel Explained

EtherChannel provides fault-tolerant, high-speed links between switches, routers, and servers, as shown in Figure 3-49. The term heard most often in the context of EtherChannel is "resiliency." Cisco defines resiliency as "the ability to recover from any network failure or issue, whether it is related to a disaster, link, hardware, design, or network service." Recall STP and how it handles link failures within a Layer 2 topology. With EtherChannel, resiliency refers to EtherChannel's ability to continue to operate when one of the links in a "bundle" goes down as well as its ability to restore the full bundle should the downed link come back into service. Chapter 2, "VLANs and VTP," discussed trunking technologies. In particular, it looked at the IEEE 802.1Q and ISL Ethernet trunking technologies. What might not have been made clear at that time is that Ethernet trunks frequently go hand in hand with EtherChannel links. The reason for this should be clear. Trunk links carry more traffic and require more bandwidth than access links.

Figure 3-49 EtherChannel Enables Logical Links with Aggregate Bandwidth of Up to 160 Gbps

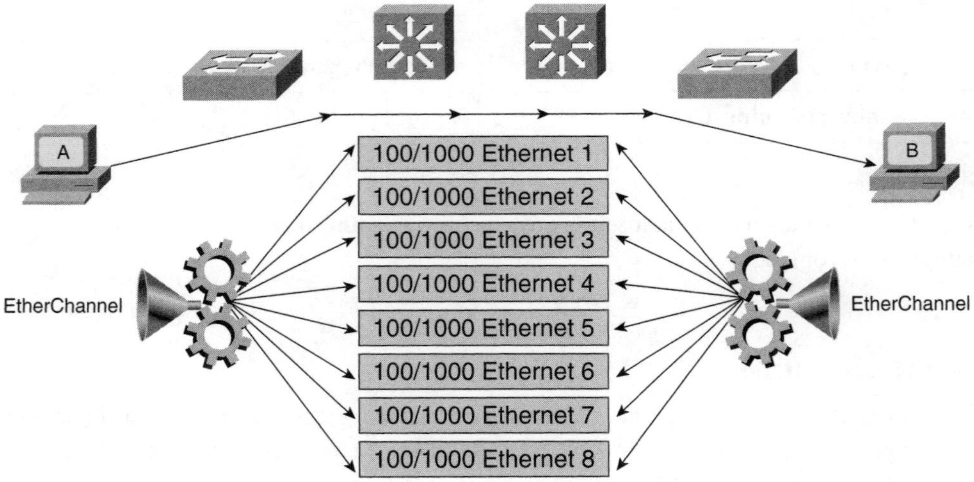

EtherChannel bundles segments into groups of two to eight links. This lets links scale at rates between 100 Mbps and a healthy fraction of 1 Tbps. T1 or 1.544 Mbps used to be the fastest WAN link available. Now it is at least 16 Tbps for up to a 50-kilometer stretch with single-mode fiber, using the Catalyst 6500 10GBASE-EX4 Metro 10 Gigabit Ethernet module. EtherChannel operates as either an access link or trunk link. For example, EtherChannel can be deployed between the wiring closet and the data center, as illustrated in Figure 3-50. In the data center, EtherChannel links can be deployed between servers and the network backbone to provide scalable incremental bandwidth.

Figure 3-50 EtherChannel Can Be Deployed Between the Wiring Closet and the Data Center

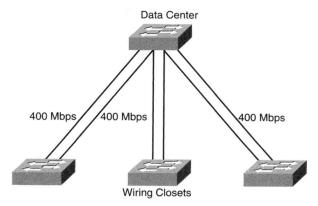

Some of the benefits of EtherChannel are as follows:

- EtherChannel does not require any changes because it is transparent to networked applications. For support of EtherChannel on enterprise-class servers and NICs, smart software drivers can coordinate distribution of loads across multiple network interfaces.
- When EtherChannel is used within the campus, switches and routers provide load distribution transparently across multiple links to network users. Unicast, multicast, and broadcast traffic is distributed across the links in the channel.
- EtherChannel provides automatic recovery for loss of a link by redistributing loads across remaining links. If a link does fail, EtherChannel redirects traffic from the failed link to the remaining links in less than a second. This convergence is transparent to the end user. No host protocol timers expire, so no sessions are dropped.

Figure 3-51 shows a typical EtherChannel network configuration.

Now that you have a fair understanding of EtherChannel technology, you can investigate how it works and how to configure it in a network. The following section explains how Ether-Channel uses frame distribution.

Figure 3-51 *All Catalyst Switches Support EtherChannel. Catalyst 6500 Switches Support 10 Gigabit EtherChannel (10 GEC). Catalyst 2950-T, Catalyst 3550, and Catalyst 4500 Switches Support Gigabit EtherChannel (GEC). Other Catalyst Switches Support Only Fast EtherChannel (FEC) or EtherChannel.*

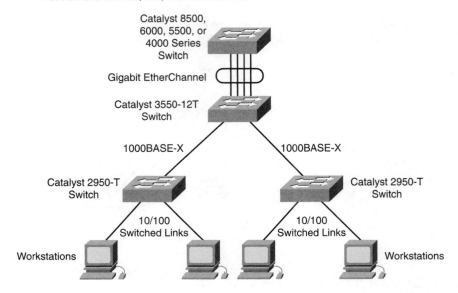

Frame Distribution

EtherChannel balances the traffic load across the links in a channel by applying an algorithm to a portion of the binary pattern extracted from addresses in the Ethernet frame or encapsulated data packets. The algorithm output is a numeric value that is then associated with one of the links in the channel. On IOS-based switches, Catalyst 4000 series switches, and Catalyst 5000/5500 family switches, EtherChannel load distribution can be based on either source MAC or destination MAC addresses. On the Catalyst 6000 family of switches, the load-balancing policy (frame distribution) can be based on a MAC address, IP address, or Port Number. With source MAC address forwarding, when packets are forwarded to an Ether-Channel, they are distributed across the ports in the channel based on the incoming packet's source MAC address. Therefore, to provide load distribution, frames from different hosts use different ports in the channel, but frames from the same host use the same port in the channel.

With destination MAC address forwarding, when frames are forwarded to an EtherChannel, they are distributed across the ports in the channel based on the MAC address of the destination host in the incoming frame. Therefore, frames to the same destination are forwarded over the same port, and frames to a different destination might be sent on a different port in the channel.

The most recent EtherChannel frame distribution process is based on a Cisco-proprietary hashing algorithm. Hash algorithms, such as Message Digest 5 (MD5), are normally used to ensure that traffic arriving at the destination is identical to that generated at the source; however, the hash algorithm used with EtherChannel is designed to consistently and somewhat randomly distribute Ethernet frames across member links in an EtherChannel. The algorithm is deterministic, meaning that given the same addresses and session information, it always hashes to the same port in the channel, preventing out-of-order frame delivery.

Although EtherChannel frame distribution based on a MAC address, IP address, or Layer 4 Port Number is possible, the configurable options allow for distribution based on source only (MAC, IP, or port), destination only (MAC, IP, or port), or both source and destination (MAC, IP, or port). The mode selected applies to all EtherChannels configured on the switch. Use the option that provides the greatest variety in the configuration. For example, if the traffic on a channel is going to a single MAC address only, using source addresses, IP addresses, or Layer 4 Port Numbers as the basis for frame distribution might provide better frame distribution than selecting MAC addresses as the basis.

In Figure 3-52, an EtherChannel connects a Catalyst 2950 to a router. The switch is also connected to four workstations. Because the router is referenced by the switch with a single MAC address, source-based forwarding on the switch EtherChannel ensures that the switch uses all available bandwidth to the router. The router is configured for destination-based forwarding because the large number of workstations ensures that the traffic is evenly distributed from the router EtherChannel.

Cisco 7000, 7200, 7500, 7600, and 8500 routers support Fast EtherChannels via logical port channel interfaces binding Fast Ethernet interfaces. Cisco 7600 and 8500 routers also support Gigabit EtherChannel.

EtherChannel Methods

EtherChannel uses two methods to negotiate bundles:

- Port Aggregation Protocol (PAgP): Cisco-proprietary
- Link Aggregation Control Protocol (LACP): IEEE 802.3ad

Figure 3-52 Source-Based Frame Distribution Is Used on the Switch, and Destination-Based Frame Distribution Is Used on the Router

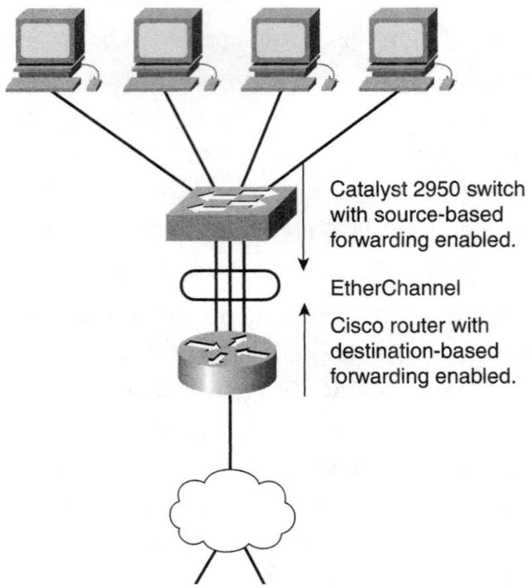

Catalyst 2950 switch with source-based forwarding enabled.

EtherChannel

Cisco router with destination-based forwarding enabled.

Port Aggregation Protocol (PAgP)

Port Aggregation Protocol (PAgP) is a Cisco-proprietary technology that facilitates the automatic creation of EtherChannels by exchanging packets between Ethernet interfaces. By using PAgP, the switch learns the identity of partners that can support PAgP and learns the capabilities of each interface. It then dynamically groups similarly configured interfaces into a single logical link (channel or aggregate port). These interfaces are grouped based on hardware, administrative, and port parameter constraints. For example, PAgP groups the interfaces with the same speed, duplex mode, native VLAN, VLAN range, and trunking status and type. After grouping the links into an EtherChannel, PAgP adds the group to the spanning tree as a single switch port.

Table 3-31 lists and defines the various PAgP modes.

Table 3-31 PAgP Modes

Mode or Keyword	Description
on	The mode that forces the port to channel without PAgP. With the on mode, a usable EtherChannel exists only when a port group in on mode is connected to another port group in on mode.
off	The mode that prevents the port from channeling.

Table 3-31 PAgP Modes (Continued)

Mode or Keyword	Description
auto	The mode that places a port in a passive negotiating state, in which the port responds to PAgP packets it receives but does not initiate PAgP packet negotiation. This is the default setting.
desirable	The mode that places a port in an active negotiating state, in which the port initiates negotiations with other ports by sending PAgP packets.
silent	The keyword that is used with auto or desirable mode when no traffic is expected from the other device. This option prevents the link from being reported to STP as down. This is the default, secondary PAgP setting.
non-silent	The keyword that is used with auto or desirable mode when traffic is expected from the other device.

As described in Table 3-31, EtherChannel includes the four user-configurable modes of on, off, auto, and desirable. Only auto and desirable are PAgP modes. The auto and desirable modes can be modified with the **silent** and **non-silent** keywords. By default, ports are in auto-silent mode. Both the auto and desirable modes allow ports to negotiate with connected ports to determine if they can form an EtherChannel, based on criteria such as port speed, trunking state, and VLAN numbers.

The on mode forces the port to channel without PAgP. With the on mode, a usable EtherChannel exists only when a port group in on mode is connected to another port group in on mode. The off mode prevents the port from channeling. The auto mode places a port in a passive negotiating state, in which the port responds to PAgP packets it receives but does not initiate PAgP packet negotiation. This is the default setting. The desirable mode places a port in an active negotiating state, in which the port initiates negotiations with other ports by sending PAgP packets.

Ports can form an EtherChannel when they are in different PAgP modes as long as the modes are compatible. For example, a port in desirable mode can form an EtherChannel successfully with another port that is in desirable or auto mode. A port in auto mode can form an EtherChannel with another port in desirable mode. A port in auto mode cannot form an EtherChannel with another port that is also in auto mode, because neither port initiates negotiation, as shown in Table 3-32.

Table 3-32 Different Combinations of PAgP Modes on Either End of a Potential EtherChannel Might or Might Not Result in a Valid EtherChannel Bundle

Valid EtherChannel Modes	Invalid EtherChannel Modes
on-on	off-any
auto-desirable	auto-auto
desirable-desirable	on-desirable
	on-auto

On CatOS switches, configuring an EtherChannel automatically creates an administrative group, designated by an integer between 1 and 1024, to which the EtherChannel belongs. If preferred, specify the administrative group number. Forming a channel without specifying an administrative group number creates a new automatically numbered administrative group. An administrative group can contain a maximum of eight ports. In addition, on CatOS switches, each EtherChannel is automatically assigned a unique EtherChannel ID.

Link Aggregation Control Protocol (LACP)

The open-standard equivalent to PAgP is *Link Aggregation Control Protocol (LACP)*. Defined in IEEE 802.3ad, LACP allows Cisco switches to manage Ethernet channels with non-Cisco devices conforming to the 802.3ad specification. It is likely that LACP will become the norm for Catalyst switches, just as Cisco migrated from ISL to IEEE 802.1Q. (Cisco cannot always wait for the IEEE to complete its standards process before incorporating new features on its devices.) To have LACP handle channeling, use the active and passive channel modes. To start automatic Ethernet channel configuration with LACP, configure at least one end of the link to active mode to initiate channeling, because ports in passive mode passively respond to initiation and never initiate the sending of LACP packets. Table 3-33 lists and defines the various LACP modes.

Table 3-33 LACP Modes

Mode	Description
on	Forces the port to channel without LACP. With the on mode, a usable EtherChannel exists only when a port group in on mode is connected to another port group in on mode.
off	Prevents the port from channeling.

Table 3-33 LACP Modes (Continued)

Mode	Description
passive	Similar to the auto mode for PAgP, passive mode places a port in a passive negotiating state, in which the port responds to LACP packets it receives but does not initiate LACP packet negotiation. Passive is the default mode.
active	Similar to the desirable mode for PAgP, active mode places a port in an active negotiating state, in which the port initiates negotiation with other ports by sending LACP packets.

The on mode forces the port to channel without LACP. With the on mode, a usable EtherChannel exists only when a port group in on mode is connected to another port group in on mode. The off mode prevents the port from channeling. The passive mode is similar to the PAgP auto mode, because it places the port in a passive negotiating state, in which the port responds to LACP packets it receives but does not initiate LACP packet negotiation. Passive mode is the default LACP mode.

When enabled, LACP always tries to configure the maximum number of compatible ports in a channel, up to the maximum allowed by the hardware (eight ports for Catalyst switches). If LACP cannot aggregate all the ports that are compatible (for example, if the remote system has more restrictive hardware limitations), all the ports that cannot be actively included in the channel are put in hot-standby state and are used only if one of the channeled ports fails.

Modifying Port Cost for EtherChannel Groups

If Port Cost is not specified, the STP Port Cost is updated based on the current Port Costs of the channeling ports. However, if channel Port Cost is specified, the Port Costs of member ports in the channel are modified to reflect the new cost. This enables load sharing of VLAN traffic across multiple channels configured with trunking, because some VLANs in the channel have Port VLAN Cost values and the others have Port Cost values. This might not sound useful (or meaningful), but it allows, for example, the configuration of VLAN traffic to load-share between one EtherChannel connected to one core switch and another EtherChannel connected to another core switch.

EtherChannel Configuration Guidelines

There are a host of guidelines for configuring EtherChannels. Figure 3-53 shows a Fast EtherChannel. The EtherChannel configuration guidelines relate to trunks, dynamic VLANs, STP, and otherwise. If improperly configured, some EtherChannel interfaces are automatically disabled to avoid network loops and other problems.

Figure 3-53 Fast EtherChannel Topology

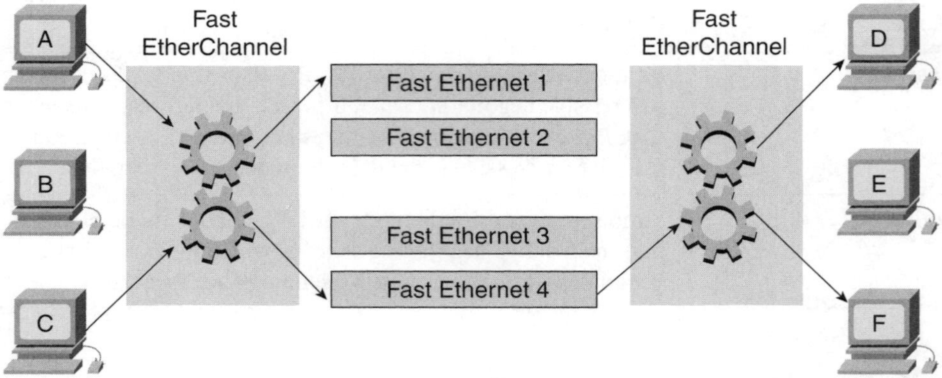

To minimize time spent troubleshooting EtherChannel, adhere to the following recommendations:

- Assign all ports in an EtherChannel to the same VLAN, or configure them as trunk ports. If the EtherChannel is configured as a trunk, configure the same trunk mode on all the ports in the EtherChannel. Configuring ports in an EtherChannel in different trunk modes can have unexpected results. An EtherChannel supports the same allowed range of VLANs on all the ports in a trunking EtherChannel. If the allowed range of VLANs is not the same for a port list, the ports do not form an EtherChannel even when set to auto or desirable mode.

- Do not configure the ports in an EtherChannel as dynamic VLAN ports. Doing so can adversely affect switch performance. An EtherChannel does not form with ports that have different GARP, GVRP, or QoS configurations. GARP and GVRP are industry-standard protocols described in IEEE 802.1p. If a broadcast limit is configured on the ports, configure it as a percentage limit for the channeled ports. With a packets-per-second broadcast limit, unicast packets might get dropped for 1 second when the broadcast limit is exceeded.

- An EtherChannel does not form with ports that have the port security feature enabled. The port security feature cannot be enabled for ports in an EtherChannel. If Internet Group Management Protocol (IGMP) multicast filtering is using one port in an Ether-Channel, set the EtherChannel mode for both PAgP and LACP to off. No other mode can be used.

- An EtherChannel does not form if one of the ports is a Switched Port Analyzer (SPAN) destination port. An EtherChannel does not form if protocol filtering is set differently on any of the ports. Each EtherChannel can have up to eight compatibly configured

Ethernet interfaces. Configure all interfaces in an EtherChannel to operate at the same speed and duplex modes.

- Enable all interfaces in an EtherChannel. If an interface in an EtherChannel is shut down, it is treated as a link failure, and its traffic is transferred to one of the remaining interfaces in the EtherChannel.

- Interfaces with different STP Port Costs can form an EtherChannel as long they are otherwise compatibly configured. Setting different STP Port Costs does not, by itself, make interfaces incompatible for the formation of an EtherChannel. However, it is preferable to set STP Port Costs to be equal for all ports in an EtherChannel.

Beyond the restrictions listed here, the only remaining concern is what ports can be used when configuring an EtherChannel. Catalyst 4000 and 6000 line cards have newer chipsets that allow the use of an even or odd number of links in the EtherChannel. The ports do not have to be contiguous or even on the same line card, as is true with some Catalyst devices and line modules. The newer chips on the Catalyst 4000s and 6000s are not available on all Catalyst hardware.

Older Catalyst switches use an Ethernet Bundle Controller (EBC) to manage aggregated EtherChannel ports (for example, performing frame distribution). The EBC communicates with the Enhanced Address Recognition Logic (EARL) application-specific integrated circuit (ASIC). The EARL is responsible for, among other things, learning MAC addresses. For example, the EARL ages out all addresses learned on a link in an EtherChannel bundle when it fails. After a link failure, the EBC and the EARL work together to recalculate in hardware the "lost" source-destination address pairs on a different link. On the older switches, when selecting ports to group for an EtherChannel process, ports that belong to the same EBC must be selected. A 24-port module has three groups of eight ports, and a 12-port module has three groups of four ports, as shown in Figure 3-54.

Figure 3-54 Groups of Four or Eight Ports Are Managed by Ethernet Bundle Controllers on Older Catalyst Switches

1	2	3	4	5	6	7	8	9	10	11	12	13	14	15	16	17	18	19	20	21	22	23	24
1	1	1	1	1	1	1	1	2	2	2	2	2	2	2	2	3	3	3	3	3	3	3	3
1	1	1	1	2	2	2	2	3	3	3	3												

Be sure to check the hardware documentation before attempting to create EtherChannel bundles. Older Catalyst switches restrict which ports are used in a given bundle. The remainder of the material in this section pertains primarily to Catalyst 5000 line modules.

In a 12-port module, up to two dual-segment EtherChannel configurations can be created within each group of four ports, as illustrated in Example A in Table 3-34. One dual-segment EtherChannel configuration can be created within each group, as shown in Example B. Example C illustrates a four-segment and two-segment EtherChannel configuration.

Table 3-34 Some Combinations of Ports Are Invalid for EtherChannel Formation on Older Catalyst Switches

Port		1	2	3	4	5	6	7	8	9	10	11	12
Example A	OK	1	1	2	2	3	3	4	4	5	5	6	6
Example B	OK	1	1			2	2			3	3		
Example C	OK	1	1	1	1	2	2						
Example D	Not OK			1	1								
Example E	Not OK	1	1	2	2	2	2						
Example F	Not OK	1		1									
Example G	Not OK		1	1									

Some EtherChannel configurations must be avoided on older Catalyst devices, including most Catalyst 5000 line cards. Example D illustrates an invalid two-segment EtherChannel configuration using Ports 3 and 4 of a group. The EBC must start its bundling with the first ports of a group. This does not mean that the first group has to be used. In contrast, a valid dual-segment EtherChannel configuration can use Ports 5 and 6 with no EtherChannel segment on the first group. Example E illustrates another invalid configuration. In this example, two EtherChannel segments are formed. One is a dual-segment EtherChannel configuration, and the other is a four-segment EtherChannel configuration. The dual-segment EtherChannel configuration is valid. The four-segment EtherChannel configuration, however, violates the rule that all ports must belong to the same group (EBC). This EtherChannel configuration uses two ports from the first group and two ports from the second group.

Finally, Example G is an invalid EtherChannel configuration because it does not use the first ports on the module to start the EtherChannel process (like Example D). The EtherChannel process cannot be started with middle ports on the line module. All the examples in Table 3-34 apply to 24-port modules as well. The only difference between 12- and 24-port modules is the number of EtherChannel segments that can be formed within a group. The 12-port module allows only two (two-port) EtherChannel segments in a group, whereas the 24-port module supports up to four (two-port) EtherChannel segments per group.

Configuring Fast EtherChannel

To configure EtherChannel on an IOS-based switch, on each of the participating interfaces (up to eight), enter the following command:

```
channel-group channel-group-number mode {auto [non-silent] | desirable
  [non-silent] | on}
```

The **channel-group** command replaces the **port group** command, which was used before Cisco IOS Release 12.1.

To remove an interface from the EtherChannel group, use the **no channel-group** interface configuration command.

Example 3-2 demonstrates the configuration of EtherChannel on an IOS-based switch. A shortcut is available, beginning with Cisco IOS Release 12.1(5)T. Identical commands can be entered once for a range of interfaces, rather than being entered separately for each interface, using the **interface range** command.

Example 3-2 *A Gigabit EtherChannel Is Configured Just as a Fast EtherChannel Is Configured*

```
Switch(config)#interface range gigabitethernet0/1 - 2
Switch(config-if)#channel-group 1 mode desirable
```

To verify the EtherChannel configuration and view EtherChannel information, use the following command:

```
show etherchannel [channel-group-number] {brief | detail | load-balance | port |
  port-channel | summary}
```

Example 3-3 demonstrates some sample output from this command.

Example 3-3 *The* **show etherchannel** *Command Replaces the Previous* **show port group** *Command*

```
Switch#show etherchannel 1 summary

Flags:  D - down        P - in port-channel
        I - stand-alone  s - suspended
        R - Layer3       S - Layer2
        U - port-channel in use

Group  Port-channel   Ports
.............................................................
1      Po1(SU)        Ci0/1(P)   Gi0/2(P)
```

The **show etherchannel** command replaces the **show port group** command, which was used before Cisco IOS Release 12.1.

To specify the technique for load distribution (frame distribution) among links comprising an EtherChannel, use the following command:

```
port-channel load-balance {dst-mac | src-mac}
```

A sample configuration using this command would be as follows:

```
Switch(config)#port-channel load-balance dst-mac
```

Verify the configuration with the command **show etherchannel load-balance**. Finally, to view PAgP status information, use the following command:

```
show pagp [channel-group-number] {counters | internal | neighbor}
```

Example 3-4 demonstrates some sample output from this command.

Example 3-4 *Use the* **show pagp counters** *Command to View PAgP Status Information*

```
Switch#show pagp counters


                 Information          Flush
    Port       Sent     Recv      Sent      Recv
    ...............................................
    Channel group: 1
      Gi0/1     45        42        0         0
      Gi0/2     45        41        0         0
```

Lab 3.10.5 Configuring Fast EtherChannel

In this lab exercise, you provide more bandwidth between Ethernet switches. You combine two 100-Mbps links to form a full-duplex 200-Mbps link.

Summary

This chapter discussed Layer 2 techniques and technologies designed to optimize network reliability, resiliency, and redundancy within a campus network.

In particular, this chapter explored

- The importance of STP as a key Layer 2 network protocol
- Scaling issues with STP as they pertain to VLANs

STP enables Layer 2 reliability, resiliency, and redundancy in a campus network. STP dynamically configures a Layer 2 topology that blocks physical loops in a switched network while at the same time providing a number of configuration options for tailoring the flow of traffic in a network.

A Root Switch serves as the focal point of the topology for each VLAN configured in PVST+ STP mode. With Path Cost, Port Priority, Bridge Priority, STP timers, PortFast, UplinkFast, and BackboneFast, the tools are available to design a robust Layer 2 topology.

EtherChannel provides the finishing touch to the Layer 2 switched infrastructure. EtherChannel provides for incremental bandwidth Ethernet link options, ranging from 10 Mbps (half-duplex) 100-m links to 160 Gbps (full-duplex) 70-km links. EtherChannel relies on PAgP to dynamically manage bundles of Ethernet links.

Several protocols are important for Layer 2 switched design and deployment. This chapter focused on STP and PAgP.

Key Terms

BackboneFast   A Catalyst feature that is initiated when a Root Port or Blocked Port on a switch receives inferior BPDUs from its Designated Bridge. Max Age is skipped to allow appropriate Blocked Ports to transition quickly to Forwarding state in the case of an indirect link failure.

Blocking state   The STP state in which a bridge listens for BPDUs. This state follows the Disabled state.

Bridge ID (BID)   An 8-byte field consisting of an ordered pair of numbers—a 2-byte decimal number called the Bridge Priority and a 6-byte (hexadecimal) MAC address.

Bridge Priority   A decimal number used to measure the preference of a bridge in the Spanning Tree Algorithm. The possible values range between 0 and 65,535.

Bridge Protocol Data Unit (BPDU)   A frame used by switches and bridges to communicate spanning-tree information.

Common Spanning Tree (CST)   A spanning-tree implementation specified in the IEEE 802.1Q standard. CST defines a single instance of spanning tree for all VLANs with BPDUs transmitted over VLAN 1.

Designated Bridge   The Designated Bridge for a segment is the bridge containing the Designated Port for that segment.

Designated Port   The Designated Port for a segment is the bridge port connected to the segment that both sends traffic toward the Root Switch and receives traffic from the Root Switch over that segment.

Disabled state   The administratively shut-down STP state.

edge port   With RSTP, an edge port is functionally equivalent to a port configured with PortFast under PVST+. An edge port immediately transitions to the Forwarding state. An edge port should be configured only on ports that connect to a single end station.

EtherChannel   A Cisco-proprietary technology that, by aggregating links into a single logical link, provides incremental trunk speeds ranging from 100 Mbps to 160 Gbps.

forward delay   How much time the bridge spends in the Listening and Learning states.

Forwarding state   The STP state in which data traffic is both sent and received on a port. It is the last STP state, following the Learning state.

hello time   The time interval between the sending of Configuration BPDUs.

Learning state   The STP state in which the bridge does not pass user data frames but builds the bridging table and gathers information, such as the source VLANs of data frames. This state follows the Listening state.

Link Aggregation Control Protocol (LACP)   Allows Cisco switches to manage Ethernet channels with non-Cisco devices conforming to the 802.3ad specification. Defined in IEEE 802.3ad.

Listening state   The STP state in which no user data is passed, but the port sends and receives BPDUs in an effort to determine the active topology. It is during the Listening state that the three initial convergence steps take place—elect a Root Switch, elect Root Ports, and elect Designated Ports. This state follows the Blocking state.

Max Age   An STP timer that controls how long a bridge stores a BPDU before discarding it. The default is 20 seconds.

Mono Spanning Tree (MST)   The spanning-tree implementation used by non-Cisco 802.1Q switches. One instance of STP is responsible for all VLAN traffic.

Multiple Instances of Spanning Tree Protocol (MISTP)   Lets you group multiple VLANs under a single instance of spanning tree. MISTP combines the Layer 2 load-balancing benefits of PVST+ with the lower CPU load of IEEE 802.1Q.

Multiple Spanning Tree (MST)   Extends the IEEE 802.1w Rapid Spanning Tree (RST) algorithm to multiple spanning trees, as opposed to the single CST of the original IEEE 802.1Q specification. This extension provides for both rapid convergence and load sharing in a VLAN environment.

Path Cost   An STP measure of how close bridges are to each other. Path Cost is the sum of the costs of the links in a path between two bridges.

Per-VLAN Spanning Tree (PVST)   A Cisco-proprietary spanning-tree implementation requiring ISL trunk encapsulation. PVST runs a separate instance of STP for each VLAN.

PortFast   A Catalyst feature that, when enabled, causes an access or trunk port to enter the spanning-tree Forwarding state immediately, bypassing the Listening and Learning states.

Port Aggregation Protocol (PAgP)   A Cisco-proprietary technology that facilitates the automatic creation of EtherChannels by exchanging packets between Ethernet interfaces.

Port ID   A 2-byte STP parameter consisting of an ordered pair of numbers—the Port Priority and the Port Number.

Port Number   A numerical identifier used by Catalyst switches to enumerate the ports.

Port Priority   A configurable STP parameter with values ranging from 0 to 63 on a CatOS switch (the default is 32) and from 0 to 255 on an IOS-based switch (the default is 128). Port Priority is used to influence Root Switch selection when all other STP parameters are equal.

PVST+   A Cisco-proprietary implementation that allows CST and PVST to exist on the same network.

Rapid Spanning Tree Protocol (RSTP)   An evolution of STP (802.1D standard) that provides for faster spanning-tree convergence after a topology change. The standard also includes features equivalent to Cisco PortFast, UplinkFast, and BackboneFast for faster network reconvergence.

Root Bridge   The bridge/switch with the lowest Bridge ID for that VLAN. Each VLAN has a Root Bridge. Also called the Root Switch.

Root Path Cost   The cumulative cost of all links to the Root Switch.

Root Port   A port on a bridge closest to the Root Switch in terms of Path Cost.

Root Switch   See *Root Bridge*.

Spanning Tree Protocol (STP)   A Layer 2 protocol that uses a special-purpose algorithm to discover physical loops in a network and effect a logical loop-free topology.

UplinkFast   A Catalyst feature that accelerates the choice of a new Root Port when a link or switch fails.

Check Your Understanding

Use the following review questions to test your understanding of the concepts covered in this chapter. Answers are listed in Appendix A, "Check Your Understanding Answer Key."

1. Which of the following is used in Root Switch election?

   A. Port ID

   B. Path Cost

   C. BID

   D. Port Priority

2. What are the three steps of STP convergence?

   A. Elect a Root Switch

   B. Elect Designated Ports

   C. Elect Blocking Ports

   D. Elect Root Ports

3. On an IOS-based switch, the Port ID is a 16-bit ordered pair composed of what two values?

   A. Port Preference

   B. Port Priority

   C. Port Number

   D. Port Cost

4. The BID is an 8-byte ordered pair composed of what two values?

   A. Bridge Priority

   B. Bridge Preference

   C. Bridge Number

   D. MAC Address

5. Every active trunk port on the Root Switch is which of the following?

   A. Root Port

   B. Non-Designated Port

   C. Designated Port

   D. Blocking Port

6. Which of the following are IEEE 802.1D spanning-tree states?

   A. Blocking

   B. Discarding

   C. Learning

   D. Forwarding

   E. Listening

7. Which of the following are IEEE 802.1w spanning-tree states?

   A. Blocking

   B. Listening

   C. Learning

   D. Forwarding

   E. Discarding

8. Multiple Spanning Tree is specified by which IEEE standard?

   A. 802.1D

   B. 802.1w

   C. 802.1Q

   D. 802.1s

9. Which of the following spanning-tree parameters can be used to enable load sharing?

   A. Port Priority

   B. Bridge Priority

   C. EtherChannel

   D. Path Cost

10. Which of the following are the two protocols used to create Ethernet channels or bundles?

   A. LACP

   B. VQP

   C. DTP

   D. PAgP

Objectives

After completing this chapter, you will be able to perform tasks related to the following:

- Explain the role of each type of VLAN.
- Understand the methods of routing between VLANs: adding a route processor to a switch by way of a daughter card or module, using router-on-a-stick, using one router-to-switch link per VLAN, and using fixed-chassis (nonmodular) multilayer switches.
- Understand the advantages and disadvantages of each inter-VLAN routing method.
- Configure inter-VLAN routing using each inter-VLAN routing method, with emphasis on switch virtual interfaces and routed ports.
- Troubleshoot inter-VLAN routing.

Chapter 4

Inter-VLAN Routing

Configuring virtual LANs (VLANs) helps you control the size of broadcast domains and keeps local traffic local. The downside of this benefit is that devices in different VLANs are unable to communicate without the presence of some form of Layer 3 routing.

This chapter focuses on the alternative inter-VLAN routing solutions that may be used within Layer 2 switched environments.

Methods of Inter-VLAN Routing

Over the years, the methods of routing traffic between VLANs have changed. The method is dependent on the particular Catalyst switch platforms and the version of the operating system. Basically, the evolution has gone from requiring a one-to-one mapping of switch ports to router ports (one per VLAN), to router-on-a-stick (one switch port trunked to one router port populated with subinterfaces—one per VLAN), and finally to routing via switch virtual interfaces on the Catalyst switch. Also, not too long ago, the ability to configure switch ports as Layer 3 interfaces, totally independent of any VLAN association, became available on switches such as the Catalyst 3550 and 6500.

Key Components of Inter-VLAN Routing

To provide routing between VLANs, three key components must be present:

- A VLAN-capable switch
- A router
- Some form of connectivity between the switch and the router

Figure 4-1 illustrates a legacy method of inter-VLAN routing.

Figure 4-1 The First Form of Inter-VLAN Routing Required a Separate Physical Connection Between the Layer 2 Switch and the Router for Each VLAN

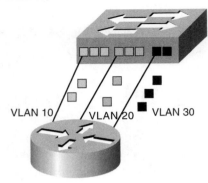

The router can be an external standalone unit, or it can be integrated within the switch hardware. Common names used to describe routers that are integrated within the switch itself include

- Route Switch Module
- Route Processor
- Route Switch Processor
- *Route Switch Feature Card (RSFC)*
- *Multilayer Switch Module (MSM)*
- Multilayer Switch Feature Card
- Layer 3 Services Module

Or, the switch is simply called a Layer 3 switch.

If an external router is employed to perform inter-VLAN routing, connection to the switch can be via a separate Ethernet/Fast Ethernet/Gigabit Ethernet link for each VLAN, or a single trunking link can be used. Figure 4-2 illustrates the single-trunk option.

Layer 3 switches integrate the *route processor* within the switch itself, either in the form of a daughter card or module added to a chassis-based (modular) switch or in the form of an embedded processor in a nonmodular switch, as shown in Figure 4-3. The Catalyst 6509 switch with an MSFC2 daughter card is an example of a chassis-based switch with a route processor added by way of a daughter card. The Catalyst 3550-24 switch is an example of a nonmodular switch with an embedded route processor.

Figure 4-2 The Second Generation of Inter-VLAN Routing Was Implemented by Connecting a Layer 2 Switch to a Router with a Trunk Link

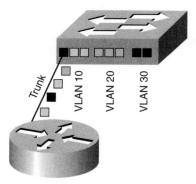

Figure 4-3 The Third Generation of Inter-VLAN Routing Came in the Form of Route Processors Integrated Within the Switches

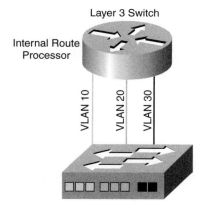

The brains of a newly purchased chassis-based Catalyst switch, called the Supervisor Engine, now come with embedded route processors, so it is no longer necessary to purchase separate daughter cards or modules to add Layer 3 switching functionality. Examples of these are the Supervisor Engine III and IV used with the Catalyst 4500 series switches and the Supervisor Engine 720 used with the Catalyst 6500 switches.

Comparison of Layer 2 and Layer 3 Operations in the Core

The core is a crucial component of every network. Failure of a core device or link can isolate large sections of a network from one another. For this reason, both core links and devices should be designed with adequate redundancy.

In a LAN environment, it is possible to implement the core as a switched or routed layer. Although both methods provide redundancy, they differ significantly in operation.

The Layer 2 or switched core manages its redundant links using Spanning Tree Protocol (STP), as shown in Figure 4-4. This means that some links are not used because one or more ports are in a blocking state. Not only does this underutilize the available bandwidth, but it also often results in inefficient traffic paths.

Figure 4-4 Spanning Tree Protocol Handles Redundant Connections in a Switched Core

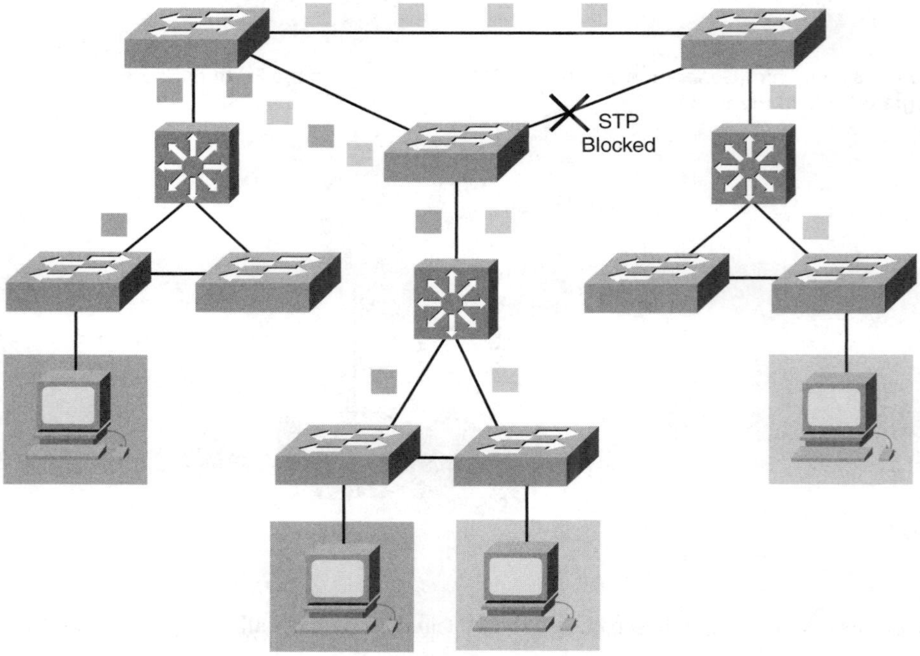

A routing protocol is used to manage redundant links in a routed core, as shown in Figure 4-5. The routing protocol can select the optimal path for traffic and can make use of redundant links through load balancing. Furthermore, implementing the core using Layer 3 allows more flexibility and control over packet flows, permitting additional benefits, such as quality of service (QoS), to be implemented.

Figure 4-5 A Routing Protocol Is Used in a Routed Core to Handle Redundant Connections

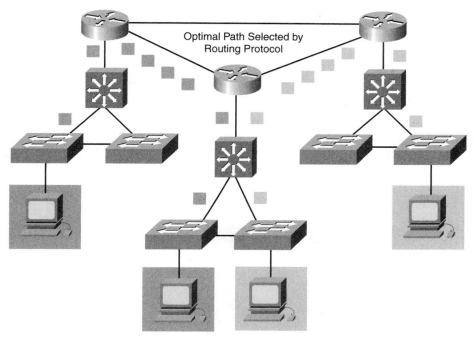

Inter-VLAN Routing Performance and Scalability Issues

For networks with just a couple of VLANs, using a physical interface for each VLAN can be a viable inter-VLAN routing strategy, as shown in Figure 4-6.

Figure 4-6 The One-Link-Per-VLAN Inter-VLAN Routing Method Theoretically Could Still Be Used in a Network with Only a Few Data VLANs

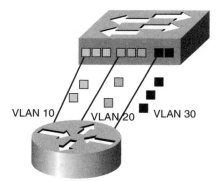

For networks with more than a few VLANs, however, a routing strategy that uses virtual interfaces becomes a must. Both an external and internal router can be used with subinterfaces. The difference between the two solutions involves a trade-off between cost and performance. An entry-level external router is generally cheaper than a switch with Layer 3 functionality, but the lack of integration between the Layer 2 and Layer 3 elements of the network and the "up and back" nature of external routers limit performance, as shown in Figure 4-7. As soon as the 100-Mbps capacity of the external router's link is exceeded, the use of an integrated route processor becomes the only realistic option for providing inter-VLAN routing, as shown in Figure 4-8.

Figure 4-7 The Bandwidth of the Trunk Link Between a Router and a Layer 2 Switch Is One Limitation of the Second-Generation Inter-VLAN Routing Method

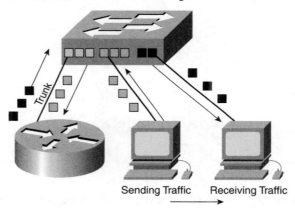

Figure 4-8 An Integrated Route Processor Is the Ideal Solution for Inter-VLAN Routing

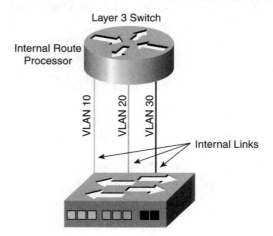

Regardless of the routing technique chosen, it is essential that the switched elements of the access and distribution layer be aligned with the routing functionality at the distribution layer. In particular, you should ensure that the distribution switch is the root of the spanning tree for each VLAN that is routed by the distribution router. This step is easily overlooked. Although a network will provide connectivity with an access layer switch acting as the STP root, the inefficient traffic flow will seriously limit the throughput of the distribution layer links.

Roles of the Different Types of VLANs

Various types of VLANS exist:

- VLAN 1
- The default VLAN
- The user VLANs
- The native VLAN
- The management VLAN

By default, all Ethernet interfaces on Cisco switches are on VLAN 1. On Catalyst switches, all the VLAN types in the preceding list default to VLAN 1, which can add to the difficulty of understanding their differences. This section explains the various types of VLANS to clear up some of the confusion.

VLAN 1

The reason VLAN 1 became a special VLAN is that Layer 2 devices needed to have a *default VLAN* to assign to their ports, including their management port(s). In addition, many Layer 2 protocols, such as Bridge Protocol Data Unit (BPDU), Cisco Discovery Protocol (CDP), VLAN Trunking Protocol (VTP), Port Aggregation Protocol (PAgP), and Dynamic Trunking Protocol (DTP), needed to be sent on a specific VLAN on trunk links. For all these reasons, VLAN 1 was chosen. Figure 4-9 illustrates that the control traffic is associated with VLAN 1.

BPDU, CDP, VTP, PAgP, and DTP are always transmitted over VLAN 1. This is always the case and cannot be changed. Cisco recommends that VLAN 1 be used only for these protocols. The management VLAN and user VLANs should all be configured to use VLANs other than VLAN 1.

Figure 4-9 The Default VLAN (VLAN 1), the User VLANs, the Native VLAN, and the Management VLAN Are All Important Considerations in Network Design

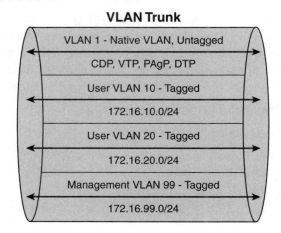

Default VLAN

By default, VLAN 1 is also the VLAN assigned to all switch ports (unless configured otherwise). VLAN 1 is also known as the default VLAN because all switch ports are in VLAN 1 when the switch boots with a clean configuration and vlan.dat file. It is possible to artificially change the default VLAN upon initial switch configuration by configuring all ports on the switch to be members of a particular VLAN other than VLAN 1. However, the Catalyst switch **show vlan** output will still display VLAN 1 as the default VLAN. The other types of VLANs—the native VLAN, the management VLAN, and the user VLANs—are all automatically members of the default VLAN unless specifically configured otherwise (see Figure 4-9).

All Ethernet interfaces on Catalyst switches default to VLAN 1. Any device connected to an interface on a switch is a member of VLAN 1 unless that interface is configured to use a different VLAN with the **switchport access vlan** interface command.

User VLANs

User VLANs are typically what people think of when referring to VLANs. A *user VLAN* is created to segment a group of users, either geographically or logically, from the rest of the network (see Figure 4-9). The **switchport access vlan** interface command is used to assign interfaces to these various user VLANs.

Native VLAN

A topic that causes considerable confusion is the native VLAN. *Native VLAN* is a term used with interfaces that are configured as VLAN trunks. When a switch port is configured as a trunk, it tags frames with the appropriate VLAN number. Frames from all VLANs are carried across the trunk link containing the 802.1Q tag, except for frames belonging to the native VLAN. With factory defaults on a Catalyst switch, frames from VLAN 1 belong to the native VLAN and are carried across the trunk untagged. Figure 4-9 illustrates this default association between the native VLAN and VLAN 1.

The IEEE committee that defined 802.1Q decided that, for backward compatibility, it was desirable to associate all untagged traffic on an 802.1Q link with a specific VLAN. This VLAN is the native VLAN and is implicitly used for all the untagged traffic received on an 802.1Q-capable port. This capability is desirable because it allows 802.1Q-capable ports to talk to old 802.3 ports directly by sending and receiving untagged traffic. However, in all other cases, leaving traffic untagged might be very detrimental. For example, identity enforcement and class of service (802.1p) bits are lost when untagged frames are transmitted over an 802.1Q link.

For these reasons—loss of means of identification and loss of classification—you should avoid the use of the native VLAN for data traffic. There are very few reasons why the native VLAN would ever need to be used explicitly for traffic.

The native VLAN can be modified to be a VLAN other than VLAN 1 with the **switchport trunk native vlan** *vlan-id* interface command.

The recommended practice is that the native VLAN should never be used as a user VLAN or the management VLAN.

As stated in the section "VLAN 1," control traffic—CDP, VTP, PAgP, and DTP—is transmitted over VLAN 1, which is the default native VLAN. If the native VLAN is changed to something other than VLAN 1, the control traffic is transmitted on VLAN 1 as tagged traffic. This has no ill effects on the control traffic.

It is fine to leave VLAN 1 as the default native VLAN, as long as it is not used as a user VLAN or as the management VLAN. Control traffic should be the only information carried across VLAN 1. However, common practice is to change the native VLAN to a dummy VLAN (other than VLAN 1) that is not used for any data or management traffic. Figure 4-10 illustrates this, with VLAN 2 configured as the native VLAN.

Figure 4-10 Common Practice Is to Create a Dummy VLAN to Be Used As the Native VLAN for IEEE 802.1Q Trunks

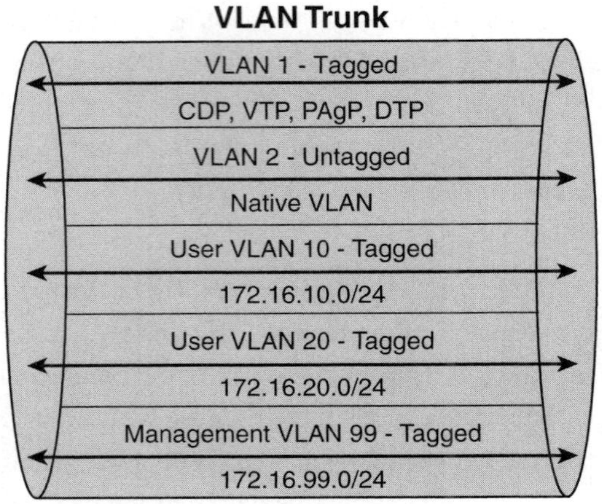

VLAN Trunk

VLAN 1 - Tagged
CDP, VTP, PAgP, DTP
VLAN 2 - Untagged
Native VLAN
User VLAN 10 - Tagged
172.16.10.0/24
User VLAN 20 - Tagged
172.16.20.0/24
Management VLAN 99 - Tagged
172.16.99.0/24

It's important to ensure that both ends of a switch-to-switch link have consistent native VLANs configured. If the native VLANs on both ends of a link are not the same, there will effectively be a bridge between them, and they will no longer be independent broadcast domains. Fortunately, recent versions of Cisco IOS software alert the user when mismatches in the native VLAN occur.

Management VLAN

Most of today's switches and routers can be accessed remotely via Telnet or SSH to the device's management Internet Protocol (IP) address. The recommended practice is to put these and other networking devices in their own VLAN, known as the *management VLAN*. The management VLAN should be a separate VLAN, independent of any user VLANs, independent of the native VLAN, and independent of VLAN 1. In case network problems occur, such as broadcast storms or spanning-tree convergence issues, an independent management VLAN still allows the network administrator to access these devices and troubleshoot the problem. In Figure 4-9, the management VLAN is configured as VLAN 99.

Another reason to keep the management VLAN independent of user VLANs is that it keeps "trusted devices" separate from "untrusted devices." This lessens the possibility, either by misconfiguration, accident, or intent, that users gain access to the routers or switches.

Configuring the Router with a Native VLAN

When a router's interface is configured as a trunk link, frames received on that interface from the native VLAN on the switch enter the interface untagged. Frames from the other nonnative VLANs enter the interface tagged as Inter-Switch Link (ISL) or 802.1Q.

Configuring the router's interface as a trunk link requires the use of subinterfaces. Each VLAN is configured on a separate subinterface. Each subinterface is configured to match the proper trunking protocol on the switch, 802.1Q or ISL using the **encapsulation [dot1q | isl]** *vlan-id* router interface command.

However, the router's subinterface that receives the native VLAN traffic must be configured to expect those frames to be untagged. This is done using the **native** option of the **encapsulation dot1q** *vlan-id* [**native**] subinterface command. Note that the **native** option is unavailable when you perform ISL trunking—it is unique to IEEE 802.1Q trunking.

Before Cisco IOS software Release 12.1(3)T, the router had to be configured with the native VLAN on the physical interface, and nonnative VLANs were configured on the subinterface with the ISL or 802.1Q tag.

Summary of VLAN Types

The following list summarizes the different VLANs and how they should be used:

- By default, VLAN 1 is the native VLAN and should only be used to carry control traffic, such as CDP, VTP, PAgP, and DTP. This information is transmitted across trunk links untagged.
- User VLANs should not include the native VLAN. VLAN 1 is the native VLAN unless this is changed. User VLAN traffic is sent as tagged frames across VLAN trunks.
- The management VLAN should be separate from the user VLANs. It should not be the native VLAN, and it should not be VLAN 1. This ensures access to networking devices in case of problems with the network.
- The subinterface on the router that is used to send and receive native VLAN traffic must be configured with the **native** option of the **encapsulation** interface command. Doing so lets the router know that any frames coming in untagged belong to that subinterface and are members of the native VLAN.

Route Switch Processors

The highest-performing inter-VLAN routing option uses an internal route switch processor. Figure 4-11 shows one type of route switch processor. In the case of a modular switch, the route switch processor resides on a router card that is plugged into the switch. On some switch platforms, the route switch processor is not modular but is an integral part of the switch hardware architecture.

Figure 4-11 Catalyst 4500 and 6500 Switches Provide Layer 3 Switching if the Appropriate Module Is Inserted in the Chassis

Integrated route switch processors perform better than external routers for the following reasons:

- The router's CPU power is well matched to the switch's capacity.
- The router has direct access to the switch's backplane. This offers more bandwidth than a physical interface.
- The router is highly integrated within the switch. This allows high-speed routing features such as Cisco Express Forwarding (CEF) to be implemented easily.

In addition to the route switch processor's high-speed routing performance, there can also be significant benefits in terms of ease of configuration and management. For most Catalyst switches, the route switch processor's interfaces are actually specified as VLAN interfaces. For example, Example 4-1 shows the commands needed to configure an IP address for the router's interface in VLAN 55.

Example 4-1 *Integrated Route Processors Make It Easy to Configure Inter-VLAN Routing*

```
Switch(config)#interface vlan 55
Switch(config-if)#ip address 10.0.1.1 255.255.255.0
```

This ease of configuration and management makes it difficult to mismatch router interfaces and VLAN IDs and produces Layer 2 and Layer 3 configuration files that are easier to interpret than when an external router is used.

Router-on-a-Stick

The technique of implementing inter-VLAN routing using a single trunk-connected Fast
Ethernet link to a router is called *router-on-a-stick* (see Figure 4-12).

Figure 4-12 Router-on-a-Stick Uses a Layer 2 Switch and an External Router Connected with an ISL
or IEEE 802.1Q Trunk

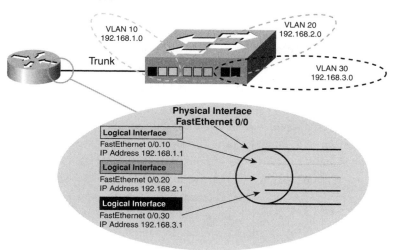

The primary advantage of using a trunk link is a reduction in router and switch ports. Doing
so not only saves money but also can reduce configuration complexity. Consequently, the
trunk-connected router approach can scale to a much larger number of VLANs than a one-
link-per-VLAN design. The number of subinterfaces on a router interface can easily accommodate the maximum number of VLANs on the connected Layer 2 switch. The Catalyst
2950T switch with the enhanced image, for example, supports up to 4094 VLANs.

However, the trunk-connected router configuration has disadvantages, including the following:

- There is a possibility of inadequate bandwidth for each VLAN.
- Additional overhead on the router can occur.
- Older versions of Cisco IOS software support only a limited set of features on trunked
  interfaces and might support only Cisco's proprietary ISL trunking encapsulation.
- Trunking is not supported on most Cisco routers with standard Ethernet interfaces and
  some lower-end routers with Fast Ethernet interfaces.

With regard to inadequate bandwidth for each VLAN, consider the situation in which all VLANs must share the Fast Ethernet 100 Mbps of bandwidth. A single VLAN could easily consume the entire capacity of the router or link, especially in the event of a broadcast storm or spanning-tree problem. Furthermore, the up-and-back nature of router-on-a-stick designs effectively doubles the link's bandwidth consumption (see Figure 4-12).

With regard to the additional overhead on the router caused by using a trunk-connected router, not only must the router perform normal routing and data-forwarding duties, it also must handle the additional encapsulation used by the trunking protocol.

When to Use the Router-on-a-Stick Design

In general, the router-on-a-stick approach to inter-VLAN routing is most appropriate when other options using internal route processors are unavailable. Internal route processors include *Route Switch Modules (RSMs)* and *Multilayer Switch Feature Cards (MSFCs)*. The router-on-a-stick design is not necessarily a poor choice; however, other options tend to provide higher throughput and functionality. Also, because the router-on-a-stick technique functions as if the router were sitting on the edge of the network (at least as far as the Layer 2 network is concerned), it tends to be less tightly integrated with the rest of the campus network, as illustrated in Figure 4-13. Newer approaches, employing embedded route processors, seek to place routing in the middle of the network, where it can have a greater influence on the network's overall scalability and stability.

Figure 4-13 The Router-on-a-Stick Technique Functions As If the Router Were Sitting on the Edge of the Network

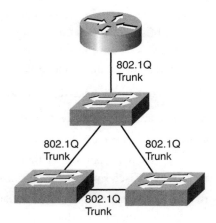

Cisco Layer 3 Feature Cards

Although the performance of route switch processors generally is adequate for typical applications, circumstances exist in which additional performance is required. Here are some situations that might require additional routing performance:

- A high proportion of traffic needs to cross VLAN boundaries. 80 percent is a figure that approximates this type of traffic in modern switched networks.
- A large number of interfaces are present, say 100 or more, and many are 1 Gbps or greater in speed.
- Additional switching capacity has been provided through the addition of a Switch Fabric Module on a Catalyst 6500.

Two Layer 3 feature cards available for the Catalyst 6500 Series switches are the MSFC, shown in Figure 4-14, and the *Policy Feature Card (PFC)*, shown in Figure 4-15.

Figure 4-14 The MSFC Is the Daughter Card on the Left Side of the Supervisor Engine

The MSFC provides Layer 3 functionality and enables the use of CEF for increased routing performance.

The PFC contains the application-specific integrated circuits (ASICs) for Layer 2 and Layer 3 lookups and performs many Cisco IOS features in hardware. The PFC performs IP Unicast and Multicast forwarding, QoS, and access control list (ACL) lookups in hardware. The PFC scales central forwarding to 30 Mbps.

Figure 4-15 The PFC Is the Daughter Card on the Right Side of the Supervisor Engine

Configuring Inter-VLAN Routing

The following four sections examine the configuration required to implement inter-VLAN routing on a Catalyst 3550 or 3750 switch. In all the examples, the first task should always be to turn on IP routing functionality with the **ip routing** global configuration command. The next sections detail inter-VLAN routing involving the following:

- Switch virtual interfaces
- Routed ports
- External router and internal route processor
- Routing between an external router and an internal route processor

Configuring Inter-VLAN Routing in a Switched Network

Catalyst 3550, 3750, 4000, 4500, 5000, 5500, 6000, and 6500 series switches all can perform inter-VLAN routing. The Catalyst 3550 and 3750 series switches provide fixed-chassis solutions for inter-VLAN routing, without the capability to add line cards for increasing port density.

All Cisco routers with Fast Ethernet interfaces, except the 1720 router, can support router-on-a-stick functionality. The router-on-a-stick solution is used if the distribution switches do not include an internal route processor. Cisco 2900XL, 2950, and 3500XL switches are examples of Layer 2 switches, which do not include route processors.

Configuring Inter-VLAN Routing Via the Switch Virtual Interface

By far the most common method of achieving inter-VLAN routing is to configure the switch virtual interface. Using this technique, the router has a virtual interface in every VLAN created on the switch. Rather than configuring a physical interface for each VLAN, the router uses a virtual or VLAN interface. For example, the commands shown in Example 4-2 allow the router to route traffic to and from VLAN 55.

Example 4-2 *Switch Virtual Interfaces Are Used to Configure Inter-VLAN Routing on IOS-Based Layer 3 Catalyst Switches*

```
Switch(config)#interface vlan 55
Switch(config-if)#ip address 10.0.1.1 255.255.255.0
```

These commands have the same effect as if a physical router interface were connected to a switch port in the appropriate VLAN.

Following the configuration of the IP address, the **no shutdown** interface command is required when configuring interface VLAN 1. The interface is shut down by default.

 Lab 4.3.2   Inter-VLAN Routing with the Internal Route Processor

In this lab exercise, you configure inter-VLAN routing using a switch with an internal route processor.

Configuring Inter-VLAN Routing Via the Routed Port

Although it is more common to configure inter-VLAN routing using the virtual (VLAN) interface, it is also possible to configure a physical switch port/interface as a router interface. Through this process, it is possible to turn a 12- or 24-port multilayer Ethernet switch into a 12- or 24-interface Ethernet router.

Turning a switch port into a router interface is simply a matter of turning off the switch port functionality, as shown in Example 4-3.

Example 4-3 *Routed Ports Are Used to Configure Layer 3 Catalyst Switch Ports as Router Interfaces*

```
Switch(config)#interface fa0/1
Switch(config-if)#no switchport
Switch(config-if)#ip address 10.0.1.1 255.255.255.0
```

As soon as the Layer 2 functionality is turned off, the interface can be treated as though it is a regular Fast Ethernet router interface. For example, an IP address can be configured. The switch port can now be used as a physical router port for connection to external devices.

Configuring Routing Between an External Router and an Internal Route Processor

Connecting an external router to an internal route switch processor is often necessary (see Figure 4-16). A common reason for this is to provide access to a WAN interface, because these often are not provided on a switch.

Figure 4-16 A Multilayer Switch Can Obtain WAN Connectivity Through a Routed Link Connection to an External Router

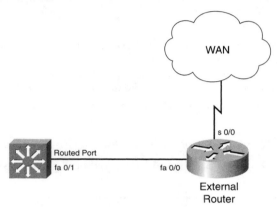

The easiest method of implementing this is to create a routed port, as shown in Example 4-4.

Example 4-4 *A Routed Link Can Be Configured Between a Multilayer Switch Port, Configured as a Routed Port, and an External Router*

```
RouteSwitch(config)#interface fa 0/1
RouteSwitch(config-if)#no switchport
RouteSwitch(config-if)#ip address 10.0.1.1 255.255.255.0


ExtRouter(config)#interface fa 0/0
ExtRouter(config-if)#ip address 10.0.1.2 255.255.255.0
```

Although a routed port is configured for connectivity with an external router, inter-VLAN routing would most likely be achieved through the use of switch virtual interfaces.

To route between VLANs 10 and 20, which have been configured on the multilayer switch, use the configuration shown in Example 4-5.

Example 4-5 *Inter-VLAN Routing with Switch Virtual Interfaces Can Be Coupled with Routing Over a Routed Link Between a Switch Port on a Multilayer Switch Configured as a Routed Port and a Router Interface on an External Router*

```
RouteSwitch(config)#interface vlan 10
RouteSwitch(config-if)#ip address 10.0.10.1 255.255.255.0
RouteSwitch(config)#interface vlan 20
RouteSwitch(config-if)#ip address 10.0.20.1 255.255.255.0
```

The internal route processor on the switch most likely will need to run a dynamic routing protocol and perhaps include some static routes. If there are network segments that are not directly connected to the switch, a dynamic routing protocol or static routes are required.

 Lab 4.3.3 Routing Between an External Router and an Internal Route Processor

In this lab exercise, you configure routing between an internal route processor and an external router.

Configuring the Router for the Native VLAN

A native VLAN is configured on the trunk link, as shown in Figure 4-17. An 802.1Q trunk requires the native VLAN for each opposing trunk port on a trunk link to match. Both the router and the switch require the native VLAN to be configured unless the default of VLAN 1 is desired (but this is not recommended).

Figure 4-17 The Native VLAN Must Be Configured on a Trunk Link Between a Router and a Catalyst Switch

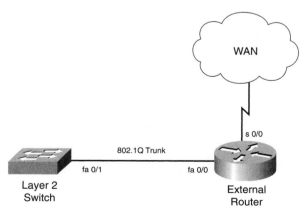

With Cisco IOS software Release 12.1(3)T and later, the router's subinterface can be configured as the native VLAN, as shown in Example 4-6.

Example 4-6 *The Native VLAN Is Configured on a Trunk Link Between a Layer 2 Switch and an External Router Using a Subinterface on the Router for the Native VLAN*

```
! Layer 2 Switch Commands:
Switch(config)#interface vlan 10
Switch(config-if)#description Management VLAN 10
Switch(config-if)#ip address 192.168.10.2 255.255.255.0
Switch(config-if)#no shutdown
Switch(config)#interface fa 0/1
Switch(config-if)#switchport mode trunk
Switch(config-if)#switchport trunk native vlan 1

! Router Commands:
Router(config)#interface fa 0/0.1
Router(config-subif)#description Control Traffic VLAN 1
Router(config-subif)#encapsulation dot1q 1 native
Router(config-subif)#ip address 192.168.1.1 255.255.255.0
Router(config)#interface fa 0/0.10
Router(config-subif)#description Management VLAN 10
Router(config-subif)#encapsulation dot1q 10
Router(config-subif)#ip address 192.168.10.1 255.255.255.0
Router(config)#interface fa 0/0.20
Router(config-subif)#description Engineering VLAN 20
Router(config-subif)#encapsulation dot1q 20
Router(config-subif)#ip address 192.168.20.1 255.255.255.0
Router(config)#interface fa 0/0.30
Router(config-subif)#description Marketing VLAN 30
Router(config-subif)#encapsulation dot1q 30
Router(config-subif)#ip address 192.168.30.1 255.255.255.0
```

The **native** option tells the router to accept any frames coming in untagged on FastEthernet0/0 as belonging to VLAN 1.

Before Cisco IOS software Release 12.1(3)T, the native VLAN had to be configured on the router's physical interface, as shown in Example 4-7.

Example 4-7 *The Native VLAN Is Configured on a Trunk Link Between a Layer 2 Switch and an External Router Using the Physical Interface on the Router for the Native VLAN*

```
Router(config)#interface fa 0/0
Router(config-if)#description VLAN 1
Router(config-if)#ip address 192.168.1.1 255.255.255.0
Router(config)#interface fa 0/0.10
Router(config-subif)#description Management VLAN 10
Router(config-subif)#encapsulation dot1q 10
Router(config-subif)#ip address 192.168.10.1 255.255.255.0
Router(config)#interface fa 0/0.20
Router(config-subif)#description Engineering VLAN 20
Router(config-subif)#encapsulation dot1q 20
Router(config-subif)#ip address 192.168.20.1 255.255.255.0
Router(config)#interface fa 0/0.30
Router(config-subif)#description Marketing VLAN 30
Router(config-subif)#encapsulation dot1q 30
Router(config-subif)#ip address 192.168.30.1 255.255.255.0
```

Configuring Router-on-a-Stick

When using an external router, you can logically divide an interface into multiple virtual sub-interfaces. Subinterfaces provide a flexible solution for routing multiple VLANs through a single physical interface, as illustrated in Figure 4-18.

Figure 4-18 Router-on-a-Stick Is Configured on a Trunk Link Between a Router and a Layer 2 Switch

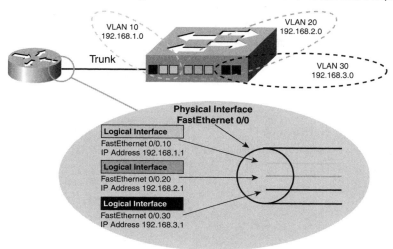

To configure subinterfaces on a physical interface, follow these steps:

Step 1   Identify the interface.

Step 2   Define the VLAN encapsulation.

Step 3   Assign an IP address to the interface.

To identify the interface, enter the global configuration command **interface FastEthernet** *slot-number/port-number.subinterface-number*, where *slot-number/port-number.subinterface-number* is the physical and logical interface.

To define the VLAN encapsulation, enter the subinterface configuration command **encapsulation dot1Q** *vlan-number*, where *vlan-number* is the VLAN for which the subinterface carries traffic.

To assign the IP address to the subinterface, enter the interface configuration command **ip address** *ip-address subnet-mask*, where *ip-address* and *subnet-mask* are the 32-bit network address and mask of the specific interface.

In Figure 4-18, the router has three subinterfaces configured on FastEthernet interface 0/0. These three interfaces are identified as FastEthernet0/0.10, FastEthernet0/0.20, and FastEthernet0/0.30. All interfaces are encapsulated for 802.1Q. Interface FastEthernet0/0.10 is routing packets for VLAN 10, whereas interface FastEthernet0/0.20 is routing packets for VLAN 20 and FastEthernet0/0.30 is routing packets for VLAN 30.

Note that the subinterface number does not have to match the VLAN number, but that is common practice.

With Cisco IOS software Release 12.1(3)T and later, the router subinterface can be configured as the native VLAN. The **native** option tells the router to accept any frames coming in untagged on FastEthernet0/0 as belonging to VLAN 1. Example 4-8 shows the configuration with Cisco IOS software Release 12.1(3)T and later.

Example 4-8 *With IOS 12.1(3)T and Later, One of the Router Subinterfaces Is Configured as the Native VLAN*

```
! Layer 2 Switch Commands:
Switch(config)#interface vlan 10
Switch(config-if)#description Management VLAN 10
Switch(config-if)#ip address 192.168.10.2 255.255.255.0
Switch(config-if)#no shutdown

Switch(config)#interface fa0/0.1
Switch(config-if)#switchport mode trunk
Switch(config-if)#switchport trunk native vlan 1
```

Example 4-8 *With IOS 12.1(3)T and Later, One of the Router Subinterfaces Is Configured as the Native VLAN (Continued)*

```
! Router Commands:
Router(config)#interface fa0/1.1
Router(config-subif)#description Control Traffic VLAN 1
Router(config-subif)#encapsulation dot1q 1 native
Router(config-subif)#ip address 192.168.1.1 255.255.255.0

Router(config)#interface fa0/0.10
Router(config-subif)#description Management VLAN 10
Router(config-subif)#encapsulation dot1q 10
Router(config-subif)#ip address 192.168.10.1 255.255.255.0

Router(config)#interface fa0/0.20
Router(config-subif)#description Engineering VLAN 20
Router(config-subif)#encapsulation dot1q 20
Router(config-subif)#ip address 192.168.20.1 255.255.255.0

Router(config)#interface fa0/0.30
Router(config-subif)#description Marketing VLAN 30
Router(config-subif)#encapsulation do1q 30
Router(config-subif)#ip address 192.168.30.1 255.255.255.0
```

Before Cisco IOS software Release 12.1(3)T, the native VLAN had to be configured on the router's physical interface, as shown in Example 4-9.

Example 4-9 *Before IOS 12.1(3)T, the Physical Interface Was Configured with the Native VLAN*

```
! Layer 2 Switch Commands:
Switch(config)#interface vlan 10
Switch(config-if)#description Management VLAN 10
Switch(config-if)#ip address 192.168.10.2 255.255.255.0
Switch(config-if)#no shutdown

Switch(config)#interface fa0/0.1
Switch(config-if)#switchport mode trunk
Switch(config-if)#switchport trunk native vlan 1
```

continues

Example 4-9 *Before IOS 12.1(3)T, the Physical Interface Was Configured with the Native VLAN (Continued)*

```
! Router Commands:
Router(config)#interface fa0/0
Router(config-if)#description VLAN 1
Router(config-if)#ip address 192.168.1.1 255.255.255.0

Router(config)#interface fa0/0.10
Router(config-subif)#description Management VLAN 10
Router(config-subif)#encapsulation dot1q 10
Router(config-subif)#ip address 192.168.10.1 255.255.255.0

Router(config)#interface fa0/0.20
Router(config-subif)#description Engineering VLAN 20
Router(config-subif)#encapsulation dot1q 20
Router(config-subif)#ip address 192.168.20.1 255.255.255.0

Router(config)#interface fa0/0.30
Router(config-subif)#description Marketing VLAN 30
Router(config-subif)#encapsulation do1q 30
Router(config-subif)#ip address 192.168.30.1
```

Lab 4.3.1   Inter-VLAN Routing with an External Router

In this lab exercise, you configure an external router (router-on-a-stick) to route inter-VLAN traffic.

Verifying the Inter-VLAN Routing Configuration

To verify that inter-VLAN routing functionality is available, use the **show ip route** command.

A useful summary of interfaces, both virtual and routed, can be obtained through the use of the command **show ip interface brief**, as shown in Example 4-10 for the topology shown in Figure 4-19.

Example 4-10 *The* **show ip interface brief** *Command Is Useful for Verifying a Router-on-a-Stick/Inter-VLAN Routing Configuration*

Interface	IP-Address	OK?	Method	Status	Protocol
Vlan1	unassigned	YES	unset	administratively down	down
Vlan10	10.0.10.1	YES	manual	up	up

Example 4-10 *The* **show ip interface brief** *Command Is Useful for Verifying a Router-on-a-Stick/Inter-VLAN Routing Configuration (Continued)*

```
Vlan20           10.0.20.1   YES  manual    up         up
FastEthernet0/1  10.0.1.1    YES  manual    up         up
FastEthernet0/2  unassigned  YES  unset     down       down
FastEthernet0/3  unassigned  YES  unset     up         up
FastEthernet0/4  unassigned  YES  unset     up         up
FastEthernet0/5  unassigned  YES  unset     up         up
FastEthernet0/6  unassigned  YES  unset     up         up
FastEthernet0/7  unassigned  YES  unset     up         up
FastEthernet0/8  unassigned  YES  unset     up         up
FastEthernet0/9  unassigned  YES  unset     up         up
FastEthernet0/10 unassigned  YES  unset     down       down
FastEthernet0/11 unassigned  YES  unset     down       down
FastEthernet0/12 unassigned  YES  unset     down       down
```

Figure 4-19 The Layer 3 Switch Is Set Up with Two User VLANs

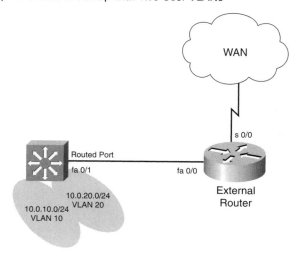

The command **show ip route** confirms that IP routing is enabled on a Layer 3-capable switch, as shown in Example 4-11.

Example 4-11 *The* **show ip route** *Command Is Used on a Layer 3 Switch Just as It Is on a Router*

```
Switch#show ip route
Codes:C - connected, S - static, I - IGRP, R - RIP, M - mobile, B - BGP
D - EIGRP, EX - EIGRP external, IA - OSPF, IA - OSPF inter area
N1 - OSPF NSSA external type1, N - OSPF NSSA external type 2
E1 - OSPF external type1, E2 - OSPF external type2, E - EGP
i - IS-IS, L1 - IS-IS level-1, L2 - IS-IS level-2, ia - IS-IS inter area
* -candidate default, U - per-user static route, o - ODR
P - periodic downloaded static route


Gateway of last resort is not set


    10.0.0.0/24 is subnetted, 3 subnets


C    10.0.10.0 is directly connected, Vlan10
C    10.0.1.0 is directly connected, FastEthernet0/1
C    10.0.20.0 is directly connected, Vlan20
```

The presence of the directly connected networks in the routing table indicates that IP routing is enabled. Without IP routing enabled, the command **show ip route** produces an empty output, as shown in Example 4-12.

Example 4-12 *The* **show ip route** *Command Yields Empty Output When IP Routing Is Disabled*

```
Switch#show ip route
Default gateway is not set
Host        Gateway       Last Use    Total Uses   Interface


ICMP redirect cache is empty
Switch#
```

To determine whether a switch port is acting as a Layer 2 member of a VLAN or is configured as a routed port, use either the **show ip interface fastethernet** *module/port* command or the **show interface fastethernet** *module/port* **switchport** command. In Example 4-13, these two commands have been applied to interface FastEthernet0/1. This interface has been configured as a routed port through the use of the interface command **no switchport**. The output illustrates that the interface has an IP status but no switchport status. This indicates that it is configured for routing.

Example 4-13 *Two Useful Commands for Verifying Whether a Switch Port Is Configured as a Routed Port*

```
Switch#show ip interface fastethernet 0/1

FastEthernet0/1 is up, line protocol is up
  Internet address is 10.0.1.1/24
  Broadcast address is 255.255.255.255
  Address determined by setup command
  MTU is 1500 bytes
  Helper address is not set
  Directed broadcast forwarding is disabled
  Outgoing access list is not set Inbound access list is not set
  Proxy ARP is enabled
  Local Proxy ARP is disabled
  Security level is default
  Split horizon is enabled
  ICMP redirects are always sent
  IP CEF Fast switching turbo vector
  IP multicast fast switching is enabled
  IP multicast distributed fast switching is disabled
  IP route-casch flags are Fast, CDF
  Router Discovery is disabled
  IP output packet accounting is disabled
  IP access violation accounting is disabled
  TCP/IP header compression is disabled
  RTP/IP header compression is disabled
  Probe proxy name replies are disabled
  Policy routing is disabled
  Network address translation is enabled, interface in domain outside
  WCCP Redirect outbound is disabled
  WCCP Redirect inboud is disabled
  WCCP Redirect exclude is disabled
  BGP Policy Mapping is disabled
Switch#
Switch#show interface fastethernet 0/1 switchport
Name: Fa0/1
Switchport: Disabled
```

When the same commands are applied to interface FastEthernet0/2, which is configured as a regular switchport and VLAN member, the output, shown in Example 4-14, clearly shows that the interface has no Layer 3 functionality but is acting as a Layer 2 interface.

Example 4-14 *The* **show ip interface fastethernet** *and* **show interface fastethernet switchport** *Commands Clarify Whether a Port Is Configured as a Layer 2 Switch Port*

```
Switch#show ip interface fastethernet

FastEthernet0/2 is down, line protocol is down
 Inbound access list is not set
Switch#

Switch#show interface fastethernet 0/2 switchport
Name: Fastethernet0/2
Switchport: Enabled
Administrative Mode: dynamic desirable
Operational Mode: down
Administrative Trunking Encapsulation: negotiate
Negotiation of Trunking: On
Access Mode VLAN: 1 (default)
Trunking Native Mode VLAN: 1 (default)
Administrative private-vlan host-association: none
Administrative private-vlan mapping: none
Operational private-vlan: none
Trunking VLANs Enabled: ALL
Pruning VLANs Enabled: 2-1001
Protected: false
Unknown unicast blocked: disabled
Unknown multicast blocked: disabled
Voice VLAN: none (Inactive)
Appliance trust: none
```

Troubleshooting Inter-VLAN Routing

The first step in troubleshooting inter-VLAN routing is to ensure that routing is actually enabled using the **show ip route** command. If the routing table displays no entries, you need to enable IP routing with the **ip routing** global configuration command.

After verifying routing, ensure that the Layer 2 VLANs and Layer 3 IP addressing are as intended using the **show ip interfaces brief** command. This command also reveals whether routing is configured for an individual switch interface or an entire VLAN. If communication with a switch seems to be a problem, check that the switch's IP address is in the appropriate VLAN and that the gateway is set.

Assuming that the VLANs are appropriately addressed, it is useful to ensure that no Layer 2 problems exist by pinging within each VLAN and verifying that it is possible to reach the router interface with every VLAN.

If communications *within* the VLAN are correct, but communications *between* the VLANs are not working, check the Layer 3 configuration. Be sure that the appropriate gateway is set on hosts and switch management interfaces. Also verify the IP network address and subnet mask.

Any remaining routing issues are likely to be the result of incorrectly configured routing protocols or the somewhat-tricky native VLAN issue. In particular, take care to prescribe the native VLAN for a trunk link. No specific **debug** or troubleshooting commands help you identify problems with the native VLAN. Some Catalyst platforms, such as the Catalyst 6000, report an error when a port receives a tagged frame for a VLAN it was expecting to be untagged, but not all models behave this way. The best strategy for dealing with native VLAN trunking problems is to maintain an awareness of the issue and to take care with the configuration.

Summary

Inter-VLAN routing is an essential component of designing a scalable switched LAN. This chapter examined the three methods of routing between VLANs and provided guidelines for choosing between the alternatives.

This chapter also demonstrated how to configure VLAN routing on both switch virtual interfaces and routed ports. It concluded with coverage of the commands needed to verify and troubleshoot inter-VLAN routing.

Key Terms

default VLAN   Upon initial switch configuration, all switch ports can be configured to be members of a particular VLAN other than VLAN 1. This particular VLAN is the default VLAN. When a user plugs a device into the switch, it automatically is associated with the default VLAN. If, upon initial switch configuration, not all switch ports are configured to be members of a VLAN other than VLAN 1, VLAN 1 is the default VLAN.

management VLAN   Most of today's switches and routers can be accessed remotely via Telnet or SSH to the device's management IP address. The recommended practice is to put these and other networking devices in their own VLAN, known as the management VLAN. The management VLAN should be a separate VLAN, independent of any user VLANs, the native VLAN, and VLAN 1.

Multilayer Switch Feature Card (MSFC)   MSFC1 and MSFC2 are daughter cards to the Catalyst 6000 Supervisor Engine. They provide multilayer switching functionality and routing services between VLANs.

Multilayer Switch Module (MSM)   A line card for Catalyst 6000 family switches that runs the Cisco IOS router software and directly interfaces with the Catalyst 6000 backplane to provide Layer 3 switching.

native VLAN   The IEEE committee that defined 802.1Q decided that, for backward compatibility, it was desirable to associate all untagged traffic on an 802.1Q link with a specific VLAN—the native VLAN. This VLAN is implicitly used for all the untagged traffic received on an 802.1Q-capable port.

Policy Feature Card (PFC)   Performs hardware-based Layer 2 to Layer 4 packet forwarding as well as packet classification, traffic management, and policy enforcement.

route processor   The main system processor in a Layer 3 networking device, responsible for managing tables and caches and for sending and receiving routing protocol updates.

Route Switch Feature Card (RSFC)   A daughter card to the Catalyst 5000/5500 Supervisor Engine IIG and IIIG that provides inter-VLAN routing and multilayer switching functionality. The RSFC runs Cisco IOS router software and directly interfaces with the Catalyst switch backplane.

Route Switch Module (RSM)   A line card that interfaces with the Supervisor Engine of a Catalyst 5000/5500 switch to provide inter-VLAN routing functionality. The RSM runs the Cisco IOS.

router-on-a-stick   A method of inter-VLAN routing consisting of an external router with a Fast Ethernet, Gigabit Ethernet, or EtherChannel trunk connecting to a switch, using ISL or 802.1Q. Subinterfaces on the trunk are created to correspond with VLANs in a one-to-one fashion.

user VLAN   A VLAN created to segment a group of users, either geographically or logically, from the rest of the network. User VLAN traffic is typically configured to be independent of VLAN 1, the native VLAN, and the management VLAN.

Check Your Understanding

Use the following review questions to test your understanding of the concepts covered in this chapter. Answers are listed in Appendix A, "Check Your Understanding Answer Key."

1. Which of the following are options that are available for inter-VLAN routing?

    A. Adding a route processor to a chassis-based switch with a daughter card or module

    B. Router-on-a-stick

    C. One router-to-switch link per VLAN

    D. Fixed chassis (nonmodular) multilayer switch

2. What is required in a Layer 2 core with physical loops?

    A. Routing protocol

    B. HSRP

    C. STP

    D. VTP

3. What is the most scalable inter-VLAN routing option?

    A. Layer 2 switch

    B. Layer 3 switch

    C. Router

    D. Router-on-a-stick

4. Which of the following are examples of modules or daughter cards that provide routing functionality in a chassis-based Catalyst switch?

    A. Multilayer Switch Module

    B. Route Switch Feature Card

    C. Route Switch Module

    D. Multilayer Switch Feature Card

5. Which of the following modules have embedded route processors?

A. Catalyst 6500 Supervisor Engine 720

B. Catalyst 4006 Supervisor Engine II

C. Catalyst 4500 Supervisor Engine III

D. Catalyst 4500 Supervisor Engine IV

6. Which of the following are required for performing router-on-a-stick?

A. Router

B. IEEE 802.1Q or ISL

C. Routing protocol

D. Layer 2 switch port

7. A switch virtual interface is configured with what command(s)?

A. Switch#**vlan database**

B. Switch(vlan)#**vlan**

C. Switch(config)#**interface vlan**

D. Switch(config)#**vlan**

8. What command is required to configure a switch port on a multilayer Catalyst switch as a routed port?

A. **ip routing**

B. **no shutdown**

C. **interface vlan**

D. **no switchport**

9. Before Cisco IOS software Release 12.1(3)T, the native VLAN was configured on which interface on a router?

A. Physical interface

B. Subinterface

C. Switch virtual interface

D. Bridge virtual interface

10. What Catalyst 3550 commands can be used to determine whether a port is a routed port or a Layer 2 switch port?

    A. show port routed

    B. show ip interface switchport

    C. show vlan

    D. show ip interface brief

Objectives

After completing this chapter, you will be able to perform tasks related to the following:

- List and understand the role of Multilayer Switching (MLS) components.
- Have a general understanding of the hardware platforms and Cisco IOS software Releases required for MLS and Cisco Express Forwarding (CEF).
- Explain MLS operation.
- Understand the advantages of CEF over MLS.
- Configure MLS and CEF.
- Verify MLS and CEF operation.

Chapter 5

Multilayer Switching

The desire for high-speed networking motivates the development of new technologies. One of the bottlenecks in high-speed networking is the decision-making process within the router. Until recently, routers forwarded traffic without the aid of specialized hardware designed to rewrite Protocol Data Unit (PDU) headers to speed up the process. In recent years, technologies and accompanying hardware have enhanced the process of rewriting PDU headers to move traffic to its ultimate destination.

A number of software and hardware combinations enable hardware-based PDU header rewrites and forwarding. Two of the methods used by Cisco devices are *Multilayer Switching (MLS)* and *Cisco Express Forwarding (CEF)*. The hardware requirements for each of these technologies are strict, so it is important to do some research before making a purchase. This chapter clarifies the hardware and software requirements for supporting MLS and CEF.

MLS is a technology used by a small number of older Catalyst switches to provide wire-speed routing. MLS is sometimes called "route once, switch many," where the first packet of a *flow* is routed by the router in software, and the remaining packets are forwarded in hardware by the switch.

CEF is the technology used by newer Cisco devices to provide wire-speed routing. MLS looks at the first packet in a flow and caches the requisite information to permit subsequent packets to be switched independent of the route processor. CEF lets packet switching circumvent the route processor altogether. This is accomplished by using specialized data structures that are dynamically updated by a communication process between the route processor and the switch processor. Therefore, the traditional routing of the first packet required by MLS is avoided. In general, CEF can be thought of as "route never, switch always," where the packet is never routed by the router in software and is always forwarded in hardware by the switch.

This chapter shows how MLS and CEF work and how to configure these technologies. This chapter also covers verifying and troubleshooting MLS and CEF and interpreting the output of various **show** commands relating to MLS and CEF.

Multilayer Switching

The term *multilayer switching* is used for two distinct things. On one hand, it is a general network design term that refers to hardware-based PDU header rewriting and forwarding, based on information specific to one or more Open System Interconnection (OSI) layers.

On the other hand, as characterized in this chapter, MLS refers to a specific technology employed by various Cisco devices to perform wire-speed PDU header rewrites and forwarding. To help differentiate between the two uses of the term multilayer switching, when the acronym MLS is used (as opposed to the expanded term), it refers to the Cisco-specific technology.

MLS was the first technological step in solving the router-as-a-bottleneck issue. MLS is also responsible for blurring the lines with respect to using the OSI model as a means of delineating per-OSI layer functions. With MLS, Layer 3 switching speeds approximate those of Layer 2 switching. This has a dramatic impact on network design. The trend is to incorporate more and more Layer 3 functionality into what are traditionally Layer 2 devices. For example, the Catalyst 3550 access layer switch uses CEF by default, making it a true multilayer switch.

The discussion of MLS in the following sections begins by detailing the hardware and software requirements, followed by an explanation of MLS components and operations.

MLS Hardware and Software Requirements

The requirements for running MLS in the network are specific. Many technologies are widely available on Cisco products. For example, most Cisco router platforms have Cisco IOS software releases that support Internetwork Packet Exchange (IPX). However, with MLS, widespread support is not the case, and options are limited.

The following sections examine the multilayer switching hardware and software requirements for switch and router platforms running MLS and CEF.

MLS

Catalyst 5000 series switches comprise the majority of MLS deployments. For Catalyst 5000 switches, the MLS requirements are as follows:

- Supervisor Engine III with *NetFlow Feature Card (NFFC)* or NFFC II, a Supervisor Engine IIG, or a Supervisor Engine IIIG (the IIG and IIIG have integrated NFFCs). The only NFFCs still available for purchase are the NFFC-A and NFFC II-A. The other NFFCs were last sold on April 30, 2000.

- Catalyst 5000 Route Switch Module (RSM), Catalyst 5000 Route Switch Feature Card (RSFC), Catalyst 6000 *Multilayer Switch Feature Card (MSFC)*, or Catalyst 6000 Multilayer Switch Module (MSM).
- CatOS 4.1(1) or later.
- Cisco IOS software Release 12.0(3c)W5(8a) or later on the RSFC.
- Cisco IOS software Release 11.3(2)WA4(4) or later on the RSM.

Catalyst 2926G switches can also work in tandem with external Cisco routers to support MLS. Catalyst 2926G switches are fixed-configuration switches. They were last sold in May 2000 and have been replaced by the 2948G switches.

The hardware and software guidelines for external routers are as follows:

- Cisco 3600, 4500, 4700, 7200, or 7500 router or Catalyst 8500 switch router externally attached to the Catalyst 5000 series switch.
- The connection between the external router and the Catalyst 5000 series switch must be a Fast Ethernet or Gigabit Ethernet link, an Inter-Switch Link (ISL) or IEEE 802.1Q trunk, or a Fast or Gigabit EtherChannel.
- Cisco IOS software Release 11.3(2)WA4(4) or later on Cisco 4500, 4700, 7200, or 7500 routers. Cisco IOS software Release 12.0 is the earliest release available on 8500 series switch routers.
- Cisco IOS software Release 12.0(2) or later on Cisco 3600 series routers.
- Catalyst 6000 MSFC on a Supervisor Engine with CatOS 6.3.
- Catalyst 6000 MSM.

For Catalyst 6000 switches, the MLS hardware and software guidelines are as follows:

- Catalyst 6000 family switches do not support an external *Multilayer Switching Route Processor (MLS-RP)*. The MLS-RP must be a MSM or MSFC. As of July 6, 2000, the MSM is no longer available for purchase and has been replaced by the MSFC.
- MSFC, Policy Feature Card (PFC), and CatOS 5.1CSX or later.
- MSM, CatOS 5.2(1)CSX or later, and Cisco MSM IOS software Release 12.0(1a)WX5(6d) or later.

CEF

Multilayer switching in the general sense is implemented with CEF in newer Catalyst 6500 products. In particular, Supervisor Engine II with Policy Feature Card 2 (PFC2), Multilayer Switch Feature Card 2 (MSFC2), and Supervisor Engine 720, comprise two standard configurations for newly purchased Catalyst 6500 switches. This configuration relies natively on CEF.

The Catalyst 4006 switch with the Layer 3 Services Module and the Catalyst 4500 switch with the Supervisor Engine III or Supervisor Engine IV also natively support CEF.

The Catalyst 3550 switch with the Enhanced Multilayer Software Image also relies on a CEF-based routing architecture to deliver high-performance dynamic IP routing. Note that the 3550 does not support IPX or AppleTalk.

With the hardware and software requirements clarified, it's important to understand how MLS works. The following sections detail the concepts of MLS flow, MLS Switching Engine (MLS-SE), and MLS Route Processor (MLS-RP).

MLS Components

The idea of MLS is simple. MLS looks at the first packet in a flow of data and caches some header information describing the flow. Subsequent packets in the flow circumvent the router, because the switch has cached the data necessary to rewrite the packet header, which it does. This is known as *wire-speed routing*.

MLS switches unicast IP data packet flows between IP subnets using advanced ASIC switching hardware, offloading processor-intensive packet routing from network routers. The packet forwarding function is moved to Layer 3 switches whenever a partial or complete switched path exists between two hosts. Packets that do not have a partial or complete switched path to reach their destinations are still forwarded in software by routers. Standard routing protocols, such as Open Shortest Path First (OSPF), Enhanced Interior Gateway Routing Protocol (EIGRP), Routing Information Protocol (RIP), and Intermediate System-to-Intermediate System (IS-IS), are used for route determination.

IP is a connectionless protocol, and every packet is delivered independent of every other packet. However, actual network traffic consists of many end-to-end conversations, or flows, between users or applications.

A flow is a unidirectional sequence of packets between a particular source and destination that share the same Layer 3 and Layer 4 information. For example, Telnet traffic transferred from a particular source to a particular destination is a flow separate from File Transfer Protocol (FTP) packets between the same source and destination. Communication from a client to a server, and from the server to the client, comprises separate and distinct flows.

If a flow is defined administratively by destination IP address alone, traffic from multiple users or applications to that destination is included in that flow.

The *MLS Switching Engine (MLS-SE)* is the set of hardware components on a Catalyst switch, excluding the route processor, necessary to support MLS. For example, a Catalyst 5000 with a Supervisor Engine IIIG is an MLS-SE. The MLS Route Processor (MLS-RP) is a Cisco device with a route processor that supports MLS. For example, a Cisco 3620 router is an MLS-RP. Only certain combinations of MLS-SEs and MLS-RPs can run MLS.

MLS Flows

An MLS-SE maintains a Layer 3 switching table (the Layer 3 MLS cache) for Layer 3 switched flows. After the MLS cache is created, packets identified as belonging to an existing flow can be switched based on the cached information. The MLS cache maintains flow information for all active flows. The maximum size of the MLS cache is 128,000 entries. The larger the active cache, the greater the likelihood that a flow will not be switched by the MLS-SE and will get forwarded to the router.

An MLS cache entry is created for the initial packet of each flow. Upon receipt of a packet that does not match any flow currently in the MLS cache, a new IP multilayer switching (IP MLS) entry is created. This first packet has special significance; it is detailed more in the next section.

A flow's state and identity are maintained while packet traffic is active. When traffic for a flow ceases, the entry ages out. The ***aging time*** for MLS entries kept in the MLS cache can be configured. If an entry is not used for the specified period of time, it ages out.

The MLS-SE uses ***flow masks*** to determine how MLS entries are created. The flow mask is a set of criteria, based on a combination of source IP address, destination IP address, protocol, and protocol ports, that describes the flow's characteristics. The MLS-SE learns the flow mask through ***Multilayer Switching Protocol (MLSP)*** messages from each MLS-RP for which the MLS-SE is performing Layer 3 switching. MLSP is the protocol used to communicate MLS information between the MLS-SE and MLS-RP. In particular, the MLS-SE populates its Layer 2 ***Content-Addressable Memory (CAM)*** table with updates received from MLSP packets. When the MLS-SE flow mask changes, the entire MLS cache is purged.

The three flow masks are as follows:

- **destination-ip**—The least-specific flow mask. The MLS-SE maintains one MLS entry for each destination IP address. All flows to a given destination IP address use this MLS entry. This mode is used if no access control lists (ACLs) are configured on any of the MLS-RP interfaces.

- **source-destination-ip**—The MLS-SE maintains one MLS entry for each source and destination IP address pair. All flows between a given source and destination use this MLS entry, regardless of the IP protocol ports. This mode is used if any of the MLS-RP interfaces has a standard access control list (ACL).

- **ip-flow**—The most-specific flow mask. The MLS-SE creates and maintains a separate MLS cache entry for every IP flow. An ip-flow entry includes the source IP address, destination IP address, protocol, and protocol ports. This mode is used if any of the MLS-RP interfaces has an extended ACL.

When a packet is Layer 3 switched from a source host to a destination host, the MLS-SE performs a packet rewrite based on information learned from the MLS-RP and stored in the MLS cache.

If Host A and Host B are on different VLANs, and Host A sends a packet to the MLS-RP to be routed to Host B, the MLS-SE recognizes that the packet was sent to the MAC address of the MLS-RP. The MLS-SE checks the MLS cache and finds the entry matching the flow in question.

When the MLS-SE receives the packet, it is formatted as shown in Figure 5-1.

Figure 5-1 The MLS-SE First Receives a Frame in a Flow with the Destination MAC Address of the MLS-RP

Frame Header		IP Header				Payload	
Destination	Source	Destination	Source	TTL	Checksum	Data	Checksum
MLS-RP MAC	Host A MAC	Host B IP	Host A IP	n	calculation1		

The MLS-SE rewrites the Layer 2 frame header, changing the destination MAC address to the MAC address of Host B and the source MAC address to the MAC address of the MLS-RP. These MAC addresses are stored in the MLS cache entry for this flow. The Layer 3 IP addresses remain the same, but the IP header Time-to-Live (TTL) is decremented, and the IP checksum is recomputed. The MLS-SE rewrites the switched Layer 3 packets so that they appear to have been routed by a router. The MLS-SE forwards the rewritten packet to the virtual LAN (VLAN) of Host B, the destination VLAN is stored in the MLS cache entry, and Host B receives the packet.

After the MLS-SE performs the packet rewrite, the packet is formatted as shown in Figure 5-2.

Figure 5-2 After a Frame Has Passed Through the MLS-SE and to the MLS-RP, It Returns to the MLS-SE with the Source MAC Address of the MLS-RP

Frame Header		IP Header				Payload	
Destination	Source	Destination	Source	TTL	Checksum	Data	Checksum
Host B MAC	MLS-RP MAC	Host B IP	Host A IP	n + 1	calculation2		

Figure 5-3 shows an IP MLS network topology. In this example, Host A is on Sales VLAN 1 (IP subnet 192.168.1.0), Host B is on Marketing VLAN 3 (IP subnet 192.168.3.0), and Host C is on Engineering VLAN 2 (IP subnet 192.168.2.0).

Figure 5-3 IP Addresses, MAC Addresses, Protocol Ports, and Destination VLANs Are Stored in the MLS Cache

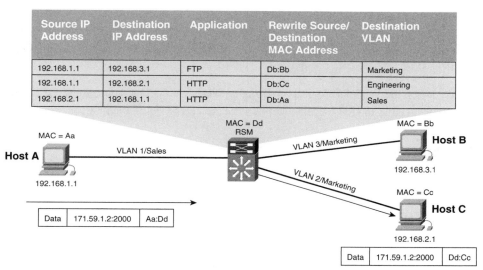

When Host A initiates an FTP file transfer to Host B, an MLS entry for this flow is created as shown. The MLS-SE stores the MAC addresses of the MLS-RP and Host B in the MLS entry when the MLS-RP forwards the first packet from Host A through the switch to Host B. The MLS-SE uses this information to rewrite subsequent packets from Host A to Host B.

Similarly, a separate MLS entry is created in the MLS cache for the HTTP traffic from Host A to Host C and for the HTTP traffic from Host C to Host A. The destination VLAN is stored as part of each MLS entry so that the correct VLAN identifier is used when encapsulating traffic on trunk links.

MLS creates flows based on ACLs configured on the MLS-RP. IP MLS allows the network administrator to enforce ACLs on every packet of the flow without compromising IP MLS performance. When IP MLS is enabled, the MLS-SE handles standard and extended ACL permit traffic at wire speed. Traffic that is denied by an ACL is always handled by the MLS-RP, not the MLS-SE. Route topology changes and the addition or modification of ACLs are reflected in the IP MLS switching path automatically on the MLS-SE.

For example, when Host A wants to communicate with Host B, it sends the first packet to the MLS-RP. If an ACL is configured on the MLS-RP to deny access from Host A to Host B, the MLS-RP receives the packet, checks the ACL to see if the packet flow is permitted, and discards the packet based on the ACL. Because the first packet for this flow does not return from the MLS-RP, an MLS cache entry is not established by the MLS-SE.

If a flow is already being Layer 3 switched by the MLS-SE, and the ACL is created on the MLS-RP, the MLS-SE learns of the change through MLSP and immediately enforces security for the affected flow by purging it from the MLS cache. New flows are created based on the restrictions imposed by the ACL.

Similarly, when the MLS-RP detects a routing topology change, the appropriate MLS cache entries are deleted in the MLS-SE. New flows are created based on the new topology.

MLS Operation

MLS operation consists of four distinct steps:

Step 1   MLSP multicast hello packets are sent every 15 seconds to inform the MLS-SE(s) of the MLS-RP MAC addresses used on different VLANs and the routing and ACL information of the MLS-RP when the router boots or after changes in ACLs. When an MLS-SE hears the MLSP hello message indicating an IP MLS initialization, the MLS-SE is programmed with a unique 1-byte *XTAG* value for each MLS-RP and with the MLS-RP MAC addresses associated with each VLAN. Figure 5-4 illustrates this step.

Figure 5-4 Step 1: The Exchange of Hello Packets Identifying the MLS-RP to the MLS-SE

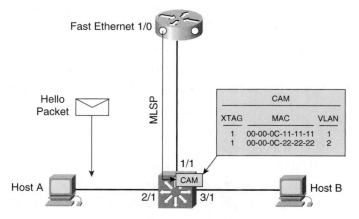

Step 2   In Figure 5-5, Host A and Host B are located on different VLANs. Host A
initiates a data transfer to Host B. When Host A sends the first packet to the
MLS-RP, the MLS-SE recognizes this packet as a *candidate packet* for Layer 3
switching, because the MLS-SE has learned the destination MAC addresses
and VLANs of the MLS-RP through MLSP. The MLS-SE learns the Layer 3
flow information (such as the destination IP address, source IP address, and
protocol port numbers) and forwards the first packet to the MLS-RP. A partial
MLS entry for this Layer 3 flow is created in MLS cache.

Figure 5-5 Step 2: The Creation of a Partial MLS Cache Entry Based on a Candidate Packet

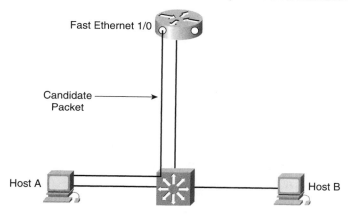

The MLS-RP receives the packet, looks at its route table to determine how to
forward the packet, and applies services such as ACLs and class of service
(CoS) policy. The MLS-RP rewrites the MAC header, adding a new destination
MAC address of Host B and its own MAC address, associated with Host
VLAN, as the source.

Step 3   The MLS-RP routes the packet to the destination host. When the switch
receives the packet, the MLS-SE recognizes that the source MAC address
belongs to the MLS-RP, that the XTAG matches that of the candidate packet,
and that the packet's flow information matches the flow for which the candidate entry was created. The MLS-SE considers this packet an *enable packet*
and completes the MLS entry in the MLS cache. Figure 5-6 illustrates this step.

Figure 5-6 Step 3: Completion of the MLS Cache Entry Based on an Enable Packet

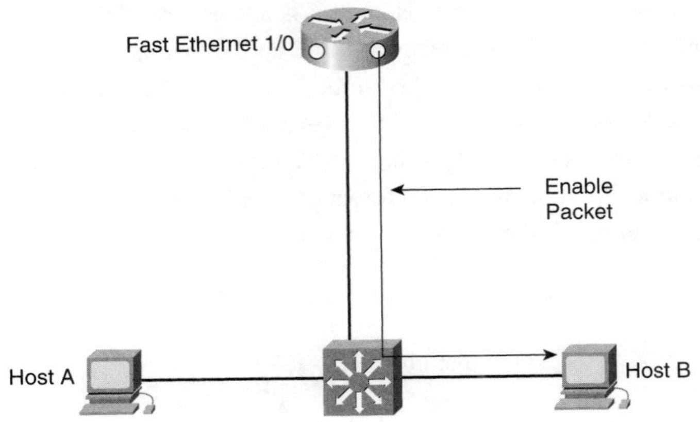

Fast Ethernet 1/0

Enable
Packet

Host A

Host B

Step 4   After the MLS entry has been completed, all Layer 3 packets in the same flow
from the source host to the destination host are Layer 3/4 switched directly by
the switch, bypassing the router. IP MLS is unidirectional. A separate Layer 3
switched path is created for traffic from Host B to Host A. Figure 5-7 illustrates
this final step of MLS operation.

Figure 5-7 Step 4: The Layer 3 Switching of Subsequent Packets in the Same Flow

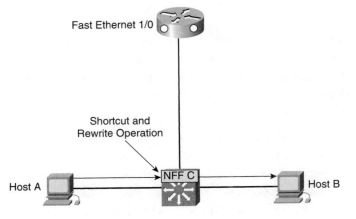

Fast Ethernet 1/0

Shortcut and
Rewrite Operation

NFF C

Host A

Host B

Finally, some Catalyst 5000 family switching line cards have onboard hardware that performs
the rewrite (as opposed to rewrites on the Supervisor Engine), maximizing IP MLS performance. This performance enhancement is also used on the Catalyst 2926G series switch

ports. When the line cards or individual ports perform the PDU header rewrites, this is called *inline rewrite*. With inline rewrite, frames traverse the switch bus only once.

The Catalyst 5000 NFFC is a daughter card for the supervisor module that enables intelligent network services, such as high-performance multilayer switching and accounting and traffic management. The NFFC contains *central rewrite engines* (one per bus) to handle PDU header rewrites when inline rewrite is not an option. If the central rewrite engines are used, this means that a frame must traverse the bus twice—first with a VLAN tag for the source, on its way to the NFFC, and second with a VLAN tag for the destination, on its way to the egress port. To determine whether a port supports packet rewrite, use the **show port capabilities** command. If the port does not support inline rewrite, the packet rewrite is done in the Supervisor Engine.

In summary, the basic MLS ingredients are the MLS-RP, MLS-SE, and MLSP. The MLS-SE creates flows in the MLS cache based on candidate and enable packets and ACLs configured on the MLS-RP. The result is wire-speed routing of packets based on criteria such as destination IP address, source IP address, and protocol port numbers.

Cisco Express Forwarding (CEF)

Cisco Express Forwarding (CEF) is a multilayer switching technology that allows for increased scalability and performance to meet the requirements of large enterprise networks. CEF has evolved to accommodate the traffic patterns realized by modern networks. These networks are characterized by an increasing number of short-duration flows. Shorter flows are common in environments with a high degree of web-based activity or other highly interactive types of traffic.

As these types of applications continue to grow in popularity, a higher-performing and more scalable forwarding methodology is required to meet the needs of these environments. Figure 5-8 outlines the architectural model that CEF uses. The following sections compare MLS and CEF technologies and provide a detailed description of CEF operation.

Comparing MLS and CEF

MLS is a flow-based model that entails software path handling of the first packet in a given flow. This, in turn, creates a cache entry that can be used by subsequent packets in the flow for accelerated performance. Although this model works extremely well, it has been shown that in environments such as those found in the core of large enterprise networks, this model might not always prove optimal. Specifically, a flow-based model is suboptimal when an enterprise network has peering problems and when the number of flows is too great for the cache size.

Figure 5-8 CEF Architectural Model

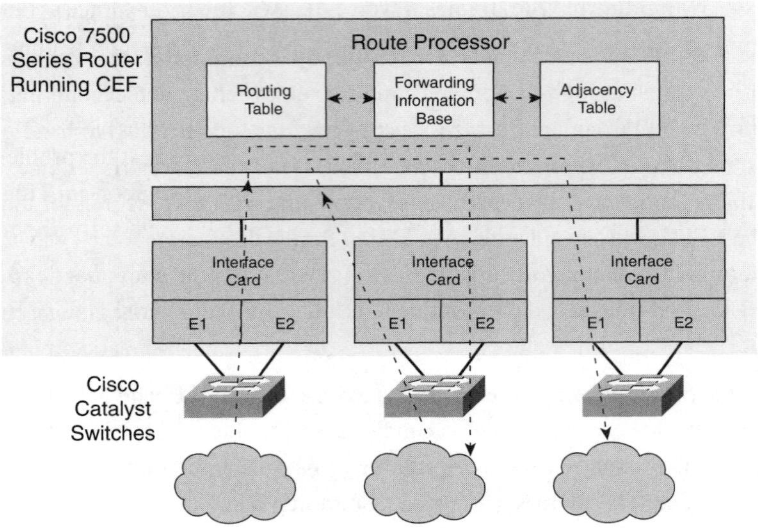

Anytime a large number of routers are controlled by a large number of independent organizations, you might encounter situations in which some devices negatively affect the stability of other devices. In this case (a peering relationship), router instability or flapping routes lead to the purging of previously cached data. In a flow-based model, the loss of cached entries requires that the first packet of a given flow be handled within the software path. In a peering situation, such as that required to support the core of an enterprise network, this means that potentially tens of thousands of flows would need to be relearned or cached by the software path to enable further hardware acceleration. However, it is difficult to scale software-based forwarding to simultaneously handle tens of thousands of concurrent flows per second. So stability, and the capability to withstand route flaps, are critical. The CEF-based forwarding model is designed to handle these situations gracefully and to minimize the impact of these events on network stability. Another area in which a flow-based model encounters scalability challenges is with respect to the actual number of flows that could be cached in the necessary lookup tables. Recall that a flow entry can be expressed in one of several ways, including destination-ip, source-destination-ip, and ip-flow. The greater the granularity selected, the more specific the flow information will be but the lower the access and storage efficiency. For example, multiple entries are likely to map to a given entry for a destination-ip flow (for example, many clients all accessing a single server). When an ip-flow mode is selected, full protocol and port information is stored in addition to the full source and destination IP addresses. This, in turn, reduces the likelihood that any two entries will be capable of sharing a given flow entry. In a large percentage of the enterprise networks in existence today, however, this is not cause for concern. The number of flows that must be supported increases as networks grow (such as in a service provider environment), consequently leading to a situation in which the number of entries exceeds the available flow cache table space. This flow cache table space limitation leads to suboptimal packet handling, in that packets not matched in the flow cache must be processed in software. One option to correct the problem is to change the flow mask to specify a less-specific mask, such as destination-ip. This solution increases cache efficiency, but it too has its limitations, beyond which software processing will be required.

Although the simple answer to the problem of exceeding the size of the flow cache would appear to be increasing the number of possible entries available, in practice it is not so simple. There is a direct relationship between the speed of hardware-based forwarding and the size of the flow cache. Simply increasing the size of the flow cache does not guarantee that the appropriate lookup engine can parse the table sufficiently fast enough to forward flows in hardware at high speed. It would then seem logical to increase the speed of the lookup engine to work against the increased flow cache table. To a certain extent, this approach could be made to work, but network administrators would have to continually upgrade equipment, an extremely costly and inefficient solution.

A cache-based forwarding model relies on actual traffic flows to establish cache entries for expedited forwarding. In a classical enterprise environment, this model has proven highly effective, because traffic patterns associate a large number of sources with a much smaller number of destinations. An example is a traditional centralized server farm, in which a large number of clients send traffic to and receive traffic from a much smaller number of servers. When comparing these traffic patterns to those of the Internet, it is far less likely to achieve the many-to-one ratio typified by the enterprise data center. Because the Internet is a global entity, it becomes increasingly difficult to maintain the flow cache and to ensure the integrity of the data therein. This means that a certain amount of cache flux must be expected in terms of the maintenance required to keep the state of the flow cache current. The variation in cache state is reflected in terms of CPU utilization.

With flow-cached models, a complete forwarding table must be maintained for the proper handling of first packets by the CPU or packets that for some other reason are incapable of being processed in hardware. After the CPU makes a forwarding decision (part of which involves a lookup against the routing table), an entry is made in the flow cache table, and subsequent packets are handled in hardware.

A CEF-based mechanism experiences greatly reduced challenges presented by flow caching models, resulting in an increase in scalability. All packets, including the first packet in a given flow, are handled in hardware. A routing table is still maintained by the router CPU, but two additional tables are created in the CEF-based model:

- *Forwarding Information Base (FIB)* **table**—The FIB table is a copy of the forwarding information from the routing table. The FIB table contains the minimum information from the routing table necessary to forward packets. The FIB table does not contain any routing protocol information.

- *Adjacency table*—The adjacency table maintains a database of node adjacencies (two nodes are said to be adjacent if they can reach each other through a single Layer 2 hop) and their associated Layer 2 MAC rewrite or next-hop information.

The *NetFlow table* is a third table. It isn't required for CEF function, but it provides network accounting data and is updated in parallel with the CEF-based forwarding mechanism provided by the FIB and adjacency tables.

By the router or switch performing a high-speed lookup against the FIB and adjacency tables, a forwarding decision along with the appropriate rewrite information can be accessed in a highly efficient and consistent manner, while also providing a mechanism offering a high degree of scalability.

CEF Support on Cisco Devices

Although high-end Cisco routers have offered support for CEF for several years now, some differences between the CEF implementations on Catalyst switches and Cisco routers exist. Specifically, both implementations provide the following:

- High-speed forwarding based on a "longest address match" lookup
- Equal-cost path load balancing
- Reverse Path Forwarding (RPF) checks
- Invalidation of less-specific routes

The CEF implementation on the Catalyst 6000 family also adds the following:

- Support for IP multicast
- Support for IPX forwarding
- Hardware-based forwarding of rates up to 210 Mbps in distributed CEF mode

Supported features of the CEF implementation only on the Cisco routers include the following:

- The capability to turn off CEF-based forwarding
- CEF per-prefix and per-prefix-length accounting
- Accounting data from load-sharing paths
- Per-packet load balancing

CEF is supported on the following Cisco devices:

- Catalyst 8500 switch routers
- Catalyst 3550 switches
- Catalyst 2948G-L3 switches
- Catalyst 4000 switches
- Catalyst 6000 switches
- Cisco routers running Cisco IOS software Release 12.2 or later
- Some routers, such as the 7500 series, beginning with Cisco IOS software Release 12.0

The Catalyst 4000 switch supports CEF in the following combinations:

- With the Layer 3 Services Module
- With the Access Gateway Module
- With Supervisor Engine III or Supervisor Engine IV

Figure 5-9 illustrates the CEF architecture for the Catalyst 4000 family Supervisor Engine III.

Figure 5-9 The Catalyst 4000 Family Supervisor Engine III and IV Provide CEF-Based Layer 2/3/4 Switching

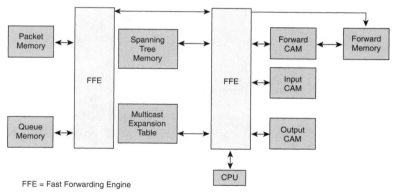

The remainder of this chapter focuses on CEF technology in the context of Catalyst 6000 family switches. In particular, the Catalyst 4000 Supervisor Engine III multilayer switching mechanism does rely on CEF, but the architecture and Layer 2/3/4 packet flow methodology are similar, but not identical, to that of the Catalyst 6000.

For Catalyst 6000 family switches, the CEF hardware requirements are Supervisor Engine II, MSFC2, and PFC2, or a Catalyst 6500 series switch with Supervisor Engine 720.

CEF Operation

Understanding how CEF functions on a Catalyst 6000 Supervisor Engine II requires a basic understanding of the architecture of the Supervisor Engine II, shown in Figure 5-10.

Figure 5-10 The Catalyst 6000 Family Supervisor Engine II with the MSFC2 and PFC2 Have CEF-Based Architectures

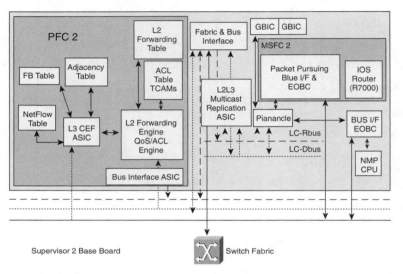

The Supervisor Engine II consists of three primary components:

- **Supervisor base board**—The Supervisor base board provides connectivity to the switching fabric, 32-Gbps bus, multicast replication ASIC, Network Management Processor (NMP), and two Gigabit Interface Converter (GBIC)-based Gigabit Ethernet ports. In addition, the base board offers connectors for attaching the PFC2 and MSFC2 daughter boards.

- **Policy Feature Card 2 (PFC2)**—PFC2 is a factory-installed daughter card of a Supervisor Engine II. It provides an array of ASICs to enable all hardware-based forwarding. The Layer 3 forwarding engine ASIC provides the actual CEF function via its inherent logic. It also provides access to the various Layer 3 tables (the FIB, adjacency table, and NetFlow table). In addition, the PFC2 daughter card also contains the ASICs that deliver hardware-based access control lists and QoS mechanisms.

- **Multilayer Switching Feature Card 2 (MSFC2)**—The MSFC2 is an optional daughter card that provides a CPU for the handling of all Layer 3 control-plane activities. The control plane is the portion of the hardware architecture that handles route calculations. The MSFC2 is responsible for handling any functions that cannot be handled in the hardware elements of the PFC2, as well as the processing of all routing protocol activities, such as OSPF and Border Gateway Protocol (BGP) routing updates. The MSFC2 is also responsible for populating the IP routing table, FIB table, and adjacency table.

Of these three elements, the Supervisor base board and PFC2 are mandatory components, and the MSFC2 element is optional (although it is effectively required for Layer 3 switching, because it contains the CPU for the population of the CEF tables).

The CPU on the MSFC2 daughter card runs all instances of whatever configured routing protocols are required. In addition, the CPU handles packets that cannot be processed in hardware. The MSFC2 is a Cisco IOS software-based router, and it is configured as such. The configuration parameters are identical to those on a Cisco 7200 series router. With the Supervisor Engine II, CEF is enabled by default. In fact, it cannot be disabled. For most common CEF functions, no specific configuration is required to enable CEF beyond the standard configuration of routing protocols, network interface addressing, and so on.

When the router is initialized, a routing table is constructed based on information in the router software configuration (such as static routes, directly connected routes, and dynamically learned routes via routing protocol exchanges). After the routing table is constructed, the CPU creates the FIB and adjacency tables automatically. The FIB and adjacency tables represent the data present within the routing table in a manner in which optimal forwarding can be performed.

Unlike a flow cache, which is based on traffic flow, the CEF table is based on the network topology. When a packet enters the switch, the switch Layer 3 forwarding engine ASIC performs a longest-match lookup based on the destination network and the most-specific netmask. For example, instead of switching based on a destination address of 172.31.10.3, the PFC2 looks for the network 172.31.10.0/24 and switches to the interface connecting to that network. This scheme is highly efficient and does not involve the software for anything other than the routing table and prepopulation of the FIB table. In addition, cache invalidation because of a route flap does not occur. As soon as a change in the routing table is made, all CEF tables are updated immediately. This makes CEF more adaptable to changes in the network topology.

CEF Forwarding Information Base

The CEF FIB table consists of a four-level hierarchical tree, as shown in Figure 5-11. The four levels are derived from the fact that IPv4 uses a 32-bit address. Each level of the hierarchy is based on 8 of the possible 32 bits. CEF relies on a longest-match forwarding algorithm, meaning that the tree is searched in descending order until the "longest match," or greatest number of bits, is matched. The FIB tree is represented hierarchically, with the least-specific address at the top of the tree and the most-specific address at the bottom. Each leaf is based on an 8-bit boundary, with more-specific entries in descending order. This tree (commonly known as a 256-way radix tree) provides a highly efficient mechanism for rapid lookups, which ensures that minimal latency is incurred during the lookup process. This tree also provides for a highly scalable architecture in that IPv4 addressing can be completely accounted for with a minimal trade-off of performance versus table efficiency. Each leaf offers a pointer to the appropriate next-hop entry in the adjacency table.

Figure 5-11 The CEF FIB Consists of a Four-Level Hierarchical Tree

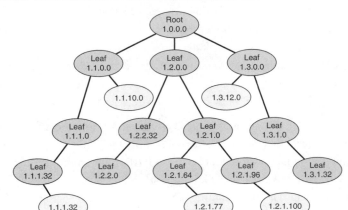

The CPU of the MSFC2 builds the FIB table from the IP routing table. The appropriate IP routing protocols first resolve the IP routing table, at which point the CEF process is invoked, and the corresponding FIB and adjacency tables are constructed. The FIB table is maintained separately from the routing table. The routing table contains additional information that is important for the purposes of routing protocols but not for the actual forwarding of packets. The FIB cannot determine which routing protocol created the route. The FIB and adjacency tables are optimized to provide only the information that is necessary for a forwarding decision to be made, and nothing more. It is also important to note that recursive routes are resolved when the FIB table is built. This resolution of recursive routes has classically been a CPU-intensive event in non-CEF implementations.

If the FIB table becomes full, subsequent entries are compared to the existing entries, and the more-specific entries are maintained at the expense of less-specific entries. This method is necessary to ensure that proper forwarding is maintained. For example, the less-specific route of 1.2.0.0 is not specific enough to ensure proper routing to 1.2.1.0. To view the contents of the FIB table, use the **show ip cef detail** command from the MSFC2.

CEF Adjacency Table

The adjacency table contents are fundamentally a function of the Address Resolution Protocol (ARP) process, whereby Layer 2 addresses are mapped to corresponding Layer 3 addresses. When the router issues an ARP request, a corresponding reply is received, and a host entry is added to the adjacency table to reflect this. In addition, the router can glean next-hop routers from routing updates and make entries in the adjacency table to reflect this. This transaction lets the router build the next-hop rewrite information necessary for Layer 3 packet forwarding. By having this data already stored in a table, CEF can perform highly efficient and consistent forwarding, because no discovery process is required. Use the **show ip cef** command to view the contents of the CEF adjacency table from the MSFC2. Use the **show ip cef summary** command to display a brief overview of the CEF process. The output from this command shows information, such as the total number of adjacencies and routes.

The third table used by CEF is the NetFlow table. It isn't discussed here, because it compiles network accounting data and does not play a role in CEF's PDU header rewrite mechanism.

Packet Flow for Layer 2 and Layer 3 Forwarding Decisions

This section details the data flow through the Layer 2 and Layer 3 forwarding process on a Catalyst 6000 Supervisor Engine II. The process is fundamentally unchanged between a Layer 2 and Layer 3 decision and is a function of whether the Layer 3 data exists. In other words, if the MSFC2 is present, the Layer 3 path is valid. Otherwise, forwarding decisions are made based purely on Layer 2 forwarding information. This discussion details the data path for Layer 2 and Layer 3 lookups.

Figure 5-12 illustrates the CEF forwarding process. The following list describes each step in detail.

Figure 5-12 The Layer 3 Portion of CEF Relies on the FIB and Adjacency Tables

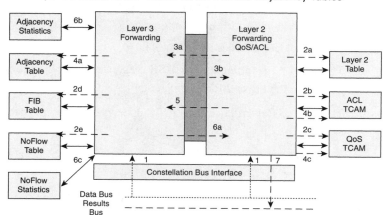

Step 1   The Layer 3 forwarding engine and Layer 2 forwarding engine ASICs receive the packet headers from the data bus.

Step 2   The following operations occur in parallel:

   a.   The Layer 2 forwarding engine performs a lookup on the destination MAC address.

   b.   The Layer 2 forwarding engine ASIC performs any necessary input security ACL lookups.

   c.   The Layer 2 forwarding engine ASIC performs any necessary input QoS/ACL lookups.

   d.   The Layer 3 forwarding engine ASIC performs a FIB table lookup.

   e.   The Layer 3 forwarding engine ASIC performs a NetFlow table lookup.

Step 3   The following operations occur in parallel:

   a.   The input ACL and QoS results from the Layer 2 forwarding engine ASIC are forwarded to the Layer 3 forwarding engine ASIC.

   b.   The Layer 3 forwarding engine ASIC sends the destination VLAN information for the packet to the Layer 2 forwarding engine ASIC.

Step 4   The following operations occur in parallel:

   a.   The Layer 3 forwarding engine ASIC performs the adjacency lookup.

   b.   The Layer 2 forwarding engine ASIC performs the outbound security ACL lookup.

   c.   The Layer 2 forwarding engine ASIC performs the outbound QoS/ACL lookup.

Step 5   The Layer 2 forwarding engine sends the results of the security and QoS/ACL lookups to the Layer 3 forwarding engine ASIC.

Step 6   The following operations occur in parallel:

   a.   The Layer 3 forwarding engine ASIC generates the rewrite result and sends it to the Layer 2 forwarding engine ASIC.

   b.   The Layer 3 forwarding engine ASIC updates the adjacency table statistics as necessary.

   c.   The Layer 3 forwarding engine ASIC updates the NetFlow table statistics as necessary.

The Layer 2 forwarding engine looks up the destination MAC address received from the Layer 3 forwarding engine ASIC. The Layer 2 forwarding engine then chooses between a

Layer 2 and a Layer 3 result and sends the result to the results bus, an out-of-band control-plane mechanism used for this purpose.

Figure 5-13 summarizes the CEF process with a traffic flow from a source workstation (on the right side of the figure) to a destination workstation (on the left side of the figure). The critical elements of the diagram are the FIB and adjacency entries of the intermediate routers along the path. All of the IP addresses and MAC addresses referenced by the FIB and adjacency tables are indicated as the packet traverses the network.

Figure 5-13 Summarization of the CEF Process with Source-to-Destination Traffic Flow

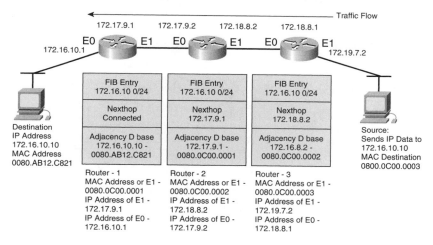

Additional Benefits of CEF-Based Forwarding

In addition to the benefits just described, CEF-based forwarding provides several other benefits:

- Enhanced scalability
- Availability
- Network stability
- Load balancing
- ACL processing
- Multicasting

Many of these benefits are supported only on the Catalyst 6500 series (a subset of the Catalyst 6000 family).

The following sections briefly describe some of these additional benefits.

Scalability

CEF increases scalability not only by the raw number of available FIB entries, but also by the replication of CEF-based forwarding technology on a per-slot basis. This distributed capability (dCEF), illustrated in Figure 5-14, allows the Catalyst 6500 series switches and Cisco 12000 series routers to provide sufficient forwarding capabilities for the largest of networks. The Catalyst 6500 series, when equipped with a Supervisor Engine II, can provide as many as 256,000 entries in the FIB table and 256,000 entries in the adjacency table. These entries are not stored via a traditional hashing algorithm, as is the case with MLS.

Figure 5-14 Cisco 12000 Series Routers Use Distributed CEF

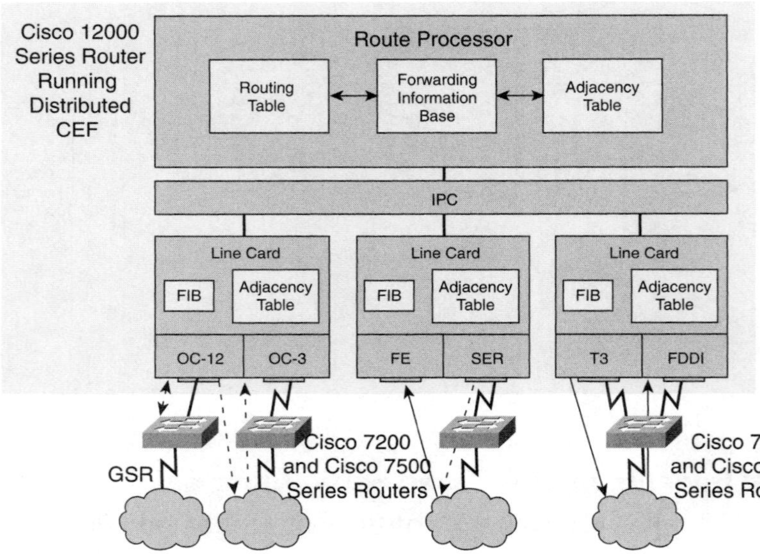

Availability

Although the Catalyst 6000 family offers a breadth of features to support high availability, the addition of CEF further increases the availability and stability demanded in today's enterprise networks. As networks increase in size, a natural side effect is the increased chance of instability and change. Network instability, whether caused by failures, configuration changes, or bursty traffic patterns, can have a tremendous impact on routing implementations, which rely on heavy CPU computations for routing-table maintenance. Because CEF employs a mechanism by which the forwarding information is constructed based on the network topology rather than a representation of traffic within the network, the CPU is no longer burdened by having to set up large numbers of entries. This also means that network availability is not directly linked to the actual size of the network.

Access Control Lists

Another manner in which various CEF implementations vary is with respect to their support of ACLs. In the case of the Catalyst 6500 series, ACLs can be handled in hardware for most common configurations. CEF-based forwarding does not have any impact on this functionality. The most notable ACL options that disable hardware processing for a given ACL are the use of the **log** keyword or enabling "IP unreachables" on a given interface (which enables the sending of Internet Control Message Protocol (ICMP) unreachable messages).

Multicasting

The CEF implementation on the Catalyst 6000 family also includes support for IP multicasting. The FIB table can hold as many as 16,000 IP multicast entries.

Summary of CEF Benefits

In conclusion, CEF provides high performance and high scalability for the largest and most demanding networks. The Supervisor Engine II offers the scalability and performance requirements necessary for both large enterprise and service-provider environments. Cisco has also managed to maintain the rich accounting support of the MLS model (using NetFlow features) while introducing CEF-based forwarding.

MLS and CEF Configuration Tasks

MLS configuration involves two components: configuring the MLS-RP and configuring the MLS-SE. CEF configuration is probably the easiest technology to configure on Cisco devices. Configuration involves only turning on the feature, and it is on by default on most platforms and with most newer IOS releases. This section also discusses monitoring and verifying MLS and CEF.

MLS-RP Configuration

Configuring MLS support on an MLS-RP has five basic steps:

Step 1   Configure the MLS-RP to globally enable MLS. This is analogous to enabling IPX or multicast routing on a router. The global configuration Cisco IOS software command to enable MLS is **mls rp ip**. A Catalyst 6000 with Supervisor Engine I and an MSFC has IP MLS globally enabled by default.

Step 2   Determine which router interfaces will be used as IP MLS interfaces, and add those interfaces to the same VLAN Trunking Protocol (VTP) domain as the MLS-SE. Remember that router interfaces will be VLAN interfaces (not physical interfaces) on the RSM, RSFC, and MSFC. The complete syntax for the command to add an IP MLS interface to a VTP domain is **mls rp vtp-domain** [*domain_name*].

On ISL or 802.1Q trunks, enter the **mls rp vtp-domain** command on the primary interface (not on the individual subinterfaces). All subinterfaces on the primary interface inherit the VTP domain assigned to the primary interface. The command **mls rp vtp-domain** is also used on physical interfaces configured as access ports (ports with only one VLAN association). On the RSFC, RSM, and MSFC, this command is entered on each VLAN interface participating in MLS.

Step 3   For Layer 3 interfaces that are not trunk ports and on which IP MLS support is desired, start by verifying that the interface has been assigned to a VLAN (as an access port). Then assign a VLAN ID to the IP MLS interface with the **mls rp vlan-id** [*vlan_id_num*] interface command.

Step 4   Enable IP MLS on the interfaces participating in IP MLS with the **mls rp ip** command. This is the same command used in global configuration mode, but here it is applied at the interface level. In the case of an ISL or 802.1Q trunk, this command must be configured on all subinterfaces (it is not entered on the physical interface itself). On the MSFC, RSM, and RSFC, this command is entered on VLAN interfaces.

Step 5   Specify an MLS-RP interface as an *MLS-RP management interface*. MLSP runs on the management interface, sending hello messages, advertising routing changes, and announcing VLANs and MAC addresses of interfaces participating in MLS. At least one router interface must be configured as a management interface (more than one is permitted, but this introduces a proportional increase in overhead). If a management interface is not specified, IP MLS does not function.

Also, the MLS-SE must have an active port in at least one VLAN that has a corresponding router interface configured as a management interface. The interface command to specify an MLS-RP interface as a management interface is **mls rp management-interface**, as shown in Example 5-1. In the case of an ISL or 802.1Q trunk, this command is applied to a particular subinterface, not to the interface itself.

Example 5-1 *Configuring MLS on an MLS-RP Is Fairly Complicated*

```
! Step 1:
Router(config)#mls rpip
! Step 2:
Router(config)#interface fa2/0
Router(config-if)#mls rp vtp-domain Cisco
! Step 3: not applicable because interface fa2/0 is a trunk interface
! Step 4:
Router(config-if)#interface fa2/0.1
Router(config-subif)#encapsulation dot1q 1
Router(config-subif)#ip address 10.1.1.1 255.255.255.0
Router(config-subif)#mls rip ip
! Step 5:
Router(config-subif)#mls rp management-interface
```

Finally, configuring output ACLs on MLS-RP interfaces works seamlessly with MLS, meaning that MLS cache entries are created that reflect the desired behavior of the ACL while still providing wire-speed packet switching. On the other hand, input ACLs on MLS-RP interfaces force every packet to be routed by the MLS-RP.

To enable MLS to cooperate with input ACL, enter the **mls rp ip input-acl** global configuration command.

MLS-SE Configuration

The configuration is platform-dependent for the MLS-SE.

IP MLS is enabled by default on Catalyst 5000 family and Catalyst 2926G series switches. If the MLS-RP is an RSM or RSFC installed in the Catalyst 5000 chassis, there is no need to configure the switch for MLS. Configuration of the switch is required only in the following circumstances:

- When an external router is the MLS-RP (this is always the case with Catalyst 2926G series switches)
- To change the IP MLS aging time parameters or packet threshold values
- To enable NetFlow Data Export (NDE) to monitor all IP MLS intersubnet traffic through the NFFC

Similarly, IP MLS is enabled by default on Catalyst 6000 family switches. Recall that the Catalyst 6000 does not support an external MLS-RP. The only options for MLS-RP are the MSM and the MSFC. Configuration of the switch is required only in the following circumstances:

- To specify MLS aging time parameters or packet threshold values
- To set the minimum IP MLS flow mask

Assuming that a Catalyst 5000 or Catalyst 2926G switch (which are CatOS, or set-based, switches) is connected to an external MLS-RP, the configuration proceeds as follows:

Step 1   Enable MLS on the switch with the **set mls enable** command. When IP MLS is enabled on the switch, the switch (MLS-SE) starts to process MLSP messages from the MLS-RPs and starts Layer 3 switching. IP MLS is enabled by default on the MLS-SE, so this step is necessary only if MLS has been disabled with the **set mls disable** command.

Step 2   Specify the external router(s) participating in MLS. Before doing so, enter the **show mls rp** command on the router to identify the MLS-RP IP address. Use the displayed address when entering the **set mls include** *ip_addr* command on the switch, the command that specifies the external router(s) participating in MLS. The MLS-SE does not process MLSP messages from external routers that have not been included as MLS-RPs. Also, the MLS-SE configured in a scenario where the MLS-RP is not an external router doesn't need the **set mls include** command, as shown in Example 5-2.

Example 5-2 *Configuring MLS on an MLS-SE Requires Just One or Two Commands, Depending on Whether the MLS-RP Is Internal or External*

```
Switch> (enable)set mls enable
Switch> (enable)set mls include 10.1.1.1
```

Configuring MLS Optional Parameters

In addition to the MLS-RP and MLS-SE commands discussed up to this point, a few optional MLS parameters are available. Two of these parameters let you configure MLS aging time and minimum flow mask. These values can be adjusted to tune MLS efficiency.

MLS Aging Time

The IP MLS aging time determines the time before an MLS entry is aged out. The default is 256 seconds. The aging time can be configured for a value in the range of 8 to 2032 seconds, in 8-second increments. Any aging-time value that is not a multiple of 8 seconds is adjusted to the closest one. For example, a value of 65 is adjusted to 64, and a value of 127 is adjusted to 128. Other events might cause MLS entries to be purged, such as routing changes or a change in link state (MLS-SE link down).

To specify the IP MLS aging time, use the CatOS **set mls agingtime** [*agingtime*] command in privileged mode.

Another useful MLS cache aging parameter is the *fast aging time*. To specify the IP MLS fast aging time and packet threshold, use the command **set mls agingtime fast** [*fastagingtime*] [*pkt_threshold*] in privileged mode.

The default *fastagingtime* value is 0 (no fast aging). The *fastagingtime* value can be set to 32, 64, 96, or 128 seconds. Any *fastagingtime* value that is not configured exactly as the indicated values is adjusted to the closest one. The *pkt_threshold* value can be set to 0, 1, 3, 7, 15, 31, or 63 packets.

Typical values for *fastagingtime* and *pkt_threshold* are 32 seconds and 0 packets (no packets switched within 32 seconds after the entry is created).

Cisco recommends keeping the number of MLS entries in the MLS cache to less than 32,000 entries. If the number of MLS entries amounts to more than 32,000, some flows are sent to the router.

To help keep the MLS cache size below 32,000, enable the IP MLS fast aging time. The IP MLS fast aging time applies to MLS entries that have no more than *pkt_threshold* packets switched within *fastagingtime* seconds after it is created. A typical cache entry that is removed is the entry for flows to and from a Domain Name System (DNS) or TFTP server; the entry might never be used again after it is created. Detecting and aging out these entries saves space in the MLS cache for other data traffic.

If IP MLS fast aging time needs to be enabled, initially set the value to 128 seconds. If the size of the MLS cache continues to grow over 32 KB, decrease the setting until the cache size stays below 32 KB. If the cache continues to grow over 32 KB, decrease the normal IP MLS aging time.

Minimum IP MLS Flow Mask

The minimum granularity of the flow mask for the MLS cache is configured on the MLS-SE. The actual flow mask used consists of the granularity specified. If a more-specific flow mask is configured, the number of active flow entries increases. To limit the number of active flow entries, you might need to decrease the MLS aging time.

If ACLs are not configured on any MLS-RP, the IP MLS flow mask on the MLS-SE is destination-ip by default (as discussed in the earlier section "MLS Flows"). However, an administrator can force the MLS-SE to use a particular flow mask granularity by setting the minimum IP MLS flow mask using the **set mls flow** {**destination** | **destination-source** | **full**} command in privileged mode (again, these are CatOS commands). Depending on the MLS-RP configuration, the actual flow mask used might be more specific than the specified minimum flow mask. For example, if the minimum flow mask of **destination-source** is configured, but an MLS-RP interface is configured with IP extended ACLs, the actual flow mask used is full (ip-flow).

The **set mls flow** command purges all existing MLS cache entries and affects the number of active entries on the MLS-SE, so use this command carefully when applying it to a production environment.

MLS Configuration Example

This example details the configuration of IP MLS for the topology shown in Figure 5-15.

Figure 5-15 A 7505 Router (MLS-RP) Connects Via an 802.1Q Trunk to an MLS-SE (a Catalyst 5509 with a Supervisor Engine III and NFFC in This Case)

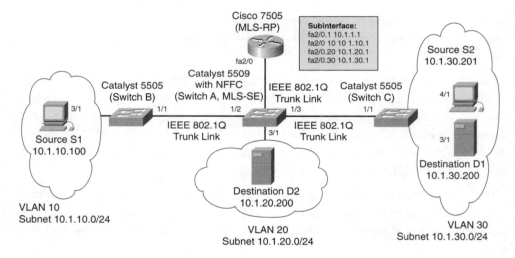

A Cisco 7505 router serves as the MLS-RP, and a Catalyst 5509 with a Supervisor Engine III and an NFFC (Switch A) serves as the MLS-SE. An IEEE 802.1Q trunk connects the two devices participating in MLS.

The IP MLS network topology shown in Figure 5-15 includes two Catalyst 5505 switches connecting via 802.1Q trunks to the MLS-SE (Switch B and Switch C). The 5505s do not play a role in MLS. The network is configured as follows:

- There are four VLANs (IP subnetworks):
    - VLAN 1 (the management VLAN), subnet 10.1.1.0/24
    - VLAN 10, subnet 10.1.10.0/24
    - VLAN 20, subnet 10.1.20.0/24
    - VLAN 30, subnet 10.1.30.0/24

- The MLS-RP is a Cisco 7505 router with a Fast Ethernet interface (interface FastEthernet 2/0)
- The subinterfaces on the router interface have these IP addresses:
  — FastEthernet 2/0.1 — 10.1.1.1 255.255.255.0
  — FastEthernet 2/0.10 — 10.1.10.1 255.255.255.0
  — FastEthernet 2/0.20 — 10.1.20.1 255.255.255.0
  — FastEthernet 2/0.30 — 10.1.30.1 255.255.255.0
- A standard output ACL is configured on subinterface FastEthernet 2/0.20 (the interface in VLAN 20) on the MLS-RP. The ACL denies all traffic from VLAN 30.
- Switch A, the MLS-SE, is a Catalyst 5509 switch with Supervisor Engine III and the NFFC.
- Switch B and Switch C are Catalyst 5505 switches.
- Switch A is the VTP server in domain "Corporate."
- Switch B and Switch C are VTP clients.

The next sections detail the inter-VLAN switching path both before and after IP MLS operation.

Operation Before IP MLS

The operation before IP MLS operation is characterized as follows:

1. Before IP MLS is implemented, when the source host S1 (on VLAN 10) transmits traffic destined for server D1 (on VLAN 30), Switch B forwards the traffic (based on the Layer 2 forwarding table) to Switch A over the 802.1Q trunk link.

2. Switch A forwards the packet to the router over the 802.1Q trunk.

3. The router receives the packet on the VLAN 10 subinterface, checks the destination IP address, and routes the packet to the VLAN 30 subinterface.

4. Switch A receives the routed packet and forwards it to Switch C.

5. Switch C receives the packet and forwards it to destination server D1. This process is repeated for each packet in the flow between source host S1 and destination server D1.

6. When source host S2 sends traffic to destination server D2, Switch C forwards the packets over the 802.1Q trunk to Switch A.

7. Switch A forwards the packet to the MLS-RP.

8. The MLS-RP receives the packet on the VLAN 30 subinterface. Because the standard ACL configured on the outgoing VLAN 20 subinterface denies all traffic from VLAN 30, the router drops the traffic to Destination D2 from Source S2.

9. Any subsequent traffic from Source S2 for Destination D2 also reaches the router and is dropped.

Operation After IP MLS

The operation after IP MLS operation is characterized as follows:

1. After IP MLS is implemented, when the source host S1 transmits traffic destined for destination server D1, Switch B forwards the traffic (based on the Layer 2 forwarding table) to Switch A (the MLS-SE) over the 802.1Q trunk link.

2. When the first packet enters Switch A, a candidate flow entry is established in the MLS cache. Switch A forwards the packet to the MLS-RP over the 802.1Q trunk.

3. The MLS-RP receives the packet on the VLAN 10 subinterface, checks the destination IP address, and routes the packet to the VLAN 30 subinterface.

4. Switch A receives the routed packet (the enable packet) and completes the flow entry in the MLS cache for destination IP address 10.1.30.200. Switch A forwards the packet to Switch C, where it is forwarded to destination server D1.

5. Subsequent packets destined for IP address 10.1.30.200 are multilayer-switched by the MLS-SE based on the flow entry in the MLS cache. For example, subsequent packets in the flow from source host S1 are forwarded by Switch B to Switch A (the MLS-SE). The MLS-SE determines that the packets are part of the established flow, rewrites the packet headers, and switches the packets directly to Switch C, bypassing the router.

Because a standard ACL is applied on subinterface FastEthernet 2/0.20, the MLS-SE must use the source-destination-ip flow mask for all MLS cache entries. When source host S2 sends traffic to destination server D2, Switch C forwards the packets over the 802.1Q trunk to Switch A. Switch A forwards the candidate packet to the MLS-RP, which receives it on the VLAN 30 subinterface. Because the standard ACL configured on the outgoing VLAN 20 subinterface denies all traffic from VLAN 30, the router drops the traffic to Destination D2 from Source S2. Switch A never receives the enable packet for the flow on VLAN 20, and no MLS cache entry is completed for the flow. Any subsequent traffic from Source S2 for Destination D2 also reaches the router and is dropped.

MLS-RP Configuration

Example 5-3 shows the MLS-RP configuration for the network shown in Figure 5-15, using the five steps outlined in the earlier section "MLS-RP Configuration."

Example 5-3 *The MLS-RP Configuration on the 7505 Router Is the Hardest Part of the MLS Configuration*

```
! MLS-RP Step 1:
Cisco7505(config)#mls rip ip
Cisco7505(config)#access-list 1 deny 10.1.30.0 0.0.0.255
Cisco7505(config)#access-list 1 permit any
Cisco7505(config-if)#interface fastethernet 2/0
Cisco7505(config-if)#speed 100
Cisco7505(config-if)#full-duplex
! MLS-RP Step 2:
Cisco7505(config-if)#mls rp vtp-domain Corporate
Cisco7505(config-subif)#interface fastethernet2/0.1
Cisco7505(config-subif)#encapsulation dot1q 1
Cisco7505(config-subif)#ip address 10.1.1.1 255.255.255.0
! MLS-RP Step 4:
Cisco7505(config-subif)#mls rp ip
! MLS-RP Step 5:
Cisco7505(config-subif)#mls rp management interface
Cisco7505(config-subif)#interface fastethernet2/0.10
Cisco7505(config-subif)#encapsulation dot1q 10
Cisco7505(config-subif)#ipo address 10.1.10.1 255.255.255.0
! MLS-RP Step 4:
Cisco7505(config-subif)#mls rip ip
Cisco7505(config-subif)#encapsulation dot1q 20
Cisco7505(config-subif)#ip address 10.1.20.1 255.255.255.0
Cisco7505(config-subif)#ip access-group 1 out
! MLS-RP Step 4:
Cisco7505(config-subif)#mls rp ip
Cisco7505(config-subif)#interface fastethernet2/0.30
Cisco7505(config-subif)#encapsulation dot1q 30
Cisco7505(config-subif)#ip address 10.1.30.1 255.255.255.0
! MLS-RP Step 4:
Cisco7505(config-subif)#mls rip ip
```

Switch A, B, and C Configuration

In some Cisco IOS software releases, traffic on the IEEE 802.1Q native VLAN is not routed. The default native VLAN on Catalyst switches is VLAN 1. If the Cisco IOS software release being used does not route traffic on the native VLAN and an administrator wants to route traffic on VLAN 1, he or she must change the native VLAN on the switch-to-router trunk link to an unused VLAN. In the Switch A, Switch B, and Switch C configuration examples, the native VLAN on all the 802.1Q trunk links is set to an unused VLAN: VLAN 5.

Example 5-4 shows the configuration for Switch A, Example 5-5 shows the configuration for Switch B, and Example 5-6 shows the configuration for Switch C.

Example 5-4 *The Catalyst 5509 Is the MLS-SE*

```
SwitchA>(enable) set vtp domain Corporate mode server
VTP domain Corporate modified
SwitchA>(enable) set vlan 5
Vlan 5 configuration successful
SwitchA>(enable) set vlan 10
Vlan 10 configuration successful
SwitchA>(enable) set vlan 20
Vlan 20 configuration successful
SwitchA>(enable) set vlan 30
Vlan 30 configuration successful
SwitchA>(enable) set trunk 1/1 on dot1q
Port(s) 1/1 trunk mode set to on.
Port(s) 1/1 trunk type set to dot1q
SwitchA>(enable) set port name 1/2 SwitchBLink
Port 1/2 name set.
SwitchA>(enable) set trunk 1/2 desirable dot1q
Port(s) 1/2 trunk mode set to desirable
Port(s) 1/2 trunk type set to dot1q
SwitchA>(enable) set port name 1/3 SwitchCLink
Port 1/3 name set
SwitchA>(enable) set trunk 1/3 desirable dot1q
Port(s) 1/3 trunk mode set to desirable
Port(s) 1/3 trunk type set to dot1q
SwitchA>(enable) set vlan 5 1/1-3
VLAN 5 modified
VLAN 1 modified
```

Example 5-4 *The Catalyst 5509 Is the MLS-SE (Continued)*

```
VLAN  Mod/Ports
----  ---------
5     1/1-3
! MLS-SE Step 1:
SwitchA>(enable) set mls enable
IP Multilayer switching is enabled
! MLS-SE Step 2:
SwitchA>(enable) set mls include 10.1.1.1
IP Multilayer switching enabled for router 10.1.1.1
SwitchA>(enable) set port name 3/1 DestinationD2
Port 3/1 name set.
SwitchA>(enable) set vlan 20 3/1
```

Example 5-5 *Switch B is a Catalyst 5505 Switch*

```
SwitchB>(enable) set port name 1/1 SwitchALink
Port 1/1 name set
SwitchB>(enable) set vlan 5 1/1
VLAN 5 modified
VLAN 1 modified
VLAN  Mod/Ports
----  ---------
5     1/1
SwitchB>(enable) set vlan 10 3/1
VLAN 10 modified
VLAN 1 modified
VLAN  Mod/Ports
----  ---------
10    3/1
```

Example 5-6 *Switch C is a Catalyst 5505 Switch*

```
SwitchC>(enable) set port name 1/1 SwitchALink
Port 1/1 name set
SwitchC>(enable) set vlan 5 1/1
VLAN 5 modified
VLAN 1 modified
```

continues

Example 5-6 *Switch C is a Catalyst 5505 Switch (Continued)*

```
VLAN  Mod/Ports
----  ----------
5     1/1
SwitchC>(enable) set port name 3/1 DesintationD1
Port 3/1 name set
SwitchC>(enable) set vlan 30 3/1
VLAN 30 modified
VLAN 1 modified
VLAN  Mod/Ports
----  ----------
30    3/1
SwitchC>(enable) set port name 4/1 SourceS2
Port 4/1 name set
SwitchC>(enable) set vlan 30 4/1
VLAN 30 modified
VLAN 1 modified
VLAN  Mod/Ports
----  ----------
30    3/1
      4/1
```

MLS Verification

The **show mls rp** command displays the following information:

- Whether MLS switching is globally enabled or disabled
- The MLS ID for this MLS-RP
- The MLS IP address for this MLS-RP
- The MLS flow mask
- The name of the VTP domain in which the MLS-RP interfaces reside
- Statistical information for each VTP domain
- The number of management interfaces defined for the MLS-RP
- The number of VLANs configured for MLS
- The ID of each VLAN configured for this MAC address
- The number of MLS-SEs to which the MLS-RP is connected
- The MAC address of each switch

Each MLS-RP is identified to the switch by both the MLS ID and the MLS IP address of the route processor. The MLS ID is the MAC address of the route processor. The MLS-RP automatically selects the IP address of one of its interfaces from MLS-enabled interfaces and uses that IP address as its MLS IP address.

The MLS-SE uses the MLS ID in the process of populating the MLS cache. This MLS IP address is used in the following situations:

- By the MLS-RP and the MLS-SE when sending MLS statistics to a data collection application
- In the included MLS-RP list on the switch

To display IP MLS information about a specific interface, use the **show mls rp interface** *type number* command. Example 5-7 shows the output of this command for interface VLAN 10.

Example 5-7 *Displaying Specific Information for an IP MLS Interface*

```
Router#show mls rp interface vlan 10
als active on Vlan10, domain Corporate
Router#
```

The **show mls rp vtp-domain** *domain-name* command displays IP MLS information for a specific VTP domain on the MLS-RP, as shown in Example 5-8.

Example 5-8 *Displaying IP MLS Information Specific to a VTP Domain*

```
Router#show mls rp vtp-domain Corporatevlan domain name: Corporate
current flow mask: ip-flow
current sequence number: 80709115
current/maximum rety count: 0/10
current domain state: no-change
current/next global purge: false/false
current/next purge count: 0/1
domain uptime: 13:07:36
keepalive timer expires in 8 seconds
retry timer not running
change timer not running
fcp subblock count = 7
1 management interface(s) current defined: vlan 1 on Vlan1
7 mac-vlan(s) configured for multi-layer switching: mac 00e0.fefc.6000
```

continues

Example 5-8 *Displaying IP MLS Information Specific to a VTP Domain (Continued)*

```
vlan id(s)
1 10 91 92 93 95 100
router currently aware of following 1 switch(es):
switch id 0010.1192.b5ff
```

On the Catalyst 6000 MSFC, the **show mls status** command displays basic MLS information, as shown in Example 5-9.

Example 5-9 *Displaying Basic MLS Information on a Catalyst 6000 Family Switch MSFC*

```
Router#show mls status
MLS global configuration status:
global mls ip:                      enabled
global mls ipx:                     enabled
global mls ip multicast:            disabled
current ip flowmask for unicast:    destination only
current ipx flowmask for unicast:   destination only
Router#
```

The **show mls** output provides the following information:

- Whether MLS is enabled on the switch
- The aging time, in seconds, for an MLS cache entry
- The fast aging time, in seconds, and the packet threshold for a flow
- The flow mask
- Total packets switched
- The number of active MLS entries in the cache
- Whether NetFlow data export is enabled and, if so, for which port and host
- The MLS-RP IP address, MAC address, XTAG, and supported VLANs

To display MLS information on an MLS-SE, enter the **show mls** command in privileged mode. Example 5-10 shows the results of this command.

Example 5-10 *Displaying MLS Information on an MLS-SE Running Catalyst OS*

```
Console>(enable) show mls

Multilayer switching enabled
Multilayer switching aging time = 256 seconds
```

Example 5-10 *Displaying MLS Information on an MLS-SE Running Catalyst OS (Continued)*

```
Multilayer switching fast aging time = 0 seconds, packet threshold = 1
Desintation-ip flow
Total packets switched = 101892
Active entries = 2153
Netflow data export enabled
Netflow data export configured for port 8010 on host 10.0.2.15
Total packets exported = 20


MLS-RIP IP   MLS-Rp ID     Xtag   MLS-RP              MAC-Vlans
............................  ....   ..........................
172.20.25.2  00008080cece  2      00-00-80-ec-e0    1-20
                                  00-00-80-ec-e1    21-30
                                  00-00-80-ec-e2    31-40
                                  00-00-80-ec-e3    41-50
                                  00-00-80-ec-e4    51-60


172.20.27.1  00008080cece  3      00-00-80-12-14    1-20, 31-40
                                  00-00-80-12-15    21-30
                                  00-00-80-12-16    41-50
```

To display information about a specific MLS-RP, enter the **show mls rp** [*ip_addr*] command. This command displays information used by the switch with regard to Layer 3 switched packets, as demonstrated in Example 5-11.

Example 5-11 *Displaying MLS-RP Information on an MLS-SE Running Catalyst OS*

```
Console>(enable) show mls rp 166.122.20.2


MLS-RP IP     MLS-Rp ID     Xtag   MLS-RP              MAC-Vlans
............................  ....   ..........................
166.122.20.2  00008080cece  2      00-00-80-ec-e0    1-20
                                   00-00-80-ec-e1    21-30
                                   00-00-80-ec-e2    31-40
                                   00-00-80-ec-e3    41-50
                                   00-00-80-ec-e4    51-60
```

Arguably, the most useful **show** commands for MLS are those that display the MLS cache entries or that use the **show mls entry** command or one of its four variations:

- **show mls entry rp**
- **show mls entry destination**
- **show mls entry source**
- **show mls entry flow**

To display all MLS entries on the switch, simply enter the command **show mls entry**, or use an option to get more specific information, as shown in Example 5-12.

Example 5-12 *Displaying MLS Cache Entries on an MLS-SE Running Catalyst OS*

```
Console>(enable) show mls entry destination 172.20.22.14/24


Destination IP  Source IP     Port  DstPrt  SrcPrt  Destination Mac    Vlan  Port


MLS-RP 172.20.25.1:
172.20.22.14   172.20.25.10   TCP   6001    Telnet  00-60-700-6c-fc-22 4    2/1
MLS-RP 172.20.25.1:
172.20.22.16   172.20.27.139  TCP   6001    Telnet  00-60-700-6c-fc-24 4    2/3
```

Finally, just as an administrator occasionally needs to clear ARP cache entries, content-addressable memory (CAM), or the routing table, sometimes there is a need to remove entries from the MLS cache. To do so, enter the **clear mls entry** command. Here's the full syntax of this command when used for IP flows:

```
clear mls entry ip [destination ip_addr_spec] [source ip_addr_spec]
  [flow protocol src_port dst_port] [all]
```

The **all** keyword clears all MLS entries. Other than the **all** keyword option, the syntax parallels that of the **show mls entry** command. Example 5-13 shows the output of a prescriptive use of the **clear mls entry ip** command.

Example 5-13 *Removing MLS Cache Entries on an MLS-SE Running Catalyst OS*

```
Console>(enable) clear mls entry ip destination 172.20.26.22 source
  172.20.22.113
  flow tcp 1652 23


MLS IP entry cleared
```

CEF Configuration and Verification

CEF configuration is straightforward. However, there are many options for verifying and monitoring CEF operation.

CEF Configuration

One of CEF's most appealing features might be its configuration. CEF for PFC2 on a Catalyst 6500 is permanently enabled on Supervisor Engine II with the PFC2 and MSFC2, so no configuration is required. However, some platforms allow CEF to be disabled or don't default to enabling CEF.

On Catalyst 3550 switches, CEF is enabled globally by default. If for some reason it is disabled, you can reenable it by using the **ip cef** global configuration command.

To enable dCEF on line cards so that the route processor can handle routing protocols or switch packets from legacy interface processors, issue the **ip cef distributed** global configuration command.

When CEF or dCEF is enabled globally, all interfaces that support CEF are enabled by default.

An administrator might want to disable CEF or dCEF on a particular interface, because that interface is configured with a feature that CEF or dCEF does not support. For example, policy routing and CEF cannot be used together. Sometimes one interface is configured to support policy routing and the other interfaces support CEF. In this case, enable CEF globally, but disable it on the interface configured for policy routing. This allows all but one interface to express forward.

To disable CEF or dCEF on an interface, use the **no ip route-cache cef** command in interface configuration mode.

When CEF or dCEF is disabled, Cisco IOS software switches packets using the next fastest switching path. In the case of dCEF, the next fastest switching path is CEF on the route processor. If CEF or dCEF is disabled on an interface, an administrator can reenable it by using the **ip route-cache cef** command while in interface configuration mode.

Verifying CEF

You can view the contents of the FIB table by issuing the **show ip cef detail** command from the MSFC2 or Supervisor Engine 720. Example 5-14 shows the output from this command.

Example 5-14 *Displaying the FIB Table on a Catalyst 6500 MSFC2 or Supervisor Engine 720*

```
MSFC2#show ip cef detail
  IP CEF with switching (Table Version 477965)
  445 routes, 0 reresolve, 0 unresolved (0 old, 0 new)
  446 leaves, 76 nodes, 132560 bytes, 477966 inserts, 477520 invalidations
  0 load sharing elements, 0 bytes, 0 references
  1 CEF resets, 2 revisions of existing leaves
  refcounts:  15824 leaf, 15038 node
  Default 192.35.86.0/24
0.0.0.0/32, version 0, receive
10.1.0.0/16, version 121980, attached, connected
0 packets, 0 bytes
  via Vlan10, 0 dependencies
    valid glean adjacency
10.1.0.0/32, version 121982, recieve
10.1.0.44/32, version 433624, connected, cached adjacency
10.1.0.44
0 packets, 0 bytes
  via 10.1.0.44, Vlan10, 0 dependencies
    next hop 10.1.0.44, Vlan10
    valid cached adjacency
10.1.0.84/32, version 122675, connected, cached adjacency
10.1.0.84
0 packets, 0 bytes
  via 10.1.0.84, Vlan10, 0 dependencies
    next hop 10.1.0.84, Vlan10
    valid cached adjacency
10.1.0.107/32, version 471278, connected, cached
adjacency 10.1.0.107
0 packets, 0 bytes
  via 10.1.0.107, Vlan10, 0 dependencies
    next hop 10.1.0.107, Vlan10
    valid cached adjacency
10.1.0.152/32, version 450780, connected, cached
adjacency 10.1.0.152
0 packets, 0 bytes
  via 10.1.0.152, Vlan10, 0 dependencies
```

Example 5-14 *Displaying the FIB Table on a Catalyst 6500 MSFC2 or Supervisor Engine 720 (Continued)*

```
     next hop 10.1.0.152, Vlan10
     valid cached adjacency
10.1.0.158/32, version 447262, connected, cached
adjacency 10.1.0.158
0 packets, 0 bytes
  via 10.1.0.158, Vlan10, 0 dependencies
    next hop 10.1.0.158, Vlan10
    valid cached adjacency
10.1.0.162/32, version 471313, connected, cached
adjacency 10.1.0.162
0 packets, 0 bytes
  via 10.1.0.162, Vlan10, 0 dependencies
    next hop 10.1.0.162, Vlan10
    valid cached adjacency
<output omitted>
```

Use the **show ip cef** command to view the contents of the CEF adjacency table from the
MSFC2 or Supervisor Engine 720, as shown in Example 5-15. The **show ip cef summary**
command, shown in Example 5-16, provides a brief overview of the CEF process with information such as the total number of adjacencies and routes.

Example 5-15 *Displaying the Contents of the CEF Adjacency Table on a Catalyst 6500 MSFC2 or Supervisor
Engine 720*

```
MSFC2#show ip cef
0.0.0/32              receive
10.1.0.0/16           attached         Vlan10
10.1.0.0/32           receive
10.1.0.44/32          10.1.0.44        Vlan10
10.1.0.84/32          10.1.0.84        Vlan10
10.1.0.107/32         10.1.0.107       Vlan10
10.1.255.253/32       10.1.255.253     Vlan10
10.1.255.254/32       receive
10.1.255.255/32       receive
10.2.0.0/16           attached         Vlan2
10.2.0.0/32           receive
10.2.0.12/32          10.2.0.12        Vlan2
```

Example 5-16 *Displaying a Brief Overview of the CEF Process on a Catalyst 6500 MSFC2 or Supervisor Engine 720*

```
MSFC2#show ip cef summary
  IP CEF with switching (Table Version 477965)
  445 routes, 0 reresolve, 0 unresolved (0 old, 0 new)
  446 leaves, 76 nodes, 132560 bytes, 477966 inserts, 477520 invalidations
  0 load sharing elements, 0 bytes, 0 references
  1 CEF resets, 2 revisions of existing leaves
  refcounts:  15824 leaf, 15038 node
  Default 192.35.86.0/24
```

Lab 5.4.1   Monitoring Cisco Express Forwarding

In this lab exercise, you monitor the default behavior of CEF.

Summary

MLS and CEF are Cisco multilayer switching technologies. CEF is newer than MLS and is supported by all the newer devices, such as the Catalyst 4000 Supervisor Engine III and IV, the Catalyst 6500 with MSFC2 and PFC2, the Catalyst 6500 Supervisor Engine 720, and Cisco routers with Cisco IOS software Release 12.2 and later. CEF has been supported on some routers since Cisco IOS software Release 12.0, such as the Cisco 7500.

Key Terms

adjacency table   One of three tables used by CEF. The adjacency table is a database of node adjacencies (two nodes are said to be adjacent if they can reach each other via a single Layer 2 hop) and their associated Layer 2 MAC rewrite or next-hop information. Each leaf of the FIB tree offers a pointer to the appropriate next-hop entry in the adjacency table.

aging time   The IP MLS aging time determines the amount of time before an MLS entry is aged out. The default is 256 seconds. You can configure the aging time in the range of 8 to 2032 seconds in 8-second increments.

candidate packet   When a source initiates a data transfer to a destination, it sends the first packet to the MLS-RP through the MLS-SE. The MLS-SE recognizes the packet as a candidate packet for Layer 3 switching, because the MLS-SE has learned the MLS-RP's destination MAC addresses and VLANs through MLSP. The MLS-SE learns the candidate packet's Layer 3 flow information (such as the destination address, source address, and protocol port numbers) and forwards the candidate packet to the MLS-RP. A partial MLS entry for this Layer 3 flow is created in the MLS cache.

central rewrite engine   The Catalyst 5000 NFFC contains central rewrite engines (one per bus) to handle PDU header rewrites when inline rewrite is not an option. If the central rewrite engines are used, this means that a frame must traverse the bus twice—first with a VLAN tag for the source (on its way to the NFFC) and second with a VLAN tag for the destination (on its way to the egress port).

Cisco Express Forwarding (CEF)   A Cisco multilayer switching technology that allows for increased scalability and performance to meet the requirements for large enterprise networks. CEF has evolved to accommodate the traffic patterns realized by modern networks, characterized by an increasing number of short-duration flows.

Content-Addressable Memory (CAM)   Memory that is accessed based on its contents, not on its memory address. Sometimes called associative memory.

enable packet   When an MLS-SE receives a packet from the MLS-RP that originated as a candidate packet, it recognizes that the source MAC address belongs to the MLS-RP, that the XTAG matches that of the candidate packet, and that the packet's flow information matches the flow for which the candidate entry was created. The MLS-SE considers this packet an enable packet and completes the MLS entry created by the candidate packet in the MLS cache.

fast aging time   The IP MLS fast aging time is the amount of time before an MLS entry is purged that has no more than *pkt_threshold* packets switched within *fastagingtime* seconds after it is created.

flow   A unidirectional sequence of packets between a particular source and destination that share the same Layer 3 and Layer 4 PDU header information.

flow mask   A set of criteria, based on a combination of source IP address, destination IP address, protocol, and protocol ports, that describes the characteristics of a flow.

Forwarding Information Base (FIB)   One of three tables used by CEF. The FIB table contains the minimum information necessary to forward packets; in particular, it does not contain any routing protocol information. The table consists of a four-level hierarchical tree, with 256 branch options per level (reflecting four octets in an IP address).

inline rewrite   Some Catalyst 5000 family switch line cards have onboard hardware that performs PDU header rewrites and forwarding, maximizing IP MLS performance. When the line card performs the PDU header rewrites, this is called inline rewrite. With inline rewrite, frames traverse the switch bus only once.

MLS Route Processor (MLS-RP)   A Cisco device with a route processor that supports MLS. For example, a Catalyst 3620 router is an MLS-RP.

MLS Switching Engine (MLS-SE)   A set of hardware components on a Catalyst switch, excluding the route processor, necessary to support MLS. For example, a Catalyst 5000 with a Supervisor Engine IIIG is an MLS-SE.

MLS-RP Management Interface   The MLS-RP interface that sends hello messages, advertises routing changes, and announces VLANs and MAC addresses of interfaces participating in MLS.

Multilayer Switch Feature Card (MSFC)   MSFC1 and MSFC2 are daughter cards to the Catalyst 6000 Supervisor Engine that provide multilayer switching functionality and routing services between VLANs.

Multilayer Switching (MLS)   A specific multilayer switching technology employed by various Cisco devices to perform wire-speed PDU header rewrites. The first packet in a flow is routed as normal, and the MLS-SE switches subsequent packets based on cached information.

Multilayer Switching Protocol (MLSP)   A protocol used to communicate MLS information between the MLS-SE and MLS-RP. In particular, the MLS-SE populates its Layer 2 CAM table with updates received from MLSP packets.

NetFlow Feature Card (NFFC)   A daughter card for a Catalyst 5000 Supervisor module that enables intelligent network services, such as high-performance multilayer switching and accounting and traffic management.

NetFlow table   One of three tables used by CEF. The NetFlow table provides network accounting data. It is updated in parallel with the CEF-based forwarding mechanism provided by the FIB and adjacency tables.

wire-speed routing   The routing of packets using a combination of hardware and data structures so that routing table lookups are circumvented and header rewrites and forwarding are handled independent of the route processor.

XTAG   A 1-byte value that the MLS-SE attaches per VLAN to all MAC addresses learned from the same MLS-RP via MLSP.

Check Your Understanding

Use the following review questions to test your understanding of the concepts covered in this chapter. Answers are listed in Appendix A, "Check Your Understanding Answer Key."

1. Which of the following describe multilayer switching?

    A. It's hardware-based.

    B. It performs PDU header rewrites and forwarding.

    C. It's platform-independent.

    D. It uses Layer 2, Layer 3, and Layer 4 header information.

2. Which of the following device combinations support Cisco Express Forwarding?

    A. Cisco 7500 router running IOS 12.0

    B. Catalyst 4500 Supervisor Engine III

    C. Catalyst 6500 MSFC2

    D. Cisco routers running IOS 12.2 or later

3. Which of the following are MLS components?

    A. MLSP

    B. MLS-RP

    C. MLS cache

    D. MLS-SE

4. Which of the following are MLS flow masks?

    A. destination-ip

    B. protocol-flow

    C. source-destination-ip

    D. ip-flow

5. After an IP MLS flow has been created, which of the following fields change in a frame traversing the MLS-SE as part of the same flow?

   A. Source MAC address

   B. Destination MAC address

   C. TTL

   D. Source IP

6. In addition to the routing table, what tables are created in the CEF-based model?

   A. Routing table

   B. Forwarding Information Base

   C. Content-flow table

   D. Adjacency table

7. How many leaves are possible in a CEF FIB?

   A. 32

   B. 64

   C. 128

   D. 256

8. How many MLS-SE commands are required to configure MLS when the MLS-RP is an external router?

   A. 1

   B. 2

   C. 3

   D. 4

9. What is the default MLS flow mask when no ACLs are configured on the MLS-RP?

   A. destination-ip

   B. protocol-flow

   C. source-destination-ip

   D. ip-flow

10. What global configuration command enables CEF?

    A. cef run

    B. enable cef

    C. cef enable

    D. ip cef

Objectives

After completing this chapter, you will be able to perform tasks related to the following:

- Explain the types of redundancy in a multilayer switched network, including hardware and software redundancy
- Implement redundant Supervisor modules in Catalyst switches
- Implement redundant Supervisor uplink modules in Catalyst switches
- Implement redundant distributed forwarding cards in Catalyst switches
- Explain how router redundancy operates
- Describe, configure, and verify Hot Standby Router Protocol (HSRP)
- Describe Virtual Router Redundancy Protocol (VRRP)
- Describe and verify Gateway Load Balancing Protocol (GLBP)
- Describe Single Router Mode (SRM) redundancy
- Describe and verify Server Load Balancing (SLB)
- Troubleshoot router redundancy using HSRP, VRRP, GLBP, SRM, and SLB

Chapter 6

Redundancy

Because many organizations are now seeking the economic benefits of campus networks for mission-critical communications, high reliability is becoming increasingly crucial. Within the campus network, much attention has been focused on providing a network infrastructure that is available 100 percent of the time. One of the greatest challenges comes not from the network infrastructure but from the workstations and network equipment at the user level.

High network availability rates rely on two key items:

- Elimination of any single point of failure
- Distribution of intelligence throughout the architecture

Availability can be increased by adding redundant components, including redundant network devices and connections to multiple WAN links, as illustrated in Figure 6-1. With the proper design, no single point of failure affects overall system availability.

The best practice is a design based on modular and hierarchical building blocks that can be replicated to support growth. The infrastructure must also be able to detect and respond quickly to any possible service, link, device, server, or software failure. Users and applications do not notice failures, because optimized resiliency technologies ensure fast convergence upon failure. To achieve optimal, fast convergence, multiple networking technologies need to interoperate and complement each other to ensure fast recovery.

The objective of this chapter is to provide an overview of hardware and software redundancy operation and implementation on the Cisco Catalyst series of switches. The Cisco-proprietary Hot Standby Router Protocol (HSRP) feature is the main focus of this module. Other redundancy technologies, such as Virtual Router Redundancy Protocol (VRRP), Gateway Load Balancing Protocol (GLBP), and Server Load Balancing (SLB) are also explored.

Figure 6-1 A Well-Designed Network Always Includes Redundancy

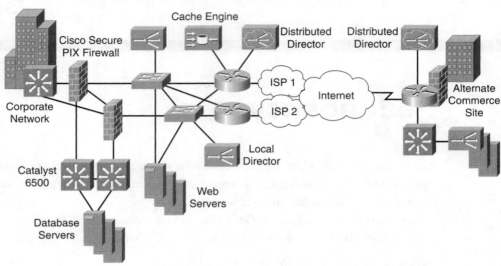

Implementing Module Redundancy in a Multilayer Switched Network

Hardware redundancy takes on many presentations with Cisco Catalyst switches. These include redundant Supervisor Engines, redundant uplink modules, redundant forwarding cards, and redundant power supplies. This section details each of these options.

Implementing Redundant Supervisor Engines in Catalyst Switches

The Catalyst 6000 family switches rely on a Supervisor Engine to manage the other modules in the chassis, as shown in Figure 6-2. Dual Supervisor Engines provide hardware redundancy for the forwarding intelligence of the Catalyst 6000 family. Catalyst 6000 family switches can support two Supervisor Engine I or II modules only in slots 1 and 2. The Catalyst 6500 can support two Supervisor Engine 720 modules only in slots 1 and 2 in a three-slot chassis, slots 5 and 6 in a six- or nine-slot chassis, and slots 7 and 8 in a 13-slot chassis. One Supervisor serves as the running, or active, Supervisor, and the other serves as the standby Supervisor. The active Supervisor Engine is the first one to come online. This can be confirmed by the "Active" Light Emitting Diode (LED) externally on the Supervisor or by entering the **show module** command at the console. The active Supervisor processes all administrative and management functions, such as Simple Network Management Protocol (SNMP), command-line interface (CLI) console, Telnet, Spanning Tree Protocol (STP), Port Aggregation Protocol (PAgP), Cisco Discovery Protocol (CDP), Dynamic Trunking Protocol (DTP), and VLAN Trunking

Protocol (VTP) functions. Redundant Supervisor Engines must be of the same type with the same model feature card. If an active Supervisor is taken offline or fails, the standby Supervisor takes over control of the system.

Figure 6-2 Catalyst Switch Supervisor Engines Manage All Other Modules in the Chassis

The two Supervisor Engines in a redundant configuration have distinct functions. The active Supervisor is responsible for controlling the system bus and all line cards. All protocols are running on the active Supervisor, and it performs all packet forwarding. The standby Supervisor does not communicate with the line cards. The standby Supervisor receives packets from the network and populates its forwarding tables with this information. However, the standby Supervisor does not participate in any packet forwarding or provide any load sharing. The relevant protocols on the system are initialized, but not active, on the standby Supervisor. The Catalyst 6500 series Supervisor Engines are hot-swappable. This means that the standby Supervisor Engine can be installed on an active system without affecting network operation. The active Supervisor provides all the packet forwarding intelligence for the system. If the active Supervisor fails, the standby Supervisor maintains the same system load. The standby Supervisor can be removed and installed without service interruption.

The standby Supervisor polls the active Supervisor on a regular interval using an out-of-band channel. The active Supervisor Engine might go offline for the following reasons:

- Hardware failures
- System overload conditions
- Memory corruption issues
- Removal from chassis
- Operator reset

The standby Supervisor detects these types of failures and becomes the active Supervisor. The software on the Supervisor Engine is responsible for restoring the protocols, line cards, and forwarding engines to normal operation. This restoration takes place using a fast switch-over or a high-availability switchover.

Implementing Redundant Supervisor Uplink Modules in Catalyst Switches

Catalyst 5000 family Supervisor Engine IIG uplink ports are modular, as shown in Figure 6-3. Modularity lets the administrator install the uplink module to deliver current bandwidth requirements. Modularity also ensures an easy migration path. Available options are as follows:

- Four-port autosensing 10/100 Fast Ethernet (RJ-45)
- Four-port 100BASE-FX (MT-RJ)
- Two-port autosensing 10/100 Fast Ethernet (RJ-45)
- Two-port 100BASE-FX (SC)
- Two-port Gigabit Ethernet SX, LX/LH (SC), or Gigabit Interface Converter (GBIC)

Any Fast Ethernet uplink port can use Fast EtherChannel technology. Fast EtherChannel provides up to 800 million packets per second (Mpps) of wire-speed, resilient, and scalable bandwidth for data center and backbone implementations.

Figure 6-3 The Catalyst 5000 Family Supervisor IIG Supports Modular Uplinks

The Catalyst 4006 Supervisor Engine III (shown in Figure 6-4), Catalyst 4500 Supervisor Engine IV (shown in Figure 6-5), and Catalyst 6500 Supervisor Engine I and II (shown in Figure 6-6) support 1000BASE-SX, 1000BASE-LX/LH, and 1000BASE-ZX uplinks via insertion of GBICs into accommodating slots on these devices.

Figure 6-4 The Catalyst 4006 Supervisor Engine III Delivers a 64-Gbps Switching Fabric with 48-Mpps Forwarding Rate in Hardware for Both Layer 2 and Layer 3/4 Traffic

Figure 6-5 The Catalyst 4000/4500 Supervisor Engine IV Delivers Integrated Resiliency and CEF-Based Layer 2/3/4 Switching at 48 Mpps

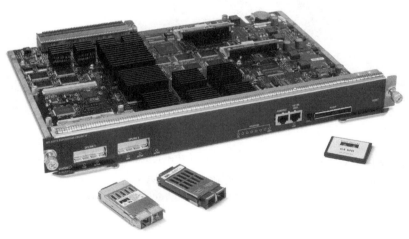

Figure 6-6 The Catalyst 6000 Family Supervisor Engine I Supports the Policy Feature Card (on the Left) and the Multilayer Switch Feature Card (on the Right)

The Catalyst 6500 Supervisor Engine 720, shown in Figure 6-7, has three physical uplink ports:

- Two Gigabit Ethernet Small Formfactor Pluggable (SFP) ports supporting 1000BASE-SX and 1000BASE-LX/LH
- One 10/100/1000 RJ-45 port

Only two of the three ports can be active at any one point in time.

NOTE

The Catalyst 6500 supports 10 Gigabit Ethernet modules. Up to eight 10 Gigabit Ethernet ports can participate in a single 10 Gigabit EtherChannel, providing 160 Gbps of bandwidth.

Figure 6-7 The Catalyst 6500 Series Supervisor Engine 720 Delivers CEF-Based Forwarding at 400 Mpps/720 Gbps

Any Gigabit Ethernet uplink port can use Gigabit EtherChannel technology. With additional Gigabit Ethernet line cards, Gigabit EtherChannel can provide up to 16 Gbps of wire-speed, resilient, and scalable bandwidth for data center and backbone implementations.

Implementing Redundant Distributed Forwarding Cards in Catalyst Switches

The distributed forwarding card (DFC) for the Catalyst 6500 series, shown in Figure 6-8, delivers high-speed distributed services and forwarding for deployment in data center backbones and server farm aggregation. The DFC complements the centralized forwarding of the Catalyst 6500 Supervisor Engine II by distributing the centralized forwarding intelligence to each DFC-enabled line card module. This capability provides localized forwarding and service decisions on each line card and accelerates the forwarding performance of the Catalyst 6500 series.

Figure 6-8 The DFC Is Installed in DFC-Enabled Line-Card Modules That Perform Distributed Forwarding, Supported by the Catalyst 6500 Supervisor Engine II

The DFC works with the Switch Fabric Module, Supervisor Engine II with Multilayer Switch Feature Card 2 (MSFC2) and fabric-enabled cards to provide a framework for a distributed CEF-based forwarding architecture, as shown in Figure 6-9. Although classic line cards cannot directly participate in distributed forwarding, CEF capabilities can still be used based on the centralized capabilities offered by Supervisor Engine II.

The Catalyst 6500 DFC-3 is installed in DFC-enabled line-card modules that perform distributed forwarding supported by the Catalyst 6500 Supervisor Engine 720 as a field upgrade.

When the DFC-3 is installed, modules that are DFC-enabled make forwarding decisions locally, leaving the Supervisor Engine free to perform routing and management functions. The DFC-3 replicates Layer 2 and Layer 3 forwarding logic of the Supervisor 720's Policy Feature Card 3 (PFC-3) on each DFC-3-equipped line card. This enables hardware acceleration of IPv6, Multiprotocol Label Switching (MPLS), Generic Routing Encapsulation (GRE), quality of service (QoS), access control list (ACL) policy enforcement, and more. The DFC-3-equipped interface modules are backward-compatible with all other Catalyst 6500 interface modules. However, the modules must be used with a Supervisor 720, and any other modules that will use distributed forwarding must also be DFC-3-equipped.

Figure 6-9 Local Forwarding Is Provided by the DFC Architecture

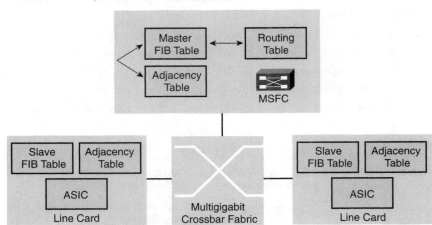

Implementing Redundant Power Supplies

To meet the need for power redundancy, Cisco has added redundant power as an option across a broad range of devices. Redundant power supplies are appropriate in situations that are considered mission-critical. In systems with redundant power supplies, both power supplies must be of the same wattage. The Catalyst 6000 family switches allow mixing of AC-input and DC-input power supplies in the same chassis.

With redundancy enabled and two power supplies of equal wattage installed, the total power drawn from both supplies is at no time greater than the capacity of one supply. If one supply malfunctions, the other supply can take over the entire system load. When two power supplies of equal wattage are used, as shown in Figure 6-10, each provides approximately half of the required power to the system. Load sharing and redundancy are enabled automatically. No software configuration is required.

With redundancy enabled and two power supplies of unequal wattage installed, both power supplies come online, but a syslog message says that the lower-wattage power supply will be disabled. If the active power supply fails, the lower-wattage power supply comes online and modules are powered down, if necessary, to accommodate the lower-wattage power supply.

In a nonredundant configuration, the power available to the system is the combined power capacity of both power supplies. The system powers up as many modules as the combined capacity allows. However, if one supply fails and there is not enough power for all previously powered-up modules, the system powers down some modules. These modules are marked as **power-deny** in the **show module status** field.

Figure 6-10 Redundant Power Supplies Are Recommended for Any Chassis-Based Catalyst Switch

You can reconfigure the configuration of the power supplies from redundant to nonredundant at any time. When switching from a redundant to a nonredundant configuration, both power supplies are enabled even if a lower-wattage power supply is present. When switching from a nonredundant to a redundant configuration, both power supplies are initially enabled. If they are of the same wattage, they remain enabled. If the power supplies are of different wattages, a syslog message appears, and the lower-wattage supply is disabled.

Implementing Router Redundancy in a Switched Network

An evolution has taken place with respect to technologies enabling router redundancy from the access and distribution layers. *Proxy ARP* was one of the first solutions designed to provide dynamic access to preferred routers on a given LAN. Other solutions over the years have included Gateway Discovery Protocol (GDP), multiple default gateways, routing protocols running on workstations, dynamic host configuration protocol (DHCP), Internet Control Message Protocol (ICMP) Router Discovery Protocol (IRDP), HSRP, VRRP, and GLBP. Many of these remain viable options. This chapter focuses mostly on HSRP, but the other options are also described.

Router Redundancy Operation

IP routing redundancy is a key component of high-availability strategy for any network, because it is a critical component of delivering reliable data, voice, and video integration. The goal of IP routing redundancy is to protect against first-hop router failure when a source host is unable to dynamically learn the IP address of an alternate first-hop router.

Some options for redundant access to routers include the following:

- Proxy Address Resolution Protocol (ARP)
- Multiple default gateways
- Dynamic routing protocols running on workstations
- DHCP

Each of these options permits a host some flexibility with respect to where traffic originating from the host exits on the local LAN segment. The focus at this point is providing redundancy to hosts, rather than to network devices, such as switches or routers.

Proxy Address Resolution Protocol

Some IP hosts use proxy ARP to select a router. When a host runs proxy ARP, an ARP request is sent with the IP address of the remote host. A router on the network replies on behalf of the remote host and provides its own MAC address. With proxy ARP, the host assumes it is connected to the same segment of the network as the remote host. If Router A fails, the host continues sending packets to Router A's MAC address. Those packets are lost until the host ARP table is updated by way of a new ARP request acquiring the MAC address of another router on the local segment. It is possible that for a significant period of time the host will be unable to communicate with the remote host, even though the routing protocol has converged, and Router B is prepared to transfer packets that would otherwise go through Router A.

Default Gateways

Specifying a *default gateway* on a host allows the workstation to simply send the packet to the default gateway. Some operating systems might have only one default gateway specified. When this gateway fails, as shown in Figure 6-11, the workstation cannot reach remote subnets.

Although the network infrastructure can quickly recover and reconverge, the host does not know about a new default gateway. With operating systems that support multiple default gateway entries, such as Microsoft Windows, failover between the entries is not dynamic. The operating system sends an echo to each gateway entry in order on bootup. The first gateway to reply is used as the default gateway. Using another listed gateway, in the event of a router failure, requires a restart of the host.

Figure 6-11 A Single Static Default Gateway on Hosts Does Not Provide an Adequate Failover
Mechanism

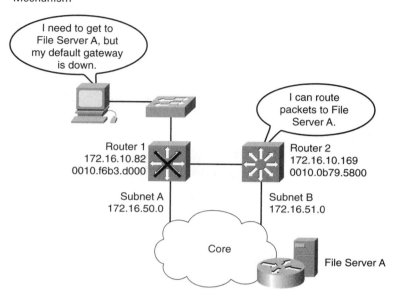

Dynamic Routing Protocol

Some IP hosts run a dynamic routing protocol, such as Routing Information Protocol (RIP) or
Open Shortest Path First (OSPF), to discover routes. Running a dynamic routing protocol on
every host might not be feasible for numerous reasons:

- Administrative and processing overhead
- Security issues
- Lack of a protocol implementation for some platforms

Dynamic Host Configuration Protocol

DHCP provides a mechanism for passing IP configuration information to hosts on a TCP/IP
network. A host joining the network requests IP configuration information from the DHCP
server. The configuration information typically consists of an IP address and a default gateway.

Interactive Media Activity   Point and Click: Router Redundancy Operation

After completing this activity, you will understand basic router redundancy operation.

ICMP Router Discovery Protocol (IRDP)

Some newer IP hosts use *ICMP Router Discovery Protocol (IRDP)*, defined in RFC 1256, to find a new router when a route becomes unavailable. A host that uses IRDP listens for hello multicast messages from the router that the host is configured to use. The host switches to an alternate router when it no longer receives those hello messages. IRDP has a default advertisement rate of once every 7 to 10 minutes. The default lifetime is 30 minutes. These default timer values mean that IRDP is not suitable to detect first-hop failures.

Enabling IRDP Processing

The only required task for configuring IRDP routing on a specified interface is to enable IRDP processing on an interface. Use the command **ip irdp** in interface configuration mode.

When enabling IRDP processing, the default parameters apply. When enabled, IRDP uses the following defaults:

- Broadcast IRDP advertisements
- Maximum interval between advertisements—600 seconds
- Minimum interval between advertisements—450 seconds
- Preference—0

To display IRDP values, use the command **show ip irdp**.

Troubleshooting IRDP

Use the **debug ip icmp** command to display information on ICMP transactions. This command helps determine whether the router is sending or receiving ICMP messages. Use this command when troubleshooting an end-to-end connection problem. The **no** form of this command disables debugging output.

Hot Standby Router Protocol (HSRP)

One way to achieve near-100-percent network uptime is to use *Hot Standby Router Protocol (HSRP)* (see RFC 2281). HSRP provides network redundancy for IP networks, ensuring that user traffic immediately and transparently recovers from first-hop failures in network edge devices or access circuits.

By sharing an IP address and a MAC address, a set of two or more routers can operate as a single router called a *virtual router*. This set of routers is known as an *HSRP group* or a standby group. A single router elected from the group is responsible for forwarding the packets that hosts send to the virtual router. To minimize network traffic, only the active and standby routers send periodic HSRP messages as soon as the protocol has completed the election process. If the local segment has only two routers, one is the active router and one is the standby router, as shown in Figures 6-12 and 6-13. If the active router fails, the standby router takes over as the active router, as shown in Figures 6-14 and 6-15. If the standby router fails or becomes the active router, another router is elected as the standby router. Hosts continue to forward IP packets to a consistent IP and virtual MAC address. The changeover between routes is transparent to the end workstation.

Figure 6-12 In a Stable Network, an Active Router Forwards All Traffic for an HSRP Group

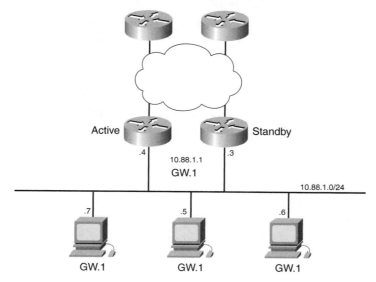

Figure 6-13 The Active Router Is Assigned the Virtual MAC Address

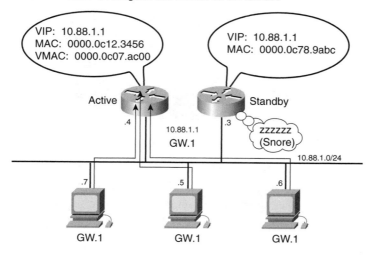

VIP = Virtual IP Address
VMAC = Virtual MAC Address

Figure 6-14 When the Active Router Goes Down, the Standby Router Immediately Takes Over

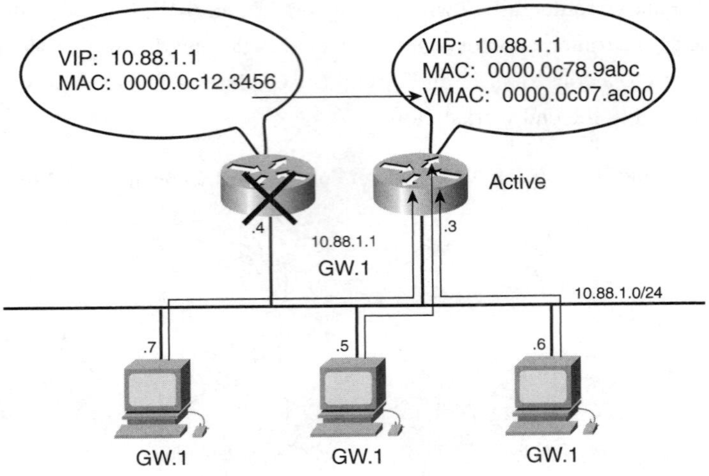

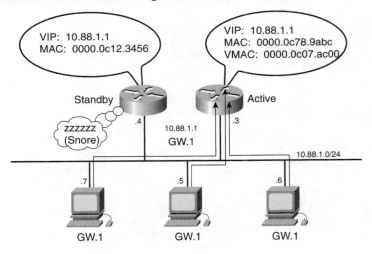

Figure 6-15 The New Active Router Is Assigned the Virtual MAC Address

On a particular LAN, multiple hot standby groups might coexist and overlap. Each standby group emulates a single virtual router. The individual routers might participate in multiple groups. In this case, the router maintains separate states and timers for each group. Each standby group has a single virtual MAC and IP address.

The HSRP MAC address is derived from the HSRP group number. The HSRP MAC address has the form 0000.0c07.ac*xx*, where *xx* is the HSRP group number.

Virtual Router Redundancy Protocol (VRRP)

Virtual Router Redundancy Protocol (VRRP) is an Internet Engineering Task Force (IETF) proposed standard (see RFC 2338) that is nearly identical to the Cisco-proprietary HSRP. As a standards-based solution introduced in 1998, VRRP is now being made available to provide interoperability using equipment from multiple vendors.

IP routing redundancy is designed to allow for transparent failover at the first-hop router.

Both HSRP and VRRP allow two or more devices to work together in a group, sharing a single virtual IP address. The virtual IP address is configured in each end-user workstation as a default gateway address and is cached in the host ARP cache.

In an HSRP or VRRP group, one router is elected to handle all requests sent to the virtual IP address. An HSRP group has an active router, a standby router, and perhaps many listening routers. A VRRP group has one master router and one or more backup routers, as shown in Figure 6-16.

Figure 6-16 VRRP Uses a Master Router and Backup Routers, Similar to HSRP Active and Standby Routers

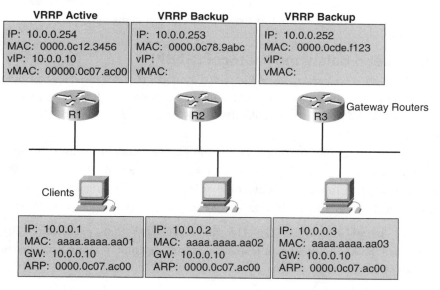

When a group initializes, messages are exchanged to elect the active or master router. Within these messages, information, such as group identifier, *priority*, virtual IP address, and hello advertisement interval, is exchanged. The routers in a group continue to exchange these messages at a configured interval. In HSRP, both the active and standby routers send periodic hello messages. In VRRP, only the master sends periodic messages, called *advertisements*.

Using the information in these messages, a standby or backup router can determine whether it needs to take over the active or master role in a group. If a hello message is not received from the active or master router in the defined interval, the standby or backup router automatically assumes the role of active or master. When the original active or master router becomes available again, it sends out a hello or advertisement message and regains the lead IP packet-forwarding role within the group. All this is transparent to the end user traversing this first-hop group. Connectivity is maintained with little or no loss of traffic and functionality.

Cisco recommends using HSRP, because it is a proven technology that has superior convergence characteristics. Use VRRP only when local subnet interoperability is required with equipment from another vendor.

VRRP is supported on Cisco 2600XM, 3600, and 3700 routers running Cisco IOS software Release 12.2T or later.

Troubleshooting VRRP

Customizing the behavior of VRRP is optional. As soon as a VRRP group is enabled, that group is operating. Always customize VRRP before enabling it. Otherwise, a router could become the master virtual router before the customization is complete.

Gateway Load Balancing Protocol (GLBP)

Like HSRP and VRRP, *Gateway Load Balancing Protocol (GLBP)* provides nonstop path redundancy for IP by sharing protocol and MAC addresses between redundant gateways. GLBP also allows a group of routers to share the load of the default gateway on a LAN. This load sharing improves performance by facilitating better use of network resources when multiple upstream paths are available and increases reliability and network availability by removing the single point of failure—the first-hop router. GLBP allows a router to automatically assume the forwarding function of another router in the group if a failure occurs in any other gateway router. The various GLBP components and concepts are defined as follows:

- **Active Virtual Gateway (AVG)**—One virtual gateway within a particular GLBP group is elected the AVG. The AVG is responsible for the operation of protocol, such as allocating MAC addresses.

- **Virtual Forwarder (VF)**—An abstract entity within a GLBP gateway that might assume responsibility for a virtual MAC address.

- **Active Virtual Forwarder (AVF)**—One VF within a particular GLBP group is elected the AVF. The AVF is responsible for forwarding packets sent to a particular virtual MAC address.

- **Primary Virtual Forwarder (PVF)**—A PVF is a VF that has been assigned the virtual MAC address by the AVG.
- **Secondary Virtual Forwarder (SVF)**—An SVF is a VF that has learned the virtual MAC address from a hello message.

Cisco generally recommends the use of GLBP in place of HSRP when more than two routers reside on a single LAN segment because of its built-in load-balancing feature. GLBP performs a similar, but not identical, function for the user as the HSRP and the VRRP. HSRP and VRRP allow multiple routers to participate in a virtual router group configured with a virtual IP address. One member is elected as the active router to forward packets sent to the virtual IP address for the group. The other routers in the group are redundant until the active router fails. These standby routers have unused bandwidth that the protocol is not using. Although multiple virtual router groups can be configured for the same set of routers, the hosts must be configured for different default gateways, which results in an extra administrative burden. GLBP provides load balancing over multiple routers (gateways) using a single virtual IP address and multiple virtual MAC addresses. Each host is configured with the same virtual IP address, and all routers in the virtual router group participate in forwarding packets. Figures 6-17 to 6-20 illustrate the operation of GLBP.

GLBP is supported on the following Cisco hardware platforms, with Cisco IOS software Release 12.2(15)T or later:

- 1700 series routers
- 2600 series routers
- 3620 routers
- 3631 routers
- 3640 routers
- 3660 routers
- 3725 routers
- 3745 routers
- 7100 series routers
- 7200 series routers
- 7400 series routers
- 7500 series routers
- Catalyst 6000 MSFC
- Catalyst 6500 Supervisor Engine 720

Figure 6-17 GLBP Lets Distinct Hosts Receive Distinct ARP Replies, with Distinct MAC Addresses Associated with the Same Virtual IP Address

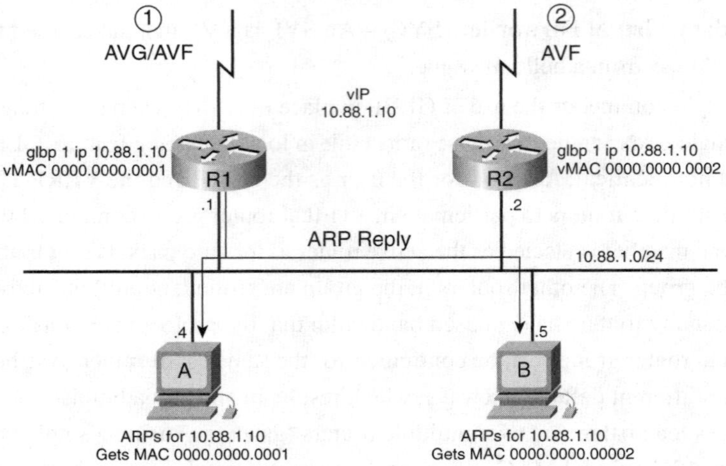

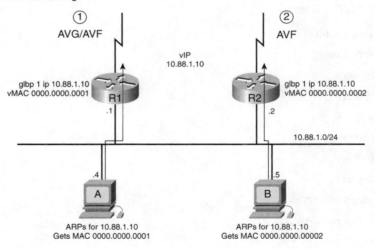

Figure 6-18 Distinct MAC Addresses Associated with the Same Virtual IP Address Permit Load Balancing

Figure 6-19 GLBP Has a Failover Mechanism, Just as VRRP and HSRP Do

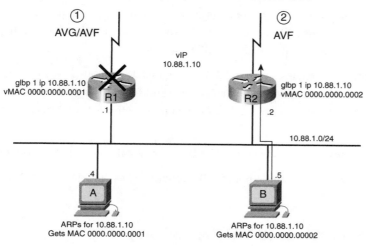

Figure 6-20 During Failover, GLBP Shifts the Role of the Virtual MAC Address Used by One Host and Associated with the Virtual IP

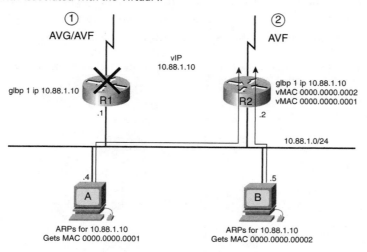

Troubleshooting GLBP

GLBP allows traffic from a single common subnet to go through multiple redundant gateways while using a single virtual IP address. GLBP provides the same level of first-hop failure recovery capability as that provided by HSRP and VRRP.

Cisco IOS software contains **show** and **debug** commands to allow network operators to determine the status of GLBP. These commands are useful for verifying the operation of GLBP and verifying that the design goals are being met relative to tracked objects and forwarder states.

Use the **show glbp** command to display GLBP operational information and statistics.

To display debugging messages about GLBP conditions, use the **debug condition glbp** command.

Single Router Mode (SRM) Redundancy

Single Router Mode (SRM) redundancy provides an alternative to having both MSFCs in a chassis active at the same time.

The designated MSFC is the MSFC that comes up first or has been up the longest. The designated MSFC can be the MSFC in slot 1 or the MSFC in slot 2. There is no mechanism to decide which MSFC is the designated one; the first to come online is the designated MSFC. Figure 6-21 shows two Catalyst 6500 switches, each with redundant MSFCs.

Figure 6-21 Single Router Mode Is the Preferred Redundancy Mechanism to Use with Dual MSFCs in a 6500 Chassis

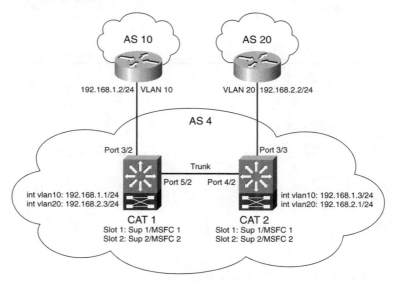

Using SRM redundancy, only the designated MSFC is visible to the network at any given time. The nondesignated MSFC is booted up completely and participates in configuration synchronization, which is automatically enabled when entering SRM. The configuration of the nondesignated MSFC is exactly the same as the designated MSFC, but its interfaces are kept in a "line down" state and are not visible to the network. Processes, such as routing protocols, are created on the nondesignated MSFC and the designated MSFC. All nondesignated MSFC interfaces are in a "line down" state and do not send updates to or receive updates from the network.

When the designated MSFC fails, the nondesignated MSFC changes its state to become the designated MSFC, and the interface states change to "link up." The MSFC builds its routing table while the existing Supervisor Engine switch processor entries are used to forward Layer 3 traffic. After the newly designated MSFC builds its routing table, the entries in the switch processor are updated.

SRM is Cisco's recommended method of internal MSFC redundancy.

Server Load Balancing (SLB)

Server Load Balancing (SLB) is an IOS-based solution defining a virtual server that represents a group of real servers in a server farm, as shown in Figure 6-22.

Figure 6-22 SLB Permits Server Redundancy by Way of a Virtual Server

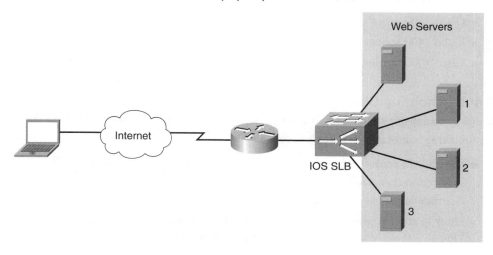

This environment connects clients to the IP address of a single virtual server. The virtual server IP address, as shown in Figure 6-23, is configured as a loopback address, or a secondary IP address, on each of the real servers.

Figure 6-23 SLB Relies on a Virtual Server with a Virtual IP Address

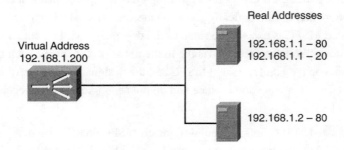

When a client initiates a connection to the virtual server, the SLB function chooses a real server for the connection based on a load-balancing algorithm. The network gains scalability and availability when virtual servers represent server farms. The addition of new servers and the removal or failure of existing servers can occur at any time without affecting the availability of the virtual server.

SLB is supported on the following platforms:

- Catalyst G-L3 series
- Catalyst 6000 series
- Cisco 7200 series
- Cisco 7400 series
- Cisco 10000 series

Troubleshooting SLB

To obtain and display runtime information when monitoring and maintaining IOS SLB, use the following commands in EXEC mode:

- **show ip slb conns** [**vserver** *virtserver-name*] [**client** *ip-address*] [**detail**]—Displays all connections handled by IOS SLB or, optionally, only those connections associated with a particular virtual server or client.
- **show ip slb dfp** [**agent** *ip_addr port*] [**detail**] [**weights**]—Displays information about Dynamic Feedback Protocol (DFP) and DFP agents and about the weights assigned to real servers.
- **show ip slb reals** [**vserver** *virtserver-name*] [**detail**]—Displays information about the real servers defined to IOS SLB.
- **show ip slb serverfarms** [**name** *serverfarm-name*] [**detail**]—Displays information about the server farms defined to IOS SLB.

- **show ip slb stats**—Displays IOS SLB statistics.

- **show ip slb sticky** [**client** *ip-address*]—Displays information about the sticky connections defined to IOS SLB.

- **show ip slb vservers** [**name** *virtserver-name*] [**detail**]—Displays information about the virtual servers defined to IOS SLB.

The **debug** commands related to the IOS SLB feature are as follows:

- **all**—Displays all debug messages for IOS SLB.

- **conns**—Displays debug messages for all connections being handled by IOS SLB, including Wireless Session Protocol (WSP) events and states.

- **dfp**—Displays debug messages for Dynamic Feedback Protocol (DFP). To display debug messages for the DFP agent subsystem, use **debug ip dfp agent**.

- **firewallfarm**—Displays debug messages related to firewall load balancing.

- **icmp**—Displays all ICMP debug messages for IOS SLB.

- **natpool**—Displays debug messages related to the IOS SLB client NAT pool.

- **probe**—Displays debug messages related to probes.

- **reals**—Displays debug messages for all real servers defined to IOS SLB.

- **replication**—Displays debug messages related to IOS SLB stateful backup virtual servers.

- **sessions**—Displays debug messages for all sessions being handled by IOS SLB.

- **vservers**—Displays debug messages for all virtual servers defined to IOS SLB.

Having taken a brief tour of VRRP, GLBP, SRM, and SLB, we now return the focus to HSRP. The operation, configuration, and monitoring of HSRP are discussed. The detailed descriptions of VRRP, GLBP, SRM, and SLB operation, configuration, and monitoring are beyond the scope of this book and course.

HSRP Operations

The main components of HSRP are an active router, a standby router, and a virtual router. In Figure 6-24, the active router forwards data packets and transmits hello messages. The standby router monitors the active router's status and quickly begins forwarding packets if the active router fails. The standby router also transmits hello messages to other routers in the HSRP group. The virtual router doesn't really exist. It simply represents a consistently available router with an IP address and MAC address to the hosts on a network.

Figure 6-24 HSRP Standby Groups Consist of Multiple Routers Performing Specific Roles

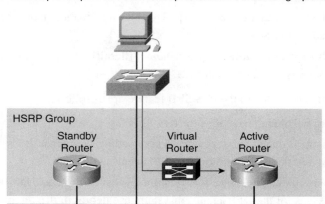

It is possible that several other routers exist in an HSRP standby group. These other routers monitor HSRP hello messages, but do not respond. They function as normal routers that forward packets sent to them but do not forward packets addressed to the virtual router. These additional HSRP routers remain in init state.

How does the standby router know when the active router fails? The standby router stops receiving hello messages from the active router and takes on the role of the active router. Because the hosts are using a virtual IP and MAC address, the hosts see minimal or no service disruption.

If both the active and standby routers fail, all other routers in the group contend for the active and standby roles. The router with the lowest MAC address becomes the active router unless an HSRP priority is configured.

To facilitate load sharing, a single router might be a member of multiple HSRP standby groups on a single segment. Each standby group emulates a single virtual router. A LAN can have up to 255 standby groups. Multiple HSRP groups are also supported on VLAN, port-channel, and Bridge Group Virtual Interface (BVI) interfaces.

In Figure 6-25, both Router A and Router B are members of Groups 1 and 2. Router A is the active forwarding router for Group 1 and the standby router for Group 2. Router B is the active forwarding router for Group 2 and the standby router for Group 1.

Routers also can simultaneously provide redundant backup and perform load sharing across different IP subnets, as shown in Figure 6-26.

Figure 6-25 Routers Can Belong to Multiple Groups on the Same Subnet in a VLAN

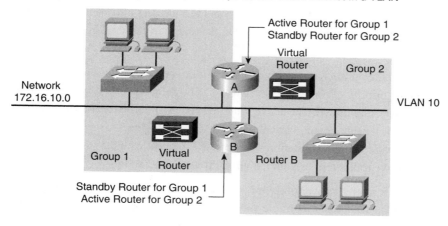

Figure 6-26 Routers Can Belong to Multiple Groups in Multiple VLANs

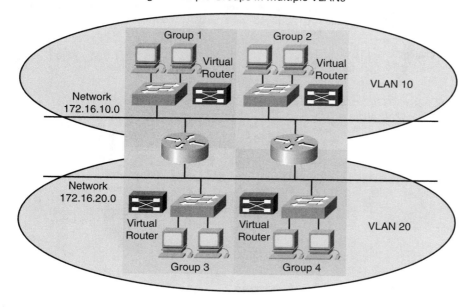

This is possible because for each standby group, an IP address and a single, well-known MAC address with a unique group identifier are allocated to the group.

A group's IP address is in the range of addresses belonging to the subnet in use on the LAN. However, the group's IP address must differ from the addresses allocated as interface addresses on all routers and hosts on the LAN, including virtual IP addresses assigned to other HSRP groups.

Initially, the standby group has no active router. Within the standby group, the router with the highest standby priority becomes the active router. The default priority for an HSRP router is 100, which can be configured. The active router responds to traffic for the virtual router. If an end station sends a packet to the virtual router MAC address, the active router receives and processes that packet. If an end station sends an ARP request with the virtual router IP address, the active router replies with the virtual router MAC address.

In Figure 6-27, Router A has a priority of 200 and Router B has a default priority of 100. Router A assumes the active router role and forwards all frames addressed to the well-known MAC address of 0000.0c07.ac*xx*, where *xx* is the HSRP group identifier. In Figure 6-27, the HSRP group number is 0x0a or 10. The well-known MAC address of 0000.0c07.ac*xx* is used for all HSRP configurations, unless HSRP is configured to use a different MAC address.

Figure 6-27   The Router with the Highest HSRP Priority Becomes the Active Router. The Active Router Responds to ARP Requests with the MAC Address of the Virtual Router.

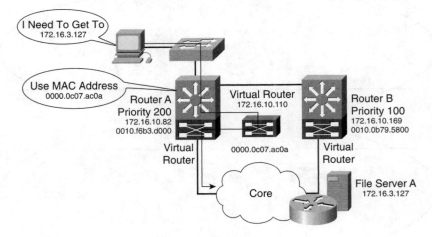

The Virtual Router MAC Address

In Figure 6-28, the MAC address used by the virtual router is made up of the following three components:

- **Vendor ID**—The first 3 bytes of the MAC address.
- **HSRP code**—2 bytes (always 07.ac) indicating that the MAC address is for an HSRP virtual router.
- **Group ID**—The last byte of the MAC address.

Figure 6-28 *The HSRP Well-Known Virtual MAC Address Is Crucial to HSRP Operation*

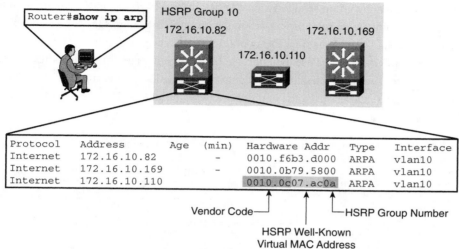

To display the virtual IP and MAC address, use the command **show standby** in privileged EXEC mode, as shown in Example 6-1.

Example 6-1 *The* **show standby** *Command Is Very Useful in Monitoring HSRP and Verifying HSRP Operation*

```
Router#show standby
FastEthernet0/0 - Group 0
  Local state is Active, priority 100
  Hellotime 3 holdtime 10
  Next hello sent in 00:00:00.630
  Hot standby IP address is 10.1.1.1 configured
  Active router is local
  Standby router is 10.1.1.3 expires in 00:00:09
  Standby virtual mac address is 0000.0c07.ac00
FastEthernet0/1 - Group 0
  Local state is Standby, priority 100
  Hellotime 3 holdtime 10
  Next hello sent in 00:00:01.542
  Hot standby IP address is 10.1.3.1 configured
  Active router is 10.1.2.3 expires in 00:00:08
  Standby router is local
  Standby virtual mac address is 0000.0c07.ac00
```

HSRP Messages

All routers in a standby group send or receive HSRP messages. These messages are used to determine and maintain the router roles within the group. HSRP messages are encapsulated in the data portion of User Datagram Protocol (UDP) packets (see Figure 6-29) and use port number 1985. HSRP messages use the interface IP address, not the virtual IP address, as the source IP address. The HSRP messages are sent to the destination multicast address (224.0.0.2). This is the multicast address used to communicate with all routers. The Time-To-Live (TTL) on the packet is set to 1.

Figure 6-29 HSRP Messages Use the Data Portion of the UDP Segment

1 Octet	1 Octet	1 Octet	1 Octet
Version	Op Code	State	Hello Time
Holdtime	Priority	Group	Reserved
Authentication Data			
Authentication Data			
Virtual IP Address			

The HSRP message fields are as follows:

- **Version**—Indicates the version of HSRP.
- **Op Code**—Describes the type of message contained in this packet:
  - **Hello = 0** Messages are sent to indicate that a router is running and can become either the active or standby router.
  - **Coup = 1** Messages are sent when a router wants to become the active router.
  - **Resign = 2** Messages are sent when a router no longer wants to be the active router.
- **State**—Describes the current state (active, standby, init) of the router sending the message.
- **Hellotime**—Meaningful only in hello messages. This field stores the approximate period, in seconds, between the hello messages that the router sends.
- *Holdtime*—Meaningful only in hello messages. This field stores the amount of time that the current hello message should be valid. The time is given in seconds.
- **Priority**—Used to elect the active and standby routers. When the priorities of two different routers are compared, the router with the numerically higher priority wins. In the case of routers with equal priority, the router with the higher IP address wins.
- **Group**—Identifies the standby group. Values of 0 to 255 are valid.
- **Reserved**—An 8-bit field reserved for future use.

- **Authentication Data**—Contains a clear-text eight-character reused password.
- **Virtual IP Address**—Contains the IP address of the virtual router used by this group.

Internally, each router in the standby group implements a state machine. Only the active and standby routers send periodic HSRP messages after the protocol has completed the election process.

HSRP States

HSRP defines six *HSRP states* in which an HSRP-enabled router can exist:

- **Initial**—The state from which the routers begin the HSRP process. This state indicates that HSRP is not running. It is entered via a configuration change or when an interface first comes up.
- **Learn**—The router has not determined the virtual IP address and has not yet seen an authenticated hello message from the active router. In this state, the router is still waiting to hear from the active router.
- **Listen**—The router knows the virtual IP address but is neither the active router nor the standby router. It listens for hello messages from those routers. Routers other than the active and standby router remain in the listen state.
- **Speak**—The router sends periodic hello messages and actively participates in the election of the active or standby router. A router cannot enter Speak state unless it has the virtual IP address.
- **Standby**—The router is a candidate to become the next active router and sends periodic hello messages. Excluding transient conditions, there must be at most one router in the group in Standby state.
- **Active**—The router is currently forwarding packets that are sent to the group virtual MAC address. The router sends periodic hello messages. Excluding transient conditions, there must be at most one router in Active state in the HSRP group.

 Interactive Media Activity   Drag and Drop: HSRP States

After completing this activity, you will have a basic understanding of HSRP states.

HSRP Configuration

To configure a router as a member of an HSRP standby group, enter the following interface configuration command:

```
standby group-number ip virtual-ip-address
```

- *group-number*—Optional. The HSRP group to which this interface belongs. Specifying a unique group number in the **standby** command lets you create multiple HSRP groups. The default group is 0.

- *virtual-ip-address*—The IP address of the virtual HSRP router.

In Cisco IOS software Release 12.1.3.T and later, HSRP has been changed to support ICMP redirect. Prior versions of IOS require disabling of ICMP redirects. While running HSRP, it is important that the end-user stations cannot discover the actual MAC addresses of the routers as the destination MAC for the default gateway. Any protocol that tells a host the router's actual address must be disabled. To ensure that the actual addresses of the participating HSRP routers are not discovered, enabling HSRP on a Cisco router interface automatically disables ICMP redirects on that interface.

The **standby ip** command changes the interface to the appropriate state. Figure 6-30 shows an example of the state message, automatically generated upon successful enabling of HSRP.

Figure 6-30 Console Messages Indicate HSRP State Changes

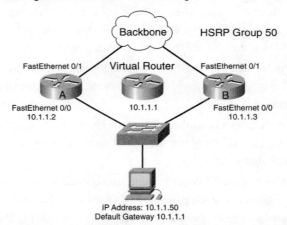

```
1w0d: %STANDBY-6-STATECHANGE: Standby: 50:
FastEthernet0/0 state
Speak     -> Standby
1w0d: %STANDBY-6-STATECHANGE: Standby: 50:
FastEthernet0/0 state
Standby    -> Active
```

Output from the **show running-config** command shows the following:

- Interface FastEthernet 0/0 is a member of HSRP standby Group 50.

- The virtual router IP address is 10.1.1.1.

- ICMP redirects are disabled.

To remove an interface from an HSRP group, enter the **no standby group ip** command.

How HSRP Addresses Redundancy Issues

HSRP provides a way for end nodes to keep communicating between networks even if individual local routers become unavailable. HSRP routers on a LAN segment or VLAN communicate among themselves to designate three possible router states:

- Active
- Standby
- Init

If an end node sends a packet to the virtual MAC address, the active router receives that packet and processes it. If an end node sends an ARP request, the active router replies with the virtual MAC address. The routers participating in HSRP can be configured to respond with their burned-in MAC address (BIA) instead of a virtual MAC address.

In Figure 6-31, Anderson is configured to use the virtual router as the default. Only the virtual router appears in the Anderson configuration. Broadway is not listed. Upon booting, the routers might elect Broadway as the active router so that Broadway will deliver packets from Anderson. If Broadway or its LAN interface goes offline, Central Park takes over as the active router, continuing with the delivery of Anderson packets. The changes taking place in the network remain transparent to Anderson. If a third HSRP router is added to the LAN segment, this router begins acting as the new standby router but remains in init state.

Figure 6-31 Only the IP Address of the Virtual Router Appears on the Anderson TCP/IP Configuration

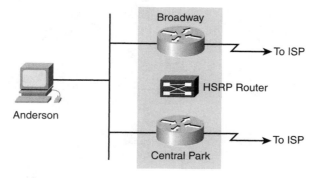

HSRP also works for proxy ARP. When an active HSRP router receives an ARP request for a node that is not on the local LAN, it replies with the virtual MAC address. If the router that originally sent the ARP reply later loses its connection, the new active router can still deliver

the traffic. Although HSRP works with proxy ARP configurations, it is not a recommended configuration for administrative and security reasons.

HSRP Standby Priority

Each standby group has its own active and standby routers. The network administrator can assign a priority value to each router in a standby group. This lets the administrator control the order in which active routers for that group are selected. To set a router's priority value, enter the following command in interface configuration mode:

standby *group-number* **priority** *priority-value*

- *group-number*—Optional. The HSRP standby group. The range is 0 to 255.
- *priority-value*—The number that prioritizes a potential hot standby router. The range is 0 to 255. The default is 100.

The router in an HSRP group with the highest priority becomes the forwarding router. The tiebreaker for matching priorities is the higher IP address.

Figure 6-32 shows that Router A FastEthernet 0/0 has a priority value of 150 in HSRP standby Group 50.

Figure 6-32 The Priority Value Determines the Active HSRP Router for an HSRP Group

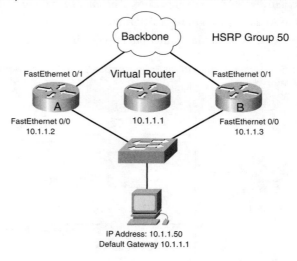

```
A (config-if) #standby 50 priority 150
```

HSRP Standby Preempt

The standby router assumes the active router role when the active router fails or is removed from service. This new active router remains as the forwarding router even when the former active router with the higher priority regains service in the network.

The former active router can be configured to resume the forwarding router role from a router with a lower priority. To make a router resume the forwarding router role, enter the command **standby** *group-number* **preempt** in interface configuration mode.

When the **standby preempt** command is issued, the interface changes to the appropriate state, as shown in Figure 6-33.

Figure 6-33 The **preempt** Option Permits a Router to Immediately Take Over as the Active Router Whenever the Priority Is Higher

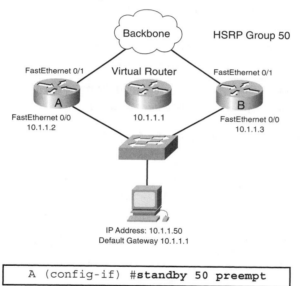

```
A (config-if) #standby 50 preempt
```

The following message is automatically generated as soon as the router becomes active in the network:

```
3w1d : %STANDBY-6-STATECHANGE: STANDBY: 50: FastEthernet0/0 state standby Active
```

HSRP Hello Timers

An HSRP-enabled router sends hello messages to indicate that it is running and that it can become either the active or standby router. The hello message contains the router's priority, as well as a hellotime and holdtime value. The hellotime value indicates the interval between the hello messages what the router sends. The holdtime value specifies how long the current hello message is considered valid. If an active router sends a hello message, receiving routers consider that hello message valid for one holdtime. The holdtime value should be at least three times the value of the hellotime.

The hellotime and holdtime parameters can be configured. To configure the time between hellos and the time before other group routers declare the active or standby router "down," enter the following command in interface configuration mode:

standby *group-number* **timers** *hellotime holdtime*

- *group-number*—Optional. The group number on the interface to which the timers apply. The default is 0.
- *hellotime*—The **hello interval** in seconds. This is an integer from 1 to 255. The default is 3 seconds.
- *holdtime*—The time before the active or standby router is declared down. This is an integer from 1 to 255. The default is 10 seconds.

In Figure 6-34, the hellotime is set to 5 seconds, and the holdtime is set to 15 seconds. To reinstate the default standby timer values, enter the **no standby group timers** command.

Figure 6-34 The HSRP Hello and Hold Timers Can Be Configured

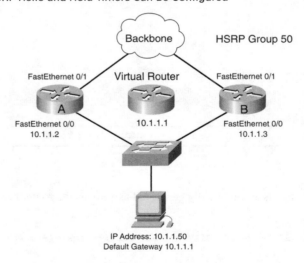

```
A (config-if) #standby 50 timers 5 15
```

HSRP Interface Tracking

In many situations, an interface's status directly affects which router needs to become the active router, particularly when each router in an HSRP group has a different path to resources within the campus network.

In Figure 6-35, Routers A and B reside in a branch office. These two routers each support a FastEthernet link to the backbone. Router A has the higher priority and is the active forwarding router for standby Group 50. Router B is the standby router for that group. Routers A and B exchange hello messages through their FastEthernet 0/0 interfaces.

Figure 6-35 The HSRP Interface Tracking Option Lets the Standby Router Become Active When an Uplink Fails on the Active Router

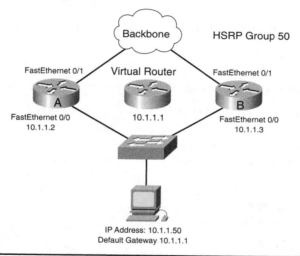

```
A (config-if) #standby 50 track fastethernet 0/1 55
```

If Router A FastEthernet 0/1 goes down, Router A loses the direct connection to the backbone. Although this doesn't prevent traffic from reaching the backbone, it does lead to an inefficient traffic flow. The FastEthernet 0/0 interface on Router A is still active, so packets destined for the core are still sent to Router A and are forwarded in turn to Router B, regardless of HSRP. The **standby track** option can be used to prevent this situation (in conjunction with the **standby preempt** command).

To configure HSRP *tracking*, enter the following command in interface configuration mode:

standby *group-number* **track** *type number interface-priority*

The value indicated by the **standby track** command is the value that gets decremented from the node's priority if the specified interface goes down. Multiple **standby track** commands can be used to list multiple interfaces. If multiple interfaces fail, the decrement values are cumulative. For example, if the FastEthernet 0/0 interface on Router A goes down, the router's HSRP priority is lowered by 55. Because this is lower than the default priority being used by Router B, Router B takes over as the active router, providing optimal flow to the backbone.

Verify HSRP Configuration

To display the status of the HSRP router, enter the following command in privileged mode:

show standby *type-number group brief*

- *type-number*—Optional. The target interface type and number for which output is displayed.
- *group*—Optional. A specific HSRP group on the interface for which output is displayed.
- *brief*—Optional. Displays a single line of output summarizing each standby group.

If none of the optional interface parameters are used, the **show standby** command displays HSRP information for all interfaces, as shown in Example 6-2.

Example 6-2 *The* **show standby** *Command Displays Useful HSRP Information*

```
ISP#show standby
FastEthernet0/0 - Group 50
  Local state is Active, priority 95, may preempt
  Hellotime 3 holdtime 10
  Next hello sent in 00:00:00.782
  Hot standby IP address is 10.1.1.1 configured
  Active router is local
  Standby router is 10.1.1.3 expires in 00:00:09
  Standby virtual mac address is 0000.0c07.ac32
  Tracking interface states for 1 interface, 0 up:
    Down FastEthernet0/1 Priority decrement: 55
```

Lab 6.5.1 Hot Standby Router Protocol

In this lab exercise, you configure HSRP on a pair of routers to provide redundant router services to a network.

Lab 6.5.2   Multigroup Hot Standby Router Protocol

In this lab exercise, you configure Multigroup Hot Standby Router Protocol
(MHSRP) on a pair of routers to provide redundant router services to a network.

HSRP over Trunk Links

To configure HSRP over an Interswitch Link (ISL) between VLANs, follow these steps:

Step 1   Define the encapsulation format.

Step 2   Define an IP address.

Step 3   Enable HSRP.

HSRP is also supported over 802.1Q trunks.

Figure 6-36 and Example 6-3 illustrate the configuration for two HSRP-enabled routers participating in two separate VLANs using ISL. Running HSRP over ISL allows users to configure redundancy between multiple routers that are configured as front ends for VLAN IP
subnets. By configuring HSRP over ISL, you can eliminate situations in which a single point
of failure causes traffic interruptions.

Figure 6-36 Network Topology for Configuring HSRP over Trunk Links

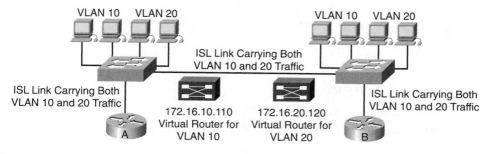

Example 6-3 *A Complete HSRP Configuration Involves HSRP Groups, Priority, and Preempt Options*

```
! Configuration for Router A:
interface FastEthernet 1/1.10
encapsulation isl 10
ip address 172.16.10.2 255.255.255.0
standby 1 ip 172.16.10.110
```

continues

Example 6-3 *A Complete HSRP Configuration Involves HSRP Groups, Priority, and Preempt Options (Continued)*

```
standby 1 priority 105
standby 1 preempt
interface FastEthernet 1/1.20
encapsulation isl 20
ip address 172.16.20.2 255.255.255.0
standby 2 ip 172.16.20.120
standby 2 priority 50
***Production, insert 2-point rule here.
! Configuration for Router B:
interface FastEthernet 1/1.10
encapsulation isl 10
ip address 172.16.10.3 255.255.255.0
standby 1 ip 172.16.10.110
standby 1 priority 50
interface FastEthernet 1/1.20
encapsulation isl 20
ip address 172.16.20.3 255.255.255.0
standby 2 ip 172.16.20.120
standby 2 priority 105
standby 2 preempt
```

Troubleshooting HSRP

To enable HSRP debugging, the **debug standby** command is used to enable output of HSRP state and packet information for all standby groups on all interfaces.

A debug condition was added in Cisco IOS software Release 12.0(2.1) that allows the output from the **debug standby** command to be filtered based on interface and group number. This command uses the debug condition paradigm introduced in Cisco IOS software Release 12.0:

```
debug condition standby interface group
```

The interface specified must be a valid interface that can support HSRP.

The debug conditions can be set for groups that do not exist, thereby allowing debug information to be captured during the initialization of a new group.

The standby debug order must be configured for any debug output to be produced. If no standby debug conditions are specified, output is produced for all groups on all interfaces. Configuring at least one standby debug condition causes the output to be filtered.

Summary

The resiliency and availability features supported by the Cisco Catalyst family of switches are well-suited to campus LAN designs that achieve high availability through a combination of device-level and network-level redundancy. The network resiliency features span Layer 2 and Layer 3 boundaries and may be deployed where needed throughout the three-tiered Access, Distribution, Core design model.

With some care in configuring the redundant network and tuning the protocol timers within the switches, interruption of network services caused by network infrastructure failures can be held in the range of 0 to 10 seconds. With these short failover times, very high network availability can be achieved by controlling the overall network failure rate.

After completing this chapter, you should be able to

- Implement hardware redundancy on the Catalyst series of switches
- Identify the virtual router for a given set of switch block devices
- Configure HSRP on the switch block devices to ensure continual inter-VLAN routing
- Maintain packet forwarding by configuring the active and standby HSRP router roles
- Ensure the role of the active router by assigning a *preempt* status

Key Terms

default gateway   Provides a definitive location for IP packets to be sent in case the source device has no IP routing functionality built into it. This is the method most end stations use to access nonlocal networks. The default gateway can be set manually or learned from a DHCP server.

Gateway Load Balancing Protocol (GLBP)   A Cisco-proprietary protocol that protects data traffic from a failed router or circuit, like HSRP and VRRP, while allowing packet load sharing between a group of redundant routers.

hello interval   The time that elapses between the sending of HSRP hello packets. The default is 3 seconds.

holdtime   The time it takes before HSRP routers in an HSRP group declare the active router to be down. The default is 10 seconds.

Hot Standby Router Protocol (HSRP)   The Layer 3 Cisco-proprietary protocol that allows a set of routers on a LAN segment to work together to present the appearance of a single virtual router or default gateway to the hosts on the segment. HSRP enables fast rerouting to alternate default gateways should one of them fail.

HSRP group   Routers on a subnet, VLAN, or subset of a subnet participating in an HSRP process. Each group shares a virtual IP address. The group is defined on the HSRP routers.

HSRP state   The descriptor for the current HSRP condition for a particular router interface and a particular HSRP group. The possible HSRP states are Initial, Learn, Listen, Speak, Standby, and Active.

ICMP Router Discovery Protocol (IRDP)   Hosts supporting IRDP dynamically discover routers to access nonlocal networks. IRDP allows hosts to locate routers (default gateways). Router discovery packets are exchanged between hosts (IRDP servers) and routers (IRDP clients).

preempt   An HSRP feature that lets a router with the highest priority immediately assume the active role at any time.

priority   An HSRP parameter used to facilitate the election of an active HSRP router for an HSRP group on a LAN segment. The default priority is 100. The router with the greatest priority for each group is elected as the active forwarder for that group.

proxy ARP   Proxy ARP allows an Ethernet host with no knowledge of routing to communicate with hosts on other networks or subnets. Such a host assumes that all hosts are on the same local segment and that it can use ARP to determine their hardware addresses. The proxy ARP function is handled by routers.

Server Load Balancing (SLB)   Balances services across numerous servers at speeds of millions of packets per second. Commonly deployed with the Cisco IOS software on Catalyst 6000 family of switches. SLB is a software solution using the advanced application-specific integrated circuits (ASICs) on the Catalyst 6000.

Single Router Mode (SRM)   Addresses the drawback of the previous HSRP-based MSFC redundancy scheme (designated MSFC versus nondesignated MSFC). When SRM is enabled, the nondesignated router is online, but all its interfaces are down. Thus, it does not hold any routing table information. This means that if the DR fails, there will be some delay before the nondesignated router coming online has a complete route table. To help account for this, the information being used before the failure by the Supervisor for Layer 3 forwarding is maintained and updated with any new information from the new designated router.

tracking   This HSRP feature allows you to specify other interfaces on the router for the HSRP process to monitor. If the tracked interface goes down, the HSRP standby router takes over as the active router. This process is facilitated by a decrement to the HSRP priority resulting from the tracked interface line protocol going down.

Virtual Router Redundancy Protocol (VRRP)   Provides functions equivalent to HSRP but is supported by multiple vendors. It is designed to eliminate a single point of failure that is unavoidable in static default routing environments.

Check Your Understanding

Use the following review questions to test your understanding of the concepts covered in this chapter. Answers are listed in Appendix A, "Check Your Understanding Answer Key."

1. With redundant Supervisor Engines and MSFCs in a Catalyst 6500 switch running SRM, which of the following statements is accurate?

    A. The nondesignated MSFC is active and has the same configuration as the designated MSFC.

    B. The nondesignated MSFC is inactive and has the same configuration as the designated MSFC.

    C. The nondesignated MSFC is inactive and has a configuration distinct from the designated MSFC.

    D. The nondesignated MSFC is active and has a configuration distinct from the designated MSFC.

2. The GLBP router responsible for allocating MAC addresses is which of the following?

   A. Active virtual gateway

   B. Active virtual forwarder

   C. Primary virtual forwarder

   D. Secondary virtual forwarder

3. The GLBP router responsible for forwarding packets sent to a particular MAC address is which of the following?

   A. Active virtual gateway

   B. Active virtual forwarder

   C. Primary virtual forwarder

   D. Secondary virtual forwarder

4. Which IETF standard introduced in RFC 2338 parallels the Cisco-proprietary HSRP?

   A. HSRP 2

   B. IRDP

   C. GLBP

   D. VRRP

5. How many virtual MAC addresses are used per HSRP group?

   A. 1

   B. 2

   C. 3

   D. 4

6. SLB is an IOS-based solution defining a virtual server that represents a group of what?

   A. Real servers in separate intranets

   B. Virtual servers in a server farm

   C. Real servers in a server farm

   D. Virtual servers in separate intranets

7. How many standby routers can there be in a given HSRP group?

   A. 1

   B. 2

   C. 3

   D. 4

8. HSRP can be configured on distribution layer Catalyst 3550 switches using switch virtual interfaces. However, on distribution layer routers, multigroup HSRP is configured on trunk links using what?

   A. Null interfaces

   B. Loopbacks

   C. Bridge virtual interfaces

   D. Subinterfaces

9. When configuring HSRP, each HSRP router interface must be configured with which of the following? (Select all that apply.)

   A. A virtual MAC address

   B. A real MAC address

   C. A virtual IP address

   D. A real IP address

10. Which HSRP option(s) is/are used to guarantee an immediate change to active state on an HSRP router?

   A. **preempt**

   B. **tracking**

   C. **priority**

   D. **hello time**

Objectives

After completing this chapter, you will be able to perform tasks related to the following:

- Describe some of the major components of a Cisco AVVID (Architecture for Voice, Video, and Integrated Data) network solution.

- Explain how Layer 2 multicast addresses map to Layer 3 multicast addresses.

- Explain the role of Internet Group Management Protocol (IGMP) in multicasting.

- Understand the purpose of IGMP snooping and Cisco Group Management Protocol (CGMP) with switched traffic.

- Understand the operation of shared trees versus source trees in multicast routing.

- List the major multicast routing protocol solutions.

- Describe the role of the auxiliary virtual LAN (VLAN) with voice traffic.

- Explain the role of class of service (CoS), type of service (ToS), and Differentiated Services Code Point (DSCP) in traffic classification.

- Understand the importance of quality of service (QoS) with IP Telephony solutions.

Chapter 7

Cisco AVVID

Traditionally, separate networks have been designed and implemented within the enterprise for data, voice, and video applications. These have been deployed in parallel and operated in isolation, often implemented and managed by separate teams.

In the past, networking vendors typically offered similar enterprise network architectures that were, almost without exception, proprietary, closed, and nonhierarchical.

These separate networks encompass enterprise local and wide-area networks. They have been built to interconnect private branch exchange (PBX) equipment, *H.320* videoconferencing equipment, and routers.

The networks have been provisioned over dedicated leased lines for PBX and H.320 video, with a combination of leased lines, Frame Relay, and ATM for data.

As client/server networking grew, the needs of enterprises were also evolving. Applying technology to business practices such as sales, support, customer response management, accounting, and supply chain was reaping tremendous benefits in increased efficiency and lower costs. Many of these new technologies supported entirely different business models (for example, business-to-consumer e-commerce, business-to-business online exchanges, and so on). In other cases, these technologies were used to reengineer existing business practices. In all cases, the needs for reliability, performance, and ease of deployment and management remain crucial, because these applications have become more critical to an enterprise's success (whether profit-making or service-oriented).

In networking today, corporations are looking for strategies to integrate disparate networking technologies over a single common network infrastructure. This trend started many years ago in the internetworking area when corporate networks began the migration of delay-sensitive, mission-critical Systems Network Architecture (SNA) data traffic across an IP infrastructure. Now, people are examining the existing and often separate data, voice, and video network infrastructures and determining the most efficient ways of bringing them together.

Most corporations have voice networks anchored around PBX systems connected to a Public Switched Telephone Network (PSTN), but most data networks are IP-based and anchored around switches and routers. Where traditional telephony in fixed 64-kbps bandwidth increments is carried across a circuit-switched PBX infrastructure, other dynamic data applications are consolidated over an intelligent IP-based backbone.

Introduction to Cisco AVVID

The Cisco Architecture for Voice, Video, and Integrated Data (AVVID) is composed of a holistic network design infrastructure. IP Telephony, campus LAN switching, wireless networks, security, storage networking, and multicasting are major components addressed by AVVID. This section discusses AVVID at a high level, describing how it is applied in production networks.

Examining the Cisco AVVID Framework

With today's separate infrastructures, two strategic directions toward the convergence of data, voice, and video are possible, as illustrated in Figures 7-1 and 7-2.

Figure 7-1 A Typical Network Infrastructure Separates the Voice and Data Components

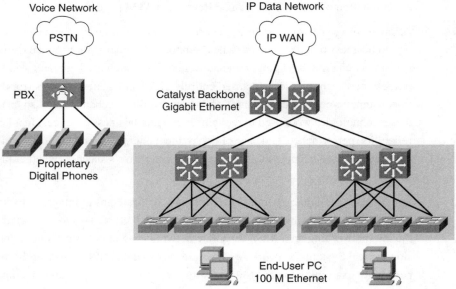

Figure 7-2 A Converged Voice and Data Network Is Now Common in Enterprise Networks

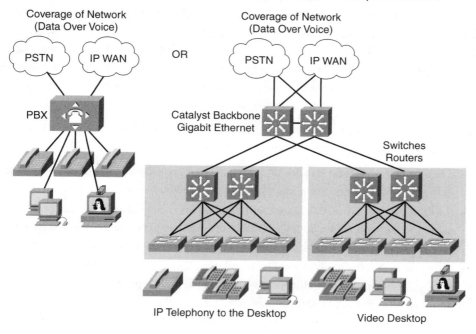

One approach calls for the use of the PBX to support the kinds of interfaces and bandwidth required by today's IP-based data applications. This means interfaces such as Ethernet, Fast Ethernet, Gigabit Ethernet, and others on PBX platforms. Most data desktops are now connected at speeds of 10 or 100 Mbps, making this a strategy without merit. Fundamentally, the PBX is a time-division multiplexing (TDM) system built on 64-kbps time slots with aggregate capacity in the tens of megabits per second. Although this is adequate for voice only, any attempt to drive data bandwidths shows that a whole new breed of platform would be required beyond the PBX.

It is also interesting to look back in history at other attempts to accomplish this integration. In the 1980s, when a 2400-bps modem was standard and a 9600-bps modem was almost unheard of, Integrated Services Digital Network (ISDN) at 64 kbps per channel was being touted as the next high-speed desktop technology. Naturally this was well-suited to be terminated on the PBX, given its conformance to the bandwidth hierarchy of the PBX systems. Interestingly, this still did not take the marketplace by storm, even before technologies such as Ethernet were on the radar screen. Vendor investment in traditional PBX technology has not scaled to meet the demands of a converged network.

Most of the networking innovation during the last ten years has been developed around IP networks because of the pervasiveness and rapid development of the Internet. This includes

World Wide Web technology, streaming video, IP Telephony, higher-speed IP transport mechanisms, and more intelligence in the network to cope with new classes of delay-sensitive, mission-critical applications. This has all lead to the future of integrated networks, one in which data, voice, and video share a common IP data network. Naturally, things will need to be done to prepare for this eventuality. The first step is to understand the architecture that will make this convergence a reality and some of the more specific considerations in the data networking infrastructure that will make this migration easier.

The Cisco solution for the convergence of data, voice, and video is Cisco AVVID. Cisco AVVID has three fundamental components, as shown in Figure 7-3:

- *Clients* are the user end stations or appliances that are used to communicate with the network or other users. Some examples are PCs, telephone devices, and video cameras.
- *Applications* for Cisco AVVID are written to an open-standards environment and, as such, will be supplied by both Cisco and third-party application developers. Some examples are interactive voice response (IVR), call center, and unified messaging.
- *Infrastructure* is the network on which both the clients and applications reside. The network is IP-based using intelligence inherent in the platforms to provide the flexibility and scalability to support the convergence of different media. Examples of network devices are Catalyst switches, Cisco routers, and voice gateways, as shown in Figure 7-4.

Cisco AVVID Network Infrastructure

Cisco AVVID network infrastructure, illustrated in Figure 7-5, is the network foundation that is recommended for rapid and seamless deployment of emerging technologies and new Internet business solutions into the retail environment.

Figure 7-3 Cisco AVVID Is Distributed, Adaptive, Open, and Manageable

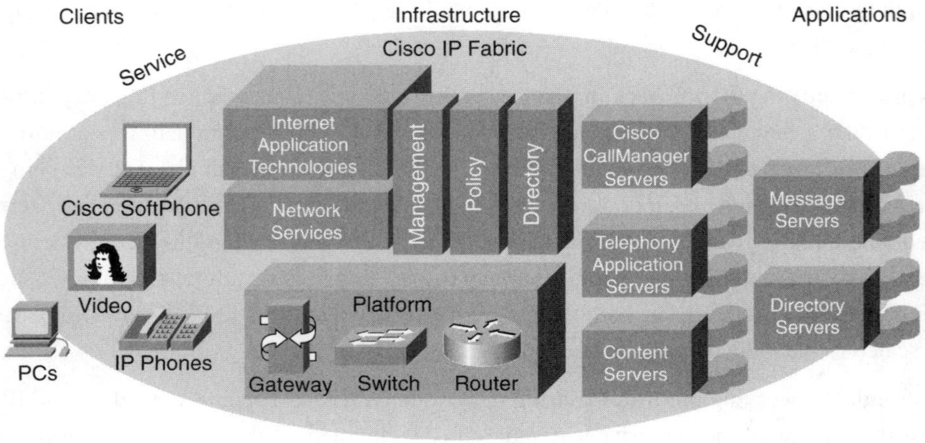

Figure 7-4 The Cisco AVVID Framework Integrates IP Networks for Large Organizations

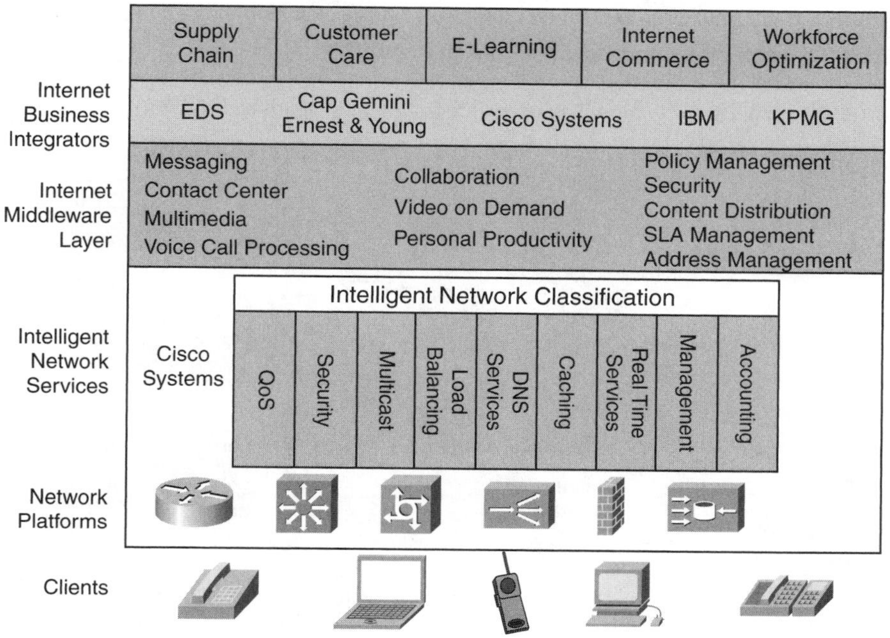

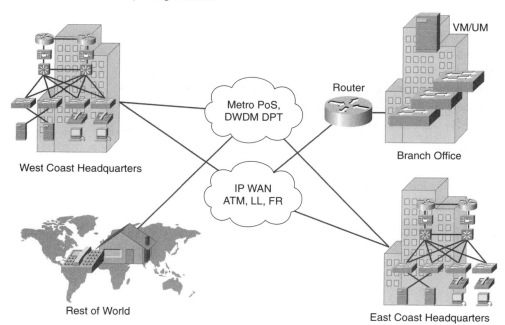

Figure 7-5 The Cisco AVVID Network Infrastructure Integrates Traditional WAN Technologies with Modern Metropolitan-Area Network (MAN) Technologies, Such as Dense Wavelength Division Multiplexing (DWDM)

As with any architecture, Cisco AVVID relies on a strong and stable foundation. This foundation is built on the multiprotocol routers and multilayer LAN switches that are used as building blocks for enterprise networks, as shown in Figure 7-6.

Figure 7-6 Cisco AVVID Provides a Cohesive, Integrated, and Optimized Network

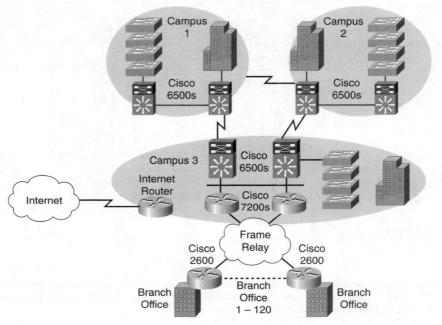

Although best-of-breed solutions might promise high performance for a specific device or application, performance is limited by the network's weakest link. Only a cohesive, integrated, optimized network can ensure the best network performance. The Cisco AVVID network infrastructure is not only tailored to the enterprise's characteristics, but it is also thoroughly lab tested and documented to provide the following benefits:

- **Speed**—A defined architectural framework and consistent services allow rapid deployment of new applications and let an enterprise quickly address change without reengineering the network.

- **Reliability**—A consistent architectural approach increases network dependability.

- **Flexibility**—The architecture allows easy transitions to changing business requirements.

- **Interoperability**—All equipment and software are configured for the ideal fit that allows seamless operation. Multiple solutions work together based on a common architectural approach.

- **Simplification**—Products are strategically deployed in alignment with the architectural framework, resulting in streamlined processes.

- **Reduced cost**—The predefined architecture minimizes the resources and time required to implement network strategies, measurements, and Resource Reservation Protocol (RSVP) signaling for admission control and reservation of resources.

- **Security**—Ensures network security through authentication, encryption, and failover. Security features include stateful, application-based filtering (context-based access control), defense against network attacks, per-user authentication and authorization, and real-time alerts.

- **High availability**—Optimizes the design and tools to ensure end-to-end availability for services, clients, and sessions.

Cisco AVVID Intelligent Network Services

The Cisco AVVID network infrastructure consists of the e-business infrastructure (physical layer) and intelligent network services, which is composed of numerous networking technologies and topologies with a corresponding large number of possible designs and architectures. Cisco lab-tested these various full-scale network designs at Research Triangle Park, North Carolina. The results are captured in Solution Reference Network Design Guides. The net result is a blueprint of optimal blending of equipment, features, and management tools that match business criteria. In addition to the physical layer, Cisco deploys Intelligent Network Services, such as quality of service (QoS) and security, to keep the network at peak performance.

QoS manages a network's delay, delay variation (jitter), bandwidth, and packet loss parameters to meet the diverse needs of voice, video, and data applications. QoS features provide value-added functionality, such as network-based application recognition (NBAR) for classifying traffic on an application basis, a service assurance agent (SAA) for end-to-end QoS measurements, and RSVP signaling for admission control and reservation of resources. Figure 7-7 illustrates queuing that prioritizes voice traffic. Low-latency queuing introduces priority queuing (PQ) for voice traffic and relies on Weighted Fair Queuing (WFQ) for the remaining traffic classes.

Figure 7-7 Low-Latency Queuing Introduces a Priority Queue for Voice Traffic and Relies on Weighted Fair Queuing for Remaining Traffic Classes

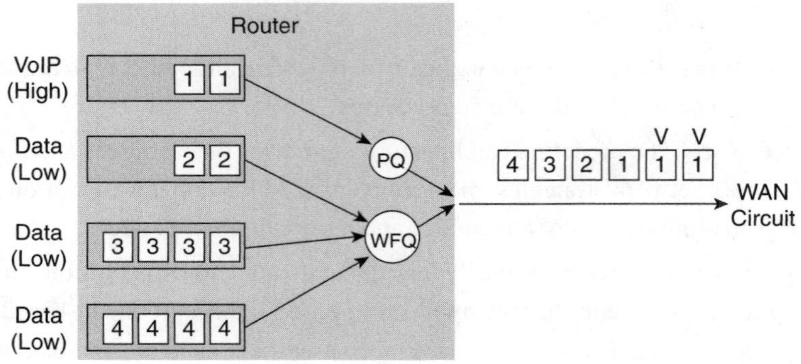

Security must be treated as an integral element of any Cisco AVVID network. An organization's communications network is the basic environment connecting all users, servers, applications, and service providers. Implementing a robust security suite provides the best defense against possible information loss, tampering, or productivity disruption. Cisco's security suite emphasizes three key areas:

- **Internal network security**—Ensuring that the internal network is secure includes tracking physical, endpoint, application, and Layer 2 security issues.
- **External network security**—External network security focuses on securing the interface between an organization's internal network and the outside world (the Internet edge).
- **Network identity**—In considering a network's overall security scheme, it is essential to establish a framework that allows the network administrator to implement identity-based network access control and policy enforcement, right down to the user and individual access port level.

Cisco AVVID network infrastructure capabilities present an array of both device-based and server-based security applications and features. Access control lists (ACLs), firewalls, server-based authentication, intrusion detection systems (IDSs), and virtual private network (VPN) capabilities can be integrated into a seamless security environment. Figure 7-8 illustrates these technologies as implemented in a network.

Figure 7-8 The Cisco AVVID Network Infrastructure Integrates an Impressive Array of Security
Technologies

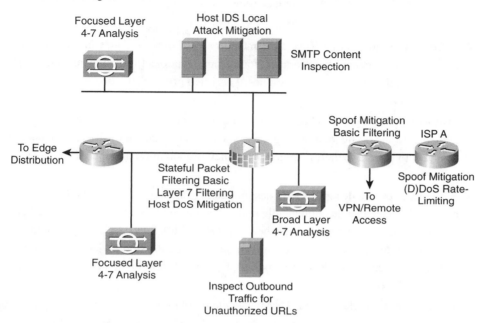

High Availability

High availability optimizes design and tools to ensure end-to-end availability for services,
clients, and sessions. Tools include reliable, fault-tolerant network devices to automatically
identify and overcome failures. Also, resilient network technologies, such as Hot Standby
Router Protocol (HSRP), bring resilience to the critical junction between hosts and backbone
links. Simple Server Redundancy Protocol (SSRP) communicates between router and ATM
switch groups to detect device failures and initiate automatic reroutes within one second of
failover time.

Determining how resilient a network is to change or disruption is a major concern for network managers. This assessment of network availability is critical. It is essential that every
network deployment emphasize, availability as the very first consideration in a baseline network design.

Availability must be viewed from the user's perspective. To the user, the network is down regardless of whether an application fails, a router dies, or a piece of fiber is cut. Here are some key availability issues to address:

- **Hardware redundancy**—This is often the first level of redundancy in the network. Cisco offers, in its modular products, for example, options for redundant supervisor engines and dual in-line power supplies. This often provides the first backstop against a network failure.

- **Protocol resiliency**—Good design practices dictate how and when to use protocol redundancy, including load sharing, convergence speed, and path redundancy handling. Contrary to popular belief, if some redundancy is good, more redundancy is not necessarily better.

- **Network capacity design**—Good design practices include capacity planning. How much traffic can a connection handle in the worst case? You must consider whether a link can handle double the traffic when a redundant link fails. Capacity planning must be included during the network design phase to ensure the smooth integration of new technologies (such as videoconferencing). Figure 7-9 shows redundant links as commonly deployed.

- **Management**—Includes the LAN Management Solution for advanced management of the Catalyst multilayer switches; the Routed WAN Management Solution for monitoring, traffic management, and access control to administer the routed infrastructure of multiservice networks; the Service Management Solution for managing and monitoring service-level agreements; and the VPN/Security Management Solution for optimizing VPN performance and security administration.

- **Multicasting**—Provides bandwidth-conserving technology that reduces traffic by simultaneously delivering a single stream of information to thousands of corporate recipients and homes. Multicasting enables distribution of videoconferencing, corporate communications, distance learning, distribution of software, and other applications. Multicast packets are replicated in the network by Cisco routers enabled with Protocol-Independent Multicast (PIM) and other supporting multicast protocols, resulting in the most efficient delivery of data to multiple receivers.

Figure 7-9 Capacity Planning Must Be Included During the Network Design Phase to Ensure the Smooth Integration of New Technologies

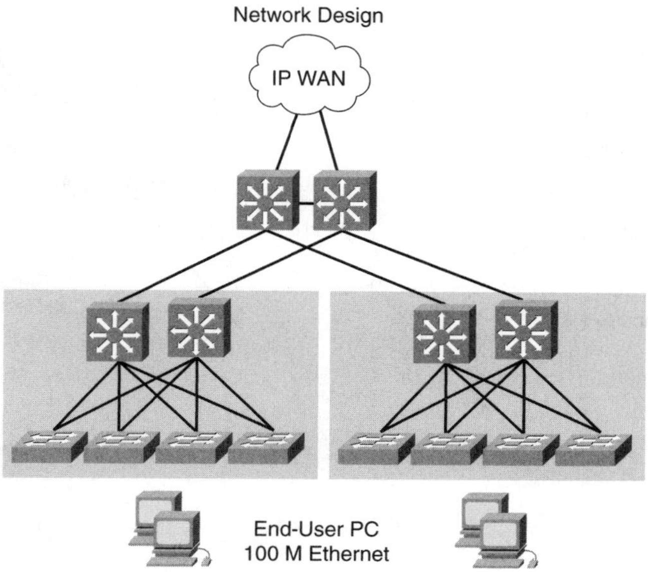

Cisco AVVID Network Solutions

Cisco AVVID network solutions include IP Telephony, IP videoconferencing, wireless LANs, security, VPNs, content networking, contact centers, and storage networking. The following sections discuss these technologies in greater detail.

IP Telephony

Built on the Cisco AVVID network infrastructure, a Cisco AVVID IP Telephony solution brings the promise of high-quality IP voice and fully integrated communications to reality. Through IP Telephony, single-site and multisite enterprises can use IP as a primary voice path with the traditional Public Switched Telephone Network (PSTN) serving as a redundant voice path. The easy-to-deploy, standards-based system delivers high voice quality while decreasing the reliance on the PSTN and significantly reducing costs (see Figure 7-10).

Figure 7-10 Cisco's IP Telephony Solution Provides an Integrated Voice and Data Network

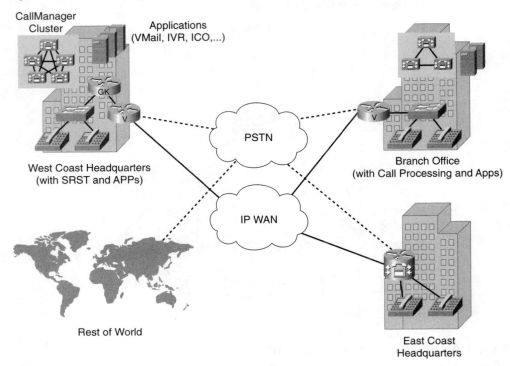

IP Videoconferencing

Using an IP-based videoconferencing solution makes it possible to run interactive video over an IP network, saving companies thousands of dollars a month by converging voice, video, and data traffic over a common path. *H.323* builds on top of existing IP data networks, ultimately saving money and scaling to larger deployments. Distance learning and business meetings are two common applications that can be deployed with H.323 over IP data networks (see Figure 7-11).

Wireless LANs

Wireless LANs let users establish and maintain a wireless network connection throughout or between buildings, without the limitations of wires or cables, as illustrated in Figure 7-12.

Figure 7-11 The Cisco AVVID Infrastructure Supports IP Videoconferencing

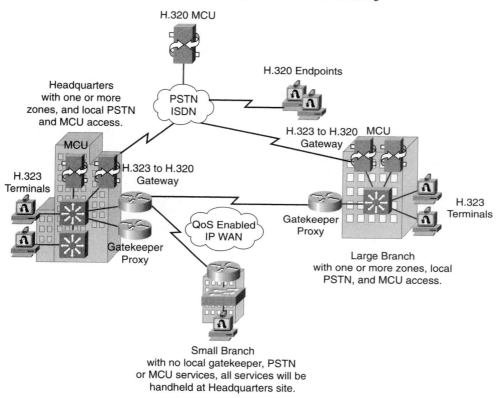

Cisco AVVID Security

Cisco offers a comprehensive array of enterprise network security solutions to make implementing and maintaining good network security easier and more cost-effective, as shown in Figure 7-13.

Virtual Private Networks

Enterprise VPN enables customer connectivity deployed on a shared (public) infrastructure with the same policies as a private network, where users expect the same application behavior, performance, and connectivity (see Figure 7-14).

Figure 7-12 Wireless LANs Are Now a Fundamental Component of Most Modern Networks

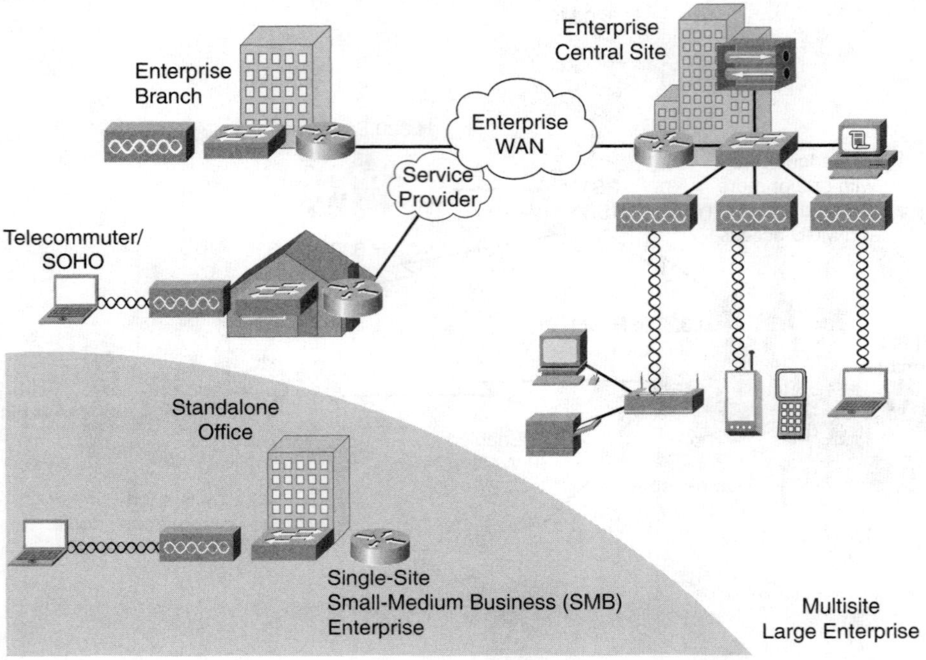

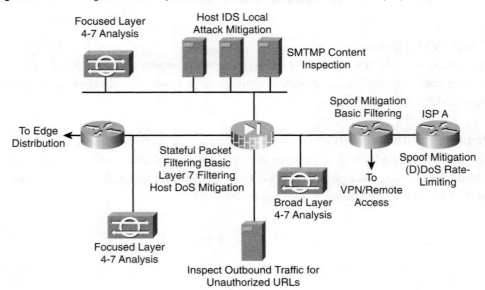

Figure 7-13 An Integrated Security Solution Is Critical in Modern Network Deployments

Figure 7-14 VPNs Are an Ideal Solution for Remote Users and Telecommuters

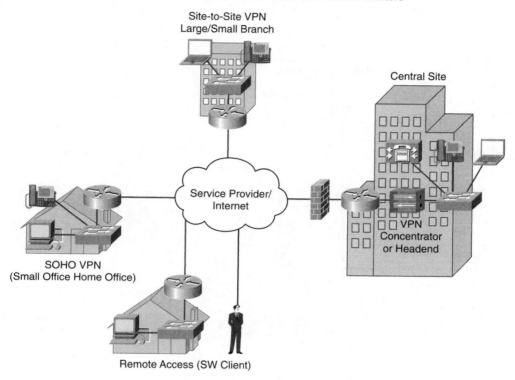

Content Networking

Content Networking, shown in Figure 7-15, allows enterprises to maximize the impact of communicating topology using the web by overcoming the modern-day bandwidth issues of delivering rich media to the desktop. Content Networking solutions guarantee that quality video, rich audio, and large graphics, as well as other high-bandwidth files, can be delivered with speed, accuracy, and consistency, dramatically increasing the impact of the communications programs.

IP Contact Center

An integral part of Cisco AVVID is the Cisco IP Contact Center (IPCC), which delivers intelligent call routing, network-to-desktop computer telephony integration (CTI), and multimedia contact management to contact center agents over an IP network. By combining software automatic call distribution (ACD) functionality with IP Telephony in a unified solution, IPCC lets companies rapidly deploy a distributed contact center infrastructure to support their global e-sales and e-service initiatives.

Figure 7-15 Content Networking Is a Relatively New Technology That Will Soon Be a Standard
Component of Enterprise Networks

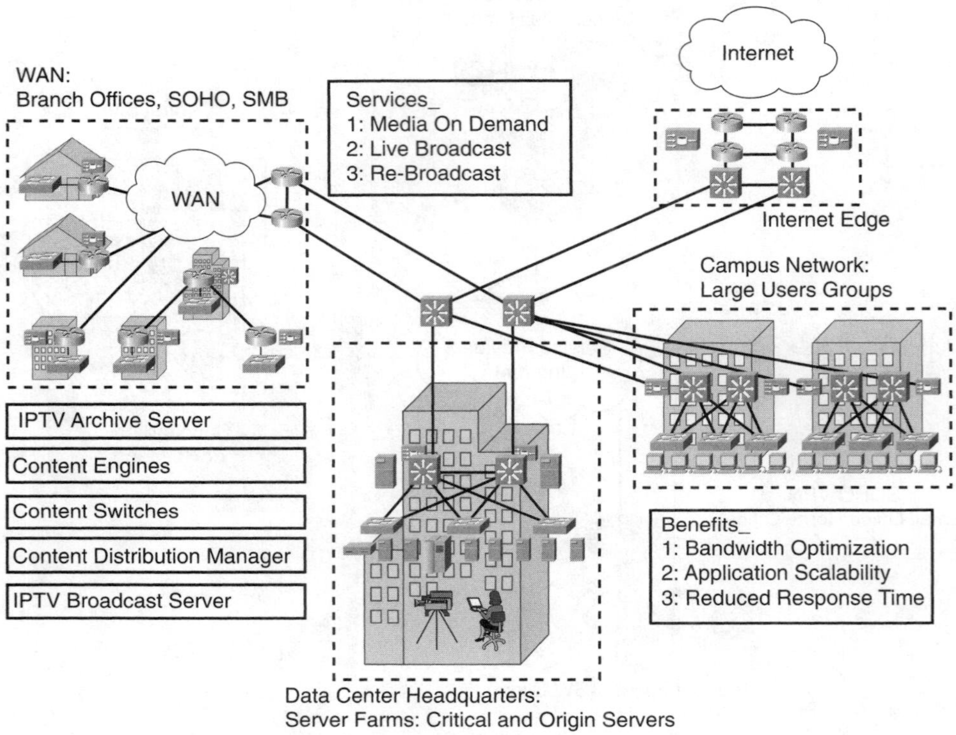

Storage Networking

The Cisco Storage Networking strategy, shown in Figure 7-16, is composed of four complementary technology areas:

- **IP access to storage**—High-speed access to block storage over IP networks
- **Network attached storage**—High-performance access, data protection, and disaster recovery for file-based storage over an IP network
- **Storage over metro optical**—Extension of storage networks across metropolitan-area networks (MANs) using an optical network infrastructure
- **Storage over WAN**—Fast, secure, and highly available storage networks interconnect over WANs

As an element of AVVID, Cisco Storage Networking allows customers to adopt a strategy for accessing, managing, and protecting their growing information resources across a consolidated IP, Gigabit Ethernet, Fiber Channel, and optical network infrastructure.

Figure 7-16 Storage Networking Is Another Relatively New Technology That Provides High-Speed
IP Access to Storage

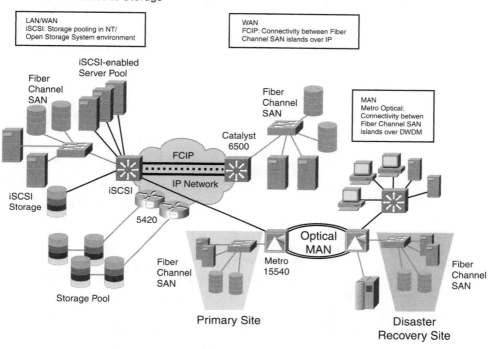

  Interactive Media Activity   Matching: Cisco AVVID Network Solutions

This Interactive Media Activity helps you better understand the Cisco AVVID
network.

Cisco AVVID Network Implementation Example

Figure 7-17 illustrates a typical deployment of a converged network combining data, voice,
and video over a single infrastructure. The network is composed of a single or several large
headquarters sites, a larger number of branch offices, and individual telecommuter sites.
From a telephony point of view, whether a physical handset or a softphone application on a
PC, the devices are treated as IP endpoints on an IP infrastructure typically serving Ethernet
to the end user. Voice calls inside a site traverse the IP LAN until the exit point from the site
where, as a first choice, the calls cross the IP WAN backbone to save on public network
toll costs. If for some reason this IP WAN is "full" or unavailable, the call is automatically
rerouted across the PSTN. Either way, the call's path is transparent to the end user. Gateways
are used at the edge of each site to provide a path to the PSTN, which is also the primary path

for local inbound and outbound calls. This level of integration allows for very simple coordinated dial plans in which an entire enterprise can use four- or five-digit dialing, as appropriate, for internal calls.

Figure 7-17 A Converged Voice, Video, and Data Cisco AVVID Solution Relies on Cisco CallManager

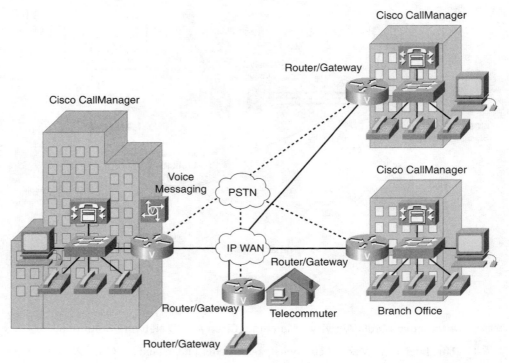

The technology used in the IP WAN allows for tremendous flexibility in the design of the intranet. Because the IP protocol is the underlying carrier of data, voice, and video, any technology such as PPP, Frame Relay, ATM, dark fiber (installed but unused fiber), digital subscriber line (DSL), Synchronous Optical Network (SONET), or wavelength division multiplexing (WDM) can be used to construct the network. This allows for maximum flexibility and agility on the part of a network manager to take advantage of new high-speed WAN services from carriers, without making major changes to the converged IP network. However, routers at the edge of the WAN must employ the proper QoS techniques to ensure that voice traffic remains high-quality, even in congested conditions. Techniques such as low-latency queuing, weighted fair queuing, and priority queuing are examples of necessary technologies in a converged network.

Familiar applications, such as voice messaging, are also easily integrated into this converged networking environment. Because the voice being carried across the network is encoded in IP, a new breed of IP-enabled unified-messaging solutions allows users to access both voice mail and e-mail from a common server. This can be accomplished with either the e-mail application or through a next-generation IP Telephony handset. Figure 7-18 illustrates unified messaging.

Figure 7-18 Unified Messaging Allows Faxes and Voice Messages to Be Accessed Through a User's E-Mail Application

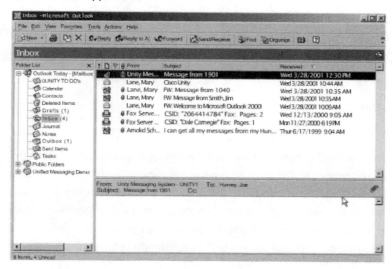

Although the nirvana of a converged network has widespread appeal to many, the reality is that every corporation already has existing voice and data networks, a scenario that requires finding simple ways to migrate to a converged network.

Legacy Migration

Although building a converged network with Cisco AVVID has obvious advantages, some existing legacy voice and video systems require a seamless migration into the New World. One example might be a scenario where an existing PBX has reached capacity and its growth is dependent on IP Telephony. In some cases, the existing voice mail system still has the capacity to sustain the additional users and it is desired to maintain the existing system in production.

In Figure 7-19, a voice mail system is connected to the PBX using multiple analog voice ports to carry voice traffic and a signaling line called a Simple Messaging Desktop Interface (SMDI) that passes information, such as whose mailbox greeting to play on which particular voice port, to the voice mail system. This is one of many ways to network voice mail to a PBX.

Figure 7-19 An Intricate Process Is Required to Migrate from a Legacy PBX Network to a Cisco AVVID Network

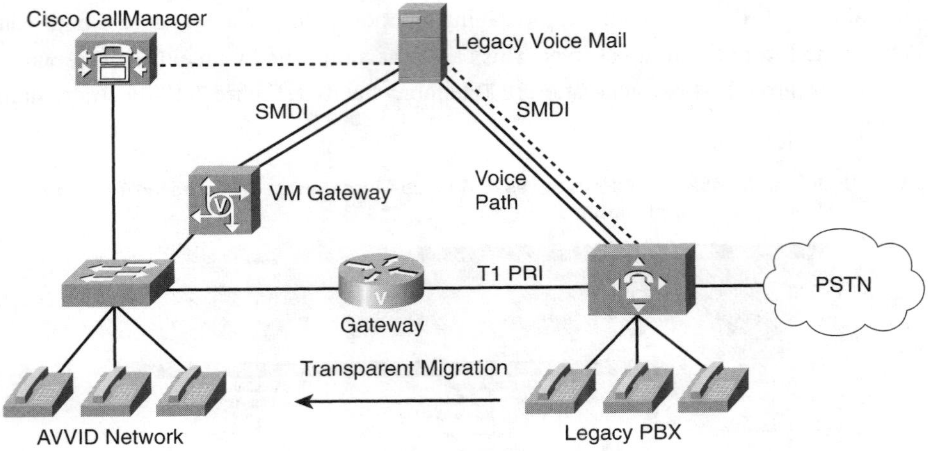

The first part of the migration to consider is establishing uniform dialing plans that are the same on both the legacy and Cisco AVVID networks. This migration is easily achieved using either a standalone gateway or one of the many router/gateway combinations available from Cisco. Regardless of which side of the network the user is on, the incoming and outgoing calls from the outside world appear exactly the same (whether direct inward dial or an operator and extensions are used). Internal dialing using a shorter dial plan (perhaps four or five digits) can also be maintained.

From a voice mail perspective, Cisco CallManager also supports SMDI for control of a voice mail system. Coupled with analog gateways connecting to the same voice mail, calls on either side of the network appear exactly the same to voice mail.

In the video world, it is common to have H.320-based videoconferencing systems, each with its own PSTN network connections. LAN-based H.323 video systems also are commonly deployed in many companies, such as Microsoft NetMeeting, which uses H.323 for video-conferencing and shared collaboration. Again, the Cisco AVVID solution provides several different ways to preserve an investment in legacy systems while investing in converged network solutions.

Figure 7-20 illustrates two different scenarios.

Figure 7-20 A Video Gateway or a Video Terminal Adapter Can Be Used to Migrate from a Legacy
H.320 Network to a Converged Video Network

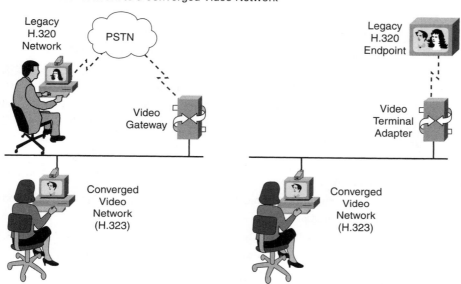

On the left side of Figure 7-20, there might be a whole network of H.320 systems deployed
by the corporation or customers. Using a Cisco video gateway enables communication
between the converged H.323 network and the legacy video network. Using a Cisco video
gateway would also allow customers or vendors who have only H.320 systems to communicate with a new network of H.323-only systems.

Additionally, on the right side of Figure 7-20, individual H.320 endpoints can be networked
seamlessly in an H.323 network with the use of a Cisco video terminal adapter.

The fact that every major networking vendor has announced plans for IP Telephony solutions
leads to the conclusion that the convergence of data, voice, and video networks is inevitable.
The only possible convergence solution is to merge the existing voice and video networks
onto the IP data network. For this to succeed, many aspects of the intelligence of the IP data
network need to be exercised.

Lastly, tools that aid in the migration from legacy voice and video networks toward networks
converged on IP make it possible for mass deployment of networks based on the Cisco
AVVID architecture.

The next section introduces IP multicast technology.

Examining Multicast in a Multilayer Switched Network

Multicasting is the process of sending a stream of data from a single source to several recipients without having to replicate a unicast stream for each recipient. Some Layer 2 and Layer 3 multicast addresses are formally associated, as described in the upcoming section "Layer 2 Multicast Addressing." IGMP is used to allow hosts to request participation in or leave particular multicast sessions. CGMP is a Cisco legacy technology used on low-end Layer 2 Catalyst switches to optimize multicast traffic flow through the switches. It has largely been replaced by a newer technology called IGMP snooping.

Multicast Overview

Most campus networks today support intranet applications that operate between one sender and one receiver. However, this paradigm is rapidly changing. In the emerging campus network, a demand exists for intranet and multimedia applications in which one sender transmits to a group of receivers simultaneously. These types of applications include the following:

- Transmitting a corporate message to employees
- Video and audio broadcasting
- Interactive video distance learning
- Transmitting data from a centralized data warehouse to multiple departments
- Communication of stock quotes to brokers
- Collaborative computing

For example, an internal technical support facility might use multicast file transfer software to send software updates to multiple users in the campus simultaneously in one stream of data.

Many corporations and industries are now realizing the potential of multimedia applications. Video and voice conferencing applications generate much of the multicast traffic today. Many websites offer video streams that transmit multicast traffic. Companies are experiencing a marked increase in multicast traffic from internal users. Because of the proliferation of multicast applications, network administrators are charged with installing and configuring devices and implementing policy to manage traffic associated with these applications. Many network designs deal efficiently with unicast traffic but neglect the impact of multicast traffic within the network. Unfortunately, this can severely affect a well-designed unicast network.

Again, it should be reiterated that it is critical in network design to take a proactive approach to controlling multicast traffic in the network. The default behavior of a switch is to flood multicast frames out all ports except the originating port. This is usually not the desired effect. Cisco has implemented the proprietary *Cisco Group Management Protocol (CGMP)* and the nonproprietary *Internet Group Management Protocol (IGMP)* snooping to help administer multicast traffic in the network. CGMP and *IGMP snooping* run on switches and routers and work hand-in-hand with IGMP, running on routers, to control the flooding of multicast traffic in a network. To control multicast traffic, either CGMP or IGMP snooping would be used, but not both.

Multicast traffic originates at sources that need to distribute the same information to multiple recipients, as illustrated in Figure 7-21.

Figure 7-21 Using Multicast Technology Greatly Reduces Unnecessary Replication of Data Traffic

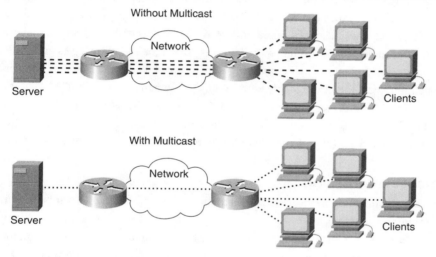

When a source creates multicast traffic, it uses special Layer 2 and Layer 3 addresses so that routers and switches know how to route or switch the frame. By default, routers do not forward multicast traffic unless they are multicast-capable and have a multicast routing protocol, such as *Distance Vector Multicast Routing Protocol (DVMRP)* or *Protocol-Independent Multicast (PIM)* enabled. DVMRP and PIM are interrouter protocols. Therefore, hosts and switches do not participate in messages for these protocols.

By default, a switch floods multicast traffic within a broadcast domain. This consumes bandwidth on both access links and trunk links. Depending on the host TCP/IP stack implementation and network interface card (NIC) attributes, the multicast frame can cause a CPU interrupt. The reason a switch floods multicast traffic is that it has no entry in the bridge table for the destination address. Multicast addresses never appear as source addresses. Therefore, the bridge/switch cannot dynamically learn multicast addresses; they must be manually configured.

IGMP is a multicast protocol that directly affects hosts. IGMP allows hosts to inform routers that they want to receive multicast traffic for a specific *multicast group* address.

Many older switches don't understand IGMP messages. As a result, Cisco developed the proprietary CGMP, which lets routers inform switches about hosts and their interest in receiving multicast traffic. This modifies the Catalyst switch default behavior of flooding the multicast frame to all hosts in the broadcast domain. Rather than flooding the frame to all hosts, the Catalyst switch limits the flooding scope to hosts in the broadcast domain that registered with the router through IGMP. If a host does not register with the router, it does not receive a copy of the multicast frame. This helps preserve access-link bandwidth.

Newer switches understand IGMP requests from hosts and implement IGMP snooping. IGMP snooping constrains the flooding of multicast traffic by dynamically configuring the interfaces so that multicast traffic is forwarded only to interfaces associated with IP multicast devices. The LAN switch snoops on the IGMP traffic between the host and the router and keeps track of multicast groups and member ports. When the switch receives an IGMP join report from a host for a particular multicast group, the switch adds the host port number to the associated multicast forwarding table entry. When the switch receives an *IGMP leave group message* from a host, the switch removes the host port from the table entry. After the switch relays the IGMP queries from the multicast router, the switch deletes entries periodically if it does not receive any *IGMP membership reports* from the multicast clients.

Multicast Addressing

Whenever an application needs to send data to more than one station but wants to restrict the distribution to stations interested in receiving the traffic, the application typically uses a multicast destination address. Whereas a broadcast targets all users in a domain, multicast addresses target a select group of stations in the network, as shown in Figure 7-22. On the other hand, if the source transmits unicast frames, it has to send multiple copies of the frame, one addressed to each intended receiver. This is a very inefficient use of network resources and does not scale well as the number of receivers increases. The disadvantage of broadcasts, on the other hand, is that even if a host is not interested in receiving the broadcast, it still has to process each frame.

By using multicast addresses, the source transmits only one copy of the frame onto the network, and routers distribute the multicast message to the other segments where interested receivers reside. As discussed previously, multicast addresses appear at Layer 2 and Layer 3. A network administrator assigns the multicast Layer 3 address for an application. The Layer 2 multicast address is then calculated from the Layer 3 multicast address. When configuring a multicast application, the NIC adds the multicast address to its list of valid Media Access Control (MAC) addresses. Usually this list consists of the built-in MAC address plus any user-configured addresses. Whenever the station receives a frame with a matching multicast destination address, the receiver sends the frame to the CPU.

Figure 7-22 A Multicast Server Sends a Single Data Stream to Multiple Clients Using a Special
Destination Address

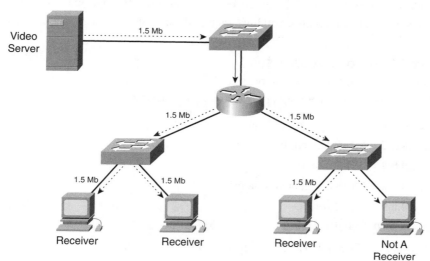

Layer 3 Multicast Addressing

IP multicast addresses at Layer 3 are characterized as Class D addresses. The first 4 bits of IP
Class D addresses are 1110. This means that IP multicast addresses have a valid range from
224.0.0.0 to 239.255.255.255. Note that multicast addresses from 224.0.0.0 to 224.0.0.255
are reserved. The following reserved addresses are specifically relevant to multicasting:

- **224.0.0.1**—All multicast-capable hosts on the segment
- **224.0.0.2**—All multicast-capable routers on the segment
- **224.0.0.4**—All DVMRP routers on the segment
- **224.0.0.5**—All Open Shortest Path First (OSPF) routers
- **224.0.0.6**—All OSPF designated routers
- **224.0.0.9**—All Routing Information Protocol version 2 (RIPv2) routers
- **224.0.0.10**—All Enhanced Interior Gateway Routing Protocol (EIGRP) routers
- **224.0.0.13**—All PIM routers

Usually, a network administrator assigns a multicast address to the application and must
select an address not used by other applications or processes. The administrator should not
use a multicast address in the reserved range.

The IP multicast address space is subdivided into several formal categories. These include reserved link local addresses, globally scoped addresses, limited scope addresses, and GLOP addressing. The following sections address each of these categories in greater detail.

Reserved Link Local Addresses

The Internet Assigned Numbers Authority (IANA) has reserved addresses from 224.0.0.0 to 224.0.0.255 to be used by network protocols on a local network segment:

- **224.0.0.1**—All systems on this subnet
- **224.0.0.2**—All routers on this subnet
- **224.0.0.5**—OSPF routers
- **224.0.0.6**—OSPF designated routers
- **224.0.0.9**—RIPv2 routers
- **224.0.0.10**—EIGRP routers
- **224.0.0.12**—Dynamic Host Configuration Protocol (DHCP) server/relay agent
- **224.0.0.13**—All PIM routers
- **224.0.0.22**—IGMP
- **224.0.0.25**—Router-to-switch (such as *Router-Port Group Management Protocol [RGMP]*)

Packets with these *link local addresses* should never be forwarded by a router. They must remain local on a particular LAN segment and are always transmitted with a time-to-live of 1.

Network protocols use these addresses for automatic router discovery and to communicate important routing information. For example, OSPF uses 224.0.0.5 and 224.0.0.6 to exchange link state information.

Globally Scoped Addresses

The address range from 224.0.1.0 to 238.255.255.255 is known as *globally scoped addresses*. This range can be used to multicast data between organizations and across the Internet.

Some of these addresses have been reserved for use by multicast applications through IANA. For example, 224.0.1.1 has been reserved for *Network Time Protocol (NTP)*, used to synchronize clocks on network devices. The IANA also assigned the two group addresses 224.0.1.39 and 224.0.1.40 for Auto-RP, a PIM sparse-mode mechanism that is discussed in the section "Configure Auto-RP (Optional)."

Limited Scope Addresses

The addresses in the range of 239.0.0.0 to 239.255.255.255 are known as *limited scope addresses* or administratively scoped addresses. These are defined by RFC 2365 to be constrained to a local group or organization. Routers are typically configured with filters to prevent multicast traffic in this address range from flowing outside an autonomous system (AS) or any user-defined domain. Within an autonomous system or domain, the limited scope address range can be further subdivided so that local multicast boundaries can be defined. This subdivision also allows for address reuse between these smaller domains.

GLOP Addressing

RFC 2770 proposes that the 233.0.0.0/8 address range be reserved for statically defined addresses, called *GLOP addresses*, by organizations that already have an AS number reserved. The term GLOP was coined by the RFC's author and is not an acronym. The domain's AS number is embedded in the second and third octets of the 233.0.0.0/8 range.

For example, AS 62010 is written in hex as F23A. Separating the two octets F2 and 3A results in 242 and 58 in decimal. This provides for a subnet of 233.242.58.0 that would be globally reserved for AS 62010 to use.

Layer 2 Multicast Addressing

When a Layer 3 multicast address is assigned, a Layer 2 address is automatically generated from the IP address. To calculate the Layer 2 address, the host copies the last 23 bits of the IP address into the last 24 bits of the MAC address. The high-order bit is set to 0.

The first 3 bytes (24 bits) of the multicast MAC address are 0x01-00-5E. This is a reserved value that indicates a multicast application. More generally, any Ethernet multicast or broadcast frame has a 1 in the last bit of the first octet.

Consider the following example:

The IP address 224.1.10.10, assigned by an administrator, has a low 23-bit value of 1.10.10. In hexadecimal format, this is 0x01-0A-0A. The MAC address takes the last 23 of the 24 bits and places them in the MAC field. The complete MAC address in this case is 01-00-5E-01-0A-0A.

Figure 7-23 illustrates another example. In this case, the IP address 224.10.8.5 translates into a MAC address of 01.00.5E.0A.08.05.

Figure 7-23 Layer 3 Multicast Addresses Map to Layer 2 Multicast Addresses in a 32-to-1 Ratio

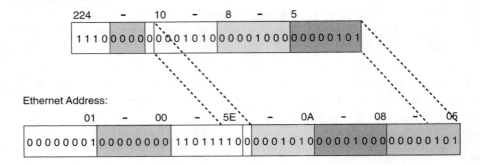

Interactive Media Activity Drag and Drop: Multicast Addressing

In this Interactive Media Activity, you gain familiarity with the key ranges of IP multicast addresses and associated terminology.

IGMP

IGMP grew out of the Host Membership Protocol. The first version, IGMPv1, was defined in RFC 1112. The most recent version, IGMPv2, was ratified in November 1997 as a standard by the Internet Engineering Task Force (IETF) and is covered in RFC 2236.

IGMP messages are used primarily by multicast hosts to signal their local multicast router when they want to join a specific multicast group and begin receiving group traffic, as shown in Figure 7-24. Hosts can also (with IGMPv2) signal to the local multicast router that they want to leave an IP multicast group and are no longer interested in receiving multicast group traffic.

Using information obtained through IGMP, routers maintain a list of multicast group memberships on a per-interface basis. A multicast group membership is active on an interface if at least one host on that interface has signaled its desire, using IGMP, to receive the multicast group traffic.

IGMP Version 1

IGMP Version 1 (IGMPv1) messages are transported within IP datagrams to transmit information about multicast groups. The datagram consists of a 20-byte IP header and an 8-byte IGMP message (see Figure 7-25).

Figure 7-24 IGMP Allows Hosts to Interactively Subscribe to and Leave IP Multicast Groups

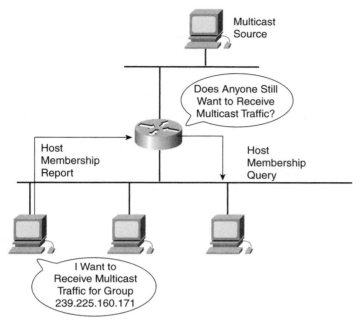

Figure 7-25 IGMP Version 1 Messages Include a Message Type Field

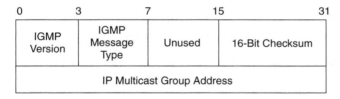

The first field of the message, IGMP Version, indicates what version of IGMP generated the message. For Version 1, this value must be 1. The IGMP Message Type field specifies the message type. Version 1 defines two messages:

- A host membership query
- A host membership report

The Checksum field carries the checksum computed by the source; the source computes the checksum for the entire IGMP message. The receiving device examines the checksum value to determine if the message was corrupted during transmission. If the checksum value doesn't match, the receiver discards the message. Finally, the IP Multicast Group Address field indicates the multicast destination group address targeted by the message.

When a host on the segment wants to receive multicast traffic, it issues an unsolicited host membership report targeting the intended multicast group.

The destination MAC address targets the multicast group it intends to join. If this were the only information in the frame to identify the group, any of 32 groups might be desired because of the address ambiguity discussed earlier. However, the Layer 3 address is included in both the IP header and the IGMP header. The Layer 3 multicast group desired by the host is 239.255.160.171; this Layer 3 multicast address is equivalent to the 32 Layer 3 multicast addresses in the ranges 224 to 239.255.160.171 and 224 to 239.127.160.171. This translates to a MAC address of 01-00-5E-7F-A0-AB. All multicast-capable devices on the shared media receive the membership report. In this situation, however, only the router is interested in the frame. The frame tells the router, "I want to receive any messages for this multicast group." The router now knows that it needs to forward a copy of any frames with this multicast address to the segment where the host that issued the report lives.

A device issues an IGMP membership report under two conditions:

- **Whenever the device first intends to receive a multicast stream**—When enabling the multicast application, the device configures the NIC, and the built-in IGMP processes send an unsolicited membership report to the router, requesting copies of the multicast frames.
- **In response to an** *IGMP membership query* **from the router**—This is a solicited membership report that helps the router confirm that hosts on the segment still want to receive multicast traffic for a particular multicast group.

Routers periodically issue host membership queries. The query period might be configured from 0 seconds to a maximum of 65,535 seconds. The default is 60 seconds.

Only one router on each segment issues the membership query message. If the segment uses IGMP Version 1, the designated router for the multicast routing protocol issues the query. If the segment uses IGMP Version 2, the multicast router with the lowest IP address on the segment issues the queries.

The host membership query message targets the all-multicast-hosts address, 224.0.0.1, in the Layer 3 address field. The Layer 2 address is 01-00-5E-00-00-01. The IGMP header uses a group address of 0.0.0.0. This translates to a query for all multicast hosts on all groups on the segment.

A host for each active multicast group must respond to this message. When multicast hosts receive the host membership query, and if the host wants to continue receiving multicast frames for a multicast group, the multicast host starts an internal random timer with an upper range of 10 seconds. The host waits for the timer to expire, and then it sends a membership report for each multicast group it wants to continue receiving.

If another station sends a membership report before the local timer expires, the host cancels the timer and suppresses the report. This behavior prevents a segment and router from experiencing host membership report floods. Only one station from each multicast group needs to respond for each group on the segment.

If the router does not receive a membership report for a particular multicast group for three query intervals, it assumes that no hosts remain that are interested in that group multicast stream. The router stops forwarding the multicast packets for this group and tells upstream routers to stop sending frames.

This process defines an implicit leave from the multicast group. No special leave mechanism is defined in IGMPv1. Instead, IGMPv1 hosts leave the group passively, without any notification to the router. A router learns that such a host is not interested in participating in a multicast group if the host does not respond to repeated queries from the router relating to that group.

IGMP Version 2

Looking at the format of *IGMP Version 2* (IGMPv2) messages in Figure 7-26, notice that the IGMP Message Type field has been merged with the IGMPv1 Version field and now occupies a full octet. The values assigned to the various message types have been chosen carefully to provide backward compatibility with IGMPv1. Another field added to IGMPv2 that is not found in IGMPv1 is Maximum Response Time.

Figure 7-26 IGMP Version 2 Messages Include a Maximum Response Time Field

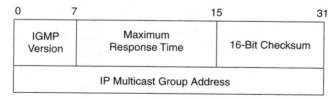

IGMP Version 2 adds two messages not found in IGMPv1 to streamline the join and leave process. RFC 2236 added a Version 2 membership report and a leave group message. The complete list of messages now consists of the following:

- **0x11**—Membership query
- **0x12**—Version 1 membership report
- **0x16**—Version 2 membership report
- **0x17**—Leave group

The membership query and Version 1 membership report carry over from IGMPv1. However, the membership query can now target specific multicast groups. In Version 1, the query message is a general query with the group address set to 0.0.0.0. All active groups respond to the general query. Version 2 allows a multicast query router to target a specific multicast group. A multicast host running Version 2 responds with a Version 2 membership report. Other multicast groups ignore the group-specific query if it is not directed at their group. The group-specific membership query works only for Version 2 systems.

If a Version 2 host leaves a multicast group, it sends an unsolicited leave group message to inform the query router that it no longer wants to receive the multicast stream. The router maintains a table of all hosts in the multicast group on the segment. If other hosts still want to receive the multicast stream, the router continues to send the multicast frames onto the segment. However, if the membership report arrives from the last host on the segment for the multicast group, the router terminates the multicast stream for that group.

In Figure 7-27, consider the multicast group shown. Hosts H2 and H3 are currently members of multicast group 224.1.1.1, although Host H2 wants to leave the group.

Figure 7-27 Host 2 Announces Its Desire to Leave the Multicast Group

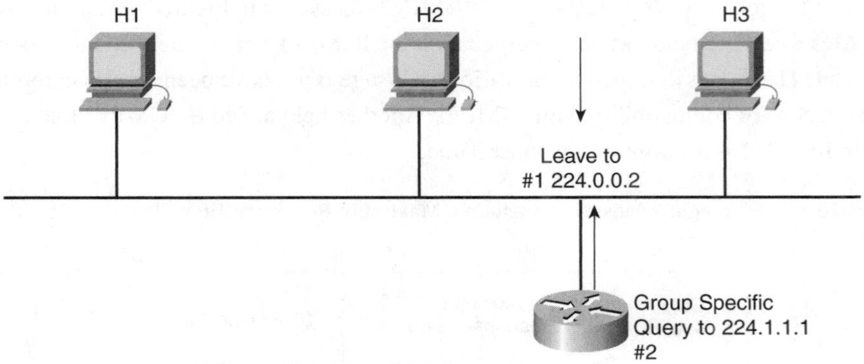

The sequence of events for Host H2 to leave the group is as follows:

1. Host H2 multicasts an IGMPv2 leave group message to the all-routes (224.0.0.2) multicast group to inform all routers on the subnet that it is leaving the group.

2. The router hears the leave group message from Host H2. However, because routers keep a list of only the group memberships that are active on a subnet, not individual hosts that are members, the router sends a group-specific query to determine whether any hosts remain for Group 224.1.1.1. Because this is a group-specific query, only hosts that are members of the group respond.

3. Host H3 is still a member of Group 224.1.1.1 and responds to the query with an IGMPv2 membership report to inform the routers on the subnet that a member of this group is still present. Host H3 is now the last remaining member of the group.

4. If Host H3 decides to leave, Steps 1 and 2 are repeated. However, when the router issues a group-specific query, no hosts respond. As a result, the router times out the group and stops forwarding packets for the group onto the subnet.

If the router wants to confirm the need to send a stream, it can transmit a general or group-specific query onto the segment. If the router does not receive any responses to a couple of query messages, it assumes that no more hosts want to receive the multicast stream.

Another feature added to IGMPv2 is the multicast router's ability to specify the hosts' response timer range. Remember that when a host receives a membership query, the host starts a random timer. The timer value is in the range of 0 to maximum response time, with the maximum response time specified in the router query message. Version 2 limits the timer's upper range to a maximum of 25 seconds. The default in a router is 10 seconds.

IGMP Version 1 and Version 2 Interoperability

The first possible combination of versions might involve hosts with a mix of versions and a Version 1 router, as shown in Figure 7-28. All IGMP operations in this scenario are driven by the version that the query router uses. When such a combination exists, the hosts must use Version 1 messages. The router does not understand Version 2 membership reports, nor does it understand Version 2 leave messages.

A second case is when the router supports IGMPv2 but hosts use IGMPv1. Although the router understands more message types than the hosts, it ultimately uses only Version 1 messages. When the Version 2 router receives the Version 1 membership report, it remembers that they are present and uses only Version 1 membership queries. Version 1 queries use the group address 0.0.0.0 and do not generate group-specific queries. If they generated group-specific queries, the Version 1 hosts would not recognize the message and would not know how to respond.

What if both Version 1 and Version 2 hosts are on the segment, with a Version 2 router? As in the previous case, the router must remember that there are Version 1 hosts and, therefore, must issue Version 1 membership queries. Additionally, if any of the Version 2 hosts send a leave message, the router must ignore it. The router ignores the message because it must still issue general queries in case a Version 1 member is still active on the segment.

Figure 7-28 IGMP Version 2 Routers Can Operate with Both IGMP Version 1 and Version 2 Hosts

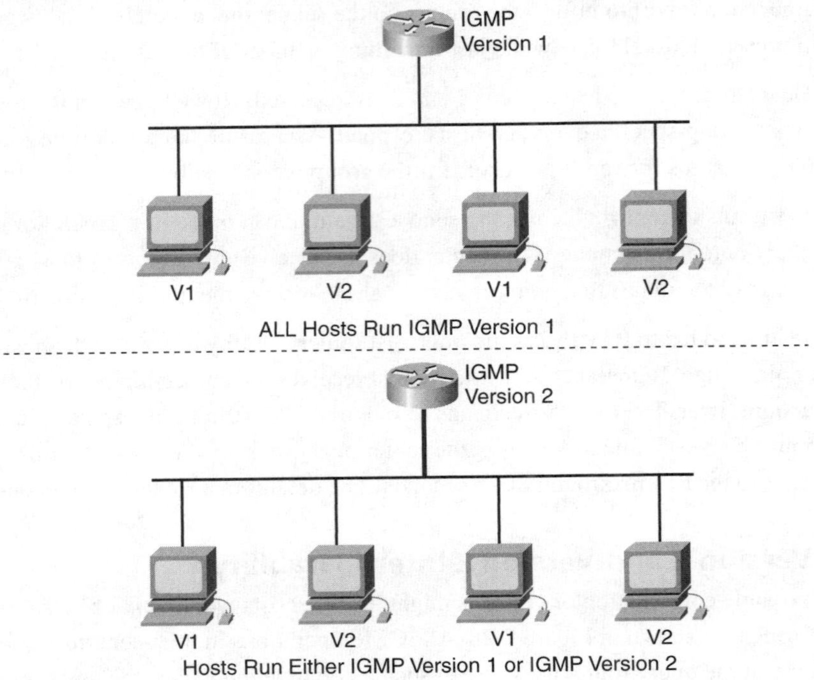

If two routers attach to the segment where one supports Version 1 and the other Version 2, the Version 2 router must be administratively configured as a Version 1 router. The Version 1 router has no way to detect the presence of the Version 2 router. Because the two versions use different methods of selecting the query router, they might not reliably agree on the query router.

IGMP Version 3

IGMP Version 3 (IGMPv3) is the next step in the evolution of IGMP. IGMPv3 adds support for *source filtering*, which lets a multicast receiver host signal to a router the groups from which it wants to receive multicast traffic, and from which sources this traffic is expected. This membership information lets Cisco IOS software forward traffic from only sources from which receivers requested the traffic. Among other things, this added feature can prevent rogue multicast servers from monopolizing the bandwidth on a segment; receivers must specifically request the servers from which multicast traffic is desired. IGMPv3 helps conserve bandwidth by allowing hosts to specify the sources of multicast traffic.

IGMPv3 supports applications that explicitly signal sources from which they want to receive traffic. With IGMPv3, receivers signal membership to a multicast host group in the following two modes:

- **INCLUDE mode**—In this mode, the receiver announces membership to a host group and provides a list of source addresses (the INCLUDE list) from which it wants to receive traffic.

- **EXCLUDE mode**—In this mode, the receiver announces membership to a multicast group and provides a list of source addresses (the EXCLUDE list) from which it does not want to receive traffic. The host receives traffic only from sources whose IP addresses are not listed in the EXCLUDE list. To receive traffic from all sources, which is the behavior of IGMPv2, a host uses EXCLUDE mode membership with an empty EXCLUDE list.

As shown in Figure 7-29, Host H1 wants to join group 224.1.1.1 but wants to receive traffic only from Source 1.1.1.1. The IGMPv3 host can signal the designated router, R3, that it is only interested in multicast traffic from Source 1.1.1.1 for Group 224.1.1.1. Router R3 could then potentially "prune" the unwanted source, 2.2.2.2.

Figure 7-29 With IGMP Version 3, a Host Can Specify Which Source(s) It Wants to Receive Multicast Traffic from for a Particular Multicast Group

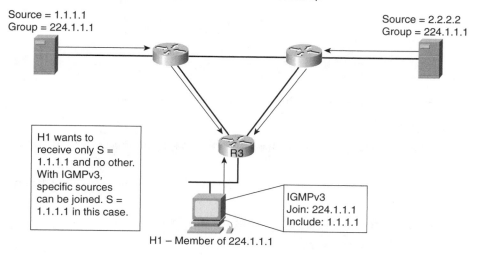

IGMP Snooping

Layer 2 switches need some degree of multicast awareness to avoid flooding multicasts to all switch ports. IGMP snooping requires the LAN switch to examine, or "snoop," some Layer 3 information in the IGMP packets sent between the hosts and the router. When the switch hears the IGMP host report from a host for a particular multicast group, it adds the host's port number to the associated multicast table entry. When the switch hears the IGMP leave group message from a host, it removes the host's port from the table entry.

When IGMP snooping is enabled, the switch responds to periodic multicast router queries to all virtual LANs (VLANs) with only one join request per MAC multicast group. Also, the switch creates one entry per VLAN in the Layer 2 forwarding table for each MAC multicast group for which it receives an IGMP join request. All hosts interested in this multicast traffic send join requests and are added to the forwarding table entry.

Because IGMP control messages are transmitted as multicast packets, they are indistinguishable from multicast data at Layer 2. A switch running IGMP snooping must examine every multicast data packet to check if it contains any pertinent IGMP control information. Enabling IGMP snooping on a low-end switch could severely affect performance when data is transmitted at high rates. Figure 7-30 shows the processes required on switches using IGMP snooping. CGMP, discussed later in this chapter, is an ideal alternative for low-end legacy switches.

Figure 7-30 IGMP Snooping Is Now the Preferred Mechanism to Avoid Unnecessary Flooding to All Switch Ports

Requirements and processes related to IGMP snooping are as follows:

- Switches become IGMP-aware
- IGMP packets are intercepted by the Network Management Processor (NMP) or by special hardware ASICs
- The switch must examine the contents of IGMP messages to determine which ports want what traffic:
  — IGMP membership reports
  — IGMP leave messages
- Impact on the switch:
  — It must process *all* Layer 2 multicast packets.
  — The administrative load increases with the multicast traffic load.
  — It requires special hardware to maintain throughput.

Configuring IGMP Snooping on a Catalyst IOS-Based Switch

By default, IGMP snooping is globally enabled. When it is globally enabled or disabled, it is also enabled or disabled in all existing VLAN interfaces. By default, IGMP snooping is enabled on all VLANs, but it can be enabled and disabled on a per-VLAN basis.

If IGMP global snooping is disabled, VLAN snooping might not be enabled. If global IGMP snooping is enabled, snooping might be enabled or disabled on a VLAN basis.

To globally enable IGMP snooping, enter the global configuration command **ip igmp snooping**. The global command **no ip igmp snooping vlan** *vlan-id* disables IGMP snooping on a particular VLAN.

To specify the next-hop interface to the multicast router, use the global configuration command **ip igmp snooping vlan** *vlan-id* **mrouter interface** *interface-id*.

When IGMP immediate-leave processing is enabled, the switch immediately removes a port from the IP multicast group when it detects an IGMPv2 leave message on that port. Immediate-leave processing allows the switch to remove an interface from the forwarding table after receiving a leave message without first sending group-specific queries from the interface. The immediate-leave feature should be implemented only when a single receiver is present on every port in the VLAN. The immediate-leave feature is disabled by default. Use the **ip igmp snooping vlan** *vlan-id* **immediate-leave** global configuration command to enable IGMP immediate-leave processing on a VLAN interface.

Example 7-1 shows a sample configuration for IGMP snooping.

Example 7-1 *IGMP Snooping Can Be Configured on Catalyst 2950, 3550, 4500, and 6500 Switches*

```
Switch(config)#ip igmp snooping
Switch(config)#ip igmp snooping vlan 1 immediate-leave
Switch(config)#ip igmp snooping vlan 2 immediate-leave
Switch(config)#exit
Switch#show ip igmp snooping

vlan 1
----------
  IGMP snooping is globally enabled
  IGMP snooping is enabled on this vlan
  IGMP snooping immediate-leave is enabled on this vlan
  IGMP snooping mrouter learn mode is pim-dvmrp on this vlan
```

continues

Example 7-1 *IGMP Snooping Can Be Configured on Catalyst 2950, 3550, 4500, and 6500 Switches (Continued)*

```
vlan 2
..........
 IGMP snooping is globally enabled
 IGMP snooping is enabled on this vlan
 IGMP snooping immediate-leave is enabled on this vlan
 IGMP snooping mrouter learn mode is cgmp on this vlan
vlan 3
..........
 IGMP snooping is globally enabled
 IGMP snooping is enabled on this vlan
 IGMP snooping immediate-leave is disabled on this vlan
 IGMP snooping mrouter learn mode is cgmp on this vlan
```

The switch might be configured to either snoop on Protocol-Independent Multicast/Distance Vector Multicast Routing Protocol (PIM/DVMRP) packets or to listen to CGMP self-join packets. By default, the switch snoops on PIM/DVMRP packets on all VLANs. PIM and DVMRP are discussed later in this chapter.

To learn of multicast router ports through only CGMP self-join packets, use the following global configuration command:

```
Switch(config)#ip igmp snooping vlan vlan-id mrouter learn cgmp
```

When this command is used, the router listens only to CGMP self-join packets and no other CGMP packets.

To learn of multicast router ports through only PIM/DVMRP packets, use the following global configuration command:

```
Switch(config)#ip igmp snooping vlan vlan-id mrouter learn pim-dvmrp
```

To view the Layer 2 multicast entries for the switch or for a VLAN, use the following command:

```
Switch#show mac-address-table multicast [vlan vlan-id] [user | igmp-snooping]
  [count]
```

The **user** option displays only the user-configured multicast entries.

CGMP Operation

CGMP is a Cisco-proprietary protocol that allows switches to learn about the existence of multicast clients from Cisco routers and older IOS-based switches. CGMP is based on a client/server model. The router is considered a CGMP server, with the switch taking on the client role. The basis of CGMP is that the IP multicast router sees all IGMP packets and, therefore, can inform the switch when specific hosts join or leave multicast groups. The switch then uses this information to construct a forwarding table.

When the router sees an IGMP control packet, it creates a CGMP packet. This CGMP packet contains the request type, a join or a leave, the multicast group address, and the client's MAC address. The packet is sent to a well-known address to which all switches listen. Each switch then interprets the packet and creates the proper entries in a forwarding table, as illustrated in Figure 7-31.

Figure 7-31 CGMP Is Used on Older Catalyst Switches, Such as the Catalyst 1900, 2820, 2900XL, 3500XL, and 5000

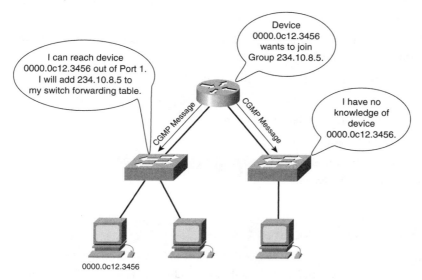

CGMP can run on an interface only if PIM is configured on the same interface. CGMP is disabled on a router by default. To enable CGMP on the router, enter the **ip cgmp** command in interface configuration mode. This command enables the CGMP for IP multicasting on a router and triggers a CGMP join message. The running configuration indicates if a specific router interface has been configured for CGMP.

For CGMP to operate correctly on a switch, the switch must have a network connection to a router running CGMP. A CGMP-capable IP multicast router detects all IGMP packets and informs the switch when specific hosts join or leave IP multicast groups. When the CGMP-capable router receives an IGMP control packet, it creates a CGMP packet that contains the request type, the multicast group address, and the host's MAC address. The router then sends the CGMP packet to a well-known address to which switches listen, as illustrated in

Figure 7-32. CGMP is no longer supported on the new series of Catalyst switches, including the 2950 and 3550 series. IGMP snooping has replaced CGMP on these models.

Figure 7-32 CGMP Frames Are Sent to a Well-Known Multicast Address

Requirements and processes related to CGMP are as follows:

- CGMP runs on both the switches and the router.
- The router sends CGMP multicast packets to the switches at a well-known multicast MAC address: 0100.0cdd.dddd.
- The CGMP packet contains the following:
  — Type field (join or leave)
  — MAC address of the IGMP client
  — Multicast address of the group
- The switch uses CGMP packet information to add or remove an entry for a particular multicast MAC address.

Routing Multicast Traffic

The campus network is composed of a collection of subnetworks connected by routers. When the source of a video data stream is located on one subnet and the host devices are located on different subnets, there needs to be a way of determining how to get from the source to the destinations. This is the function of IP.

Each host on the Internet has an IP address that identifies the host's location. Part of the address identifies the subnet on which the host resides and part identifies the individual host on that subnet. Routers periodically send routing update messages to adjacent routers, conveying the network's state as perceived by that particular router. This data is recorded in routing tables that are then used to determine optimal transmission paths for forwarding messages across the network.

Unicast transmission involves transmission from a single source to a single destination. The transmission is directed toward a single physical location that is specified by the host address. This routing procedure is relatively straightforward because of the binding of a single address to a single host.

Routing multicast traffic is a more complex problem. A multicast address identifies a particular transmission session, rather than a specific physical destination. An individual host can join an ongoing multicast session by using IGMP to communicate this desire to the subnet router, as illustrated in Figure 7-33.

Figure 7-33 Multicast Transmissions Are Particularly Useful with IP Video Transmissions

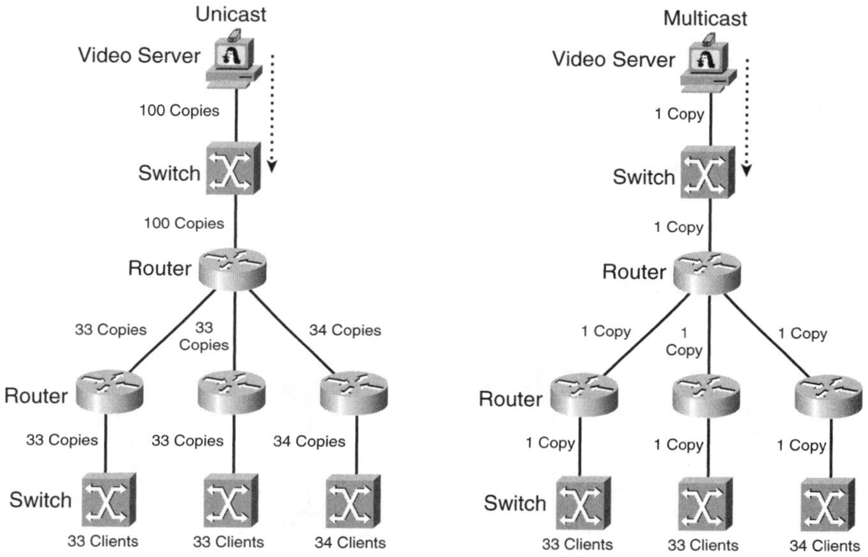

Because the number of receivers for a multicast session can potentially be quite large, the source should not need to know all the relevant addresses. Instead, the network routers must somehow be able to translate multicast addresses into host addresses. The basic principle involved in multicast routing is that routers interact with each other to exchange information about neighboring routers.

Distribution Trees

To deliver multicast packets to all receivers, designated routers construct a tree that connects all members of an IP multicast group. A *distribution tree* specifies a unique forwarding path between the subnet of the source and each subnet containing members of the multicast group.

A distribution tree has just enough connectivity so that there is only one, loop-free path between every pair of routers. Because each router knows which of its lines belong to the tree, it can copy an incoming multicast datagram onto all the outgoing branches. This action generates the minimum needed number of datagram copies. Because messages are replicated only when the tree branches, the number of copies of the messages transmitted through the network is minimized.

Because multicast groups are dynamic, with members joining or leaving a group at any time, the distribution tree must be dynamically updated. Branches that contain new members must be added. Branches in which no listeners exist must be discarded, or pruned.

As Figure 7-34 illustrates, there are two basic tree construction techniques:

- Source-specific trees
- Shared or center-specific trees

Figure 7-34 Source Distribution Trees and Shared Distribution Trees Are Used with IP Multicast Routing

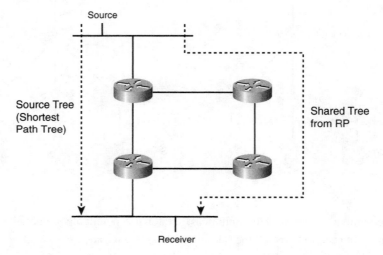

Source Distribution Tree

The simplest form of a multicast distribution tree is a *source tree*, whose root is the source of the multicast traffic and whose branches form a spanning tree through the network to the receivers. Because this tree uses the shortest path through the network, it is also often called a shortest-path tree (SPT).

Figure 7-35 shows an example of an SPT for Group 224.1.1.1 rooted at the source, Host A, and connecting two receivers, Hosts B and C.

The special notation of (S,G), pronounced "S comma G," enumerates an SPT, where S is the IP address of the source and G is the multicast group address. Using this special notation, the SPT in Figure 7-35 would be written as (192.1.1.1, 224.1.1.1). The (S,G) entries are stored on the multicast routers.

Figure 7-35 Source Distribution Trees Are Indicated with the (S,G) Notation

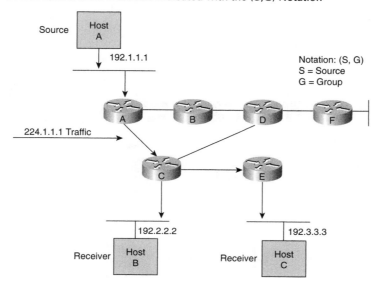

Notice that this notation implies that a separate SPT exists for every individual source originating a stream for a multicast group. Therefore, if Host B is also sending traffic to Group
224.1.1.1 and Hosts A and C are receivers, a separate (S,G) SPT would exist with a notation
of (192.2.2.2, 224.1.1.1).

Shared Distribution Tree

Unlike source trees, which have their roots at the source, shared trees use a single common
root placed at some chosen point in the network. Depending on the multicast routing protocol, this root is often called a rendezvous point (RP) or *core*, which lends itself to other common names of *shared trees*: RP Trees (RPT) or *Core-Based Trees (CBT)*.

Figure 7-36 shows a shared tree for Group 224.2.2.2 with the root located at Router D. When
using a shared tree, sources must send their traffic to the root for the traffic to reach all
receivers.

In this example, multicast group traffic from source Host A and Host D travels to the root
(Router D) and then down the shared tree to two receivers, Hosts B and Host C. Because all
sources in the multicast group use a common shared tree, a wildcard notation written as
(*,G), pronounced "star comma G," represents the tree. In this case, * means all sources, and
G represents the multicast group. Therefore, the shared tree shown in Figure 7-36 would be
written (*,224.2.2.2). The (*,G) entries are stored on the multicast routers.

Figure 7-36 Shared Distribution Trees Are Indicated with the (*,G) Notation

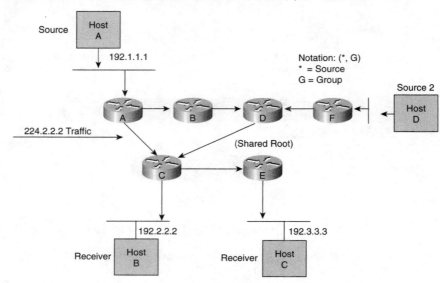

Managing Delivery of Multicast Packets

In a campus network, limiting high-bandwidth traffic to specific LANs or regions within the network is essential to containing or eliminating unnecessary consumption of resources. One method of containing multicast traffic is to impose constraints on the forwarding of that traffic by using the Time-To-Live (TTL) field in the IP packet.

As in unicast routing, the multicast TTL field controls the packet's lifetime. The function of TTL is to prevent packets from being looped forever because of routing errors. However, the TTL field in multicasting also carries the concept of a "threshold."

Multicast-enabled routers have a TTL threshold assigned to each interface. Packets with a TTL greater than the interface threshold are forwarded, and packets with a TTL equal to or less than the interface threshold are discarded. The packet TTL is compared to the interface threshold first. The router then decrements the packet TTL by a value of 1 as the packet is sent out the interface (see Figure 7-37).

A multicast packet with a TTL of less than 16 is restricted to the same department, or site, and should not be forwarded across an interface to other sites in the same region. Defining the scope of a "site" or "region" is the responsibility of the network administrator.

Figure 7-37 Assigning a TTL Threshold to Each Interface Limits the Scope of Multicast
Transmission

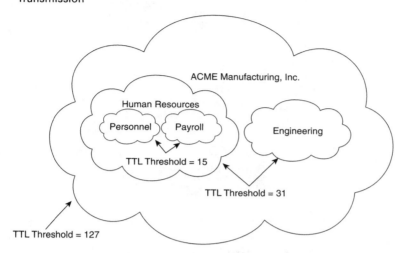

Assigning a TTL Threshold to Each Interface Limits the Scope of
Multicast Transmission

A multicast router forwards a multicast packet across an interface only if the TTL field in
the IP header is greater than the TTL threshold assigned to the interface. If the TTL field in the
packet's IP header is equal to or less than the TTL threshold assigned to the interface, the packet is
discarded. If the interface has no assigned TTL threshold, the packet is forwarded.

In Figure 7-38, the interfaces on the router have been configured with the following TTL
thresholds:

- **E1**—TTL Threshold = 16
- **E2**—TTL Threshold = 0 (none)
- **E3**—TTL Threshold = 64

An incoming multicast packet for Group XYZ is received on Interface E0 with a TTL of 24.
The outgoing interface list for Group XYZ contains Interfaces E1, E2, and E3. The TTL
threshold check is performed on each outgoing interface as follows:

- **E1**—TTL (24) > TTL Threshold (16). FORWARD
- **E2**—TTL (24) > TTL Threshold (0). FORWARD
- **E3**—TTL (24) < TTL Threshold (64). DROP

The TTL is then decremented to 23 by normal router IP packet processing.

Figure 7-38 Distinct TTL Thresholds Can Be Configured on Independent Interfaces

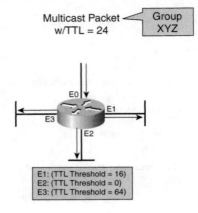

Reverse Path Forwarding (RPF)

Reverse Path Forwarding (RPF) is a fundamental concept in multicast routing that lets routers correctly forward multicast traffic down the distribution tree. RPF uses the existing unicast routing table to determine the upstream and downstream neighbors. A router forwards a multicast packet only if it is received on the upstream interface. This RPF check helps guarantee that the distribution tree is loop-free.

RPF Check

When a multicast packet arrives at a router, the router performs an RPF check on the packet. If the RPF check is successful, the packet is forwarded. Otherwise, it is dropped.

For traffic flowing down a source tree, the RPF check procedure works as follows:

1. The router looks up the source address in the unicast routing table to determine if it has arrived on the interface that is on the reverse path back to the source.

2. If the packet has arrived on the interface leading back to the source, the RPF check is successful, and the packet is forwarded.

3. If the RPF check in Step 2 fails, the packet is dropped.

Figure 7-39 shows an example of an unsuccessful RPF check.

Figure 7-39 Packets That Fail the RPF Check Are Discarded

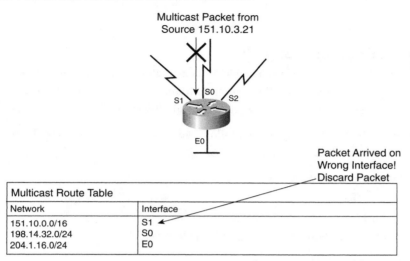

A multicast packet from source 151.10.3.21 is received on interface S0. A check of the unicast route table shows that the interface this router would use to forward unicast data to 151.10.3.21 is S1. Because the packet arrives on S0, it is discarded.

Figure 7-40 is an example of a successful RPF check.

Figure 7-40 Packets That Pass the RPF Check Are Forwarded

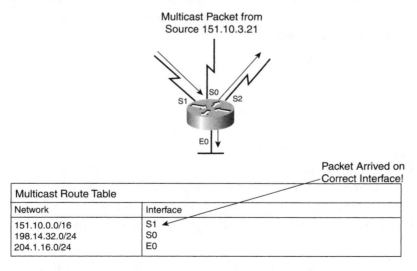

This time the multicast packet arrives on S1. The router checks the unicast routing table and finds that S1 is the correct interface.

Multicast Routing Protocols

A multicast routing protocol is responsible for constructing multicast delivery trees and enabling multicast packet forwarding. Different IP multicast routing protocols use different techniques to construct multicast spanning trees and forward packets.

IP multicast routing protocols generally follow one of two basic approaches, depending on the distribution of multicast group members on the network:

- Dense-mode routing protocols:
  - DVMRP
  - PIM Dense Mode (PIM-DM)
  - Multicast Open Shortest Path First (MOSPF)
- Sparse-mode routing protocols:
  - CBT
  - PIM Sparse Mode (PIM-SM)

Dense-Mode Routing Protocols

The dense-mode routing protocol approach is based on the assumption that the multicast group members are densely distributed throughout the network and bandwidth is plentiful, meaning that almost all hosts on the network belong to the group. These dense-mode multicast routing protocols rely on periodic flooding of the network with multicast traffic to set up and maintain the distribution tree.

To reiterate, dense-mode routing protocols include the following:

- DVMRP
- PIM-DM
- MOSPF

Dense-mode protocols employ only SPTs to deliver (S,G) multicast traffic using a push principle. The push principle assumes that every subnet in the network has at least one receiver of the (S,G) multicast traffic, and, therefore, the traffic is pushed or flooded to all points in the network. This process is analogous to a radio or TV broadcast that is transmitted over the air to all homes within the coverage area. Receivers simply need to tune in to the broadcast to receive the program.

The DM protocols are most appropriate in environments with densely clustered receivers and the bandwidth to tolerate flooding. An example of when a DM protocol might be used is when a CEO of a company wants to broadcast a message to all employees within the head-quarters campus network.

Distance Vector Multicast Routing Protocol

DVMRP was the first true multicast routing protocol to see widespread use. DVMRP is similar in many ways to Routing Information Protocol (RIP), with some variations added to support multicast. Described in RFC 1075, DVMRP is widely used on the Internet *multicast backbone (MBONE)*. The key characteristics of DVMRP are as follows:

- Distance vector-based (similar to RIP)
- Periodic route updates (every 60 seconds)
- Infinity = 32 hops
- Classless

DVMRP uses reverse-path flooding. When a router receives a packet, it floods the packet out all paths except the one that leads back to the packet source. This technique allows a data stream to reach all LANs. If a router is attached to a set of LANs that do not want to receive a particular multicast group, the router can send a prune message back up the distribution tree to stop subsequent packets from traveling where there are no members.

DVMRP periodically floods packets to reach any new hosts that want to receive traffic from a particular multicast group. There is a direct relationship between the time it takes for a new receiver to get the data stream and the frequency of flooding.

DVMRP implements its own unicast routing protocol to determine which interface leads back to the source of the data stream. This unicast routing protocol is similar to RIP and is based purely on hop counts. As a result, the path that the multicast traffic follows might not be the same as the path that the unicast traffic follows.

Protocol-Independent Multicast Dense Mode

Protocol-Independent Multicast (PIM) gets its name from the fact that it is IP routing protocol-independent. That is, regardless of which unicast routing protocol(s) is/are used to populate the unicast routing table (including static routes), PIM uses this information to perform multicast forwarding; hence, it is protocol-independent. Although PIM is typically referred to as a multicast routing protocol, it actually uses the existing unicast routing table to perform the RPF check function instead of maintaining a separate multicast route table. Because PIM doesn't have to maintain its own routing table, it doesn't send or receive multicast route updates like other protocols, such as MOSPF and DVMRP. By not having to send multicast route updates, the PIM overhead is significantly reduced in comparison to other multicast protocols.

NOTE

Cisco routers run PIM. They know enough about DVMRP to successfully forward multicast packets to and receive packets from a DVMRP neighbor. Cisco routers can also propagate DVMRP routes into and through a PIM cloud. However, only the PIM protocol uses this information. Cisco routers do not implement DVMRP to forward multicast packets.

PIM-DM is similar to DVMRP, as you can see from the following list of key characteristics:

- Protocol-independent (uses a unicast route table for RPF check)
- No separate multicast routing protocol (as with DVMRP)
- Flood-and-prune behavior (3-minute cycle)
- Classless (as long as classless unicast routing is in use)

PIM-DM works best when numerous members belong to each multimedia group. PIM floods the multimedia packet to all routers in the network and then prunes routers that do not support members of that particular multicast group.

PIM-DM is most useful when

- Senders and receivers are in close proximity to one another
- There are few senders and many receivers
- The volume of multicast traffic is high
- The stream of multicast traffic is constant

PIM-DM is no longer a widely deployed protocol because PIM-SM has proven to be the more efficient multicast solution.

Multicast Open Shortest Path First

NOTE

Cisco routers do not support MOSPF.

Described in RFC 1584, *Multicast Open Shortest Path First (MOSPF)* is intended for use within a single routing domain, such as a network controlled by a single organization. MOSPF is dependent on the use of OSPF as the accompanying unicast routing protocol. Figure 7-41 shows how MOSPF works by including multicast information in OSPF link-state advertisements. An MOSPF router learns which multicast groups are active on which LANs.

MOSPF is best suited for environments that have relatively few (S,G) pairs active at any given time. This protocol works less well in environments that have many active sources or unstable links.

Sparse Mode Routing Protocols

The second approach to multicast routing is based on the assumption that the multicast group members are sparsely distributed throughout the network and bandwidth is not necessarily widely available.

It is important to note that sparse mode does not imply that the group has few members, just that they are widely dispersed. In this case, flooding would unnecessarily waste network bandwidth and could cause serious performance problems. Therefore, sparse-mode multicast routing protocols must rely on more selective techniques to set up and maintain multicast trees. Sparse-mode protocols begin with an empty distribution tree and add branches only as the result of explicit requests to join the distribution.

Figure 7-41 MOSPF Operation

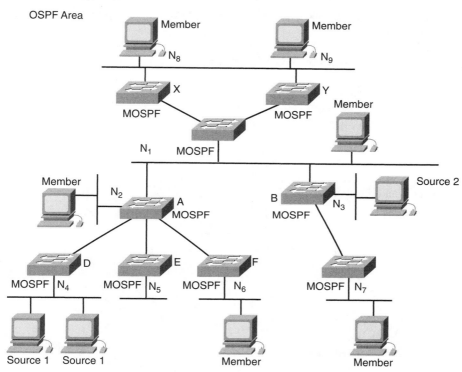

To reiterate, sparse-mode routing protocols include the following:

- CBT
- PIM-SM

Because sparse-mode protocols assume that relatively few routers in the network will be involved in each multicast, these protocols are more appropriate in WAN environments.

Core-Based Trees

RFC 2201 describes CBT. The CBT protocol constructs a single tree that is shared by all members of the group. Multicast traffic for the entire group is sent and received over the same tree, regardless of the source. This use of a shared tree can provide significant savings in terms of the amount of multicast state information that is stored in individual routers.

A CBT shared tree has a core router that is used to construct the tree, as shown in Figure 7-42. Routers join the tree by sending a join message to the core. When the core receives a join request, it returns an acknowledgment over the reverse path, thus forming a branch of the tree. Join messages need not travel all the way to the core before being acknowledged. If a join message encounters a router on the tree before the message reaches the core, that router terminates the join message and acknowledges it. The router that sent the join is then connected to the shared tree.

Figure 7-42 The CBT Protocol Core Router Constructs a Single Tree Shared by All Members of the Group

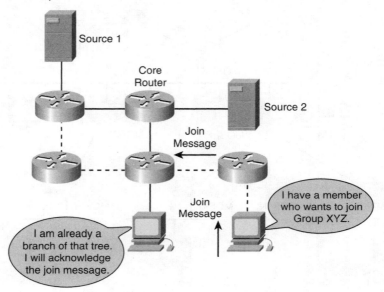

The CBT multicast routing protocol is truly a work in progress and has been so for several years. The original version, CBTv1, was superseded by CBTv2 (defined in RFC 2189), which, unfortunately, is not backward-compatible with CBTv1. However, because CBTv1 was never really implemented in any production networks to speak of, backward compatibility is not an issue. CBTv2 also has not seen significant deployment to date, which is probably good, because a new draft specification for CBTv3 is already out that supersedes and is not backward-compatible with CBTv2!

PIM-SM

Protocol-Independent Multicast Sparse Mode (PIM-SM) is optimized for environments that have many multipoint data streams. Sparse multicast is most useful when

- A group has few receivers
- The type of traffic is intermittent

In sparse mode, each data stream goes to a relatively small number of segments in the campus network. Instead of flooding the network to determine the status of multicast members, PIM-SM defines a rendezvous point. When a sender wants to send data, it first sends to the rendezvous point. When a receiver wants to receive data, it registers with the rendezvous point. When the data stream begins to flow from sender to rendezvous point to receiver, the routers in the path optimize the path automatically to remove any unnecessary hops. PIM-SM assumes that no hosts want the multicast traffic unless they specifically ask for it. PIM can simultaneously support dense mode for some multicast groups and sparse mode for others.

Configure IP Multicast Routing

The IP multicast routing tasks are divided into basic and advanced tasks. The basic tasks that must be performed to set up a multicast session are as follows:

- Enabling IP multicast routing
- Enabling PIM on an interface
- Configuring a rendezvous point (optional)
- Configuring a TTL threshold (optional)
- Joining a multicast group (optional)
- Changing the IGMP version (optional)
- Enabling CGMP or IGMP snooping (optional)

The first two basic tasks in the list are required to configure IP multicast routing; the remaining tasks are optional.

Configuring PIM-SM is really quite straightforward. On each router in the network, IP multicast routing must be enabled by using the **ip multicast-routing** global configuration command, first introduced in Cisco IOS Release 10.1.

Then, it is best to enable PIM-SM on every interface in every router in the network using the **ip pim sparse-mode** interface command.

The final step is to configure each of the routers in the network with the RP's IP address using the following global configuration command:

```
Router(config)#ip pim rp-address rp-address
```

This command tells the router where to send the (*,G) joins when it needs to join the shared tree in sparse mode.

The reason for turning on multicast on every interface is that IP multicast routing is upside-down routing that forwards (or does not forward) multicast packets based on where the packets came from (source IP address) as opposed to where they are going (multicast group address). Consequently, the control mechanism for multicast traffic paths is not quite the same as the control mechanism for unicast routing.

NOTE

Another method of enabling multicast on an interface is the use of the **ip pim sparse-dense-mode** command. This command allows the router to use either dense or sparse mode, depending on the existence of RP information for each multicast group. This makes it much easier to switch the entire network from dense mode to sparse mode (or vice versa) as needed. *PIM sparse-dense mode* is the recommended mode to use when deploying Auto-RP, as discussed later.

Not turning on multicast routing on every interface is a common mistake when network administrators are first enabling multicast routing. Failure to enable multicast on every interface often results in RPF failures, because the RPF interface for a particular source of multicast traffic is the interface that would be used if the router sent traffic to this particular source.

Verify PIM Configuration

To display information about interfaces configured for PIM, enter the **show ip pim interface** [*type number*] [*count*] privileged mode command, as shown in Example 7-2.

Example 7-2 *Displaying the IP Address of the Next-Hop Multicast Router, as Well as the Interface's PIM Mode, Can Be Useful*

```
Router#show ip pim interface
Address        Interface      Version/Mode    Nbr    Query        DR
                                                     Count Intvl
10.1.1.2       FastEthernet0/0 v2/Sparse-Dense 0      30           10.1.1.2
192.168.1.1    Serial0/0      v2/Sparse-Dense 0      30           0.0.0.0
0.0.0.0        Serial0/1      v2/Sparse-Dense 0      30           0.0.0.0
Router#
```

The output in Example 7-2 displays the following items:

- The IP address of the next-hop router
- The interface type; on a Route Switch Module (RSM), this value is the VLAN designation
- The PIM version and mode configured on each interface
- How many PIM neighbors have been discovered through this interface
- The frequency, in seconds, of PIM router-query messages
- The IP address of the designated router on the LAN

Designated Router Selection

NOTE

DR election is necessary only on multi-access networks. It is not required for point-to-point links, because the connected router is effectively the DR for directly connected host systems.

Cisco routers use the PIM routing protocol to forward multicast traffic. Two PIM routers are neighbors if there is a direct connection between them.

Each multicast-enabled router is configured to know which interfaces will use PIM. These interfaces connect either to neighboring PIM routers in the network or to host systems on a LAN. If a LAN has multiple PIM routers, they are considered neighbors.

The procedure for electing the designated router (DR) is the same for both PIM-SM and PIM-DM. Each PIM router connected to a multiaccess LAN issues periodic PIM router queries onto the LAN. The PIM router with the highest IP address becomes the DR for the LAN. If the DR becomes inoperable, a new DR is elected from the alternate PIM routers on the LAN. Figure 7-43 illustrates the DR election process.

Figure 7-43 PIM Elects a DR on a LAN

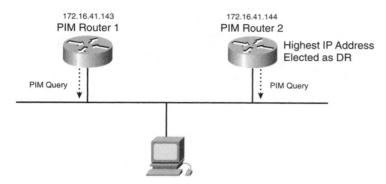

On a multiaccess LAN, one router is selected to poll the LAN for host group membership. However, all PIM routers on a single subnet receive replies from the host. The router selected to poll the LAN is called the DR. The DR is responsible for sending IGMP host-query messages to all hosts on the LAN. A campus network can have many DRs, one for each leaf subnet of the distribution tree.

Displaying PIM Neighbors

Cisco IOS software can be used to discover the PIM neighbors in the network. To display a table of the neighboring routers from a specific router, enter this privileged mode command:

```
Router#show ip pim neighbor type number
```

Configure Auto-RP (Optional)

Manually configuring multiple rendezvous points in a large campus network can result in inconsistent RP configurations and can cause connectivity problems. *Auto-RP* is a Cisco-proprietary standalone protocol that automates the distribution of group-to-RP mappings in a network running sparse-mode PIM. Auto-RP facilitates the use of multiple RPs within a network to serve different group ranges. Auto-RP also allows load splitting among different RPs and the arrangement of RPs according to the locations of group participants. With the Auto-RP mechanism, an **rp-announce** command must be entered on the router to act as an RP for a certain range of multicast group addresses. Multiple RPs can be used to serve different group ranges, or to serve as backups of each other. An *RP mapping agent* is assigned to a router to receive the RP announcement messages. The RP mapping agent then sends the consistent group-to-RP mappings to all designated routers. This method allows all designated routers to automatically discover which RP to use for attached receivers and senders, as shown in Figure 7-44.

Figure 7-44 Auto-RP Enables the Propagation of Group-to-RP Mappings

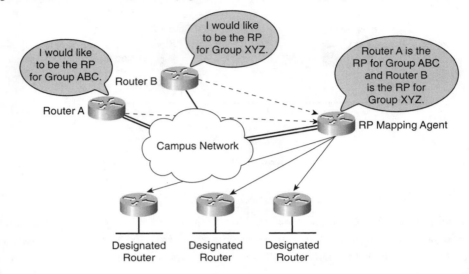

Auto-RP is disabled by default. To enable it on a router, enter the following global configuration mode command:

```
Router(config)#ip pim send-rp-announce type number scope ttl group-list
  access-list-number
```

To disable a router as a *candidate RP*, enter the **no ip pim send-rp-announce** command.

As illustrated in Figure 7-45, candidate RPs send an Auto-RP RP announcement message to the well-known group CISCO-RP-ANNOUNCE (224.0.1.39). A router configured as an RP mapping agent listens on this well-known group address to determine which RPs act for the various ranges of multicast group addresses.

The RP mapping agent then sends the RP-to-group mappings in an Auto-RP RP discovery message to the well-known group CISCO-RP-DISCOVERY (224.0.1.40). PIM DRs listen to this well-known group to determine which RPs to use.

By default, a router is not configured as a PIM RP mapping agent. To configure a router to send Auto-RP RP discovery messages, enter the following global configuration mode command:

```
Router(config)#ip pim send-rp-discovery scope ttl
```

ttl is the Time-To-Live value that limits the scope of the discovery message.

Figure 7-45 Auto-RP Relies on the Well-Known Multicast Groups 224.0.1.39 and 224.0.1.40

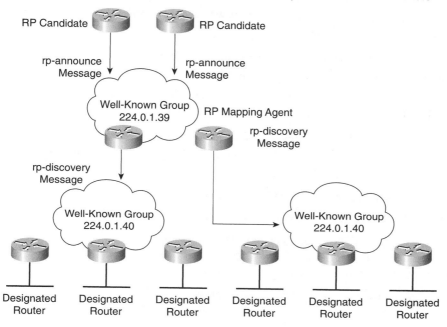

Example 7-3 shows that Nakagawa is an RP mapping agent. The scope of the discovery messages is 16 router hops.

Example 7-3 *An RP Mapping Agent Is Used to Advertise the RP-to-Group Mappings*

```
Nakagawa(config)#ip multicast-routing
Nakagawa(config)#ip pim send-rp-discovery scope 16
```

To disable a router as an RP mapping agent, enter the **no ip pim send-rp-discovery** command.

Optional IP Multicast Routing Tasks

Optional IP multicast routing tasks include the following (as described in the following sections):

- Defining the scope of delivery of multicast packets
- Joining a multicast group
- Changing IGMP versions

Defining the Scope of Delivery of Multicast Packets

The function of the TTL parameter on a multicast-enabled interface controls whether packets are forwarded out that interface.

Only multicast packets with a TTL greater than the interface TTL threshold are forwarded on the interface. Packets with a TTL equal to or less than the interface threshold are discarded. The packet TTL is compared to the interface threshold first. The router then decrements the packet TTL by a value of 1 upon sending the packet out the interface.

The default value for the TTL threshold on an interface is 0. A value of 0 means that all multicast packets are forwarded on the interface. To change the default TTL threshold value, enter the following command in interface configuration mode:

```
Router(config-if)#ip multicast ttl-threshold ttl
```

ttl signifies the TTL value in router hops; this value can range from 0 to 255 hops.

In Example 7-4, the TTL threshold is set to 16 router hops.

Example 7-4 *The TTL Threshold Can Be Set Between 0 and 255*

```
Router#show running-config

<output omitted>

interface FastEthernet0/0
 ip address 10.1.1.2 255.255.255.0
 no ip directed-broadcast
 ip pim sparse-dense-mode
 ip multicast ttl-threshold 16

<output omitted>
```

To restore the default value of 0, enter the following command in interface configuration mode:

```
Router(config-if)#no ip multicast ttl-threshold
```

Joining a Multicast Group

Cisco routers can be configured to be members of a multicast group. Being a member of a multicast group is useful in determining multicast reachability in a network. If a router is configured to be a member of a specific multicast group, that router can respond to commands,

NOTE

Because the TTL field is used to limit the range, or scope, of a multicast transmission, configure the TTL threshold only on border routers. Routers on which a TTL threshold value is configured automatically become border routers.

such as **ping** and Internet Control Message Protocol (ICMP) echo requests, addressed to that group. A group member router can also participate in multicast Cisco IOS software traceroute actions.

To have the router join a multicast group, enter the following command in interface configuration mode:

```
Router(config-if)#ip igmp join-group group-address
```

group-address is the address of the multicast group.

The configuration shown in Example 7-5 places the router in multicast Group 224.1.1.1.

Example 7-5 *A Router Interface Can Be Configured to Participate as a Host in a Distribution Tree*

```
Router#show running-config

<output omitted>

interface FastEthernet0/0
 ip address 10.1.1.2 255.255.255.0
 no ip directed-broadcast
 ip pim sparse-dense-mode
 ip multicast ttl-threshold 16
 ip igmp join-group 224.1.1.1

<output omitted>
```

> **NOTE**
>
> The term *interface* describes the primary interface on an attached network. If a router has multiple physical interfaces on a single network, this protocol needs to run on only one of the interfaces. Hosts, on the other hand, need to perform their actions on all interfaces that have memberships associated with them.

Issuing a **ping** command specifying that multicast group address causes all routers in that group to respond.

To cancel a router's membership in a multicast group, enter the **no ip igmp join-group** *group-address* command.

Changing IGMP Versions

Cisco routers do not automatically detect the IGMP version of systems on the subnet and dynamically switch between versions.

IGMP Version 2 mode is the default for all systems using Cisco IOS Release 11.3(2)T or later. IGMP Version 3 is available with Cisco IOS Release 12.0(15)S or later. To determine the current version setting for an interface, enter the following privileged command:

```
Router#show ip igmp interface type-number
```

type-number represents the name of the interface on which the IGMP protocol is configured. Example 7-6 shows sample output from the **show ip igmp interface** command to determine the IGMP version.

Example 7-6 *Determining the IGMP Version on an Interface*

```
Router#show ip igmp interface fast 0/0
FastEthernet0/0 is up, line protocol is up
  Internet address is 10.1.1.2/24
  IGMP is enabled on interface
  Current IGMP version is 2
  CGMP is disabled on interface
  IGMP query interval is 60 seconds
  IGMP querier timeout is 120 seconds
  IGMP max query response time is 10 seconds
  Last member query response interval is 1000 ms
  Inbound IGMP access group is not set
  IGMP activity: 3 joins, 1 leaves
  Multicast routing is enabled on interface
  Multicast TTL threshold is 16
  Multicast designated router (DR) is 10.1.1.2 (this system)
  IGMP querying router is 10.1.1.2 (this system)
```

To enable a specific IGMP version, enter the following interface configuration mode command:

```
ip igmp version {3 | 2 | 1}
```

To restore the default value of Version 2, enter the **no ip igmp version** command.

Because of its unique capability to send out a single data stream to multiple clients, IP multicast technologies have become the transmission method of choice for most multimedia applications.

Cisco IP Telephony

Cisco AVVID was discussed earlier in this chapter. Cisco AVVID includes the Cisco IP Telephony solution. The chapter then changed gears and explored IP multicast, which is also part of the AVVID architecture. This chapter now looks at the Cisco IP Telephony solution in more detail.

Voice over IP (VoIP) is probably the most feasible among today's technologies for data, voice, and video integration. VoIP is the technology that uses IP to transmit voice conversations over a data network, such as an intranet or the Internet.

Introducing the Cisco IP Telephony Solution

The Cisco IP Telephony solution relies on the stable foundation of Cisco multiprotocol routers and Catalyst multilayer LAN switches, which are the building blocks in enterprise networks. Cisco CallManager is the heart of an IP Telephony solution. Figures 7-46, 7-47, and 7-48 illustrate alternative CallManager deployments used in Cisco IP Telephony deployments. The uOne Messaging System is composed of three components:

- A uOne GateServer
- Two back-end servers (the directory server and the message server)

These components run on a Sun Sparc server.

Figure 7-46 No Geographic Limitations Exist for Deploying CallManager Servers

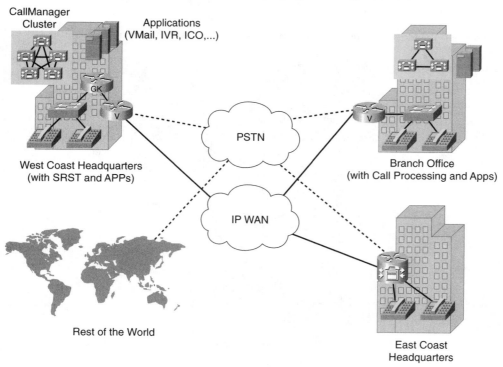

Figure 7-47 CallManager Provides a Migration Path from Legacy to Pure IP Telephony Solutions

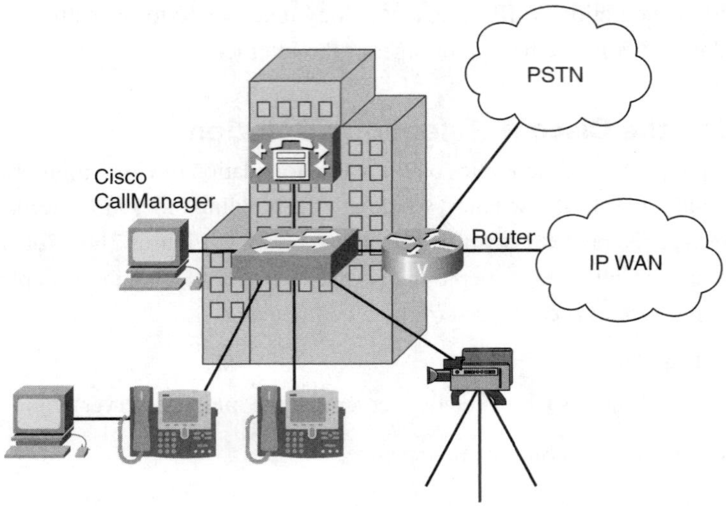

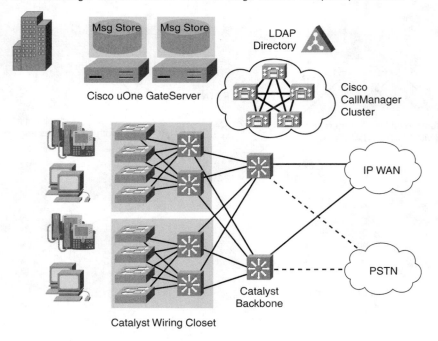

Figure 7-48 CallManager Clusters Can Be Used for Large-Scale IP Telephony Solutions

Cisco CallManager is the software-based call-processing component and essentially is the heart of the Cisco IP Telephony solution. The software extends enterprise telephony features and functions to packet telephony network devices such as IP Phones, media processing devices, voice over IP (VoIP) gateways, and multimedia applications. Additional data, voice, and video services such as unified messaging, multimedia videoconferencing, collaborative contact centers, and interactive multimedia response systems interact with the IP Telephony solution through Cisco CallManager's open telephony application programming interface (API).

The Cisco CallManager software includes a suite of integrated voice applications that perform ad hoc voice conferencing and browser-based attendant console functions. The key benefit of all these voice applications is that special-purpose voice processing hardware is not required.

Supplementary and enhanced services such as hold, transfer, forward, conference, multiple line appearances, automatic route selection, speed dial, and last-number redial are available on Cisco CallManager. It also provides extension mobility. Users can log in to any IP Phone, and the extension and the individual's dial privileges are applied to the phone regardless of his or her location. This lets users access all of their personal phone features, such as fast dials, personal contacts, voice mail, productivity applications, and more from any IP Phone when they are away from their desks.

Multiple Cisco CallManager servers are clustered and managed as a single entity. The ability to cluster multiple call-processing servers on an IP network is unique in the industry and provides scalability for up to 10,000 users per cluster. By interlinking multiple clusters, system capacity can be increased to up to 100,000 users per multiple cluster system. Clustering aggregates the power of multiple distributed Cisco CallManager servers, enhancing the scalability and accessibility of the servers to phones, gateways, and applications. Triple server redundancy improves overall system availability. Call admission control ensures that voice QoS is maintained across constricted WAN links and automatically diverts calls to alternate PSTN routes when WAN bandwidth is unavailable.

Figure 7-49 shows the availability and scalability of four Cisco hardware platforms when deployed in an IP Telephony environment. Figures 7-50, 7-51, and 7-52 show the various graphical user interface (GUI) components of CallManager and Cisco IP Phones.

Figure 7-49 Several Cisco Hardware Platforms Are Available to Enable Scalable IP Telephony Solutions

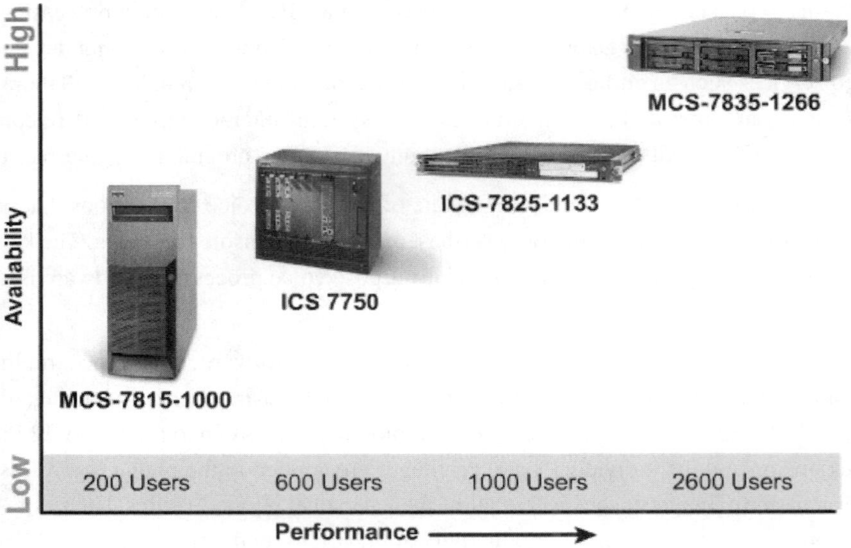

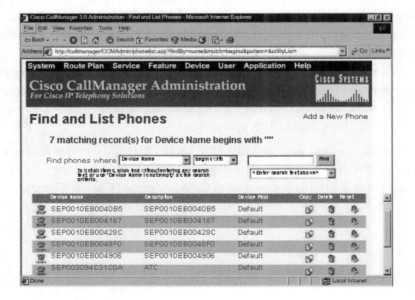

Figure 7-50 The CallManager GUI Allows for Easy Viewing of IP Phones on the Network

Figure 7-51 The CallManager GUI Can Display the Configuration on an Individual IP Phone

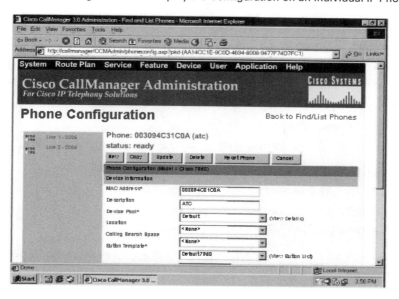

Figure 7-52 Cisco IP Phones Have a Graphical Interface Used to Enable Easy Configuration and to Display Useful Information

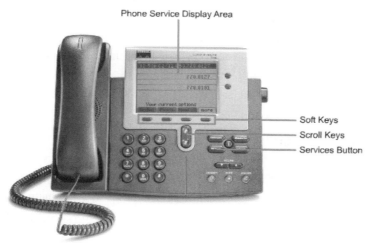

Cisco IP Telephony Designs

The overall goals of an IP Telephony network are as follows:

- End-to-end IP Telephony
- IP WAN as the primary voice path between sites, with the PSTN as the secondary voice path
- Lower total cost of ownership with greater flexibility
- Enabling of new applications

Currently, four general design models apply to the majority of implementations:

- Single-site model
- Multiple sites with independent call processing
- Multisite IP WAN with distributed call processing
- Multisite IP WAN with centralized call processing

The following sections summarize the design goals and implementation guidelines for each of these models.

Single-Site Model

The single-site model has the following design characteristics:

- A single Cisco CallManager server or CallManager cluster
- A maximum of 10,000 users per cluster
- A maximum of eight servers in a Cisco CallManager cluster (four servers for primary call processing, two for backup call processing, one database publisher, and one Trivial File Transfer Protocol [TFTP] server)
- A maximum of 2500 users registered with a Cisco CallManager server at any time
- The PSTN only for all external calls
- Digital signal processor (DSP) resources for conferencing
- Voice mail and unified messaging components
- A *G.711* codec for all IP phone calls (80 kbps of IP bandwidth per call, uncompressed)
- To guarantee voice quality, use Cisco LAN switches with a minimum of two queues.

Figure 7-53 illustrates the single-site design model for a Cisco IP Telephony network.

Figure 7-53 The Single-Site Model Uses a Single CallManager Server or CallManager Cluster

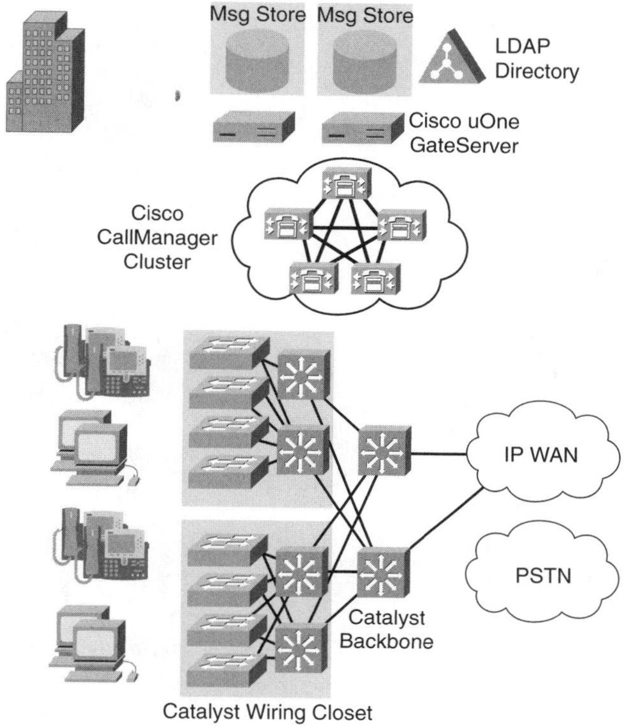

Multiple Sites with Independent Call Processing

The independent multiple sites model has the following design characteristics:

- A Cisco CallManager server or CallManager cluster at each site to provide scalable call control
- A maximum of 10,000 IP Phones per cluster
- No limit on the number of clusters
- Use of the PSTN for networking multiple sites and for all external calls
- DSP resources for conferencing at each site
- Voice messaging or unified messaging components at each site
- Voice compression is not required

Figure 7-54 illustrates the multiple site with independent call processing design model for a Cisco IP Telephony network.

Figure 7-54 *Multiple Sites with Independent Call Processing Use a CallManager Server or Cluster at Each Site*

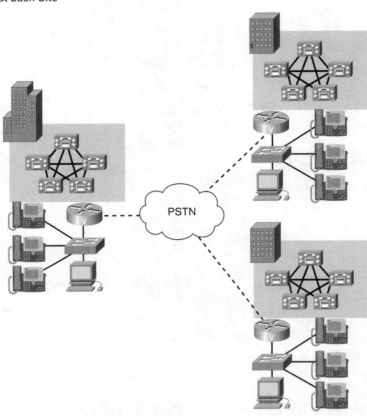

Multiple Sites with Distributed Call Processing

The multisite IP WAN with distributed call processing has the following design characteristics:

- A Cisco CallManager server or CallManager cluster at each location (10,000 users maximum per site)
- Cisco CallManager clusters are confined to a single campus and might not span the WAN.
- IP WAN as the primary voice path between sites, with the PSTN as the secondary voice path
- Transparent use of the PSTN if the IP WAN is unavailable
- Cisco IOS gatekeeper for *E.164* address resolution
- Cisco IOS gatekeeper for admission control to the IP WAN
- A maximum of 100 sites interconnected across the IP WAN using hub-and-spoke topologies

- Compressed voice calls are supported across the IP WAN.
- A single WAN codec is supported.
- DSP resources for conferencing and WAN transcoding at each site.
- Voice mail and unified messaging components at each site.
- The minimum bandwidth requirement for voice and data traffic is 56 kbps. For voice, interactive video, and data, the minimum requirement is 768 kbps. In each case, the bandwidth allocated to voice, video, and data should not exceed 75% of the total capacity.
- Remote sites can use Cisco IOS as well as gateways based on the Skinny Gateway Protocol.

Figure 7-55 illustrates the multisite IP WAN with a distributed call processing design model for a Cisco IP Telephony network.

Figure 7-55 Multiple Sites with Distributed Call Processing Use the Cisco IOS Gatekeeper for Admission Control

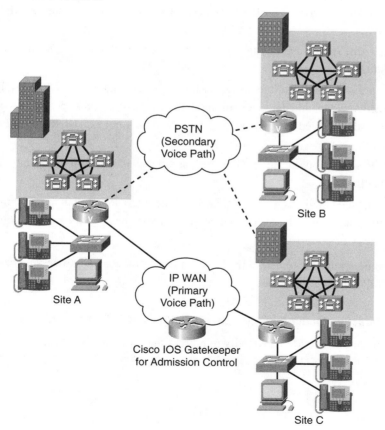

Multisite IP WAN with Centralized Call Processing

The multisite IP WAN with centralized call processing has the following design characteristics:

- The central site supports only one active Cisco CallManager server. A cluster can contain a secondary and tertiary CallManager server as long as all IP Phones served by the cluster are registered to the same CallManager server at any given time. This is called a centralized call processing cluster.
- Each centralized call processing cluster supports a maximum of 2500 users (there's no limit on the number of remote sites). Multiple centralized call processing clusters of 2500 users at a central site can be interconnected using H.323.
- IP Phones at remote sites do not have a local Cisco CallManager server.
- The call admission control mechanism is based on bandwidth by location.
- Compressed voice calls across the IP WAN are supported.
- Manual use of the PSTN is available if the IP WAN is fully subscribed for voice traffic (the PSTN access code must be dialed after a busy signal).
- Dial backup is required for IP Phone service across the WAN in case the IP WAN goes down.
- Voice mail, unified messaging, and DSP resource components are available at the central site only.
- The minimum bandwidth requirement for voice and data traffic is 56 kbps. For voice, interactive video, and data, the minimum requirement is 768 kbps. In each case, the bandwidth allocated to voice, video, and data should not exceed 75 percent of the total capacity.
- Remote sites can use Cisco IOS, as well as gateways, based on the Skinny Station Protocol.
- If using voice mail, each site must have unique internal dial plan number ranges. Internal dial plans cannot be overlapped among remote sites if voice mail is required—no two sites can share 1XXX.

Figure 7-56 illustrates the multisite IP WAN with a centralized call processing design model for a Cisco IP Telephony network.

 Interactive Media Activity   Checkbox: Cisco IP Telephony Designs

This Interactive Media Activity reinforces the goals of Cisco IP Telephony.

Figure 7-56 Multisite IP WAN with Centralized Call Processing Relies on a Centralized CallManager
Cluster

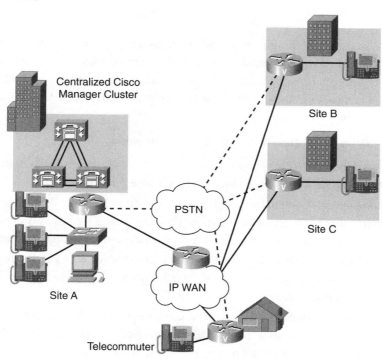

Voice Quality Issues

Although VoIP is one of the most useful technologies in recent history, its effective deployment is strongly dependent on the quality of service implemented for the voice traffic. IP phones sit at the access layer, normally connected to Layer 2 switches. From the access layer to the WAN, QoS features must be implemented to optimize voice quality.

Common Voice Issues

Two major factors affect voice quality:

- **Delayed packets**—Packet delay can cause either voice quality degradation because of the end-to-end voice latency or packet loss if the delay is variable. If the end-to-end voice latency becomes too long (250 milliseconds (ms), for example), the conversation begins to sound like two parties talking on a CB radio. If the delay is variable, there is a risk of jitter buffer overruns at the receiving end.
- **Lost packets**—Packet loss causes voice clipping and skips.

The next sections explore common voice issues in more detail.

Delay

One of the most important design considerations in implementing voice is minimizing one-way, end-to-end delay. Voice traffic is real-time traffic; if there is too long a delay in voice packet delivery, speech becomes unrecognizable. Delay is inherent in voice networking and is caused by a number of different factors, such as low-bandwidth links. An acceptable delay is less than 200 ms.

Two kinds of delay are inherent in today's telephony networks:

- **Propagation delay**—Propagation delay is caused by the characteristics of the speed of light traveling via a fiber-optic-based or copper-based medium.

- **Handling delay**—Sometimes called serialization delay, handling delay is caused by the devices that handle voice information. Handling delays significantly degrade voice quality in a packet network. Delays caused by codecs are considered handling delays.

  Another handling delay is the time it takes to generate a voice packet. In VoIP, the DSP generates a frame every 10 ms. Two of these frames are then placed within one voice packet, so the packet delay is 20 ms.

  A third source of handling delay is the time it takes to move the packet to the output queue. Cisco IOS software expedites the process of determining packet destination and getting the packet to the output queue. The actual delay at the output queue is another source of handling delay and should be kept under 10 ms whenever possible by using queuing methods that are optimal for the network.

Jitter

Jitter is another factor that affects delay. Jitter is the difference between when a voice packet is expected to be received and when it actually is received, causing discontinuity in the real-time voice stream. Voice devices compensate for jitter by setting up a playout buffer to play back voice smoothly. Jitter can be caused by thermal noise, bandwidth limitations, improper impedance termination, asymmetries in clock cycles, and EMI problems.

End-to-End Delay

Figuring out the end-to-end delay is not difficult if the end-to-end signal paths/data paths, the codec, and the packets' payload size are known factors. Adding the delays from the endpoints to the codecs at each end, the encoder delay (which is 5 ms for the G.711 and *G.726* codecs and 10 ms for the *G.729* codec), the packet delay, and the fixed portion of the network delay yields the connection's end-to-end delay. Table 7-1 describes common *codecs*.

Table 7-1 Codecs Are Critical Variables in Configuring VoIP Solutions

Codec	Bit Rate (kbps)	Framing Size	Compression Delay (ms)
G.711 PCM	64	0.125	5
G.729 *CS-ACELP*	8	10	15
G.729a CS-ACELP	8	10	15

Echo

Echo is voice feedback in the telephone receiver when talking. When timed properly, echo is reassuring to the speaker. But if the echo exceeds approximately 25 ms, it can be distracting and cause breaks in the conversation.

In a traditional telephony network, echo is normally caused by a mismatch in impedance from the four-wire network switch conversion to the two-wire local loop and is controlled by echo cancellers. In voice-packet-based networks, echo cancellers are built into the low bit-rate codecs and are operated on each DSP. Echo cancellers are, by design, limited by the total amount of time they will wait for the reflected speech to be received. This amount of time is called an *echo trail*. The echo trail is normally 32 ms. VoIP has configurable echo trails of 8, 16, 24, and 32 ms.

Voice, as a class of IP network traffic, has strict requirements concerning packet loss, delay, and delay variation (also known as jitter). To meet these requirements for voice traffic, the Cisco IP Telephony solution includes QoS features such as classification, queuing, traffic shaping, scheduling, Compressed Real-Time Transport Protocol (CRTP), and Transmission Control Protocol (TCP) header compression. The QoS components of the Cisco AVVID IP Telephony solution are provided through the rich IP traffic management, queuing, and shaping capabilities of the Cisco AVVID network infrastructure.

Implementing QoS for Voice

Voice, video, and mission-critical data applications are important underlying productivity tools that make a business successful. Ensuring that these applications are effectively delivered requires skillful traffic management, particularly within the context of an integrated networking solution. QoS is a key Cisco AVVID network infrastructure enabling the capability for such an environment. Figure 7-57 shows various WAN environments for which VoIP QoS needs to be implemented.

Figure 7-57 QoS Configuration Is an Integral Piece of the Integration of Voice, Video, and Data

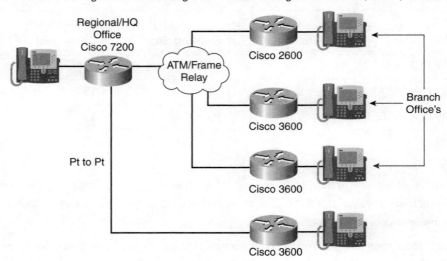

QoS

In a converged environment, all types of traffic travel over a single transport infrastructure. Yet not all traffic types are the same. Data is bursty, loss-intolerant, and latency-insensitive. Voice, on the other hand, is nonbursty and has some tolerance to loss but is latency-sensitive. The challenge is in providing the required level of service for each of these traffic types.

Running both voice and data on a common network requires the proper QoS tools to ensure that the delay and loss parameters of voice traffic are satisfied. These tools are available as features in IP phones, switches, and routers.

Application Considerations for QoS

The specific QoS requirements for given applications are generally determined by the three parameters of latency, jitter, and loss. Depending on the type of application to be implemented over a Cisco AVVID network infrastructure, the importance and effects of these considerations can differ.

One-way latency for voice or videoconferencing should be no more than 150 to 200 ms, and streaming video can tolerate up to 4- to 5-second latency. Similarly, jitter is not an issue for streaming video, but it should be limited to 30 ms for voice and videoconferencing applications.

Bandwidth effects also differ. For example, to support videoconferencing, the minimum bandwidth guarantee is the size of the videoconferencing session plus 20 percent. (For example, a 384-kbps videoconferencing session requires 460 kbps of guaranteed priority bandwidth.) Voice requires 17 to 106 kbps of guaranteed priority bandwidth per call (depending on the sampling rate, codec, and Layer 2 overhead), and 150 bps (plus Layer 2 overhead) per phone of guaranteed bandwidth is required for voice control traffic.

Although planning requirements certainly vary depending on the application, Cisco AVVID network infrastructure capabilities have the flexibility to concurrently support QoS requirements of voice, streaming video, video content distribution, videoconferencing, and mission-critical data traffic all carried over a common IP-based networking environment.

Traffic Classification Types

The goal of protecting voice traffic from being run over by data traffic is accomplished by classifying voice traffic as high-priority and then allowing it to travel in the network before low-priority traffic, as shown in Figure 7-58. Classification can be done at Layer 2 or Layer 3.

Figure 7-58 Prioritizing Voice Traffic Is Standard Operating Procedure with QoS Configuration

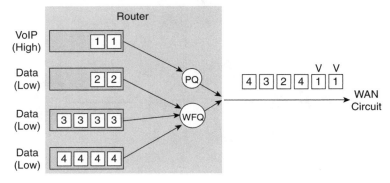

Classification is the first step toward achieving QoS. Ideally, this step should be done as close to the source as possible, usually at the network's access layer, and often at the edge of the network.

Trust Boundaries

The concept of trust is an important and integral one to implementing QoS. As soon as the end devices have a set class of service (CoS) or type of service (ToS), the switch has the option of trusting them or not. If the switch does not trust the settings, it must perform reclassification for appropriate QoS (see Figure 7-59); if the switch trusts the settings, it does not need to do any reclassification (see Figure 7-60).

Figure 7-59 The Switch Might Not Trust the Host Station's CoS Configuration

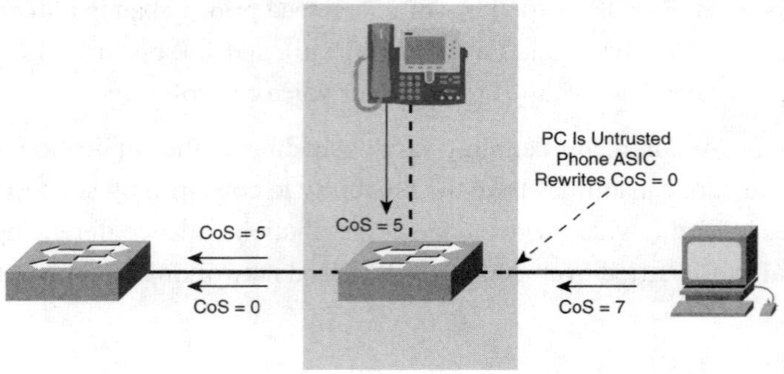

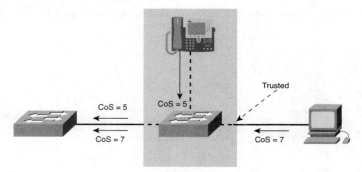

Figure 7-60 A Switch May Be Configured to Trust a Host's CoS Configuration

The notion of trusting or not trusting forms the basis of the *trust boundary*. Ideally, classification should be done as close to the source as possible. If the end device can perform this function, the trust boundary for the network is at the access layer in the wiring closet. If the device cannot perform this function, or the wiring closet switch does not trust the classification done by the end device, the trust boundary might shift. How this shift happens depends on the switch's capabilities in the wiring closet. If the switch can reclassify the packets, the trust boundary remains in the wiring closet. If the switch cannot perform this function, the task falls to other devices in the network going toward the backbone. In this case, the rule of thumb is to perform reclassification at the distribution layer. This means that the trust boundary has shifted to the distribution layer. It is more than likely that a high-end switch is in the distribution layer with features to support this function. If possible, try to avoid performing this function in the network core.

Traffic Classification

Equally important as queuing, however, is a QoS mechanism called *classification*. It is important to differentiate at all points in the network between voice and data traffic so that queuing techniques can be applied in places such as the WAN edge. Therefore classification "marks" voice and data frames differently so that they can be treated differently by the other switches and routers that make up the intelligent IP network. Two standards-based methods are used:

- At Layer 2, 802.1p defines classes of service pertaining to that Ethernet segment, as shown in Figure 7-61.

- At Layer 3, the IP layer, the IP ToS field can carry different values end to end through the network.

Figure 7-61 A Switch Can Reclassify CoS Values of Transit Voice and Data Traffic

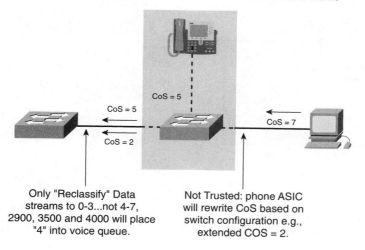

Only "Reclassify" Data streams to 0-3...not 4-7, 2900, 3500 and 4000 will place "4" into voice queue.

Not Trusted: phone ASIC will rewrite CoS based on switch configuration e.g., extended COS = 2.

The capability to change the Layer 2 and Layer 3 classification parameters to values desired by the network designer is a function inherent in the Cisco AVVID architecture. It is available in the IP Phone integrated switch and some Catalyst switching platforms. The ability of the network manager to manipulate these values at different points in the network defines a parameter called the *trust boundary*. For example, if it is trusted that the end stations and phones will set their QoS values correctly so that end-to-end QoS can be maintained, the trust boundary includes the end stations. However, if it cannot be guaranteed that all end stations behave properly and set their own priority values correctly, the capability to properly manipulate these parameters is available in the Catalyst switch infrastructure.

Traffic Classification at Layer 2

Cisco IP Phones can mark voice packets as high-priority using CoS as well as ToS. By default, the phone sends 802.1Q tagged packets with the CoS and ToS set to a value of 5.

Because most PCs do not have an 802.1Q-capable network interface card (NIC), they send the packets untagged without an 802.1Q field (see Figure 7-62). Unless the applications running on the PC send packets with a specific CoS value, this field is 0. A special case is where the TCP/IP stack in the PC has been modified to send all packets with a ToS value other than 0. Typically this does not happen, and the ToS value is 0.

Figure 7-62 IEEE 802.1Q Frames Include 3 Bits for IEEE 802.1p Tagging

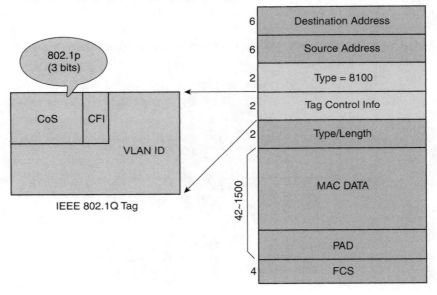

Even if the PC is sending tagged frames with a specific CoS value, Cisco IP Phones can zero out this value before sending the frames to the switch. This is the default behavior. Frames coming from the phone have a CoS of 5, and frames coming from the PC have a CoS of 0. When the switch receives these frames, it can take into account these values for further processing based on its capabilities.

The switch uses its queues (available on a per-port basis) to buffer incoming frames before sending them to the switching engine. (It is important to remember that input queuing comes into play only when there is congestion.) The switch uses the CoS value(s) to put the frames in appropriate queues. The switch can also employ mechanisms such as Weighted Random Early Detection (WRED) to make intelligent drops within a queue (also known as congestion avoidance) and Weighted Round-Robin (WRR) to provide more bandwidth to some queues than to others (also known as congestion management).

There might be times, however, when it is desirable to trust the PC CoS (if sending tagged packets), such as when there is absolute certainty that the PC CoS has the desired value. Or there might be times when it is desirable to assign a value other than 0. This can be achieved on Catalyst switches as well.

Traffic Classification at Layer 3

Using the 802.1p bits within the 802.1Q tag provides the desired QoS results at Layer 2. When traffic has to cross a Layer 3 boundary, however, it becomes imperative to implement these mechanisms using Layer 3 parameters, such as the 3 IP precedence bits (commonly called ToS) or the new Differentiated Services Code Point (DSCP) parameter, which uses the 6 most significant bits within the IP header's ToS byte (see Figure 7-63 and Table 7-2). Traffic crosses a Layer 3 boundary when packets are routed between subnets by Layer 3 switches or routers. Traffic also crosses a Layer 3 boundary when packets need to go out of the campus network onto the WAN through edge routers. When this happens, Layer 2 classification does not help. Layer 3 classification is needed to achieve the desired level of QoS. All the QoS techniques employed by the routers (including the very important WAN QoS) rely on Layer 3 classification.

Figure 7-63 8 Bits for Differentiated Code Point Classification Are Included in the IPv4 ToS Byte

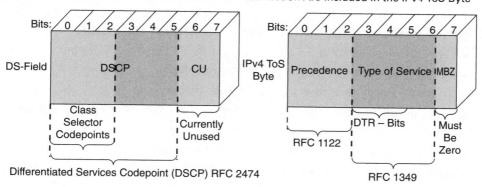

Table 7-2 lists IP Precedence and ToS values.

Table 7-2 IP Precedence and ToS Values

Bits (0 to 2): IP Precedence Defined	Bits (3 to 6): Type of Service Defined
111 (Network Control)	0000 (all normal)
110 (Internetwork Control)	1000 (minimize delay)
101 (CRITIC/ECP)	0100 (maximize throughput)
100 (Flash)	0010 (maximize reliability)
101 (Immediate)	0001 (minimize monetary cost)
001 (Priority)	
000 (Routine)	

Layer 3 classification can be achieved by using the appropriate platforms in the campus. Beginning with the IP phones, packets are already presented to the switch with CoS = ToS = 5. This Layer 3 classification is preserved even if the packets travel all the way through to the WAN edge router where the Layer 2 header is removed. So, if the trust boundary is at the source (IP phone), voice traffic has the ToS bits set to 5 and is presented to the network devices for appropriate treatment. WAN routers can use this classification to employ any of the queuing techniques. If the trust boundary is not at the source and packets need to be reclassified, the device performing this function should be able to do it at Layer 3 before it can cross a Layer 3 boundary.

Summary Recommendations for QoS Implementation

- Create a trust boundary at the network edge in the wiring closet. Make ports trusted on the wiring closet switch where IP phones are attached.
- Reclassify ToS at the edge if devices cannot be trusted.
- Shrink the trust boundary to the distribution layer and reclassify ToS there if reclassification is not possible at the edge.
- Use a priority queue if possible for delay-sensitive traffic.
- Use QoS ACLs for more granular classification of packets using Layer 4 information.
- Use policing if necessary to limit traffic for individual flows as well as aggregate flows.
- Have traffic going to the WAN edge classified at Layer 3 so that the router can use it for advanced WAN queuing mechanisms.
- Use a WAN edge router as the classifier for very small remote site networks where a Layer 3-capable switch is unavailable.

Network Design Issues for Voice

Implementing an IP Telephony solution must be preceded by a major design effort. Issues to consider involve the method of powering IP phones, how voice and data traffic are categorized into VLANs, redundancy, and QoS. The following sections cover each of these considerations in greater detail.

IP Phone Physical Connectivity

Cisco IP Phones, which connect to a switch port, also provide connectivity for an attached computer. The phone electronics, which include a three-port switch, preserve the switched connectivity model for the computer and ensure quality of service for both the IP Phone and the downstream computer.

Several options exist for physically connecting the IP Phone to the network. The first option is to connect the IP Phone to the switch and to connect the data device (computer or workstation) to the switched Ethernet port on the IP Phone. This is the most common connectivity option, and it helps with rapid deployment with minimal modifications to the existing environment. This arrangement has the advantage of using a single port on the switch to provide connectivity to both devices. Also, no changes to the cabling plant are required if the IP Phone is line-powered. In this case, the switch must be able to provide ample power to all the phones and must receive sufficient power from the AC outlet.

The second option is to connect the IP Phone and the computer using different switch ports. Although this option doubles the switch port count for every user, it provides a level of redundancy for the user. If the IP Phone goes down, the PC is unaffected, and vice versa. Also, the IP Phone and PC ports can be connected on different modules, thus achieving another layer of redundancy by providing protection for one of the devices if either module goes down.

The third option differs from the others in that the phone is not a hardware device, but a Java Telephony Application Programming Interface (JTAPI) application running on a computer. This option, the Cisco IP SoftPhone, could be particularly useful in environments where the need for a separate handset is minimal.

Power/Protection Options

Reliable power is vital to IP Telephony. An uninterruptible power supply (UPS) can be used to ensure a reliable and highly available infrastructure by protecting it from power failures. Each UPS has some amount of battery that keeps the equipment running for a certain period of time. The UPS can be configured with the appropriate amount of battery for desired results. Most Cisco AVVID products do not ordinarily come with a backup power supply.

Here are some common strategies for using a UPS:

- Back up the wiring closet switches and downstream data center using UPS. Although this strategy ensures that power is maintained to the phones, wall-powered devices such as PCs can still go down.

- Back up the whole building using UPS. This protects all devices and equipment from power failures. Protecting PCs in this fashion is useful because of the new breed of highly available data applications.

- Provide a separate generator for power (besides the feed from the utility company) and use it as backup. In this case, a UPS should be added because it usually takes a few minutes for the generator to ramp up. The advantage of this strategy is that less battery time is needed for each UPS.

In addition, UPS can be configured with options such as Simple Network Management Protocol (SNMP), remote monitoring, alarm reporting, and so on.

Power to IP Phones

Cisco IP Phones support a variety of power options:

- **Inline power**—The advantage of inline power is that it does not require a local power outlet. Power is provided by the Ethernet switch and is passed to the IP Phone through the four-pair unshielded twisted-pair (UTP) cabling. This also permits centralization of power management facilities.

- **External patch panel power**—If the switch does not have a power-enabled line card, or if one is not available for the switch being used, a Cisco power patch panel can be used. The power patch panel can be inserted in the wiring closet between the Ethernet switch and the Cisco IP Phone.

  The patch panel has a 250 W power supply and draws its power from a 110 volts alternating current (VAC) source. It can accommodate 48 ports and can supply power to each of the 48 ports at 6.3 W (see Table 7-3). A UPS is recommended for backup in the event of a power failure.

Table 7-3 Various Power Supplies Are Available to Handle Different Numbers of IP Phones

Power Supply (Watts)	IP Phones Supported at 6.3 W Per Phone
1050	60 IP Phones
1300	96 IP Phones (two modules)
2500	240 IP Phones (five modules)

The actual conductors used are pins 4 and 5 (pair 1) and pins 7 and 8 (pair 4) for power and ground return. This means that all four pairs in the Category 5 cable need to be terminated at the user's desk and in the wiring closet.

■ **Wall power**—A third option is to power the Cisco IP Phone from a local transformer module plugged into a nearby outlet. The obvious drawback to individually powering the IP Phones is the absence of centralized power protection and backup.

A combination of these power options can provide redundant power to the Cisco IP Phone.

Infrastructure Considerations

Building an end-to-end IP Telephony system requires an IP infrastructure based on Layer 2 and Layer 3 switches and routers, with switched connections to the desktop. Network designers must ensure that the endpoints are connected using switched 10/100 Ethernet ports. The use of hubs for shared connectivity to the switches is not recommended, because they can interfere with the correct operation of the IP Telephony system.

High Availability

The distributed architecture of a Cisco IP Telephony solution provides the inherent availability that is a prerequisite for voice networking. Cisco IP Telephony solutions are also inherently scalable, allowing seamless provisioning of additional capacity for infrastructure, services, and applications.

In the world of converged networking, in contrast to the world of the PBX, availability is designed into a distributed system rather than into a box. Redundancy is available in the individual hardware components for services such as power and supervisor modules. Network redundancy, however, is achieved with a combination of hardware, software, and intelligent network design practices.

Network redundancy is achieved at many levels. Physical connections exist from the edge devices where IP phones and computers are attached to two spatially diverse aggregation devices. In the event that an aggregation device fails, or connectivity is lost for any reason (such as a broken fiber or a power outage), failover of traffic to the other device is possible. By provisioning clusters of Cisco CallManager servers to provide resilient call control, other servers can pick up the load if any device within the cluster fails.

Advanced Layer 3 protocols such as HSRP or fast converging routing protocols, such as OSPF and EIGRP, can be used to provide optimum network layer convergence around failures.

Advanced tools are also available for the MAC layer (Layer 2). Tunable spanning-tree parameters and the new 802.1s standards allow fast convergence. Value-added features, such as UplinkFast and BackboneFast, allow intelligently designed networks to further optimize network convergence.

High availability of the underlying network plays a major role in ensuring a successful deployment. This translates into redundancy, resiliency, and fast convergence.

IP Addressing and Management

Each IP phone requires an IP address, along with associated information such as subnet mask, default gateway, and so on. Essentially, this means that an organization's need for IP addresses doubles as IP phones are assigned to all current PC users. This information can be configured statically on the IP phone or can be provided by DHCP. Figures 7-64 and 7-65 illustrate the private and public IP addressing options for IP phones.

Figure 7-64 Using Private Addressing for IP Phones

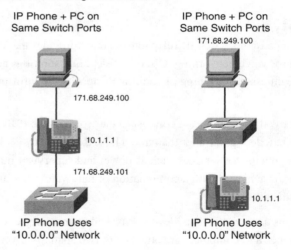

A straightforward solution to provide IP addresses to the IP phones might be to use the same subnet as data devices. However, many sites have IP subnets with more than 50 percent of subnet addresses already allocated. This would require the addition of address ranges or reallocation of the existing ranges.

Figure 7-65 Using Public IP Addressing with an IP Phone or Using the Same IP Address with a
Cisco IP SoftPhone

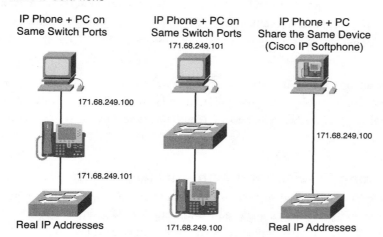

IP phones can be placed on a separate IP subnet. The new subnet could be in a registered
address space or a private address space, such as network 10.0.0.0. Using this scheme, the PC
would be on a subnet reserved for data devices and the phone would be on a subnet reserved
for voice. Configuration on the IP phone can be minimized by having the phone learn as
much information dynamically as possible. Therefore, when the IP phone powers up, it
should get its voice subnet automatically and then send a DHCP request on that subnet for
an IP address.

The automated mechanism by which the IP phone gets its voice subnet is provided through
enhancements to the Cisco Discovery Protocol (CDP).

Cisco IP Phones use CDP to interact with the switch so that it knows that an IP phone is connected to it. To provide this level of support, three new fields have been added to CDP:

- A Voice VLAN ID (VVID) field for communicating the voice subnet to the IP phone
- A Trigger field for soliciting a response from the connected device
- A Power Requirement field for getting the exact power requirement from the phone

A VLAN (Layer 2) maps to a subnet (Layer 3) as a broadcast domain such that a VLAN is
equivalent to a subnet. The VVID was introduced with Release 5.5 of the Catalyst software.
This is the voice VLAN that the switch assigns to the IP phone inside the CDP message. It
allows the IP phone to get its VLAN ID automatically when it is plugged into the switch if a
VLAN is configured for the phone. If no VLAN is configured for the IP phone, the phone
resides in the switch's native VLAN (data subnet).

The Trigger field is used to force a response from the connected device. Under normal circumstances, a device sends CDP update messages at a configured interval (the default is 1 minute). If an IP phone is connected between CDP messages, it cannot receive its VVID. In this case, the IP phone issues a trigger in the CDP message it sends to the switch, forcing the switch to respond with a VVID.

When the switch provides inline power to an IP phone, it has no way of knowing how much power the phone needs (this varies by model). Initially, the switch allocates 10 W and then adjusts the delivered power according to the requirements sent by the IP phone in the CDP message.

Implementing IP Telephony with Auxiliary VLANs

The new voice VLAN is called an auxiliary VLAN in the Catalyst software command-line interface (CLI). In the traditional switched world, data devices reside in a data VLAN. The new auxiliary VLAN is used to represent other types of devices collectively. Today, those devices are IP phones (hence, the notion of a voice VLAN), but in the future, other types of nondata devices will also be part of the auxiliary VLAN. Just as data devices come up and reside in the native VLAN (the default VLAN), IP phones come up and reside in the auxiliary VLAN if one has been configured on the switch. Figure 7-66 illustrates data and auxiliary VLANs used for a workstation and IP phone, respectively.

Figure 7-66 Auxiliary VLANs Can Be Used for Cisco IP Phones and Other Nondata Devices

Phone VLAN = 200   PC VLAN = 3

When the IP phone powers up, it communicates with the switch using CDP. The switch then provides the phone with its configured VLAN ID (voice subnet), also known as the voice VLAN ID or VVID. Meanwhile, data devices continue to reside in the switch's native VLAN (default VLAN). A data device VLAN (data subnet) is called a port VLAN ID (PVID).

Voice VLAN Configuration

The voice VLAN is disabled and the CoS value is not trusted by default on Catalyst IOS switches, such as the Catalyst 2950 and Catalyst 3550.

Before you enable the voice VLAN, you should enable QoS on the switch by entering the **mls qos** global configuration command. You also must configure the port trust state to trust by entering the **mls qos trust** interface configuration command.

You configure the voice VLAN using the following interface configuration mode command:

```
switchport voice vlan {vlan-id | dot1p | none | untagged}
```

The argument and keyword options for this command are as follows:

- *vlan-id*—The VLAN used for voice traffic. Valid IDs are from 1 to 4094. Do not enter leading 0s.
- **dot1p**—The phone uses priority tagging and VLAN 0 (the native VLAN). By default, the Cisco IP Phone forwards the voice traffic with an 802.1p priority of 5.
- **none**—The phone is not instructed through the CLI about the voice VLAN. The phone uses the configuration from the phone keypad.
- **untagged**—The phone does not tag frames and uses VLAN 4095.

To instruct the Cisco IP Phone to forward all voice traffic through a specified VLAN, use the interface command **switchport voice vlan** *vlan-id*.

By default, the Cisco IP Phone forwards the voice traffic with an 802.1Q priority of 5. Valid VLAN IDs are from 1 to 4094.

An alternative to specifying a particular voice VLAN on the switch is to instruct the switch port to use 802.1p priority tagging for voice traffic and to use the default native VLAN (VLAN 0) to carry all traffic. By default, if enabled, the Cisco IP Phone forwards the voice traffic with an 802.1p priority of 5. Use the interface command **switchport voice vlan dot1p** to specify 802.1p priority tagging of voice traffic.

To display the voice VLAN for an interface, use the **show interfaces** *interface-id* **switchport** privileged EXEC command.

Connecting to the Network with Auxiliary VLANs

The following steps outline the process that takes place when an IP phone is powered up and plugged into the network:

1. The IP phone begins a CDP exchange with the switch. The phone issues a trigger CDP to force a response from the switch. That response contains the phone's VVID.

2. If the IP phone is configured to use DHCP (the default), it issues a DHCP request on the voice subnet it got from the switch. This is the recommended mode of operation. Static addressing can be used, but it prevents mobility.

3. The IP phone gets a response from the DHCP server in the network. Along with the DHCP response, which provides the IP address to the telephone, it is also possible to supply the address of the TFTP server from which the phone gets its configuration. This is done by configuring option 150 on the DHCP server and specifying the address of

the TFTP server; Cisco DHCP server supports this feature. Again, it is possible to specify the TFTP server address manually, but this would limit adds, moves, and changes, as well as remove some other benefits.

4. The IP phone contacts the TFTP server and receives a list of addresses of Cisco CallManager servers. Up to three Cisco CallManager servers can be specified in the list. This provides redundancy in case the first Cisco CallManager server in the list is unavailable.

5. The IP phone contacts the Cisco CallManager server and registers itself, receiving in return a configuration file and runtime code necessary for the phone to operate. For each configuration, the IP phone receives a directory number (DN) from the Cisco CallManager server to be used for calling that particular IP phone.

6. The IP phone is ready to make and receive calls.

Summary

Corporations are looking for strategies to integrate disparate networking technologies over a single common network infrastructure. This trend started many years ago.

Cisco AVVID solutions are heavy in design and include the following:

- IP Telephony, IP Video Conferencing, Wireless, Enterprise Mobility, Security, Virtual Private Networks
- Content networking
- IP Contact Centers
- Storage networking

Familiar applications, such as voice messaging, are also easily integrated into the AVVID environment.

A new breed of IP-enabled unified-messaging solutions allows users to access both voice mail and e-mail from a common server.

IP multicasting is the transmission of an IP data frame to a host group, which is identified by a single IP address. Because the host group is identified by a single IP address rule, the IP multicast contains a specific combination of the destination MAC address and a destination IP address.

Because of their unique capability to send a single data stream to multiple clients, IP multicast technologies have become the transmission methods of choice for most multimedia applications.

Multicast routing protocols fall into two categories: dense mode (DM) and sparse mode (SM). DM protocols assume that almost all routers in the network will need to distribute multicast traffic for each multicast group. SM protocols assume that relatively few routers in the network will be involved in each multicast. The hosts belonging to the group are widely dispersed, as might be the case for most multicasts in the Internet. SM protocols are recommended for use in today's networks.

IGMP is used between hosts on a LAN and the router(s) on that LAN to track of which multicast groups the hosts are members.

PIM is used between routers so that they can track which multicast packets to forward to each other and to their directly connected LANs.

Cisco CallManager is the software-based call-processing component of the Cisco IP Telephony solution and essentially is the heart of the IP Telephony solution. The key benefit of CallManager and the supporting applications is that special-purpose voice-processing hardware is not required. Supplementary and enhanced services are seamlessly added without incurring major expense.

IP Telephony designs include the following:

- Single-site model
- Multiple sites with independent call processing
- Multisite IP WAN with distributed call processing
- Multisite IP WAN with centralized call processing

A trust boundary should be maintained in the wiring closet. If necessary, move it to the distribution layer on a case-by-case basis, but avoid moving it to the network core. This advice conforms with the general guidelines to keep the trust boundary as close to the source as possible.

IP phone connectivity, backup power, and IP addressing are considerations of IP Telephony design.

You can purchase line cards that can apply power to the IP phone. If you deploy IP phones using the existing switches, you should install line cards that can apply power. Alternatively, you could use the external Cisco power patch panel to power the phones if powered line cards are not available for the switch. As a final option, you could use wall power.

The Catalyst software can be easily configured to support enhanced features, such as auxiliary/voice VLANs. Figure 7-67 summarizes Cisco AVVID technologies.

Figure 7-67 Cisco AVVID Provides a Complete, Integrated Solution for Voice, Video, and Data

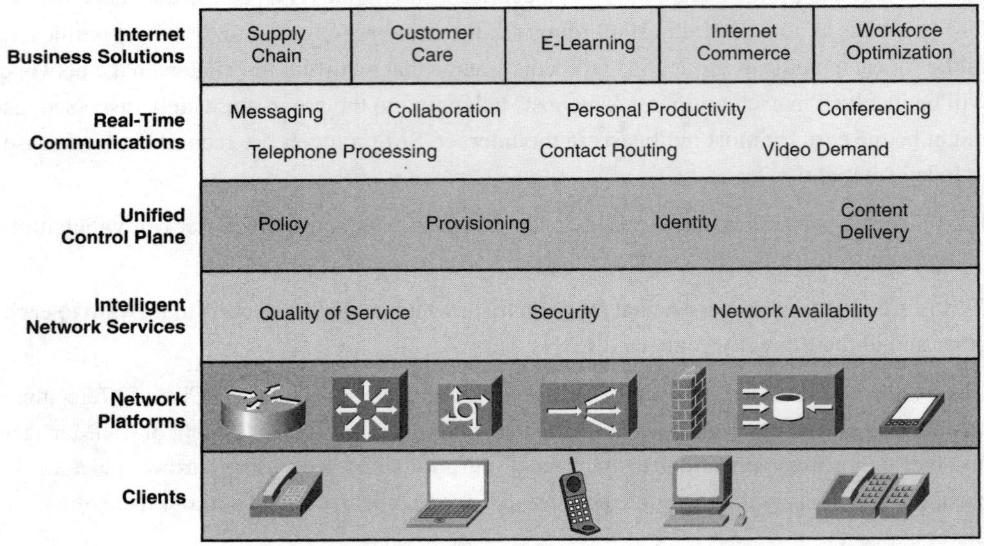

Internet Business Solutions	Supply Chain	Customer Care	E-Learning	Internet Commerce	Workforce Optimization
Real-Time Communications	Messaging	Collaboration	Personal Productivity		Conferencing
	Telephone Processing		Contact Routing		Video Demand
Unified Control Plane	Policy	Provisioning		Identity	Content Delivery
Intelligent Network Services	Quality of Service		Security	Network Availability	
Network Platforms					
Clients					

Key Terms

Auto-RP   A PIM feature that automates the distribution of group-to-RP mappings.

candidate RP   A router that announces its candidacy to be an RP for a PIM-SM network via the Cisco-Announce group, 224.0.1.39.

Cisco Group Management Protocol (CGMP)   A Cisco-developed protocol that runs between Cisco routers and Catalyst switches to leverage IGMP information on Cisco routers to make Layer 2 forwarding decisions on Catalyst switches. With CGMP, IP multicast traffic is delivered only to Catalyst switch ports that are attached to interested receivers.

classification   Using a traffic descriptor to categorize a packet within a specific group to define that packet and make it accessible for QoS handling on the network.

codec   Coder-decoder. An integrated circuit device that typically uses pulse code modulation to transform analog signals into a digital bit stream and digital signals back into analog signals. In voice over IP, voice over Frame Relay, and voice over ATM, a codec refers to a DSP software algorithm used to compress/decompress speech or audio signals.

Conjugate Structure Algebraic Code Excited Linear Prediction (CS-ACELP)   A CELP voice compression algorithm providing 8 kbps, or 8:1 compression. Standardized in ITU-T Recommendation G.729.

core   In CBT, the router that serves as the root of the shared tree. Similar to PIM-SM's RP.

Core-Based Trees (CBT)   A multicast routing protocol introduced in September 1997 in RFC 2201 CBT builds a shared tree like PIM-SM. CBT uses information in the IP unicast routing table to calculate the next-hop router in the direction of the core.

Distance Vector Multicast Routing Protocol (DVMRP)   The first multicast routing protocol, publicized in RFC 1075 in 1998. Unlike PIM, DVMRP builds a separate multicast routing table from the unicast routing table.

distribution tree   A unique forwarding path for a multicast group between the source and each subnet containing members of the multicast group.

E.164   An ITU-T recommendation for international telecommunication numbering, especially in ISDN, BISDN, and SMDS. An evolution of standard telephone numbers. Also, the name of the field in an ATM address that contains numbers in E.164 format.

G.711   Describes the 64-kbps PCM (Pulse Code Modulation) voice-coding technique. In G.711, encoded voice is already in the correct format for digital voice delivery in the PSTN or through PBXs. Described in the ITU-T standard in its G-series recommendations.

G.726 Describes Adaptive Differential Pulse Code Modulation (ADPCM) coding at 40, 32, 24, and 16 kbps. ADPCM-encoded voice can be interchanged between packet voice, PSTN, and PBX networks if the PBX networks are configured to support ADPCM. Described in the ITU-T standard in its G-series recommendations.

G.729 Describes CELP compression in which voice is coded into 8-kbps streams. This standard has two variations (G.729 and G.729 Annex A) that differ mainly in computational complexity; both provide speech quality similar to 32-kbps ADPCM. Described in the ITU-T standard in its G-series recommendations.

globally scoped addresses A multicast address space in the range from 224.0.1.0 to 238.255.255.255. These addresses can be used to multicast data between organizations and across the Internet.

GLOP address RFC 2770 proposes that the 233.0.0.0/8 address range be reserved for statically defined addresses by organizations that already have an AS number reserved. The second and third octets are populated with the decimal equivalents of the first and second bytes of the hexadecimal representation of the AS number.

H.320 A suite of ITU-T standard specifications for videoconferencing over circuit-switched media such as ISDN, fractional T1, and switched-56 lines.

H.323 An extension of ITU-T standard H.320 that enables videoconferencing over LANs and other packet-switched networks, as well as video over the Internet. H.323 is a set of communications protocols used by programs such as Microsoft NetMeeting and equipment such as Cisco routers to transmit and receive audio and video information over the Internet.

IGMP leave group message A message used by IGMPv2 to allow a host to announce its intention to leave a multicast group. The leave message is sent to the all-routers multicast address, 224.0.0.2.

IGMP membership query A message used by IGMP and sent to the all-hosts multicast address, 224.0.0.1, to verify that at least one host on the subnet is still interested in receiving traffic directed to that group. Also referred to as a general query.

IGMP membership report A message used by IGMP to indicate a host's interest in receiving traffic for a particular multicast group.

IGMP snooping A Layer 2 multicast constraining mechanism (like CGMP) used by switches, allowing only multicast traffic to be forwarded to those interfaces associated with IP multicast devices. The switch snoops on the IGMP traffic between the host and the router and keeps track of multicast groups and member ports.

IGMP Version 1 A version of IGMP that relies solely on membership query messages and membership report messages.

IGMP Version 2   A version of IGMP that adds the ability of a host to proactively leave a multicast group and the ability of a router to send a group-specific query (as opposed to a general query).

IGMP Version 3   A version of IGMP that adds support for source filtering.

Internet Group Management Protocol (IGMP)   A protocol used to allow hosts to communicate to local multicast routers their desire to receive multicast traffic.

limited scope address   Also called an administratively scoped address. It falls in the range from 239.0.0.0 to 239.255.255.255 and is limited for use by a local group or organization.

link local address   An IANA reserved multicast address space in the range from 224.0.0.0 to 224.0.0.255 to be used by network protocols on a local network segment.

multicast backbone (MBONE)   A multicast backbone across the public Internet, built with tunnels between DVMRP-capable Sun workstations running the mroute daemon (process).

multicast group   An arbitrary group of hosts that expresses an interest in receiving a particular data stream via multicast. This group has no physical or geographic boundaries. Hosts that are interested in receiving data flowing to a particular group must join the group using IGMP.

Multicast OSPF (MOSPF)   A multicast routing protocol specified in RFC 1584. MOSPF is a set of extensions to OSPF enabling multicast forwarding decisions.

Network Time Protocol (NTP)   Used to synchronize clocks on network devices. The multicast address 224.0.1.1 is reserved for NTP operation.

PIM sparse-dense mode   An alternative to pure dense mode or pure sparse mode for a router interface. Sparse-dense mode allows individual groups to be run in either sparse or dense mode, depending on whether RP information is available for that group. If the router learns RP information for a particular group, it is treated as sparse mode; otherwise, that group is treated as dense mode.

Protocol-Independent Multicast (PIM)   An IP multicast routing protocol that derives its information using RPF checks based on the unicast routing table. PIM has several variations, including dense mode, sparse mode, sparse-dense mode, source-specific mode, and bidirectional mode.

Protocol-Independent Multicast Dense Mode (PIM-DM)   A PIM variation that builds a source tree for each multicast source and uses flood-and-prune behavior.

Protocol-Independent Multicast Sparse Mode (PIM-SM)   A PIM variation that builds shared trees. The root of the tree is called the rendezvous point, similar to CBT's core.

Reverse Path Forwarding (RPF)   An algorithm used to forward multicast datagrams. It functions as follows:

- If a router receives a datagram on an interface it uses to send unicast packets to the source, the packet has arrived on the RPF interface.
- If the packet arrives on the RPF interface, a router forwards the packet out the interfaces present in the outgoing interface list of a multicast routing table entry.
- If the packet does not arrive on the RPF interface, the packet is silently discarded to prevent loops.

Router-Port Group Management Protocol (RGMP)   Lets a router communicate to a switch the IP multicast group for which the router wants to receive or forward traffic. RGMP is designed for switched Ethernet backbone networks running PIM.

RP mapping agent   A router that receives the RP-announcement messages from the candidate RPs and arbitrates conflicts. The RP mapping agent sends the group-to-RP mappings to all multicast-enabled routers via the Cisco-Discovery group, 224.0.1.40.

shared tree   A multicast distribution tree using a root placed at some chosen point in the network. PIM-SM and CBT both use shared trees. When using a shared tree, sources must send their traffic to the root for the traffic to reach the receivers.

source filtering   A capability added to IGMPv3 that lets a multicast host signal to a router the groups for which it wants to receive multicast traffic and the sources from which it wants to receive the traffic.

source tree   A multicast distribution tree with root at the source of the multicast traffic and whose branches form a spanning tree through the network to the receivers. Also called the shortest-path tree (SPT). For every source of a multicast group, there is a corresponding SPT.

trust boundary   When classifying traffic types in an enterprise network, a trust boundary must be established. The boundary is established by the access device, which either classifies traffic it allows into the network itself or trusts classification that has already been applied by an end station, such as an IP phone.

Check Your Understanding

Use the following review questions to test your understanding of the concepts covered in this chapter. Answers are listed in Appendix A, "Check Your Understanding Answer Key."

1. What type of VLAN is commonly used with Catalyst switches to support IP phones?

    A. User VLAN

    B. Native VLAN

    C. Auxiliary VLAN

    D. Management VLAN

2. Which of the following is an indispensable software-based call-processing component required for a Cisco IP Telephony solution?

    A. LDAP

    B. Gateserver

    C. IOS Gatekeeper

    D. CallManager

3. Different codecs have different encoding delays. These delays are added to the end-point-to-codec delays to determine which of the following?

    A. Propagation delay

    B. Latency

    C. Initialization delay

    D. End-to-end delay

4. A priority queue is established for what type of traffic when implementing QoS for an IP Telephony solution?

    A. TCP

    B. UDP

    C. Data

    D. Voice

5. Layer 2 traffic classification uses which of the following?

    A. Type of service

    B. Class of service

    C. Differentiated Services Code Point

    D. Voice queue

6. Layer 3 traffic classification uses which of the following?

    A. Type of service

    B. Class of service

    C. Differentiated Services Code Point

    D. Voice queue

7. What is used to ensure that multicast traffic is correctly forwarded down the distribution tree?

    A. LCP

    B. CRTP

    C. RTP

    D. RPF

8. What are the two types of multicast distribution trees?

    A. CBT trees

    B. Shared trees

    C. Shortest-path trees

    D. Rendezvous trees

9. What Layer 2 multicast address corresponds to the Layer 3 multicast address 224.10.8.5?

    A. FF.FF.FF.FF.FF.FF

    B. 01.00.22.44.10.05

    C. 01.00.5E.0A.08.05

    D. 01.00.5E.10.08.05

10. What multicast protocol is used to optimize multicast traffic between hosts and routers participating in multicast traffic flows?

    A. RGMP

    B. IGMP

    C. CGMP

    D. PIM-SM

Objectives

After completing this chapter, you will be able to perform tasks related to the following:

- Understand loss, latency, and jitter
- Understand the quality of service (QoS) models
- Understand class of service (CoS), type of service (ToS), IP Precedence, and Differentiated Services Code Point (DSCP)
- Configure CoS trust and rewrite on Catalyst switches
- Describe and configure Committed Access Rate (CAR)
- Describe and configure Class-Based Weighted Fair Queuing (CBWFQ)
- Describe and configure Weighted Random Early Detection (WRED)
- Describe and configure Low Latency Queuing (LLQ)
- Describe and configure Generic Traffic Shaping (GTS) and Frame Relay traffic shaping
- Describe Link Fragmentation and Interleaving (LFI)
- Describe and configure Compressed Real-Time Transport Protocol (CRTP)
- Verify QoS configurations

Chapter 8

Quality of Service

Increasingly, data networks are being called on to support communications for traffic with varied delivery requirements. Previously an organization used separate networks for voice, video, and data traffic. Now, it is common practice to combine these into a single multiservice network in which the varied traffic types coexist. There are many circumstances in which these quality of service (QoS) requirements have not been met or even addressed at a rudimentary level:

- The long delay in speech transmission when calling by way of an international satellite link
- Stop-start and choppy Internet streaming video performance
- Unclear audio when using an Internet-based IP phone
- Messenger applications

For applications such as file and print services, Internet browsing, e-mail, and peer-to-peer messaging products, the "best-effort" delivery attempts of the Internet and many corporate networks might be adequate. However, for organizations seeking to integrate their voice and data networks using voice over IP (VoIP), IP telephony, or high-quality streaming video for corporate communications, it is essential that QoS be built into the network design.

To provide QoS within a network, it is critical that you understand the network characteristics that make up QoS and the QoS requirements of the varied traffic and applications using the network. As soon as you can state application and traffic requirements in QoS terms, you can use classification techniques to identify streams of traffic as having a particular QoS requirement. For example, you could use a standard access list to identify a user who requires priority access to network resources. After you have classified traffic into classes of service, you can use many scheduling and congestion management techniques to provide the desired service characteristics. The key to effective QoS design is knowing how these techniques operate and the benefits and limitations of each.

Quality of Service Requirements

QoS is affected by an array of variables, including loss, delay, and jitter. QoS requirements are unique to the type of traffic, such as voice, video, and data. This section defines QoS, the motivation behind it, and the specific requirements to optimize voice, video, and data traffic.

Quality of Service Defined

QoS refers to a network's ability to provide improved service to selected network traffic over various underlying technologies, including Frame Relay, Asynchronous Transfer Mode (ATM), Ethernet and 802.3 networks, Synchronous Optical Network (SONET), and IP-routed networks. QoS can be applied in a central office or branch office or in between (see Figure 8-1), especially to support IP telephony.

Figure 8-1 QoS Can Be Applied to Networks Regardless of the Underlying Technology. IP Telephony Is a Major Motivator for Implementing QoS.

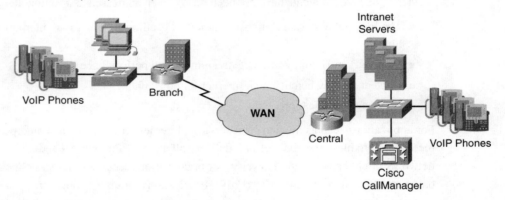

QoS features provide improved and more predictable network service by offering the following services:

- Dedicated bandwidth
- Improved loss characteristics
- Congestion management
- Congestion avoidance
- Traffic shaping
- Traffic prioritization

In a network, the goal is to move information from one point to another. The characteristics that define the quality of this movement are

- Loss
- Delay or latency
- Delay variation (also called jitter)

The following three sections discuss each of these characteristics in greater detail.

Loss

Loss refers to the percentage of packets that fail to reach their destination. Loss can result from errors in the network, corrupted frames, and congested networks. With modern switched and optical-based networks, corrupted frames and packet losses caused by network noise, interference, and collisions are becoming rare. Many of the packets lost in an optimized network are deliberately dropped by networking devices to avoid congestion. For many Transmission Control Protocol/Internet Protocol (TCP/IP)-based traffic flows, such as those associated with file and print services, small numbers of lost packets are of little concern because TCP/IP's retransmission mechanism ensures their eventual arrival. However, for User Datagram Protocol (UDP) traffic associated with real-time applications such as streaming media and voice, retransmission is not feasible and losses are less tolerable. As a guideline, a highly available network should suffer less than 1% loss. For voice traffic, the loss should approach 0 percent.

Delay or Latency

Delay or *latency* refers to the time it takes a packet to travel from the source to the destination. Delay is composed of fixed and variable delays. Fixed delays include such events as serialization and encoding/decoding. For example, a bit takes a fixed 100 nanoseconds (ns) to exit a 10-Mbps Ethernet interface. Variable delays are often the result of congestion. They include the time packets spend in network buffers waiting for access to the media. In general, delay resulting from bidirectional network traffic is a more significant problem, because it tends to be additive. Examples of bidirectional traffic include voice traffic and Telnet sessions to a remote host, in which delay manifests itself as the slow acceptance of keystrokes. The resulting latency makes it difficult to conduct a conversation without talking over the other party.

As a design rule, a voice packet should cross the network in less than 150 milliseconds (ms).

Delay Variation or Jitter

Delay variation or *jitter* is the difference in the delay times of consecutive packets. A jitter buffer is often used to smooth out arrival times, but buffering capabilities have instantaneous and total limits. Any type of buffering used to reduce jitter directly increases total network delay. In general, traffic requiring low latency also requires a minimum variation in latency.

As a design rule, voice networks cannot cope with more than 30 ms of jitter. Jitter greater than 30 ms results in degraded audio performance. Excessive jitter in a streaming video environment results in jerky motion, loss of video quality, or loss of video.

Network Availability

Providing QoS requires maximizing network uptime. Low loss, small delays, and minimal jitter are meaningless if the network is down. Redundancy, dynamic routing protocols, Hot Standby Router Protocol (HSRP), and Spanning Tree Protocol (STP) are all used to create a highly available network and to form the foundation of a network that can fulfill QoS requirements. Figure 8-2 illustrates the redundancy and maximizing of network availability as provided by HSRP and STP.

Figure 8-2 Maximizing Network Availability with STP and HSRP by Providing Layer 2 and Layer 3 Redundancy

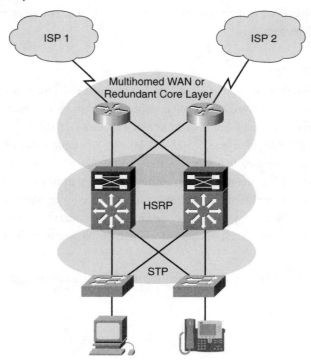

Provisioning

You might find it surprising that bandwidth is not listed as an element of QoS. Inadequate bandwidth inflates latency as packets spend increasing amounts of time queued in network devices. In seriously congested networks, inadequate bandwidth results in loss of data as queues overflow. Meeting QoS requirements is impossible if network LAN and wide area network (WAN) links have insufficient bandwidth. Adding bandwidth, also known as over-provisioning, does not solve the problem. The possibility of an overprovisioned network becoming congested is reduced. If the network does become congested, it might not perform as well as a lower-bandwidth, lower-cost network that makes use of sophisticated QoS features. Figure 8-3 illustrates provisioning.

Figure 8-3 Sometimes a Lower-Bandwidth Network with Intelligent QoS Performs Better Than an Overprovisioned Network That Becomes Congested

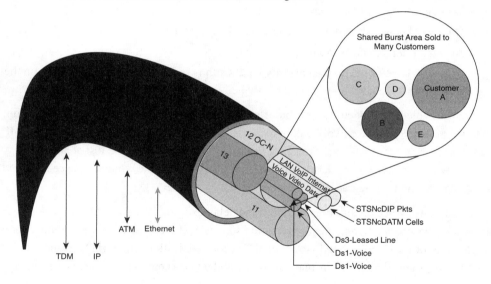

Quality of Service Requirements for Data

Different applications, protocols, and traffic types have different QoS requirements in terms of the amount of loss, latency, and jitter they can tolerate. Recognizing these differences is an essential element in designing and configuring a network that delivers the required QoS.

When addressing the QoS needs of data application traffic, profile the applications to get a basic understanding of the network requirements. It is not necessary to overengineer the provisioning of bandwidth, because some traffic can usually tolerate lower QoS levels. Instead, use the proven relative priority model to divide traffic into no more than four classes:

- **Gold (mission-critical)**—Transactional and business software
- **Silver (guaranteed bandwidth)**—Streaming video, messaging, and intranet
- **Bronze (best-effort and default class)**—Internet browsing, e-mail
- **Less-Than-Best-Effort (Optional; higher-drop preferences)**—File Transfer Protocol (FTP), backups, and applications (such as Napster or KaZaa)

Quality of Service Requirements for Voice

Voice quality is directly affected by all three QoS factors—loss, delay, and delay variation. Recommended parameters are as follows:

- Loss should be no more than 1 percent
- One-way latency should be no more than 150 to 200 ms
- Average jitter should be no more than 30 ms
- 21 to 106 kbps of guaranteed priority bandwidth is required per call, depending on the sampling rate, codec, and Layer 2 overhead

Loss causes voice clipping and skips. Industry-standard codec algorithms can correct for up to 30 ms of lost voice. Cisco VoIP technology uses 20-ms samples of voice payload per VoIP packet. Only a single Real-Time Transport Protocol (RTP) packet can be lost at any given time. If two successive voice packets are lost, the 30-ms correctable window is exceeded, and voice quality begins to degrade.

Delay can cause voice quality degradation if the delay exceeds 200 ms. If the end-to-end voice delay becomes too long, the conversation sounds as if the two parties are talking over a satellite link or a CB radio. The International Telecommunication Union (ITU) standard for VoIP, G.114, states that a 150-ms one-way delay budget is acceptable for high voice quality.

With respect to delay variation, adaptive jitter buffers exist within IP Telephony devices that can usually compensate for 20 to 50 ms of jitter.

Quality of Service Requirements for Video

Streaming video applications have more-lenient QoS requirements because they are delay-insensitive. A video can take several seconds to cue up and is largely delay variation-insensitive because of application buffering. Streaming video might contain valuable content, as in the case of an e-learning application, and might require service guarantees using QoS. Streaming video would be appropriately provisioned in the "Silver" class of data traffic. When provisioning for streaming video, take into account the video content distribution requirements. Recommended QoS parameters for streaming video traffic are as follows:

- Loss should be no more than 2 percent
- Latency should be no more than 4 to 5 seconds
- There are no significant jitter requirements
- Bandwidth requirements depend on the encoding and rate of the video stream
- Non-entertainment streaming video should be provisioned into the "Silver" data traffic class

Video file distribution is very similar to FTP traffic and can have a major impact on network performance because of the file size. Distribution traffic should be managed to avoid affecting the network using the following QoS parameters for video content transfers:

- Streaming video content is delay- and delay-variation insensitive.
- Streaming video requires large file transfers.
- Try to restrict distribution to less-busy times of day.
- Provision as "less-than-best-effort" data.
- The minimum bandwidth guarantee is the size of the videoconferencing session plus 20 percent.

When addressing the QoS needs of videoconferencing traffic, the basic requirements are similar to those for voice (see Figure 8-4):

- Loss should be no more than 1%.
- One-way latency should be no more than 150 to 200 ms.
- The average jitter should be no more than 30 ms.
- Because of its bursty nature, the minimum bandwidth guarantee is the size of the videoconferencing session plus 20 percent.

As Figure 8-4 illustrates, this means that a 384-kbps videoconferencing session requires 460 kbps guaranteed priority bandwidth.

Figure 8-4 Videoconferencing Bandwidth Requirements for a 384-kbps Session

Video conferencing Bandwidth Requirements for a 384-Kbps Session

"I" Frame (Full-Sample Video) 1024 to 1518 Bytes

"I" Frame (Full-Sample Video) 1024 to 1518 Bytes

600 kbps

30 pps

"P" and "B" Frames Differential/Predicted Frames 128 to 256 Bytes

15 pps

35 kbps

I = Intra-Frame
P = Predictive
B = Bidirectional

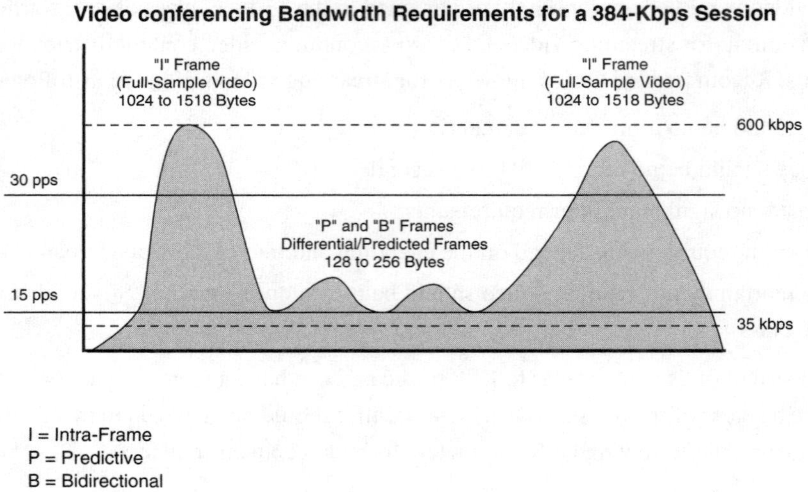

Quality of Service Mechanisms

After you've defined the network's QoS requirements, the next step is to select an appropriate service model. A service model is a general approach or a design philosophy for handling the competing streams of traffic within a network. There are three service models from which to choose:

- Best-effort
- Integrated
- Differentiated

The service model you select must be capable of meeting the network's QoS requirements and integrating any networked applications.

Best-Effort Service

Best-effort is a single service model in which an application sends data whenever it must, in any quantity, without requesting permission or first informing the network. The characteristics of the best-effort service model are as follows:

- Data is delivered if resources exist.
- All traffic has an equal chance of being dropped because of congestion.
- It is implemented using first-in, first-out (FIFO) queues.

For best-effort service, the network delivers data if it can, without any assurance of reliability, delay bounds, or throughput. The Cisco IOS QoS feature that implements best-effort service is FIFO queuing. FIFO is the default method of queuing for LAN and high-speed WAN interfaces on switches and routers. Best-effort service is suitable for a wide range of networked applications, such as general file transfers, e-mail, and web browsing.

Integrated Services Model

The Integrated Services or IntServ architecture is a multiple-service model that can accommodate multiple QoS requirements. Its characteristics are as follows:

- An application makes an explicit request for network resources.
- An application must be QoS-aware.
- It is implemented using Resource Reservation Protocol (RSVP).
- It uses Guaranteed Rate Service or Controlled Load Service.

In this model, the application requests a specific kind of service from the network before it sends data. The request is made by explicit signaling. The application informs the network of its traffic profile and requests a particular kind of service that can encompass its bandwidth and delay requirements. The application is expected to send data only after it gets a confirmation from the network. The application is also expected to send data that lies within its described traffic profile.

The network performs admission control based on information from the application and available network resources. The network also commits to meeting the application's QoS requirements as long as the traffic remains within the profile specifications. The network fulfills its commitment by maintaining a per-flow state and then performing packet classification, policing, and intelligent queuing based on that state.

The Cisco IOS IntServ model allows applications to make use of the Internet Engineering Task Force (IETF) RSVP, which applications can use to signal their QoS requirements to the router. However, the IntServ model does not scale well as additional streams are added. Each reservation is analogous to a phone call with a guaranteed end-to-end connection.

Routers, in conjunction with RSVP, can use intelligent queuing mechanisms to provide two types of services:

- **Guaranteed Rate Service**—Allows applications to reserve bandwidth to meet their requirements. Adaptive real-time applications, such as playback of a recorded conference, can use this kind of service.
- **Controlled Load Service**—Allows applications to have low delay and high throughput even during times of congestion. For example, adaptive real-time applications, such as playback of a recorded conference, can use this kind of service. Cisco IOS QoS uses RSVP with Weighted Random Early Detection (WRED) to provide this kind of service.

Differentiated Services Model

NOTE

For additional information, go to Cisco.com and search for the document "Implementing DiffServ for End-to-End Quality of Service Overview."

The Differentiated Services or DiffServ architecture is an emerging standard from the IETF. Its characteristics are as follows:

- Packets are classified upon entering the network.
- QoS is classified at Layer 2 using 802.1Q/p CoS.
- QoS is classified at Layer 3 using IP Precedence or DSCP.
- Network devices use the classification to queue, shape, and police traffic flows.
- Applications do not need to be QoS-aware.

The DiffServ architecture specifies that each packet is classified upon entry into the network. The classification is carried in the IP packet header using either *IP Precedence* or the preferred *Differentiated Services Code Point (DSCP)*. These are represented using the first 3 or 6 bits of the *Type of Service (ToS)* field, respectively. Classification can also be carried in the Layer 2 frame in the form of the *Class of Service (CoS)* field embodied in ISL and 802.1Q frames.

After packets are classified at the edge by access layer switches or border routers, the network uses the classification to determine how the traffic should be queued, shaped, and policed.

Per-hop behaviors (PHBs) are often used to describe the DiffServ model. The default PHB specifies that a packet marked with a DSCP value of 000000 (recommended) receives the traditional best-effort service from a DiffServ-compliant node. Also, if a packet arrives at a DiffServ-compliant node, and the DSCP value is not mapped to any other PHB, the packet is mapped to the default PHB. Other PHBs include the Class Selector PHB, the Assured Forwarding PHB, and the Expedited Forwarding PHB.

Unlike the IntServ model, DiffServ does not require network applications be QoS-aware.

Traffic Marking

To provide QoS to varying packets and frames, you must mark them to indicate their QoS requirements. Specific fields are used for QoS marking or classification in frames or packets, as shown in Figure 8-5.

At the data-link layer, a raw Ethernet frame has no fields to signify its QoS requirements. If QoS marking is required, ISL or 802.1Q/p must be used because they provide a 3-bit CoS field. At the network layer, an IP packet contains a 1-byte ToS field, of which the first 3 bits form the IP-Precedence field and the first 6 bits form the DSCP fields. Either of these can be used to signify an IP packet's QoS requirements.

Figure 8-5 It Is Important to Understand That QoS Can Be Implemented at Both Layer 2 and Layer 3

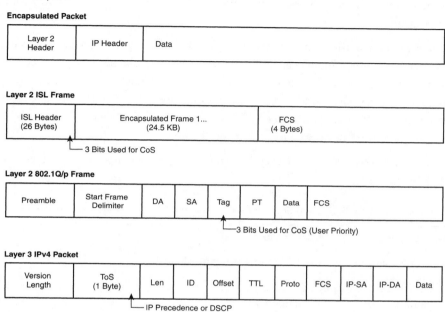

The marking of traffic at Layer 2 or 3 is crucial to providing QoS within a network. Network devices use this marking to determine traffic's relative priority. The decision of whether to mark traffic at Layers 2 or 3 or both is not trivial and should be made after considering the following points:

- Layer 2 marking of frames can be performed for non-IP traffic.
- Layer 2 marking of frames is the only QoS option available for switches that are not IP-aware.
- Layer 3 marking carries the QoS information end-to-end.
- Older IP equipment might not understand DSCP.

Although it might seem confusing to have three options for marking traffic, in practice the way to proceed is often determined by the capabilities of hosts, switches, and routers within the network. In many instances, it might be necessary to use different marking techniques at different points within a network. For this reason, it is common to do both of the following:

- Use DSCP to mark the packets' QoS requirements through the network's routed layers
- Use CoS to mark the frames to allow Layer 2 devices, such as switches, to provide for the packets' QoS requirements at the data-link layer

The 3-bit CoS field present in the Layer 2 ISL and 802.1Q/p frames allows eight levels of priority to be set for each frame. These values range from 0 for the lowest priority to 7 for the highest priority.

Although the CoS field can be used to influence the QoS treatment of packets, it does not have the flexibility or end-to-end capability of the IP marking schemes using IP Precedence or DSCP. For this reason, it is common to have switches set a Layer 2 CoS value for traffic based on their ingress port and to have a router translate the CoS value into an equivalent IP Precedence or DSCP value. This Layer 3 ToS is then used to influence the QoS as the packet passes through network devices en route to its destination.

Table 8-1 compares associating a packet with an IP Precedence to associating a packet with an IP DSCP QoS level.

Table 8-1 Packet Association: Comparing IP Precedence and IP DSCP QoS Level Associations

IP Precedence	IP DSCP QoS Level
Layer 3 QoS marking mechanism	Layer 3 QoS marking mechanism
Relevant only to IP traffic	Relevant only to IP traffic
Superseded by DSCP	
3-bit field	6-bit field (the first 3 bits are ToS)
0 = low priority	0 = low priority
7 = highest priority	63 = highest priority

Associating a packet with either IP Precedence level or an IP DSCP QoS level allows network devices to classify traffic based on the packet's IP Precedence and IP DSCP value, depending on which value is marked. These markings can be used to identify traffic with similar QoS requirements within the network, and traffic classes can be created. Traffic types that have similar QoS requirements can be given equivalent treatment.

The IP DSCP value is the first 6 bits in the ToS byte, and the IP Precedence value is the first 3 bits in the ToS value. The IP Precedence value is actually part of the IP DSCP value. Therefore, both values cannot be set simultaneously. If they are, the packet is marked with the IP DSCP value. Essentially, DSCP supersedes IP Precedence.

If it is necessary to provide QoS through packet marking, and all the devices in the network support IP DSCP marking, it is best to use the IP DSCP marking. IP DSCP markings provide more packet-marking options than IP Precedence.

DSCP marking might be undesirable because some older devices in the network do not support IP DSCP values. In this case it might be necessary to use the IP Precedence value to mark the packets. A maximum of eight different IP Precedence markings and 64 different IP DSCP markings may be set.

Modular QoS Command-Line Interface (MQC)

The Modular QoS command-line interface (MQC) is central to Cisco's model for implementing IOS-based QoS solutions. The MQC breaks down the tasks associated with QoS into modules that

- Identify traffic flows.
- Classify traffic flows as belonging to a common class of QoS.
- Apply QoS policies to that class.
- Define the interfaces on which the policy should be enforced.

The modular nature of MQC allows the reuse of common traffic classes and policies, which provides the following benefits:

- It simplifies the configuration.
- It makes it more efficient to implement changes.
- It reduces the chance of error.

MQC has three steps:

Step 1   Classify traffic using the **class-map** command.

Step 2   Apply QoS policies to the traffic using the **policy-map** command.

Step 3   Apply policies to an interface using the **service-policy** command.

Using the class-map Command to Define Traffic Classes

The **class-map** command defines a traffic class. The purpose of a traffic class is to classify traffic that should be given a particular QoS. A traffic class contains three major elements:

- A name
- A series of **match** commands
- If more than one **match** command exists in the traffic class, instructions on how to evaluate these **match** commands

The traffic class is named in the **class-map** command line. For example, if you enter the **class-map cisco** command while configuring the traffic class in the command-line interface (CLI), the traffic class is named **cisco**, as shown in Example 8-1.

Example 8-1 *The* **class-map** *Defines a Traffic Class*

```
Switch(config)#class-map cisco
Switch(config-cmap)#
```

match commands specify various criteria for classifying packets. Packets are checked to determine whether they match the criteria specified in the **match** commands. If a packet matches the specified criteria, that packet is considered a member of the class and is forwarded according to the QoS specifications set in the traffic policy. Packets that fail to meet any of the matching criteria are classified as members of the default traffic class and are subject to a separate traffic policy.

The actual criteria that can be used to establish a match vary considerably between hardware platforms and versions of Cisco IOS software. Table 8-2 compares the supported **match** commands on the Catalyst 2950 and Catalyst 3550.

Table 8-2 Several Match Parameters Are Available on the Catalyst 3550

Match On	Catalyst 2950	Catalyst 3550	Description
access-group	✓	✓	Access group
ip dscp	✓	✓	A specific DSCP value or a list of values
ip precedence		✓	A specific IP Precedence value or a list of values
any		✓	Any packet
class-map		✓	A nested class map
destination-address		✓	A destination MAC address
input-interface		✓	Selects an input interface to match on
mpls		✓	Multiprotocol Label Switching values
protocol		✓	Matches on a protocol type
source-address		✓	A source MAC address
vlan		✓	VLAN ID

In Example 8-2, any traffic that is permitted by the named ACL **test** is considered part of the traffic class known as **cisco**.

Example 8-2 *The* **match** *Command Defines What Traffic to Permit*

```
Switch(config)#class-map cisco
Switch(config-cmap)#match access-group name test
```

The instruction on how to evaluate these **match** commands needs to be specified if more than one **match** statement exists in the traffic class. You specify the evaluation instruction with one of the following two options:

```
class-map match-any
```

or

```
class-map match-all
```

If **match-any** is specified as the evaluation instruction, the traffic being evaluated by the traffic class must match one of the specified criteria. If **match-all** is specified as the evaluation instruction, the traffic being evaluated by the traffic class must match all the specified criteria. Example 8-3 illustrates the **match-any** option.

NOTE

The Catalyst 2950 has no **match-any** option. The default behavior of the 2950 is to match any. This can be overridden using the **match-all** command.

Example 8-3 *The* **match-any** *Command Allows for a Match of Any Single Criteria in a List of Matchable Options*

```
Switch(config)#class-map match-any cisco
Switch(config-cmap)#match access-group name test
Switch(config-cmap)#match input-interface fastethernet 0/1
```

If traffic matches a permit statement in the ACL **test** or the traffic originates from FastEthernet 0/1, it is considered part of the class of traffic known as **cisco**.

On the Catalyst 3550 and Catalyst 6500 the MQC allows multiple traffic classes to be configured as a single traffic class; this includes nested traffic classes, also called nested class maps. This nesting can be achieved with the use of the **match class-map** command.

Defining the QoS Policy Using the Policy Map

The **policy-map** command is used to create a traffic policy. The purpose of a traffic policy is to configure the QoS features that should be associated with the traffic that has been classified in a user-specified traffic class. A traffic policy contains three elements:

- Policy name
- Traffic class specified with the **class** command
- QoS policies to be applied to each class

The policy map shown in Example 8-4 creates a traffic policy named policy1. The policy applies to all traffic classified by the previously defined traffic class **cisco** and specifies that traffic in this example should be allocated bandwidth of 3000 kbps. Any traffic that does not belong to the class **cisco** forms part of the catchall **class-default** class and is given a default bandwidth of 2000 kbps.

NOTE

The actual policies that can be implemented are platform-dependent. Example 8-4 is relevant for a Catalyst 3550 or Catalyst 6500; however, the Catalyst 2950 does not support the **bandwidth** command. Table 8-3 describes the QoS policy parameters for 2950s and 3550s.

Example 8-4 *The* **policy-map** *Command Creates a Traffic Policy That Configures the QoS Features*

```
Switch(config)#policy-map policy1
Switch(config-pmap)#class cisco
Switch(config-pmap-c)#bandwidth 3000
Switch(config-pmap-c)#exit
Switch(config-pmap)#class class-default
Switch(config-pmap-c)#bandwidth 2000
Switch(config-pmap-c)#exit
```

Table 8-3 QoS Policy Parameters on the Catalyst 2950 and 3550

Action	Catalyst 2950	Catalyst 3550	Description
bandwidth		✓	Limits bandwidth to kbps.
set ip dscp	✓	✓	Marks frames with a specific DSCP value.
set ip precedence		✓	Marks frames with a specific IP Precedence value.
trust cos		✓	Trusts the frame's CoS.
trust dscp		✓	Trusts the packet's DSCP.
ip-precedence		✓	Trusts the packet's IP Precedence.
police		✓	Enforces bandwidth and flow characteristics on traffic.

The MQC does not necessarily require that users associate only one traffic class to one traffic policy. When packets match more than one match criterion, multiple traffic classes can be associated with a single service policy.

Applying the Policy to an Interface Using the Service Policy

The **service-policy** command attaches the traffic policy, as specified with the **policy-map** command, to an interface. Because the elements of the traffic policy can be applied to packets entering and leaving the interface, it is necessary to specify whether the traffic policy characteristics should be applied to incoming or outgoing packets. For instance, the **service-policy output policy1** command shown in Example 8-5 attaches all the characteristics of the traffic policy named policy1 to the specified interface. All packets leaving the specified interface are evaluated according to the criteria specified in the traffic policy named **policy1**.

Example 8-5 *The* **service-policy** *Command Attaches a Policy to an Interface*

```
Switch(config)#interface fastethernet 0/1
Switch(config-if)#service-policy output policy1
Switch(config-if)#exit
```

Classification at the Access Layer

To be effective, QoS should be implemented end-to-end within a network. Best practice is to classify traffic as soon as possible and ideally at the network edge or access layer. Some network devices can signify their traffic's QoS requirements directly, and others rely on access layer switches or border routers to perform this function on their behalf. Specifically:

> End devices can specify their own CoS, IP Precedence, and DSCP QoS parameters.
>
> or
>
> These parameters can be classified by the switch based on the ingress port.

Frames and packets can be marked as important by using Layer 2 CoS settings in the User Priority bits of the 802.1p portion of the 802.1Q header or the IP Precedence/DSCP bits in the ToS byte of the Internet Protocol version 4 (IPv4) header. The following sections outline the various classification techniques that can be applied at the ingress port of an access layer switch.

Trusting the CoS

The 3-bit CoS field in an ISL or 802.1Q/p frame allows for a range of CoS values between 0 and 7, where 0 is the lowest priority and 7 is the highest priority. If the edge device, such as an IP phone or PC application, can set the CoS bits, the network designer must decide whether to trust the device. The default action is for a switch with QoS features activated not to trust edge devices, and any frames that enter the switch have their CoS rewritten to the lowest priority of 0. If the edge device can be trusted, this default behavior must be overridden, and the access switch must be configured to switch the frame, leaving the CoS bits untouched, as shown in Figure 8-6.

Figure 8-6 Trusting the CoS of the Edge Devices Is One Option for Access Layer Switch Configuration

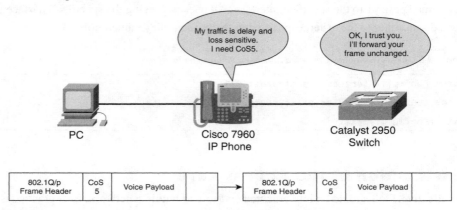

Configuring CoS Trust Using the IOS

Depending on the switch model, it might be necessary to first activate QoS using the global configuration command **mls qos**.

The **mls qos** command is required on both the Catalyst 3550 and the Catalyst 6500. The Catalyst 2950 has QoS enabled by default.

The trust is configured on the switch port using the interface command **mls qos trust cos**. Example 8-6 demonstrates configuring trust (with comments for each step) on Catalyst switches.

Example 8-6 *Configuring Trust on Catalyst Switches Is Straightforward*

```
switch(config)#mls qos
! Enables QoS functionality
switch(config-if)#mls qos trust cos
! Allows the switch to pass CoS values without changing them
switch(config-if)#mls qos cos default-cos
! Unmarked frame is given a default CoS when entering a port
```

Any ISL or 802.1Q/p frames that enter the switch port now have their CoS passed, untouched, through the switch. If an untagged frame arrives at the switch port, the switch assigns a default CoS to the frame before forwarding it. By default, untagged frames are assigned a CoS of 0. This can be changed using the interface configuration command **mls qos cos** *default-cos,* where *default-cos* is a number between 0 and 7.

Assigning CoS on a Per-Port Basis

For most network devices, such as PCs and printers, switch access ports can be assigned a default port CoS value of 0, because they have no special QoS requirements. For devices requiring a specific QoS that are unable to set the CoS value, an appropriate CoS value should be applied to the switch port. After a switch port is configured with a default CoS, traffic that passes through the port is automatically tagged with the required CoS value.

The CoS value assigned by the switch can be changed on a port-by-port basis using the interface configuration command **mls qos cos** *default-cos.*

After you apply the **mls qos cos** *default-cos* command, and assuming that the switch has been configured to trust the frames' existing CoS value, the switch's behavior is as follows:

- If the incoming frame has no CoS, apply the default CoS.
- If the incoming frame has a CoS, maintain the same CoS.

Rewriting the CoS

In some cases, it might be desirable not to trust any CoS value that might be present in frames sourced from an edge device. For example, an office PC used for general applications, such as web browsing, e-mail, and file and print services, does not require special QoS treatment. Allowing it to request higher levels of QoS might adversely affect applications that require guarantees of bandwidth and latency, such as voice and video.

For this reason, it is possible to use the **override** parameter to tell the switch to ignore any existing CoS value that might be in the frame and apply the default value. This effectively disables any trust configuration that might have been applied to the port previously.

The CoS value assigned by the switch can be changed on a port-by-port basis using the interface configuration command **mls qos cos override**, as shown in Figure 8-7.

Figure 8-7 The CoS of Incoming Frames Can Be Overridden

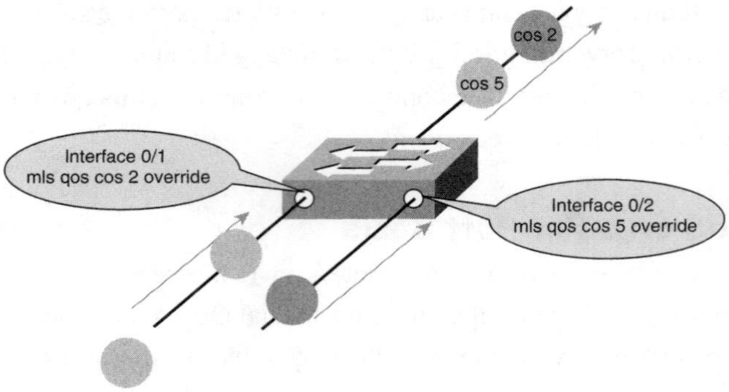

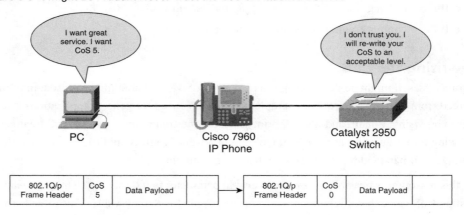

After you apply the **mls qos cos override** command, the switch rewrites the CoS value for all incoming frames to the configured default value, regardless of any existing CoS value, as shown in Figure 8-8.

Figure 8-8 It Might Be Prudent Not to Trust the CoS of Attached Devices

Using a MAC ACL to Assign a DSCP Value

Classifying a frame's CoS based on an ingress port is not always possible. An example of where ingress port classification would be a problem is where an ingress port is connected to multiple hosts through a hub or a simple workgroup switch that does not support QoS classification, as shown in Figure 8-9.

Figure 8-9 Not All Frames Can Be Meaningfully Assigned a CoS Based on the Ingress Port

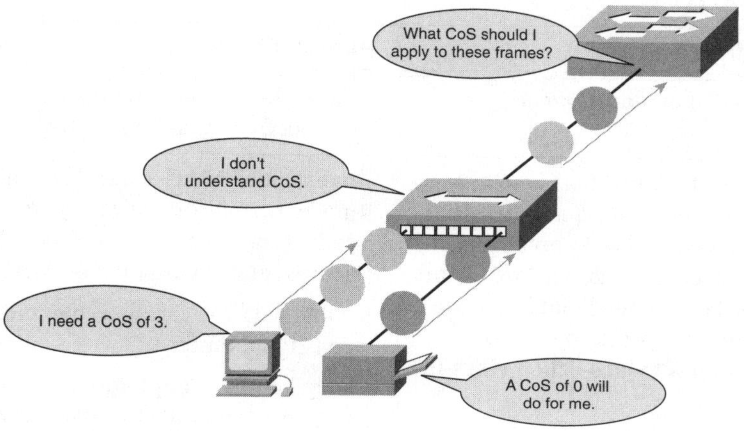

An IP access list could be a way of identifying traffic; however, this practice would limit QoS classification to IP traffic. IP access lists are also problematic when equipment must move between VLANs or when the IP address is dynamically allocated, such as DHCP. In this case, a possible solution would be to use a Layer 2 MAC-based ACL.

The syntax for a MAC ACL is similar to that required for an IP-based ACL. Use the global configuration command **mac access-list extended** *name*. Table 8-4 shows the syntax for creating MAC ACLs.

In the QoS context, the permit and deny actions in the access control entries (ACEs) have different meanings than with security ACLs:

- If a match with a permit action is encountered, known as the first-match principle, the specified QoS-related action is taken.
- If a match with a deny action is encountered, the ACL being processed is skipped, and the next ACL is processed.
- If no match with a permit action is encountered and all the ACLs have been examined, no QoS processing occurs on the packet.
- If multiple ACLs are configured on an interface, the lookup stops after the packet matches the first ACL with a permit action, and QoS processing begins.

NOTE

When creating an access list, remember that, by default, the end of the access list contains an implicit deny statement for everything if no match is found before the end is reached.

Table 8-4 Named MAC ACLs Are Useful When Multiple Devices Are Connected to a Single
Switch Port

Command/Parameters	Description
mac access-list extended *name*	From global configuration mode, defines an extended MAC access list using a name.
{**deny** | **permit**} {**any** | **host** *source MAC address*} {**any** | **host** *destination MAC address*} [**aarp** | **amber** | **appletalk** | **dec-spanning** | **decnet-iv** | **diagnostic** | **dsm** | **etype-6000** | **etype-8042** | **lat** | **lavc-sca** | **mop-console** | **mop-dump** | **msdos** | **mumps** | **netbios** | **vines-echo** | **vines-ip** | **xns-idp**]	In extended MAC access list configuration mode, permits or denies any source MAC address or a specific host source MAC address and any destination MAC address. (Optional) You can also enter the following non-IP options: **aarp** | **amber** | **appletalk** | **dec-spanning** | **decnet-iv** | **diagnostic** | **dsm** | **etype-6000** | **etype-8042** | **lat** | **lavc-sca** | **mop-console** | **mop-dump** | **msdos** | **mumps** | **netbios** | **vines-echo** | **vines-ip** | **xns-idp**
show access-lists [*number* | *name*]	Displays the access list configuration.

After a traffic class has been defined with a MAC-based ACL, a policy can be attached to that
class. A policy can contain multiple classes with different QoS actions specified for each of
them. For classification purposes, the policy class can be used to set a CoS at Layer 2 or
DSCP at Layer 3.

Lab 8.9.1 Classifying Traffic Using Class of Service at the Access Layer

This lab introduces the use of the Layer 2 CoS field as a means of classifying traffic
entering the network at the access layer.

Configuring DSCP Using a MAC ACL

In Figure 8-10, a MAC ACL is used to set the DSCP field of packets coming from a single IP
Phone, called **receptionphone**, within a switched network. Given that the MAC address of
the IP Phone is known to be 000.0a00.0111, a MAC ACL can be configured to identify traffic
sourced from this device.

Figure 8-10 MAC ACLs Can Be Used As a Basis for DSCP Marking

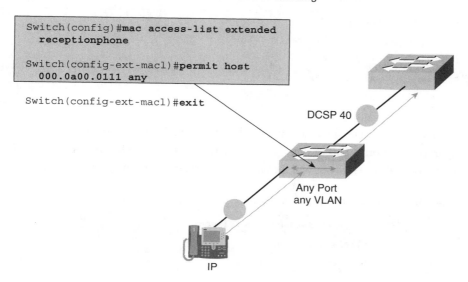

```
Switch(config)#mac access-list extended
   receptionphone

Switch(config-ext-macl)#permit host
   000.0a00.0111 any
```

```
Switch(config-ext-macl)#exit
```

DCSP 40

Any Port
any VLAN

IP

Verify the access list configuration using the **show access-lists** command, as shown in Example 8-7.

Example 8-7 *Verifying Access List Configuration*

```
Switch#show access-lists
Extended MAC access list receptionphone permit host 0000.0a00.0111 any
  permit host 0000.0a00.0111 any
```

After the traffic is identified, a class map is used to link the identified traffic to a particular class of service. In this case, a class of service called **ipphone** is created, as shown in Example 8-8.

Example 8-8 *Traffic Defined by a MAC ACL Can Be Referenced in a Class Map*

```
Switch(config)#class-map match-all ipphone
Switch(config-cmap)#match access-group name receptionphone
```

Verify the class map configuration using the **show class-map** command, as shown in Example 8-9.

Example 8-9 *Verifying Class Map Configuration*

```
Switch#show class-map
class map match-any class-default (id 0)
match any
class map match-all ipphone (id 2)
match access-group name receptionphone
```

Now that the traffic is classified, a policy map is used to define the action that should be taken on any traffic that forms part of that class, as shown in Example 8-10. In this case, the policy is called **inbound-accesslayer**, and the action is to set DSCP for the packets to 40.

Example 8-10 *A Policy Map Defines the Action to Take on the Traffic Defined by the MAC ACL*

```
Switch(config)#policy-map inbound-accesslayer
Switch(config-pmap)#class ipphone
Switch(config-pmap-c)#set ip dscp 40
```

Verify the policy map configuration using the **show policy-map** command, as shown in Example 8-11.

Example 8-11 *Verifying the Policy Map Configuration*

```
Switch#show policy-map
Policy Map inbound-accesslayer
class ipphone
set ip dscp 40
```

Now that the action to be taken on packets coming from the IP Phone is defined, the only remaining step is to tell the switch to apply the policy to the appropriate interface. In this case, the policy is applied to all the interfaces (as shown in Example 8-12) so that QoS is maintained regardless of the interface the IP Phone is connected to.

Example 8-12 *Applying the Policy Map to All Interfaces*

```
Switch(config)#interface range fastethernet 0/1 - 24
Switch(config-if-range)#service-policy input inbound-accesslayer
```

Determine the policies that are bound to a particular interface on the switch using the **show mls qos interface** command, as shown in Example 8-13.

Example 8-13 *Determining Policies Bound to an Interface*

```
Switch#show mls qos interface fastethernet 0/1
FastEthernet0/1
Attached policy-map for Ingress: inbound-accesslayer
trust state: not trusted
trust mode: not trusted
COS override: dis
default COS: 0
pass-through: none
trust device: none
```

Using an IP ACL to Define the DSCP or Precedence

Using the MQC, it is possible to classify traffic based on its IP or TCP properties, as shown in Figure 8-11.

Figure 8-11 A Named Extended IP ACL Is Commonly Used as a Basis for DSCP Marking

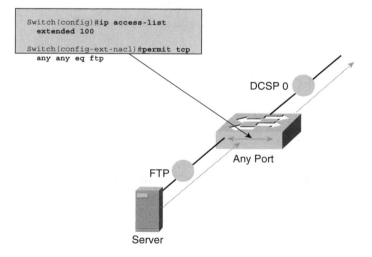

For instance, to prevent large FTP downloads from disrupting more critical services, the network administrator tags all FTP packets entering an access layer switch with either a low IP Precedence of 0 or a DSCP of 0 so that the traffic can be subjected to QoS policies within the network. In Figure 8-11, an IP ACL is used to identify the packets.

Using the MQC command **class-map**, a class can be defined; in this case it is called **reduced-service**, for traffic that does not require high levels of QoS. Traffic is classified as **reducedservice** if it is permitted by the access list, as shown in Example 8-14.

Example 8-14 *A Class Map Classifies the FTP Traffic*

```
Switch(config)#class-map reducedservice
Switch(config-cmap)#match access-group 100
```

NOTE

Both the Catalyst 2950 and the Catalyst 3550 support the setting of the DSCP. However, only the Catalyst 3550 supports the setting of Precedence. This is not a serious problem, because the IP Precedence field forms the first 3 bits of the DSCP. Therefore, by choosing and setting the appropriate DSCP value, you can still set the IP Precedence.

The MQC command **policy-map** is used in Example 8-15 to set the DSCP to 0 for this class of traffic.

Example 8-15 *Setting the DSCP Value to 0*

```
Switch(config)#policy-map inbound-accesslayer
Switch(config-pmap)#class reducedservice
Switch(config-pmap-c)#set ip dscp 0
```

Alternatively, the IP Precedence can be set using a policy map, as shown in Example 8-16.

Example 8-16 *Setting the IP Precedence to 0 on a Catalyst 3550*

```
Switch(config)#policy-map inbound-accesslayer
Switch(config-pmap)#class reducedservice
Switch(config-pmap-c)#set ip precedence 0
```

Now that the action to be taken on FTP packets is defined, the only remaining step is to tell the switch which interfaces to apply the policy to. In the case of Example 8-17, the policy is applied to all the interfaces so that QoS is maintained regardless of which interface an FTP source might be connected to.

Example 8-17 *Applying the Policy Map to All Interfaces*

```
Switch(config)#interface range fastethernet 0/1 - 24
Switch(config-if-range)#service-policy input inbound-accesslayer
```

 Lab 8.9.2   Introduction to the Modular QoS Command-Line Interface

This lab introduces the concept of the DSCP, which is used to mark packets with a QoS identifier.

Policing and Marking

Traffic policing involves placing a constraint on the maximum traffic rate. When the traffic rate reaches the configured maximum rate, excess traffic is dropped or remarked. The result is an output rate that appears as a saw tooth with crests and troughs, as illustrated in Figure 8-12.

Figure 8-12 Policing Makes It Possible to Act on Nonconforming Packets, Such as by Dropping Them

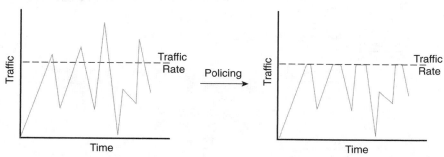

Policers define bandwidth limits for traffic. Packets that exceed the limits are said to be "out of profile" or nonconforming. Each policer specifies the action to take for packets that are in or out of profile. These actions, carried out by the "marker," include the following:

- Passing the packet through the switch without modification
- Dropping the packet
- Marking down the packet with a new DSCP value that is obtained from the configurable policed-DSCP map

Figure 8-13 provides a useful flow chart that describes policing.

Individual Policers

Individual policers apply the bandwidth limits specified in the policer separately to each matched traffic class. This type of policer is configured within a policy map using the **police** policy map configuration command.

The format of the **police** command on the Catalyst 3550 is as follows:

```
Switch(config-pmap-c)#police rate-bps burst-byte [exceed-action
  {drop | policed-dscp-transmit}]
```

The **police** command on an IOS-based router operates in a similar fashion, except that the actual DSCP values are specified as part of the command line rather than being specified as a separate translation table, as is the case on a Catalyst switch. IOS-based routers also permit IP Precedence to be set.

Figure 8-13 Policed Packets Can Be Passed Through, Marked, or Dropped

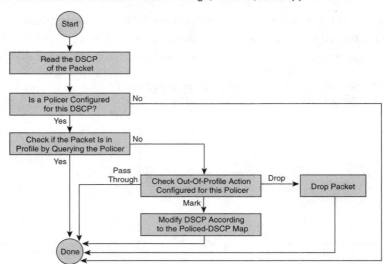

Aggregate Policers

Aggregate policers apply the bandwidth limits specified in an aggregate policer cumulatively to all matched traffic flows. You configure this type of policer by specifying the aggregate policer name within a policy map by using the **police aggregate** *policy-map* configuration command. Specify the policer's bandwidth limits by using the **mls qos aggregate-policer** global configuration command. In this way, the aggregate policer is shared by multiple classes of traffic within a policy map.

Example 8-18 demonstrates the operation of an aggregate policer.

Example 8-18 *An Aggregate Policer on a Catalyst 3550 Applies Bandwidth Limits Cumulatively to All Matched Traffic*

```
mls qos
mls qos aggregate-policer pol_1mbps 1000000 16000
  exceed-action drop
!---Defines the ACLs to select taffic
access-list 123 permit udp any any eq 111
access-list 145 permit tcp any eq 20 any
!---Defines the traffic classes to be policed
class-map match-all cl_udp111
 match access-group 123
class-map match-all cl_tcp20
 match access-group 145
```

Example 8-18 *An Aggregate Policer on a Catalyst 3550 Applies Bandwidth Limits Cumulatively to All*
Matched Traffic (Continued)

```
!---Defines the QoS policy and attaches the policer to the traffic classes
policy-map po_test
 class cl_udp111 polic aggregate pol_1mbps
 class cl_tcp20 polic aggregate pol_1mpbs
```

Token Bucket

Policing uses a token bucket algorithm. As the switch receives each frame, a token is added to
the bucket. The bucket has a hole in it and leaks at a rate that is specified as the average traffic
rate in bits per second. Each time a token is added to the bucket, the switch performs a check
to determine if the bucket has enough room. If there is not enough room, the packet is marked
as nonconforming, and the specified policer action is taken—dropped or marked down—as
illustrated in Figure 8-14.

Figure 8-14 Token Buckets Are Often Used to Describe QoS Operation

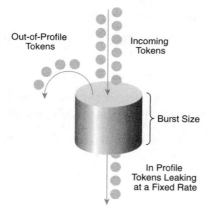

How quickly the bucket fills is a function of the bucket depth, or burst-byte, the rate at which
the tokens are removed (rate-bps), and the duration of the burst above the average rate. The
bucket's size imposes an upper limit on the burst length and determines the number of frames
that can be transmitted back-to-back. If the burst is short, the bucket does not overflow, and
no action is taken against the traffic flow. However, if a burst is long and at a higher rate, the
bucket overflows and the policing actions are taken against the frames in that burst.

The bucket depth, the maximum burst that is tolerated before the bucket overflows, is configured by using the **burst-byte** option of the **police** policy map class configuration command or
the **mls qos aggregate-policer** global configuration command. The rate or average at which

tokens are removed is configured using the *rate-bps* option of the **police** policy map class configuration command or the **mls qos aggregate-policer** global configuration command.

Classification and Policing Using Committed Access Rate (CAR)

Committed Access Rate (CAR) is a multifaceted feature that implements both classification services and policing through rate limiting. This section describes its classification capability.

CAR's classification services allow traffic flow limits to be placed on incoming traffic. These limits specify the average rate, *rate-bps,* and the burst rate, *burst-byte,* that are permissible. Traffic that is nonconforming because it exceeds either the average rate or the burst rate specified can be marked down in terms of DSCP. As traffic flows through the network, networking devices can use the adjusted DSCP to determine how the traffic should be treated. For example, congestion management and avoidance techniques can be used to selectively drop packets from traffic that was previously marked down in terms of DSCP.

The policy map command that enables CAR and that defines a policer for the classified traffic is as follows:

```
police rate-bps burst-byte [exceed-action {drop | policed-dscp-transmit}]
```

- *rate-bps* specifies the average traffic rate in bits per second (bps). The range is 8000 to 2,000,000,000.
- *burst-byte* specifies the normal burst size in bytes. The range is 8000 to 512,000,000.

You can configure up to 128 policers on ingress Gigabit-capable Ethernet ports, up to eight policers on ingress 10/100 Ethernet ports, and up to eight policers on egress ports.

The **exceed-action** option specifies the action to take when the rates are exceeded. Use the **exceed-action drop** keywords to drop the packet. Use the **exceed-action policed-dscp-transmit** keywords to mark down the DSCP value (by using the policed DSCP map) and send the packet.

Configuring the Policed DSCP Map

To mark down the DSCP value of nonconforming traffic, the switch uses a map to translate between the initial DSCP value and the marked-down DSCP.

The global configuration command **mls qos map policed-dscp** on a Catalyst 3550 modifies the default condition of mapping the inbound DSCP value to the same outbound DSCP.

The global configuration command syntax is as follows:

```
mls qos map policed-dscp dscp-list to mark-down-dscp
```

dscp-list consists of up to eight DSCP values to be mapped to a single *mark-down-dscp* value.

The **show mls qos maps policed-dscp** command displays the current mapping, as shown in
Example 8-19. The map can be returned to its defaults with the **no mls qos policed-dscp**
command.

Example 8-19 *Displaying DSCP Mappings with the* **show mls qos maps policed-dscp** *Command*

```
Switch#show mls qos maps policed-dscp
Policed-dscp map:
d1:   d2  0   1   2   3   4   5   6   7   8   9
    ------------------------------------------
0:    00  01  02  03  04  05  06  07  08  09
1:    10  11  12  13  14  15  16  17  18  19
2:    20  21  22  23  24  25  26  27  28  29
3:    30  31  32  33  34  35  36  37  38  39
4:    40  41  42  43  44  45  46  47  48  49
5:    00  00  00  00  00  00  00  00  58  59
6:    60  61  62  63
```

Example 8-20 shows how to map DSCPs 50 to 57 to a marked-down DSCP value of 0.

Example 8-20 *Many-to-One DSCP Mappings Are Possible*

```
Switch#configure terminal
Switch(config)#mls qos map policed-dscp 50 51 52 53 54 55 56 57 to 0
Switch(config)#end
Switch#show mls qos maps policed-dscp
Policed-dscp map:
d1  d2  0   1   2   3   4   5   6   7   8   9
    -----------------------------------------
0:  00  01  02  03  04  05  06  07  08  09
1:  10  11  12  13  14  15  16  17  18  19
2:  20  21  22  23  24  25  26  27  28  29
3:  30  31  32  33  34  35  36  37  38  39
4:  40  41  42  43  44  45  46  47  48  49
5:  00  00  00  00  00  00  00  00  58  59
6:  60  61  62  63
```

You read the map by taking the original DSCP in the form of "d1 d2" and reading the new
DSCP value from the intersection of the "d1" row and the "d2" column.

Configuring Classification Using CAR

Example 8-21 shows how to create a policy map on a Catalyst 3550 by using CAR and attaching it to an ingress interface.

Example 8-21 *MQC Is Used to Configure CAR*

```
Switch(config)#access-list 1 permit 10.1.0.0 0.0.255.255
Switch(config)#class-map ipclass1
Switch(config-cmap)#match access-group 1
Switch(config-cmap)#exit
Switch(config)#policy-map flow1t
Switch(config-pmap)#class ipclass1
Switch(config-pmap-c)#trust dscp
Switch(config-pmap-c)#police 48000 8000 exceed-action policed-dscp-transmit
Switch(config-pmap-c)#exit
Switch(config-pmap)#exit
Switch(config)#interface gigabitethernet0/1
Switch(config-if)#service-policy input flow1t
```

In the configuration, an IP standard ACL permits traffic from network 10.1.0.0, as shown in Figure 8-15. For traffic matching this classification, the DSCP value in the incoming packet is trusted. If the matched traffic exceeds an average traffic rate of 48000 bps and a normal burst size of 8000 bytes, its DSCP is marked down based on the previously defined policed-DSCP map and then is sent.

Figure 8-15 CAR Is Configured for Incoming Traffic from the 10.1.0.0/16 Subnet

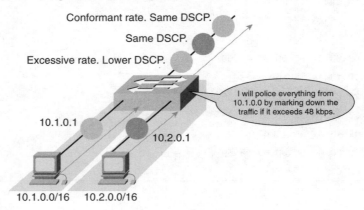

Configuring Policing Using CAR

Example 8-22 demonstrates a policy that is strictly enforced on a Catalyst 3550 for the setup shown in Figure 8-16.

Example 8-22 *CAR Can Be Used to Strictly Enforce a Policy by Dropping Packets*

```
Switch(config)#access-list 1 permit 10.1.0.0 0.0.255.255
Switch(config)#class-map ipclass1
Switch(config-cmap)#match access-group 1
Switch(config-cmap)#exit
Switch(config)#policy-map flow1t
Switch(config-pmap)#class ipclass1
Switch(config-pmap-c)#trust dscp
Switch(config-pmap-c)#police 48000 8000 exceed-action drop
Switch(config-pmap-c)#exit
Switch(config-pmap)#exit
Switch(config)#interface gigabitethernet0/1
Switch(config-if)#service-policy input flow1t
```

Figure 8-16 CAR Can Be Configured to Be Strictly Enforced by Dropping Nonconforming Packets

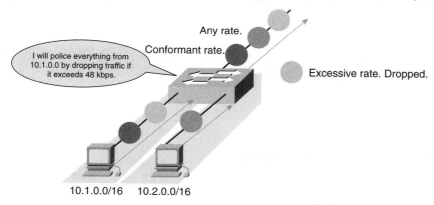

Rather than merely marking down the DSCP value of nonconforming packets, the packets are dropped. An IP standard ACL permits traffic from network 10.1.0.0. For traffic matching this classification, the DSCP value in the incoming packet is trusted, and the packet is forwarded

with the DSCP intact. If the matched traffic exceeds an average traffic rate of 48000 bps and a normal burst size of 8000 bytes, the traffic is dropped.

 Lab 8.9.3   QoS Classification and Policing Using CAR

In this lab, you use CAR to classify and police traffic.

Scheduling

The process of assigning packets to one of multiple queues, based on classification, for priority treatment through the network, is called *scheduling*. Here, traffic that has been subject to classification at the network edge receives any preferential QoS treatment requested. Options include FIFO, WFQ, and CBWFQ.

FIFO Queue

The simplest form of scheduling and the default for interfaces 2 Mbps and faster is the FIFO queue, illustrated in Figure 8-17. The FIFO queue offers no preferential service for traffic; packets are merely forwarded in the order they are received.

Figure 8-17   FIFO Is the Default Queuing Method on Serial Interfaces with Speeds Greater Than T1/E1

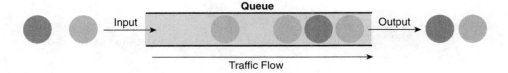

Weighted Fair Queuing (WFQ)

Weighted Fair Queuing (WFQ) classifies traffic entering the queue based on traffic flows, as shown in Figure 8-18. The actual flow classification can be based on the following:

- Source and destination addresses
- Protocol
- Session identifier (port/socket)

Figure 8-18 WFQ Is the Default Queuing Method on Serial Interfaces with Speeds Less Than T1/E1

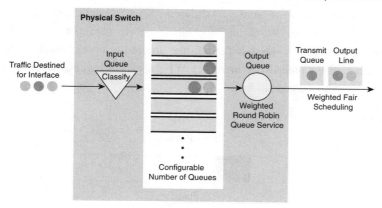

Each flow is given its own queue. In its simplest form, WFQ services each of these queues on a round-robin basis. This means that every flow of traffic has an equal share of the available bandwidth if it is required—hence the term, "fair" queue. The benefit for low-volume traffic is reduced and predictable latency. For many applications, this default behavior of WFQ is sufficient. However, some applications need specific QoS guarantees that require more than simply "fair" access to the bandwidth. In this case, the "weight" needs to be modified so that WFQ does not share bandwidth on a round-robin basis but is influenced by the class or priority of the traffic in the flow. Weight is determined by the following:

- Requested QoS (IP Precedence, RSVP)
- Frame Relay forward explicit congestion notification (FECN), backward explicit congestion notification (BECN), discard eligible (DE) (for Frame Relay traffic)
- Slow throughput (weighted fair)

Weighted fair queuing is activated on an interface using the **fair-queue** interface command.

Note that the queuing strategies described here apply to packets at Layer 3. Consequently, these techniques can be used only on router interfaces. Physical interfaces on the Catalyst 3550 and Catalyst 6500 switches are used as router interfaces after the interface command **no switchport** is applied.

These features are unavailable on regular Layer 2 switch ports and Layer 2 switches, such as the Catalyst 2950.

WFQ and IP Precedence

WFQ is IP Precedence-aware. Figure 8-19 shows the IPv4 ToS field, which includes 3 bits for specifying the IP Precedence. WFQ can detect higher-priority packets marked with precedence by the IP Forwarder and can schedule them faster, providing superior response time for this traffic. Therefore, as the precedence increases, WFQ allocates more bandwidth to the conversation during periods of congestion.

Figure 8-19 ToS Field in an IPv4 Packet

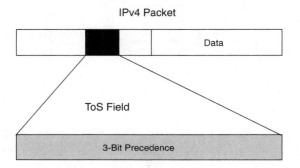

WFQ assigns a weight to each flow that determines the transmit order for queued packets. In this scheme, lower weights are served first. For standard Cisco IOS WFQ, the IP Precedence serves as a divisor to this weighting factor. For each cycle through all flows, WFQ effectively services queues such that the proportion of bandwidth given to any IP Precedence level is the IP Precedence plus 1. For example, if there is one flow at each precedence level, each flow gets precedence + 1 parts of the link:

$$1 + 2 + 3 + 4 + 5 + 6 + 7 + 8 = 36$$

Therefore, precedence 0 traffic gets 1/36 of the bandwidth, precedence 1 traffic gets 2/36, and precedence 7 traffic gets 8/36.

However, for 18 precedence-1 flows and one of each of the rest, the total is now

$$1 + (2*18) + 3 + 4 + 5 + 6 + 7 + 8 = 70$$

So an individual precedence-1 flow receives 2/70 or 1/35 of the bandwidth.

The actual allocated bandwidth changes continuously as flows are added or ended.

Lab 8.9.4   Weighted Fair Queuing

In this lab, you configure and optimize weighted fair queuing.

Class-Based Weighted Fair Queuing (CBWFQ)

Class-Based Weighted Fair Queuing (CBWFQ) extends the standard WFQ functionality to provide support for user-defined traffic classes as follows:

- CBWFQ provides for up to 64 classes. Flow-based WFQ is limited to seven classifications or weights.
- CBWFQ allows for coarser granularity. Multiple IP flows can belong to a single class.

For CBWFQ, the traffic classes are defined using match criteria including protocols, access control lists, and input interfaces. Packets satisfying the match criteria for a class constitute the traffic for that class, and a FIFO queue is reserved for each class. Traffic belonging to a class is directed to the queue for that class the same way WFQ directs traffic belonging to different flows.

After you have defined a class according to its match criteria, you can assign characteristics to it. To characterize a class, you specify bandwidth, weight, and maximum packet limit. The bandwidth assigned to a class is the guaranteed bandwidth delivered to that class during congestion. Packets belonging to a class are subject to the bandwidth and queue limits that characterize the class, as shown in Figure 8-20. After a queue has reached its configured queue limit, queuing of additional packets to the class causes further packets to be dropped.

Figure 8-20 The WFQ Algorithm Is Applied to Classes Rather Than to Flows

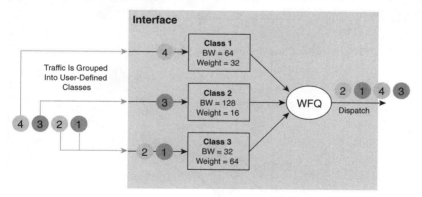

If a default class is configured with the **bandwidth** policy map class configuration command, all unclassified traffic is put in a single FIFO queue and is treated according to the configured bandwidth. If a default class is configured with the **fair-queue** command, all unclassified traffic is flow-classified and given best-effort treatment. If no default class is configured, by default the traffic that does not match any of the configured classes is flow-classified and given best-effort treatment. As soon as a packet is classified, all the standard mechanisms that can be used to differentiate service among the classes apply.

For CBWFQ, the weight specified for the class becomes the weight of each packet that meets the class's match criteria. Packets that arrive at the output interface are classified according to the match criteria filters specified. Each packet is then assigned the appropriate weight. The weight for a packet belonging to a specific class is derived from the bandwidth assigned to the class when configured. In this case, the user can configure a class's weight.

Configuring CBWFQ

CBWFQ can be configured on Cisco routers, Catalyst 3550 switches, and Catalyst 6500 switches. The appropriate image must be loaded in each case. For example, 12.2 Enterprise Plus or Advanced IP Services images work on Cisco routers. Recent EMI images do the trick on 3550 switches.

In Example 8-23, incoming traffic that has been marked with a DSCP of 50 is given 40 percent of the outbound link available bandwidth. All other traffic shares the remaining 60 percent of bandwidth using WFQ, as illustrated in Figure 8-21. Configuring CBWFQ begins with turning on QoS functionality and defining the traffic that belongs to a particular class.

Example 8-23 *The Traffic Is Defined as Packets That Have a DSCP Value of 50*

```
Router(config)#mls qos
Router(config)#class-map prioritytraffic
Router(config)#match dscp 50
```

Figure 8-21 CBWFQ Permits Per-Class Bandwidth Allocation

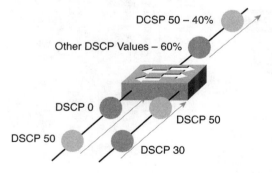

Example 8-24 configures a policy map defining the QoS requirements for both the priority traffic identified and all other traffic (default).

Example 8-24 *The Policy Limits the DSCP-Defined Traffic to 40 Percent of the Bandwidth*

```
Router(config)#policy-map prioritybw
Router(config-pmap)#class class-default
Router(config-pmap-c)#fair-queue
Router(config-pmap-c)#exit
Router(config-pmap)#class prioritytraffic
Router(config-pmap-c)#bandwidth percent 40
Router(config-pmap-c)#queue-limit 200
```

The **queue-limit** option specifies the depth of the queue for that class. Specifying a queue limit tells the router that a tail-drop policy is to be used. Inbound traffic is placed in the queue until it is full. As soon as the queue is full, all further packets are dropped until space is again available. The section "Congestion Avoidance" explores an alternative way to handle congested queues.

Finally, the policy has to be actually implemented by applying it to an interface, as shown in Example 8-25.

Example 8-25 *The Policy Is Applied to Outgoing Traffic on the GigabitEthernet0/1 Interface*

```
Router(config)#interface fastethernet0/1
Router(config)#no fair-queue
Router(config-if)#service-policy output prioritybw
```

Configuring CBWFQ on a physical interface is possible only if the interface is in the default queuing mode. Serial interfaces at E1 (2.048 Mbps) and below use WFQ by default, and other interfaces use FIFO by default. Enabling CBWFQ on a physical interface overrides the default interface queuing method.

Several useful router **show** commands are available for CBWFQ verification:

- **show policy-map** *policy-map*—Displays the configuration of all classes that make up the specified policy map.

- **show policy-map** *policy-map* **class** *class-name*—Displays the configuration of the specified class of the specified policy map.

- **show policy-map interface** *interface-name*—Displays the configuration of all classes configured for all policy maps on the specified interface.

- **show queue** *interface-type interface-number*—Displays queuing configuration and statistics for a particular interface.

NOTE

CBWFQ cannot be configured on the Catalyst 2950 switch. However, it is supported on Catalyst 6500 switches and IOS-based routers.

The counters displayed after the **show policy-map interface** command is issued are updated only if congestion is present on the interface.

CBWFQ Bandwidth Allocation

The sum of all bandwidth allocation on an interface cannot exceed 75 percent of the total available interface bandwidth. The remaining 25 percent is used for other overhead, including Layer 2 overhead, routing traffic, and best-effort traffic. Bandwidth for the CBWFQ class-default class is taken from the remaining 25 percent. However, under aggressive circumstances in which it is necessary to configure more than 75 percent of the interface bandwidth to classes, the 75 percent maximum can be overridden using the **max-reserved-bandwidth** *percent* interface command.

Congestion Avoidance

Up to this point, this chapter has covered methods of dealing with congestion. When networks are heavily congested and the aggregate flows through a network device exceed the bandwidth of its links or its capability to keep up, packets inevitably are dropped. TCP/IP uses lost packets as a way of telling the sender that congestion is occurring in the network. TCP/IP responds to lost packets by reducing the size of its congestion window, which results in a reduced rate of transmission and alleviates congestion in the network.

The problem with dropped packets is that packets for all flows are dropped simultaneously. This is called tail-drop, and it occurs when the ingress queue on a network device becomes full. Consequently, all TCP/IP senders reduce their transmission speed simultaneously and might underutilize the available bandwidth for a period of time. Eventually the TCP/IP senders increase the size of their congestion window until congestion occurs again. As this cycle continues, the TCP/IP senders tend to synchronize with one another. This symptom is called *global synchronization*. This leads to several problems:

- Bursty network traffic that makes QoS more difficult to achieve
- Excessive retransmissions of lost packets
- Periods of underutilization of the available bandwidth

Furthermore, although it is possible to prioritize traffic as it flows through a network device, it is not possible to prioritize traffic when an ingress queue is full. QoS requires that ingress queues always have some space available so that priority traffic can be received. A technique is needed to ensure that ingress queues are never allowed to completely fill. This technique is called congestion avoidance.

Weighted Random Early Detection (WRED)

Weighted Random Early Detection (WRED) is a queuing technique for congestion avoidance. WRED manages how packets are handled when an interface starts becoming congested. When traffic begins to exceed the interface traffic thresholds before any congestion, the interface starts dropping packets from selected flows. If the dropped packets are TCP, the TCP source recognizes that packets are getting dropped and lowers its transmission rate. The lowered transmission rate then reduces the traffic to the interface, avoiding congestion. Because TCP retransmits dropped packets, no actual data loss occurs.

When the average queue size is above the maximum threshold, all packets are dropped. The mark probability denominator is the fraction of packets dropped when the average queue size is at the maximum threshold. For example, if the denominator is 512, one out of every 512 packets is dropped when the average queue is at the maximum threshold. When the average queue size is above the maximum threshold, all packets are dropped. Figure 8-22 summarizes packet drop probability.

Figure 8-22 Packet Drop Probability

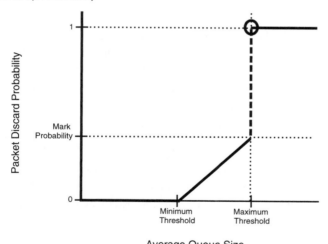

WRED drops packets according to the following criteria:

- RSVP flows are given precedence over non-RSVP flows to ensure that time-critical packets are transmitted as required.
- Using IP Precedence or the DSCP value of the packets, packets with higher precedence are less likely to be dropped. If the default settings are preventing QoS, the precedence value can be used to control how WRED determines when and how often to drop packets.

- The amount of bandwidth used by the traffic flow. Flows that use the most bandwidth are more likely to have packets dropped.
- The weight factor defined for the interface determines how frequently packets are dropped.

WRED chooses the packets to drop after considering these factors in combination. The net result is that the highest-priority and lowest-bandwidth traffic is preserved. WRED differs from standard random early detection (RED) in that RED ignores IP Precedence and instead drops packets from all traffic flows, not selecting low-precedence or high-bandwidth flows. By selectively dropping packets before congestion occurs, WRED prevents an interface from getting flooded, necessitating a large number of dropped packets. This increases the overall bandwidth usage for the interface.

An effective use of WRED is to avoid congestion on a predominantly TCP/IP network, one that has minimal UDP traffic and no significant traffic from other networking protocols. WRED is especially effective on core devices rather than edge devices, because the traffic marking performed on edge devices can then affect the WRED interfaces throughout the network.

The disadvantage of WRED is that only predominantly TCP/IP networks can benefit. WRED has no effect on UDP traffic, though. Other protocols, such as NetWare Internetwork Packet Exchange (IPX)/Sequenced Packet Exchange (SPX), do not respond to dropped packets by lowering their transmission rates; they just retransmit the packets at the same rate. WRED treats all non-TCP/IP packets as having precedence 0. In a mixed-protocol environment, WRED might not be the best choice for queuing traffic.

WRED interfaces automatically favor high-priority, low-bandwidth traffic flows. No specific policies are needed. However, because WRED automatically uses the IP Precedence settings in packets, consider marking all traffic that enters the device or mark the traffic at the point where it enters the network. Marking all traffic ensures that packets receive the service level intended.

Configuring WRED on a Physical Interface

To enable WRED on an interface, use the interface command **random-detect**.

No other commands or parameters need to be specified to configure WRED on the interface with the default parameter values.

The defaults can be changed with the following interface commands:

- **random-detect exponential-weighting-constant** *exponent min-threshold max-threshold mark-prob-denominator*—This command configures the weight factor used in calculating the average queue length.

- **random-detect precedence** *precedence min-threshold max-threshold mark-prob-denominator*—This command configures parameters for packets with a specific IP Precedence. The minimum threshold for IP Precedence 0 corresponds to half the maximum threshold for the interface. The command must be issued for each precedence. To configure RED, use the same parameters for each precedence. The default WRED parameter values are based on the best available data.

Lab 8.9.5   Configuring WRED on a Physical Interface

In this lab, you configure WRED in its simplest form using the default IP Precedence bits in a packet to determine the weighting.

Verifying WRED Configuration

The following commands can be used to verify the configuration and operation of WRED:

- **show interfaces** [*type slot | port-adapter | port*]—Displays the WRED configuration on an interface.
- **show queueing random-detect**—Displays the queuing configuration for WRED.
- **show queue** *interface-type interface-number*—Displays the header information of the packets inside a queue.

Configuring WRED with CBWFQ

WRED can be combined with CBWFQ. In this combination, CBWFQ provides a guaranteed percentage of the output bandwidth, and WRED ensures that TCP traffic is not sent faster than CBWFQ can forward it.

The abbreviated configuration shown in Example 8-26 shows how WRED can be added to a policy map specifying CBWFQ.

Example 8-26 *WRED Can Be Combined with CBWFQ*

```
Router(config)#policy-map prioritybw
Router(config-pmap)#class class-default
Router(config-pmap-c)#fair-queue
Router(config-pmap-c)#exit
Router(config-pmap)#class prioritytraffic
Router(config-pmap-c)#bandwidth percent 40
Router(config-pmap-c)#random-detect
```

The **random-detect** parameter specifies that WRED is used rather than the default tail-drop action.

 Lab 8.9.6   Configuring WRED with CBWFQ

In this lab, you learn to configure CBWFQ in conjunction with WRED.

Low Latency Queuing (LLQ)

The *Low Latency Queuing (LLQ)* feature brings strict priority queuing (PQ) to CBWFQ. Strict PQ allows delay-sensitive data, such as voice, to be sent before packets in other queues are sent. Without LLQ, CBWFQ provides WFQ based on defined classes with no strict priority queue available for real-time traffic. For CBWFQ, the weight for a packet belonging to a specific class is derived from the bandwidth assigned to the class. Therefore, the bandwidth assigned to the packets of a class determines the order in which the packets are sent. All packets are serviced fairly based on weight, and no class of packets may be granted strict priority. This scheme poses problems for voice traffic, which is largely intolerant of delay, especially variation in delay. For voice traffic, variations in delay introduce irregularities of transmission manifesting as jitter in the heard conversation. LLQ provides strict priority queuing for CBWFQ, reducing jitter in voice conversations, as illustrated in Figure 8-23.

Figure 8-23 LLQ Provides for Strict Priority Queuing of Voice Traffic (V)

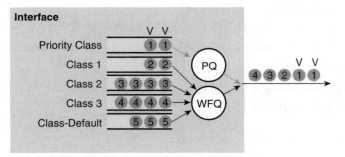

LLQ enables the use of a single, strict priority queue within CBWFQ at the class level. Any class can be made a priority queue by adding the **priority** keyword. Within a policy map, one or more classes can be given priority status. When multiple classes within a single policy map are configured as priority classes, all traffic from these classes is sent to the same, single, strict priority queue.

Although it is possible to queue various types of real-time traffic to the strict priority queue, it is strongly recommended that only voice traffic be sent to the strict priority queue because voice traffic is well-behaved, whereas other types of real-time traffic are not. Moreover, voice traffic requires that delay be nonvariable to avoid jitter. Real-time traffic, such as video, could introduce variation in delay, thereby thwarting the steadiness of delay required for successful voice traffic transmission.

When the **priority** command is specified for a class, it takes a *bandwidth* argument that gives maximum bandwidth in kbps. This parameter specifies the maximum amount of bandwidth allocated for packets belonging to the class configured. The *bandwidth* parameter both guarantees bandwidth to the priority class and restrains the flow of packets from the priority class. In the event of congestion, policing is used to drop packets when the bandwidth is exceeded.

Voice traffic queued to the priority queue is UDP-based and therefore is not adaptive to the early packet drop characteristic of WRED. Because WRED is ineffective, the WRED **random-detect** command cannot be used with the **priority** command. In addition, because policing is used to drop packets and a queue limit is not imposed, the **queue-limit** command cannot be used with the **priority** command.

Lab 8.9.7   Configuring Low Latency Queuing (LLQ)

In this lab, LLQ enables the use of a single, strict-priority queue within CBWFQ at the class level.

Configuring LLQ

To give priority to a class within a policy map, use the policy map class configuration mode command **priority** *bandwidth,* which offers the following benefits:

- It adds strict priority queuing to CBWFQ.
- It offers better treatment for delay-sensitive data, such as voice over IP.
- It's very useful on slow links.
- It's also called priority queuing/CBWFQ.

Example 8-27 shows the configuration for a policy map that provides 80 kbps for the traffic class **llqtraffic**.

Example 8-27 *CBWFQ with a Priority Queue: LLQ*

```
Router(config)#class-map llqtraffic
Router(config-cmap)#exit
Router(config)#policy-map prioritybw
Router(config-pmap)#class llqtraffic
```

continues

Example 8-27 *CBWFQ with a Priority Queue: LLQ (Continued)*

```
Router(config-pmap-c)#priority 80
Router(config-pmap)#class class-default
Router(config-pmap-c)#fair-queue
Router(config-pmap-c)#exit
```

The configuration and operation of LLQ can be verified with the following commands:

- **debug priority**—Displays priority queuing output if packets are dropped from the priority queue.

- **show queue** *interface-type interface-number*—Displays the queuing configuration and statistics for a particular interface.

- **show policy-map** *interface interface-name*—Displays the configuration of all classes configured for all traffic policies on the specified interface. Tells you whether packets and bytes were discarded or dropped for the priority class in the traffic policy attached to the interface.

Traffic Shaping

Traffic shaping allows rate control of traffic leaving an interface to match its flow to the speed of the remote target interface and to ensure that the traffic conforms to policies defined for it. Therefore, traffic adhering to a particular profile can be shaped to meet downstream requirements, eliminating bottlenecks in topologies with data-rate mismatches.

Traffic shaping prevents packet loss. Its use is important in Frame Relay networks, because a Frame Relay switch cannot determine which packets take precedence and which packets should be dropped when congestion occurs. Traffic shaping is of critical importance for real-time traffic, such as voice over Frame Relay. Latency must be minimized by bounding the amount of traffic and traffic loss in the data-link network and by keeping the data in the router that is making the guarantees.

Retaining the data in the router through the use of queuing allows the router to prioritize traffic according to the guarantees it is making.

Cisco IOS QoS software has three types of traffic shaping:

- *Generic Traffic Shaping (GTS)*
- *Class-based*
- *Frame Relay Traffic Shaping (FRTS)*

All three of these traffic-shaping methods are similar in implementation, although the CLIs differ somewhat and they use different types of queues to contain and shape traffic that is deferred. The underlying code that determines whether enough credit is in the token bucket for a packet to be sent or whether that packet must be delayed is common to each feature. If a packet is deferred, GTS and class-based shaping use a weighted fair queue to hold the delayed traffic. FRTS uses either a custom queue or a priority queue for the same, depending on what has been configured.

More Information
The remainder of this section focuses on GTS.
For further information on class-based shaping, refer to http://www.cisco.com/univercd/cc/td/doc/product/software/ios122/122cgcr/fqos_c/fqcprt4/qcfcbshp.htm.
For more information on Frame Relay traffic shaping, see http://www.cisco.com/univercd/cc/td/doc/product/software/ios122/122cgcr/fwan_c/wcffrely.htm#wp1001623.

Generic Traffic Shaping (GTS)

Traffic shaping lets you control traffic going out an interface to match its transmission to the speed of the remote target interface and to ensure that the traffic conforms to the policies contracted for it. Traffic adhering to a particular profile can be shaped to meet downstream requirements, thereby eliminating bottlenecks in topologies with data-rate mismatches.

Generic Traffic Shaping (GTS) shapes traffic by reducing outbound traffic flow to avoid congestion by constraining traffic to a particular bit rate using the token bucket mechanism, as shown in Figure 8-24.

Figure 8-24 GTS Constrains Traffic Using the Token Bucket Mechanism

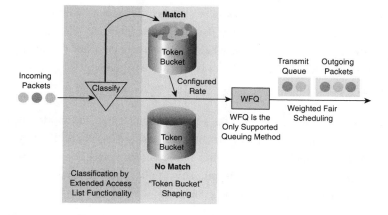

GTS is applied on a per-interface basis and can use access lists to select the traffic to shape. GTS works with a variety of Layer 2 technologies, including

- Frame Relay
- ATM
- Switched Multimegabit Data Service (SMDS)
- Ethernet

On a Frame Relay subinterface, you can set up GTS to adapt dynamically to available bandwidth by integrating Backward Explicit Congestion Notification (BECN) signals, or simply to shape to a specified rate.

A service provider can use GTS to define the data rate independently of the physical link clock rate. An ISP might provide customers with a physical T1, regardless of the data rate they are paying for. The actual rate supplied can then be 128 kbps, configured using GTS. If the customer wants to upgrade to a 1-Mbps service, this can be achieved with a minor configuration change.

Configuring GTS for an Interface

GTS can be configured to shape traffic for all traffic exiting an interface using the following interface command:

traffic-shape rate *bit-rate* [*burst-size* [*excess-burst-size*]]

Alternatively, traffic defined by an ACL can be shaped independently of other traffic exiting an interface using the following interface command:

traffic-shape group *access-list-number bit-rate* [*burst-size* [*excess-burst-size*]]

The *bit-rate* determines the average data rate that is permitted out of the specified interface. The *burst-size* is the number of bits that can be sent as a single burst within a time period. The instantaneous *bit-rate* can be much higher than the average bit rate. The *burst-size* should be configured so that any peaks do not overwhelm the input queue of the destination interface. The time period (T_c) over which the bit rate is measured is given by this formula:

$$T_c = \text{burst size} / \text{bit rate}$$

From this formula, you can deduce that the smaller the burst size, the shorter the measurement time period, and consequently the smoother, or less bursty, the traffic flow. A small T_c also ensures more consistent latency, which is important for voice. For voice applications, T_c should be as small as possible—about 10 ms. This implies that the burst size should be no more than one one-hundredth of the average bit rate.

The *excess-burst-size* allows more traffic to be sent in a given time interval than the *burst-size* would allow if in a previous time period the maximum amount was not sent. Whenever less than the *burst-size* is sent during an interval, the remaining number of bits, up to the *excess-burst-size,* can be used to send more than the burst size in a later interval. Configuring the *excess-burst-size* to be the same as the *burst-size* effectively disables any excess burst capability. Example 8-28 demonstrates traffic shaping configuration on an interface.

Example 8-28 *Interface Ethernet 0 Is Configured to Limit UDP Traffic to 1 Mbps, and Interface Ethernet 1 Is Configured to Limit All Output to 5 Mbps*

```
access-list 101 permit udp any any
interface Ethernet0
traffic-shape group 101 1000000 125000 125000
!
interface Ethernet1
traffic-shape rate 5000000 625000 625000
```

GTS for Frame Relay Networks

User-specified traffic shaping can be performed on a Frame Relay interface or subinterface with the **traffic-shape rate** command. The **traffic-shape adaptive** command can be specified to allow the shape of the traffic to dynamically adjust to congestion experienced by the Frame Relay provider. This is achieved through the receipt of BECNs from the Frame Relay switch. When a Frame Relay switch becomes congested, it sends BECNs in the direction the traffic is coming from, and it generates FECNs in the direction the traffic is flowing to.

If the **traffic-shape fecn-adapt** command is configured at both ends of the link, as shown in Example 8-29, the far end reflects FECNs as BECNs. BECNs tell the sender to decrease the transmission rate. If the traffic is one-way only, such as multicast traffic, there is no reverse traffic with BECNs to notify the sender to slow down. Therefore, when a data terminal equipment (DTE) device receives a FECN, it first determines if it is sending any data in return. If it is sending return data, this data gets marked with a BECN on its way to the other DTE device. However, if the DTE device is not sending any data, it can send a Q.922 TEST RESPONSE message with the BECN bit set.

Example 8-29 *In the Presence of BECN Bits from the Network, the Flow Is Throttled Back to the Committed Information Rate of 64 kbps*

```
interface serial 2
  traffic-shape rate 1544000
  traffic-shape adaptive 64000
  traffic-shape fecn-adapt
```

Configuring GTS for Frame Relay Networks

The following interface commands are used to configure GTS in a Frame Relay environment (as shown in Example 8-29):

- **traffic-shape rate** *bit-rate* [*burst-size* [*excess-burst-size*]]—The standard GTS configuration command that can be applied to any interface to enable outbound traffic shaping.
- **traffic-shape adaptive** [*bit-rate*]—Configures the minimum bit rate that traffic is shaped to when BECNs are received on an interface. It is common to set this to the committed information rate (CIR) of the Frame Relay link.
- **traffic-shape fecn-adapt**—Configures the reflection of BECN signals as FECNs are received.

With adaptive GTS, the router uses BECNs to estimate the available bandwidth and adjust the transmission rate accordingly. The actual maximum transmission rate is between the rate specified in the **traffic-shape adaptive** command and the rate specified in the **traffic-shape rate** command.

Verifying GTS Configuration

The following commands can be used to verify the configuration and operation of GTS:

- **show traffic-shape**
- **show traffic-shape statistics**

Examples 8-30 and 8-31 demonstrate sample output from each of these commands.

Example 8-30 *Verifying GTS Configuration with the* **show traffic-shape** *Command*

```
Router#show traffic-shape
           Access Target   Byte    Sustain   Excess     Interval  Increment Adapt
I/F        List   Rate     Limit   bits/int  bits/int   (ms)      (bytes)   Active
Fa0/0      101    1000000  31250   125000    125000     125       15625     -
Fa0/1             5000000  156250  625000    625000     125       78125     -
```

Example 8-31 *Displaying GTS Statistics with the* **show traffic-shape statistics** *Command*

```
Router#show traffic-shape statistics
           Access Queue   Packets  Bytes   Packets   Bytes     Shaping
I/F        List   Depth                    Delayed   Delayed   Active
Fa0/0      101    0        0        0       0         0         no
Fa0/1             0        0        0       0         0         no
```

Lab 8.9.8   Configuring Generic Traffic Shaping (GTS)

In this lab, you configure GTS on an interface.

 Lab 8.9.9   QoS Manually Configured Frame Relay Traffic Shaping

In this lab, you use FRTS to shape traffic exiting a Frame Relay interface so that it matches the CIR, Bc, and Be provided by the ISP.

 Lab 8.9.10   QoS Dynamically Configured Frame Relay Traffic Shaping

In this lab, you use Dynamic FRTS to shape traffic exiting a Frame Relay interface such that the traffic flow responds to BECNs received from the Frame Relay switch.

QoS Using Low-Speed Links

Up to this point, QoS issues within a switched LAN environment have been considered. Some traffic needs to find its way across lower-speed WAN links. Although many of the QoS features explored in the LAN environment can be applied in the WAN, low-bandwidth WAN links are significant contributors to latency and require special attention. Figure 8-25 illustrates several low-speed WAN links. Figure 8-26 illustrates dial-up connections.

Figure 8-25   QoS Is Just as Important on Low-Speed WAN Links As Anywhere Else in a Network

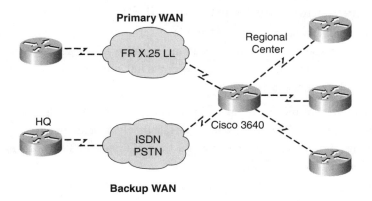

Figure 8-26 *Terminal Server and Remote-Access Applications Enjoy the Benefits of QoS*

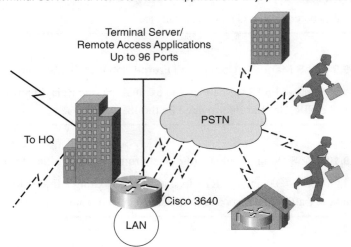

Link Efficiency Mechanisms

A significant problem associated with low-speed WAN links is the possibility of vital traffic becoming trapped behind streams of less-important traffic. Link efficiency mechanisms can be used to give priority to one class of traffic over another. WFQ is one such mechanism that can be used to reduce the latency for low-volume traffic streams. However, if the WAN bandwidth is very low, even being trapped behind a single large packet might introduce too much latency for delay-sensitive voice traffic.

Link Fragmentation and Interleaving (LFI)

In addition to network congestion, one of the primary contributors to both delay and jitter is serialization delay, which is often caused by a time-sensitive packet getting "stuck in traffic" behind a large data packet, such as FTP. The lower the link's speed, the more significant the serialization delay, as shown in Table 8-5.

Link fragmentation is the process of breaking up large packets to allow smaller, more time-sensitive packets to proceed through the network in a timely manner. Interleaving is the process of "weaving" time-sensitive packets into the train of fragmented data packets, as shown in Figure 8-27—thus, the term *Link Fragmentation and Interleaving (LFI)*.

Table 8-5 Serialization Delay Is the Frame Size in Bits Divided by the Link Bandwidth in Bits Per Second

	1 Byte	64 Bytes	128 Bytes	256 Bytes	512 Bytes	1024 Bytes	1500 Bytes
56 kbps	$143\,\mu s$	9 ms	18 ms	36 ms	72 ms	144 ms	214 ms
64 kbps	$125\,\mu s$	8 ms	16 ms	32 ms	64 ms	126 ms	187 ms
128 kbps	$62.5\,\mu s$	4 ms	8 ms	16 ms	32 ms	64 ms	93 ms
256 kbps	$31\,\mu s$	2 ms	4 ms	8 ms	16 ms	32 ms	46 ms
512 kbps	$15.5\,\mu s$	1 ms	2 ms	4 ms	8 ms	16 ms	32 ms
768 kbps	$10\,\mu s$	$640\,\mu s$	1.28 ms	2.56 ms	5.12 ms	10.24 ms	15 ms
1536 kbps	$5\,\mu s$	$320\,\mu s$	$640\,\mu s$	1.28 ms	2.56 ms	5.12 ms	7.5 ms

Figure 8-27 LFI Breaks Up Large Packets and Weaves Them into the Train of Fragmented Data

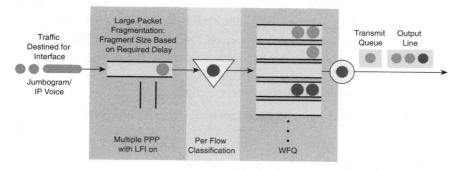

Link Fragmentation and Interleaving (LFI): Multilink PPP

Although 1500 bytes is a common size for data packets, a typical VoIP packet carrying G.729 voice frames can be about 66 bytes—20 bytes voice payload, 6 bytes Layer 2 header, 20 bytes RTP and UDP header, and 20 bytes IP header.

Now imagine a 56-kbps leased line link where voice and data traffic coexist. If a voice packet is ready to be serialized just when a data packet starts being transmitted over the link, a problem occurs. The delay-sensitive voice packet has to wait 214 ms before being transmitted.

Large data packets can delay the delivery of small voice packets, reducing speech quality. Fragmenting these large data packets into smaller ones and interleaving voice packets among the fragments reduces jitter and delay. The Cisco IOS LFI feature helps satisfy the real-time delivery requirements of VoIP on a multilink PPP link, as shown in Figure 8-28.

NOTE

In cases with a WAN link of more than 768 kbps, the fragmentation feature is unneeded. However, there is still a need for some type of QoS mechanism, such as LLQ or IP RTP Priority. Seven hundred sixty-eight kbps offers enough bandwidth to allow voice packets to enter and leave the queue without delay issues.

Figure 8-28 LFI Can Work in Conjunction with Multilink PPP

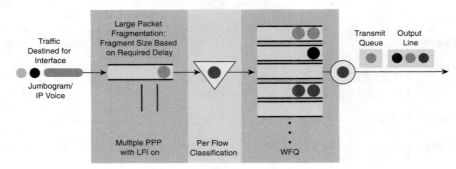

The amount of serialization delay (the time it takes to place the bits on an interface) introduced on low-speed WAN links can be significant, particularly when you consider that the target end-to-end one-way delay should not exceed 150 ms. For voice applications, the recommended serialization delay, on a per-hop basis, is 10 ms and should not exceed 20 ms.

Lab 8.9.11 Link Fragmentation and Interleaving

In this lab, you configure LFI to control latency over a low-speed WAN link.

Compressed Real-Time Protocol (CRTP)

RTP is the Internet-standard protocol for the transport of real-time data, including audio and video. It can be used for media on demand as well as interactive services, such as Internet telephony. RTP consists of a data part and a control part, called Real-Time Control Protocol (RTCP). The data part of RTP is a thin protocol that provides support for applications with real-time properties such as continuous media, audio and video, timing reconstruction, loss detection, and content identification.

Compressed Real-Time Transport Protocol (CRTP) is used on a link-by-link basis to compress the IP/UDP/RTP header. In a packet voice environment when framing speech samples every 20 ms, this scenario generates a payload of 20 bytes. The total packet size is made up of the following:

- An IP header of 20 bytes
- A UDP header of 8 bytes

- An RTP header of 12 bytes
- A payload of 20 bytes

It is evident that the header size is twice the size of the payload. When generating packets every 20 ms on a slow link, the header consumes a large portion of the bandwidth. To avoid the unnecessary consumption of available bandwidth, CRTP is used on a link-by-link basis.

This compression scheme, illustrated in Figure 8-29, reduces the IP/UDP/RTP header to 2 bytes most of the time when no UDP checksums are being sent or to 4 bytes when UDP checksums are used.

NOTE

Cisco recommends using CRTP only with links lower than 768 kbps, unless the router is running at a low CPU utilization rate. Monitor the router CPU utilization and disable CRTP if it is above 75%. If CRTP needs to be disabled, it is likely that a higher-performance router or additional capacity is required.

Figure 8-29 CRTP Efficiently Compresses IP/UDP/RTP Header Combinations

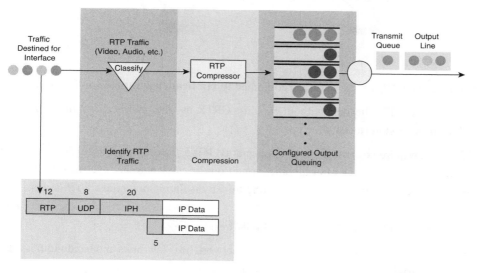

Efficiencies	Payload	Packet Size Reduction*
VoIP	20 Bytes	~240%
SQL Queuing	256 Bytes	~13%
FTP	1500 Bytes	~2.3%

*Also -5 ms Reduction in Serialization Delay at 64 kbps

Configuring CRTP

CRTP is a hop-by-hop compression scheme. It must be configured on both ends of the link, unless the passive option is configured. A typical implementation involves a Frame Relay permanent virtual circuit (PVC), as shown in Figure 8-30.

Figure 8-30 CRTP Is a Hop-by-Hop Compression Scheme

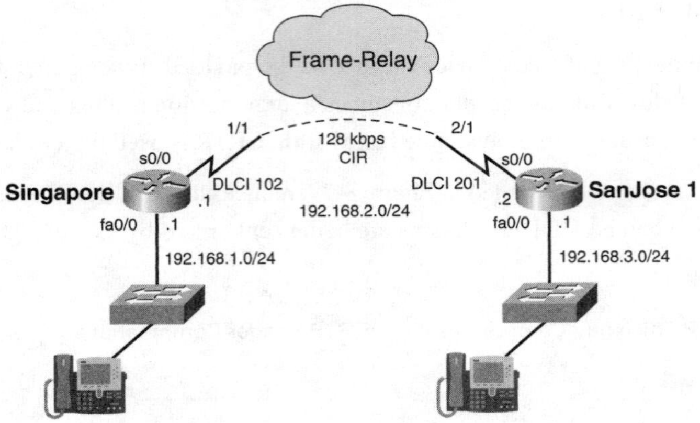

NOTE

When the command **ip rtp header-compression** is used, the router adds the command **ip tcp header-compression** to the configuration by default. This is used to compress the headers of TCP/IP packets. Header compression is particularly useful on networks with a large percentage of small packets, such as those supporting many Telnet connections. The TCP header compression technique is supported on serial lines using HDLC or PPP encapsulation.

To configure CRTP, use the interface command **ip rtp header-compression** [**passive**].

To compress the TCP headers without enabling CRTP, use the interface command **ip tcp header-compression** [**passive**].

CRTP is not required to ensure good voice quality. It is a feature that reduces bandwidth consumption. Configure CRTP after all other conditions are met, and the voice quality is good. This procedure can save you troubleshooting time by isolating potential CRTP issues.

Lab 8.9.12 QoS Compressed Real-Time Protocol

In this lab, you configure CRTP if the network has slow links and bandwidth needs to be saved.

Summary

This chapter outlined the components of QoS and the IOS mechanisms for delivering end-to-end QoS through classification, marking, policing, traffic shaping, and link efficiency mechanisms. Although the general principles for implementing QoS are quite straightforward, there are many types of QoS, and sometimes several can be used in combination. In many cases, QoS features are specific to the Cisco hardware platform.

Key Terms

class of service (CoS)   802.1Q frame headers have a 2-byte Tag Control Information field that carries the CoS value in the 3 most-significant bits. Layer 2 CoS values range from 0 for low priority to 7 for high priority. CoS is used with QoS, especially at the network's access layer.

class-based traffic shaping   Allows you to control the traffic going out an interface to match its transmission to the speed of the remote, target interface and to ensure that the traffic conforms to policies contracted for it. Traffic adhering to a particular profile can be shaped to meet downstream requirements, thereby eliminating bottlenecks in topologies with data-rate mismatches. Can be enabled on any interface that supports GTS.

Class-Based Weighted Fair Queuing (CBWFQ)   Extends the standard WFQ functionality to provide support for user-defined traffic classes. For CBWFQ, you define traffic classes based on match criteria including protocols, access control lists (ACLs), and input interfaces. Packets satisfying the match criteria for a class constitute the traffic for that class. A FIFO queue is reserved for each class, and traffic belonging to a class is directed to the queue for that class.

Committed Access Rate (CAR)   A rate-limiting feature for policing traffic. It manages a network's access bandwidth policy by ensuring that traffic falling within specified rate parameters is sent, while dropping packets that exceed the acceptable amount of traffic or sending them with a different priority. The exceed action for CAR is to drop or mark down packets.

Compressed Real-Time Transport Protocol (CRTP)   An RTP header compression feature used on a link-by-link basis.

delay   Also known as latency. Refers to the time it takes a packet to travel from the source to the destination.

delay variation   See *jitter*.

Differentiated Services Code Point (DSCP)   The first 6 bits of the ToS field. Used to classify IP traffic.

Frame Relay Traffic Shaping (FRTS)   Eliminates bottlenecks in Frame Relay networks that have high-speed connections at the central site and low-speed connections at branch sites. You configure rate enforcement, a peak rate configured to limit outbound traffic, to limit the rate at which data is sent on the VC at the central site. Using FRTS, you can configure rate enforcement to either the CIR or some other defined value, such as the excess information rate, on a per-VC basis. The ability to allow the transmission speed used by the router to be controlled by criteria other than line speed (that is, by the CIR or the excess information rate) provides a mechanism for multiple VCs to share media. You can allocate bandwidth to each VC, creating a virtual time-division multiplexing (TDM) network.

Generic Traffic Shaping (GTS)   Shapes traffic by reducing outbound traffic flow to avoid congestion by constraining traffic to a particular bit rate using the token bucket mechanism. GTS applies on a per-interface basis and can use access lists to select the traffic to shape. It works with a variety of Layer 2 technologies, including Frame Relay.

IP Precedence   3 bits in the ToS field of the IP header used to specify a packet's class of service.

jitter   Also known as delay variation. The difference in the delay times of consecutive packets.

latency   See *delay*.

Link Fragmentation and Interleaving (LFI)   A feature that reduces delay on slower-speed links by breaking up large datagrams and interleaving low-delay traffic packets with the smaller packets resulting from the fragmented datagram.

loss   The percentage of packets that fail to reach their destination.

Low Latency Queuing (LLQ)   Brings strict priority queuing to CBWFQ. Strict priority queuing allows delay-sensitive data, such as voice, to be dequeued and sent first (before packets in other queues are dequeued), giving delay-sensitive data preferential treatment over other traffic.

scheduling   The process of assigning packets to one of multiple queues, based on classification, for priority treatment through the network.

type of service (ToS)   A 1-byte field in the IP header used for traffic classification. Specifies the parameters for the type of service requested. Networks can use the parameters to define the handling of the datagram during transport.

Weighted Fair Queuing (WFQ)   A dynamic scheduling method that provides fair bandwidth allocation to all network traffic. WFQ applies priority, or weights, to identified traffic to classify traffic into conversations and to determine how much bandwidth each conversation is allowed relative to other conversations. WFQ is a flow-based algorithm that simultaneously schedules interactive traffic to the front of a queue to reduce response time. It fairly shares the remaining bandwidth among high-bandwidth flows.

Weighted Random Early Detection (WRED)   A mechanism designed to avoid the global synchronization problems that occur when tail-drop is used as the congestion avoidance mechanism on the router. WRED is a queuing technique for congestion avoidance. WRED manages how packets are handled when an interface starts becoming congested. When traffic begins to exceed the interface traffic thresholds before any congestion, the interface starts dropping packets from selected flows. If the dropped packets are TCP, the TCP source recognizes that packets are getting dropped and lowers its transmission rate. The lowered transmission rate then reduces the traffic to the interface, avoiding congestion. Because TCP retransmits dropped packets, no actual data loss occurs.

Check Your Understanding

Use the following review questions to test your understanding of the concepts covered in this chapter. Answers are listed in Appendix A, "Check Your Understanding Answer Key."

1. What QoS characteristics define the quality of the movement of traffic from one point to another?

   A. Bandwidth

   B. Jitter

   C. Loss

   D. Delay

2. Loss for voice traffic should not exceed what percentage?

   A. .5 percent

   B. 1 percent

   C. 2 percent

   D. 4 percent

3. Latency for video traffic should be no more than how many seconds?

   A. 2 to 3 seconds

   B. 3 to 4 seconds

   C. 4 to 5 seconds

   D. 5 to 6 seconds

4. Which of the following are the three QoS service models?

   A. Deterministic

   B. Best-effort

   C. DiffServ

   D. IntServ

5. How many bits are used to indicate IP Precedence?

    A. 2

    B. 3

    C. 6

    D. 8

6. How many bits are used to indicate IP DSCP?

    A. 2

    B. 3

    C. 6

    D. 8

7. The CoS is set to which of the following values on traffic sourced by a Cisco IP Phone?

    A. 0

    B. 1

    C. 5

    D. 7

8. What type of QoS is used to prevent tail drop from causing traffic irregularities?

    A. RSVP

    B. GTS

    C. WRED

    D. CAR

9. Where in a network should traffic be marked? (Select all that apply.)

    A. Edge router

    B. Core router

    C. Access router

    D. Distribution router

10. What type of queuing is designed specifically for voice traffic?

    A. CBWFQ

    B. FIFO

    C. WFQ

    D. LLQ

Objectives

After completing this chapter, you will be able to perform tasks related to the following:

- Understand and configure Switched Port Analyzer (SPAN), VLAN-based Switched Port Analyzer (VSPAN), and Remote Switched Port Analyzer (RSPAN).
- Understand the role and implementation of the Network Analysis Module (NAM).
- Understand the role and implementation of the Switch Fabric Module (SFM).
- Explain access control policy.
- Configure password protection, privilege levels, and remote-access restrictions.
- Configure Secure Shell (SSH).
- Configure virtual LAN (VLAN) maps.
- Configure router access control lists (ACLs) and port ACLs.
- Configure port security and protected ports.
- Configure authentication, authorization, and accounting (AAA) with Terminal Access Controller Access Control System Plus (TACACS+) and Remote Authentication Dial-In User Service (RADIUS).
- Understand 802.1x port-based authentication.

Chapter 9

Monitoring and Security

This chapter covers two main areas:

- The first part discusses mechanisms for monitoring traffic in a multilayer switched network using the Cisco Switched Port Analyzer (SPAN) feature set. This discussion includes the following topics:
  - How to use VLAN-based Switched Port Analyzer (VSPAN) to monitor traffic in a VLAN
  - How to use Remote Switched Port Analyzer (RSPAN) to monitor traffic across multiple switches
  - How to use the Network Analysis Module (NAM) and Switch Fabric Module (SFM) to improve switch monitoring and performance
- The second part discusses securing devices in a multilayer switched network. Topics discussed in this part include the following:
  - Security concepts
  - Security and remote device management
  - Technologies available for controlling user traffic

Monitoring Switched Network Performance with SPAN and VSPAN

SPAN is a method of monitoring network traffic by copying source port or VLAN-specific traffic to a destination port for analysis. Figure 9-1 illustrates a SPAN in which all traffic on port 5, the source port, is mirrored to port 10, the destination port. A network analyzer on port 10 receives all network traffic from port 5 without being physically attached to port 5.

Figure 9-1 SPAN in Action

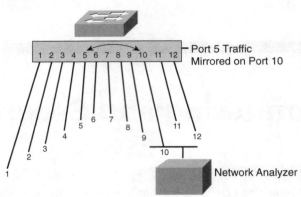

VLAN-based SPAN (VSPAN) is the analysis of the network traffic in one or more VLANs. You can configure VSPAN to monitor only received traffic, which applies to all the ports for that VLAN.

SPAN can be used to monitor all network traffic, including

- Multicast and Bridge Protocol Data Unit (BPDU) frames
- Cisco Discovery Protocol (CDP) frames
- VLAN Trunking Protocol (VTP) frames
- Dynamic Trunking Protocol (DTP) frames
- Spanning Tree Protocol (STP) frames
- Port Aggregation Protocol (PAgP) frames

In some SPAN configurations, multiple copies of the same source packet are sent to the SPAN destination port. For example, suppose a bidirectional SPAN session is configured for sources a1 and a2 to destination port d1, as shown in Figure 9-2. A bidirectional SPAN session monitors both incoming and outgoing traffic for a port. If a packet enters the switch through a1 and gets switched to a2, both incoming and outgoing packets are sent to destination port d1. In this case, both packets are the same. However, if the data is re-encapsulated at Layer 3, the frames are different.

Monitoring with SPAN on a Port Basis

SPAN can be used to analyze network traffic passing through ports. This occurs by sending a copy of the traffic to a destination port on the switch that has been connected to a network analyzer or protocol analyzer. SPAN can be used to mirror traffic for later analysis. Mirrored traffic is all traffic sent to and/or received from one or more SPAN source ports defined in the SPAN configuration.

Figure 9-2 The Destination Port Sees Multiple Copies of Frames When Unicast Traffic Passes Between Two SPAN Source Ports

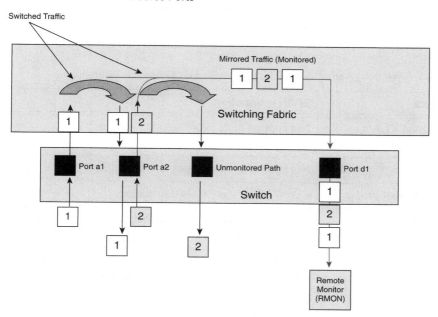

SPAN does not affect the switching of network traffic on source ports, although it might affect the behavior of some features on source and destination ports. A copy of the packets received or sent by the source interfaces is sent to the destination interface. The only traffic sent or received by SPAN destination ports is related to the SPAN process.

A source port is a Layer 2 or Layer 3 port from which the SPAN process copies traffic. Data forwarded from a SPAN source port to a SPAN destination port can include all frames transmitted by the port and/or all frames received by the port.

A SPAN destination port is a Layer 2 or Layer 3 port to which the SPAN process copies traffic. When a port is configured as a SPAN destination port, it can no longer forward any traffic other than SPAN traffic, and it becomes dedicated for use by the SPAN process. A SPAN destination port does not forward any traffic except that required for the SPAN session.

Beginning with switch Cisco IOS Release 12.1(13)E, trunk ports can be configured as SPAN destination ports. This allows SPAN destination ports to transmit traffic encapsulated for multiple VLANs. With earlier switch IOS releases, a trunk port automatically reverted to access mode when configured as a SPAN destination port.

SPAN Interaction with Other Features

SPAN might affect the behavior of features configured on source and destination ports. SPAN disables some destination port features, which are restored when the SPAN session is removed from the switch. Table 9-1 summarizes the features and interactions.

Table 9-1 SPAN Does Not Work Seamlessly with Some LAN Switch Technologies

Feature	SPAN Interaction
Change in VLAN membership	Not applied until the session is disabled.
Trunk settings	Not applied until the session is disabled.
EtherChannel groups	Cannot become a SPAN destination.
EtherChannel port members	Removed from the EtherChannel group for the duration of the SPAN session.
QoS-classified traffic	Packets could differ from source port ingress traffic. The destination port receives packets after classification and policing.
Multicast traffic	Only a single, unedited packet is sent to the destination port, not one for each multicast session member.

SPAN Interaction with VLANs and CDP

Changes in VLAN membership can be made, but they are not applied to SPAN destination ports. For source ports, VLAN or trunk settings take effect immediately, and the SPAN session automatically adjusts accordingly.

A SPAN destination port does not participate in CDP.

SPAN Interaction with an EtherChannel Member or Trunked Port

If a port is added to a monitored EtherChannel group, it is added to the SPAN source port list. If a port is removed from a monitored EtherChannel group, it is automatically removed from the source port list.

An EtherChannel group can be configured as a source port, but not as a SPAN destination port. When a group is configured as a SPAN source, the entire group is monitored.

VLAN membership or trunk settings can be modified for source or destination ports at any time. However, changes in VLAN membership or trunk settings for a destination port do not take effect until the SPAN session is disabled.

If a physical port that belongs to an EtherChannel group is configured as a SPAN source or destination port, that port is removed from the group. After the port is removed from the SPAN session, it rejoins the EtherChannel group. Ports removed from an EtherChannel group remain members of the group, but they are in the down or standalone state.

If a physical port that belongs to an EtherChannel group is a destination port and the EtherChannel group is a source, the port is removed from the EtherChannel group and from the list of monitored ports.

SPAN Interaction with QoS Classified and Multicast Traffic

For ingress, or incoming, traffic monitoring, the packets sent to the SPAN destination port might be different from the packets actually received at the SPAN source port. The packets are forwarded after ingress QoS classification and policing. The Differentiated Services Code Point (DSCP) value of the sent packet might not be the same as that for the received packet.

Multicast traffic can be monitored. For egress (or outgoing) traffic and ingress port monitoring, only a single unedited packet is sent to the SPAN destination port.

A port with port security configured on it cannot be a SPAN destination port. Port security is discussed in the section "Using Port Security, Protected Ports, and Private VLANs."

SPAN Configuration Limitations

Only one local SPAN session can be configured and stored in nonvolatile random-access memory (NVRAM) on a Catalyst 2950 switch.

Consider the following issues when configuring SPAN or VSPAN:

- A port cannot double as a destination port and a source port. It must be one or the other.
- An EtherChannel port can be only a SPAN source port.
- For SPAN source ports, sent and received traffic can be monitored for a single port or for a range of ports.
- A switch port configured as a SPAN destination port is no longer a normal switch port. Only monitored traffic passes through the SPAN destination port.
- A SPAN destination port does not participate in any VLAN spanning tree, although spanning-tree BPDUs on source ports or VLAN traffic are copied to SPAN destination ports.

A Catalyst 3550 or Catalyst 6500 can have two local SPAN sessions with two different destination ports. Also, with these switches, a source port can be included in two different sessions and monitored by two different destination ports.

Configuring SPAN Sessions

The procedure to create a SPAN session and specify the source (or monitored) port and the destination (or monitoring) port is relatively simple, as shown in Table 9-2.

Table 9-2 Configuring SPAN Involves Specifying the Source and Destination Ports

Step	Command	Description
1	**configure terminal**	Enters global configuration mode.
2	**no monitor session** {*session-number* | **all** | **local** | **remote**}	Clears any existing SPAN configuration for the session. Specify **all** to remove all SPAN sessions, **local** to remove all local sessions, or **remote** to remove all remote SPAN sessions.
3	**monitor session** *session-number* **source interface** *interface-id* [**,** | **-**] [**both** | **rx** | **tx**]	Specifies the SPAN session and source port (monitored port). For *interface-id,* specify the source port, interface, or logical interface (**port-channel** *port-channel-number*). The optional keywords [**,** | **-**] specify a series or range of interfaces. The optional keywords [**both** | **rx** | **tx**] specify the direction of traffic to monitor (**rx** = received; **tx** = sent). The default is bidirectional (**both**).
4	**monitor session** *session-number* **destination interface** *interface-id*	Specifies the SPAN session and destination port (monitoring port). For *interface-id,* specify the destination port. Physical interfaces are valid. (Optional) Specify the encapsulation header for outgoing packets.
5	**end**	Returns to privileged EXEC mode.
6	**show monitor** [**session** *session-number*]	Verifies entries.
7	**copy running-config startup-config**	(Optional) Saves entries in the configuration file.

Initially, clear any previous SPAN session from the active configuration:

```
no monitor session session_number
```

Next, define the source port being monitored:

```
monitor session session-number source interface interface-id module/interface
```

Finally, specify the destination port for the mirrored traffic:

```
monitor session session-number destination interface interface-id
   module/interface [encapsulation {dot1q | isl}]
```

Example 9-1 shows how to set up a SPAN session, session 1, to monitor source port traffic to a destination port. First, any existing SPAN configuration for session 1 is cleared, and then bidirectional traffic is mirrored from source port 1 to destination port 10.

Example 9-1 *A Basic SPAN Session Is Simple to Set Up*

```
Switch(config)#no monitor session 1
Switch(config)#monitor session 1 source interface fastethernet 0/1
Switch(config)#monitor session 1 destination interface fastethernet 0/10
  encapsulation dot1q
Switch(config)#end
```

Table 9-3 documents how to remove a source port from a SPAN session.

Table 9-3 Removing a SPAN Session Is Straightforward

Step	Command	Description
1	**configure terminal**	Enters global configuration mode.
2	**no monitor session** *session-number* **source interface** *interface-id* [**,**	**-**] [**both**	**rx**	**tx**]	Specifies the characteristics of the source port (monitored port) and SPAN session to remove. For *interface-id,* specify the source port to no longer monitor. This operation is valid only when monitoring received traffic. The optional keywords [**both**	**rx**	**tx**] specify the direction of traffic to no longer monitor. The default is to disable both **rx** and **tx**.
3	**end**	Returns to privileged EXEC mode.
4	**show monitor** [**session** *session-number*]	Verifies entries.
5	**copy running-config startup-config**	(Optional) Saves entries in the configuration file.

Example 9-2 shows how to remove source port FastEthernet0/1 from SPAN session 1.

Example 9-2 *Removing a Source Port from a SPAN Session*

```
Switch(config)#no monitor session 1 source interface fastethernet 0/1
Switch(config)#end
```

To remove a destination port from a SPAN session, use the following global configuration command:

no monitor session *session-number* **destination interface** *interface-id*

Example 9-3 shows how to remove destination port FastEthernet 0/10 from SPAN session 1.

Example 9-3 *Removing a Destination Port from a SPAN Session*

```
Switch(config)#no monitor session 1 destination interface fastethernet 0/10
Switch(config)#end
```

Lab 9.9.1 Creating a Switched Port Analyzer (SPAN) Session

In this lab exercise, you create a SPAN session to remotely monitor network traffic.

VSPAN—SPAN Using VLANs as Monitored Source

SPAN can also be applied on a VLAN basis. A source VLAN is a VLAN monitored for network traffic analysis. VSPAN uses one or more VLANs as the SPAN source. All the ports in the source VLAN(s) become source ports. For VSPAN, only incoming traffic can be monitored (rx traffic). VSPAN cannot be implemented on 2950 switches.

VLAN monitoring is similar to port monitoring, as shown in Table 9-4.

Table 9-4 SPAN Can Be Used to Monitor All Traffic from One or More VLANs

Step	Command	Description
1	**configure terminal**	Enters global configuration mode.
2	**no monitor session** {*session-number* | **all** | **local** | **remote**}	Clears any existing SPAN configuration for the session. Specify **all** to remove all SPAN sessions, **local** to remove all local sessions, or **remote** to remove all remote SPAN sessions.

Table 9-4 SPAN Can Be Used to Monitor All Traffic from One or More VLANs

Step	Command	Description
3	**monitor session** *session-number* **source vlan** *vlan-id* [**,** I **-**] **rx**	Specifies the SPAN session and the source VLANs (monitored VLANs). You can monitor only received (rx) traffic on VLANs. (Optional) Use a comma (**,**) to specify a series of VLANs, or use a hyphen (**-**) to specify a range of VLANs. Enter a space before and after the comma or hyphen.
4	**monitor session** *session-number* **destination interface** *interface-id*	Specifies the SPAN session and the destination port (monitoring port). For *interface-id,* specify the destination port. Physical interfaces are valid.
5	**end**	Returns to privileged EXEC mode.
6	**show monitor** [**session** *session-number*]	Verifies entries.
7	**copy running-config startup-config**	(Optional) Saves entries in the configuration file.

First, you clear any previous SPAN session from the active configuration using the **no monitor session** *session_number* command.

This is followed by defining the VLANs being monitored using the **monitor session** *session_number* **source vlan** *vlan-id* [**,** I **-**] **rx** command. Note that other directions are unavailable for use when setting a VLAN as the SPAN source.

Finally, you specify a destination port for the mirrored traffic using the command **monitor session** *session_number* **destination interface** *interface-id module/interface* [**encapsulation** {*dot1q* I *isl*}]. Note that ISL cannot be specified on 2950 switches.

Example 9-4 shows how to clear any existing configuration on SPAN session 2, configure SPAN session 2 to monitor received traffic on all ports belonging to VLANs 1 to 3, and send it to destination port 7. The configuration is then modified to also monitor received traffic on all ports belonging to VLAN 10.

Example 9-4 *Specifying SPAN Source Traffic by VLAN*

```
Switch(config)#no monitor session 2
Switch(config)#monitor session 2 source vlan 1 - 3 rx
Switch(config)#monitor session 2 destination interface gigabitethernet 0/7
Switch(config)#monitor session 2 source vlan 10 rx
Switch(config)#end
Switch#show monitor session 2
```

To remove one or more source VLANs or destination ports from the SPAN session, use the following global configuration command:

no monitor session *session_number* **source vlan** *vlan-id*

To remove the destination interface, use the following global configuration command:

no monitor session *session_number* **destination interface** *interface-id*

To display the status of the current SPAN configuration, use the **show monitor** privileged EXEC command, as shown in Example 9-5.

Example 9-5 *Verifying the SPAN Configuration*

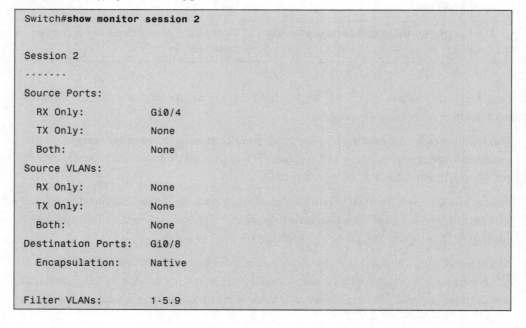

```
Switch#show monitor session 2


Session 2
-------
Source Ports:
  RX Only:           Gi0/4
  TX Only:           None
  Both:              None
Source VLANs:
  RX Only:           None
  TX Only:           None
  Both:              None
Destination Ports:   Gi0/8
  Encapsulation:     Native

Filter VLANs:        1-5.9
```

 Lab 9.9.2 Creating a VSPAN Session

In this lab exercise, you create a VSPAN session to remotely monitor network traffic.

RSPAN

RSPAN is an implementation of SPAN designed to support source ports, source VLANs, and destination ports across different switches. RSPAN allows remote monitoring of multiple switches across a network, as shown in Figure 9-3. An RSPAN requirement is that participating switches must have the enhanced software image (EI) installed. A significant difference in RSPAN from SPAN and VSPAN is that RSPAN cannot be used to monitor Layer 2 protocols including BPDUs.

Figure 9-3 RSPAN Enables the Monitoring of Traffic from Remote Switches

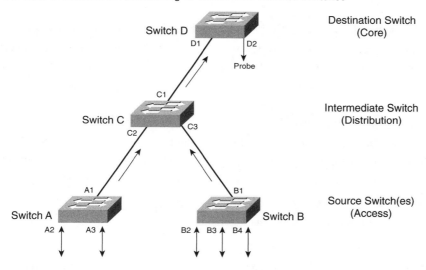

The first step in creating an RSPAN session is to create an RSPAN VLAN dedicated to that particular session in all participating switches.

RSPAN uses reflector ports to be able to reproduce traffic from source ports residing on remote switches to the destination port on the local switch. Except for traffic that is required for the RSPAN session, RSPAN reflector ports work just like RSPAN destination ports. Reflector ports forward only packets received from or sent by source ports. They do not receive or forward any other network traffic, as shown in Figure 9-4.

RSPAN source ports can be trunks carrying the RSPAN VLAN. Local SPAN and RSPAN do not monitor the RSPAN traffic in the RSPAN VLAN seen on a source trunk.

RSPAN traffic from source ports or source VLANs is switched to the RSPAN VLAN and is then forwarded to destination ports that are also in the RSPAN VLAN. The source, port or VLAN, in an RSPAN session can be different on different source switches. However, if Internet routers, such as the Cisco 7600 series routers, are used as sources for an RSPAN session, they must have the same VLANs as RSPAN sources.

Figure 9-4 Reflector Ports Are Dedicated to Forwarding SPAN Traffic

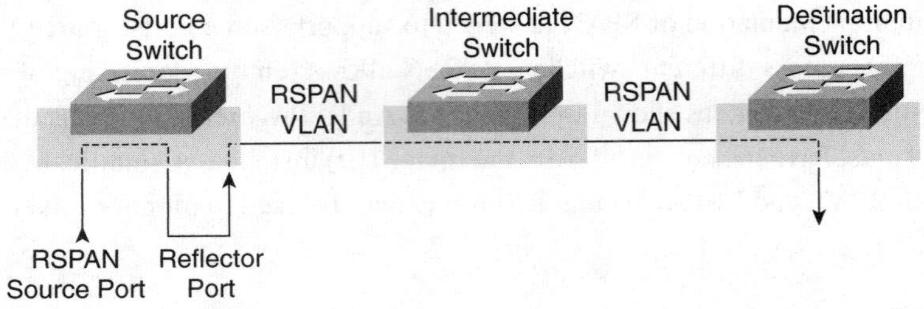

Like SPAN, RSPAN does not affect the switching of network traffic on source ports. Copies of the packets received or sent by the source interfaces are sent to the destination interface. Except for traffic that is required for the RSPAN session, reflector ports and destination ports do not receive or forward traffic.

RSPAN Reflector Ports

Reflector ports are used as a mechanism to copy monitored packets onto an RSPAN VLAN. The reflector port forwards only the traffic from the RSPAN source session with which it is affiliated. Any device connected to a port set as a reflector port loses connectivity until the RSPAN source session is disabled.

The reflector port has the following characteristics:

- It is a port set to loopback.
- It cannot be an EtherChannel group, it does not trunk, and it cannot do protocol filtering.
- It can be a physical port that is assigned to an EtherChannel group, even if the Ether-Channel group is specified as a SPAN source. The port is removed from the group while it is configured as a reflector port.
- A port used as a reflector port cannot be a SPAN source or destination port, nor can a port be a reflector port for more than one session at a time.
- It is invisible to all VLANs.
- The native VLAN for looped-back traffic on a reflector port is the RSPAN VLAN.
- The reflector port loops back untagged traffic to the switch. The traffic is then placed on the RSPAN VLAN and flooded to any trunk ports that carry the RSPAN VLAN.
- STP is automatically disabled on a reflector port.
- If the reflector port's bandwidth is insufficient to handle the traffic from the corresponding source ports, the excess packets are dropped. A 10/100 port reflects at 100 Mbps. A Gigabit port reflects at 1 Gbps.

The global configuration command necessary to assign an existing port as a reflector port is as follows:

```
monitor session session-number destination remote vlan vlan-id reflector-port
  interface
```

- *session-number* is the RSPAN monitoring session.
- *vlan-id* identifies the unique RSPAN VLAN.
- *interface* specifies the interface that will flood the RSPAN traffic to the RSPAN VLAN.

RSPAN Interaction with Other Features

In addition to SPAN interaction characteristics, RSPAN interacts in the following way with other switch features:

- **Spanning Tree Protocol (STP)**—A reflector port does not participate in STP while its RSPAN session is active. STP can be active on trunk ports carrying an RSPAN VLAN.
- **VLAN Trunking Protocol (VTP)**—VTP can be used to prune an RSPAN VLAN between switches.
- **VLANs and trunking**—VLAN membership or trunk settings can be modified for reflector ports at any time. However, changes in VLAN membership or trunk settings for a destination or reflector port do not take effect until the RSPAN session is disabled.
- **EtherChannel groups**—If a physical port belonging to an EtherChannel group is a reflector port and the EtherChannel group is a source, the port is removed from the EtherChannel group and from the list of monitored ports.

RSPAN and RSPAN VLANs

The following restrictions apply when you configure SPAN and RSPAN sessions on a 2950 series switch:

- There is a limit of one active source session for either SPAN or RSPAN.
- A 2950 switch cannot support both SPAN and RSPAN source processes simultaneously.
- RSPAN source sessions have one destination per session with an RSPAN VLAN associated for that session.
- Each RSPAN destination session has one or more destination interfaces for each RSPAN VLAN it supports.
- RSPAN destination sessions are limited to two, or one if a local SPAN or source RSPAN session is configured on the same switch.

On a 3550 series switch, a maximum of two SPAN or RSPAN sessions can be configured and stored in NVRAM on each switch. The two sessions can be divided between SPAN, RSPAN source, and RSPAN destination sessions. Multiple source ports or source VLANs can be configured for each session.

The Catalyst 6500 series switch, configured as an RSPAN source switch, can support up to 30 RSPAN destination sessions.

In a network consisting of only Catalyst 2950 series switches, each RSPAN source switch should be configured with a unique RSPAN VLAN. If two or more switches use the same RSPAN VLAN, they can act only as RSPAN source switches to ensure the delivery of all monitored traffic to the RSPAN destination switch.

Any VLAN on either the Catalyst 2950 series or 3550 series switch can be configured as an RSPAN VLAN as long as the following conditions are met:

- The RSPAN VLAN cannot be configured as a native VLAN on a Catalyst 2950 series switch.
- Extended range RSPAN VLANs configured on a Catalyst 2950 series switch are not propagated to other switches using VTP.
- No access port is configured in the RSPAN VLAN.
- All participating switches support RSPAN.
- The same RSPAN VLAN is used for an RSPAN session in all Catalyst 3550 series switches.

An RSPAN VLAN (a VLAN reserved for use by an RSPAN) should be created and propagated through the switch network before an RSPAN source or destination session is configured. If VTP is enabled in the network, the RSPAN VLAN can be created on a single VTP server switch, and it is propagated to other VTP switches in the VTP domain. If VTP pruning is also enabled, RSPAN traffic is pruned by the VLAN trunks to prevent any unwanted flooding of RSPAN traffic across the network for VLAN-IDs lower than 1005. Also, MAC address learning is disabled on the RSPAN VLAN.

Configuring RSPAN

Configuring an RSPAN session is similar to the procedure you follow when configuring SPAN and VSPAN, as shown in Table 9-5.

An initial configuration step is to create an RSPAN VLAN. A unique RSPAN VLAN must be created for each monitoring session.

Source ports and session IDs are configured as they are in a SPAN session. On the source switch, an RSPAN VLAN and reflector port are nominated with the following global configuration command:

```
monitor session-number destination remote vlan vlan-number reflector-port port-id
```

Table 9-5 Configuring RSPAN Involves Defining an RSPAN VLAN

Step	Command	Description
1	**configure terminal**	Enters global configuration mode.
2	**vlan** *vlan-id* **name** *vlan-name* **exit**	Sets a unique RSPAN VLAN on the server switch with VTP enabled.
3	**no monitor session** {*session-number* | **all** | **local** | **remote**}	Clears any existing SPAN configuration for the session. Specify **all** to remove all SPAN sessions, **local** to remove all local sessions, or **remote** to remove all remote SPAN sessions.
4	**monitor session** *session-number* **source interface** *interface-id* [**,** | **-**] [**both** | **rx** | **tx**]	Specifies the RSPAN session and the source port (monitored port). For *interface-id*, specify the source port to monitor. Valid interfaces include physical interfaces and port-channel logical interfaces (**port-channel** *port channel-number*). (Optional) Specify the direction of traffic to monitor. The default is both sent and received traffic.
5	**monitor session** *session-number* **destination remote vlan** *vlan-id* **reflector-port** *interface*	Specifies the RSPAN session, the destination remote VLAN, and the reflector port. For *vlan-id,* specify the RSPAN VLAN to carry the monitored traffic to the destination port. For *interface,* specify the interface that will flood the RSPAN traffic onto the RSPAN VLAN.
6	**end**	Returns to privileged EXEC mode.
7	**show monitor** [**session** *session-number*]	Verifies entries.
8	**copy running-config startup-config**	(Optional) Saves entries in the configuration file.

On the destination switch, the RSPAN VLAN must be nominated as the source of monitored traffic with the following global configuration command, as shown in Table 9-6:

```
monitor session session-number source remote vlan vlan-id
```

Table 9-6 The RSPAN VLAN Is the Source VLAN Specified on the Destination Switch

Step	Command	Description
1	**configure terminal**	Enters global configuration mode.
2	**monitor session** *session-number* **source remote vlan** *vlan-id*	Specifies the RSPAN session and the source RSPAN VLAN. For *vlan-id,* specify the source RSPAN VLAN to monitor.
3	**monitor session** *session-number* **destination interface** *interface-id* [**encapsulation** {**dot1q**}]	Specifies the RSPAN session and destination interface. For *interface-id,* specify the destination interface. (Optional) Specify the encapsulation header for outgoing packets. The default is native form.
4	**end**	Returns to privileged EXEC mode.
5	**show monitor** [**session** *session-number*]	Verifies entries.
6	**copy running-config startup-config**	(Optional) Saves entries in the configuration file.

A destination interface is then selected in the same way as it is for SPAN sessions.

Ports can be removed from the monitoring session in the same way as for SPAN sessions, as shown in Table 9-7.

To display the status of the current RSPAN configuration, use the **show monitor session** command, as shown in Example 9-6.

Table 9-7 Removing RSPAN Ports Is Similar with RSPAN and Basic SPAN

Step	Command	Description
1	**configure terminal**	Enters global configuration mode.
2	**no monitor session** *session-number* **source interface** *interface-id* [**,** | **-**] [**both** | **rx** | **tx**]	Specifies the characteristics of the RSPAN source port (monitored port) to remove. For *interface-id,* specify the source port to no longer monitor. Valid interfaces include physical interfaces and port-channel logical interfaces (**port-channel** *port-channel-number*). (Optional) Specify the direction of traffic (**both, rx**, or **tx**) to no longer monitor. The default is to disable both receive (**rx**) and transmit (**tx**).
3	**end**	Returns to privileged EXEC mode.
4	**show monitor** [**session** *session-number*]	Verifies entries.
5	**copy running-config startup-config**	(Optional) Saves entries in the configuration file.

Example 9-6 *The* **show monitor** *Command Displays a Remote Source Session*

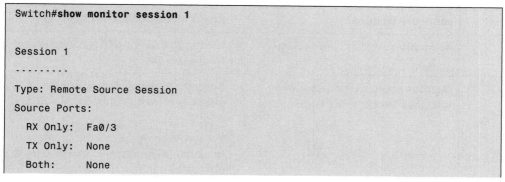

```
Switch#show monitor session 1

Session 1
---------
Type: Remote Source Session
Source Ports:
  RX Only:  Fa0/3
  TX Only:  None
  Both:     None
```

continues

Example 9-6 *The* **show monitor** *Command Displays a Remote Source Session (Continued)*

```
Source VLANS:
  RX Only:  None
  TX Only:  None
  Both:     None
Source RSPAN VLAN:  None
Destination Ports:  None
Encapsulation:  Native
Reflector Port:  Fa0/4
```

Configuring RSPAN to Filter Trunks for Specific VLAN Traffic

Trunk VLAN filtering allows analysis of network traffic on a selected set of VLANs on trunk source ports. Trunk VLAN filtering can be combined with other source ports that belong to any of the selected VLANs. Based on the traffic type (ingress, egress, or both), SPAN sends a copy of the network traffic from the selected VLANs to the destination port.

Use trunk VLAN filtering only with trunk source ports. If trunk VLAN filtering is combined with other source ports that belong to VLANs not included in the selected list of filter VLANs, SPAN includes only ports that belong to one or more of the selected VLANs in the operational sources. Table 9-8 outlines the steps to configure VLAN filtering.

Table 9-8 VLANs Can Be Filtered from the List of Mirrored VLANs on Source Trunk Ports

Step	Command	Description
1	**configure terminal**	Enters global configuration mode.
2	**no monitor session** *session-number*	Clears any existing SPAN configuration for the session.
3	**monitor session** *session-number* **interface** *interface-id* **rx**	Specifies the characteristics of the source port (monitored port) and SPAN session. For *interface-id,* specify the source port to monitor. The interface specified must already be configured as a trunk port.
4	**monitor session** *session-number* **filter vlan** *vlan-id* [,	-]	Limits the SPAN source traffic to specific VLANs. For *vlan-id,* the range is 1 to 4094; do not enter leading 0s.

Table 9-8 VLANs Can Be Filtered from the List of Mirrored VLANs on Source Trunk
Ports (Continued)

Step	Command	Description
5	**monitor session** *session-number* **destination interface** *interface-id*	Specifies the characteristics of the destination port (monitoring port) and SPAN session. For *interface-id,* specify the destination port. Physical interfaces are valid.
6	**end**	Returns to privileged EXEC mode.
7	**show monitor** [**session** *session-number*]	Verifies entries.
8	**copy running-config startup-config**	(Optional) Saves entries in the configuration file.

When a VLAN is cleared, it is removed from the VLAN filter list. A SPAN session is disabled if the VLAN filter list becomes empty.

Trunk VLAN filtering is not applicable to VSPAN sessions.

To monitor all VLANs on the trunk port, use the following global configuration command:

```
no monitor session session_number filter
```

Example 9-7 shows how to clear any existing configuration on SPAN session 2, configure SPAN session 2 to monitor traffic received on trunk port 4, and send traffic for only VLANs 1 to 5 and 9 to destination port 8.

Example 9-7 *VLAN Trunk Traffic Can Be Filtered in a SPAN Session*

```
Switch(config)#no monitor session 2
Switch(config)#monitor session 2 source interface gigabitethernet 0/4 rx
Switch(config)#monitor session 2 filter vlan 1 - 5 , 9
Switch(config)#monitor session 2 destination interface gigabitethernet0/8
Switch(config)#end
```

Lab 9.9.3   Creating an RSPAN Session

In this lab exercise, you create an RSPAN session on two switches to remotely monitor network traffic.

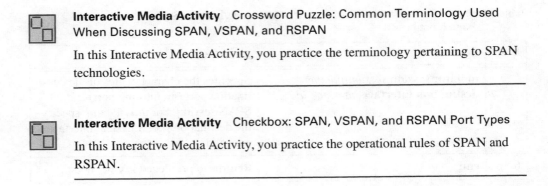

Interactive Media Activity   Crossword Puzzle: Common Terminology Used When Discussing SPAN, VSPAN, and RSPAN

In this Interactive Media Activity, you practice the terminology pertaining to SPAN technologies.

Interactive Media Activity   Checkbox: SPAN, VSPAN, and RSPAN Port Types

In this Interactive Media Activity, you practice the operational rules of SPAN and RSPAN.

Network Analysis Modules and Switch Fabric Modules

With the increased capability of access, distribution, and core layer switches to monitor network traffic, it is desirable to capture this monitored traffic at switching aggregation points. In this way the data can be recorded and analyzed at a central location.

Extra data flow generated by monitored traffic puts additional load on a network's switching bandwidth. A trend toward integration of time-sensitive voice over IP (VoIP) and interactive multimedia services into data networks further exacerbates the situation. These developments make it imperative that the switching fabric at aggregation points have sufficient bandwidth to ensure that latency does not become an issue with mission-critical, time-sensitive traffic.

The preceding issues have been addressed by the introduction of two modules for the Catalyst 6500 series chassis:

- The *Network Analysis Module (NAM)* contains features that let it store and analyze multiple monitored traffic streams in real time. This enhances the network engineer's ability to capture valuable information and to fast-track problem solving. Figure 9-5 shows the recommended NAM placement in a campus network.

- The *Switch Fabric Module (SFM)*, illustrated in Figure 9-6, is designed to address the requirement for increased switching bandwidth, catering to traffic monitoring and the increasing integration of high-priority time-sensitive traffic into the data network.

The following sections explore the NAM and SFM features and installation and configuration issues in greater depth.

Figure 9-5 NAMs Enable Prescriptive Traffic Monitoring as Appropriate for Distinct Parts of the Network

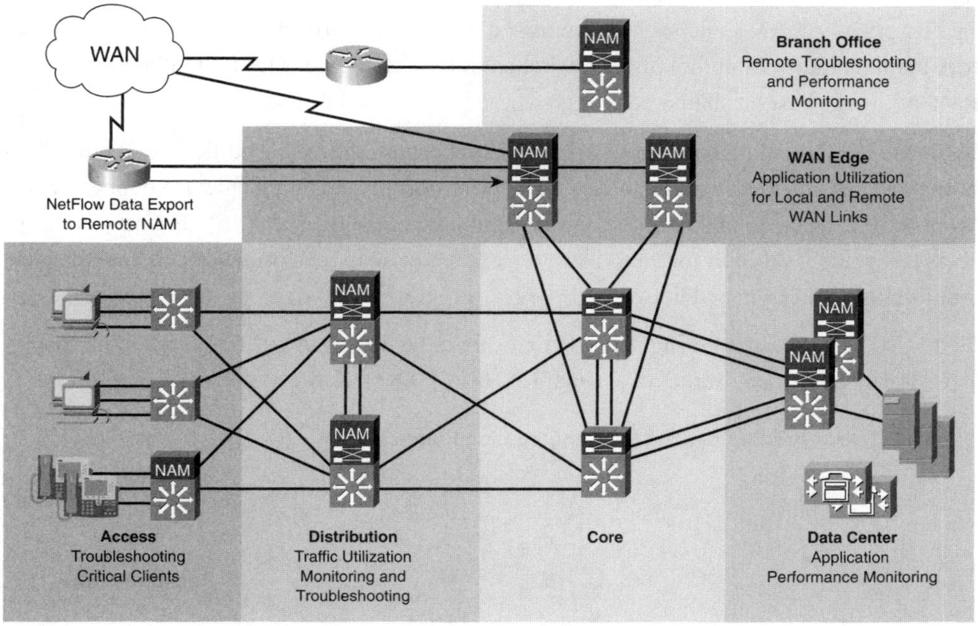

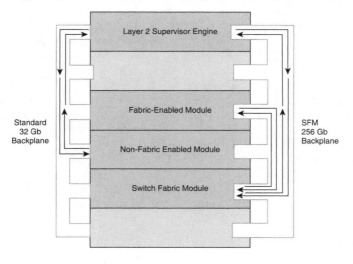

Figure 9-6 The Switch Fabric Module Enables Increased Bandwidth to Fabric-Enabled Line Cards

The Network Analysis Module

Network managers rely on a variety of tools for efficient network management and monitoring. Historically, LAN switches have improved network performance but have prevented network administrators from monitoring switched traffic. This is because remote monitoring (RMON) works best on shared networks, where it can see all traffic.

LAN switches demand greater monitoring control because they filter traffic so that it does not show on a port unless it is either destined for, or has originated from, a device connected to that port. The need for "increased visibility" into network activity for different network segments has made it difficult for administrators to tune network performance and has impeded troubleshooting in switched networks.

The NAM is a LAN monitoring solution that should be deployed at LAN aggregation points where it can see critical traffic and virtual LANs (VLANs), as illustrated in Figure 9-7.

Figure 9-7 NAMs Are Deployed at LAN Aggregation Points

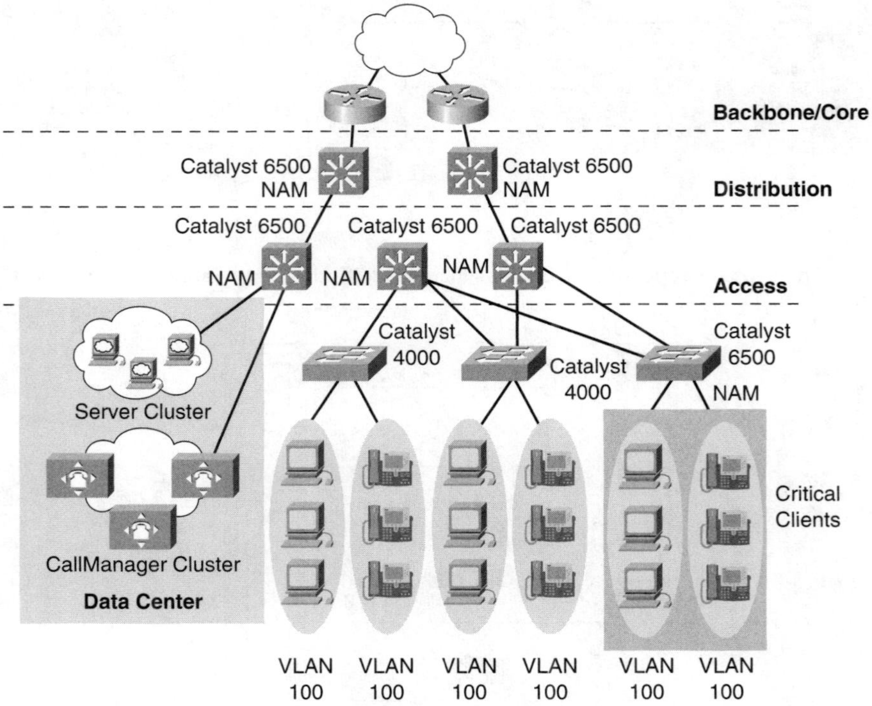

Remote Monitoring (RMON) is a standard monitoring specification that lets various network monitors and console systems exchange network-monitoring data. RMON gives network administrators more freedom to select network-monitoring probes and consoles with features that meet their particular networking needs.

The Cisco Catalyst 6500 series switches already have built-in RMON features with data collection in the statistics, history, alarm, and event groups. Additional RMON and RMON2 features require the use of network monitoring instrumentation.

The NAM provides remote monitoring functions that are based on RMON and RMON2 Management Information Bases (MIBs). The NAM collects data at all layers so that network managers can obtain a broad spectrum of analyses. NAM uses range from fault isolation and troubleshooting to capacity planning and management, performance management, application monitoring, and debugging.

The NAM occupies one full slot in any Cisco Catalyst 6500 series chassis.

The NAM can collect statistics from both data and voice streams, simplifying overall management. The NAM uses SPAN or RSPAN to accept data from physical ports, VLANs, EtherChannel, and NetFlow data export frames. The NAM simultaneously monitors multiple switch ports or VLANs and provides separate RMON/RMON2 statistics for each data source.

Using the NAM

The NAM can be used for network analysis for a variety of functions, including, but not limited to, TACACS, SNMP, and the capture of SPAN information. The remainder of this section discusses the use of NAMs in relation to SPAN sessions.

The NAM Traffic Analyzer, shown in Figure 9-8, is a web-based monitoring application embedded in the NAM software. The application provides comprehensive traffic monitoring and analysis capabilities on board the NAM in addition to its traffic statistics collection functionality. This functionality combines the roles of the monitoring agent and analysis application in the same device.

The NAM Traffic Analyzer runs on a web server on the NAM itself and is accessible through a web browser (Microsoft Internet Explorer 5.0 and above, Netscape 4.7 and above). The NAM Traffic Analyzer enables troubleshooting and monitoring of applications, such as IP Telephony and quality of service (QoS).

The NAM automatically learns VLANs from the switch but does not automatically SPAN them. The Active SPAN Sources window in the NAM graphical user interface (GUI) must be used to SPAN them.

Figure 9-8 The NAM Traffic Analyzer Is Viewed on a Web Browser

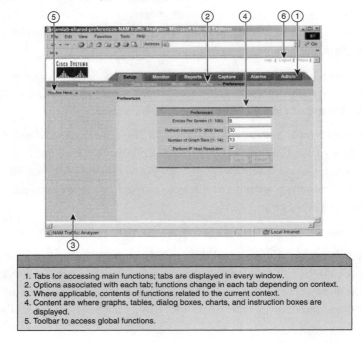

1. Tabs for accessing main functions; tabs are displayed in every window.
2. Options associated with each tab; functions change in each tab depending on context.
3. Where applicable, contents of functions related to the current context.
4. Content are where graphs, tables, dialog boxes, charts, and instruction boxes are displayed.
5. Toolbar to access global functions.

Key features of the NAM Traffic Analyzer include the following:

- **Monitoring capabilities**—It supports full RMON and RMON2 monitoring to analyze network traffic up to the application layer for hosts, conversations, applications.

- **Voice and QoS monitoring**—It offers Differentiated Services Monitoring (DSMON) and IP telephony monitoring capabilities, including protocol utilization, call and phone attributes, and violations of QoS policies.

- **Troubleshooting capabilities**—The NAM Traffic Analyzer can capture and decode data and voice packets in real time to troubleshoot network problems, including alarm capabilities and drill-down views of traffic to identify potential problems before they occur.

- **Web access**—It provides instant access to traffic statistics.

- **Secure web access**—Users can enable the HTTP over Secure Socket Layer (HTTPS) server on the NAM and use up to 168-bit encryption for data exchange.

- **Role-based user administration**—Provides local and remote (TACACS+) authentication and authorization capabilities to assign different levels of roles and privileges to users.

The NAM has no network interfaces. Monitored packets are forwarded to the line module using SPAN or RSPAN functionality that mirrors any switch port or VLAN on the NAM. The NAM supports simultaneous monitoring of multiple ports or VLANs and maintains independent group statistics for each data source. Any data source, such as physical ports, VLANs, EtherChannel, or NetFlow data export frames, that can be directed to the NAM using the SPAN or RSPAN function is supported for RMON data collection.

With the help of SPAN configuration on the Supervisor, the NAM can also monitor Ether-Channel. On the Supervisor, each physical port in the bundle is mirrored into the NAM.

 Interactive Media Activity   Checkbox: Network Analysis Module (NAM)

In this Interactive Media Activity, you reinforce your knowledge of the basic facts pertaining to the NAM.

Benefits of Deploying a NAM

The NAM Traffic Analyzer interface becomes a key element in expediting the network troubleshooting process.

The NAM can be deployed in any Cisco Catalyst 6500 series chassis. It offers the following benefits:

- **An integrated solution**—By occupying a single slot within the Cisco Catalyst 6500 chassis, the NAM helps administrators conserve rack space. NAM gets its data from the switch's backplane, and the spanned traffic does not flow out the switch.
- **A complete LAN network monitoring solution**—The NAM includes the web browser-accessible Traffic Analyzer application for monitoring and troubleshooting.
- **Scalable performance**—Multiple NAMs can be deployed within a switch chassis. Network monitoring capacity can be increased as needed.
- **Standards-based**—The NAM is completely standards-compliant, including full RMON-1 (RFC 2819), RMON-2 (RFC 2021), High-capacity Remote Monitoring (HCRMON), and Switch Monitoring (SMON) (RFC 2613) support for monitoring in LAN environments. It also implements DSMON and the RFC 2074 protocol directory standard.

NAM Troubleshooting

The NAM has no network interfaces. Troubleshooting for the NAM occurs using the web-based interface NAM Traffic Analyzer. Most troubleshooting generally occurs at the SPAN/ VSPAN/RSPAN configuration level. The NAM Traffic Analyzer aids in fast-tracking the troubleshooting process. Figure 9-9 shows a NAM troubleshooting flowchart.

Figure 9-9 Troubleshooting the NAM Depends on Whether the Problem Is Hardware-Based

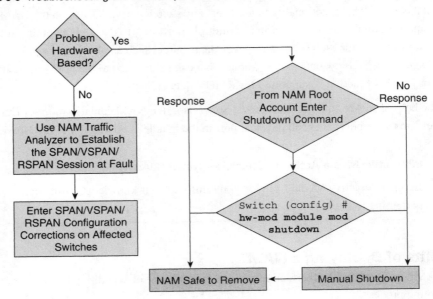

From the root account on the NAM, enter the **shutdown** command.

In privileged mode from the CLI, enter the **hw-mod module mod shutdown** command.
(When this command is used, the **hw-mod module mod reset** command must be entered to
restart the NAM.)

If the NAM does not respond to any commands from the NAM prompt or the Supervisor
Engine, use a small, pointed object to access the SHUTDOWN button, similar to how you
press the inset button on a Cisco Aironet 350 series wireless bridge.

Increasing Switching Fabric in Catalyst 6500 Series Switches

The Catalyst 6500 series Switch Fabric Module (SFM), in combination with the Supervisor
Engine 2, delivers an increase in available system bandwidth from the default 32 Gbps on the
forwarding bus to 256 Gbps. Including an SFM in a Catalyst 6500 chassis increases the speed
at which switching, routing, and network monitoring modules can transfer data between each
other. The SFM reduces latency and the incidence of packet drop caused by bandwidth bottlenecks at traffic aggregation points within the network.

The SFM creates a dedicated connection between fabric-enabled modules and provides unin-
terrupted transmission of frames between these modules. The SFM also provides fabric-
enabled modules with a direct connection to the Catalyst 6500 32-Gbps forwarding bus. If

two SFMs are installed in the chassis, the secondary module acts as a backup in the event of failure of the first module.

The SFM, shown in Figure 9-10, does not have a console. A two-line LCD display on the front panel shows fabric utilization, software revision, and basic system information.

Figure 9-10 The SFM Can Effect a Seven-Fold Increase in Forwarded Packets Per Second and an Eight-Fold Increase in Available System Bandwidth on a Catalyst 6500

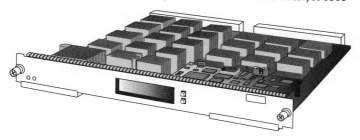

The following are the key features of the SFM:

- It enables 30 Mpps Cisco Express Forwarding (CEF)-based central forwarding on Supervisor Engine 2.
- It enables up to 210 Mpps distributed forwarding on supported line cards.
- It supports advanced services, such as QoS and security in hardware, through access control lists (ACLs).

Fabric-enabled modules in a Catalyst 6500 are modules whose capacity is enhanced by the introduction of the SFM. When an SFM is installed, the traffic is forwarded to and from modules in one of the following modes:

- **Bus mode**—Data passes between the local bus and the Supervisor Engine bus. This mode is used for traffic to or from non-fabric-enabled modules and between fabric-enabled and non-fabric-enabled modules.
- **Truncated mode**—Only the truncated data (the first 64 bytes of the frame) is sent over the switch fabric channel if both the destination and the source are fabric-enabled modules. If either the source or destination is not a fabric-enabled module, the data goes through the switch fabric channel and the data bus. The SFM does not get involved when traffic is forwarded between non-fabric-enabled modules.
- **Compact mode**—A compact version of the DBus header is forwarded over the switch fabric channel, delivering the best possible switching rate. Non-fabric-enabled modules do not support the compact mode and generate cyclic redundancy check (CRC) errors if they receive frames in compact mode. This mode is used only when no non-fabric-enabled modules are installed in the chassis.

Interactive Media Activity   Drag and Drop: The Mode Type Used to Forward Traffic Internally on a Catalyst 6500 with SFM

After completing this Interactive Media Activity, you will understand the mode type on a Catalyst 6500 with an SFM.

Configuring the Switch Fabric Module

The SFM does not require any user configuration. A fully automated startup sequence brings the module online and runs the connectivity diagnostics on the ports. Based on the other modules in the chassis, the SFM determines which mode to operate in.

To manually configure the switching mode (supported in Cisco IOS Release 12.1(11b)E and later), use the following global configuration command:

`fabric switching-mode allow {bus-mode | {truncated [{threshold [number]}]}}`

To configure fabric-required mode, which prevents all switching modules from operating unless an SFM is installed, use the global configuration command **fabric required**.

This effectively turns off all modules except the Supervisor Engine if no SFM is installed.

Use the **no fabric required** command to clear fabric required mode.

Monitoring the Switch Fabric Module

The SFM supports a number of **show** commands for monitoring purposes, as shown in Table 9-9. A fully automated startup sequence brings the module online and runs the connectivity diagnostics on the ports.

Table 9-9 A Number of **show** Commands Are Available to Monitor the SFM

Command	Description
show module {5 | 6 | 7 | 8}	Displays module information.
show fabric active	Displays SFM redundancy status.
show fabric switching-mode [**module** {*slot-number*} | **all**]	Displays the fabric channel switching mode for one or all of the modules.
show fabric status [*slot-number* | **all**]	Displays the fabric status for one or all of the modules.
show fabric utilization [*slot-number* | **all**]	Displays the fabric utilization for one or all of the modules.
show fabric errors [*slot-number* | **all**]	Displays fabric errors for one or all of the modules.

The SFM **show** commands monitor the SFM in the following ways:

- Display module information (see Example 9-8)
- Display the active fabric cards (see Example 9-9)
- Display fabric channel switching modes (see Example 9-10)
- Display fabric status (see Example 9-11)
- Display the fabric utilization (see Example 9-12)
- Display any fabric errors (see Example 9-13)

Example 9-8 **show module** *Displays Module Information*

```
Router#show module 5

Mods  Ports  Card Type             Model         Serial No.
----  -----  --------------------  ------------  -----------
5     0      Switching Fabric Module  WS-c6500-SFM  SAD04420JR5



Mod   MAC addresses                   Hw   Fw      Sw        Status
---   ------------------------------  --   -----   --------  ------
5     0001.0002.0003 to 0001.0002.0003  1.0  6.1(3)  6.2(0.97)  Ok
```

Example 9-9 **show fabric active** *Displays the Active Fabric Cards*

```
Router#show fabric active
Active fabric card in slot 5
No backup fabric card in the system
```

Example 9-10 **show fabric switching-mode all** *Displays Fabric Channel Switching Modes*

```
Router#show fabric switching-mode all
bus-only mode is allowed
Module  Slot          Switching Mode
1 Bus
2 Bus
3 DCEF
4 DCEF
5 No Interfaces
6 DCEF
```

Example 9-11 **show fabric status all** *Displays Fabric Status*

```
Router#show fabric status all

slot   channel  module   fabric
                status   status
1      0        OK       OK
3      0        OK       OK
3      1        OK       OK
4      0        OK       OK
```

Example 9-12 **show fabric utilization all** *Displays Fabric Utilization*

```
Router#show fabric utilization all
slot   channel  Ingress%  Egress%
1      0        0         0
3      0        0         0
3      1        0         0
4      0        0         0
4      1        0         0
6      0        0         0
6      1        0         0
7      0        0         0
7      1        0         0
```

Example 9-13 **show fabric errors** *Displays Any Fabric Errors*

```
Router#show fabric errors
slot   channel  module   module   module   fabric
                crc      hbeat    sync     sync
1      0        0        0        0        0
3      0        0        0        0        0
3      1        0        0        0        0
4      0        0        0        0        0
4      1        0        0        0        0
6      0        0        0        0        0
6      1        0        0        0        0
7      0        0        0        0        0
7      1        0        0        0        0
```

Basic Security

A number of rudimentary security measures are available on Catalyst switches to prevent unauthorized access. Both out-of-band and in-band management connections to Catalyst switches are possible. Basic password protection is simple to configure. Restricting physical access to switches must also be taken into account.

Access Control Policy

Implementation of any access control begins with the creation of a standard access policy. An access policy defines access rights and privileges for the network users. The access policy should provide guidelines for connecting external networks, connecting devices to a network, and adding new software to systems.

Most access policies outline the following information:

- Network device management issues, such as physical security and access control
- User access to the network
- Traffic-flow policies
- Route filtering

Each layer of a hierarchical network will probably have a different access policy, because each layer is responsible for different tasks. Figure 9-11 illustrates a campus network where an access policy should be defined.

Figure 9-11 A Network Policy Can Be Implemented at the Access Layer

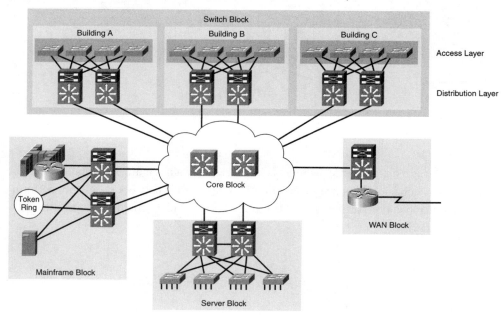

The access layer, highlighted in Figure 9-11, is the point at which local end users are allowed into the network. Port security can be used to control traffic at the access layer. Passwords can be used to protect network devices. The access layer can also use VLANs, access lists, or filters to further optimize traffic control for a particular set of users.

The network's distribution layer is the demarcation point between the access and core layers, as shown in Figure 9-12. This layer helps define and differentiate the core. Providing boundary definition, the distribution layer is where packet manipulation should take place. The distribution layer should be responsible for ensuring that only necessary traffic makes it to the core or another switch block. The distribution layer can be summarized as the layer that provides policy-based connectivity.

Figure 9-12 A Network Policy Can Be Implemented at the Distribution Layer

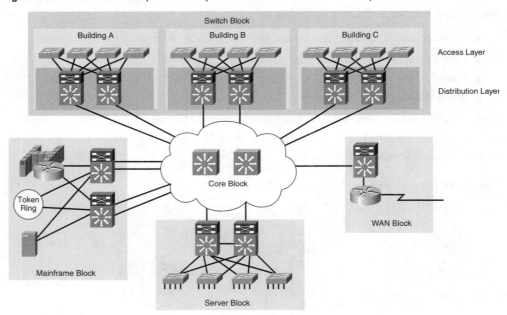

The core layer is a high-speed switching backbone, as shown in Figure 9-13, and it should be designed to switch packets as fast as possible. This layer of the network should not perform any packet manipulation, such as access lists and filtering, which would slow down the switching of packets.

Figure 9-13 A Network Policy Is Rarely Implemented at the Core Layer

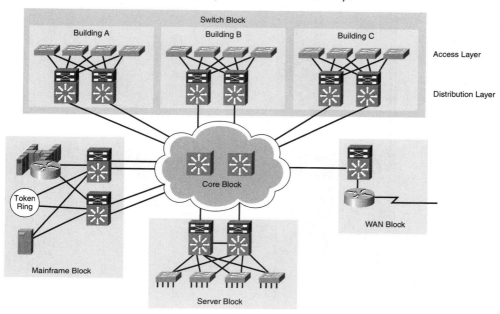

Basic Security Measures

Controlling access to network devices, such as switches and routers, should be one of the first priorities of an access policy. Every device at every layer of the hierarchical model should have a plan for physical security, password protection, privilege levels, and remote control (Telnet/SSH/HTTP) access. The following sections address these issues.

Physical Security

Physical access to a router or switch gives a sufficiently sophisticated user total control over that device. Nearly all switches and routers have "password-recovery techniques" or other backdoors to access the device without a password. These techniques are publicly documented on the Internet. Installing software security measures makes no sense when access to the hardware is not controlled.

Physically secure network devices by doing the following:

- **Provide the proper physical environment**—This includes lockable doors and backup power supplies, as shown in Figure 9-14.
- **Control direct access to the device**—This includes lockable racks (see Figure 9-15) and password protection to console and auxiliary ports. Ports that are not being used should also be disabled.

Figure 9-14 Lockable Doors Let You Secure Network Equipment

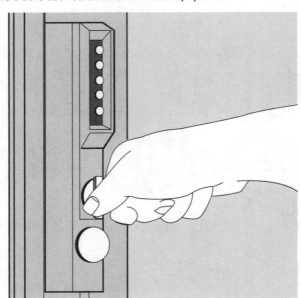

Figure 9-15 Lockable Racks Control Direct Access to Network Devices

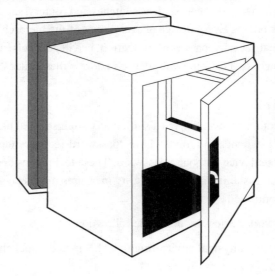

Connecting to the Switch

Cisco devices may be accessed using in-band management or out-of-band management.

- **Out-of-band management**—Using a separate communications channel for management traffic and data traffic. These channels can be physically or logically separate.
- **In-band management**—Using a common communications channel for both data and management traffic.

Out-of-Band Management

Out-of-band management options include the following:

- Console 0 (con0)
- Auxiliary 0 (aux0)

Figures 9-16, 9-17, and 9-18 illustrate the location of the console port on various Cisco switching devices.

Figure 9-16 The Console Port Is on the Supervisor Engine on a Catalyst 6500

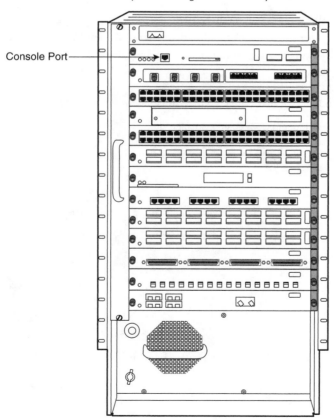

Figure 9-17 The Console Port Is on the Back of a Catalyst 3550

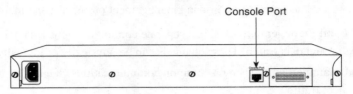

Figure 9-18 The Console Port Is on the Back of a Catalyst 2950

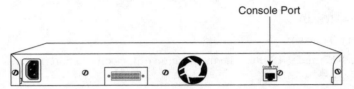

NOTE

Connecting modems to the switch console port can allow network administrators to access remote devices during data network outages. Because connecting modems to remote devices allows access to the device console or auxiliary port from anyone using the public telephone network, the phone number used to dial into the device should be kept secret.

Console and auxiliary ports can be directly attached to local management terminals using serial connections for local out-of-band management. Modems can also be connected to console and auxiliary ports to support out-of-band management from remote locations, as illustrated in Figure 9-19.

Figure 9-19 A Modem Can Be Connected to a Console Port for Remote Administration

Switch with Modem Connected Console Port

Remote Out-of-Band Management Station

Remote devices with modems connected to console or auxiliary ports should also be configured with complex passwords. That is, passwords should not use real words and should be made up using a combination of numbers (0 to 9), upper- and lowercase letters (a to z, A to Z), and special characters (! @ # $ % ^ & * { } [ ]).

In-Band Management

In-band management options include the following:

- Virtual terminal (vty) ports used for remote terminal access, as shown in Figure 9-20.
- Web interface (HTTP) used for remote monitoring and control
- TFTP
- Network management protocols, such as Simple Network Management Protocol (SNMP) and network management software, such as CiscoWorks

Figure 9-20 Virtual Terminal Access Is Provided Via Telnet

Unencrypted vty console sessions can be established using Telnet. Encrypted vty terminal console sessions can be established using a Secure Shell (SSH) client. Using encrypted communications for vty console sessions wherever possible provides better security for network devices.

Cisco IOS devices can be configured to allow remote monitoring and control functions through a normal web browser using HTTP. The web interface is inherently insecure and should be disabled if possible, especially in large networks with sophisticated users.

A TFTP server can be used to load a common configuration script onto Cisco IOS devices. This can be used as an efficient mechanism to manage a large number of network devices.

Access to the TFTP server implicitly provides console access to a large number of IOS devices in the network at the same time. Because of this, the TFTP server must be secured and managed appropriately to prevent accidental or malicious misconfiguration of any shared configuration scripts.

Cisco IOS devices support monitoring and management functions provided by SNMP. Because SNMP was not originally designed with built-in security, using SNMP should be restricted to monitoring functions wherever possible.

You can gain additional control over these in-band management options using a management VLAN and access lists. Use of the advanced in-band management features is covered in the section "Securing User Access."

Interactive Media Activity   Checkbox: Direct Access to Cisco Devices

After completing this Interactive Media Activity, you will better understand in-band and out-of-band access to Cisco devices.

Basic Password Protection

The factory-default configuration for Cisco IOS devices does not contain any passwords.

Cisco IOS-based devices support three types of local passwords for use with both out-of-band and in-band connections:

- Enable and secret passwords
- Line passwords
- Local usernames and passwords

By default, all passwords in a Cisco IOS device are stored in clear text, as shown in Figure 9-21, with the exception of the optional **enable secret** password.

The **enable** password is unencrypted, as shown in Example 9-14.

Passwords can be encrypted using the global configuration **service password-encryption** command, as shown in Example 9-15. Notice that the enable password line in the configuration script now has the number 7 before the encrypted password. This tells the IOS that the string of numbers and letters is an encrypted password.

Figure 9-21 Passwords Are Not Encrypted by Default

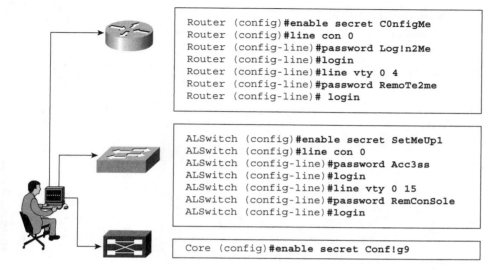

```
Router (config)#enable secret C0nfigMe
Router (config)#line con 0
Router (config-line)#password Log!n2Me
Router (config-line)#login
Router (config-line)#line vty 0 4
Router (config-line)#password RemoTe2me
Router (config-line)# login
```

```
ALSwitch (config)#enable secret SetMeUp1
ALSwitch (config)#line con 0
ALSwitch (config-line)#password Acc3ss
ALSwitch (config-line)#login
ALSwitch (config-line)#line vty 0 15
ALSwitch (config-line)#password RemConSole
ALSwitch (config-line)#login
```

```
Core (config)#enable secret Conf!g9
```

Example 9-14 *The Enable Password Is Unencrypted*

```
Access1#show running-config
Building configuration...

Current configuration : 947 bytes
!
version 12.1
no service pad
service timestamps debug uptime
service timestamps log uptime
no service password-encryption
!
hostname Access1
!
enable password SetMeUp1
!
```

Example 9-15 *Passwords Can Be Encrypted with the* **service password-encryption** *Command*

```
Access1#show running-config
Building configuration...

Current configuration : 956 bytes
!
version 12.1
no service pad
service timestamps debug uptime
service timestamps log uptime
service password-encryption
!
hostname Access1
!
enable password 7 06350A35614B3C0954
!
```

Every method of accessing the device should have a password applied to prevent unauthorized access. By default, console and auxiliary ports have no password protection. The enable password is the password used to restrict access to privileged EXEC mode.

Passwords defined for individual console, auxiliary, or vty lines are called *line passwords*.

Cisco IOS devices can also store locally defined usernames as passwords. Using local usernames and passwords allows the network administrator to create individual logins for users and define additional options and controls on a per-user basis. Using the advanced options with local usernames is covered in the section "Advanced Username Options."

It is better to have users log in to the system using an individual username and password, rather than having everyone use the line password. Having users log in to the device using their own usernames makes it easier to track down who is accessing the device and what changes they have made.

Lab 9.9.4 Setting Encrypted Passwords

In this lab exercise, you configure passwords on switch console ports and virtual terminal lines.

Securing Remote Management

Several options are available for remote management of Catalyst switches. These include Telnet, SSH, web browsing, and SNMP. SSH is commonly used nowadays as a secure means of administering devices remotely. Using Telnet is generally not an option anymore because of its use of plain text. Web management is also a security risk but is commonly used in a localized fashion. Many Cisco GUIs, such as the Security Device Manager, rely on web access and provide a user-friendly means of configuring complicated technologies. Access lists and judicious VLAN usage add another level of security to the remote management solution.

Remote Management Security Options

Out-of-band connections from remote locations need to have a modem connected to the console or auxiliary port of the device being managed. You can control who has access to the modem by combining advanced local username options with callback technology to ensure that specific users can establish dial-in modem sessions from only specific locations. Configuring modem callback security is covered in the CCNP 2 Remote Access course.

In-band management traffic shares bandwidth with user traffic and can be segregated from user traffic using the following features:

- Local usernames
- SSH session encryption
- VLANs
- Access lists

In-band management connections can also be controlled using advanced local username options. The next section covers advanced local username options for controlling both out-of-band and in-band connections.

Lab 9.9.5   Using Local Usernames and Passwords

In this lab exercise, you configure multiple local usernames with passwords. These are used for login authentication on the console port and virtual terminal lines.

Advanced Username Options

A variety of user-specific options are available for configuration in the Cisco IOS. These commands can be used either singularly or in combination to provide granular control over connections to the device. These options can be entered individually or together in a single command.

NOTE

These commands are stored in the running configuration as a single command.

Storing a User Password Using Strong Encryption

The first of these commands is **username** *name* **secret** *password*. This command is used to store a user's password using strong encryption, even if **service password-encryption** is not enabled. For example:

```
username cde secret xyz
```

The result in the running config appears as follows:

```
username cde secret 5 $1$HgUN$q150B5AxLvpT7w/zp2vn
```

Creating a Generic User Account

Using the **username** *name* **nopassword** command creates a user account that does not require a password to log on. This feature might be used for a generic account and should be implemented only in conjunction with a limited privilege level associated with that username. For example:

```
ALSwitch(config)#username Helpdesk nopassword
```

The result in the running config appears as follows:

```
username Helpdesk nopassword
```

Use of this feature in a production environment is not recommended.

Limiting the Scope of Commands Available to a User Account

The **username** *name* **privilege** *level* command is used to limit the scope of commands available to a particular user. Consider the following example:

```
ALSwitch(config)#username Helpdesk privilege 1
ALSwitch(config)#username Bob privilege 15
```

The command **username Helpdesk privilege 1** gives Alice user-mode access after she authenticates with the server. The command **username Bob privilege 15** gives Bob privileged-mode access after he authenticates with the server.

The result in the running config appears as follows:

```
username Helpdesk privilege 1 no password
Username Bob privilege 15 secret 5
$1$f3mK$C5PuyHwjT0T0fvNgPDwT60
```

Limiting the Maximum Number of Simultaneous Sessions Available to a User Account

The **username** *name* **user-maxlinks** *number* command is used to limit the maximum number of sessions a particular username can establish simultaneously. This can be used to control the use of resources by users, giving different user accounts different levels of access to resources.

For example:

```
ALSwitch(config)#username Helpdesk user-maxlinks 2
```

The result in the running config appears as follows:

```
username Helpdesk privilege 1 nopassword user-maxlinks 2
```

Binding Access Lists to a User Account

Access lists can be bound to specific usernames using the **username** *name* **access-class** *access-list* command. This forces session traffic from a specific user to match **permit** statements defined in an access list to establish a successful connection.

For example, with these commands, an administrator has a large degree of flexibility. A guest login account can be created that requires no password, has user-mode access only, is limited to a maximum of two simultaneous sessions, and can be used only from a defined IP host or subnet on the network. For example:

```
ALSwitch(config)#username Carol access-class 99
```

The result in the running config appears as follows:

```
username Carol access-class 99 secret 5
$1$808J$XeiJBlrFTCLUaZhBcE/y..
```

Lab 9.9.6 Using Advanced Username Options

In this lab exercise, you configure multiple user accounts with advanced options to limit privilege levels and use strong encryption to secure passwords.

Interactive Media Activity Checkbox: Username Options for Accessing Cisco Devices

After completing this Interactive Media Activity, you will better understand username options for accessing Cisco devices.

Encrypting Communications Using Secure Shell

Recall that Ethernet is a broadcast-based technology. This means that all nodes sharing an Ethernet segment, or nodes attached to a SPAN port in a switched environment, receive a copy of all frames on the network at Layer 2. This means that the Ethernet network is inherently insecure. Also recall that computers can be configured to use promiscuous mode network drivers, which allow the computers to ignore the Layer 3 information in the packet header, and record the packets for later examination and analysis.

Telnet allows administrators and users to connect to Cisco IOS devices from remote locations through the production data network. Because Telnet packets are transmitted across the network in clear text (that is, without encryption), these packets can be captured and their contents easily read, including the capture of usernames and passwords.

SSH allows administrators and users to securely connect to Cisco IOS devices from remote locations through the production data network. Because the data payload in SSH packets is protected by encryption, the contents of any captured SSH packets cannot be easily read, as illustrated in Figure 9-22. The recommended practice is that SSH encryption be configured at the minimum for securing in-band management traffic where possible.

Figure 9-22 SSH Encrypts a Session So That Intercepted Traffic Cannot Be Read

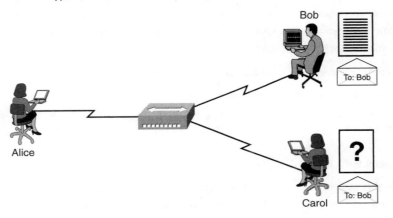

Secure Shell (SSH) is an application and a protocol that provides a secure replacement to the Berkeley r-tools. This protocol secures the sessions using standard cryptographic mechanisms.

Two versions of SSH currently are available:

- **SSH Version 1**—Implemented in the Cisco IOS software. Consists of an application and a protocol. The application includes both a server and a client.
- **SSH Version 2**—The Catalyst switch supports an SSHv2 server.

The SSH Server feature lets an SSH client make a secure, encrypted connection to a Cisco IOS device. This connection provides functionality that is similar to that of an inbound Telnet connection. SSH allows strong encryption to be used in conjunction with Cisco IOS authentication features. The SSH server in Cisco IOS software works with any commercially available SSH-compliant client software.

The SSH Integrated Client feature is an application running over the SSH protocol to provide device authentication and encryption. The SSH client lets a Cisco IOS device make a secure, encrypted connection to another Cisco IOS device or to any other device running the SSH server. This connection provides functionality that is similar to a Telnet connection, except that this connection is encrypted. With authentication and encryption, the SSH client allows for secure communications over an insecure network.

The SSH client in Cisco IOS software works with any commercially available SSH-compliant server software. The SSH integrated client supports the Data Encryption Standard (DES) and Triple-DES (3DES) ciphers and also supports password-based authentication. User authentication is performed like that in a Telnet session to a router. The user authentication mechanisms supported by the SSH integrated client include RADIUS, TACACS+, and locally stored usernames and passwords.

The following are some basic SSH restrictions:

- Rivest, Shamir, and Adelman (RSA) authentication, available in SSH clients, is not supported in the SSH server for Cisco IOS Release 12.2.
- SSH server and SSH client are available on DES (56-bit) and 3DES (168-bit) data encryption IOS images only. In DES IOS images, DES is the only encryption algorithm available to be used by SSH. In 3DES IOS images, both the DES and 3DES encryption algorithms are available.

The command execution shell is the only application supported on Cisco IOS devices running the SSH server process.

Interactive Media Activity   Crossword Puzzle: Device Access Control Policy: Definitions

After completing this Interactive Media Activity, you will better understand definitions involving device access control policy.

Encryption Key Pairs

The most common understanding of a data encryption system is based on preshared secret-key cryptography. Preshared secret-key cryptography is where two parties share the same secret. This secret is used to both encrypt and decrypt data before sending or reading the actual data. Anyone who knows the preshared secret key can encrypt and decrypt data.

The problem with a preshared secret-key system is in transferring knowledge of the preshared secret key to all participating parties while keeping the key secret. This problem was solved with the development of asymmetric key pair systems, also known as public/private key pairs or Public Key Infrastructure (PKI).

With asymmetric key pairs, the public-key portion is designed to be distributed freely. The private-key portion must be kept secret. If data is encrypted with the public key, it can be decrypted only using the corresponding private key. For example, a message encrypted with the public key cannot be decrypted with the public key. Only the private key can be used to decrypt the message. This ensures that an eavesdropper cannot decrypt the message without the secret private key.

Table 9-10 compares the characteristics of asymmetric and symmetric key pairs.

Table 9-10 Asymmetric Key Pairs (Public Key Infrastructure) Are More Secure Than Symmetric Keys (Preshared Keys)

Symmetric Keys	Asymmetric Key Pairs
The same key is used for all encryption and decryption.	Pairs of keys are generated—one key for encryption (public) and another for decryption (private).
The cryptographic process is mathematically simpler and faster to process.	The cryptographic process is mathematically more complex and slower to process.
The cryptographic process is more easily compromised.	The cryptographic process is more difficult to compromise.
The cryptographic process is two-way: the key used for encryption can also be used for decryption, which is less secure.	The cryptographic process is one-way: the key used for encryption cannot be used for decryption, and the key used for decryption cannot be used for encryption, which is more secure.
Keeping the key secret (secure) is crucial.	Only the decryption key needs to be kept secure.
Distributing the key securely can be complex.	The encryption (public) key can be distributed over insecure media.
Also known as the preshared secret key.	Also known as the public key infrastructure.
	Systems used by digital certificates and Open-PGP standards.

When an RSA key pair is generated on a Cisco IOS device, both a private key and a public key are created. After they are generated, these keys can be used to encrypt communications between the SSH server running on the IOS device and the SSH client. The first time an SSH client connects to an SSH server, the client is given a copy of the server's public key. Any data encrypted using the public key can only be decrypted using the matching private key, which is kept secret on the SSH server. Even if many people have copies of the public key, only the SSH server has the private key, and only the SSH server can decrypt the encrypted communications. This allows authentication details and session traffic to be exchanged between the SSH server and client securely.

Using VLANs to Restrict Remote Management

Virtual LANs (VLANs) can be used to control who can establish in-band communications with the switch. The switch uses VLAN 1 as the management VLAN, unless it is explicitly configured to be on another VLAN. The management VLAN on a switch is the only VLAN from which in-band management sessions can be established. When shipped from the factory, all ports on the switch are configured as members of VLAN1. At factory default settings, the switch accepts management traffic from any port.

Network administrators should separate management traffic and user traffic. The recommended practice for managing network devices (router and switches) is to establish separate logical networks for user traffic and management traffic using multiple VLANs and subnets, as shown in Figure 9-23. The management VLAN should not carry any user traffic. It is also important that the management VLAN be included in the list of VLANs propagated by the VLAN Trunking Protocol (VTP) processes. Separating management and user traffic helps protect the network infrastructure against attacks from network users.

Figure 9-23 VLANs Can Be Used to Separate Management Traffic from User Traffic

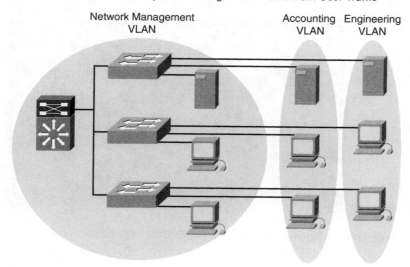

Note that in a multilayer switched network, a switch does not need to have a port that is a member of the management VLAN to accept traffic from the management VLAN. Because a

trunk port normally passes traffic for all VLANs, the switch accepts management traffic over a trunked connection.

Lab 9.9.7   Configuring the Management VLAN on a Single Switch

In this lab exercise, you configure and use a nondefault management VLAN. You use the **config-vlan** and **vlan database** modes to configure VLANs.

Securing the Web Management Interface

Cisco switches and routers have the capacity to host a web interface to simplify remote monitoring and management, as shown in Figure 9-24. Because this interface uses insecure protocols, it is not recommended that it be used for remote management. This interface can still be used to provide access where security is less important, such as for usage monitoring, but it should still be secured as much as possible. To enable the web interface, use the **ip http server** command from global configuration mode.

Figure 9-24 The Catalyst 2950 Web Interface Provides User-Friendly Management

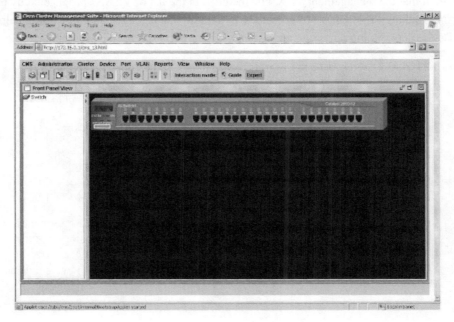

One of the settings for the web interface is the configuration of the TCP port number. The HTTP server process running on the switch normally listens for connection requests on port

TCP:80. To configure the HTTP server process to listen on a different port, use the global configuration command **ip http port** *http-port,* where *http-port* is a number between 1 and 65535.

You also can establish a connection to the switch's web interface using access control lists. The global configuration command **ip http access-class** *acl-number* is used to bind a standard access list to the HTTP server process, where *acl-number* must be between 1 and 99.

Lab 9.9.9   Restricting Web Interface Sessions with Access Lists

In this lab exercise, you define and apply access lists to restrict access to the switch's web interface.

Using Access Lists to Restrict Remote Management

Table 9-11 describes the commands you can use to restrict various remote management methods. The following sections cover each in detail.

Table 9-11 Telnet, HTTP, SNMP, and NTP Access Can Be Restricted

Command	Configuration Mode	Description
access-class *access-list* **in** I **out**	Line configuration mode	Evaluates inbound or outbound virtual terminal traffic against a standard access list.
ip http access-class *access-list*	Global configuration mode	Evaluates inbound connections to the HTTP server against a standard access list.
username *name* **access-class** *access-list*	Global configuration mode	Evaluates inbound traffic against a standard or extended access list during user authentication.
snmp community *string* [**ro** I **rw** I **view**] *access-list*	Global configuration mode	Evaluates SNMP traffic for a particular community against a standard access list. Level of access (read only, read-write, view only) to a single community string can be controlled using multiple access lists.
ntp access-group peer I **query-only** I **serve** I **serve-only** *access-list*	Global configuration mode	Grants appropriate permissions to Network Time Protocol (NTP) processes according to access list membership.

Restricting vty Connections

Remote access to a switch can be controlled using access lists. The line configuration command **access-class** *access-list* can be used to limit virtual terminal sessions to those matching a predefined standard or extended access list.

Restricting Web Interface Connections

Web management interface sessions can be controlled using the global configuration command **ip http access-class** *access-list,* where *access-list* refers to a standard access list number between 1 and 99. It is not possible to control access to the web management interface using extended access lists.

Restricting Specific Users

The global configuration command **user** *username* **access-class** *access-list* is used to limit a specific user to traffic patterns defined by an access list. The parameter *access-list* can refer to a standard access list in the ranges 1 to 99 or 1300 to 1999, or to an extended access list in the ranges 100 to 199 or 2000 to 2699. This feature can also be used to control user access to a dial-in access server.

Restricting Access to SNMP and NTP Processes

Standard access lists can also be used to control traffic relating to other management processes running on the switch. Access to SNMP community strings can be restricted to read-only, read-write, or view-only according to membership of standard access lists. Access to NTP processes can also be controlled using standard access lists.

Lab 9.9.8   Restricting Virtual Terminal Sessions with Access Lists

In this lab exercise, you define and apply access lists to restrict access to virtual terminal sessions on the switch.

Interactive Media Activity   Checkbox: Security for Web Management Interface

After completing this Interactive Media Activity, you will better understand security for the web management interface.

Additional Remote Management Session Options

Remote management sessions can be enhanced using the following optional messages:

- Message-of-the-day
- Vacant message
- Refuse message

These messages are usually defined as explanatory notes to users. They can be applied to console, auxiliary, and vty lines, as defined in Table 9-12. Note that these message settings are superseded if the switch has AAA enabled, because AAA can display similar messages.

Table 9-12 Message-of-the-Day, Vacant Messages, and Refuse Messages Are Used to Further Define User Access

Command	Configuration Mode	Description
banner motd *$ Message $*	Global configuration mode	Defines the message-of-the-day banner message.
motd-banner	Line configuration mode	Enables the use of the message-of-the-day banner message on one or more lines.
vacant-message *$ Message $*	Line configuration mode	Defines the vacant message for one or more lines.
refuse-message *$ Message $*	Line configuration mode	Defines the refuse message for one or more lines.

Message-of-the-Day Banner

The message-of-the-day banner is displayed when a user establishes a connection to the switch. The actual message is defined using the global configuration command **banner motd**. Example 9-16 shows a sample message-of-the-day banner. It is not recommended that the name of the organization that owns the device be included in the banner message.

Example 9-16 *The Message-of-the-Day Banner Is Normally Used to Warn Users of Unauthorized Access*

```
This is a protected system
Any attempt at unauthorized access will be logged and reported to the relevant
  authorities


User Access Verification


Username:
```

After you create the message-of-the-day banner, you need to bind it to one or more lines using the line configuration command **motd-banner**.

Vacant Message

The vacant message is displayed when the user session is disconnected:

```
ALSwitch1#exit
```

```
Session Disconnected.
```

The message displayed is defined using the **vacant-message** line configuration command.

Refuse Message

The refuse message is displayed to the user when his or her authentication fails at login. The refuse message is defined using the line configuration command **refuse-message**.

Note that these message options may not be displayed for users connecting to the switch over SSH.

Configuring, Verifying, and Troubleshooting SSH Server

Before you configure SSH, perform the following tasks:

Step 1   Download the required image on the device. The SSH server requires the IPSec (DES or 3DES) encryption software image. The SSH client requires the IPSec (DES or 3DES) encryption software image.

Step 2   Configure a host name and host domain for the device using the following commands:

```
hostname host-name
ip domain-name domain-name
```

For example:

```
switch(config)#hostname ALSwitch1
ALSwitch1#ip domain-name abc.com
```

The results in the running config are as follows:

```
hostname ALSwitch1
!
ip domain-name abc.com
```

Step 3   Generate an RSA key pair for the device using the configuration line command **crypto key generate rsa**. This also automatically enables SSH.

Step 4   Configure a local username and password on the device using the following commands:

```
username name secret password
login local
```

For example:

```
ALSwitch1(config)#username Alice secret fantastic
ALSwitch1(config)#line vty 0 15
ALSwitch1(config-line)#login local
```

The results in the running config are as follows:

```
username Alice secret 5
$1$vBnC$kw40PgOX0yQQyM1KzOmv71

line vty 0 4
 login local
line vty 5 15
 login local
```

The device may also be configured with TACACS+ or RADIUS protocols for user authentication.

You can verify SSH configuration using the following commands:

- **show ip ssh**—Verifies that the SSH server is enabled, and displays the version and configuration data.

- **show ssh**—Displays details of users connected to the SSH server process running on the device.

SSH Configuration Errors

SSH configuration commands are rejected if an RSA key pair was not successfully generated first. To resolve this problem, generate a new RSA key pair. If necessary, zeroize any existing RSA key pair using the **crypto key zeroize rsa** command first.

The error messages **no hostname specified** and **no domain specified** during the generation of an RSA key pair are caused by the lack of a hostname or host domain in the switch's running configuration. These elements of a device's configuration are used to generate an RSA key pair. This problem can be resolved by ensuring that both the hostname and the host domain have been configured before an RSA key pair is generated.

Because an SSH session uses a vty resource on an SSH server, the number of simultaneous SSH sessions is limited by the number of vty lines available on the device. Cisco IOS-based switches support up to 16 simultaneous vty sessions.

SSH Connection Errors

There are two main reasons for an SSH server to refuse a connection request:

- No vty resources remain to allocate to a new vty session. The maximum number of vty sessions hosted by the SSH server has been reached.

- The public portion of the RSA key pair held on the client no longer matches the private portion of the RSA key pair held on the server. This is the case only when the RSA key pair on the SSH server has been zeroized and regenerated. This problem is resolved by deleting the old public key on the client and downloading a copy of the new public key from the SSH server on the switch.

Securing User Access

Management traffic is not the only traffic that needs to be secured in corporate networks. Different types of user traffic, such as user traffic from different parts of the organization, should be separated from each other. User traffic should also be kept separate from management traffic.

User traffic can be controlled using

- VLANs
- Port security
- Protected ports and private VLANs
- ACLs

Using Port Security, Protected Ports, and Private VLANs

Port security is an IOS feature available on the 6500 series, 3550 series, and 2950 series of Catalyst switches. The port security feature can be used to restrict input to an interface by limiting and identifying the MAC addresses of the stations allowed access to the port. When secure MAC addresses are assigned to a secure port, the port does not forward packets with source addresses outside the group of defined addresses. By limiting the number of secure MAC addresses to one and assigning a single secure MAC address to the port, the workstation attached to that port is assured the port's full bandwidth.

If a port is configured as a secure port and the maximum number of secure MAC addresses is reached, when an additional station attempts to access the port, a security violation is logged. Also, if a station with a secure MAC address configured or learned on one secure port attempts to access a different secure port, a violation is flagged.

Operation of Port Security

After the maximum number of secure MAC addresses on a port (the range is 1 to 128 with a default of 128) has been configured, the secure addresses are included in an address table in one of the following ways:

- Manual configuration of all secure MAC addresses by using the **switchport port-security mac-address** *mac_address* interface configuration command.

- The port dynamically configures secure MAC addresses with the MAC addresses of connected devices.

- Manual configuration of a number of addresses, with the remainder to be configured dynamically.

NOTE

If a port shuts down, all dynamically learned addresses for that port are removed.

As soon as the maximum number of secure MAC addresses is configured, they are stored in an address table. Setting the maximum number of addresses to 1 and configuring the MAC address of an attached device ensures that the device has the port's full bandwidth.

Port Security Violations

A security violation occurs in the following situations:

- The maximum number of secure MAC addresses has been added to the address table, and a station whose MAC address is not in the address table attempts to access the interface.

- A station whose MAC address is configured as secure on another secure port attempts to access the interface.

The interface can be configured for one of three violation modes, based on the action to be taken if a violation occurs:

- **Shutdown**—A port security violation causes the interface to shut down immediately, and send an SNMP trap notification. After it is shut down, the interface must be manually re-enabled by using the **no shutdown** interface configuration command. This is the default mode when port security is enabled.

- **Protect**—When the number of secure MAC addresses reaches the maximum limit allowed on the port, packets with unknown source addresses are dropped until secure MAC addresses are manually removed from the port's address table to create a free slot.

- **Restrict**—A port security violation causes a trap notification to be sent to the SNMP network management station.

By default, port security is disabled on a port. Port security defaults are a maximum of 128 secure MAC addresses per port and shutdown on security violation.

Protected Ports

Protected ports do not forward any traffic to other protected ports on the same switch. This means that all traffic passing between protected ports (unicast, broadcast, and multicast) must be forwarded through a Layer 3 device. Protected ports can forward any type of traffic to unprotected ports, and they forward as usual to all ports on other switches.

This functionality is available on the Catalyst 2950 series and 3550 series switches. The Catalyst 6500 series switch uses a technology called private VLANs. Although protected ports and private VLANs are conceptually the same, configuring private VLANs on the Catalyst 6500 series switch is significantly different from configuring protected ports on the Catalyst 2950 series and Catalyst 3550 series switches.

This section covers the configuration of protected ports on 2950 series and 3550 series switches. Refer to Cisco.com for information on configuring private VLANs on Catalyst 6500 series switches.

Protected ports provide Layer 2 isolation between ports within the same VLAN and have two common features:

- A protected port that does not forward any traffic (unicast, multicast, or broadcast) to any other port that is also a protected port. Traffic cannot be forwarded between protected ports at Layer 2. All traffic passing between protected ports must be forwarded through a Layer 3 device.
- Forwarding behavior between a protected port and an unprotected port proceeds as usual.

The factory default is that no protected ports are configured.

There could be times when unknown unicast or multicast traffic from an unprotected port is flooded to a protected port, because a MAC address has timed out or has not been learned by the switch. Using the commands **switchport block unicast** and **switchport block multicast** guarantees that no unicast and multicast traffic is flooded to the port under these conditions.

Using Access Lists

Packet filtering can help limit network traffic and restrict network use by certain users or devices. ACLs can filter traffic as it passes through a switch and permit or deny packets at specified interfaces. This chapter has also shown how ACLs can be deployed to control management sessions for remote control of the switch.

Recall that an ACL is a sequential collection of permit and deny conditions that apply to packets. When a packet is received on an interface, the switch compares the packet's fields against any applied ACLs to verify that the packet has the required permissions to be forwarded, based on the criteria specified in the access lists. The switch tests packets against the conditions in an access list one by one. The first match determines whether the switch accepts or rejects the packets. Because the switch stops testing conditions after the first match, the order of conditions in the list is critical. If no conditions match, the switch rejects the packets. If there are no restrictions, the switch forwards the packet; otherwise, the switch drops the packet.

Switches traditionally operate at Layer 2 only, switching traffic within a VLAN, whereas routers route traffic between VLANs. The Catalyst 3550 switch can accelerate packet routing between VLANs by using Layer 3 switching. The switch bridges the packet, the packet is then routed internally without going to an external router, and then the packet is bridged again to send it to its destination. During this process, the switch can use ACLs to filter all data it switches, including data bridged within a VLAN.

ACLs can be configured on a router or switch to provide basic security for a network. If ACLs are not configured, all packets passing through the switch could be allowed onto all parts of the network. ACLs can be used to control which hosts can access different parts of a network or to decide which types of traffic are forwarded or blocked at router interfaces. For example, an ACL might be configured to allow e-mail traffic but not Telnet traffic. Layer 3 ACLs can be configured to filter inbound traffic, outbound traffic, or both. ACLs on Layer 2 interfaces can filter only inbound traffic.

An ACL contains an ordered list of access control entries (ACEs). Each ACE specifies a set of conditions the data must match and a **permit** or **deny** action to perform when a match is found. The meaning of the **permit** or **deny** action depends on the context in which the ACL is used.

The 3550 switch supports two types of ACLs:

- IP ACLs to filter IP traffic at Layer 3, including TCP, UDP, Internet Group Management Protocol (IGMP), and Internet Control Message Protocol (ICMP).
- Ethernet or MAC ACLs to filter traffic at Layer 2.

The switch supports three applications of ACLs to filter traffic:

- Router ACLs filter routed traffic between VLANs and are applied to Layer 3 interfaces based on the following criteria:
  - Source address(es)
  - Destination address(es)
  - Source IP port(s)
  - Destination IP port(s)
  - Individual host address
  - Address range or pattern
  - Port range
  - Inbound/outbound/bidirectional traffic

One router ACL can be applied in each direction on an interface.

- Port ACLs filter traffic entering a Layer 2 interface. The switch does not support port ACLs in the outbound direction. Only one IP access list and one MAC access list to a Layer 2 interface can be applied.

- VLAN ACLs or VLAN maps filter all packets (bridged and routed). VLAN maps are used to filter traffic between devices in the same VLAN or to provide Layer 3 access control based on IP addresses. Unsupported protocols are filtered through MAC addresses by using Ethernet ACEs. After a VLAN map is applied to a VLAN, all packets (routed or bridged) entering the VLAN are checked against the VLAN map. Packets can enter the VLAN either through a switch port at Layer 2 or through a routed port after being routed at Layer 3.

Both router ACLs and VLAN maps can be used on the same switch. However, port ACLs cannot be used on a switch that contains VLAN maps or inbound router ACLs.

When a switch has a Layer 2 interface with an applied IP ACL or MAC ACL, IP ACLs and VLAN maps can be created. However, an IP ACL cannot be applied to an input Layer 3 interface on that switch. Also, a VLAN map cannot be applied to any of the switch VLANs; an error message is generated if this is attempted. An IP ACL can still be applied to an output Layer 3 interface on a switch with port ACLs.

When a switch has an input Layer 3 ACL or a VLAN map applied to it, an IP ACL or MAC ACL cannot be applied to a Layer 2 interface on that switch; an error message is generated if this is attempted. However, a port ACL can be applied if the switch has an ACL applied only to an output Layer 3 interface.

If 802.1Q tunneling is configured on an interface, any 802.1Q encapsulated IP packets received on the tunnel port can be filtered by MAC ACLs at Layer 2, but not by IP ACLs at Layer 3. This is because the switch does not recognize the protocol inside the 802.1Q header. This restriction applies to router ACLs, port ACLs, and VLAN maps.

Router ACLs

Router ACLs can be applied on the following interface types:

- Switch virtual interfaces (SVIs), which are Layer 3 interfaces to VLANs
- Physical Layer 3 interfaces
- Layer 3 EtherChannel interfaces

Router ACLs are applied on interfaces for specific directions (inbound or outbound). One IP ACL in each direction can be specified.

One ACL can be used with multiple features (such as QoS) for a given interface, and one feature can use multiple ACLs. When a single router ACL is used by multiple features, it is examined multiple times.

Standard IP ACLs use source addresses for matching operations.

Extended IP ACLs use source and destination addresses and optional protocol type information for matching operations.

The switch examines ACLs associated with features configured on a given interface and direction. As packets enter the switch on an interface, ACLs associated with all inbound features configured on that interface are examined. After packets are routed and before they are forwarded to the next hop, all ACLs associated with outbound features configured on the egress interface are examined.

ACLs permit or deny packet forwarding based on how the packet matches the entries in the ACL. For example, ACLs can be used to allow one host to access part of a network and prevent another host from accessing the same part. As shown in Figure 9-25, ACLs applied at the router input allow Host A to access the Human Resources network and prevent Host B from accessing the same network.

Figure 9-25 Routed Traffic Is Filtered with a Router ACL

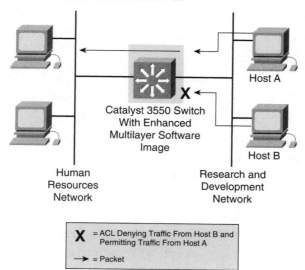

Port ACLs

ACLs can also be applied to Layer 2 interfaces on a switch. *Port ACLs* are supported on physical interfaces only, not on EtherChannel interfaces. Port ACLs are applied on interfaces for inbound traffic only.

The following port ACLs are supported on Layer 2 interfaces:

- Standard IP ACLs using source addresses
- Extended IP ACLs using source and destination addresses and optional protocol type information
- MAC extended ACLs using source and destination MAC addresses and optional protocol type information

Similar to router ACLs, with port ACLs, the switch examines ACLs associated with features configured on a given interface and permits or denies packet forwarding based on how the packet matches the entries in the ACL.

However, ACLs can be applied only to Layer 2 interfaces in the inbound direction. For instance, in the network setup shown in Figure 9-25, if all workstations were in the same VLAN, ACLs applied at the Layer 2 input would allow Host A to access the Human Resources network and prevent Host B from accessing the same network.

When a port ACL is applied to a trunk port, the ACL filters traffic on all VLANs present on the trunk port. When a port ACL is applied to a port with voice VLAN, the ACL filters traffic on both data and voice VLANs.

With port ACLs, IP traffic can be filtered using IP ACLs. Using MAC ACLs permits non-IP traffic to be filtered. Both IP and non-IP traffic can be filtered on the same Layer 2 interface by applying both an IP ACL and a MAC ACL to the interface.

Only one IP ACL and one MAC ACL can be applied to a Layer 2 interface. If an IP ACL or MAC ACL is already configured on a Layer 2 interface and a new IP ACL or MAC ACL is applied to the interface, the new ACL replaces the previously configured one.

VLAN ACLs and VLAN Maps

VLAN maps, also known as *VLAN ACLs* or *VACLs*, can filter all traffic traversing a switch. VLAN maps can be configured on the switch to filter all packets that are routed into or out of a VLAN or that are bridged within a VLAN. VLAN maps are used strictly for security packet filtering. Unlike router ACLs, VLAN maps are not defined by direction (input or output).

VLAN maps can be configured to filter on packet characteristics and Layer 3 and Layer 4. All non-IP protocols are filtered through MAC addresses and Ethertype using MAC VLAN maps (IP traffic is not filtered by MAC VLAN maps). VLAN maps can be enforced only on packets going through the switch; VLAN maps cannot be enforced on traffic between hosts on a hub or on another switch connected to this switch.

With VLAN maps, forwarding of packets is permitted or denied based on the action specified in the map. VLAN maps use **match** clauses to select traffic and perform operations on it. Each clause contains one or more access lists, each of which uses permit and deny actions to select or ignore traffic. VLAN maps are like access lists made up of other access lists. Figure 9-26 illustrates how a VLAN map is applied to deny a specific type of traffic from Host A in VLAN 10 from being forwarded.

Figure 9-26 Intra-VLAN Traffic Is Filtered with VLAN Maps

Host A
(VLAN 10)

Catalyst 3550 Switch
Bridging Traffic

Host B
(VLAN 10)

VLAN maps are the only way to control filtering within a VLAN. VLAN maps have no direction. That is, unlike IP ACLs, VLAN maps do not differentiate between inbound and outbound traffic. To filter traffic in a specific direction using a VLAN map, you need to include an ACL with specific source or destination addresses. If there is a **match** clause for a type of packet (IP or MAC) in the VLAN map, and that packet does not match any of the entries in the map, the default VLAN map action is to drop the packet. If there is no **match** clause for that type of packet, the default is to forward the packet.

Before creating the VLAN map, create the standard or extended IP ACLs or named MAC extended ACLs to be applied to the VLAN. This ACL selects the traffic that will be either forwarded or dropped by the access map. Only traffic matching the **permit** condition in an ACL is passed to the access map for further processing.

To create a VLAN map and apply it to one or more VLANs, follow the steps shown in Table 9-13.

Table 9-13 Configuring VLAN Maps

Step	Command	Description
1	**configure terminal**	Enters global configuration mode.
2	**vlan access-map** *name* [*number*]	Creates a VLAN map and gives it a name and (optionally) a number.
		Each VLAN map can have multiple entries. The order of these entries is determined by the *number*. If no sequence number is entered, access map entries are added with sequence numbers in increments of 10.
		When modifying or deleting maps, enter the number of the map entry to be modified or deleted.
		Entering this command puts the command-line interface into access map configuration mode.
3	**action {drop | forward}**	In access map configuration mode, optionally enter an **action forward** or **action drop**. The default is to forward traffic.
4	**match {ip | mac} address** {*access-list name/number*} [*access-list name/ number*]	Enter the **match** command to specify an IP packet or a non-IP packet (with only a known MAC address) and to match the packet against one or more ACLs (standard or extended).
		Note that packets are matched only against access lists or the correct protocol type. IP packets are matched against standard or extended IP access lists. Non-IP packets are matched only against named MAC extended access lists.
5	**vlan filter** *access-map-name* **vlan-list** *vlan-list*	Use this global configuration command to apply a VLAN map to one or more VLANs. A single access map can be used on multiple VLANs.

Note that a VLAN map cannot be applied to a VLAN on a switch that has ACLs applied to Layer 2 interfaces (port ACLs).

 Lab 9.9.11   Configuring VLAN Maps

In this lab exercise, you configure VACLs for IP addresses in a common VLAN.

Configuring and Verifying Port Security

Follow these guidelines when configuring port security:

- A protected port cannot be a routed port.
- A secure port cannot be a dynamic access port or a trunk port.
- A protected port cannot be a secure port.
- A secure port cannot be a destination port for a SPAN.
- A secure port cannot belong to a Fast EtherChannel or Gigabit EtherChannel port group.
- A secure port cannot be an 802.1x port. Attempting to enable 802.1x on a secure port results in an error message, and 802.1x is not enabled. Attempting to change an 802.1x-enabled port to a secure port also results in an error message, and the security settings are not changed.

Beginning in privileged EXEC mode, follow the steps listed in Table 9-14 to restrict input to an interface using port security.

Table 9-14 Port Security Can Be Used to Shut Down a Port Upon Unauthorized Access Attempts

Step	Command	Description
1	**configure terminal**	Enters global configuration mode.
2	**interface** *interface-id*	Enters interface configuration mode for the physical interface to be configured (GigabitEthernet0/1, for example).
3	**switchport mode** *access*	Sets the interface mode as access; an interface in the default mode (dynamic desirable) cannot be configured as a secure port.
4	**switchport port-security** *maximum-number-of-addresses*	(Optional) Sets the maximum number of secure MAC addresses for the interface. The range is 1 to 128. The default is 128.

continues

Table 9-14 Port Security Can Be Used to Shut Down a Port Upon Unauthorized Access
Attempts (Continued)

Step	Command	Description
5	**switchport port-security violation {protect	restrict	shutdown}**	(Optional) Sets the violation mode, the action to be taken when a security violation is detected as one of the following: **shutdown**—The interface shuts down immediately, and an SNMP trap notification is sent. When shut down, the interface must be manually re-enabled by using the **no shutdown** interface configuration command. **shutdown** is the default mode. **restrict**—A trap notification is sent to the network management station. **protect**—When the number of port secure MAC addresses reaches the maximum limit allowed on the port, packets with unknown source addresses are dropped until you remove a sufficient number of secure MAC addresses to drop below the maximum value.
6	**switchport port-security mac-address** *mac-address*	(Optional) Enters a secure MAC address for the interface. You can use this command to enter the maximum number of secure MAC addresses. If you configure fewer secure MAC addresses than the maximum, the remaining MAC addresses are dynamically learned.
7	**end**	Returns to privileged EXEC mode.
8	**show port-security interface** *interface-id*	Verifies the entries.
	show port-security address	Verifies the entries.
9	**copy running-config startup-config**	(Optional) Saves the entries in the configuration file.

To return the interface to the default condition (a nonsecure port), use the **no switchport port-security** interface configuration command.

To return the interface to the default number of secure MAC addresses (128), use the **no switchport port-security maximum** *maximum-number-of-addresses* interface configuration command.

To delete a MAC address from the address table, use the **no switchport port-security mac-address** *mac_address* command.

To return the violation mode to the default condition (shutdown mode), use the **no switchport port-security violation {protect | restrict}** command.

The **show interfaces** *interface-id* **switchport** privileged EXEC command displays the interface traffic suppression and control configuration.

The **show interfaces counters** privileged EXEC command displays the count of discarded packets.

The **show storm control** and **show port-security** privileged EXEC commands display those features.

Lab 9.9.10   Configuring Protected Ports

In this lab exercise, you configure private VLAN edge protected ports.

Interactive Media Activity   Drag and Drop: Catalyst Port Security

After completing this Interactive Media Activity, you will better understand port security configuration.

Configuring and Verifying Protected Ports

Starting in privileged EXEC mode, follow the steps listed in Table 9-15 to define a port as a protected port.

Table 9-15 By Default, Traffic Is Not Forwarded Between Protected Ports Without the Intervention of a Layer 3 Device

Step	Command	Description
1	**configure terminal**	Enters global configuration mode.
2	**interface** *interface-id*	Enters interface configuration mode for the physical interface to be configured (GigabitEthernet0/1, for example).
3	**switchport protected**	Configures the interface to be a protected port.
4	**end**	Returns to privileged EXEC mode.
5	**show interface** *interface-id* **switchport**	Verifies your entries.

To disable a protected port, use the **no switchport protected** interface configuration command.

 Interactive Media Activity   Checkbox: Catalyst Protected Port

After completing this Interactive Media Activity, you will better understand the configuration of protected ports.

Configuring and Verifying Access Lists

This section describes how to create switch ACLs. Recall that the switch tests packets against the conditions in an ACL one by one. The first match determines whether the switch accepts or rejects the packet. Because the switch stops testing conditions after the first match, the order of the conditions is critical. If no conditions match, the switch denies the packet.

Follow these steps to use ACLs:

Step 1   Create an ACL by specifying an access list number (see Table 9-16) or name and access conditions.

Step 2   Apply the ACL to interfaces or terminal lines.

Cisco IOS-based switches support the following types of IP ACLs:

■ Standard IP ACLs using source addresses for matching operations.

■ Extended IP ACLs using source and destination addresses for matching operations and optional protocol-type information for finer granularity of control.

Table 9-16 At Least 15 Different ACL Ranges Are Available for IOS Filtering

ACL Number	Type	Supported?
1 to 99	IP standard access list	Yes
100 to 199	IP extended access list	Yes
200 to 299	Protocol type-code access list	No
300 to 399	DECnet access list	No
400 to 499	XNS standard access list	No
500 to 599	XNS extended access list	No
600 to 699	AppleTalk access list	No
700 to 799	48-bit MAC address access list	No
800 to 899	IPX standard access list	No
900 to 999	IPX extended access list	No
1000 to 1099	IPX SAP access list	No
1100 to 1199	Extended 48-bit MAC address access list	No
1200 to 1299	IPX summary address access list	No
1300 to 1399	IP standard access list (expanded range)	Yes
2000 to 2699	IP extended access list (expanded range)	Yes

MAC extended ACLs use source and destination MAC addresses and optional protocol type information for matching operations.

In addition to numbered standard and extended ACLs, named standard and extended IP ACLs can be created. The advantage of using named ACLs instead of numbered lists is that individual entries can be deleted from a named list.

ACLs can be applied to any management interface, such as the switch virtual interface on a Catalyst 2950T.

The limitations that apply to ACLs on physical interfaces do not apply to ACLs on management interfaces.

After creating an ACL, you can apply it to one or more interfaces or terminal lines. You can also apply ACLs on inbound interfaces. This section describes how to accomplish this task for both terminal lines and network interfaces. Keep the following guidelines in mind:

- When controlling access to a line, numbered IP ACLs or MAC extended ACLs must be used.
- When controlling access to an interface, named or numbered ACLs can be used.
- Set identical restrictions on all the virtual terminal lines, because a user can attempt to connect to any of them.
- If applying ACLs to a management interface, the ACL filters only packets that are intended for the CPU, such as SNMP, Telnet, or web traffic.

Beginning in privileged EXEC mode, follow the steps listed in Table 9-17 to restrict incoming connections between a virtual terminal line and the addresses in an ACL.

Table 9-17 The Access Class Can Be Used to Restrict Access on Console and vty Lines

Step	Command	Description
1	**configure terminal**	Enters global configuration mode.
2	**line** | **console** | **vty** | *line-number*	Identifies a specific line for configuration and enters in-line-configuration mode. Enter **console** for the console terminal line. The console port is DCE. Enter **vty** for a virtual terminal for remote console access. The *line-number* is the first line number in a contiguous group that you want to configure when the line type is specified. The range is from 0 to 16.
3	**access-class** *access-list-number* {**in**}	Restricts incoming and outgoing connections between a particular virtual terminal line (into a device) and the address in an access list.
4	**end**	Returns to privileged EXEC mode.
5	**show running-config**	Displays the access list configuration.

Beginning in privileged EXEC mode, follow the steps listed in Table 9-18 to control access to a Layer 2 interface.

Table 9-18 A Port ACL Is Applied to a Layer 2 Interface

Step	Command	Description
1	**configure terminal**	Enters global configuration mode.
2	**interface** *interface-id*	Identifies a specific line for configuration and enters in-line-configuration mode. The interface must be a Layer 2 or management interface or a management interface VLAN ID.
3	**ip access-group** {*access-list-number/ name*} {**ia**}	Controls access to the specified interface.
4	**end**	Returns to privileged EXEC mode.
5	**show running-config**	Displays the access list configuration.

Use the commands listed in Table 9-19 to display the ACLs that are configured on the switch and to display the ACLs that have been applied to physical and management interfaces.

Table 9-19 The **show access-lists** Command Is Extremely Useful for Displaying Configured Access List Information

Command	Description
show access-lists [*number/name*]	Displays information about all IP and MAC address access lists or about a specific access list (numbered or named).
show ip access-lists [*number/name*]	Displays information about all IP address access lists or about a specific access list (numbered or named).

Authentication, Authorization, and Accounting (AAA)

AAA is an architectural framework for configuring three different security features:

- **Authentication**—Supplying user credentials to gain access to a system. Authentication asks the user who he is.

- **Authorization**—Limiting a user's access to certain "authorized" commands and options. Authorization asks the user what privileges he has.

- **Accounting**—Recording user activity for security, billing, or other purposes. Accounting records what the user did and when he did it.

Configuring a local database of usernames and passwords on the switch has already been covered in this chapter. AAA can also be used for login authentication. Using AAA for device logins offers three main advantages:

- **AAA provides scalability**—Many Cisco IOS devices can use AAA to refer to a common set of usernames and passwords on a central security server.

- **AAA supports standardized protocols**—Cisco IOS devices running AAA can communicate securely with security servers using protocols such as TACACS+ and RADIUS.

- **AAA allows for multiple backup systems**—Cisco IOS devices can consult a second or third source of information if the primary source of security information is offline.

Overall, these benefits mean that AAA provides scalability as well as increased flexibility and control of access configuration.

Network hosts are often configured to use a security protocol, as shown in Figure 9-27.

Figure 9-27 A Network Access Server Configured for AAA Can Authenticate and Authorize Remote Users Via TACACS+ or RADIUS

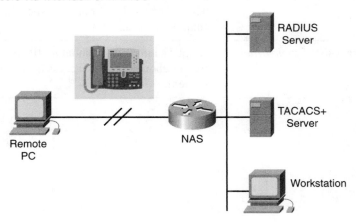

Hosts use a security protocol to communicate with a specialized security server. The security server maintains a password and username database, as well as authorization configurations, and stores accounting information. Cisco IOS supports three key security protocols:

- TACACS+
- RADIUS
- Kerberos

TACACS+ is a security application used with AAA that provides centralized validation of users attempting to gain access to a router or network access server. TACACS+ services are maintained in a database on a TACACS+ daemon running, typically, on a UNIX or Windows NT workstation. TACACS+ provides for separate and modular authentication, authorization, and accounting facilities.

RADIUS is a distributed client/server system used with AAA that secures networks against unauthorized access. In the Cisco implementation, RADIUS clients run on Cisco routers and send authentication requests to a central RADIUS server that contains all user authentication and network service access information.

Kerberos is a secret-key network authentication protocol used with AAA that uses the Encryption Standard (DES) cryptographic algorithm for encryption and authentication. Kerberos was designed to authenticate requests for network resources. It is based on the concept of a trusted third party that performs secure verification of users and services. The primary use of Kerberos is to verify that users and the network services they use are really who and what they claim to be. To accomplish this, a trusted Kerberos server issues tickets to users. These tickets, which have a limited life span, are stored in a user's credentials cache and can be used in place of the standard username and password authentication mechanism.

Of the three protocols, TACACS+ and RADIUS offer the most comprehensive AAA support. Kerberos provides a highly secure method of authentication, in which passwords are never sent over the wire. Kerberos does not support the authorization and accounting components of AAA and, therefore, is not covered in any detail in this chapter.

The following sections examine TACACS+ and RADIUS in detail. Table 9-20 compares the features of each.

TACACS+

TACACS+ provides the most comprehensive and flexible security configurations when using Cisco routers and switches. TACACS+ is derived from the TACACS and extended TACACS protocols. Both of these older protocols are considered "deprecated" protocols, which means that they are no longer seen as viable solutions. A Cisco-proprietary protocol, TACACS+ is incompatible with TACACS and extended TACACS.

Table 9-20 TACACS+ Versus RADIUS

TACACS+	RADIUS
A Cisco-proprietary enhancement to the original TACACS protocol.	An open standard developed by Livingston Enterprises.
Supports AAA functions.	Supports AAA functions.
Uses the AAA architecture, which separates authentication, authorization, and accounting.	Combines the functions of authentication, authorization, and accounting.
Provides two ways to control the authorization of router commands on a per-user or per-group basis.	Does not allow administrators to control which commands can be executed on a router.
Uses TCP.	Uses UDP.
Normal operation fully encrypts the body of the packet for more secure communications.	Encrypts only the password in the access request packet. Information such as username, authorization services, and accounting could be captured by a third party.

TACACS+ uses TCP to communicate between a TACACS+ server and a TACACS+ client, as shown in Figure 9-28. Use of TACACS+ is required to take advantage of all the features of AAA. Unlike RADIUS, TACACS+ separates the functions of authentication, authorization, and accounting.

RADIUS

The RADIUS protocol is a client/server protocol developed by Livingston Enterprises as an authentication and accounting protocol for use with access servers. RADIUS is specified in RFCs 2865, 2866, and 2868. Even though TACACS+ offers more flexible AAA configurations, RADIUS is a popular AAA solution. Because it is an open standard, it typically uses fewer CPU cycles and is less memory-intensive than the proprietary TACACS+. RADIUS is currently the only security protocol supported by emerging wireless authentication protocols.

Communication between a network device and a RADIUS server is based on UDP. Generally, the RADIUS protocol is considered a connectionless service. Issues related to server availability, retransmission, and timeouts are handled by the RADIUS-enabled devices rather than by the transmission protocol. Typically, the RADIUS protocol retries a transmission if a response is not received within a specified timeout period.

Figure 9-28 By Default, Traffic Is Not Forwarded Between Protected Ports Without the Intervention of a Layer 3 Device

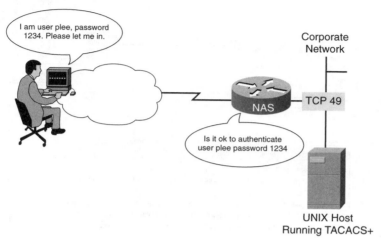

The RADIUS client is typically a network device, such as a network access server (NAS), a LAN switch, or a network router. The RADIUS server is usually a daemon process running on a UNIX machine or a service running on a Windows machine. The client passes user information to designated RADIUS servers and waits for a response. The RADIUS server receives the user connection request, authenticates the user, and returns the configuration information—accept, reject, or challenge—necessary for the client to deliver service to the user. Figure 9-29 illustrates the transactions between a client and a RADIUS server. A RADIUS server can also act as a proxy client to other RADIUS servers and other kinds of authentication servers.

Today, the emerging Extensible Authentication Protocol (EAP) relies on RADIUS services. EAP with RADIUS makes it possible to use various authentication methods on a network that are not supported by the NAS. This means that customers can use standard authentication mechanisms, such as random key tokens, smart cards, and public keys, to strengthen end-user and device-authenticated access to networks.

Variants of EAP, such as Cisco Lightweight Extensible Authentication Protocol (LEAP) and the standards-based Protected Extensible Authentication Protocol (PEAP), provide dynamic per-user, per-session Wired Equivalent Privacy (WEP) key enhancements to mitigate a variety of wireless network attacks. As more network professionals turn to EAP, LEAP, and PEAP to better secure their networks, RADIUS deployments will increase.

Figure 9-29 RADIUS Was Originally Designed for Dialup Clients

- User initiates PPP authentication to the NAS.
- NAS prompts for username and password (if PAP or challenge (if CHAP).
- User replies.
- RADIUS client sends username and encrypted password to the RADIUS server.
- RADIUS server responds with Accept, Reject, or Challenge.
- RADIUS client acts upon service and services parameters bundled with Accept or Reject.

Cisco Secure Access Control Server (ACS)

The Cisco Secure Access Control Server (ACS), shown in Figure 9-30, is specialized security software that runs on Windows 2000. Earlier versions of ACS (before ACS 3.1) ran on Windows NT and UNIX. The software simplifies and centralizes control of access control and accounting for dialup access servers, virtual private networks (VPNs) and firewalls, voice over IP (VoIP) solutions, broadband access, content networks, and wireless networks. Cisco ACS employs a web-based graphical interface and can distribute the AAA information to hundreds or even thousands of access points in a network.

The Cisco Secure ACS software uses either the TACACS+ or RADIUS protocol to provide network security and tracking.

Each network device can be configured to communicate with ACS. Service providers can use ACS to centralize control of dialup access. With a CiscoSecure ACS, system administrators may use a variety of authentication methods that are aligned with a varying degree of authorization privileges. Centralizing control of network access simplifies access management and helps establish consistent provisioning and security policies. For example, ACS can automatically disable accounts to prevent brute-force password-guessing attacks.

Cisco Secure ACS also acts as a central repository for accounting information. Each user session that is granted by the ACS can be fully accounted for and stored in the server. This accounting information can be used for billing, capacity planning, and security audits.

Figure 9-30 Cisco Secure Access Control Server Is Used for Enterprise Access Control

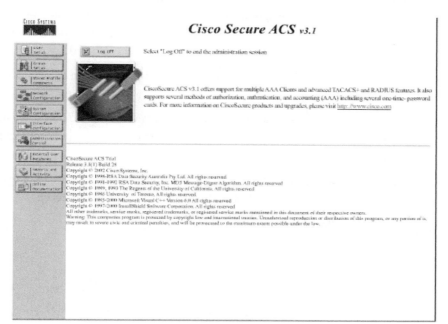

The web-based interface can be used to log in to the Cisco Secure ACS database and easily create user or group accounts, set passwords, or configure access controls.

Configuring AAA

Configuring AAA can be a complex process. It is imperative that security policies are well planned before beginning to configure AAA.

To enable AAA, issue the following command in global configuration mode:

```
Router(config)#aaa new-model
```

The **aaa new-model** command enables the AAA feature so that other AAA commands can be entered. To disable AAA, use the **no aaa new-model** command.

Do not issue the **aaa new-model** command unless you're prepared to configure AAA authentication. In some cases, just issuing this command forces Telnet users to authenticate with a username, even if no username database or authentication method is configured. If access to the router console is unavailable, access to the router is blocked.

The following sections describe how to configure the three elements of AAA using TACACS+, RADIUS, and local databases.

Configuring TACACS+ and RADIUS Clients

If a TACACS+ server is used in conjunction with AAA, the device must be configured with the address(es) of the server(s) and the TACACS+ encryption key. The encryption key must be the same on both the TACACS+ server and its clients.

To configure the address of a TACACS+ server, use the global configuration command **tacacs-server host** *ip-address*.

Use multiple **tacacs-server host** commands to specify multiple hosts. Cisco IOS software searches for the hosts in the order specified. The **tacacs-server key** *word* global configuration command configures the encryption key.

The following commands would be used to configure the router shown in Figure 9-31 to communicate with a TACACS+ server at 192.168.0.11 using the shared key **topsecret**:

```
RTA(config)#tacacs-server host 192.168.0.11
RTA(config)#tacacs-server key topsecret
```

Figure 9-31 Configuring a Router to Communicate with a TACACS+ Server

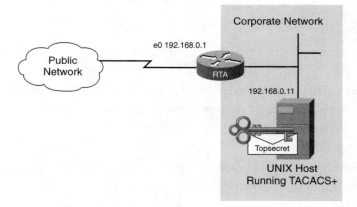

Use the **show tacacs** command to verify TACACS+ configuration and connection, as demonstrated in Example 9-17.

Example 9-17 *The **show tacacs** Command Displays the IP Address of the TACACS+ Server*

```
RTA#show tacacs
Server:192.168.0.11/49; opens=4 closes=4 aborts=0 errors=0
        packets in=6 packets out=6
        no connection
```

Like TACACS+, devices are configured to use RADIUS by specifying a server address and shared key.

Use the **radius-server host** *ip-address* global configuration command to specify an IP address for the server.

Use multiple **radius-server host** commands to specify multiple hosts. Cisco IOS software searches for the hosts in the order specified. Use the **radius-server key** *word* global configuration command to specify the encryption key.

To configure a router to communicate with a RADIUS server at 192.168.0.22, using the shared key **topsecret**, enter the following commands:

```
RTA(config)#radius-server host 192.168.0.22
RTA(config)#radius-server key topsecret
```

Configuring AAA Authentication

Authentication provides the method of identifying users, including

- Login and password dialog
- Challenge and response
- Messaging support

A Cisco Catalyst switch has several different types of authentication:

- When logging into the switch
- When accessing privileged EXEC mode
- When establishing a PPP connection to a router

A username and password that successfully authenticates for one type of access might not work for another.

The basic steps to follow when configuring AAA authentication are as follows:

Step 1   Turn on **aaa new-model** in the switch.

Step 2   Configure AAA server group(s).

Step 3   Configure AAA login method(s).

Step 4   Attach login methods to server groups.

Step 5   Attach AAA login method(s) to line(s).

AAA authentication can be used on Cisco Catalyst 6500 series, 3550 series, and 2950 series switches to configure the following configuration types:

- Access to the console
- Access to virtual terminals through Telnet and SSH connections
- Access to privileged EXEC mode (enable mode)

To configure access to the console, use the global configuration command **aaa authentication** *login method*.

Specify which type of authentication to configure (login, enable, PPP) when using this command. Table 9-21 lists some of the keywords used with the **aaa authentication** command.

Table 9-21 AAA Authentication Can Be Applied to Users Connecting Via PPP, Accessing a Line, or Entering Privileged Mode

Keyword	Description
arap	Sets the authentication method for ARAP.
enable	Sets the authentication method for privileged EXEC mode.
login	Sets the authentication method for logins and terminal lines, virtual terminal lines, and the console.
nasi	Sets the authentication method for NetWare Access Server Interface (NASI).
ppp	Sets the authentication method for any authentication protocol supported by PPP (Challenge Handshake Authentication Protocol [CHAP], Password Authentication Protocol [PAP], Microsoft CHAP [MS-CHAP]).

After an authentication type has been specified, define either a default method list or a named method list. Named method lists must be applied to a specific interface before any of the defined authentication methods are performed. The default method list is automatically applied to all interfaces if no other method list is defined.

These lists are called "method lists," because they list the types of authentication to be performed and the sequence in which they are performed. Authentication methods include the following:

- Using a password already configured on the router, such as the enable password or a line password
- Using the local username/password database
- Consulting a Kerberos server
- Consulting a RADIUS server or a group of RADIUS servers
- Consulting a TACACS+ server or group of TACACS+ servers

Note that a FAIL response is significantly different from an ERROR. A FAIL means that the user has not met the criteria contained in the applicable authentication database to be successfully authenticated. Authentication ends with a FAIL response. An ERROR means that the security server has not responded to an authentication query. Because of this, no authentication has been attempted. Only when an ERROR is detected does AAA select the next authentication method defined in the authentication method list.

One of the advantages of AAA is that more than one of these methods can be configured, and they are tried in sequence. For example, the router can be configured to authenticate PPP users by first consulting a group of RADIUS or TACACS+ servers. If the router is unable to connect to a server, a backup method, such as using the local username/password database, can be configured.

Using AAA, you can configure up to four methods in a method list, as illustrated in Figure 9-32. If all the defined methods return an error, the user is not authenticated.

Figure 9-32 Use the **aaa authentication** Command to Specify the Authentication Type, Method List Type, and Authorization Methods

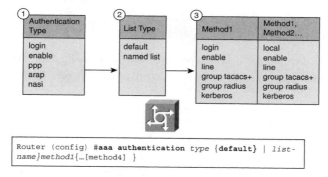

AAA commands can be confusing because there are so many syntax possibilities. When configuring AAA authentication, as illustrated in Figure 9-32, it is best to follow a three-step process for each **aaa authentication** command:

Step 1   Specify the authentication type (login, enable, PPP, and so on).

Step 2   Specify the method list as default or give it a name.

Step 3   List the authentication methods to be tried in order.

For example, the syntax for creating a method list to be used for PPP authentication is

```
aaa authentication ppp {default | list-name} method1 [...[method4]]
```

The **aaa authentication login** command enables AAA authentication for logins on terminal lines (ttys), virtual terminal lines (vtys), and the console (con 0). To create one or more lists that are tried at login, use the following command:

```
aaa authentication login {default | list-name} method1 [...[method4]]
```

The default list is applied to all lines. If a named list is configured, apply it to a specific line or group of lines using the **aaa authentication login** command.

The additional methods of authentication are used only if the previous method returns an ERROR, not a FAIL.

A typical ERROR is a failure to connect with a member of a server group because of link failure or a server-side problem.

To ensure that the user is granted access, even if all methods return an ERROR, specify **none** as the final method in the command line. If all defined methods end with an ERROR and **none** is not specified as the final method, the user is not authenticated. If authentication is not specifically set for a line, the default is to deny access, and no authentication is performed.

Depending on the network security policy, **none** may be configured as the final method. Alternatively, the security policy might dictate that denying access when all other methods return an ERROR is the most secure course of action.

Because this authentication method list specifies TACACS+ as the first method, the **tacacs-server host** and **tacacs-server key** commands are used to configure RTA as a TACACS+ client.

The **aaa new-model** command enables the AAA feature. Finally, the **aaa authentication login** command defines the method list. The method list configures RTA to attempt to contact the TACACS+ servers first. If neither server is reached, this method returns an ERROR and AAA tries to use the second method, the **enable** password. If this attempt also returns an ERROR (because no **enable** password is configured on the router), the user is allowed access with no authentication.

The default list is applied to the console (con 0), all tty lines (including the auxiliary line or AUX port), and all vty lines. The default method list can be overridden by a named list to one or more of these lines. Example 9-18 shows how to configure a named list for the network shown in Figure 9-33.

RTA is configured with the **radius-server host** and **radius-server key** commands, because the named method list relies on RADIUS. The **aaa authentication login default local** command configures the default method as the local username/password database. This method is applied to all ttys, vtys, and the console by default.

The **aaa authentication login PASSPORT group radius local none** command creates a named method list called **PASSPORT**. The first method in this list is the group of RADIUS servers. In the event that RTA cannot contact any RADIUS server, the local username/password database is tried. The **none** keyword ensures that, if no usernames exist in the local database, the user is granted access.

Figure 9-33 A Named List Can Be Used to Authenticate with a RADIUS Server

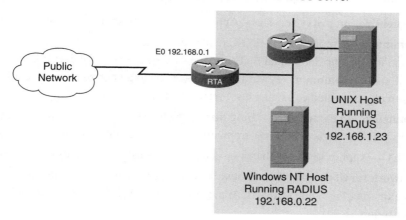

Example 9-18 *Configuring a Named List to Authenticate with a RADIUS Server*

```
RTA(config)#radius-server host 192.168.0.22
RTA(config)#radius-server host 192.168.1.23
RTA(config)#radius-server key top secret
RTA(config)#aaa new-model
RTA(config)#aaa authentication login default local
RTA(config)#aaa authentication login PASSPORT group radius local none
```

Apply named method lists for login authentication by using the line login authentication command **login authentication** *listname*.

To apply the **PASSPORT** method list to all five vty lines for the network shown in Figure 9-33, you would enter the following commands:

```
RTA(config)#line vty 0 4
RTA(config-line)#login authentication PASSPORT
```

Configuring AAA Authorization

AAA authorization enables service limits available to a user. When AAA authorization is enabled, the router uses information retrieved from the user's profile, which is located either in the local user database or on the security server, to configure the user's session. After this is done, the user is granted access to a requested service only if the information in the user profile allows it.

Cisco IOS Release 12.05T supports eight different options of authorization on a 2600 router:

- **Authentication proxy services**—Applies specific security policies on a per-user basis.
- **Commands**—Applies to the EXEC mode commands a user issues. To enable authorization for specific, individual EXEC commands associated with a specific privilege level, use the **command** keyword. This allows you to authorize all commands associated with a specified command level from 0 to 15.
- **Configuration commands**—Using **no aaa authorization** configuration commands stops the network access server from attempting configuration command authorization.
- **EXEC**—Applies to the attributes associated with a user EXEC terminal session.
- **Network services**—Applies to network connections. This can include a PPP, Serial Line Internet Protocol (SLIP), or AppleTalk Remote Access Protocol (ARAP) connection.
- **Reverse Telnet access**—Applies to reverse Telnet sessions.
- **Configuration**—Applies to downloading configurations from the AAA server.
- **IP mobile**—Applies to authorization for IP mobile services.

AAA authorization is configured with the **aaa authorization** command. You must specify the type of authorization when using this command. Table 9-22 lists and describes some of the keywords used with the **aaa authorization** command.

Table 9-22 A Number of Options Are Available for Defining Authorization to Switch Commands and Services

Keyword	Description
auth-proxy	Configures authorization for authentication proxy services.
commands	Configures authorization for EXEC commands.
config-commands	Configures authorization for configuration mode commands.
exec	Configures authorization for starting an EXEC session.
ipmobile	Configures authorization for Mobile IP services.
network	Configures authorization for network services.
reverse-access	Configures authorization for reverse Telnet connections.

As soon as an authorization type has been specified, define either a default method list or a named method list. Named method lists must be applied to a specific interface before any of the defined authorization methods are performed. The default method list is automatically applied to all lines and interfaces if no other method list is defined.

Table 9-23 lists the authorization methods and their IOS keywords.

Table 9-23 Authorization Methods Are Specified as Arguments to the **aaa authorization** Command

Keyword	Description
group tacacs+	TACACS+ authorization defines specific rights for users by associating attribute-value pairs, which are stored in a database on the TACACS+ security server, with the appropriate user.
group radius	RADIUS authorization defines specific rights for users by associating attributes, which are stored in a database on the RADIUS server, with the appropriate user.
if-authenticated	The user is allowed to access the requested function provided that he or she has been authenticated successfully.
none	The router does not request authorization information; authorization is not performed over this line/interface.
local	The router consults its local database, as defined by the **username** command, for example, to authorize specific rights for users. Only a limited set of functions can be controlled via the local database.

Before configuring AAA authorization, perform the following tasks:

Step 1   Enable AAA using the **aaa new-model** command.

Step 2   Configure AAA authentication. Authorization generally takes place after authentication and relies on authentication to work properly.

Step 3   Configure the router as a TACACS+ or RADIUS client if necessary.

Step 4   Configure the local username/password database if necessary. Using the **username** command, rights associated with specific users can be defined.

After TACACS+ and authentication are configured, configure authorization using the following global configuration command:

aaa authorization *type* {**default** | *list-name*} [*method1* [...[*method4*]]]

Figure 9-34 shows AAA authorization configuration.

The highlighted command shown in Example 9-19 configures authorization for reverse Telnet sessions for the network shown in Figure 9-35.

Figure 9-34 Use the **aaa authorization** Command to Specify the Authorization Type, Method List Type, and Authorization Methods

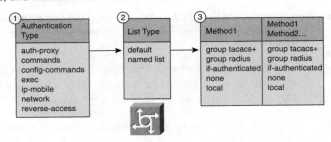

Example 9-19 *Configuring Authorization for Reverse Telnet Sessions*

```
RTA(config)#tacacs-server host 192.168.0.11 255.255.255.0
RTA(config)#tacacs-server host 192.168.1.23 255.255.255.0
RTA(config)#tacacs-server key topsecret
RTA(config)#aaa new-model
RTA(config)#aaa authentication login default group tacacs+ enable none
RTA(config)#aaa authorization reverse-access default group tacacs+
```

Figure 9-35 Authorization Can Even Be Configured for Reverse Telnet Sessions

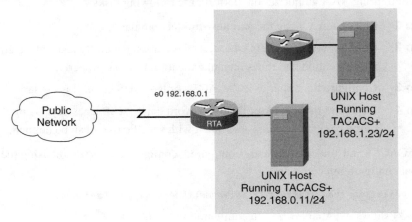

Users attempting to reverse Telnet from the router must be authorized to issue the command first by a TACACS+ server.

Example 9-20 presents a sample EXEC authorization configuration for the network shown in Figure 9-35. When configured with the highlighted command, the router contacts a TACACS+ server to determine if users are permitted to start an EXEC shell when they log in.

Example 9-20 *The Ability to Start an EXEC Shell Can Be Restricted Using AAA Authorization*

```
RTA(config)#tacacs-server host 192.168.0.11 /24
RTA(config)#tacacs-server host 192.168.1.23 /24
RTA(config)#tacacs-server key topsecret
RTA(config)#aaa new-model
RTA(config)#aaa authentication login default group tacacs+ enable none
RTA(config)#aaa authorization exec default group tacacs+ local
```

The **aaa authorization** command is used to control exactly which commands a user is allowed to enter on the router. Users can enter commands only at or beneath their privilege level. All IOS router commands are assigned a privilege level from 0 to 15. By default, the router has three privilege levels:

- **privilege level 1**—Nonprivileged (the prompt is router>), the default level for login.
- **privilege level 15**—Privileged (the prompt is router#), the level after going into enable mode.
- **privilege level 0**—Includes five commands: **disable**, **enable**, **exit**, **help**, and **logout**.

When a user logs in to the router EXEC via the console or a vty line, he or she can issue any command in **privilege level 1** and/or **privilege level 0** by default. After the user authenticates using the **enable** command and **enable** password, he or she has **privilege level 15**.

Levels 2 to 14 are not used in a default configuration, but commands that are normally at level 15 can be moved down to one of those levels, and commands that are normally at level 1 can be moved up to one of those levels. Obviously, this security model involves some administration on the router. To determine the privilege level as a logged-in user, use the **show privilege** command.

To determine what commands are available at a particular privilege level for the Cisco IOS software release being used, enter a **?** at the command line when logged in at that privilege level.

Instead of assigning privilege levels, command authorization can be done if the authentication server supports TACACS+. The RADIUS protocol does not support command authorization.

Which commands belong to which privilege levels can be precisely configured, including manually defined levels. The commands shown in Example 9-21 move the **snmp-server** commands from **privilege level 15** (the default) to **privilege level 7**. The **ping** command is moved up from **privilege level 1** to **privilege level 7**.

Example 9-21 *Commands Can Be Moved to a Lower Privilege Level*

```
RTA(config)#privilege configure level 7 snmp-server host
RTA(config)#privilege configure level 7 snmp-server enable
RTA(config)#privilege configure level 7 snmp-server
RTA(config)#privilege exec level 7 ping
RTA(config)#privilege exec level 7 configure terminal
RTA(config)#privilege exec level 7 configure
```

Use the **aaa authorization** command to grant access to commands by privilege level, as demonstrated in Example 9-22.

Example 9-22 *Access to Different Commands as a Function of Privilege Level Can Be Affected by Using the* **aaa authorization** *Command*

```
RTB(config)#aaa authorization commands 0 default group tacacs+ local
RTB(config)#aaa authorization commands 15 default group tacacs+ local
RTB(config)#aaa authorization commands 7 default group tacacs+ local
```

The user who logs in with level 7 privileges can **ping** and do **snmp-server** configuration in configuration mode. Other configuration commands are unavailable.

A user's privilege level can be determined by the security server or the local username/password database. To configure a local user for a specific privilege, use the following global configuration command:

username *name* **privilege** *level* **password** *password*

For example, the command used to create a user named **flannery** with a privilege level of 7 is

username flannery privilege 7 password letmein

When this user logs in, she has access only to commands in privilege level 7 and below.

Configuring AAA Accounting

Like authentication and authorization method lists, method lists for accounting define how accounting is performed and the sequence in which these methods are performed.

Named accounting method lists are used to designate a particular security protocol to be used on specific lines or interfaces for accounting services. The default method list is automatically applied to all interfaces except those that have a named method list explicitly defined.

As with AAA authentication and authorization, a defined method list overrides the default method list.

Accounting method lists are specific to the type of accounting being requested. AAA supports six different types of accounting:

- **Network**—Provides information for all PPP, SLIP, or ARAP sessions, including packet and byte counts.

- **EXEC**—Provides information about user EXEC terminal sessions of the network access server.

- **Commands**—Provides information about the EXEC mode commands that a user issues. Command accounting generates accounting records for all EXEC mode commands, including global configuration commands, associated with a specific privilege level.

- **Connection**—Provides information about all outbound connections made from the network access server, such as Telnet, local-area transport (LAT), TN3270, packet assembler/disassembler (PAD), and rlogin.

- **System**—Provides information about system-level events.

- **Resource**—Provides "start" and "stop" records for calls that have passed user authentication, and provides "stop" records for calls that fail to authenticate.

To configure AAA accounting, issue the **aaa accounting** command. When using this command, specify which type of accounting to configure. Table 9-24 lists some of the keywords associated with the **aaa accounting** command.

Table 9-24 A Number of Options Are Available to Account for Switch Commands, Connections, and Services

Keyword	Description
commands	Configures AAA accounting for EXEC commands.
connection	Configures AAA accounting for outbound connections, such as Telnet and rlogin.
exec	Configures AAA accounting for starting an EXEC session.
nested	Configures AAA accounting to generate NETWORK records before the EXEC-STOP records. This keyword formats accounting logs so that start and stop events are kept together, which might be useful for billing purposes.
network	Configures AAA accounting for networking services.

continues

Table 9-24 A Number of Options Are Available to Account for Switch Commands, Connections, and Services (Continued)

Keyword	Description
suppress	Configures AAA accounting to not generate accounting records for a specific type of user.
system	Configures AAA accounting for systems events.
update	Enables periodic interim accounting records to be sent to the accounting server.

NOTE

Note that the **system** option of AAA accounting does not support named method lists.

After an accounting type has been specified, define either a default method list or a named method list. Named method lists must be applied to a specific interface before any of the defined authorization methods are performed. The default method list is automatically applied to all lines and interfaces if no other method list is defined.

After specifying a named or default list, indicate the accounting record type using one of the following four keywords, one for each accounting record type:

- **none**—To stop all accounting activities on this line or interface, use the **none** keyword.
- **start-stop**—For more accounting information, use the **start-stop** keyword to send a start accounting notice at the beginning of the requested event and a stop accounting notice at the end of the event.
- **stop-only**—For minimal accounting, use the **stop-only** keyword, which instructs the specified method (RADIUS or TACACS+) to send a stop record accounting notice at the end of the requested user process.
- **wait-start**—As in **start-stop**, **wait-start** sends both a start and a stop accounting record to the accounting server. However, if the **wait-start** keyword is used, the requested user service does not begin until the start accounting record is acknowledged. A stop accounting record is also sent.

Finally, after specifying the accounting type and the accounting record type, configure the accounting method using the following command:

```
Router(config)aaa accounting type {{default} | list-name} record-type
    method1 [...[method4]]}
```

Figure 9-36 shows the AAA accounting configuration.

Figure 9-36 Use the **aaa accounting** Command to Specify the Accounting Type, Method List Type, Record Type, and Accounting Methods

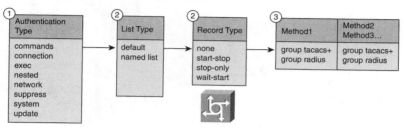

Before configuring AAA accounting, perform the following tasks:

Step 1   Enable AAA using the **aaa new-model** command.

Step 2   Configure the router as a TACACS+ or RADIUS client. This is required for AAA accounting. A server is needed to act as a repository for the accounting data.

Example 9-23 shows a possible AAA accounting configuration for the network shown in Figure 9-37.

Example 9-23 *Configuring AAA Accounting*

```
RTA(config)#tacacs-server host 192.168.0.11 255.255.255.0
RTA(config)#tacacs-server host 192.168.1.23 255.255.255.0
RTA(config)#tacacs-server key topsecret
RTA(config)#aaa new-model
RTA(config)#aaa authentication login default group tacacs+ local enable
RTA(config)#aaa accounting network default start-stop group tacacs+
```

The **aaa accounting network** command enables accounting for network services, which includes information for all PPP, SLIP, and ARAP sessions, including packet and byte counts.

Figure 9-37 Accounting Can Be Configured for Network Services, Such as PPP

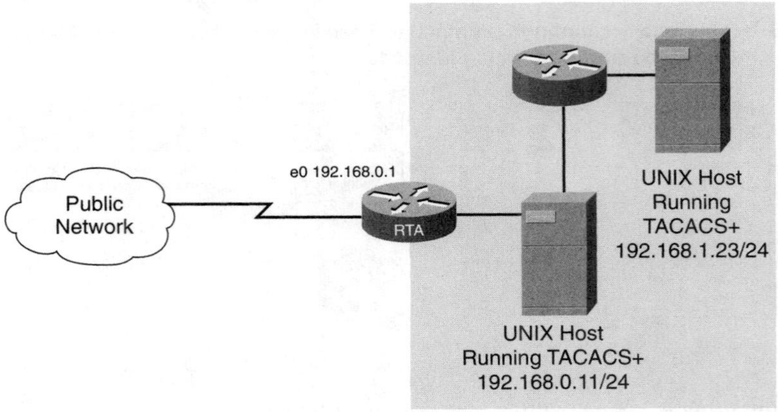

As shown in Example 9-23, RTA sends accounting information for PPP sessions to a TACACS+ server. The format of the output stored on the server varies, depending on the TACACS+ or RADIUS implementation. Example 9-24 presents sample TACACS+ output from a UNIX TACACS+ daemon.

Example 9-24 *Accounting Is Typically Logged on a TACACS+ or RADIUS Server*

```
Wed Jun 27 04:02:19 2001 172.16.25.15       fgeorge Async5
562/4327528 starttask_id=35
service=ppp
Wed Jun 27 04:02:25 2001 172.16.25.15       fgeorge Async5
562/4327528 update_task_id=35  service+ppp  protocol=ip
addr=10.1.1.2
Wed Jun 27 04:05:03 2001 172.16.25.15       fgeorge Async5
562/4327528 stoptask_id=35  service=ppp  protocol=ip
addr=10.1.1.2  bytes_in=3366  bytes_out=2149  paks_in=42
packs_out=28  elapsed_time=164
```

IEEE 802.1x Port-Based Authentication

The *IEEE 802.1x* standard defines a client/server-based access control and authentication protocol that restricts unauthorized clients from connecting to a LAN through publicly accessible ports. The authentication server authenticates each client connected to a switch port before making available any services offered by the switch or LAN.

Until the client is authenticated, 802.1x access control allows only Extensible Authentication Protocol over LAN (EAPOL) traffic through the port to which the client is connected. After authentication is successful, normal traffic can pass through the port.

With 802.1x port-based authentication, the devices in the network have specific roles.

A client is the device (workstation) that requests access to the LAN and switch services and responds to requests from the switch. The workstation must be running 802.1x-compliant client software, such as that offered in the Microsoft Windows XP operating system. (The client is the supplicant in the IEEE 802.1x specification.)

The authentication server performs the actual authentication of the client. The authentication server validates the client's identity and tells the switch whether the client is authorized to access the LAN and switch services. Because the switch acts as the proxy, the authentication service is transparent to the client. In this release, the RADIUS security system with EAP extensions is the only supported authentication server; it is available in Cisco Secure Access Control Server version 3.0. RADIUS operates in a client/server model in which secure authentication information is exchanged between the RADIUS server and one or more RADIUS clients.

A switch (edge switch or wireless access point) controls the physical access to the network based on the client's authentication status. The switch acts as an intermediary (proxy) between the client and the authentication server, requesting identity information from the client, verifying that information with the authentication server, and relaying a response to the client. The switch includes the RADIUS client, which is responsible for encapsulating and decapsulating the EAP frames and interacting with the authentication server.

When the switch receives EAPOL frames and relays them to the authentication server, the Ethernet header is stripped and the remaining EAP frame is re-encapsulated in the RADIUS format. The EAP frames are not modified or examined during encapsulation, and the authentication server must support EAP within the native frame format. When the switch receives frames from the authentication server, the server's frame header is removed, leaving the EAP frame, which is then encapsulated for Ethernet and sent to the client.

The devices that can act as intermediaries include the Catalyst 3550 multilayer switch, the Catalyst 2950 switch, or a wireless access point. These devices must be running software that supports the RADIUS client and 802.1x.

Authentication Initiation and Message Exchange

The switch or the client can initiate authentication. If authentication is enabled on a port by using the **dot1x port-control auto** interface configuration command, the switch must initiate authentication when it determines that the port link state transitions from down to up. The switch then sends an EAP-request/identity frame to the client to request its identity. (Typically, the switch sends an initial identity/request frame followed by one or more requests for authentication information.) Upon receipt of the frame, the client responds with an EAP-response/identity frame.

However, if during bootup the client does not receive an EAP-request/identity frame from the switch, the client can initiate authentication by sending an EAPOL-start frame. This prompts the switch to request the client's identity.

If 802.1x is not enabled or supported on the network access device, any EAPOL frames from the client are dropped. If the client does not receive an EAP-request/identity frame after a defined number of attempts to start authentication, the client sends frames as if the port were in the authorized state. A port in the authorized state effectively means that the client has been successfully authenticated.

When the client supplies its identity, the switch begins its role as the intermediary, passing EAP frames between the client and the authentication server until authentication succeeds or fails. If the authentication succeeds, the switch port becomes authorized.

The specific exchange of EAP frames depends on the authentication method being used. Figure 9-38 shows a message exchange initiated by the client using the One-Time Password (OTP) authentication method with a RADIUS server.

Figure 9-38 Authentication Initiation and Message Exchange Are Used with the One-Time Password Authentication Method with a RADIUS Server

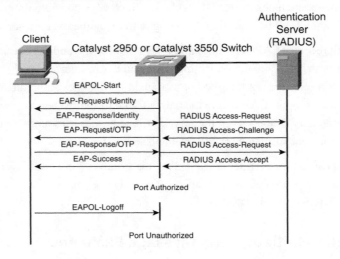

Ports in Authorized and Unauthorized States

The switch port state determines whether the client is granted access to the network. As shown in Figure 9-39, the port starts in the unauthorized state. While in this state, the port disallows all ingress and egress traffic except for 802.1x protocol packets. When a client is successfully authenticated, the port transitions to the authorized state, allowing all traffic for the client to flow normally.

Figure 9-39 IEEE 802.1x Port States Determine Whether the Client Is Granted Access to the Network

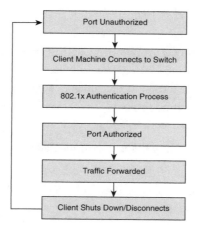

If a client that does not support 802.1x is connected to an unauthorized 802.1x port, the switch requests the client's identity. In this situation, the client does not respond to the request, the port remains in the unauthorized state, and the client is not granted access to the network.

In contrast, when an 802.1x-enabled client connects to a port that is not running the 802.1x protocol, the client initiates the authentication process by sending the EAPOL-start frame. When no response is received, the client sends the request for a fixed number of times. Because no response is received, the client begins sending frames as if the port were in the authorized state.

To control the port authorization state, use the **dot1x port-control** interface configuration command. Several keywords are associated with this command.

With the **force-authorized** keyword, 802.1x authentication is disabled and the port transitions to the authorized state without any authentication exchange required. The port sends and receives normal traffic without 802.1x-based authentication of the client. This is the default setting.

The **force-unauthorized** keyword causes the port to remain in the unauthorized state, ignoring all attempts by the client to authenticate. The switch cannot provide authentication services to the client through the interface.

The **auto** keyword enables 802.1x authentication and causes the port to begin in the unauthorized state, allowing only EAPOL frames to be sent and received through the port. The authentication process begins when the port's link state transitions from down to up or when an EAPOL-start frame is received. The switch requests the client's identity and begins relaying authentication messages between the client and the authentication server. Each client that attempts to access the network presents its MAC address to the switch for unique identification.

If the client is successfully authenticated (if it receives an Accept frame from the authentication server), the port state changes to authorized, and all frames from the authenticated client are allowed through the port. If the authentication fails, the port remains in the unauthorized state, but authentication can be retried. If the authentication server cannot be reached, the switch can resend the request. If no response is received from the server after the specified number of attempts, authentication fails, and network access is not granted.

When a client logs off, it sends an EAPOL-logoff message, causing the switch port to transition to the unauthorized state.

If a port's link state transitions from up to down, or if an EAPOL-logoff frame is received, the port returns to the unauthorized state.

Supported Topologies

The 802.1x port-based authentication is supported in two topologies:

- Point-to-point
- Wireless LAN

In a point-to-point configuration, only one client can be connected to the 802.1x-enabled switch port. The switch detects the client when the port link state changes to the up state.

If a client leaves or is replaced with another client, the switch changes the port link state to down, and the port returns to the unauthorized state.

Figure 9-40 shows 802.1x port-based authentication in a wireless LAN. The 802.1x switch port is configured as a multiple-host port that becomes authorized as soon as one client is authenticated. When the port is authorized, all other hosts indirectly attached to it are granted access to the network. If the port becomes unauthorized (if reauthentication fails or an EAPOL-logoff message is received), the switch denies network access to all the attached clients. In this topology, the wireless access point is responsible for authenticating the clients attached to it, and the wireless access point acts as a client to the switch.

Figure 9-40 IEEE 802.1x Is Frequently Used as a Component of an Enterprise Wireless LAN
Security Policy

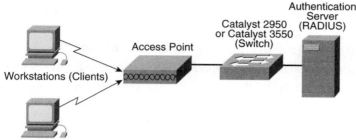

802.1x Configuration Guidelines

When the 802.1x protocol is enabled, ports are authenticated before any other Layer 2 feature
is enabled.

The 802.1x protocol is supported on Layer 2 static-access ports, but it is not supported on the
following port types:

- **Trunk ports**—Attempting to enable 802.1x on a trunk port generates an error message,
  and 802.1x is not enabled. The port mode does not change if the mode of an 802.1x
  enabled port is changed to trunk.

- **Dynamic ports**—A port in dynamic mode can negotiate with its neighbor to become a
  trunk port. Attempting to enable 802.1x on a dynamic port results in an error message,
  and 802.1x is not enabled. The port mode does not change if the mode of an 802.1x-
  enabled port is changed to dynamic.

- **VQP ports**—Attempting to enable 802.1x on a dynamic-access (VLAN Query Protocol [VQP]) port generates an error message, and 802.1x is not enabled. Attempting to
  change an 802.1x-enabled port to dynamic VLAN assignment generates an error message, and the VLAN configuration is not changed.

- **Active EtherChannel ports**—Before enabling 802.1x on the port, first remove the
  port from the EtherChannel before enabling 802.1x on it. Attempting to enable 802.1x
  on an EtherChannel or on an active port in an EtherChannel generates an error message, and 802.1x is not enabled. A port does not join the EtherChannel if 802.1x is
  enabled on a not-yet-active port of an EtherChannel.

- **Secure ports**—A secure port cannot be configured as an 802.1x port. Attempting to
  enable 802.1x on a secure port generates an error message, and 802.1x is not enabled.
  Port security settings do not change if an 802.1x-enabled port is changed to a secure
  port, and an error message is generated.

- **SPAN destination ports**—802.1x can be enabled on a port that is a SPAN destination port. However, 802.1x is disabled until the port is removed as a SPAN destination. 802.1x can be enabled on a SPAN source port.

Configuring 802.1x Port-Based Authentication

To enable 802.1x port-based authentication, AAA must be enabled. An authentication method list must also be specified. Recall that a method list describes the sequence and authentication methods to be queried to authenticate a user.

Table 9-25 lists the default 802.1x configuration settings.

Table 9-25 The Default 802.1x Configuration Settings Include a 60-Minute Delay for Reauthentication Attempts

Feature	Default Setting
AAA authentication	Disabled
RADIUS server IP address UDP authentication port Key	 None specified 1812 None specified
Per-interface 802.1x enable state	Disabled (force-unauthorized). The port transmits and receives normal traffic without 802.1x-based client authentication.
Periodic reauthentication	Disabled
Number of seconds between reauthentication attempts	3600 seconds
Quiet period	60 seconds (how long the switch remains in the quiet state following a failed authentication exchange with the client)
Retransmission time	30 seconds (how long the switch should wait for a response to an EAP request/identity frame from the client before retransmitting the request)

Table 9-25 The Default 802.1x Configuration Settings Include a 60-Minute Delay for Reauthentication Attempts (Continued)

Feature	Default Setting
Maximum retransmission number	2 times (the number of times the switch sends an EAP request/identify frame before restarting the authentication process)
Multiple host support	Disabled
Client timeout period	30 seconds (when relaying a request from the authentication server to the client, how long the switch waits for a response before retransmitting the request to the client). This setting cannot be configured.
Authentication server timeout period	30 seconds (when relaying a request from the client to the authentication server, how long the switch waits for a reply before retransmitting the response to the server). This setting cannot be configured.

The software uses the first method listed to authenticate users. If that method fails to respond, the software selects the next authentication method in the method list. This process continues until there is successful communication with a listed authentication method or until all defined methods are exhausted. If authentication fails at any point in this cycle, the authentication process stops, and no other authentication methods are attempted.

Beginning in privileged EXEC mode, follow the steps shown in Table 9-26 to configure 802.1x port-based authentication.

Table 9-26 AAA Must Be Configured Before 802.1x Is Enabled

Step	Command	Description
1	**configure terminal**	Enters global configuration mode.
2	**aaa new-model**	Enables AAA.

continues

Table 9-26 AAA Must Be Configured Before 802.1x Is Enabled (Continued)

Step	Command	Description
3	**aaa authentication dot1x {default}** *method1* [*method2*...]	Creates an 802.1x authentication method list. To create a default list that is used when a named list is not specified in the **authentication** command, use the **default** keyword followed by the methods that are to be used in default situations. The default method list is automatically applied to all interfaces. Enter at least one of these keywords: **group radius**—Uses the list of all RADIUS servers for authentication. **none**—Uses no authentication. The client is automatically authenticated without the switch using the information supplied by the client.
4	**interface** *interface-id*	Enters interface configuration mode and specifies the interface to be enabled for 802.1x authentication.
5	**dot1x port-control auto**	Enables 802.1x on the interface.
6	**end**	Returns to privileged EXEC mode.
7	**show dot1x**	Verifies your entries. Check the Status column in the display's 802.1x Port Summary section. An enabled status means that the port-control value is set to either **auto** or **force-authorized**.
8	**copy running-config startup-config**	(Optional) Saves your entries in the configuration file.

Summary

The requirement for monitoring and securing multilayered networks has increased with the advent of data-rich technology, such as voice over IP and streaming multimedia. This chapter covered discussing and implementing mechanisms for monitoring traffic and securing switches in a multilayer switched network to improve the quality of service delivered by the network.

The following traffic-monitoring technologies were discussed:

- SPAN
- VSPAN
- RSPAN
- Specialist traffic monitoring and control hardware

The following security-related technologies were discussed:

- Access control policy
- Basic security measures
- Communications encryption
- Securing remote management
- Securing user access
- Authentication, authorization, and accounting
- Port security
- Protected ports
- 802.1x port-based authentication

Key Terms

IEEE 802.1x   A standard defining a client/server-based access control and authentication protocol that restricts unauthorized clients from connecting to a LAN through publicly accessible ports. The authentication server authenticates each client connected to a switch port before making available any services offered by the switch or the LAN. Until the client is authenticated, 802.1x access control allows only Extensible Authentication Protocol over LAN (EAPOL) traffic through the port to which the client is connected. After authentication is successful, normal traffic can pass through the port.

Kerberos   A secret-key network authentication protocol used with AAA that uses the DES cryptographic algorithm for encryption and authentication. Kerberos was designed to authenticate requests for network resources. It is based on the concept of a trusted third party that performs secure verification of users and services.

Network Analysis Module (NAM)   A LAN monitoring solution that should be deployed at LAN aggregation points where it can see critical traffic and virtual LANs (VLANs).

Port ACL   ACLs can be applied to Layer 2 interfaces on a switch. Port ACLs are supported on Layer 2 physical interfaces only, not on EtherChannel interfaces. Port ACLs are applied on interfaces for inbound traffic only. They support standard IP access lists using source addresses, extended IP access lists using source and destination addresses and optional protocol type information, and MAC extended access lists using source and destination MAC addresses and optional protocol type information.

RADIUS   A client/server authentication and accounting protocol for use with access servers. RADIUS is specified in RFCs 2865, 2866, and 2868.

Remote Monitoring (RMON)   A monitoring specification that lets various network monitors and console systems exchange network-monitoring data. RMON gives network administrators more freedom in selecting network-monitoring probes and consoles with features that meet their particular networking needs.

Router ACL   An ACL that can be applied to SVIs, physical Layer 3 interfaces, and Layer 3 EtherChannel interfaces. Router ACLs are applied on interfaces for specific directions (inbound or outbound). One IP access list in each direction can be specified.

RSPAN   An implementation of SPAN designed to support source ports, source VLANs, and destination ports across different switches. RSPAN allows remote monitoring of multiple switches across a network.

Secure Shell (SSH)   A program to log into another computer over a network, to execute commands in a remote machine, and to move files from one machine to another. It provides strong authentication and secure communications over insecure channels.

Switch Fabric Module (SFM)   A line card that delivers an increase in available system bandwidth on a Catalyst 6500 switch from the default 32 Gbps on the forwarding bus to 256 Gbps. Including an SFM in a Catalyst 6500 chassis increases the speed at which switching, routing, and network monitoring modules can transfer data between each other. The SFM reduces latency and the incidence of packet drop caused by bandwidth bottlenecks at traffic aggregation points within the network.

Switched Port Analyzer (SPAN)   A tool used with Catalyst switches to enable the capture of traffic. A SPAN session is an association of a destination port with a set of source ports, configured with parameters that enable the monitoring of network traffic.

TACACS+   A Cisco-proprietary protocol used to authenticate users against a database. TACACS+ uses TCP to communicate between a TACACS+ server and a TACACS+ client.

VLAN access control list (VACL)   See *VLAN map*.

VLAN-based SPAN (VSPAN)   An analysis of network traffic in one or more VLANs.

VLAN map   Also called a VLAN ACL or VACL. Can filter all traffic traversing a switch. VLAN maps can be configured on the switch to filter all packets that are routed into or out of a VLAN or that are bridged within a VLAN. VLAN maps are used strictly for security packet filtering. Unlike router ACLs, VLAN maps are not defined by direction (input or output).

Check Your Understanding

Use the following review questions to test your understanding of the concepts covered in this chapter. Answers are listed in Appendix A, "Check Your Understanding Answer Key."

1. Which of the following are valid SPAN source ports?

    A. Layer 2 port

    B. Layer 3 port

    C. EtherChannel

    D. Trunk port

2. An RSPAN session requires the use of what type of port(s)?

    A. Source port

    B. Destination port

    C. Trunk port

    D. Reflector port

3. What Catalyst 6500 module is used to store and modify monitored traffic?

   A. Intrusion Detection Sensor

   B. Switch Fabric Module

   C. Network Analysis Module

   D. Supervisor Engine

4. What is the web interface used with the NAM called?

   A. Netsys Baseliner

   B. RMON 2 Viewer

   C. RMON Viewer

   D. NAM Traffic Analyzer

5. The Switch Fabric Module is used on which Catalyst switches?

   A. 2950

   B. 3550

   C. 6500

   D. 7600

6. Basic security measures include which considerations?

   A. Physical security

   B. Privilege level

   C. Remote access

   D. Password protection

7. The CoS is set to what value on traffic sourced by a Cisco IP Phone?

   A. 0

   B. 1

   C. 5

   D. 7

8. Out-of-band management is performed on what lines or interfaces?

   A. Ethernet

   B. Console

   C. Auxiliary

   D. vty

9. Secure Shell requires the use of what command(s)?

   A. **ip domain-name**

   B. **crypto key generate rsa**

   C. **ssh**

   D. **login local**

10. What type of access list filters both routed and bridged traffic?

   A. MAC ACL

   B. Port ACL

   C. VLAN map

   D. Router ACL

Objectives

After completing this chapter, you will be able to perform tasks related to the following:

- Identify the characteristics of an Ethernet service
- Describe the transparent local area network (LAN) services architecture
- Compare the benefits of transparent LAN service over legacy services
- Describe Cisco transparent LAN service solutions
- Describe transparent LAN service implementations

Chapter 10

Transparent LAN Services

This chapter introduces the characteristics of transparent LAN architectures and services in a metropolitan-area network (MAN). This chapter examines how transparent LAN services (TLS) enhance the services previously provided by existing technologies and describes the Cisco solutions.

Ethernet Solutions for Transparent LAN Services (TLS)

Cisco is committed to supporting the latest technologies in metropolitan optical networking, including TLS, dense wavelength division multiplexing (DWDM), course wavelength division multiplexing (CWDM), metro (Gigabit and 10 Gigabit) Ethernet, and Synchronous Optical Network (SONET)/Synchronous Digital Hierarchy (SDH) deployments. Several Cisco products are used to implement these technologies and services; in particular, the Optical Networking System (ONS) and the Carrier Routing System (CRS) product lines supports these diverse technologies.

VLAN tunneling is useful for extending and differentiating campus VLANs in a metro optical environment. This section introduces VLAN tunneling and contains an overview of the architecture used for metro optical networking, including points of presence (POPs) and the SONET/SDH/DWDM interconnections.

Same Network, New Services

Customers today have moved beyond the need for basic point-to-point Internet circuits and legacy voice lines connecting private branch exchanges (PBXs). With the steadily growing acceptance of voice over IP (VoIP) systems, increased demand for virtual private networks (VPNs), and expanding distributed mesh networking, as with mobile wireless, new systems have to be in place to support these infrastructures.

Transparent LAN Services (TLS) let the service provider offer the customer native LAN services over wide-area links without the need to implement complicated and costly Asynchronous Transfer Mode (ATM) networks. Figure 10-1 shows a TLS solution connecting gigabit service through a SONET/DWDM infrastructure. The same optical infrastructure is being used to carry IP over Gigabit Ethernet services, a feature that lets the service provider increase its offering over a common infrastructure. TLS can be incorporated into existing optical infrastructures.

Figure 10-1 Transparent LAN Services Include a Solution Connecting Gigabit Service Through a SONET/DWDM Infrastructure

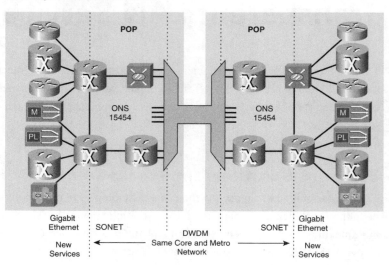

The Cisco ONS 15327 (see Figure 10-2) and Cisco ONS 15454 platforms (see Figure 10-3) support TLS today through the addition of Ethernet service cards. This support enables the migration or addition of TLS service offerings by service providers to existing optical network infrastructures without the need for costly equipment replacement. Through the addition of a single card, service providers can now offer additional TLS services to their clients.

Figure 10-2 The Cisco ONS 15327 Platform

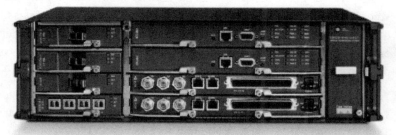

Figure 10-3 The Cisco ONS 15454 Platform

Figure 10-3 The Cisco ONS 15454 Platform

The following sections explore these concepts:

- VLAN tunneling
- Intermetro LAN transport
- Interservice point of presence (POP) connectivity
- Metro segmentation

These topics are all discussed in the context of TLS.

VLAN Tunneling

VLAN tunneling in the metro environment allows customers to extend their logical network topology across wide geographic areas. This comes into play especially when VoIP technologies are implemented. Without VLAN tunneling, customers are forced to renumber their existing VLANs, or the service provider is forced to provide some sort of VLAN translation at the access point to support multiple customers with overlapping VLAN numbers.

However, through DWDM and separate wavelength routing solutions, each customer is completely segmented from the others, allowing complete autonomy.

Figure 10-4 illustrates VLAN service for Customers A and B. VLAN tunneling allows the service provider to support overlapping VLAN numbers on the same physical port, as shown in Table 10-1.

Figure 10-4 VLAN Tunneling Permits Intra-VLAN Communication Over a MAN

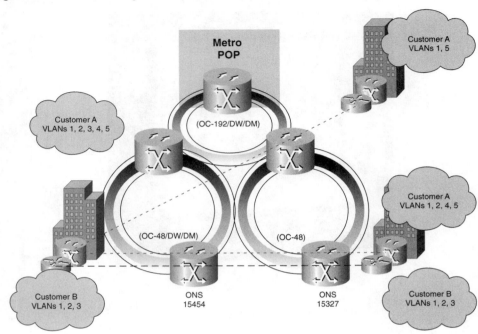

Table 10-1 VLAN Tunneling Allows the Service Provider to Support Overlapping VLAN Numbers on the Same Physical Port

Customer	VLANs
A	1, 2, 3, 4, 5
B	1, 2, 3

VLAN tunneling supports the isolation of Customer A's VLANs 1, 2, and 3 from Customer B's VLANs 1, 2, and 3 over the same physical optical interface. Therefore, support is provided for VLANs 1, 2, 3, 4, and 5 for Customer A and VLANs 1, 2, and 3 for Customer B over the same fiber.

Intermetro LAN Transport

As applications evolve, bandwidth needs increase. This increases the need for customer bandwidth across the wide area as well as internally. TLS allows the service provider to offer high-speed wide-area connectivity in a native LAN technology that the customer understands and already supports.

Speeds up to OC-192 can provide wire-speed gigabit connectivity (see the upcoming section "Defining SONET and SDH"). Gigabit Ethernet and 10 Gigabit Ethernet (10 GbE) over optical connections between two enterprise locations are now quite common (see Figure 10-5).

Figure 10-5 10 GbE Transports Over Optical Connections Are Becoming More Common in Intermetro Networks

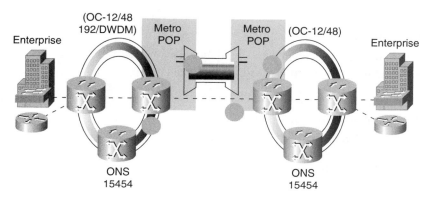

Interservice POP Connectivity

As multiple service providers team up to offer extended service offerings to their customers, the need for better interconnectivity increases also, as illustrated in Figure 10-6. TLS allows for high-speed interconnections in an easy-to-support technology, as well as providing point-to-multipoint connectivity.

Figure 10-6 Service Providers Can Work Together to Improve Interconnectivity with TLS and Better Service Customers

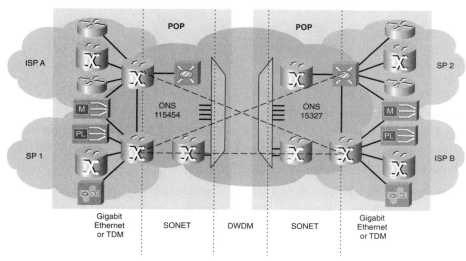

The benefits provided by TLS allow for the seamless interconnectivity of multiple service providers, which in turn allows for increased service offerings and support to the end customer.

Again, TLS enables the use of Gigabit Ethernet as a shared LAN in a metro optical environment. In Figure 10-6, ISPA and ISPB, along with service providers SP1 and SP2, can mutually share content as a result of Gigabit Ethernet over optical usage.

Metro Segmentation

Transparent LAN services integrate into a full metro-segmentation network architecture, as shown in Figure 10-7. The metro network is segmented into three areas:

- Customer premises equipment (CPE)
- Aggregation point for forwarding
- POP, used to interconnect to other networks, such as the core of other metro networks

Figure 10-7 TLS Services Integrate into a Full Metropolitan-Area Network Architecture

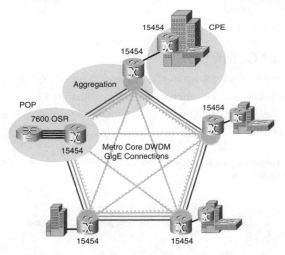

TLS provides for an economical, scalable, and established technology for connecting customers who require extended wide-area bandwidth. In addition, with its native quality of service (QoS) and VLAN support, customers have the advantage of advanced traffic shaping and flexibility in logical network design.

TLS can provide CPE user VLANs with QoS at gigabit speeds. At the aggregation point, TLS can provide a method to create shared multipoint connectivity that feeds into the POP. At the

POP, TLS can provide an access point for content networking, as well as an interconnecting point to transfer VLAN tunnels to the core network.

The benefits of integrating transparent LAN services into a full metro segmentation network architecture can be summarized as follows:

- Multiple service options:
    - Dedicated point-to-point Ethernet
    - Shared distributed multipoint Ethernet
    - Internet-scaled tiered bandwidth sharing
- One platform:
    - Access wavelength redundancy
    - Core route redundancy
    - Full-method Gigabit Ethernet data backbone
- Economical and scalable:
    - Pack wavelengths and bits
    - VLAN and Multiprotocol Label Switching (MPLS) VPN-enabled

Introducing Transparent LAN Services Architecture

The TLS architecture encompasses a wide range of services. Metro Ethernet services, such as Gigabit or 10 GbE Internet access and high-speed virtual private network (VPN) access, are available. IP+Optical is an emerging technology that provides high-speed man without relying on SONET/SDH or ATM. Point-to-point and multipoint Transparent LAN Services (TLS) circuits are options for providing bandwidth to the customer. The multipoint option has a greater reliance on QoS to provide guaranteed bandwidth to the customer.

Metro Ethernet Services

Understanding TLS architecture helps to facilitate network design and installation, as well as long-term operations and support. It is important to understand where TLS fits into an overall optical network architecture, as illustrated in Figure 10-8.

TLS is an ideal solution for providing shared bandwidth across a wide area, such as a distributed campus design, or for providing high bandwidth, where a LAN-based technology would facilitate operations. Typically, TLS falls within the metro-to-customer access role.

Figure 10-8 TLS Fits into an Overall Optical Network Architecture

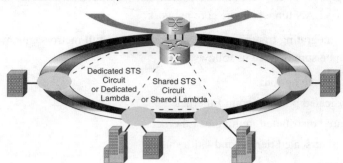

Four services can be offered by a metro Ethernet service provider:

- **High-speed Internet access**—Gigabit Ethernet to the POP for Internet access
- **High-speed VPN access**—Gigabit Ethernet connected into an MPLS backbone using a local MPLS provider edge router
- **Transparent LAN services**—Gigabit connectivity over a shared multipoint metro LAN
- **Point-to-point LAN services**—Gigabit point-to-point connectivity

The following section covers how TLS can be used in existing SONET-based networks and natively with the optical layer. The following sections elaborate on TLS in the metro environment in terms of

- IP+Optical efficiency
- Point-to-point dedicated
- Point-to-multipoint shared
- QoS

IP+Optical

IP+Optical removes the need to layer SONET or ATM technologies between the Layer 3 protocol and the optical physical layer, as shown in Figure 10-9. Removing this additional technology greatly increases overhead efficiency.

The Layer 3 protocol is required to provide end-to-end error checking and recovery, as well as any QoS. However, these functions are already built into the IP protocol.

Figure 10-9 IP+Optical Removes the Need to Layer Technologies Between Layer 3 and Layer 1

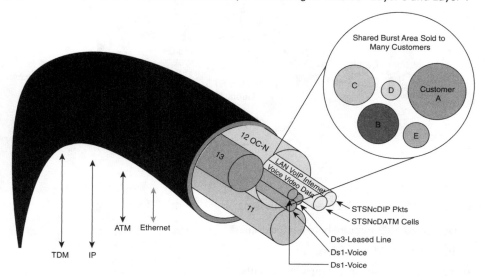

Some of the key benefits to IP+Optical technology are as follows:

- Efficient transport of time-division multiplexing (TDM), packets, cells, and frames through the reduction of packet overheads

- Services aggregated on Synchronous Transport Signal level 1 (STS-1), the basic building block signal of SONET, operating at 51.84 Mbps (nxSTS1) and wavelengths providing for easy manageability and bandwidth management

- Strong QoS and statistical multiplexing of bursty data traffic through existing support in the IP protocol

- Maintains existing Ethernet/IP/MPLS methods because these technologies are not changed at all—merely layered directly onto the optical layer

Point-to-Point Dedicated

Dedicated point-to-point TLS circuits provide guaranteed bandwidth to the customer. This allows for easily monitored service level agreement (SLA) offerings and network capacity planning. Ethernet bandwidth is layered directly onto an STS circuit running across the optical network.

A point-to-point Ethernet service can be sent over an optical STS core, as shown in Figure 10-10. The service is available with speeds of 10 Mbps, 100 Mbps, or 1000 Mbps. It can be purchased in 1-Mbps increments.

Figure 10-10 Point-to-Point Ethernet Service Can Be Sent Over an Optical STS Core

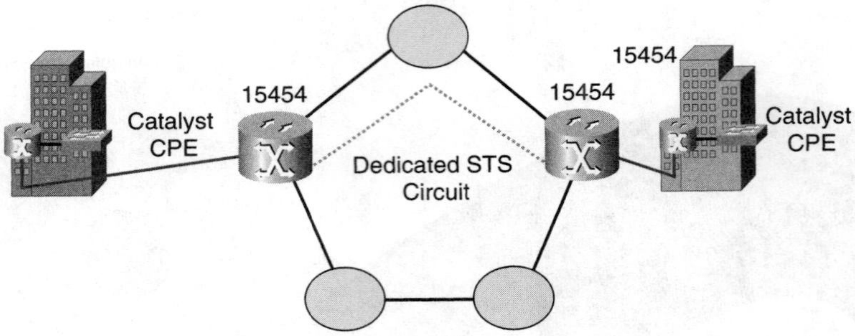

The optical STS core can include the following:

- Dedicated STS circuits between customers
- 10/100/1000-Mbps connecting
- Rate-limit service in 1-Mbps increments
- STS-24c capacity for line-rate Gigabit Ethernet
- STS-3c for Fast Ethernet
- Unidirectional path-switched ring (UPSR) wavelength redundancy

Point-to-Multipoint Shared

Shared point-to-multipoint TLS circuits provide greater flexibility from the service provider's perspective. Shared point-to-multipoint TLS circuits allow for a large bandwidth circuit to be created and additional drops to be added, necessitated by the acquisition of new customers. Careful monitoring of bandwidth requirements prevents one drop from starving the others, which is why QoS is important.

One of the best solutions for this design is in distributed campus models, where the customer needs a large bandwidth connection between multiple geographically dispersed sites.

Figure 10-11 illustrates a shared multipoint TLS solution interconnecting three remote sites on the right with the central site on the left. The shared multipoint TLS solution supports the following options or features:

- Hub-and-spoke connectivity
- Same lambda for multiple links
- VLAN association secures data
- VLAN- and MPLS-VPN-enabled

Figure 10-11 A Shared Multipoint TLS Solution Is an Option

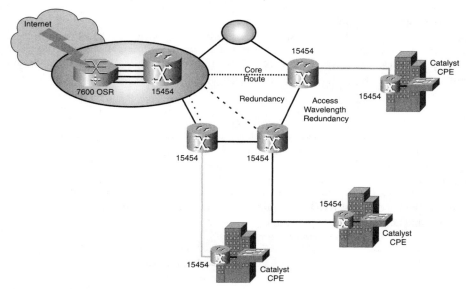

Role of QoS in TLS

QoS becomes an important part of the optical network with the implementation of TLS, especially with shared-bandwidth circuits. QoS is used to prevent one shared-bandwidth node from starving the bandwidth from others and can also be used to guarantee certain levels of service for all drops during times of peak usage (see Figure 10-12).

Figure 10-12 QoS Can Be Used to Guarantee Levels of Service for Customers

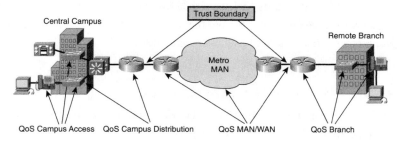

Table 10-2 defines the characteristics of QoS at the campus access layer, the campus distribution layer, in the MAN/wide area network (WAN), and within the remote branch.

Table 10-2 QoS Characteristics in an Optical Network Implementing TLS

QoS Campus Access	QoS Campus Distribution	QoS MAN/WAN	QoS Branch
Speed and duplex settings	Layer 3 policing	Multiple queues	Classification and trust boundaries on IP phone, access layer switch, and router
Classification/trust on IP phone and access switch	Multiple queues on all ports; priority queuing for VoIP	Low-latency queuing	Multiple queues on IP phone and all access ports
Multiple queues on IP phone and access ports	WRED within data queue for congestion management	Link fragmentation and interleave	
		Bandwidth provisioning	
		Call admission control	

Customers using private shared bandwidth services to connect a distributed campus network might also benefit from the implementation of QoS, because it allows customers to extend their own QoS model across the WAN network to other sites.

To summarize, TLS provides for either dedicated point-to-point or shared point-to-multipoint communication. IP+Optical reduces packet overhead, allowing increased bandwidth efficiency and allowing TLS to be layered directly onto the optical layer. QoS plays a large role in TLS networks, guaranteeing bandwidth to customers and nodes.

Examining Fiber-Optic Transports

This section discusses running Gigabit Ethernet over various transport mechanisms, such as SONET, Dynamic Packet Transport (DPT), and DWDM.

Defining SONET and SDH

Synchronous Optical Network (SONET) and *Synchronous Digital Hierarchy (SDH)* are standards for interfacing operating telephone company (OTC) optical networks. Together they are a set of global standards that interface equipment from different vendors, as documented in Table 10-3.

Table 10-3 SONET and SDH Are Standards for Interfacing Optical Networks

Optical Level	SONET Electrical Level	SDH Equivalent	Line Rate (Mbps)	Payload Rate (Mbps)	Overhead Rate (Mbps)	SONET Capacity	SDH Capacity
OC-1	STS-1	—	51.840	50.112	1.728	28 DS-1s or 1 DS-3s	21 E1s
OC-3	STS-3	STM-1	155.520	150.336	5.148	84 DS-1s or 3 DS-3s	63 E1s or 1 E4
OC-12	STS-12	STM-4	622.080	601.344	20.736	336 DS-1s or 12 DS-3s	252 E1s or 4 E4s
OC-48	STS-48	STM-16	2488.320	2405.376	82.944	1344 DS-1s or 192 DS-3s	1008 E1s or 16 E4s
OC-192	STS-192	STM-64	9953.280	9621.504	331.776	5376 DS-1s or 192 DS-3s	—
OC-768	STS-768	STM-256	39813.120	38486.016	1327.104	21504 DS-1s or 768 DS-3s	4032 E1s or 164 E4s

Although an SDH STM-1 has the same bit rate as the SONET STS-3, the two signals contain different frame structures.

STM = Synchronous Transport Module (ITU-T)

STS = Synchronous Transport Signal (ANSI)

OC = Optical Carrier (ANSI)

DS = Digital Signal

SDH is basically the international version of SONET, and SONET can be thought of as the North American version of SDH. SDH is growing in popularity and is currently the main concern, with SONET being considered as the variation. SONET's popularity is not shrinking, but SDH is gaining more and more popularity.

Both SONET and SDH can transport signals for all the networks in existence today, and they have the flexibility to accommodate any networks defined in the future. They are used in three traditional telecommunications areas: long-haul networks, local networks, and loop carriers. They can also be used to carry cable TV (CATV) video traffic.

There are some slight differences between SONET and SDH. The main differences are in the basic SDH and SONET frame formats, but SDH and SONET are essentially identical beyond the STS-3 signal level. The base signal for SONET is STS-1, and the base signal for SDH is STM-1. STS-3c is equivalent to STM-1, and the lower tributaries can be mapped interchangeably between the two formats from that point on.

STS-1

The Synchronous Transport Signal level 1 (STS-1) is SONET's basic signal rate. SONET adopts a frame length of 125 microns or a frame rate of 8000 octets per frame. Figure 10-13 shows the frame structure.

Figure 10-13 STS-1 Is the Basic Signal Rate for SONET

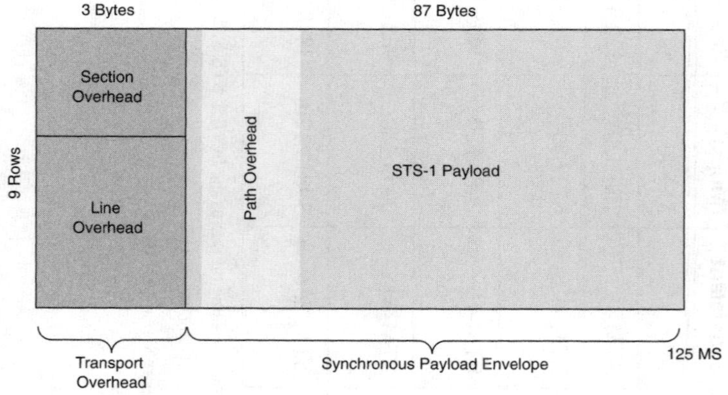

Each frame has 9 rows by 90 columns of octets, or bytes, forming a total of 810 octets per frame. This gives SONET a basic transmission rate of 51.840 Mbps. Of the 810 total octets, 27 are dedicated overhead. The first 3 columns make up the transport overhead, where 9 bytes are used for section overhead and 18 are used for line overhead. Columns 4 to 90 contain the Synchronous Payload Envelope (SPE), where the STS-1 path overhead is found. Because the first 3 columns are overhead, the actual data rate is 50.112 Mbps, rather than 51.840 Mbps. The STS-1 frame is transmitted starting from the byte in row 1 column 1 to the byte in row 9 column 90. The most significant bit of a byte is transmitted first.

Higher line rates are obtained by synchronous multiplexing of the lower line rates. The STS-1 signal can be repeated N times, where valid values of N are 1, 3, 12, 48, and 192. Therefore, STS-192 has a line rate as follows:

$\qquad$ 51.84 Mbps * 192 = 9953.28 Mbps

STM-1

The Synchronous Transport Module level 1 (STM-1) is the basic signal rate of SDH. Figure 10-14 shows the STM-1 frame structure.

Figure 10-14 STM-1 Is the Basic Signal Rate for SDH

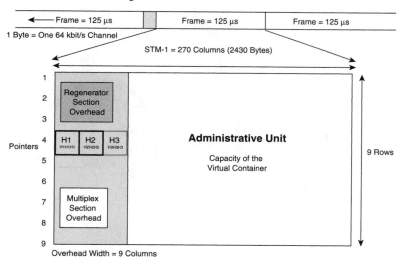

SDH also uses a frame length of 125 microns or a frame rate of 8000 octets per frame. The STM-1 frame consists of overhead plus a virtual container (VC) capacity. Each frame has 9 rows by 270 columns of octets, or bytes, structure totaling 2430 octets per frame. Of the 2430 total octets, 81 are dedicated section overhead. The first 9 columns make up the section overhead, and columns 10 to 270 make up the VC. The VC plus the pointers, H1, H2, and H3 bytes, is called the administrative unit (AU).

Carried within the VC capacity, which has its own frame structure of 9 rows and 261 columns, are the path overhead and the container. The first column is for path overhead, and the payload container follows it.

The STM frame is transmitted in a byte-serial fashion, row by row, like STS frames, and is scrambled immediately before transmission to ensure adequate clock timing content for downstream regenerators.

Regenerators extend a line's maximum distance and quality by decomposing it into multiple sections.

Applications for SONET/SDH

Optical networking has emerged as the foundation for campus, MAN, and WAN networking with the capability to integrate voice, video, data, and storage over a single network, as illustrated in Figure 10-15.

Figure 10-15   Optical Networking Is Becoming the Foundation of Virtually All Networks Beyond the Campus LAN Access Layer

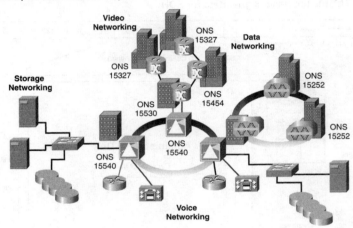

SONET/SDH provides increased bandwidth and performance while facilitating data center, application server, storage, and network infrastructure consolidation to optimize resources and reduce costs. In addition, optical networking supports storage-area networking (SAN) and IP-based network-attached storage (NAS) solutions to effectively access, manage, and protect corporate data and to provide the foundation of business resilience applications.

Implementing SONET/SDH Within a Metropolitan Network

High-speed MAN services can be layered over an existing SONET infrastructure. This allows for the smooth addition of services for the service provider and support for either point-to-point dedicated bandwidth or point-to-multipoint shared bandwidth to downstream devices.

The network shown in Figure 10-16 depicts the construction of a SONET-based transparent LAN network. The core is a SONET network, and the edge supports Ethernet. The Transport Layer Security data traffic can be metered as well as supported under various SLAs.

Figure 10-16 Routers Are Connected to a SONET/SDH Infrastructure by Way of a Third Party

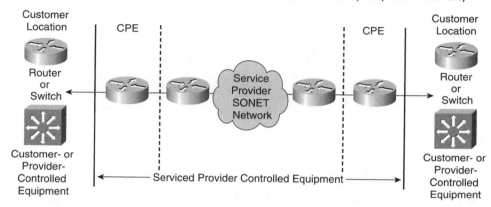

The SONET/SDH infrastructure includes the following features:

- Intrametro and intermetro
- Dedicated secure bandwidth
- STS-based circuits
- 10/100/1000-Mbps access ports
- Traffic metering via CPE
- End-to-end SLA planning

Defining Dynamic Packet Transport (DPT)

Dynamic Packet Transport (DPT), illustrated in Figure 10-17, is a resilient packet ring technology designed to deliver scalable Internet service, reliable IP-aware optical transport, and simplified network operations. For MAN applications, DPT-based solutions allow service providers to scale and distribute their Internet and IP services across a reliable optical packet ring infrastructure in a cost-effective manner. DPT is based on Spatial Reuse Protocol (SRP), a Cisco-developed MAC-layer protocol for ring-based packet internetworking. Cisco has submitted SRP to the IEEE 802.17 Resilient Packet Ring (RPR) Working Group for consideration as a standard.

Figure 10-17 Dynamic Packet Transport Is a Resilient Packet Ring Technology

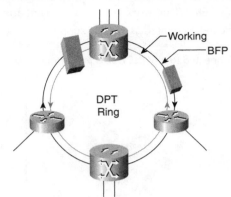

Some of the benefits of DPT are as follows:

- It replaces the complexity of SONET/SDH with the simplicity of Ethernet but retains the main benefits of SONET/SDH.
- It is an implementation of the Big Fat Pipe (BFP) concept. Bandwidth allocation is not fixed. The system tries to use all available bandwidth as much as possible using statistical time-domain multiplexing.
- It extends rich IP functionality over the metro area by replacing the legacy TDM nodes with DPT nodes and mapping the physical topology into IP.
- It significantly reduces the configuration management requirements because, from the IP perspective, a DPT ring is as simple to handle as an Ethernet segment.

At the time this chapter was written, the IEEE 802.17 standards were still in draft form. The new standard will use existing physical layer specifications (PHYs) and will develop new PHYs where appropriate.

Defining CWDM and DWDM

Dense wavelength division multiplexing (DWDM) employs multiple light wavelengths to transmit signals over a single optical fiber. Today, DWDM is a crucial component of optical networks, because it maximizes the use of installed fiber cable and allows new services to be quickly and easily provisioned over existing infrastructure. Flexible add/drop modules allow individual channels to be dropped and inserted along a route. An open-architecture system allows a variety of devices to be connected, including SONET terminals, ATM switches, and IP routers. Figure 10-18 shows this.

Figure 10-18 CWDM and DWDM Permit Multiple Channels to Share the Same Optical Fiber, with the Number of Channels Varying According to the Spacing of the Wavelengths

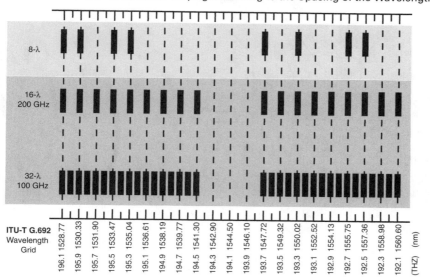

Coarse wavelength division multiplexing (CWDM) employs multiple light wavelengths to transmit signals over a single optical fiber. CWDM technology is a crucial component of Ethernet LAN and MAN networks, because it maximizes the use of installed fiber infrastructure at a very attractive price point.

CWDM technology is based on the same WDM concept as DWDM technology. The two technologies differ primarily in the spacing of the wavelengths, number of channels, and the capability to amplify signals in the optical space.

Implementing DWDM Over a MAN

The two largest problems facing service providers today in the metro environment are bandwidth scalability and fiber exhaustion. Figure 10-19 illustrates unused portions of bandwidth available on fiber links, or dark fiber.

DWDM addresses these needs through the use of wavelength multiplexing, as shown in Figure 10-20. Wavelength multiplexing allows a service provider to offer virtual dark fiber to individual wavelengths or lambdas as individual dark fibers. One fiber ring supports 16 individual lambdas. In addition, each lambda can support up to OC-48 speeds, allowing for unprecedented scalability and future growth.

Figure 10-19 Virtual Dark Fiber (Unused Fiber-Optic Bandwidth) and Bandwidth Scalability Are Important Variables for Service Providers

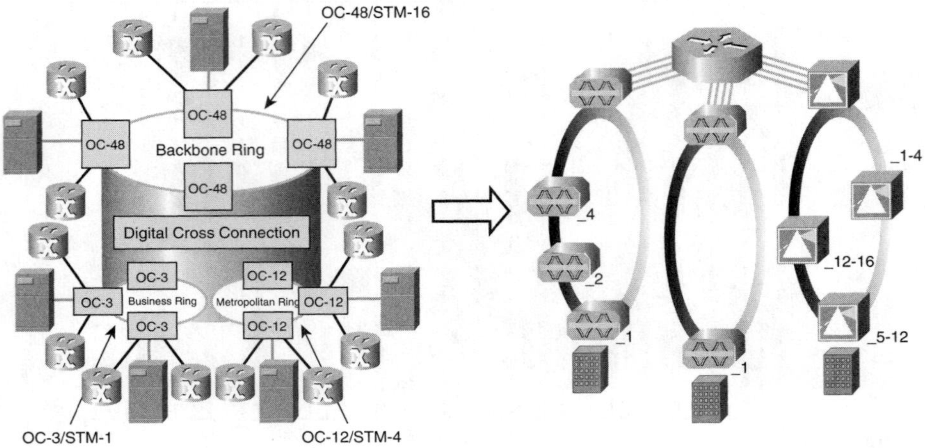

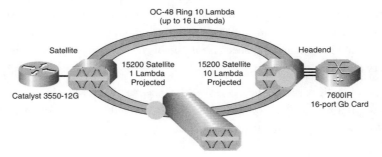

Figure 10-20 DWDM Uses Wavelength Multiplexing

Through the use of virtual fiber by DWDM, an existing fiber infrastructure can be segmented to allow multiple service offerings, as shown in Figure 10-21. This allows for flexible network topology offerings to the client and lower infrastructure costs to the service provider.

Figure 10-21 DWDM Optimizes the Use of the Existing Fiber Infrastructure

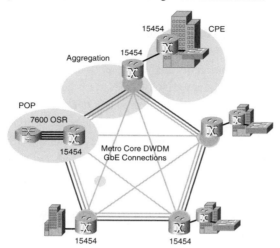

One fiber infrastructure can support a variety of service offerings and topologies:

- Dedicated point-to-point Ethernet
- Shared point-to-multipoint Ethernet
- Internet-scale tiered bandwidth sharing
- Access wavelength redundancy
- Core route redundancy
- Fully meshed Gigabit Ethernet backbones
- VLAN and MPLS support for QoS offerings

10 Gigabit Ethernet Standards

Positioned as a high-speed technology for networking applications in LANs, MANs, and WANs, 10 GbE provides very high bandwidth with simplicity and relatively low cost. In LAN applications, 10 GbE lets network managers scale their packet-based networks from 10 Mbps to 10,000 Mbps and, thereby, leverage their investments in Ethernet as they increase their networks' performance. In MAN and WAN applications, 10 GbE lets Internet service providers (ISPs) and network service providers (NSPs) create very high-speed links at very low cost between collocated carrier-class switches and routers.

In the Open System Interconnection (OSI) model, Ethernet is fundamentally a Layer 2 protocol. 10 GbE uses the IEEE 802.3 Ethernet Media Access Control (MAC) protocol, the IEEE 802.3 Ethernet frame format, and the minimum and maximum IEEE 802.3 frame size. Just as 1000BASE-X and 1000BASE-T (Gigabit Ethernet) remained true to the Ethernet model, 10 GbE continues the natural evolution of Ethernet in speed and distance. Because it is a full duplex-only and fiber-only technology, 10 GbE does not need the carrier sense multiple access/collision detect (CSMA/CD) access method that defines slower, half-duplex Ethernet technologies. In every other respect, 10 GbE remains true to the original Ethernet model. An Ethernet physical layer device, which corresponds to Layer 1 of the OSI model, connects the media, optical or copper, to the MAC layer, which corresponds to OSI Layer 2. Ethernet architecture further divides Layer 1 into a physical media dependent (PMD) and a physical coding sublayer (PCS). Optical transceivers, for example, are PMDs. The PCS is made up of coding algorithms and a serializer and often implements multiplexing functions.

The 802.3ae 10 Gigabit Ethernet specification defines two physical layer types, such as the LAN and WAN PHYs illustrated in Figure 10-22. The WAN PHY has an extended feature set added onto the functions of a LAN PHY. These PHYs are solely distinguished by the PCS.

Figure 10-22 The LAN and WAN PHY for 10 GbE Are Specified in the IEEE 802.3ae Specification

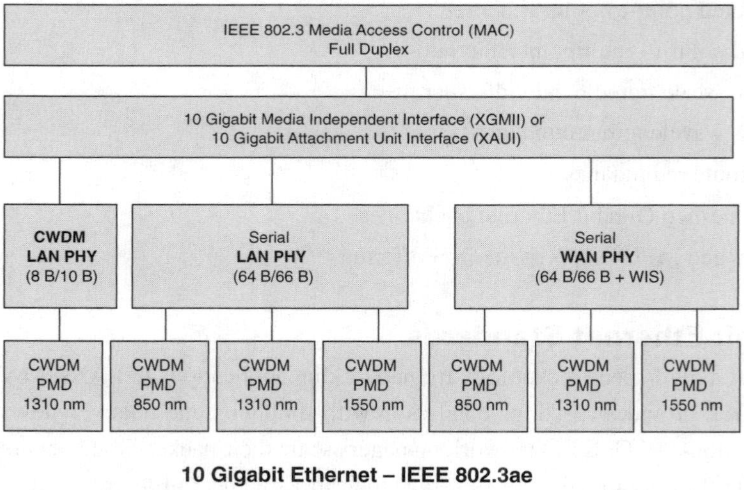

10 Gigabit Ethernet – IEEE 802.3ae

The WAN PHY differs from the LAN PHY by the inclusion of a simplified SONET framer. Because SONET OC-192 is within a few percent of 10 Gbps, it is simple to implement a MAC to be able to operate with a LAN PHY at 10 Gbps or a WAN PHY at the SONET OC-192 payload rate. To enable low-cost WAN PHY implementations, the IEEE 802.3ae committee specifically rejected conformance to SONET jitter, stratum clock, and other

SONET optical specifications. Therefore, the WAN interface sublayer (WIS) does not render a 10 GbE WAN PHY compliant with either SONET or SDH at any rate or format.

The LAN PHY is the most cost-effective solution to support the existing 10 GbE applications across LAN and MAN distances on dark fiber and dark wavelengths. However, it lacks the capability to speak the same language as the synchronous TDM gear most prevalent in the WAN environment. The WAN PHY can be used to connect Ethernet-based networks to the existing SONET/SDH TDM and DWDM infrastructure and support lit wavelengths and lit fiber over WAN distances.

The expectation is that the LAN PHY will also be used in pure optical switching environments extending over long-haul distances. This is possible because, by using optical equipment that incorporates the capability to transparently carry any higher-level technologies, such as 10 GbE, ATM, SONET, SDH, and so on, LAN and TDM services will seamlessly converge into a single optical infrastructure. This infrastructure will provide Layer 1 transport across MAN/WAN distances and will offer carrier-grade reliability while remaining completely technology-agnostic. Therefore, the importance of the WAN PHY for long-haul applications will also diminish.

Summary

Transparent LAN services provide up to 10-Gbps WAN connectivity across a wide geographic region, typically comprising a metropolitan area. The connectivity provided by TLS has the appearance of being realized over a local LAN while actually covering a wide geographic area. In particular, TLS lets VLANs span a MAN.

TLS can run over most high-speed WAN transports, such as SONET, SDH, and DPT. The Cisco implementation of TLS features Gigabit Ethernet or 10 GbE running over the underlying WAN transport.

Key Terms

coarse wavelength division multiplexing (CWDM) A technology that employs multiple light wavelengths to transmit signals over a single optical fiber. CWDM technology is based on the same WDM concept as DWDM technology. The two technologies differ primarily in the spacing of the wavelengths, the number of channels, and the capability to amplify signals in the optical space.

dense wavelength division multiplexing (DWDM) A technology that employs multiple light wavelengths to transmit signals over a single optical fiber.

Dynamic Packet Transport (DPT) A resilient packet ring technology designed to deliver scalable Internet service, reliable IP-aware optical transport, and simplified network operations.

Synchronous Digital Hierarchy (SDH) A standard for interfacing operating telephone company optical networks. SDH and SONET form a set of global standards that interface equipment from different vendors.

Synchronous Optical Network (SONET) A standard for interfacing operating telephone company optical networks. SONET and SDH form a set of global standards that interface equipment from different vendors.

Transparent LAN Services (TLS) A set of technologies that lets the service provider offer the customer native LAN services over wide-area links without the need to implement complicated and costly ATM networks.

VLAN tunneling A technology that allows customers in a metro environment to extend their logical network topology across wide geographic areas.

Check Your Understanding

Use the following review questions to test your understanding of the concepts covered in this chapter. Answers are listed in Appendix A, "Check Your Understanding Answer Key."

1. TLS solutions can be much less costly than which of the following traditional WAN solutions while providing equivalent or improved service?

   A. ATM

   B. ISDN

   C. Frame Relay

   D. X.25

2. What can be used to connect Ethernet-based networks to an existing SONET/SDH and TDM and DWDM infrastructure?

   A. PCS

   B. CSMA/CD

   C. WAN PHY

   D. PMD

3. Which two LAN and WAN technologies can be integrated relatively easily because of their comparable bandwidths?

   A. Fast Ethernet and OC-3

   B. Gigabit Ethernet and STS-1

   C. 10 Gigabit Ethernet and OC-192

   D. Standard Ethernet and STS-3

4. What is the maximum speed available with SONET?

   A. OC-48

   B. OC-192

   C. OC-384

   D. OC-768

5. What three areas are defined by a segmented metro network?

   A. Aggregation point for forwarding

   B. CPE

   C. LAN

   D. POP

6. What three service options are available with metro Ethernet?

   A. High-speed Internet access

   B. High-speed VPN access

   C. Remote access

   D. Point-to-point LAN service

7. Which of the following technologies removes the need to layer SONET or ATM technologies between a Layer 3 protocol and the optical physical layer?

   A. TLS

   B. 10 GEC

   C. IP+Optical

   D. TDM+Optical

8. What Cisco device can be configured to provide shared point-to-multipoint TLS?

   A. Catalyst 6500 NAM

   B. PIX 515

   C. ONS 15454

   D. Cisco 7600 router

9. Which of the following is a QoS feature commonly implemented in metro optical networks?

   A. Bandwidth provisioning

   B. CoS-to-DSCP mapping

   C. Priority queuing

   D. Compression

10. How many bytes are there per SONET frame?

   A. 210

   B. 410

   C. 810

   D. 1610

Check Your Understanding Answer Key

Chapter 1

1. Which of the following are key requirements in a modern campus network?

   A. Redundancy

   B. Scalability

   C. 80/20 rule

   D. Multicasting

   Answer: A, B, D

2. Which of the following is not a category of service in a campus network?

   A. Local

   B. Geographic

   C. Remote

   D. Enterprise

   Answer: B

3. Which of the following layers typically involve Layer 3 switching?

   A. Access

   B. Distribution

   C. Session

   D. Core

   Answer: B, D

4. What layer is the point at which end users are allowed into the network?

   A. Access

   B. Distribution

   C. Session

   D. Core

   Answer: A

5. Which of the following are backbone campus network solutions?

   A. Layer 2 switching

   B. Layer 3 switching

   C. Layer 4 switching

   D. ATM

   Answer: A, B, D

6. What type of cable is used to configure Catalyst 2950 switches through a console connection?

   A. Coaxial

   B. Straight-through

   C. Crossover

   D. Rollover

   Answer: D

7. What type of UTP cable can be used to connect FastEthernet ports on two Catalyst 3550 switches?

   A. Coaxial

   B. Straight-through

   C. Crossover

   D. Rollover

   Answer: C

8. What two commands are used to restore a Catalyst 3550 switch to a default configuration?

   A. **delete startup-config**

   B. **erase startup-config**

   C. **delete vlan.dat**

   D. **erase vlan.dat**

   Answer: B, C

9. Which of the following commands are used with password recovery on a Catalyst 2950 switch?

   A. **flash_init**

   B. **load_helper**

   C. **rename**

   D. **boot**

   Answer: A, B, C, D

10. What command is used to set the port speed to 100 on a Catalyst 3550 10/100 interface?

   A. **set speed**

   B. **speed**

   C. **bandwidth**

   D. **set bandwidth**

   Answer: B

Chapter 2

1. For which of the following VTP modes does a Catalyst switch listen to VTP advertisements?

   A. Client

   B. Server

   C. Transparent

   D. Peer

   Answer: A, B

2. Which of the following are Cisco-proprietary protocols?

   A. CDP

   B. VQP

   C. VTP

   D. ISL

   Answer: A, B, C, D

3. Which of the following are VLAN trunking methods?

   A. ATM LANE

   B. IEEE 802.10

   C. IEEE 802.1Q

   D. ISL

   Answer: A, B, C, D

4. Two devices in the same VLAN require a Layer 3 switch to communicate. What campus design model is used?

   A. Remote VLANs

   B. Campus VLANs

   C. Local VLANs

   D. End-to-end VLANs

   Answer: C

5. Which of the following are required for dynamic VLAN assignment to ports with VMPS?

   A. VQP

   B. VMPS server

   C. VMPS client

   D. TFTP server

   Answer: A, B, C, D

6. Which VLAN database configuration mode command is used to remove VLAN 20?

   A. **erase vlan 20**

   B. **clear vlan 20**

   C. **delete vlan 20**

   D. **no vlan 20**

Answer: D

7. What is the operational mode of a link when both ends are configured as dynamic desirable?

   A. Trunk

   B. Static access

Answer: A

8. What three commands are used to restore a Catalyst 3550 switch to a default configuration?

   A. **copy running-config startup-config**

   B. **erase startup-config**

   C. **delete vlan.dat**

   D. **reload**

Answer: B, C, D

9. Which construct can be used to filter both intra-VLAN and inter-VLAN traffic?

   A. Router ACL

   B. VLAN map

   C. IOS ACL

   D. Port ACL

Answer: B

10. Which of the following messages are used with VTP?

   A. Join messages

   B. Advertisement requests

   C. Subset advertisements

   D. Summary advertisements

Answer: A, B, C, D

Chapter 3

1. Which of the following is used in Root Switch election?

   A. Port ID

   B. Path cost

   C. Bridge ID

   D. Port priority

   Answer: C

2. What are the three steps of STP convergence?

   A. Elect a Root Switch

   B. Elect Designated Ports

   C. Elect Blocking Ports

   D. Elect Root Ports

   Answer: A, B, D

3. On an IOS-based switch, the Port ID is a 16-bit ordered pair composed of what two values?

   A. Port Preference

   B. Port Priority

   C. Port Number

   D. Port Cost

   Answer: B, C

4. The Bridge ID is an 8-byte ordered pair composed of what two values?

   A. Bridge Priority

   B. Bridge preference

   C. Bridge number

   D. MAC address

   Answer: A, D

5. Every active trunk port on the Root Switch is which of the following?

   A. Root Port

   B. Non-Designated Port

   C. Designated Port

   D. Blocking Port

   Answer: C

6. Which of the following are IEEE 802.1D spanning-tree states?

   A. Blocking

   B. Discarding

   C. Learning

   D. Forwarding

   E. Listening

   Answer: A, C, D, E

7. Which of the following are IEEE 802.1w spanning-tree states?

   A. Blocking

   B. Listening

   C. Learning

   D. Forwarding

   E. Discarding

   Answer: C, D, E

8. Multiple Spanning Tree is specified by which IEEE standard?

   A. 802.1D

   B. 802.1w

   C. 802.1Q

   D. 802.1s

   Answer: D

9. Which of the following spanning-tree parameters can be used to enable load sharing?

   A. Port Priority

   B. Bridge Priority

   C. EtherChannel

   D. Path Cost

   Answer: A, B, D

10. Which of the following are the two protocols used to create Ethernet channels or bundles?

    A. LACP

    B. VQP

    C. DTP

    D. PAgP

    Answer: A, D

Chapter 4

1. Which of the following are options that are available for inter-VLAN routing?

    A. Adding a route processor to a chassis-based switch with a daughter card or module

    B. Router-on-a-stick

    C. One router-to-switch link per VLAN

    D. Fixed chassis (nonmodular) multilayer switch

    Answer: A, B, C, D

2. What is required in a Layer 2 core with physical loops?

    A. Routing protocol

    B. HSRP

    C. STP

    D. VTP

    Answer: C

3. What is the most scalable inter-VLAN routing option?

    A. Layer 2 switch

    B. Layer 3 switch

    C. Router

    D. Router-on-a-stick

    Answer: B

4. Which of the following are examples of modules or daughter cards that provide routing functionality in a chassis-based Catalyst switch?

A. Multilayer Switch Module

B. Route Switch Feature Card

C. Route Switch Module

D. Multilayer Switch Feature Card

Answer: A, B, C, D

5. Which of the following modules have embedded route processors?

A. Catalyst 6500 Supervisor Engine 720

B. Catalyst 4006 Supervisor Engine II

C. Catalyst 4500 Supervisor Engine III

D. Catalyst 4500 Supervisor Engine IV

Answer: A, C, D

6. Which of the following are required for performing router-on-a-stick?

A. Router

B. IEEE 802.1Q or ISL

C. Routing protocol

D. Layer 2 switch port

Answer: A, B, D

7. A switch virtual interface is configured with what command(s)?

A. Switch#**vlan database**

B. Switch(vlan)#**vlan**

C. Switch(config)#**interface vlan**

D. Switch(config)#**vlan**

Answer: C

8. What command is required to configure a switch port on a multilayer Catalyst switch as a routed port?

   A. **ip routing**

   B. **no shutdown**

   C. **interface vlan**

   D. **no switchport**

   Answer: D

9. Before Cisco IOS software Release 12.1(3)T, the native VLAN was configured on which interface on a router?

   A. Physical interface

   B. Subinterface

   C. Switch virtual interface

   D. Bridge virtual interface

   Answer: A

10. What Catalyst 3550 commands can be used to determine whether a port is a routed port or a Layer 2 switch port?

    A. **show port routed**

    B. **show ip interface switchport**

    C. **show vlan**

    D. **show ip interface brief**

    Answer: B, D

Chapter 5

1. Which of the following describe multilayer switching?

   A. It's hardware-based.

   B. It performs PDU header rewrites and forwarding.

   C. It's platform-independent.

   D. It uses Layer 2, 3, and 4 header information.

   Answer: A, B, D

2. Which of the following device combinations support Cisco Express Forwarding?

   A. Cisco 7500 router running IOS 12.0

   B. Catalyst 4500 Supervisor Engine III

   C. Catalyst 6500 MSFC2

   D. Cisco routers running IOS 12.2 or later

   Answer: A, B, C, D

3. Which of the following are MLS components?

   A. MLSP

   B. MLS-RP

   C. MLS cache

   D. MLS-SE

   Answer: A, B, D

4. Which of the following are MLS flow masks?

   A. **destination-ip**

   B. **protocol-flow**

   C. **source-destination-ip**

   D. **ip-flow**

   Answer: A, C, D

5. After an IP MLS flow has been created, which of the following fields change in a frame traversing the MLS-SE as part of the same flow?

   A. Source MAC address

   B. Destination MAC address

   C. TTL

   D. Source IP

   Answer: A, B, C

6. In addition to the routing table, what tables are created in the CEF-based model?

   A. Routing table

   B. Forwarding Information Base

   C. Content flow table

   D. Adjacency table

   Answer: A, B, D

7. How many leaves are possible in a CEF Forwarding Information Base?

A. 32

B. 64

C. 128

D. 256

Answer: D

8. How many MLS-SE commands are required to configure MLS when the MLS-RP is an external router?

A. 1

B. 2

C. 3

D. 4

Answer: B

9. What is the default MLS flow mask when no ACLs are configured on the MLS-RP?

A. destination-ip

B. protocol-flow

C. source-destination-ip

D. ip-flow

Answer: A

10. What global configuration command enables CEF?

A. cef run

B. enable cef

C. cef enable

D. ip cef

Answer: D

Chapter 6

1. With redundant Supervisor Engines and MSFCs in a Catalyst 6500 switch running SRM, which of the following statements is accurate?

A. The nondesignated MSFC is active and has the same configuration as the designated MSFC.

B. The nondesignated MSFC is inactive and has the same configuration as the designated MSFC.

C. The nondesignated MSFC is inactive and has a configuration distinct from the designated MSFC.

D. The nondesignated MSFC is active and has a configuration distinct from the designated MSFC.

Answer: B

2. The GLBP router responsible for allocating MAC addresses is which of the following?

A. Active virtual gateway

B. Active virtual forwarder

C. Primary virtual forwarder

D. Secondary virtual forwarder

Answer: A

3. The GLBP router responsible for forwarding packets sent to a particular MAC address is which of the following?

A. Active virtual gateway

B. Active virtual forwarder

C. Primary virtual forwarder

D. Secondary virtual forwarder

Answer: B

4. Which IETF standard introduced in RFC 2338 parallels the Cisco-proprietary HSRP?

A. HSRP 2

B. IRDP

C. GLBP

D. VRRP

Answer: D

5. How many virtual MAC addresses are used per HSRP group?

A. 1

B. 2

C. 3

D. 4

Answer: A

6. SLB is an IOS-based solution defining a virtual server that represents a group of what?

   A. Real servers in separate intranets

   B. Virtual servers in a server farm

   C. Real servers in a server farm

   D. Virtual servers in separate intranets

   Answer: C

7. How many standby routers can there be in a given HSRP group?

   A. 1

   B. 2

   C. 3

   D. 4

   Answer: A

8. HSRP can be configured on distribution layer Catalyst 3550 switches using switch virtual interfaces. However, on distribution layer routers, multigroup HSRP is configured on trunk links using what?

   A. Null interfaces

   B. Loopbacks

   C. Bridge virtual interfaces

   D. Subinterfaces

   Answer: D

9. When configuring HSRP, each HSRP router interface must be configured with which of the following? (Select all that apply.)

   A. A virtual MAC address

   B. A real MAC address

   C. A virtual IP address

   D. A real IP address

   Answer: C, D

10. Which HSRP option(s) is/are used to guarantee an immediate change to active state on an HSRP router?

    A. **preempt**

    B. **tracking**

C. **priority**

D. **hello time**

Answer: A, C

Chapter 7

1. What type of VLAN is commonly used with Catalyst switches to support IP phones?

    A. User VLAN

    B. Native VLAN

    C. Auxiliary VLAN

    D. Management VLAN

    Answer: C

2. Which of the following is an indispensable software-based call-processing component required for a Cisco IP Telephony solution?

    A. LDAP

    B. Gateserver

    C. IOS Gatekeeper

    D. CallManager

    Answer: D

3. Different codecs have different encoding delays. These delays are added to the end-point-to-codec delays to determine which of the following?

    A. Propagation delay

    B. Latency

    C. Initialization delay

    D. End-to-end delay

    Answer: D

4. A priority queue is established for what type of traffic when implementing QoS for an IP telephony solution?

   A. TCP

   B. UDP

   C. Data

   D. Voice

Answer: D

5. Layer 2 traffic classification uses which of the following?

   A. Type of service

   B. Class of service

   C. Differentiated Services Code Point

   D. Voice queue

Answer: B

6. Layer 3 traffic classification uses which of the following?

   A. Type of service

   B. Class of service

   C. Differentiated Services Code Point

   D. Voice queue

Answer: A, C

7. What is used to ensure that multicast traffic is correctly forwarded down the distribution tree?

   A. LCP

   B. CRTP

   C. RTP

   D. RPF

Answer: D

8. What are the two types of multicast distribution trees?

   A. CBT trees

   B. Shared trees

   C. Shortest-path trees

   D. Rendezvous trees

Answer: B, C

9. What Layer 2 multicast address corresponds to the Layer 3 multicast address 224.10.8.5?

   A. FF.FF.FF.FF.FF.FF

   B. 01.00.22.44.10.05

   C. 01.00.5E.0A.08.05

   D. 01.00.5E.10.08.05

Answer: C

10. What multicast protocol is used to optimize multicast traffic between hosts and routers participating in multicast traffic flows?

   A. RGMP

   B. IGMP

   C. CGMP

   D. PIM-SM

Answer: B

Chapter 8

1. What QoS characteristics define the quality of the movement of traffic from one point to another?

   A. Bandwidth

   B. Jitter

   C. Loss

   D. Delay

Answer: B, C, D

2. Loss for voice traffic should not exceed what percentage?

   A. .5 percent

   B. 1 percent

   C. 2 percent

   D. 4 percent

Answer: B

3. Latency for video traffic should be no more than how many seconds?

   A. 2 to 3 seconds

   B. 3 to 4 seconds

   C. 4 to 5 seconds

   D. 5 to 6 seconds

   Answer: C

4. Which of the following are the three QoS service models?

   A. Deterministic

   B. Best-effort

   C. DiffServ

   D. IntServ

   Answer: B, C, D

5. How many bits are used to indicate IP Precedence?

   A. 2

   B. 3

   C. 6

   D. 8

   Answer: B

6. How many bits are used to indicate IP DSCP?

   A. 2

   B. 3

   C. 6

   D. 8

   Answer: C

7. The CoS is set to which of the following values on traffic sourced by a Cisco IP Phone?

   A. 0

   B. 1

   C. 5

   D. 7

   Answer: C

8. What type of QoS is used to prevent tail drop from causing traffic irregularities?

   A. RSVP

   B. GTS

   C. WRED

   D. CAR

   Answer: C

9. Where in a network should traffic be marked? (Select all that apply.)

   A. Edge router

   B. Core router

   C. Access router

   D. Distribution router

   Answer: A, C

10. What type of queuing is designed specifically for voice traffic?

   A. CBWFQ

   B. FIFO

   C. WFQ

   D. LLQ

   Answer: D

Chapter 9

1. Which of the following are valid SPAN source ports?

   A. Layer 2 port

   B. Layer 3 port

   C. EtherChannel

   D. Trunk port

   Answer: A, B, C, D

2. An RSPAN session requires the use of what type of port(s)?

   A. Source port

   B. Destination port

    C. Trunk port

    D. Reflector port

    Answer: A, B, C, D

3. What Catalyst 6500 module is used to store and modify monitored traffic?

    A. Intrusion Detection Sensor

    B. Switch Fabric Module

    C. Network Analysis Module

    D. Supervisor Engine

    Answer: C

4. What is the web interface used with the NAM called?

    A. Netsys Baseliner

    B. RMON 2 Viewer

    C. RMON Viewer

    D. NAM Traffic Analyzer

    Answer: D

5. The Switch Fabric Module is used on which Catalyst switches?

    A. 2950

    B. 3550

    C. 6500

    D. 7600

    Answer: C

6. Basic security measures include which considerations?

    A. Physical security

    B. Privilege level

    C. Remote access

    D. Password protection

    Answer: A, B, C, D

7. The CoS is set to what value on traffic sourced by a Cisco IP Phone?

    A. 0

    B. 1

C. 5

D. 7

Answer: C

8. Out-of-band management is performed on what lines or interfaces?

   A. Ethernet

   B. Console

   C. Auxiliary

   D. vty

   Answer: B, C

9. Secure Shell requires the use of what command(s)?

   A. **ip domain-name**

   B. **crypto key generate rsa**

   C. **ssh**

   D. **login local**

   Answer: A, B

10. What type of access list filters both routed and bridged traffic?

    A. MAC ACL

    B. Port ACL

    C. VLAN map

    D. Router ACL

    Answer: C

Chapter 10

1. TLS solutions can be much less costly than which of the following traditional WAN solutions while providing equivalent or improved service?

   A. ATM

   B. ISDN

   C. Frame Relay

   D. X.25

   Answer: A

2. What can be used to connect Ethernet-based networks to an existing SONET/SDH and TDM and DWDM infrastructure?

   A. PCS

   B. CSMA/CD

   C. WAN PHY

   D. PMD

   Answer: C

3. Which two LAN and WAN technologies can be integrated relatively easily because of their comparable bandwidths?

   A. Fast Ethernet and OC-3

   B. Gigabit Ethernet and STS-1

   C. 10 Gigabit Ethernet and OC-192

   D. Standard Ethernet and STS-3

   Answer: C

4. What is the maximum speed available with SONET?

   A. OC-48

   B. OC-192

   C. OC-384

   D. OC-768

   Answer: D

5. What three areas are defined by a segmented metro network?

   A. Aggregation point for forwarding

   B. CPE

   C. LAN

   D. POP

   Answer: A, B, D

6. What three service options are available with metro Ethernet?

   A. High-speed Internet access

   B. High-speed VPN access

C. Remote access

D. Point-to-point LAN service

Answer: A, B, D

7. Which of the following technologies removes the need to layer SONET or ATM technologies between a Layer 3 protocol and the optical physical layer?

A. TLS

B. 10 GEC

C. IP+Optical

D. TDM+Optical

Answer: C

8. What Cisco device can be configured to provide shared point-to-multipoint TLS?

A. Catalyst 6500 NAM

B. PIX 515

C. ONS 15454

D. Cisco 7600 router

Answer: C

9. Which of the following is a QoS feature commonly implemented in metro optical networks?

A. Bandwidth provisioning

B. CoS-to-DSCP mapping

C. Priority queuing

D. Compression

Answer: A

10. How many bytes are there per SONET frame?

A. 210

B. 410

C. 810

D. 1610

Answer: C

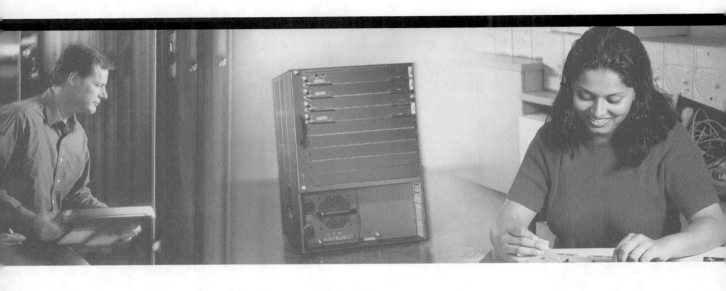

Appendix B

Gigabit Ethernet and 10 Gigabit Ethernet Standards and Operation

The demand for bandwidth continues to grow as new applications and services are added to existing networks. More than 85 percent of workstations are presently running Fast Ethernet, driving the need for servers with Gigabit connections. Industry expectation is that autonegotiating 10/100/1000-Mbps network interface cards (NICs) will enjoy almost complete market share by 2005. With users simultaneously editing a remote Structured Query Language (SQL) database, downloading MP3 files, sending an e-mail with a 10-MB attachment, and conducting a NetMeeting conference call over a multicast-enabled IP network, it's not surprising that Gigabit Ethernet is making its way to the desktop.

In the late 1990s, Gigabit Ethernet standards were approved for copper cable (IEEE 802.3ab) and fiber media (IEEE 802.3z), carrying on a 25-year tradition. Gigabit Ethernet options are now common for campus network devices, including switches, routers, servers, and desktops.

With more than 85 percent of the installed base of network ports using Ethernet, the job of the network engineer is in some sense simplified with the increased availability of Gigabit Ethernet products. As the standards for Ethernet evolve, backward compatibility with 10-Mbps and 100-Mbps Ethernet installations continues to be maintained. More than 90 percent of existing Category 5 installations already meet the minimum requirements for deploying Gigabit Ethernet, so upgrading to Gigabit Ethernet is often just a matter of adding or swapping modules in a switch chassis.

The familiarity of Ethernet also serves as a psychological advantage for deploying Gigabit Ethernet. Most network engineers are much more comfortable with Ethernet deployments as compared to other LAN/MAN technologies. Ethernet is easy to use and easy to upgrade. The process of upgrading typically proceeds from the campus backbone to the server farm to the desktop.

Another advantage of Gigabit Ethernet is its support of quality of service (QoS) features such as IEEE 802.1p traffic prioritization that enhance audio and video communication. QoS is now pervasive in modern networks as voice, video, and data networks converge. This book does not delve into the array of QoS options for optimizing network traffic flow, but you are strongly encouraged to begin your study of QoS as soon as possible to stay current in the field.

More than increased bandwidth, ease of upgrades, or QoS options, the small cost-versus-bandwidth ratio of Gigabit Ethernet is the primary reason for its success. The bottom line generally serves as the deciding factor in major network upgrades.

Gigabit Ethernet Standards

The original 10-Mbps Ethernet standards were devised more than 25 years ago. Among these is 10BASE-T (supported by Category 3, 4, and 5 cable).

The 10BASE-T standards were followed by the IEEE 802.3u Fast Ethernet standards. Fast Ethernet includes specifications for 100BASE-T (Category 5 cable with pins 1 and 2 for transmission and pins 3 and 6 for receiving and collision detection), 100BASE-T4 (Category 3 cable using all four wire pairs), and 100BASE-FX (multimode or single-mode fiber used, for example, between buildings or in areas where there are high levels of radiated electrical noise).

Gigabit Ethernet standards have been in place since the late 1990s. Gigabit Ethernet ports are now as commonplace as 10-Mbps ports were in the early 1990s. The IEEE 802.3z standard specifies 1000 Mbps over fiber, and the IEEE 802.3ab standard specifies 1000 Mbps over Category 5 cable (1000BASE-T). The 802.3ab standard also supports 1000 Mbps over the EIA/TIA Category 5e specification. Figure B-1 summarizes the Gigabit Ethernet standards.

History of the Gigabit Ethernet Standards Process

More than a decade ago, the old 10BASE5 and 10BASE2 Ethernet networks were replaced by 10BASE-T hubs, allowing for greater manageability of the network and the cable plant. As applications increased the demands on the network, newer high-speed protocols such as Fiber Distributed Data Interface (FDDI) and Asynchronous Transfer Mode (ATM) became available. However, Fast Ethernet became the backbone of choice because of its simplicity and its backward compatibility with Ethernet. The primary goal of Gigabit Ethernet was to build on that topology and knowledge base to create a higher-speed technology without forcing customers to throw away existing networking equipment.

Figure B-1 IEEE 802.3z and IEEE 802.3ab Comprise the Gigabit Ethernet Standards

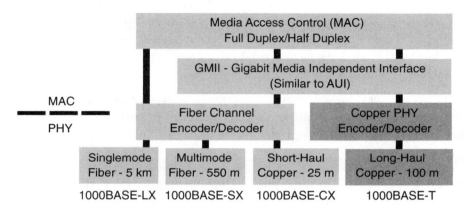

The standards body that worked on Gigabit Ethernet was called the Institute of Electrical and Electronics Engineers (IEEE) 802.3z Task Force. The possibility of a Gigabit Ethernet Standard was raised in mid-1995 after the final ratification of the Fast Ethernet standard. By November 1995, there was enough interest to form a high-speed study group. This group met at the end of 1995 and several times during early 1996 to study the feasibility of Gigabit Ethernet. The meetings grew in attendance, reaching 150 to 200 individuals. Numerous technical contributions were offered and evaluated.

In July 1996, the 802.3z Task Force was established with the charter to develop a standard for Gigabit Ethernet. Basic concept agreement on technical contributions for the standard was achieved at the November 1996 IEEE meeting. The first draft of the standard was produced and reviewed in January 1997, and the final standard was approved in June 1998. The IEEE 802.3ab standard for Gigabit Ethernet over copper cable was approved one year later in June 1999.

IEEE 802.3ab

IEEE 802.3ab describes the specifications for running Gigabit Ethernet over unshielded twisted-pair copper cabling. 1000BASE-T provides 1-Gbps throughput via four pairs of Category 5 unshielded twisted-pair (UTP) cable (250 Mbps per wire pair). (Note that all eight wires are used, as opposed to 10BASE-T and 100BASE-T.) Cabling distances for such an installation cannot exceed 100 meters.

Before you upgrade to Gigabit Ethernet, you should test existing Category 5 cable for far-end crosstalk and return loss. If the cable fails the test, the ANSI/TIA/EIA TSB-95 standard details options for correcting the problems. For new installations, Category 5e cable is recommended.

The standard supports both half-duplex and full-duplex operation, but full-duplex implementations are far more common. The carrier sense multiple access collision detect (CSMA/CD) access method is used when Gigabit Ethernet is operating in half-duplex mode. In full-duplex mode, CSMA/CD is out of the picture, but flow-control mechanisms are used to handle buffering.

Gigabit Ethernet over Category 5 cable is presently the most common medium for horizontal cabling in ceilings and floors. However, as with Fast Ethernet, fiber-optic cabling is the medium of choice between buildings and between floors of a building.

1000BASE-T can be deployed in three parts of a network:

- **Switch uplinks**—1000BASE-T provides high-bandwidth connectivity from desktop switches to the next point of aggregation. With such uplinks, switches can be linked to servers and other resources at gigabit speeds. These connections can substantially relieve network congestion, improving access to high-bandwidth applications and data.

- **Server connectivity**—1000BASE-T links can be used to connect high-performance servers to the switch. This use dramatically improves traffic flow. Moreover, the price of 1000BASE-T network interface cards has been falling at the same time availability has been increasing.

- **Desktop connectivity**—As desktop network interface cards become available, users will begin implementing 1000BASE-T at the desktop. At first, only power users will require such performance on the desktop. However, over time, 1000BASE-T is expected to migrate more to the desktop as prices continue to decrease.

IEEE 802.3z

The Gigabit interface converter (GBIC) allows network engineers to configure each gigabit port on a port-by-port basis for short wavelength (SX), long wavelength (LX), and long-haul (LH) interfaces. Figure B-1 shows the various distances allowed for the 1000BASE-SX and 1000BASE-LX Gigabit Ethernet standards. Vendor-specific LH GBICs extend the single-mode fiber distance from the standard 5 km up to 70 km. The LH option is a value-add; although it's not part of the 802.3z standard, LH allows switch vendors to build a single physical switch or switch module that the customer can configure for the required laser/fiber topology.

The 802.3z specification calls for media support of multimode fiber-optic cable, single-mode fiber-optic cable, and a special balanced shielded 150-ohm copper cable. The current connector for Gigabit Ethernet is the SC connector for both single-mode and multimode fiber.

The signaling rate for Gigabit Ethernet is 1.25 Gbps. With the 8B/10B encoding scheme, data transmission amounts to 1.0 Gbps.

10 Gigabit Ethernet

10 Gigabit Ethernet was formally ratified as an IEEE 802.3 Ethernet standard in June 2002. This technology is the next step in scaling the performance and functionality of enterprise and service provider networks, because it combines multigigabit bandwidth and intelligent services to achieve scaled, intelligent, multigigabit networks with network links that range in speed from 10 Mbps to 10,000 Mbps. Since March 1999, the Ethernet industry has been working to increase the speed of Ethernet from 1 Gbps to 10 Gbps. This technology is very significant because not only will Ethernet run at 10 Gbps and serve as a LAN connection, but it also will work in metropolitan-area networks (MANs) and WANs. With 10 Gigabit Ethernet, network managers will be able to build LANs, MANs, and WANs using Ethernet as the end-to-end Layer 2 transport.

10 Gigabit Ethernet is a full-duplex technology that targets the LAN, MAN, and WAN application spaces. Prestandard 10 Gigabit Ethernet products entered the market in 2001. 10 Gigabit Ethernet supports multimode and single-mode fiber-optic installations (note the fiber-only options). Coupled with devices supporting wave division multiplexing, 10 Gigabit Ethernet extends Ethernet to the WAN, allowing a common technology to run over both private and public networks. LAN applications support distances of up to 40 km with single-mode fiber, connecting multiple campus locations within a 40-km range (see Figure B-2).

Figure B-2 10 Gigabit in the LAN Permits Links Ranging Up to 40 km

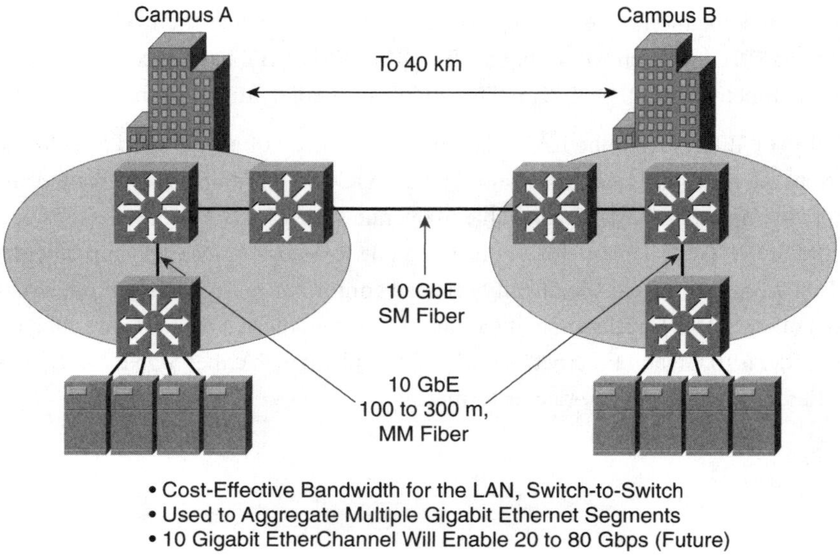

- Cost-Effective Bandwidth for the LAN, Switch-to-Switch
- Used to Aggregate Multiple Gigabit Ethernet Segments
- 10 Gigabit EtherChannel Will Enable 20 to 80 Gbps (Future)

Positioned as a high-speed technology for networking applications in LANs, MANs, and WANs, 10 Gigabit Ethernet will provide very high bandwidth with simplicity and relatively low cost. In LAN applications, 10 Gigabit Ethernet will let network managers scale their packet-based networks from 10 Mbps to 10,000 Mbps and thereby leverage their investments in Ethernet as they increase their networks' performance. In MAN and WAN applications, 10 Gigabit Ethernet will allow Internet service providers (ISPs) and network service providers (NSPs) to create very high-speed links at very low cost between colocated carrier-class switches and routers.

10 Gigabit Ethernet Standards

In the Open System Interconnection (OSI) model, Ethernet is fundamentally a Layer 2 protocol. 10 Gigabit Ethernet uses the IEEE 802.3 Ethernet Media Access Control (MAC) protocol, the IEEE 802.3 Ethernet frame format, and the minimum and maximum IEEE 802.3 frame size. Just as 1000BASE-X and 1000BASE-T (Gigabit Ethernet) remained true to the Ethernet model, 10 Gigabit Ethernet continues the natural evolution of Ethernet in speed and distance. Because it is a full-duplex-only and fiber-only technology, 10 Gigabit Ethernet does not need the carrier sense multiple access collision detect (CSMA/CD) access method that defines slower, half-duplex Ethernet technologies. In every other respect, 10 Gigabit Ethernet remains true to the original Ethernet model. An Ethernet physical layer device, which corresponds to Layer 1 of the OSI model, connects the medium, optical or copper, to the MAC layer, which corresponds to OSI Layer 2. The Ethernet architecture further divides Layer 1 into a physical medium dependent (PMD) and a physical coding sublayer (PCS). An optical transceiver is an example of a PMD. The PCS is made up of coding algorithms and a serializer. It often implements multiplexing functions.

The 802.3ae specification defines two physical layer types, such as the LAN and WAN physical sublayers (PHYs), as shown in Figure B-3. The WAN PHY has an extended feature set added to the functions of a LAN PHY. These PHYs are solely distinguished by the PCS.

The WAN PHY differs from the LAN PHY by the inclusion of a simplified Synchronous Optical Network (SONET) framer. Because SONET OC-192 is within a few percent of 10 Gbps, it is simple to implement a MAC to be able to operate with a LAN PHY at 10 Gbps or a WAN PHY at the SONET OC-192 payload rate. To enable low-cost WAN PHY implementations, the IEEE 802.3ae committee specifically rejected conformance to SONET jitter, stratum clock, and other SONET optical specifications. Therefore, the WAN interface sublayer (WIS) does not render a 10 Gigabit Ethernet WAN PHY compliant with either SONET or Synchronous Digital Hierarchy (SDH) at any rate or format.

Figure B-3 IEEE 802.3ae Specifies a LAN and WAN PHY

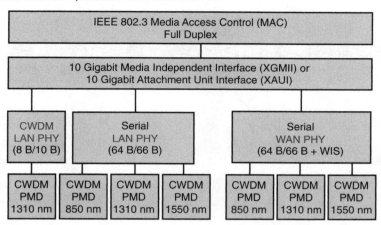

The LAN PHY is the most cost-effective solution to support the existing 10 Gigabit Ethernet applications across LAN and MAN distances on dark fiber and dark wavelengths. However, it lacks the ability to speak the same language as synchronous time-division multiplexing (TDM) gear, most prevalent in the WAN environment. The WAN PHY can be used to connect Ethernet-based networks to the existing SONET/SDH TDM and dense wavelength division multiplexing (DWDM) infrastructure and support lit wavelengths and lit fiber over WAN distances.

It is expected that the LAN PHY will also be used in pure optical switching environments extending over long-haul distances. This is possible because, by using optical equipment that incorporates the capability to transparently carry higher-level technologies such as 10 Gigabit Ethernet, ATM, SONET, SDH, and so on, LAN and TDM services will seamlessly converge into a single optical infrastructure. This infrastructure will provide a Layer 1 transport across MAN/WAN distances and will offer carrier-grade reliability while being technology-agnostic. Therefore, the importance of the WAN PHY for long-haul applications will also diminish. When dark wavelengths are available, 10 Gigabit Ethernet can be transmitted directly across the optical infrastructure, reaching distances of 70 to 100 km!

Appendix C

Using the Catalyst Operating System

Cisco routers run on Cisco IOS software. The command-line interface (CLI) embedded in Cisco IOS software is by now quite familiar to you. However, you might not be as familiar with the Catalyst operating system.

There are two major Catalyst switch operating systems. One of these is called Catalyst OS, CatOS, Catalyst set command-based OS, or set-based OS. The CatOS is distinguished by its reliance on **set** commands.

The other major Catalyst operating system is the one used on switches, such as the Catalyst 2950 and 3550. This is an IOS-like operating system, a hybrid OS that evolved from Cisco's acquisition of Kalpana in 1994. This Catalyst switch operating system is normally referred to as command-based or IOS-based. In fact, executing a **show version** command on a Catalyst 2950 switch reveals "Cisco Internetwork Operating System software" in the first line of output. The IOS-based Catalyst operating system is very similar to the router IOS to which you're accustomed.

Catalyst 6500 series switches have an optional "native IOS." It is a single Cisco IOS image that simultaneously controls the Layer 2, 3, and 4 configuration. Native IOS is also called Catalyst IOS, Cat IOS, or Supervisor IOS. In this case, the Supervisor module and the Multilayer Switch Feature Card (MSFC) both run a single bundled Cisco IOS image. The Catalyst 6500 Supervisor Engine 720 has an integrated Policy Feature Card 3 (PFC3) and a Multilayer Switch Feature Card 3 (MSFC3), and all can be managed with a single bundled IOS image. The Supervisor Engine III and IV for Catalyst 4500 series switches also use an integrated native IOS image. The IOS commands used in these hardware combinations are similar, if not identical, to the IOS switch commands used throughout this book.

Companies over the years have deployed Catalyst switches, such as the 4000, 5000, and 6000 family switches, using the CatOS. Many of these companies opt not to migrate to the IOS-based alternatives to the CatOS, so Cisco continues to support CatOS options for these switches. However, the trend is clearly in the direction of an integrated, strictly IOS-based solution for Cisco routers and switches.

In this appendix, you'll learn the following basic system administration tasks for Catalyst switches using the CatOS:

- Accessing the switch CLI
- Configuring idle timeouts
- Configuring passwords
- Recovering passwords
- Erasing configurations
- Saving configurations
- Naming the switch
- Configuring Telnet access
- Setting the port speed and duplex
- Setting port/interface descriptors
- Using command history options
- Using help features
- Using the **ping** command
- Executing TFTP downloads
- Using basic **show** commands

Preparing to Access the Switch

Before you can begin configuring your switch, you'll need to access the switch's operating system using a console connection, a modem connection, or a Telnet session. You also need a terminal emulation program to access the command line for the switch OS.

Console Access

When your switch is right out of the box, the first step of configuring it is connecting to it via the console port from a workstation. Your switch documentation details which connectors and cables to use. Your switch will arrive with the connectors and cables you need for console access. Should you need to terminate cables or adapters for console access, the pinouts for each Catalyst switch can be found at http://www.Cisco.com.

For example, to console in to a Supervisor Engine on a Catalyst 4000/5000/6000 switch from a PC, use an RJ-45-to-RJ-45 rollover cable and the DB-9-to-RJ-45 serial adapter supplied with the switch, and follow these steps (as you would with most Cisco routers):

Step 1   Connect one end of the rollover cable to the console port.

Step 2   Attach the supplied DB-9-to-RJ-45 serial adapter (labeled "Terminal") to a "Comm" port on the PC.

Step 3   Attach the other end of the rollover cable to the RJ-45 port on the serial adapter.

Connecting via the console port gives you direct physical access to the switch's operating system, whether it be a fixed-chassis switch or a switch chassis with 13 modules. On chassis switches, you often have the option of *consoling* directly into various modules populating the chassis. Normally, though, you'll console into the Supervisor module on these switches and access modules indirectly via the switch's backplane.

Terminal Emulation

Many applications, such as Tera Term, HyperTerminal (shown in Figure C-1), and SecureCRT, include terminal emulation programs that can be used for console access to a Catalyst switch. These applications typically provide other access options, such as Telnet (TCP port 23) and Secure Shell (TCP port 22). In addition, these applications give you a wide range of fine-tuning options, such as scrollback buffer size, function keys, scripting, window size, and line delay.

Figure C-1 HyperTerminal Is a Terminal Emulation Application That Can Be Used for Console Access to a Catalyst Switch

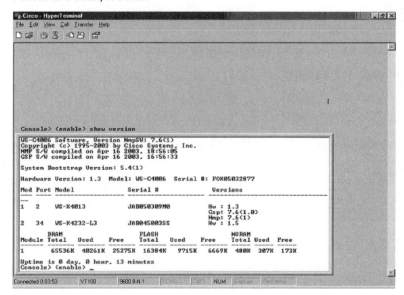

Fundamentals of Switch Configuration

As soon as you have access to the switch's operating system, you need to understand how to navigate through the system and perform basic tasks, just as you would on a PC.

Entering the Switch and Changing Modes

On CatOS, the CLI supports two modes of operation:

- Normal (also called login or user mode)
- Privileged (also called enable mode)

Both modes are password-protected. Use normal-mode commands for system monitoring, similar to a Cisco router's user EXEC mode. Normal mode allows you to view most switch parameters, but you're unable to make configuration changes. Privileged-mode commands are used to change the system configuration, unlike on a Cisco router, where you need to enter global configuration mode to make system changes.

When you first connect to the switch (with the proper physical media and a terminal emulation program), you see the following prompt:

```
Enter password:
```

On a new switch, the normal-mode password is null. If you are connecting to a new switch, press **Enter** at the prompt. Otherwise, enter the normal-mode password for the switch.

After you enter the correct password

```
Enter Password: normal_mode_password
```

you see the following user-level command-line prompt:

```
Console>
```

To disconnect from the switch CLI, enter the **exit** command:

```
Console> exit
Session Disconnected...


Cisco Systems, Inc. Console          Fri Dec 27 2002, 02:47:02
```

Many commands (such as commands that modify the configuration) can be entered only in privileged mode. To enter privileged command mode from normal mode, enter the **enable** command. On a new switch, the privileged-mode password is null. If you're connecting to a new switch, press **Enter** at the Enter password prompt. Otherwise, enter the privileged-mode password for the switch as follows:

```
Console> enable

Enter password: privileged_mode_password
Console> (enable)
```

Note the change in the prompt for privileged mode. To exit privileged mode and return to normal mode, enter the **disable** command.

As with a router, switch commands are additive in that making a configuration change does not completely overwrite the existing configuration.

Command-Line Processing and Editing

Switch commands are not case-sensitive. You can abbreviate commands and parameters as long as they contain enough letters to be different from any other currently available commands or parameters. You can scroll through the last 20 commands stored in the history buffer and enter or edit the command at the prompt. Table C-1 lists command-line processing and editing keystroke shortcuts.

Table C-1 Command-Line Processing and Editing

Keystroke	Function
Ctrl-A	Jumps to the first character of the command line.
Ctrl-B or the left arrow key	Moves the cursor back one character.
Ctrl-C	Escapes and terminates prompts and tasks.
Ctrl-D	Deletes the character at the cursor.
Ctrl-E	Jumps to the end of the current command line.
Ctrl-F or the right arrow key	Moves the cursor forward one character.
Ctrl-K	Deletes from the cursor to the end of the command line.
Ctrl-L; Ctrl-R	Repeats the current command line on a new line.
Ctrl-N or the down arrow key	Enters the next command line in the history buffer.
Ctrl-P or the up arrow key	Enters the previous command line in the history buffer.
Ctrl-U; Ctrl-X	Deletes from the cursor to the beginning of the command line.
Ctrl-W	Deletes the last word typed.
Esc B	Moves the cursor back one word.
Esc D	Deletes from the cursor to the end of the word.
Esc F	Moves the cursor forward one word.
Delete key or Backspace key	Erases a mistake when you enter a command. Reenter the command after pressing this key.

Just as with the Cisco router IOS, if you cannot remember a complete command name, press the **Tab** key to allow the system to complete a partial entry. If you enter a set of characters that could indicate more than one command, the system beeps to indicate an error. Enter a question mark (**?**) to obtain a list of commands that begin with that set of characters. Do not leave a space between the last letter and the question mark. For example, suppose that three commands in privileged mode start with **co**. To see what they are, enter **co?** at the privileged prompt. The system displays all commands (and their descriptions) that begin with **co**. Note that you don't need to press the **Enter** key after the question mark.

When the output is longer than the terminal screen can display, a **--More--** prompt is displayed at the bottom of the screen. Press the **Enter** key to see the next line, or press the **Spacebar** to see the next screen of output. If you enter /*text* and press the **Enter** key at the **--More--** prompt, the display starts two lines above the line containing the *text* string. If the text string is not found, **Pattern Not Found** is displayed. You can also enter **n** at the **--More--** prompt to search for the last entered *text* string.

Command History

Several shortcuts are available for repeating and/or editing previously entered commands. Table C-2 lists the various combinations.

Table C-2 Command History

Command	Function
To repeat recent commands:	
!!	Repeats the most recent command.
!-*nn*	Repeats the *nn*th most recent command.
!*n*	Repeats the command *n*.
!*aaa*	Repeats the command beginning with string *aaa*.
!?*aaa*	Repeats the command containing the string *aaa*.
To modify and repeat the most recent command:	
^*aaa***^***bbb*	Replaces the string *aaa* with the string *bbb* in the most recent command.

Table C-2 Command History (Continued)

Command	Function
To add a string to the end of a previous command and repeat it:	
!!*aaa*	Adds the string *aaa* to the end of the most recent command.
!*n aaa*	Adds the string *aaa* to the end of command *n*.
!*aaa bbb*	Adds the string *bbb* to the end of the command beginning with string *aaa*.
!?*aaa bbb*	Adds the string *bbb* to the end of the command containing string *aaa*.

Help Features

To see a list of commands and command categories, enter **help** in normal or privileged mode. Also, you can get context-sensitive help (usage and syntax information) for individual commands by appending **help** to any specific command (as opposed to a Cisco router, where output is displayed on a parameter-by-parameter basis, with no context-sensitive help). If you enter a command using the wrong number of arguments or inappropriate arguments, usage and syntax information for that command is displayed. Additionally, appending **help** to a command category displays a list of commands in that category. Example C-1 displays these options (note that the output of **clear help** is truncated).

Example C-1 *The Syntax of the* **help** *Command Differs from That of IOS*

```
Console> (enable) help
Commands:
-------------------------------------------------------------------
cd                       Set default flash device
clear                    Clear, use 'clear help' for more info
configure                Configure system from network
copy                     Copy files between TFTP/RCP/module/flash devices
delete                   Delete a file on flash device
dir                      Show list of files on flash device
disable                  Disable privileged mode
```

continues

Example C-1 *The Syntax of the* **help** *Command Differs from That of IOS (Continued)*

```
disconnect                      Disconnect user session
download                        Download code to a processor
enable                          Enable privileged mode
format                          Format a flash device
help                            Show this help screen
history                         Show contents of history substitution buffer
l2trace                         Layer2 trace between hosts
ping                            Send echo packets to hosts
pwd                             Show default flash device
quit                            Exit from the Admin session
reconfirm                       Reconfirm VMPS
reset                           Reset system or module
session                         Tunnel to ATM or Router module
set                             Set commands, use 'set help' for more info
show                            Show commands, use 'show help' for more info
slip                            Attach/detach Serial Line IP interface
squeeze                         Reclaim space used by deleted files
telnet                          Telnet to a remote host
test                            Test command, use 'test help' for more info
traceroute                      Trace the route to a host
undelete                        Undelete a file on flash device
upload                          Upload code from a processor
verify                          Verify checksum of file on flash device
wait                            Wait for x seconds
whichboot                       Which file booted
write                           Write system configuration to terminal/network
```

```
Console> (enable) copy help
Usage: copy file-id <tftp | rcp | flash | file-id | config>
       copy <tftp | rcp > <flash | file-id | config>
       copy flash <tftp | rcp | file-id | config>
       copy config <flash | file-id | tftp | rcp> [all]
       file-id has the format of [[m/]device:][filename]
       (example of file-id : bootflash:new_image, 1/bootflash:old_image)
```

```
Console> (enable) clear help
```

Example C-1 *The Syntax of the* **help** *Command Differs from That of IOS (Continued)*

```
Clear commands:

- - - - - - - - - - - - - - - - - - - - - - - - - - - - - - - - - - - - - - - - - - -
clear alias                   Clear aliases of commands
clear arp                     Clear ARP table entries
clear banner                  Clear Message Of The Day banner
clear boot                    Clear booting environment variable
clear cam                     Clear CAM table entries
clear cgmp                    Clear CGMP statistics
clear channel                 Clear PagP statistical information
clear config                  Clear configuration and reset system
clear counters                Clear MAC and Port counters
clear dot1x                   Clear Dot1x feature
clear gmrp                    Clear GMRP statistics
clear gvrp                    Clear GVRP statistics
clear igmp                    Clear IGMP filter
clear ip                      Clear IP, use 'clear ip help' for more info
clear kerberos                Clear Kerberos configuration information
clear key                     Clear config-key string
clear lacp-channel            clear LACP statistical information
clear localuser               Clear localuser record
clear log                     Clear log information
clear logging                 Clear system logging information
clear multicast               Clear multicast router port
clear netstat                 Clear network statistics
clear ntp                     Clear NTP servers and timezone
clear port                    Clear port features
clear pvlan                   Clear Private Vlan Mappings
clear qos                     Clear QoS features
clear radius                  Clear radius information
clear rcp                     Clear RCP information for other copy
clear snmp                    Clear SNMP trap receiver address
clear spantree                Clear spantree parameters
clear tacacs                  Clear TACACS server host/key
clear timezone                Clear timezone
clear top                     Clear TopN report
```

continues

Example C-1 *The Syntax of the **help** Command Differs from That of IOS (Continued)*

```
clear trunk              Clear trunk ports
clear vlan               Clear VLAN information
clear vmps               Clear VMPS information
clear vtp                Clear VTP statistics
Console> (enable)
```

Notice that when the console displays help, it returns the command line with a blank line (where the command **copy help** was entered in Example C-1). The command string you entered so far is not displayed for you as it is on a router.

Erasing and Saving the Configuration

On a Catalyst CatOS-based switch, as with a Cisco router, commands are additive. This means that adding configuration statements to an existing file does not completely overwrite the existing configuration. To ensure that a new configuration completely overwrites an existing configuration, enter the **clear config all** command. When you clear the configuration using the **clear config all** command, the factory default switch configuration is restored. The **all** keyword specifies clearing of all modules and system configuration information, including the IP address (so if you are accessing the switch via Telnet, you lose your connection to the switch). With the **all** keyword, all ports are restored to virtual LAN (VLAN) 1, VLAN Trunking Protocol (VTP) is not configured, and all spanning-tree parameters revert to their default values.

Example C-2 shows how to clear the configuration for the entire switch.

Example C-2 *Restoring the Default Configuration on a CatOS Switch*

```
Console> (enable) clear config all
This command will clear all configuration in NVRAM.
This command will cause ifIndex to be reassigned on the next system startup.
Do you want to continue (y/n) [n]? y
........
............................

System configuration cleared.
Console> (enable)
```

To clear the configuration on an individual module, use the **clear config** *mod_num* command in privileged mode. Example C-3 shows how to clear the configuration for module 2.

Example C-3 *Erasing the Configuration for Module 2 in a CatOS Switch*

```
Console> (enable) clear config 2
This command will clear module 2 configuration.
Do you want to continue (y/n) [n]? y
............................
Module 2 configuration cleared.
Console> (enable)
```

The **clear config all** command affects only modules that are directly configured from the Supervisor module. To clear the configurations on the router modules, you need to access the modules with the **session** *module_number* command. This command performs the equivalent of an internal Telnet to the module so that you can make configuration changes. To display which slot the router module is in, use the **show module** command. The router modules on a switch use Cisco IOS commands to change, save, and clear configurations.

Configuring the switch through the console and via Telnet allows you to save commands in real-time. Unlike a router, the switch immediately stores commands in nonvolatile random-access memory (NVRAM). Any command entered into a Catalyst switch is immediately stored and remembered, even through a power cycle. This presents a challenge when you attempt to reverse a series of commands. On a router, you can reverse a series of commands with **reload**, as long as you didn't write the running configuration into NVRAM. You'll find that many times the most challenging tasks with CatOS involve removing configured items.

Passwords

One of the first tasks you should perform when configuring a networking device is to secure it against unauthorized access. The simplest form of security in a campus network is to limit access to the switches in the switch block with passwords. By setting passwords, you can limit the level of access or completely exclude a user from logging on to an access, distribution, or core layer switch.

You can apply two types of passwords to your devices. The login password requires that you verify authorization before accessing any line, including the console. The enable password requires authentication before you can set or change the system operating parameters.

NOTE

The default login and enable passwords are null on CatOS. Just press **Enter** at the prompt.

To set the normal (login) mode password on a CatOS switch, use the **set password** command. You're prompted to enter the old password and the new password and to reenter the new password. Passwords are case-sensitive and might be 0 to 30 characters in length, including spaces. You do not see any output as you enter the passwords, as shown in Example C-4.

Example C-4 *Changing the CatOS Login Password*

```
Console> (enable) set password
Enter old password:
Enter new password:
Retype new password:
Password changed.
Console> (enable)
```

Example C-5 demonstrates how to change the privileged (enable) mode password on the switch using the command **set enablepass**.

Example C-5 *Changing the CatOS Enable Password*

```
Console> (enable) set enablepass
Enter old password:
Enter new password:
Retype new password:
Password changed.
Console> (enable)
```

Example C-6 displays a portion of the CatOS **show config** output. This command is used to display the nondefault system and module configuration. You can see the login and enable passwords displayed as encrypted text.

Example C-6 *The **show config** Output Is Extremely Lengthy. The Login and Enable Passwords Appear as Encrypted Text.*

```
Console> (enable) show config
This command shows non-default configurations only.
Use 'show config all' to show both default and non-default configurations.
************
******************
```

Example C-6 *The* **show config** *Output Is Extremely Lengthy. The Login and Enable Passwords Appear as Encrypted Text. (Continued)*

```
*********************

**

begin
!
# ***** NON-DEFAULT CONFIGURATION *****
!
!
#time : Fri Dec 21 2001, 15 :33 :14
!
#version 6.2(1)
!
!
#system web interface version(s)
set password $2$FxA/$KIPORCd/9ocXmtxpXQaFA/
set enablepass $2$vgI.$.OXPfwpUqD5QvC9FtCWPL1
!
```

Password Recovery

Each networking device has its own procedure for recovering passwords. For Cisco devices, the procedures are conveniently organized by platform in the article "Password Recovery Procedures" (Document ID: 6130) at http://www.cisco.com/warp/public/474/.

As demonstrated in the following password recovery process, an attacker simply needs to reboot the Catalyst switch and to access the console to get into privileged mode. When in privileged mode, the attacker can make any changes desired. It is extremely important that you maintain physical security of your equipment. It really does pay to keep wiring closets secured and console access restricted.

The CatOS password recovery procedure is the easiest to perform of all Cisco devices:

Step 1 Connect to the switch with the appropriate console cable, adapter, terminal emulation program, and terminal settings.

Step 2 Turn the switch off and on.

Step 3 Within 30 seconds of turning on the switch, perform the following sequence:

a. Press **Enter** at the password prompt to enter a null password.

b. Enter **enable** at the prompt to enter enable mode.

c. Press **Enter** at the password prompt to enter a null password.

d. Change the password using the **set password** command or the **set enablepass** command.

e. Press **Enter** at the prompt to enter the old password.

Setting System Name, Contact, and Location

The system name on a CatOS switch is similar to the host name on a Cisco router. It can be manually configured or assigned via Domain Name System (DNS). To manually set the system name, use the command **set system name** *name_string*. When you set the system name, the first 20 characters of the name are used as the system prompt. You can override this with the **set prompt** *prompt_string* command. To clear the system name, use the command **set system name** with no arguments.

You can specify the contact name and location to help you with resource management tasks. The system contact and location are set with the commands **set system contact** and **set system location**. Example C-7 demonstrates the name, contact, and location system commands.

Example C-7 *Setting the System Name, Contact, and Location*

```
Console> (enable) set system name Cat6506
System name set.
Cat6506> (enable) set system name
System name cleared.
Console> (enable) set system contact Nakagawa@EandC.com
System contact set.
Console> (enable) set system location Newtown
System location set.
```

The system name, contact, and location can be viewed with the **show system** command.

Remote Access

Before you can Telnet to, ping, or globally manage a switch, you need to assign the switch an IP address, associate the switch with the management VLAN, and define a default gateway. Although many LAN switches are primarily Layer 2 devices, these switches maintain an IP stack for administrative purposes. Assigning an IP address to the switch associates that switch with the management VLAN, provided that the subnet portion of the switch IP address matches the subnet number of the management VLAN.

The in-band (sc0) management interface on the Supervisor Engines of Catalyst 4500, 5500, and 6500 series switches is connected to the switching fabric and participates in all the functions of a normal switch port, such as spanning tree, Cisco Discovery Protocol (CDP), and VLAN membership. When you configure the IP address, subnet mask, broadcast address, and VLAN membership of the sc0 interface, you can access the switch through Telnet or Simple Network Management Protocol (SNMP).

All IP traffic generated by the switch (for example, a Telnet session opened from the switch to a host) is forwarded according to the entries in the switch IP routing table. For network communication to occur, you must configure at least one default gateway for the sc0 interface. The switch IP routing table is used to forward traffic originating on the switch only, not to forward traffic sent by devices connected to the switch.

The switch can be configured to obtain its IP configuration automatically via Dynamic Host Configuration Protocol (DHCP) or Reverse Address Resolution Protocol (RARP), but the focus here is on manual configuration.

The default IP settings are as follows for the sc0 interface:

- The IP address, subnet mask, and broadcast address are 0.0.0.0.
- sc0 is assigned to VLAN 1.
- The default gateway address defaults to 0.0.0.0 with a metric of 0.

To assign an IP address to the sc0 interface, use the command **set interface sc0** [*ip_addr*[*/netmask*] [*broadcast*]]. You can specify the subnet mask (*netmask*) using the number of subnet bits or using the subnet mask in dotted-decimal format. Example C-8 illustrates these two options.

Example C-8 *Setting the IP Address and Subnet Mask for the Management Interface*

```
Console> (enable) set interface sc0 128.1.2.3/24
Interface sc0 IP address and netmask set.
```

continues

Example C-8 *Setting the IP Address and Subnet Mask for the Management Interface (Continued)*

```
Console> (enable) show interface
sl0: flags=50<DOWN,POINTOPOINT,RUNNING>
        slip 0.0.0.0 dest 0.0.0.0
sc0: flags=63<UP,BROADCAST,RUNNING>
        vlan 1 inet 128.1.2.3 netmask 255.255.255.0 broadcast 128.1.2.255
me1: flags=62<DOWN,BROADCAST,RUNNING>
        inet 0.0.0.0 netmask 0.0.0.0 broadcast 0.0.0.0

Console> (enable) set interface sc0 128.1.2.3/255.255.255.0
Interface sc0 IP address and netmask set.

Console> (enable) show interface
sl0: flags=50<DOWN,POINTOPOINT,RUNNING>
        slip 0.0.0.0 dest 0.0.0.0
sc0: flags=63<UP,BROADCAST,RUNNING>
        vlan 1 inet 128.1.2.3 netmask 255.255.255.0 broadcast 128.1.2.255
me1: flags=62<DOWN,BROADCAST,RUNNING>
        inet 0.0.0.0 netmask 0.0.0.0 broadcast 0.0.0.0
```

NOTE

To assign ports 2/3, 2/4, 2/5, and 5/7 to VLAN 3, for example, use the command **set vlan 3 2/3-5, 5/7**.

To associate the in-band logical interface to a specific VLAN, enter the **set interface sc0** *vlan* command. If you do not specify a VLAN, the system automatically defaults to VLAN1 and the management VLAN. Example C-9 shows how to assign interface sc0 to VLAN 1 and administratively bring it up.

Example C-9 *Assigning the Management Interface to a VLAN*

```
Console> (enable) set interface sc0 1
Interface sc0 vlan set.
Console> (enable) set interface sc0 up
Interface sc0 administratively up.
```

Finally, you need to configure the default gateway. The Supervisor Engine sends IP packets destined for other IP subnets to the default gateway (a router interface in the same subnet as the switch IP address). The switch does not use the IP routing table to forward traffic from connected devices, only IP traffic generated by the switch itself (for example, Telnet, Trivial File Transfer Protocol [TFTP], and ping).

You can define up to three default IP gateways. Use the **primary** keyword to make a gateway the primary gateway. If you do not specify a primary default gateway, the first gateway configured is the primary gateway. If more than one gateway is designated as primary, the last primary gateway configured is the primary default gateway.

The switch sends all off-network IP traffic to the primary default gateway. If connectivity to the primary gateway is lost, the switch attempts to use the backup gateways in the order they were configured. The switch sends periodic ping messages to determine whether each default gateway is up or down. If connectivity to the primary gateway is restored, the switch resumes sending traffic to the primary.

To specify one or more default gateways, use the **set ip route default** *gateway* [*metric*] [**primary**] command. To remove default gateway entries, use the **clear ip route default** *gateway* command, or use **clear ip route all** to remove all default gateways and static routes. Example C-10 provides an example of configuring and removing default gateways.

Example C-10 *Setting and Removing a Default Gateway*

```
Console> (enable) set ip route default 128.1.2.1 primary
Route added.
Console> (enable) set ip route default 128.1.2.2
Route added.
Console> (enable) show ip route
Fragmentation   Redirect   Unreachable
-------------   --------   -----------
enabled         enabled    enabled


The primary gateway: 128.1.2.1
Destination     Gateway           RouteMask    Flags   Use       Interface
-------------   ---------------   ----------   -----   --------  ---------
default         128.1.2.2         0x0          G       0         sc0
default         128.1.2.1         0x0          UG      0         sc0
128.1.2.0       128.1.2.3         0xffffff00   U       14        sc0


Console> (enable) clear ip route default 128.1.2.1
Route deleted.
Console> (enable) show ip route
Fragmentation   Redirect   Unreachable
-------------   --------   -----------
```

continues

Example C-10 *Setting and Removing a Default Gateway (Continued)*

```
enabled          enabled     enabled


The primary gateway: 128.1.2.2
Destination       Gateway            RouteMask     Flags   Use       Interface
---------------   ---------------    ----------    -----   --------  ----------
default           128.1.2.2          0x0           UG      0         sc0
128.1.2.0         128.1.2.3          0xffffff00    U       332       sc0
```

After the switch is configured for IP, it can communicate with other nodes on the network (beyond simply switching traffic). To test connectivity to remote hosts, use the **ping** *destination ip address* command. The **ping** command returns one of the following responses:

- **Success rate is 100 percent or ip address is alive**—This response occurs in 1 to 10 seconds, depending on network traffic and the number of Internet Control Message Protocol (ICMP) packets sent.

- **Destination does not respond**—No answer message is returned if the host does not respond.

- **Unknown host**—This response occurs if the targeted host does not exist.

- **Destination unreachable**—This response occurs if the default gateway cannot reach the specified network.

- **Network or host unreachable**—This response occurs if there is no entry in the route table for the host or network.

Finally, because the focus of this discussion is remote access, it's useful to be able to adjust idle timeouts. The idle timeout specifies how long the connection stays active without any keystrokes taking place. The idea is that, if you forget to log out and leave your terminal unattended, the idle timeout prevents someone from gaining unauthorized access to the switch by using the terminal. Although this feature's default setting is 5 minutes, you can alter it with the **set logout** *number of minutes* command. If you use the **0** argument (**set logout 0**), sessions are not automatically logged out.

Loading Images to Flash

One of the more common administrative tasks is to load images to Macromedia Flash memory. The procedure is similar for all Cisco network devices. The idea is to set up a TFTP server and download a new image to the device via Ethernet using the IP address configuration of the appropriate management interface.

The Supervisor Engine implements a file system that can hold several images. Supervisors have at least a Flash device named bootflash:. Depending on the number of PCMCIA slots on the Supervisor, you can also have a slot0: and a slot1: Flash device available. Most basic operations such as listing, copying, and deleting files on these devices are available, with commands similar in name and syntax to DOS commands. Here's a list of common commands:

- Formatting Flash—**format** *device***:**
- Listing files on Flash—**dir** [*device***:**] [**all**]
- Changing the default Flash device—**cd** *device*
- Copying files—**copy** [*device***:**] *filename* [*device***:**] *filename*
- Marking files as deleted—**delete** [*device***:**] *filename*
- Squeezing Flash—**squeeze** *device***:**

The Catalyst 5000 and 6000 family switches support two IP management interfaces—the in-band management interface (sc0) and the Serial Line Internet Protocol (SLIP) interface (sl0). The sc0 interface is attached to the switch's switching fabric. The sc0 interface is an internal management interface that participates in all the functions of a normal switch port, such as Spanning Tree Protocol (STP), CDP, and VLAN membership. The SLIP interface is an out-of-band management port because it is not attached to the switching fabric and no traffic is switched over it.

The Catalyst 4000 family switches support three IP management interfaces:

- sc0
- sl0
- me1, which is an out-of-band management Ethernet interface

The 10/100 me1 interface is not attached to the switching fabric. If both the sc0 and me1 interfaces are configured, the Supervisor Engine software determines which interface to use when performing standard transmission and reception of IP packets based on the local routing table. Operations that use this functionality include TFTP, ping, Telnet, and SNMP.

When you configure the IP address, subnet mask, and broadcast address (and, on the sc0 interface, VLAN membership) of the sc0 or me1 interface, you can access the switch through Telnet or SNMP. When you configure the SLIP (sl0) interface, you can open a point-to-point connection to the switch from a workstation through the console port.

sc0 does not have an external port for direct connection. It exists as a logical interface inside the switch and is accessible via any of the physical ports on the switch.

me1 is actually a physical Ethernet port on the Supervisor module on the Catalyst 4000 family switches. This interface is used for network management only and does not support network switching.

NOTE

Use a straight-through patch cable to connect the Supervisor module me1 port to the TFTP server's NIC. In this sense, the me1 port acts like a regular switch port. This requirement is often a source of confusion, considering that TFTP downloads to routers are normally done with crossover cables.

The me1 or sc0 management interface must be assigned an address in the same subnet as the TFTP server.

Example C-11 shows a TFTP download via the me1 interface. (The procedure is the same for the sc0 interface.) Example C-11 shows the commands to set the me1 from the enable prompt.

Example C-11 *Configuring the IP for the me1 Interface on a Catalyst 4006*

```
Console> (enable) set interface me1 172.16.0.5 255.255.255.0
Interface me1 IP address and netmask set.
Console> (enable)
```

NOTE

On some versions of the CatOS, you get a **172.16.0.2 is alive** message instead of the typical Cisco **ping** output.

You should confirm IP connectivity with the TFTP server by pinging the server as shown in Example C-12.

Example C-12 *Confirming Connectivity to the TFTP Server*

```
Console> (enable) ping 172.16.0.2
!!!!!
----172.16.0.2 PING Statistics----
5 packets transmitted, 5 packets received, 0% packet loss
round-trip (ms)  min/avg/max = 14/15/17
Console> (enable)
```

Example C-13 demonstrates using the **show flash** command to check the contents of Flash to confirm that space is available for the new image. In this case, the new image is 4,089,736 bytes.

Example C-13 *Checking the Contents of Flash*

```
Console> (enable) show flash
-#- ED --type-- --crc--- -seek-- nlen -length- -----date/time------ name
  1 .. ffffffff 548c8f9c  39cf70   17  3526384 --- -- ---- --:--:--
   cat4000.5-4-2.bin
12071928 bytes available (3526384 bytes used)
Console> (enable)
```

You are ready to copy the image from the TFTP server, as shown in Example C-14.

Example C-14 *Copying the Image to Flash*

```
Console> (enable) copy tftp flash
IP address or name of remote host [172.16.0.2]?
Name of file to copy from []? cat4000.6-2-1.bin
Flash device [bootflash]?
Name of file to copy to []? cat4000.6-2-1.bin
7981064 bytes available on device bootflash, proceed (y/n) [n]? y
CCCCCCCCCCCCCCCCCCCCCCCCCCCCCCCCCCCCCCCCCCCCCCCCCCCCCCCCCCCCCCCCCCCCCCCCCCCCCCCCC
CCCCCCCCCCCCCCCCCCCCCCCCCCCCCCCCCCCCCCCCCCCCCCC
File has been copied successfully.

Console> (enable)
```

To confirm that the file was downloaded, use the **show flash** or **dir** command, as shown in
Example C-15. You will see that both images are now present.

Example C-15 *Verifying the New Image in Flash*

```
Console> (enable) show flash
-#- ED --type-- --crc--- -seek-- nlen -length- -----date/time------ name
  1 .. ffffffff 548c8f9c  39cf70  17  3526384 --- -- ---- --:--:--
  cat4000.5-4-2.bin
  2 .. ffffffff d39d5c46  783778  17  4089736 Apr 17 2001 14:40:15
  cat4000.6-2-1.bin

7981192 bytes available (7616376 bytes used)

Console> dir
-#- -length- -----date/time------ name
  1  3526384 --- -- ---- --:--:-- cat4000.5-4-2.bin
  2  4089736 Apr 17 2001 14:40:15 cat4000.6-2-1.bin

7981192 bytes available (7616376 bytes used)
```

Use the **set boot system flash bootflash:** *image_name* **prepend** command to tell the switch which image to use. It is critical that you use the **prepend** option to force the switch to load the new image by default. Example C-16 illustrates the impact of the **prepend** option.

Example C-16 *Reordering the Images in Flash*

```
Console> (enable) set boot system flash bootflash:cat4000.6-2-1.bin prepend

Console> (enable) show config
<output omitted>
#set boot command
set boot config-register 0x2
set boot system flash bootflash:cat4000.6-2-1.bin
set boot system flash bootflash:cat4000.5-4-2.bin
<output omitted>
```

To delete the old image, use the **delete** command. Using the **dir** command shows you that the file is gone, but actually it's just marked as deleted (note that the "bytes available" and "bytes used" have not changed). The file still appears in the output of the **dir deleted** command. To really get rid of the image, you need to execute the command **squeeze bootflash:**. Example C-17 demonstrates this sequence of commands.

Example C-17 *Deleting an Old Image*

```
Console> (enable) delete cat4000.5-4-2.bin
Console> (enable) dir
-#- -length- -----date/time------ name
  2  4089736 Apr 17 2001 14:40:15 cat4000.6-2-1.bin

7981192 bytes available (7616376 bytes used)
Console> (enable) dir deleted
-#- ED --type-- --crc--- -seek-- nlen -length- ----date/time---- name
  1 .. ffffffff 548c8f9c 39cf70  17  3526384 -- -- ---- --:-:- cat4000.5-4-2.bin

7981192 bytes available (7616376 bytes used)

Console> (enable) squeeze bootflash:

All deleted files will be removed, proceed (y/n) [n]? y
```

Example C-17 *Deleting an Old Image (Continued)*

```
Squeeze operation may take a while, proceed (y/n) y

Console> (enable) dir
-#- -length- -----date/time------ name
   1  4089736 Apr 17 2001 14:40:15 cat4000.6-2-1.bin

12070928 bytes available (4089736 bytes used)
```

You can use the same method to download configuration files from or upload configuration files to a TFTP server. If you want to restore a previous configuration to a CatOS switch, enter **clear config all** and then load the previous configuration. Note that the command **write network** has the same effect as the **copy config tftp** command on a CatOS switch.

Port Descriptors

You can add a description to an interface or port to help facilitate switch administration, such as documenting what access or distribution layer device the interface services. The **set port name** command is very useful in an environment in which a switch has numerous connections and the network engineer needs to check a link to a specific location. This description is meant solely as a comment to help identify how the interface is being used or where it is connected (such as which floor, which office, and so on). This description appears in the output when you display the configuration information.

To assign a name to a port, use the command **set port name** *mod_num/port_num* [*name_string*]. Verify the configuration with the **show port** [*mod_num*[*/port_num*]] command. Note that the **show port** command can have a module number as an argument.

Example C-18 shows how to set the name for ports 1/1 and 1/2 and how to verify that the port names are configured correctly.

Example C-18 *Configuring and Verifying Descriptive Identifiers for Ports*

```
Console> (enable) set port name 1/1 Router Connection
Port 1/1 name set.
Console> (enable) set port name 1/2 Server Link
Port 1/2 name set.
Console> (enable) show port 1
```

continues

Example C-18 *Configuring and Verifying Descriptive Identifiers for Ports (Continued)*

```
Port  Name                Status      Vlan        Level   Duplex  Speed  Type
----- ------------------- ----------  ----------  ------  ------  -----  ------------
 1/1  Router Connection   connected   1           normal  full    1000   1000BaseSX
 1/2  Server Link         connected   1           normal  full    1000   1000BaseSX


<output omitted>


Last-Time-Cleared

-------------------------

Tue Dec 28 2002, 16:25:57
Console> (enable)
```

Port Speed and Duplex

You can configure the port speed on 10/100-Mbps Fast Ethernet modules. To set the port
speed for a 10/100-Mbps port, perform this task in privileged mode. Use the **set port speed**
mod num/port num {**10** | **100** | **auto**} command. Verify the port speed configuration with the
show port [*mod_num*[/*port_num*]] command.

Example C-19 shows how to set the port speed to 100 Mbps on port 2/3.

Example C-19 *Setting and Verifying Port Speed*

```
Console> (enable) set port speed 2/3 100
Port(s)  2/3 speed set to 100Mbps.
Console> (enable) show port 2/3
Port  Name                Status      Vlan        Level   Duplex  Speed  Type
----- ------------------- ----------  ----------  ------  ------  -----  ------------
 2/3                      connected   1           normal  half    100    10/100BaseTX
<output omitted>


Console> (enable) set port speed 2/3 auto
Port(s)  2/3 speed set to auto detect.
Console> (enable) show port 2/3
Port  Name                Status      Vlan        Level   Duplex  Speed  Type
----- ------------------- ----------  ----------  ------  ------  -----  ------------
 2/3                      connected   1           normal  a-half  a-100  10/100BaseTX
<output omitted>
```

You can set the port duplex mode to full- or half-duplex for Ethernet and Fast Ethernet ports. You cannot change the duplex mode of ports configured for auto-negotiation. To set a port's duplex mode, use the command **set port duplex** *mod num/port num* {**full** | **half**}, and verify with the **show port** command, as shown in Example C-20.

Example C-20 *Setting and Verifying Port Duplex*

```
Console> (enable) set port duplex 2/3 half
Port(s)  2/3 set to half-duplex.
Console> (enable) show port 2/3
Port  Name              Status      Vlan       Level  Duplex Speed Type
----- ----------------- ----------- ---------- ------ ------ ----- ------------
 2/3                    connected   1          normal half    100 10/100BaseTX
<output omitted>
```

NOTE

On 1000BASE-T Gigabit Ethernet ports, you cannot configure speed or duplex mode. 1000BASE-T ports operate only in the default configuration, where the speed is 1000 and the duplex mode is full. You cannot disable auto-negotiation.

In general, for Catalyst switches, Gigabit Ethernet and 10 Gigabit Ethernet are full-duplex only. You cannot change the duplex mode on Gigabit Ethernet and 10 Gigabit Ethernet ports. To determine which features an Ethernet port supports, enter the **show port capabilities** *mod_num* command.

access port   A switch port that connects to an end-user device or a server.

adjacency table   One of three tables used by CEF. The adjacency table is a database of node adjacencies (two nodes are said to be adjacent if they can reach each other via a single Layer 2 hop) and their associated Layer 2 MAC rewrite or next-hop information. Each leaf of the FIB tree offers a pointer to the appropriate next-hop entry in the adjacency table.

aging time   The IP MLS aging time determines the amount of time before an MLS entry is aged out. The default is 256 seconds. You can configure the aging time in the range of 8 to 2032 seconds in 8-second increments.

Application-Specific Integrated Circuit (ASIC)   A chip designed for a particular application (as opposed to the integrated circuits that control functions such as RAM).

ATM LAN Emulation (ATM LANE)   A standard defined by the ATM Forum that gives two stations attached via ATM the same capabilities they normally have with Ethernet and Token Ring.

Auto-RP   A PIM feature that automates the distribution of group-to-RP mappings.

BackboneFast   A Catalyst feature that is initiated when a Root Port or Blocked Port on a switch receives inferior BPDUs from its Designated Bridge. Max Age is skipped to allow appropriate blocked ports to transition quickly to Forwarding state in the case of an indirect link failure.

Blocking state   The STP state in which a bridge listens for BPDUs. This state follows the Disabled state.

Bridge ID (BID)   An 8-byte field consisting of an ordered pair of numbers—a 2-byte decimal number called the Bridge Priority and a 6-byte (hexadecimal) MAC address.

Bridge Priority   A decimal number used to measure the preference of a bridge in the Spanning Tree Algorithm. The possible values range between 0 and 65,535.

Bridge Protocol Data Unit (BPDU)   A frame used by switches and bridges to communicate spanning-tree information.

broadcast domain   The set of all devices that receive broadcast frames originating from any device in the set. Broadcast domains are typically bounded by routers because routers do not forward broadcast frames.

candidate packet   When a source initiates a data transfer to a destination, it sends the first packet to the MLS-RP through the MLS-SE. The MLS-SE recognizes the packet as a candidate packet for Layer 3 switching, because the MLS-SE has learned the MLS-RP's destination MAC addresses and VLANs through MLSP. The MLS-SE learns the candidate packet's Layer 3 flow information (such as the destination address, source address, and protocol port numbers) and forwards the candidate packet to the MLS-RP. A partial MLS entry for this Layer 3 flow is created in the MLS cache.

candidate RP   A router that announces its candidacy to be an RP for a PIM-SM network via the Cisco-Announce group, 224.0.1.39.

central rewrite engine   The Catalyst 5000 NFFC contains central rewrite engines (one per bus) to handle PDU header rewrites when inline rewrite is not an option. If the central rewrite engines are used, this means that a frame must traverse the bus twice—first with a VLAN tag for the source (on its way to the NFFC) and second with a VLAN tag for the destination (on its way to the egress port).

Cisco Express Forwarding (CEF)   A Cisco multilayer switching technology that allows for increased scalability and performance to meet the requirements for large enterprise networks. CEF has evolved to accommodate the traffic patterns realized by modern networks, characterized by an increasing number of short-duration flows.

Cisco Group Management Protocol (CGMP)   A Cisco-developed protocol that runs between Cisco routers and Catalyst switches to leverage IGMP information on Cisco routers to make Layer 2 forwarding decisions on Catalyst switch ports that are attached to interested receivers. With CGMP, IP multicast traffic is delivered only to Catalyst switch ports that are attached to interested receivers.

class of service (CoS)   802.1Q frame headers have a 2-byte Tag Control Information field that carries the CoS value in the 3 most significant bits. Layer 2 CoS values range from 0 for low priority to 7 for high priority. CoS is used with QoS, especially at the network's access layer.

class-based traffic shaping   Allows you to control the traffic going out an interface to match its transmission to the speed of the remote, target interface and to ensure that the traffic conforms to policies contracted for it. Traffic adhering to a particular profile can be shaped to meet downstream requirements, thereby eliminating bottlenecks in topologies with data-rate mismatches. Can be enabled on any interface that supports GTS.

Class-Based Weighted Fair Queuing (CBWFQ)   Extends the standard WFQ functionality to provide support for user-defined traffic classes. For CBWFQ, you define traffic classes based on match criteria including protocols, access control lists (ACLs), and input interfaces. Packets satisfying the match criteria for a class constitute the traffic for that class. A FIFO queue is reserved for each class, and traffic belonging to a class is directed to the queue for that class.

classification   Using a traffic descriptor to categorize a packet within a specific group to define that packet and make it accessible for QoS handling on the network.

clustering   A method of managing a group of switches without having to assign an IP address to every switch.

Coarse Wavelength Division Multiplexing (CWDM)   A technology that employs multiple light wavelengths to transmit signals over a single optical fiber. CWDM technology is based on the same WDM concept as DWDM technology. The two technologies differ primarily in the spacing of the wavelengths, the number of channels, and the capability to amplify signals in the optical space.

codec   Coder-decoder. An integrated circuit device that typically uses pulse code modulation to transform analog signals into a digital bit stream and digital signals back into analog signals. In voice over IP, voice over Frame Relay, and voice over ATM, a codec refers to a DSP software algorithm used to compress/decompress speech or audio signals.

collision domain   In Ethernet, the network area within which frames that have collided are propagated. Repeaters and hubs propagate collisions; LAN switches, bridges, and routers do not.

Committed Access Rate (CAR)   A rate-limiting feature for policing traffic. It manages a network's access bandwidth policy by ensuring that traffic falling within specified rate parameters is sent, while dropping packets that exceed the acceptable amount of traffic or sending them with a different priority. The exceed action for CAR is to drop or mark down packets.

Common Spanning Tree (CST)   A spanning-tree implementation specified in the IEEE 802.1Q standard. CST defines a single instance of spanning tree for all VLANs with BPDUs transmitted over VLAN 1.

Compressed Real-Time Transport Protocol (CRTP)   An RTP header compression feature used on a link-by-link basis.

Conjugate Structure Algebraic Code Excited Linear Prediction (CS-ACELP)   A CELP voice compression algorithm providing 8 kbps, or 8:1 compression. Standardized in ITU-T Recommendation G.729.

Content-Addressable Memory (CAM)   Memory that is accessed based on its contents, not on its memory address. Sometimes called associative memory.

core   In CBT, the router that serves as the root of the shared tree. Similar to PIM-SM's RP.

Core-Based Trees (CBT)   A multicast routing protocol introduced in September 1997 in RFC 2201, CBT builds a shared tree like PIM-SM. CBT uses information in the IP unicast routing table to calculate the next-hop router in the direction of the core.

default gateway   Provides a definitive location for IP packets to be sent in case the source device has no IP routing functionality built into it. This is the method most end stations use to access nonlocal networks. The default gateway can be set manually or learned from a DHCP server.

default VLAN   Upon initial switch configuration, all switch ports can be configured to be members of a particular VLAN other than VLAN 1. This particular VLAN is the default VLAN. When a user plugs a device into the switch, it automatically is associated with the default VLAN. If, upon initial switch configuration, not all switch ports are configured to be members of a VLAN other than VLAN 1, VLAN 1 is the default VLAN.

delay   Also known as latency. Refers to the time it takes a packet to travel from the source to the destination.

delay variation   See *jitter*.

Dense Wavelength Division Multiplexing (DWDM)   A technology that employs multiple light wavelengths to transmit signals over a single optical fiber.

Designated Bridge   The Designated Bridge for a segment is the bridge containing the Designated Port for that segment.

Designated Port   The Designated Port for a segment is the bridge port connected to the segment that both sends traffic toward the Root Switch and receives traffic from the Root Switch over that segment.

Differentiated Services Code Point (DSCP)   The first 6 bits of the ToS field. Used to classify IP traffic.

Disabled state   The administratively shut-down STP state.

Distance Vector Multicast Routing Protocol (DVMRP)   The first multicast routing protocol, publicized in RFC 1075 in 1998. Unlike PIM, DVMRP builds a separate multicast routing table from the unicast routing table.

distribution tree   A unique forwarding path for a multicast group between the source and each subnet containing members of the multicast group.

Dynamic Packet Transport (DPT)   A resilient packet ring technology designed to deliver scalable Internet service, reliable IP-aware optical transport, and simplified network operations.

Dynamic Trunking Protocol (DTP)   A Cisco-proprietary protocol that autonegotiates trunk formation for either ISL or 802.1Q trunks.

Dynamic VLAN   A VLAN in which end stations are automatically assigned to the appropriate VLAN based on their MAC address. This is made possible via a MAC address-to-VLAN mapping table contained in a VLAN Management Policy Server (VMPS) database.

E.164   An ITU-T recommendation for international telecommunication numbering, especially in ISDN, BISDN, and SMDS. An evolution of standard telephone numbers. Also, the name of the field in an ATM address that contains numbers in E.164 format.

edge port   With RSTP, an edge port is functionally equivalent to a port configured with Port-Fast under PVST+. An edge port immediately transitions to the Forwarding state. An edge port should be configured only on ports that connect to a single end station.

Emulated LAN (ELAN)   A logical construct, implemented with switches, that provides Layer 2 communication between a set of hosts in a LANE network. See *ATM LAN Emulation (ATM LANE)*.

enable packet   When an MLS-SE receives a packet from the MLS-RP that originated as a candidate packet, it recognizes that the source MAC address belongs to the MLS-RP, that the XTAG matches that of the candidate packet, and that the packet's flow information matches the flow for which the candidate entry was created. The MLS-SE considers this packet an enable packet and completes the MLS entry created by the candidate packet in the MLS cache.

end-to-end VLAN   Also known as a campus-wide VLAN. An end-to-end VLAN spans a campus network. It is characterized by the mapping to a group of users carrying out a similar job function (independent of physical location).

EtherChannel   A Cisco-proprietary technology that, by aggregating links into a single logical link, provides incremental trunk speeds ranging from 100 Mbps to 160 Gbps.

fast aging time   The IP MLS fast aging time is the amount of time before an MLS entry is purged that has no more than *pkt_threshold* packets switched within *fastagingtime* seconds after it is created.

flow   A unidirectional sequence of packets between a particular source and destination that share the same Layer 3 and Layer 4 PDU header information.

flow mask   A set of criteria, based on a combination of source IP address, destination IP address, protocol, and protocol ports, that describes the characteristics of a flow.

forward delay   How much time the bridge spends in the Listening and Learning states.

Forwarding Information Base (FIB)   One of three tables used by CEF. The FIB table contains the minimum information necessary to forward packets; in particular, it does not contain any routing protocol information. The table consists of a four-level hierarchical tree, with 256 branch options per level (reflecting four octets in an IP address).

Forwarding state   The STP state in which data traffic is both sent and received on a port. It is the last STP state, following the Learning state.

Frame Relay Traffic Shaping (FRTS)   Eliminates bottlenecks in Frame Relay networks that have high-speed connections at the central site and low-speed connections at branch sites. You configure rate enforcement, a peak rate configured to limit outbound traffic, to limit the rate at which data is sent on the virtual circuit (VC) at the central site. Using FRTS, you can configure rate enforcement to either the CIR or some other defined value, such as the excess information rate, on a per-VC basis. The ability to allow the transmission speed used by the router to be controlled by criteria other than line speed (that is, by the CIR or the excess information rate), which provides a mechanism for multiple VCs to share media. You can allocate bandwidth to each VC, creating a virtual time-division multiplexing (TDM) network.

G.711   Describes the 64-kbps PCM (Pulse Code Modulation) voice-coding technique. In G.711, encoded voice is already in the correct format for digital voice delivery in the PSTN or through PBXs. Described in the ITU-T standard in its G-series recommendations.

G.726   Describes Adaptive Differential Pulse Code Modulation (ADPCM) coding at 40, 32, 24, and 16 kbps. ADPCM-encoded voice can be interchanged between packet voice, PSTN, and PBX networks if the PBX networks are configured to support ADPCM. Described in the ITU-T standard in its G-series recommendations.

G.729   Describes CELP compression in which voice is coded into 8-kbps streams. This standard has two variations (G.729 and G.729 Annex A) that differ mainly in computational complexity; both provide speech quality similar to 32-kbps ADPCM. Described in the ITU-T standard in its G-series recommendations.

Gateway Load Balancing Protocol (GLBP)   A Cisco-proprietary protocol that protects data traffic from a failed router or circuit, like HSRP and VRRP, while allowing packet load sharing between a group of redundant routers.

Generic Traffic Shaping (GTS)   Shapes traffic by reducing outbound traffic flow to avoid congestion by constraining traffic to a particular bit rate using the token bucket mechanism. GTS applies on a per-interface basis and can use access lists to select the traffic to shape. It works with a variety of Layer 2 technologies, including Frame Relay.

globally scoped addresses   A multicast address space in the range from 224.0.1.0 to 238.255.255.255. These addresses can be used to multicast data between organizations and across the Internet.

GLOP address   RFC 2770 proposes that the 233.0.0.0/8 address range be reserved for statically defined addresses by organizations that already have an AS number reserved. The second and third octets are populated with the decimal equivalents of the first and second bytes of the hexadecimal representation of the AS number.

H.320   A suite of ITU-T standard specifications for videoconferencing over circuit-switched media such as ISDN, fractional T1, and switched-56 lines.

H.323   An extension of ITU-T standard H.320 that enables videoconferencing over LANs and other packet-switched networks, as well as video over the Internet. H.323 is a set of communications protocols used by programs, such as Microsoft NetMeeting, and equipment, such as Cisco routers, to transmit and receive audio and video information over the Internet.

Hello interval   The time that elapses between the sending of HSRP Hello packets. The default is 3 seconds.

Hello time   The time interval between the sending of Configuration BPDUs.

holdtime   The time it takes before HSRP routers in an HSRP group declare the active router to be down. The default is 10 seconds.

Hot Standby Router Protocol (HSRP)   The Layer 3 Cisco-proprietary protocol that allows a set of routers on a LAN segment to work together to present the appearance of a single virtual router or default gateway to the hosts on the segment. HSRP provides high network availability and transparent network topology changes. It creates a hot standby router group with a lead router that services all packets sent to the hot standby address. HSRP enables fast rerouting to alternate default gateways should one of them fail. The lead router is monitored by other routers in the group, and if it fails, one of these standby routers inherits the lead position and the hot standby group address.

HSRP group   Routers on a subnet, VLAN, or subset of a subnet participating in an HSRP process. Each group shares a virtual IP address. The group is defined on the HSRP routers.

HSRP state   The descriptor for the current HSRP condition for a particular router interface and a particular HSRP group. The possible HSRP states are Initial, Learn, Listen, Speak, Standby, and Active.

ICMP Router Discovery Protocol (IRDP)   Hosts supporting IRDP dynamically discover routers to access nonlocal networks. IRDP allows hosts to locate routers (default gateways). Router discovery packets are exchanged between hosts (IRDP servers) and routers (IRDP clients).

IEEE 802.10   The IEEE standard that provides a method for transporting VLAN information inside the IEEE 802.10 frame (FDDI). The VLAN information is written to the security association identifier (SAID) portion of the 802.10 frame. This allows for transporting VLANs across FDDI backbones.

IEEE 802.1Q   The IEEE standard for identifying VLANs associated with Ethernet frames. IEEE 802.1Q trunking works by inserting a VLAN identifier into the Ethernet frame header.

IEEE 802.1x   A standard defining a client/server-based access control and authentication protocol that restricts unauthorized clients from connecting to a LAN through publicly accessible ports. The authentication server authenticates each client connected to a switch port before making available any services offered by the switch or the LAN. Until the client is authenticated, 802.1X access control allows only Extensible Authentication Protocol over LAN (EAPOL) traffic through the port to which the client is connected. After authentication is successful, normal traffic can pass through the port.

- If a router receives a datagram on an interface it uses to send unicast packets to the source, the packet has arrived on the RPF interface.
- If the packet arrives on the RPF interface, a router forwards the packet out the interfaces present in the outgoing interface list of a multicast routing table entry.
- If the packet does not arrive on the RPF interface, the packet is silently discarded to prevent loops.

IGMP leave group message   A message used by IGMPv2 to allow a host to announce its intention to leave a multicast group. The leave message is sent to the all-routers multicast address, 224.0.0.2.

IGMP membership query   A message used by IGMP and sent to the all-hosts multicast address, 224.0.0.1, to verify that at least one host on the subnet is still interested in receiving traffic directed to that group. Also referred to as a general query.

IGMP membership report   A message used by IGMP to indicate a host's interest in receiving traffic for a particular multicast group.

IGMP snooping   A Layer 2 multicast constraining mechanism (like CGMP) used by switches, allowing only multicast traffic to be forwarded to those interfaces associated with IP multicast devices. The switch snoops on the IGMP traffic between the host and the router and keeps track of multicast groups and member ports.

IGMP Version 1   A version of IGMP that relies solely on membership query messages and membership report messages.

IGMP Version 2   A version of IGMP that adds the ability of a host to proactively leave a multicast group and the ability of a router to send a group-specific query (as opposed to a general query).

IGMP Version 3   A version of IGMP that adds support for source filtering.

inline rewrite   Some Catalyst 5000 family switch line cards have onboard hardware that performs PDU header rewrites and forwarding, maximizing IP MLS performance. When the line card performs the PDU header rewrites, this is called inline rewrite. With inline rewrite, frames traverse the switch bus only once.

Internet Control Message Protocol (ICMP)   A network layer Internet protocol that reports errors and provides other information relevant to IP packet processing. Documented in RFC 792.

Internet Group Management Protocol (IGMP)   A protocol used by IP hosts to communicate to local multicast routers their desire to receive multicast traffic. The hosts report their multicast group memberships to an adjacent multicast router.

Inter-Switch Link (ISL)   A Cisco-proprietary encapsulation protocol for creating trunks. ISL prepends a 26-byte header and appends a 4-byte CRC to each data frame.

IP Precedence   3 bits in the ToS field of the IP header used to specify a packet's class of service.

jitter   Also known as delay variation. The difference in the delay times of consecutive packets.

Kerberos   A secret-key network authentication protocol used with AAA that uses the Data Encryption Standard (DES) cryptographic algorithm for encryption and authentication. Kerberos was designed to authenticate requests for network resources. It is based on the concept of a trusted third party that performs secure verification of users and services.

LAN Emulation (LANE)   An ATM Forum standard used to transport VLANs over ATM networks.

latency   See *delay.*

Learning state   The STP state in which the bridge does not pass user data frames but builds the bridging table and gathers information, such as the source VLANs of data frames. This state follows the Listening state.

limited scope address   Also called an administratively scoped address. It falls in the range 239.0.0.0 to 239.255.255.255 and is limited for use by a local group or organization.

Link Aggregation Control Protocol (LACP)   Allows Cisco switches to manage Ethernet channels with non-Cisco devices conforming to the 802.3ad specification. Defined in IEEE 802.3ad.

Link Fragmentation and Interleaving (LFI)   A feature that reduces delay on slower-speed links by breaking up large datagrams and interleaving low-delay traffic packets with the smaller packets resulting from the fragmented datagram.

link local address   An IANA reserved multicast address space in the range from 224.0.0.0 to 224.0.0.255 to be used by network protocols on a local network segment.

Listening state   The STP state in which no user data is passed, but the port sends and receives BPDUs in an effort to determine the active topology. It is during the Listening state that the three initial convergence steps take place—elect a Root Switch, elect Root Ports, and elect Designated Ports. This state follows the Blocking state.

local VLAN   Also known as a geographic VLAN. A local VLAN is defined by a restricted geographic location, such as a wiring closet.

loss   The percentage of packets that fail to reach their destination.

Low Latency Queuing (LLQ)   Brings strict priority queuing to CBWFQ. Strict priority queuing allows delay-sensitive data, such as voice, to be dequeued and sent first (before packets in other queues are dequeued), giving delay-sensitive data preferential treatment over other traffic.

management VLAN   Most of today's switches and routers can be accessed remotely via Telnet or SSH to the device's management IP address. The recommended practice is to put these and other networking devices in their own VLAN, known as the management VLAN. The management VLAN should be a separate VLAN, independent of any user VLANs, the native VLAN, and VLAN 1.

Max Age   An STP timer that controls how long a bridge stores a BPDU before discarding it. The default is 20 seconds.

MBONE   A multicast backbone across the public Internet, built with tunnels between DVMRP-capable Sun workstations running the mroute daemon (process).

MLS Route Processor (MLS-RP)   A Cisco device with a route processor that supports MLS. For example, a Catalyst 3620 router is an MLS-RP.

MLS Switching Engine (MLS-SE)   A set of hardware components on a Catalyst switch, excluding the route processor, necessary to support MLS. For example, a Catalyst 5000 with a Supervisor Engine IIIG is an MLS-SE.

MLS-RP Management Interface   The MLS-RP interface that sends hello messages, advertises routing changes, and announces VLANs and MAC addresses of interfaces participating in MLS.

Mono Spanning Tree (MST)   The spanning-tree implementation used by non-Cisco 802.1Q switches. One instance of STP is responsible for all VLAN traffic.

multicast group   An arbitrary group of hosts that expresses an interest in receiving a particular data stream via multicast. This group has no physical or geographic boundaries. Hosts that are interested in receiving data flowing to a particular group must join the group using IGMP.

Multicast OSPF (MOSPF)   A multicast routing protocol specified in RFC 1584. MOSPF is a set of extensions to OSPF, enabling multicast forwarding decisions.

Multilayer Switch Feature Card (MSFC)   MSFC1 and MSFC2 are daughter cards to the Catalyst 6000 Supervisor Engine. They provide multilayer switching functionality and routing services between VLANs.

Multilayer Switch Module (MSM)   A line card for Catalyst 6000 family switches that runs the Cisco IOS router software and directly interfaces with the Catalyst 6000 backplane to provide Layer 3 switching.

Multilayer Switching (MLS)   A specific multilayer switching technology employed by various Cisco devices to perform wire-speed PDU header rewrites. The first packet in a flow is routed as normal, and the MLS-SE switches subsequent packets based on cached information.

Multilayer Switching Protocol (MLSP)   A protocol used to communicate MLS information between the MLS-SE and MLS-RP. In particular, the MLS-SE populates its Layer 2 CAM table with updates received from MLSP packets.

Multiple Instances of Spanning Tree Protocol (MISTP)   Lets you group multiple VLANs under a single instance of spanning tree. MISTP combines the Layer 2 load-balancing benefits of PVST+ with the lower CPU load of IEEE 802.1Q.

Multiple Spanning Tree (MST)   Extends the IEEE 802.1w Rapid Spanning Tree (RST) algorithm to multiple spanning trees, as opposed to the single CST of the original IEEE 802.1Q specification. This extension provides for both rapid convergence and load sharing in a VLAN environment.

native VLAN   The IEEE committee that defined 802.1Q decided that, for backward compatibility, it was desirable to associate all untagged traffic on an 802.1Q link with a specific VLAN—the native VLAN. This VLAN is implicitly used for all the untagged traffic received on an 802.1Q-capable port. A trunk port reverts to the native VLAN if trunking is disabled on the port.

NetFlow Feature Card (NFFC)   A daughter card for a Catalyst 5000 Supervisor module that enables intelligent network services, such as high-performance multilayer switching and accounting and traffic management.

NetFlow table   One of three tables used by CEF. The NetFlow table provides network accounting data. It is updated in parallel with the CEF-based forwarding mechanism provided by the FIB and adjacency tables.

Network Analysis Module (NAM)   A LAN monitoring solution that should be deployed at LAN aggregation points where it can see critical traffic and virtual LANs (VLANs).

Network Time Protocol (NTP)   Used to synchronize clocks on network devices. The multicast address 224.0.1.1 is reserved for NTP operation.

nonblocking   The ability to switch a packet immediately without encountering a busy condition.

Path Cost   An STP measure of how close bridges are to each other. Path Cost is the sum of the costs of the links in a path between two bridges.

Per-VLAN Spanning Tree (PVST)   A Cisco-proprietary spanning-tree implementation requiring ISL trunk encapsulation. PVST runs a separate instance of STP for each VLAN.

PIM sparse-dense mode   An alternative to pure dense mode or pure sparse mode for a router interface. Sparse-dense mode allows individual groups to be run in either sparse or dense mode, depending on whether RP information is available for that group. If the router learns RP information for a particular group, it is treated as sparse mode; otherwise, that group is treated as dense mode.

Policy Feature Card (PFC)   Performs hardware-based Layer 2 to 4 packet forwarding as well as packet classification, traffic management, and policy enforcement.

Port ACL   ACLs can be applied to Layer 2 interfaces on a switch. Port ACLs are supported on Layer 2 physical interfaces only, not on EtherChannel interfaces. Port ACLs are applied on interfaces for inbound traffic only. They support standard IP access lists using source addresses, extended IP access lists using source and destination addresses and optional protocol type information, and MAC extended access lists using source and destination MAC addresses and optional protocol type information.

Port Aggregation Protocol (PAgP)   A Cisco-proprietary technology that facilitates the automatic creation of EtherChannels by exchanging packets between Ethernet interfaces.

Port ID   A 2-byte STP parameter consisting of an ordered pair of numbers—the Port Priority and the Port Number.

Port Number   A numerical identifier used by Catalyst switches to enumerate the ports.

Port Priority   A configurable STP parameter with values ranging from 0 to 63 on a CatOS switch (the default is 32) and from 0 to 255 on an IOS-based switch (the default is 128). Port Priority is used to influence Root Switch selection when all other STP parameters are equal.

port-based VLAN   Also known as a static VLAN. A port-based VLAN is configured manually on a switch, where ports are mapped, one by one, to the configured VLAN. This hard-codes the mapping between ports and VLANs directly on each switch.

PortFast   A Catalyst feature that, when enabled, causes an access or trunk port to enter the spanning-tree Forwarding state immediately, bypassing the Listening and Learning states.

preempt   An HSRP feature that lets a router with the highest priority immediately assume the active role at any time.

priority   An HSRP parameter used to facilitate the election of an active HSRP router for an HSRP group on a LAN segment. The default priority is 100. The router with the greatest priority for each group is elected as the active forwarder for that group.

private VLAN   A VLAN you configure to have some Layer 2 isolation from other ports within the same private VLAN. Ports belonging to a private VLAN are associated with a common set of supporting VLANs that create the private VLAN structure.

Protocol-Independent Multicast (PIM)   An IP multicast routing protocol that derives its information using RPF checks based on the unicast routing table. PIM has several variations, including dense mode, sparse mode, sparse-dense mode, source-specific mode, and bidirectional mode.

Protocol-Independent Multicast Dense Mode (PIM-DM)   A PIM variation that builds a source tree for each multicast source and uses flood-and-prune behavior.

Protocol-Independent Multicast Sparse Mode (PIM-SM)   A PIM variation that builds shared trees. The root of the tree is called the rendezvous point, similar to CBT's core.

proxy ARP   Proxy ARP allows an Ethernet host with no knowledge of routing to communicate with hosts on other networks or subnets. Such a host assumes that all hosts are on the same local segment and that it can use ARP to determine their hardware addresses. The proxy ARP function is handled by routers.

PVST+   A Cisco-proprietary implementation that allows CST and PVST to exist on the same network.

RADIUS   A client/server authentication and accounting protocol for use with access servers. RADIUS is specified in RFCs 2865, 2866, and 2868.

Rapid Spanning Tree Protocol (RSTP)   An evolution of Spanning Tree Protocol (802.1D standard) that provides for faster spanning-tree convergence after a topology change. The standard also includes features equivalent to Cisco PortFast, UplinkFast, and BackboneFast for faster network reconvergence.

Remote Monitoring (RMON)   A monitoring specification that lets various network monitors and console systems exchange network-monitoring data. RMON gives network administrators more freedom in selecting network-monitoring probes and consoles with features that meet their particular networking needs.

Reverse Path Forwarding (RPF)   An algorithm used to forward multicast datagrams.

Root Bridge   The bridge/switch with the lowest Bridge ID for that VLAN. Each VLAN has a Root Bridge. Also called the Root Switch.

Root Path Cost   The cumulative cost of all links to the Root Switch.

Root Port   A port on a bridge closest to the Root Switch in terms of Path Cost.

Root Switch   See *Root Bridge*.

route processor   The main system processor in a Layer 3 networking device, responsible for managing tables and caches and for sending and receiving routing protocol updates.

Route Switch Feature Card (RSFC)   A daughter card to the Catalyst 5000/5500 Supervisor Engine IIG and IIIG that provides inter-VLAN routing and multilayer switching functionality. The RSFC runs Cisco IOS router software and directly interfaces with the Catalyst switch backplane.

Route Switch Module (RSM)   A line card that interfaces with the Supervisor Engine of a Catalyst 5000/5500 switch to provide inter-VLAN routing functionality. The RSM runs the Cisco IOS.

Router ACL   An ACL that can be applied to SVIs, physical Layer 3 interfaces, and Layer 3 EtherChannel interfaces. Router ACLs are applied on interfaces for specific directions (inbound or outbound). One IP access list in each direction can be specified.

router-on-a-stick   A method of inter-VLAN routing consisting of an external router with a Fast Ethernet, Gigabit Ethernet, or EtherChannel trunk connecting to a switch, using ISL or 802.1Q. Subinterfaces on the trunk are created to correspond with VLANs in a one-to-one fashion.

Router-Port Group Management Protocol (RGMP)   Lets a router communicate to a switch in the IP multicast group for which the router wants to receive or forward traffic. RGMP is designed for switched Ethernet backbone networks running PIM.

RP mapping agent   A router that receives the RP-announcement messages from the candidate RPs and arbitrates conflicts. The RP mapping agent sends the group-to-RP mappings to all multicast-enabled routers via the Cisco-Discovery group, 224.0.1.40.

RSPAN   An implementation of SPAN designed to support source ports, source VLANs, and destination ports across different switches. RSPAN allows remote monitoring of multiple switches across a network.

scheduling   The process of assigning packets to one of multiple queues, based on classification, for priority treatment through the network.

Secure Shell (SSH)   A program to log into another computer over a network, to execute commands in a remote machine, and to move files from one machine to another. It provides strong authentication and secure communications over insecure channels.

Server Load Balancing (SLB)   Balances services across numerous servers at speeds of millions of packets per second. Commonly deployed with the Cisco IOS software on Catalyst 6000 family of switches. SLB is a software solution using the advanced application-specific integrated circuits (ASICs) on the Catalyst 6000.

shared tree   A multicast distribution tree using a root placed at some chosen point in the network. PIM-SM and CBT both use shared trees. When using a shared tree, sources must send their traffic to the root for the traffic to reach the receivers.

Single Router Mode (SRM)   Addresses the drawback of the previous HSRP-based MSFC redundancy scheme (designated MSFC versus nondesignated MSFC). When SRM is enabled, the nondesignated router is online, but all its interfaces are down. Thus, it does not hold any routing table information. This means that if the DR fails, there will be some delay before the nondesignated router coming online has a complete route table. To help account for this, the information being used before the failure by the Supervisor for Layer 3 forwarding is maintained and updated with any new information from the new designated router.

source filtering   A capability added to IGMPv3 that lets a multicast host signal to a router the groups for which it wants to receive multicast traffic and the sources from which it wants to receive the traffic.

source tree   A multicast distribution tree with root at the source of the multicast traffic and whose branches form a spanning tree through the network to the receivers. Also called the shortest path tree (SPT). For every source of a multicast group, there is a corresponding SPT.

Spanning Tree Protocol (STP)   A Layer 2 bridge protocol that uses the spanning-tree algorithm, allowing a learning bridge to dynamically work around loops in a network topology by creating a spanning tree. Bridges exchange BPDU messages with other bridges to detect loops and then remove the loops by shutting down selected bridge interfaces. STP refers to both the IEEE 802.1 Spanning Tree Protocol standard and the earlier Digital Equipment Corporation Spanning Tree Protocol on which it is based. The IEEE version supports bridge domains and allows the bridge to construct a loop-free topology across an extended LAN. The IEEE version is generally preferred over the digital version.

Switch Fabric Module (SFM)   A line card that delivers an increase in available system bandwidth on a Catalyst 6500 switch from the default 32 Gbps on the forwarding bus to 256 Gbps. Including an SFM in a Catalyst 6500 chassis increases the speed at which switching, routing, and network monitoring modules can transfer data between each other. The SFM reduces latency and the incidence of packet drop caused by bandwidth bottlenecks at traffic aggregation points within the network.

Switched Port Analyzer (SPAN)   A tool used with Catalyst switches to enable the capture of traffic. A SPAN session is an association of a destination port with a set of source ports, configured with parameters that enable the monitoring of network traffic.

Synchronous Digital Hierarchy (SDH)   A standard for interfacing operating telephone company optical networks. SDH and SONET form a set of global standards that interface equipment from different vendors.

Synchronous Optical Network (SONET)   A standard for interfacing operating telephone company optical networks. SONET and SDH form a set of global standards that interface equipment from different vendors.

TACACS+   A Cisco-proprietary protocol used to authenticate users against a database. TACACS+ uses TCP to communicate between a TACACS+ server and a TACACS+ client.

tracking   This HSRP feature allows you to specify other interfaces on the router for the HSRP process to monitor. If the tracked interface goes down, the HSRP standby router takes over as the active router. This process is facilitated by a decrement to the HSRP priority resulting from the tracked interface line protocol going down.

Transparent LAN Services (TLS)   A set of technologies that lets the service provider provide native LAN services over wide-area links without the need to implement complicated and costly ATM networks.

trunk   A point-to-point link connecting a switch to another switch, router, or server. A trunk carries traffic for multiple VLANs over the same link. The VLANs are multiplexed over the link with a trunking protocol.

trust boundary   When classifying traffic types in an enterprise network, a trust boundary must be established. The boundary is established by the access device, which either classifies traffic it allows into the network itself or trusts classification that has already been applied by an end station, such as an IP phone.

type of service (ToS)   A 1-byte field in the IP header used for traffic classification. Specifies the parameters for the type of service requested. Networks can use the parameters to define the handling of the datagram during transport.

UplinkFast   A Catalyst feature that accelerates the choice of a new Root Port when a link or switch fails.

user VLAN   A VLAN created to segment a group of users, either geographically or logically, from the rest of the network. User VLAN traffic is typically configured to be independent of VLAN 1, the native VLAN, and the management VLAN.

virtual LAN (VLAN)   A group of end stations with a common set of requirements, independent of their physical location, that communicate as if they were attached to the same wire. A VLAN has the same attributes as a physical LAN but allows you to group end stations even if they are not located physically on the same LAN segment.

Virtual Router Redundancy Protocol (VRRP)   Provides functions equivalent to HSRP but is supported by multiple vendors. It is designed to eliminate a single point of failure that is unavoidable in static default routing environments.

VLAN access control list (VACL)   See *VLAN map*.

VLAN Management Policy Server (VMPS)   A Cisco-proprietary solution for enabling dynamic VLAN assignments to switch ports within a VTP domain.

VLAN map   Also called a VLAN ACL or VACL in the context of Catalyst 6500 switches. It can filter all traffic traversing a switch. VLAN maps can be configured on the switch to filter all packets that are routed into or out of a VLAN or that are bridged within a VLAN. VLAN maps are used strictly for security packet filtering. Unlike router ACLs, VLAN maps are not defined by direction (input or output).

VLAN Trunking Protocol (VTP)   A Cisco-proprietary protocol that uses Layer 2 trunk frames to communicate VLAN information among a group of Catalyst switches and to manage the addition, deletion, and renaming of VLANs across the network from a central point of control.

VLAN tunneling   A technology that allows customers in a metro environment to extend their logical network topology across wide geographic areas.

VLAN-based SPAN (VSPAN)   An analysis of network traffic in one or more VLANs.

VTP domain   Also called a VLAN management domain. A network's VTP domain is the set of all contiguously trunked switches with the same VTP domain name.

VTP pruning   A switch feature used to dynamically eliminate, or prune, unnecessary VLAN traffic.

Weighted Fair Queuing (WFQ)   A dynamic scheduling method that provides fair bandwidth allocation to all network traffic. WFQ applies priority, or weights, to identified traffic to classify traffic into conversations and to determine how much bandwidth each conversation is allowed relative to other conversations. WFQ is a flow-based algorithm that simultaneously schedules interactive traffic to the front of a queue to reduce response time. It fairly shares the remaining bandwidth among high-bandwidth flows.

Weighted Random Early Detection (WRED)   A mechanism designed to avoid the global synchronization problems that occur when tail-drop is used as the congestion avoidance mechanism on the router. WRED is a queuing technique for congestion avoidance. WRED manages how packets are handled when an interface starts becoming congested. When traffic begins to exceed the interface traffic thresholds before any congestion, the interface starts dropping packets from selected flows. If the dropped packets are TCP, the TCP source recognizes that packets are getting dropped and lowers its transmission rate. The lowered transmission rate then reduces the traffic to the interface, avoiding congestion. Because TCP retransmits dropped packets, no actual data loss occurs.

wire-speed routing   The routing of packets using a combination of hardware and data structures so that routing table lookups are circumvented and header rewrites and forwarding are handled independent of the route processor.

XTAG   A 1-byte value that the MLS-SE attaches per VLAN to all MAC addresses learned from the same MLS-RP via MLSP.

Index